MATHEMATICS

FOR CCEA AS LEVEL

OLOURPOINT
UCATIONAL

Rewarding Learning

Luke Robinson

First Edition
Second Impression, 2015

ISBN: 978-1-78073-022-6

Layout and design: April Sky Design, Newtownards
Printed by: GPS Colour Graphics Ltd, Belfast

Colourpoint Educational
An imprint of Colourpoint Creative Ltd
Colourpoint House
Jubilee Business Park
21 Jubilee Road
Newtownards
County Down
Northern Ireland
BT23 4YH

Tel: 028 9182 6339
Fax: 028 9182 1900
E-mail: sales@colourpoint.co.uk
Web site: www.colourpointeducational.com

The Author
Luke Robinson took a mathematics degree, followed by an MSc and PhD in meteorology. He taught at Northwood College in London before becoming a freelance mathematics tutor and writer. He now lives in County Down with his wife and son.

Rewarding Learning

Approved/endorsed by CCEA on 19 November 2013. If in any doubt about the continuing currency of CCEA endorsement, please contact Heather Clarke at CCEA, 29 Clarendon Road, Belfast, BT1 3BG.

Whilst the publisher has taken all reasonable care in the preparation of this book CCEA makes no representation, express or implied, with regard to the accuracy of the information contained in this book. CCEA does not accept any legal responsibility or liability for any errors or omissions from the book or the consequences thereof.

Publisher's Note: This book has been written to help students preparing for the AS Mathematics specification from CCEA. While Colourpoint Educational and the authors have taken every care in its production, we are not able to guarantee that the book is completely error-free. Additionally, while the book has been written to closely match the CCEA specification, it is the responsibility of each candidate to satisfy themselves that they have fully met the requirements of the CCEA specification prior to sitting an exam set by that body. For this reason, and because specifications change with time, we strongly advise every candidate to avail of a qualified teacher and to check the contents of the most recent specification for themselves prior to the exam. Colourpoint Creative Ltd therefore cannot be held responsible for any errors or omissions in this book or any consequences thereof.

Contents

Chapter 1

Indices and Surds

1.1 Introduction

Keywords

Index (plural indices): a power. For example in a^2 the index is 2.

Base: the number raised to a power. For example in 4^2, the base is 4.

Reciprocal: means 'one over'. For example the reciprocal of 2 is ½. And the reciprocal of ½ is 2.

Surd: any root. For example the square root of 2, $\sqrt{2}$, or the cube root of 10, $\sqrt[3]{10}$.

Before You Start

You should know how to:

Recognise some common squares and cubes, e.g.

$$4^2 = 4 \times 4 = 16$$

$$2^3 = 2 \times 2 \times 2 = 8$$

Evaluate powers of 2, e.g.

$$2^5 = 2 \times 2 \times 2 \times 2 \times 2 = 32$$

Use the Difference of Two Squares, e.g.

$$a^2 - b^2 = (a - b)(a + b)$$

EXERCISE

REVISION EXERCISE 1A

1. Evaluate:

   a) The squares of 4, 12, 15 and 20 b) 3^3, 5^3, 10^3,

   c) The cube roots of 64 and 8 d) 2^n where $n = 2, 3, 6, 9$

2. Use the difference of two squares to rewrite the following:

   a) $x^2 - 9$ b) $a^2 - b^2$ c) $1 - c^2$

   d) $(d + 10)(d - 10)$ e) $e^2f^2 - (gh)^2$

EXERCISE

What You Will Learn

In this chapter you will learn:

- How to understand and use **index notation;**
- More about using the **laws of indices;**
- How to manipulate **surds** and simplify expressions involving surds;
- The laws of indices and surds.

This chapter provides the basis for a lot of the mathematics used in all the Core modules. You will use indices a lot in the chapters on differentiation and integration. You will often use surds when you need to give an exact answer to a problem. For example, they are often used when solving quadratic equations.

1.2 Indices

In this section you will learn how to simplify expressions and solve equations using the rules of indices (powers). Some of this chapter will be revision of the work you did at GCSE.

5^3 (**Say it out loud:** '5 cubed' or '5 to the power of 3') and 7^2 (**Say it out loud:** '7 squared' or '7 to the power of 2') are example of numbers in index form.

The powers ^{1}, ^{2} and ^{3} are known as indices. Indices are useful (for example, they allow us to represent numbers in standard form) and have a number of important properties.

As a reminder: $7^1 = 7$

$7^2 = 7 \times 7$

$7^3 = 7 \times 7 \times 7$

EXERCISE

EXERCISE 1B

1. Evaluate:

a) 2^8 b) 3^4 c) 4^4 d) 14^2 e) $2^3 + 3^2$

f) $3^4 + 4^3$ g) $6^2 + 5^2$ h) $(3^2)^2$ i) $\left(\frac{2}{3}\right)^3$ j) $(0.2)^4$

2. Write the following in index form:

a) 49 b) 100 c) 0.01 d) 121 e) 0.001

f) $\frac{9}{49}$ g) 0.09 h) $\frac{1}{100000}$ i) 0.16

EXERCISE

IN THE REAL WORLD

The population of the world is 7 billion or 7,000,000,000 people.

Doesn't it look much easier and neater to write 7×10^9 ?

1.3 The Laws of Indices

There are several rules for dividing and multiplying numbers written in index form. These properties only hold, however, when the same base is being used. For example, we cannot easily work out what $2^3 \times 5^2$ would be, but we can simplify $3^2 \times 3^3$.

Multiplication

When we multiply numbers with indices, we add the powers. So for example:

$$z^a \times z^b = z^{a+b}$$

Remember, this doesn't work if the base changes. For example, we cannot simplify:

$$z^a \times w^b$$

There is no easy way of simplifying:

$$7^5 \times 2^{-3}$$

because 7 and 2 are different bases. This is true for all our laws of indices.

EXAMPLES

1. $x^2 \times x^6 = x^8$

2. $5^5 \times 5^{-2} = 5^3$

   (because $5 + (-2) = 3$)

3. $x^2 \times x^3 = x^{2+3}$

   $= x^5$

4. $2y^2 \times 4y^5$

   $= 2 \times 4 \times y^2 \times y^5$

   $= 8y^7$ (adding the powers of y)

5. As noted above, you cannot simplify an expression involving indices if the bases are different. However, sometimes it is possible to make the bases the same:

   $9^3 \times 3^4 = (3^2)^3 \times 3^4$

   $= 3^6 \times 3^4$

   $= 3^{10}$

Division

If we divide two numbers with indices, we subtract the powers. So for example:

$$p^a \div p^b = p^{a-b}$$

EXAMPLES

1. $\dfrac{r^2}{r^3} = r^{-1}$

2. $t^2 \div t^4 = t^{-2}$

3. $6^2 \div 6^{-5} = 6^7$

   (because $2 - (-5) = 7$)

4. $6z^6 \div 2z^2$

   $= (6 \div 2) \times (z^6 \div z^2)$

   $= 3z^4$

Brackets

If we have a number with an index, all raised to another power, this is the only time we multiply our indices:

$$(x^a)^b = x^{ab}$$

EXAMPLES

1. $(x^2)^3 = x^6$ 2. $(5^3)^2 = 5^6$

EXERCISE

EXERCISE 1C

1. Simplify these expressions:

a) $x^2 \times x^4$ b) $2x^2 \times 4x^{-3}$ c) $6p^3 \div 2p^2$ d) $6r^3 \times 2r^{-2}$
e) $8s^3 \div 2s^{-2}$ f) $(3a^3)^3 \div a^4$ g) $(3b^3)^2 \div b^2$ h) $6c^3 \times 2c^2 \times c$
i) $6r^3 \times 2r^2 \div r^2$ j) $(4d^3)^3 \div 2d^4$

EXERCISE

A Special Index: 0

Anything to the power 0 is equal to 1. The table below may help you see why this is true. Looking only at the second row, try to fill in the missing number from the sequence.

3^{-1}	3^0	3^1	3^2	3^3
$\frac{1}{3}$		3	9	27

EXAMPLES

1. $4^0 = 1$ 2. $(-124)^0 = 1$ 3. $x^0 = 1$

Negative Indices

A negative index means "one over" (or **reciprocal**). In other words, we take 1 over the base, then raise it to the index made positive.

EXAMPLES

1. $n^{-1} = \frac{1}{n}$ 2. $n^{-a} = \frac{1}{n^a}$

3. $3^{-2} = \frac{1}{3^2} = \frac{1}{9}$ 4. $\left(\frac{1}{2}\right)^{-3} = 2^3 = 8$ *(Remember: the reciprocal of ½ is 2)*

Note: the negative power does not make your answer negative!
2^{-1} = ½ not –½

Fractional Indices

If the index is a fraction, we must take a root of the number. For example, $4^{½}$ means take the square root of 4. Similarly, an index of $^1/_3$ means take the cube root.

EXAMPLES

1. $\left(\frac{9}{64}\right)^{\frac{1}{2}} = \sqrt{\frac{9}{64}} = \frac{3}{8}$ Note: in this example, we must take the positive square root of **each** value, numerator and denominator.

2. $8^{\frac{1}{3}} = \sqrt[3]{8} = 2$ (the cube root of 8)

3. $8^{-\frac{1}{3}} = \left(\frac{1}{8}\right)^{\frac{1}{3}} = \frac{1}{2}$ (the cube root of $\frac{1}{8}$)

4. $\left(\frac{1}{8}\right)^{-\frac{1}{3}} = \left(\frac{1}{1/8}\right)^{\frac{1}{3}} = 8^{\frac{1}{3}} = 2$

Remember that the **reciprocal** of 8 is $^1/_8$ and the **reciprocal** of $^1/_8$ is 8.

More Complicated Fractional Indices

If the index is a more complicated fraction, for example $^2/_3$, we must take the cube root of the number, then raise it to the power 2. For example, $8^{\frac{2}{3}}$ means take the cube root of 8, which is 2, then square it, which gives 4.

EXAMPLES

1. $a^{\frac{2}{3}} = \left(\sqrt[3]{a}\right)^2$

2. $8^{\frac{2}{3}} = \left(\sqrt[3]{8}\right)^2 = (2)^2 = 4$

3. $a^{\frac{5}{2}} = \left(\sqrt{a}\right)^5$

EXERCISE

EXERCISE 1D

1. Find the value of:

a) $8^{\frac{4}{3}}$ b) $9^{\frac{5}{2}}$ c) $16^{\frac{3}{2}}$ d) $16^{\frac{5}{2}}$

e) $16^{\frac{5}{4}}$ f) $27^{\frac{4}{3}}$ g) $64^{\frac{4}{3}}$ h) $81^{\frac{5}{4}}$

2. Simplify:

a) $\dfrac{8x^{\frac{3}{2}}}{4x}$ b) $-\dfrac{7x^{\frac{3}{2}}}{14x^{\frac{5}{2}}}$

3. Simplify these expressions:

a) 5^{-2} b) $4^{-2} \times 4^{-3}$ c) $g^{-3} \times g^{-3}$

d) $\dfrac{1}{t^{-2}}$ e) 64^0 f) $(q^3)^0$

g) $\left(\frac{1}{16}\right)^{\frac{1}{2}}$ h) $\left(\frac{1}{64}\right)^{-\frac{1}{2}}$ i) $\left(f^{\frac{3}{2}}\right)^2$

j) $64^{\frac{2}{3}}$ k) $\left(b^{\frac{1}{a}}\right)^a$

EXERCISE

Solving Equations

Sometimes we need to solve equations containing indices. You will often use the fact that:

$$\text{If } a^b = a^c \text{ then } b = c$$

EXAMPLE 1

Solve for y: $8^y = 64^4$

$$8^y = (8^2)^4$$

$$8^y = 8^8$$

$$y = 8$$

EXAMPLE 2

Solve for x: $\dfrac{6^x}{36^{x-2}} = \sqrt{6}$

$$6^x = (\sqrt{6})(36^{x-2})$$

$$6^x = \left(6^{\frac{1}{2}}\right)(6^2)^{x-2}$$

$$6^x = \left(6^{\frac{1}{2}}\right)6^{2x-4}$$

$$6^x = 6^{2x-7/2}$$

$$x = 2x - \frac{7}{2}$$

$$x = \frac{7}{2}$$

EXERCISE

EXERCISE 1E

1. Solve for the variable in the equation:

a) $\sqrt{2} = \dfrac{2^g}{4^2}$

b) $\sqrt{3} = \dfrac{9^4}{3^t}$

c) $\dfrac{\sqrt{3}}{3^{5f+2}} = 3^{-1/4}$

d) $\dfrac{2^y}{4^5} = \sqrt{2}$

e) $3^k = \dfrac{3^{2k+6}}{\sqrt{3}}$

f) $\dfrac{\sqrt{2}}{4^2} = 2^d$

g) $\sqrt{2} = \dfrac{2^w}{4^3}$

h) $\sqrt{3} = \dfrac{3^{4q+3}}{9^5}$

i) $\dfrac{4^2}{2^z} = \sqrt{2}$

j) $4^3 = \dfrac{2^g}{2^{6g+6}}$

EXERCISE

1.4 Surds

Introduction

A surd is a root, for example a square root or a cube root. You cannot usually find a simple integer answer for a surd, so they are often left in the solutions to equations, for example:

$$x = 1 + \sqrt{3} \quad \text{or} \quad z = \frac{\sqrt[3]{2}}{2}$$

Say it out loud: We would say "x equals 1 plus root 3" or "z equals the cube root of 2 over 2". In this way we can give more accurate answers to some problems.

EXAMPLE

What is the length of the diagonal of a square whose sides are 1 cm?

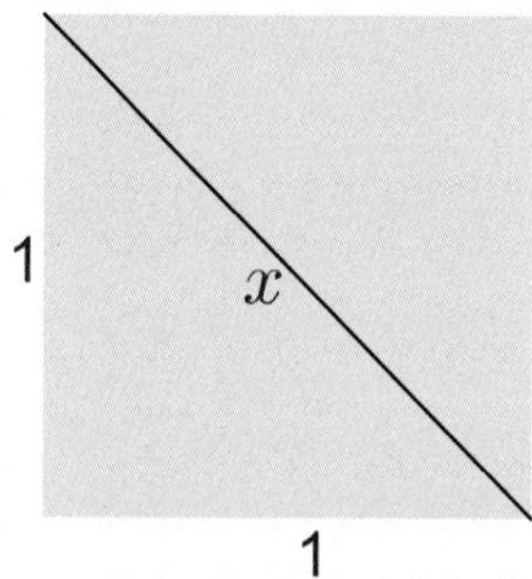

Using Pythagoras' Theorem:

$$x = \sqrt{1^2 + 1^2} = \sqrt{2} \text{ cm}$$

IN THE REAL WORLD – THE GOLDEN RATIO

One very famous use of surds is in the **Golden Ratio.** The Golden Ratio appears frequently in art and nature, as well as in mathematics and science. It is sometimes given the Greek letter phi Φ and has the equation:

$$\Phi = \frac{1 + \sqrt{5}}{2}$$

$$\Phi \approx 1.61$$

When it is used in art and architecture, the Golden Ratio is said to give the most beautiful results. The Acropolis in Greece was built over 2000 years ago. Some studies of this ancient building suggest that the Golden Ratio was used throughout, for example the width divided by the height of the front façade.

We also see the Golden Ratio in flower petals, pine cones, cauliflower florets, snails' shells and weather systems.

Use and Manipulation of Surds

In this section you will learn how to use and manipulate surds. There are two important rules to remember when using surds:

Rule 1: $\sqrt{a \times b} = \sqrt{a}\sqrt{b}$ Rule 2: $\sqrt{\frac{a}{b}} = \frac{\sqrt{a}}{\sqrt{b}}$

EXAMPLES

1. Simplify $\sqrt{30}$

$$\sqrt{30} = \sqrt{3}\sqrt{10}$$
$$= \sqrt{3}\sqrt{5}\sqrt{2}$$

2. Simplify $\sqrt{98}$

$$\sqrt{98} = \sqrt{49}\sqrt{2}$$
$$= 7\sqrt{2}$$

3. Simplify $\sqrt{\frac{121}{100}}$

$$\sqrt{\frac{121}{100}} = \frac{\sqrt{121}}{\sqrt{100}}$$
$$= \frac{11}{10}$$

4. Simplify $\sqrt{48} + \sqrt{108}$

$$\sqrt{48} + \sqrt{108} = \sqrt{3}\sqrt{16} + \sqrt{3}\sqrt{36}$$
$$= 4\sqrt{3} + 6\sqrt{3}$$
$$= 10\sqrt{3}$$

Rationalise the Denominator

Usually, we do not leave a surd in the denominator of a fraction. For example, we would **not** give the answer to a question like this:

$$y = \frac{1}{\sqrt{3}} \qquad \text{or this:} \qquad x = \frac{4}{\sqrt{5} + 2}$$

Instead, we must multiply both numerator and denominator by something to make the surd appear only in the numerator.

Method 1: If the denominator is a simple surd, multiply the top and bottom by this surd.

Method 2: If the denominator is the sum of a surd and a number, $a + \sqrt{b}$, multiply the top and bottom by $a - \sqrt{b}$ or $\sqrt{b} - a$.

EXAMPLE

Rationalise the denominator: $y = \frac{1}{\sqrt{3}}$

$$y = \frac{1}{\sqrt{3}} = \frac{1 \times \sqrt{3}}{\sqrt{3} \times \sqrt{3}} = \frac{\sqrt{3}}{3}$$

At the beginning of this chapter you revised the difference of two squares: $a^2 - b^2 = (a - b)(a + b)$. This can be applied to some surd problems.

EXAMPLE

Simplify: $(7 - \sqrt{5})(7 + \sqrt{5})$

This is an expression of the form: $(a - b)(a + b)$.

We can use the difference of two squares: $(a - b)(a + b) = a^2 - b^2$.

Therefore: $(7 - \sqrt{5})(7 + \sqrt{5}) = 7^2 - (\sqrt{5})^2$

$$= 49 - 5 = 45$$

EXAMPLE

Rationalise the denominator: $\dfrac{4-\sqrt{5}}{\sqrt{5}-2}$

$$\frac{4-\sqrt{5}}{\sqrt{5}-2}=\frac{(4-\sqrt{5})(\sqrt{5}+2)}{(\sqrt{5}-2)(\sqrt{5}+2)}=\frac{4\sqrt{5}-5+8-2\sqrt{5}}{5-2\sqrt{5}+2\sqrt{5}-4}=\frac{2\sqrt{5}+3}{1}=2\sqrt{5}+3$$

EXERCISE 1F

EXERCISE

1. Express $\sqrt{450}$ in the form $a\sqrt{2}$ where a is an integer.
2. Express $\sqrt{180}$ in the form $a\sqrt{5}$ where a is an integer.
3. Express $(5-\sqrt{2})^2$ in the form $b+c\sqrt{2}$ where b and c are integers.
4. Express $(6-\sqrt{5})^2$ in the form $b+c\sqrt{5}$ where b and c are integers.
5. Express $\sqrt{18}$ in the form $a\sqrt{2}$ where a is an integer.
6. Express $\sqrt{245}$ in the form $a\sqrt{5}$ where a is an integer.
7. Express $\dfrac{3(2+\sqrt{2})}{2-\sqrt{2}}$ in the form $b+c\sqrt{2}$ where b and c are integers.
8. Express $\dfrac{2(3+\sqrt{5})}{3-\sqrt{5}}$ in the form $b+c\sqrt{5}$ where b and c are integers.
9. Giving your answers in the form $a+b\sqrt{2}$, where a and b are rational numbers, find:

   a) $(6-\sqrt{8})^2$ b) $(1+\sqrt{8})^2$ c) $\dfrac{1}{5-\sqrt{8}}$ d) $\dfrac{1}{3+\sqrt{8}}$

10. Giving your answers in the form $a+b\sqrt{3}$, where a and b are rational numbers, find:

    a) $(7-\sqrt{27})^2$ b) $\dfrac{1}{6-\sqrt{27}}$

11. Expand and simplify:

    a) $(4+\sqrt{2})(4-\sqrt{2})$ b) $(7+\sqrt{2})(7-\sqrt{2})$ c) $(4+\sqrt{3})(4-\sqrt{3})$
    d) $(6+\sqrt{3})(6-\sqrt{3})$ e) $(3+\sqrt{5})(3-\sqrt{5})$ f) $(3+\sqrt{6})(3-\sqrt{6})$
    g) $(7+\sqrt{6})(7-\sqrt{6})$ h) $(7+\sqrt{7})(7-\sqrt{7})$ i) $(8+\sqrt{7})(8-\sqrt{7})$
    j) $(4+\sqrt{8})(4-\sqrt{8})$

12. Express in the form $a+b\sqrt{c}$, where a, b and c are integers:

    a) $\dfrac{6}{3+\sqrt{6}}$ b) $\dfrac{20}{3+\sqrt{5}}$ c) $\dfrac{24}{4+\sqrt{8}}$ d) $\dfrac{28}{2+\sqrt{2}}$

EXERCISE

SUMMARY

The laws of indices are:

Rule 1: $a^p \times a^q = a^{p+q}$

Rule 2: $a^p \div a^q = a^{p-q}$

Rule 3: $(a^p)^q = a^{pq}$

Rule 4: $a^0 = 1$

Rule 5: $a^{-p} = \dfrac{1}{a^p}$

Rule 6: $a^{\frac{1}{p}} = \sqrt[p]{a}$

Rule 7: $a^{\frac{p}{q}} = \sqrt[q]{a^p}$

You can use the following two rules to manipulate surds:

Rule 1: $\sqrt{a \times b} = \sqrt{a}\sqrt{b}$

Rule 2: $\sqrt{\dfrac{a}{b}} = \dfrac{\sqrt{a}}{\sqrt{b}}$

If there is a surd in the denominator you can **rationalise the denominator** by multiplying top and bottom by a surd expression:

Method 1: If the denominator is a simple surd, multiply top and bottom by this surd.

Method 2: If the denominator is the sum of a surd and a number, $a + \sqrt{b}$, multiply top and bottom by $a - \sqrt{b}$ or $\sqrt{b} - a$.

Chapter 2

Quadratic Functions and Simultaneous Equations

2.1 Introduction

Keywords

Quadratic: an equation containing x^2 or y^2, or sometimes both.

Parabola: the shape of some quadratic curves when plotted on a graph.

Vertex: The point at which a parabola is at its minimum or maximum.

Perfect Square: A quadratic expression that has two identical factors.

Root: A solution to an equation.

Repeated Root: The solution to an equation if there are two solutions that are identical.

Discriminant: In a quadratic expression, the value of $b^2 - 4ac$.

Before You Start

You should know how to:

Simplify surds, e.g. $\sqrt{98} = \sqrt{49}\sqrt{2} \quad = 7\sqrt{2}$

Expand brackets, e.g. $(x + 3)(2x - 4) = 2x^2 - 4x + 6x - 12 \quad = 2x^2 + 2x - 12$

EXERCISE

REVISION EXERCISE 2A

1. Simplify:

   a) $\sqrt{20}$ b) $\sqrt{80}$ c) $\sqrt{72}$ d) $(3 + \sqrt{5})(3 - \sqrt{5})$ e) $\dfrac{1}{2 - \sqrt{6}}$

2. Expand the following double brackets:

   a) $(x + 1)(x - 2)$ b) $(2x + 1)(2x - 3)$ c) $(1 - x)(1 - 3x)$

   d) $(1 - x)(1 + x)$ e) $(2p + 3)(3 - 5p)$

EXERCISE

What You Will Learn

In this chapter you will learn how to:

- Solve quadratic equations by:
  - Factorising
  - Completing the Square
  - Using the Quadratic Formula;
- Solve three simultaneous linear equations;
- Solve simultaneous equations involving powers;
- Solve linear and quadratic simultaneous equations;
- Solve quadratic inequalities;
- Solve simultaneous inequalities.

2.2 Quadratic Functions and Their Graphs

The general quadratic equation is:

$$y = ax^2 + bx + c \quad \text{or} \quad f(x) = ax^2 + bx + c$$

If $a > 0$, the shape of the curve is like this:

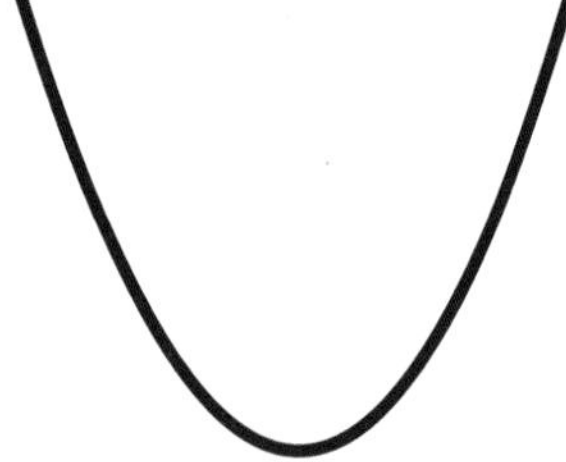

If $a < 0$, the shape of the curve is like this:

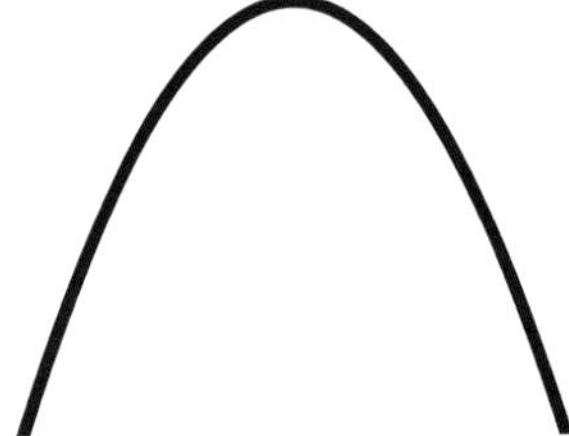

The shape of the quadratic curve is called a **parabola**.

An example of a quadratic is: $f(x) = 3x^2 - 2x + 4$

Another would be: $f(x) = x^2$

This is the simplest of all quadratic equations. It occurs when $a = 1, b = 0, c = 0$

If we want to find out where a quadratic curve cuts the x-axis, we must solve the equation

$$f(x) = 0$$

Often, we can do this by factorising the quadratic. You learnt at GCSE that if $a = 1$, we must find two numbers that add up to b and multiply to make c.

IN THE REAL WORLD – THE TELESCOPE

The reflecting telescope was invented by Isaac Newton in 1668 and similar mirrors are still in use today in astronomy. If you took a cross section through any of these mirrors, you would get the shape of a **parabola**, the curve we know from GCSE maths, described by a quadratic equation. The same parabolic shape is also used for the bowls of the giant radio telescopes, and even the satellite TV dish on the side of a house. Quadratic equations are at the heart of modern communications!

EXAMPLE 1

Where does the curve defined by: $f(x) = x^2 - 3x + 2$ intersect the x-axis?

We must solve: $x^2 - 3x + 2 = 0$

The two numbers that add up to −3 and multiply to make 2 are −1 and −2.

So factorising gives: $(x - 1)(x - 2) = 0$

Remember, if two terms multiplied make zero, one or both of them must equal zero.

So either $(x - 1) = 0$ or $(x - 2) = 0$ giving either $x = 1$ or $x = 2$.

Sometimes factorising and solving a quadratic equation leaves you with the same solution twice. This solution is known as a **repeated root.**

EXAMPLE 2

Where does the curve defined by $y = x^2 + 6x + 9$ meet the x-axis?

We must solve: $x^2 + 6x + 9 = 0$

Factorising gives: $(x + 3)(x + 3) = 0$

$$x + 3 = 0$$

$$x = -3$$

This curve meets the x-axis only once at the point (−3, 0), as shown in the diagram:

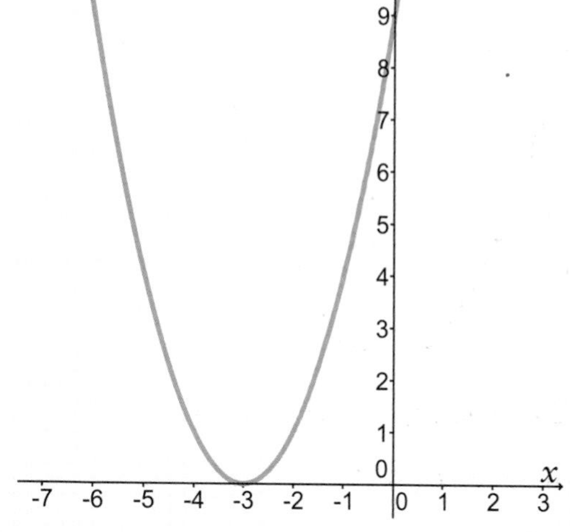

Note: Sometimes you will not be able to factorise and solve a quadratic equation.

Before solving a quadratic equation, you may need to re-arrange it to make the right-hand side zero.

EXAMPLE 3

Solve for x: $x(x - 1) = 2(x + 2)$

$$x^2 - x = 2x + 4$$

$$x^2 - 3x - 4 = 0$$

$$(x - 4)(x + 1) = 0$$

$$x = 4 \text{ or } x = -1$$

However, you may not need to expand the brackets.

EXAMPLE 4

Solve for x: $3x(x-1) = 2(x-1)$

Note that the brackets are the same on each side of the equation.

$$3x(x-1) - 2(x-1) = 0$$

$$(3x-2)(x-1) = 0$$

$$x = \frac{2}{3} \text{ or } x = 1$$

If the coefficient of the x^2 term is greater than one, factorising may be more difficult. The next example demonstrates one technique for solving this type of problem.

EXAMPLE 5

Factorise and solve: $2x^2 + 3x - 2 = 0$

Looking at the coefficients of the three terms, $a = 2, b = 3, c = -2$.

$$\Rightarrow ac = -4, b = 3.$$

We attempt to find two numbers whose product is –4 and whose sum is 3.

These numbers are 4 and –1.

Now take the quadratic equation and split the term in x, using these numbers:

$$2x^2 + 4x - x - 2 = 0$$

Factorise each pair of terms:

$$2x(x+2) - 1(x+2) = 0$$

The terms inside the brackets should be the same for each pair.

$$(2x-1)(x+2) = 0$$

$$x = \frac{1}{2} \text{ or } x = -2$$

Watch out for the **difference of two squares:** $a^2 - b^2 = (a-b)(a+b)$

EXAMPLE 6

Solve for x: $9x^2 - 64 = 0$

$$(3x)^2 - 8^2 = 0$$

Use the difference of two squares formula: $(3x-8)(3x+8) = 0$

$$x = \frac{8}{3} \text{ or } x = -\frac{8}{3}$$

EXERCISE

EXERCISE 2B

1. Solve the following quadratic equations:

a) $x^2 + 12x + 27 = 0$ b) $x^2 + 14x + 33 = 0$ c) $x^2 + 12x + 20 = 0$
d) $x^2 + 10x + 25 = 0$ e) $x^2 + 10x + 24 = 0$ f) $x^2 + 2x - 3 = 0$
g) $x^2 + 6x - 7 = 0$ h) $x^2 + x - 42 = 0$ i) $x^2 - 7x + 10 = 0$
j) $x^2 + 16x + 63 = 0$

2. Solve these equations for x:

a) $(x - 3)(x - 4) = 0$ b) $(2x - 5)(2x + 5) = 0$ c) $x(x - 4) = 0$
d) $3x(x - 1) = 0$ e) $2(x + 6)(x - 4) = 0$ f) $(x - 3)^2 = 0$
g) $7(1 - x)(x + 1) = 0$ h) $-5(1 - x)^2 = 0$ i) $(2x + 1)(2x - 7) = 0$
j) $x(x - 91) = 0$ k) $4(x + 6)(x + 8) = 0$ l) $(x + 1)^2 = 0$
m) $5(1 + x)(x - 1) = 0$ n) $-9(-1 - x)^2 = 0$ o) $(4x - 1)(8x + 1) = 0$

3. Expand the brackets to solve these quadratic equations for x:

a) $x(x - 6) = 2(x - 8)$ b) $x(x - 8) = 3(x - 6)$ c) $x(x - 9) = 3(x - 12)$
d) $x(x + 3) = 2(3x + 5)$ e) $x(x - 11) = 4(x - 14)$ f) $x(x - 8) = 4(15 - x)$
g) $x(x - 13) = 5(x - 16)$ h) $x(x - 7) = 3(x - 3)$ i) $x(x + 11) = -6(x + 12)$
j) $x(x - 7) = 6(x - 5)$ k) $x(x - 10) = 2(x - 18)$ l) $x^2 = 4(x - 1)$

4. Factorise these equations and hence solve for x. Leave your answers as fractions where appropriate.

a) $2(x + 1) - x(x + 1) = 0$ b) $5(3x - 2) - 2x(3x - 2) = 0$
c) $6(x + 2) = x(x + 2)$ d) $4(6x + 3) = -9x(6x + 3)$
e) $8(2x + 1) = -5x(2x + 1)$ f) $7(7x + 3) = 3x(7x + 3)$
g) $-8(-x - 5) = 3x(-x - 5)$ h) $4(5x - 5) = 7x(5x - 5)$
i) $-3(7x - 5) = 8x(7x - 5)$ j) $2(-8x - 4) = 2x(-8x - 4)$
k) $6(-5x - 9) = 2x(-5x - 9)$ l) $2(6x - 7) = 6x(6x - 7)$
m) $6(-5x + 7) = 9x(-5x + 7)$ n) $-7(7x + 6) = -2x(7x + 6)$
o) $-6(8x - 3) = -4x(8x - 3)$

5. Factorise these equations and solve:

a) $2x^2 + 5x - 3 = 0$ b) $2n^2 - 11n + 12 = 0$
c) $2z^2 - 19z + 24 = 0$ d) $3p^2 - 4p + 1 = 0$

6. Use the difference of two squares to solve the following:

a) $x^2 - 49 = 0$ b) $y^2 - 81 = 0$ c) $p^2 - 4 = 0$ d) $9z^2 - 49 = 0$
e) $q^2 - 9 = 0$ f) $25b^2 - 9 = 0$ g) $25c^2 - 16 = 0$ h) $64x^2 - 1 = 0$
i) $16y^2 - 4 = 0$ j) $64z^2 - 16 = 0$ k) $25m^2 - 49 = 0$ l) $49n^2 - 16 = 0$
m) $\frac{x^2}{36} - 1 = 0$ n) $\frac{y^2}{16} - 36 = 0$ o) $\frac{z^2}{36} - 25 = 0$ p) $\frac{p^2}{64} - 36 = 0$
q) $\frac{q^2}{81} - 16 = 0$ r) $\frac{r^2}{9} - 25 = 0$ s) $\frac{s^2}{64} - 49 = 0$ t) $\frac{t^2}{9} - 49 = 0$

EXERCISE

2.3 Completing the Square

We referred earlier to quadratic expressions that are perfect squares, which contain two identical factors. Some expressions of this type are:

$$(x-6)^2 \qquad (x+5)(x+5) \qquad x^2-6x+9$$

EXAMPLE 1

Solve the equation:

$$x^2-6x+9=25$$

$$x^2-6x+9=25$$
$$(x-3)^2=25$$
$$(x-3)=\pm 5$$
$$x=-2 \quad \text{or} \quad x=8$$

You can use a technique called **Completing the Square** for any quadratic expression. It will give you a perfect square term and a single number. The next example demonstrates this technique.

EXAMPLE 2

Complete the square for the expression: x^2+6x

The **coefficient** of x is 6. We take half of this coefficient and use it in our square term. We must also subtract the square of this number. So:

$$x^2+6x=(x+3)^2-9$$

(You could expand the brackets to check that this is correct.)

You can solve any quadratic equation using the Completing the Square technique. We make the left hand side of the equation a perfect square.

EXAMPLE 3

Solve the equation:

$$x^2+14x+10=7$$

Half the coefficient of x is +7. We use this in our square term. We must also subtract 7^2:

$$(x+7)^2-49+10=7$$

(You could expand the brackets to check that the left-hand side has not changed.)
Now collect all the number terms on the right-hand side:

$$(x+7)^2=46$$
$$x+7=\pm\sqrt{46}$$
$$x=-7\pm\sqrt{46}$$

You can also use Completing the Square when the coefficient of x is not 1.

EXAMPLE 4

Solve the equation: $2x^2 - 16x - 3 = 0$

Take the number term to the right-hand side. Factorise the left-hand side:

$$2(x^2 - 8x) = 3$$

$$x^2 - 8x = \frac{3}{2}$$

Complete the square for the left-hand side. The coefficient of x is –8.

$$(x - 4)^2 - 16 = \frac{3}{2}$$

$$(x - 4)^2 = \frac{35}{2}$$

$$(x - 4) = \pm\sqrt{\frac{35}{2}}$$

$$x = 4 \pm \sqrt{\frac{35}{2}}$$

$$x = 4 \pm \frac{1}{2}\sqrt{70}$$

EXERCISE 2C

EXERCISE

1. Solve the following equations for x by taking square roots:

a) $(6x + 15)^2 = 9$
b) $(5x - 3)^2 = 100$
c) $(7x - 12)^2 = 100$
d) $(8x + 8)^2 = 49$
e) $(5x + 9)^2 = 1$
f) $(6x - 13)^2 = 16$
g) $\left(\frac{x}{4} - 3\right)^2 = 4$
h) $\left(\frac{x}{5} - 13\right)^2 = 9$
i) $\left(\frac{x}{6} + 10\right)^2 = 64$
j) $\left(\frac{x}{5} - 2\right)^2 = 4$
k) $\left(\frac{x}{3} - 11\right)^2 = 1$
l) $\left(\frac{x}{6} + 12\right)^2 = 1$
m) $\left(\frac{x}{5} - 9\right)^2 = 4$
n) $\left(\frac{x}{3} + 3\right)^2 = 64$
o) $\left(\frac{x}{6} - 6\right)^2 = 36$

2. Solve these equations by completing the square.

a) $x^2 + 6x - 4 = 0$
b) $2x^2 + 8x + \frac{3}{2} = 0$
c) $x^2 + 2x + 3 = 7$
d) $2x^2 + 12x + 9 = 11$
e) $4x^2 - 16x + 3 = 7$
f) $2x^2 + 18x + 3 = 1 - 2x$
g) $3x^2 + 6x + 3 = 11 - 2x - x^2$
h) $-x^2 + 4x + 16 = 0$
i) $-7x^2 - 28x - 2 = -9$

EXERCISE

Discussion

Completing the Square is a powerful tool when you are asked to sketch the graph of a quadratic. You can quickly find the minimum or maximum value of the function and for which value of x it occurs.

EXAMPLE 1

Consider the quadratic: $y = x^2 + 6x + 2$

a) Complete the square to write this in the form $y = (x + a)^2 + b$

b) Find the minimum value of y.

c) What value of x gives this minimum value of y?

d) Find the points of intersection with both axes. Give **exact** answers.

---

a) $y = x^2 + 6x + 2$

$y = (x + 3)^2 - 9 + 2$

$y = (x + 3)^2 - 7$

b) The minimum value of y must be –7. The brackets squared will always be zero or more.

c) The brackets are zero when $x = -3$. So the coordinates of the minimum point are (–3, –7).

d) When $x = 0$, $y = 2$, so the curve crosses the y-axis at (0, 2). When $y = 0$:

$(x + 3)^2 = 7$

$x = -3 \pm \sqrt{7}$

So the curve crosses the x-axis at $(-3 + \sqrt{7}, 0)$ and $(-3 - \sqrt{7}, 0)$

You do not have a calculator in the C1 exam, so these coordinates must be left as surds.

Remember: if the **coefficient** of x^2 is negative, there will be a maximum point, not a minimum.

EXAMPLE 2

Consider the quadratic: $y = -x^2 + 4x + 12$

a) Complete the square to write this in the form

b) Find the maximum value of y.

c) What value of x gives this maximum value of y?

d) Sketch the curve, showing the points of intersection with the axes and the maximum point.

---

a) The solution:

$y = -x^2 + 4x + 12$

$y = -[x^2 - 4x - 12]$

$y = -[(x - 2)^2 - 4 - 12]$

$y = -(x - 2)^2 + 16$

b) The maximum value of y is 16, which occurs when the brackets are 0.

c) The brackets are zero when $x = 2$. So the coordinates of the maximum point are (2, 16). (Try some other values of x to convince yourself.)

d) When $x = 0$, $y = 12$, so the curve crosses the y-axis at (0, 12).

continued...

Example 2... When $y = 0$: $(x - 2)^2 = 16$

$$x - 2 = \pm 4$$

$$x = 6 \text{ or } x = -2$$

So the curve crosses the x-axis at $(6, 0)$ and $(-2, 0)$.

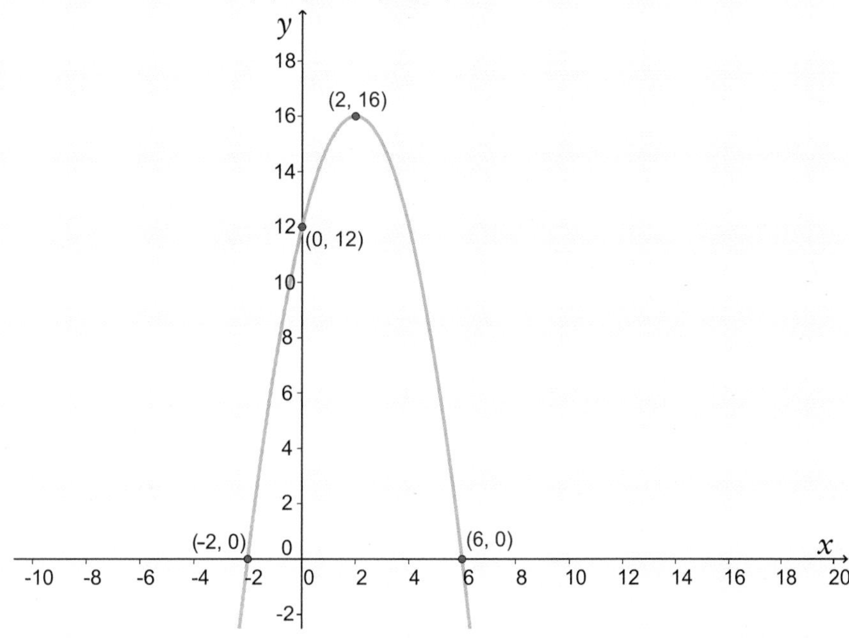

EXERCISE

EXERCISE 2D

1. For each of the following quadratic curves, find the coordinates of
   i) the point of intersection with the y-axis;
   ii) the minimum point.

   a) $y = x^2 - 2x + 20$
   b) $y = x^2 - 4x + 16$
   c) $y = x^2 - 10x + 12$
   d) $y = x^2 - 8x + 20$
   e) $y = x^2 - 6x + 16$
   f) $y = x^2 + 10x + 16$
   g) $y = x^2 - 18x + 16$
   h) $y = x^2 + 6x + 12$
   i) $y = x^2 - 14x + 20$
   j) $y = x^2 + 16x + 16$
   k) $y = x^2 + 12x + 16$

2. For each of the following quadratic curves, find the coordinates of
   i) the point of intersection with the y-axis;
   ii) the maximum point.

   a) $y = -x^2 + 10x + 8$
   b) $y = -x^2 - 6x + 16$
   c) $y = -x^2 - 8x + 16$
   d) $y = -x^2 + 10x + 16$
   e) $y = -x^2 + 12x + 8$
   f) $y = -x^2 - 14x + 12$
   g) $y = -x^2 - 16x + 20$
   h) $y = -x^2 + 18x + 20$
   i) $y = -x^2 - 4x + 12$
   j) $y = -x^2 - 6x + 14$
   k) $y = -x^2 + 18x + 10$
   l) $y = -x^2 + 14x + 14$
   m) $y = -x^2 - 12x + 6$
   n) $y = -x^2 + 14x + 8$
   o) $y = -x^2 + 16x + 14$

EXERCISE

2.4 The Quadratic Formula and the Discriminant

The Quadratic Formula

Apart from completing the square, there is another way to solve a quadratic equation, which uses a formula:

$$x = \frac{-b \pm \sqrt{b^2 - 4ac}}{2a}$$

You have probably seen this before at GCSE.
This formula is so frequently used, it is sometimes simply referred to as "The Formula"!

PROOF OF THE QUADRATIC FORMULA

Don't worry: you will not have to remember this proof!

We wish to find a solution to a general quadratic equation: $ax^2 + bx + c = 0$

Factorising gives: $$a\left(x^2 + \frac{b}{a}x + \frac{c}{a}\right) = 0$$

which means: $$x^2 + \frac{b}{a}x + \frac{c}{a} = 0$$

Completing the square gives: $$\left(x + \frac{b}{2a}\right)^2 - \left(\frac{b}{2a}\right)^2 + \frac{c}{a} = 0$$

Re-arranging gives: $$\left(x + \frac{b}{2a}\right)^2 = \left(\frac{b}{2a}\right)^2 - \frac{c}{a}$$

$$x + \frac{b}{2a} = \pm\sqrt{\left(\frac{b}{2a}\right)^2 - \frac{c}{a}}$$

$$x = -\frac{b}{2a} \pm \sqrt{\frac{b^2}{4a^2} - \frac{4ac}{4a^2}}$$

$$x = -\frac{b}{2a} \pm \sqrt{\frac{b^2 - 4ac}{4a^2}}$$

$$x = -\frac{b}{2a} \pm \frac{\sqrt{b^2 - 4ac}}{2a}$$

$$x = \frac{-b \pm \sqrt{b^2 - 4ac}}{2a}$$

Using the quadratic formula is a good idea if you cannot easily factorise a quadratic.

EXAMPLE 1

Solve: $x^2 + 2x - 7 = 0$

We cannot factorise this, so we use the formula. We use $a = 1, b = 2, c = -7$

continued...

Example 1...

$$x = \frac{-b \pm \sqrt{b^2 - 4ac}}{2a}$$

$$x = \frac{-2 \pm \sqrt{2^2 - 4(1)(-7)}}{2}$$

$$x = \frac{-2 \pm \sqrt{32}}{2}$$

$$x = -1 \pm 2\sqrt{2}$$

So there are two solutions to this equation:

$$x = -1 + 2\sqrt{2}$$

$$x = -1 - 2\sqrt{2}$$

EXERCISE

EXERCISE 2E

1. Solve these equations using the quadratic formula. Give your answers in simplified surd form.

a) $x^2 + x - 1 = 0$ b) $x^2 + 5x - 5 = 0$ c) $x^2 - x - 11 = 0$

d) $x^2 + x - 31 = 0$ e) $2x^2 - 2x - 2 = 0$ f) $2x^2 - 4x + 1 = 0$

g) $x^2 + 3x - 9 = 0$ h) $3x^2 + 4x - 1 = 0$ i) $x^2 + 2x - 6 = 0$

j) $2x^2 + 4x + 1 = 0$

2. Re-arrange these equations into the form $ax^2 + bx + c = 0$. Using the quadratic formula, find solutions to the equation, giving your answer in surd form.

a) $x^2 + 1 + 4x = 0$ b) $2x^2 - 1 + 5x = 0$ c) $-x + 3x^2 - 1 = 0$

d) $4x + 5 - 2x^2 = 0$ e) $4x - 1 + 4x^2 = 0$ f) $-2 + 3x^2 + 4x = 0$

g) $-2x - 1 + 2x^2 = 0$ h) $3x + 4 - 3x^2 = 0$ i) $-4x - 4 + x^2 = 0$

j) $-4x + 3 - 3x^2 = 0$

EXERCISE

The Discriminant

You probably remember from GCSE that some quadratic equations do not have a real solution. This occurs when $b^2 - 4ac < 0$.

Note: In the quadratic formula, we take the square root of $b^2 - 4ac$. You cannot find the square root of a negative number.

Because $b^2 - 4ac$ is so important, we give it a special name: **the discriminant.** The rules are as follows:

Discriminant $b^2 - 4ac$	
< 0	No solutions
$= 0$	Two solutions that are the same (a **repeated root**)
> 0	Two different solutions

EXERCISE

EXERCISE 2F

1. For each of the following equations, calculate the value of the discriminant. From this, decide whether the equation has two solutions, only one, or none at all. If there are solutions, calculate them, leaving your answer in surd form where appropriate.

a) $x^2 + 2x - 2 = 0$ b) $x^2 - 3x + 39 = 0$ c) $4x^2 + 2x - 1 = 0$

d) $x^2 - x + 19 = 0$ e) $3x^2 + 2x + 1 = 0$ f) $4x^2 + x + 2 = 0$

g) $4x^2 + x - 2 = 0$ h) $x^2 - x + 3 = 0$ i) $x^2 - 4x + 4 = 0$

j) $3x^2 - 3x - 3 = 0$ k) $x^2 + 2x - 4 = 0$ l) $3x^2 - 3x + 4 = 0$

m) $2x^2 - x + 4 = 0$ n) $5x^2 - 2x - 1 = 0$

2. The equation $x^2 + px + (p + 8) = 0$
where p is a constant, has two different real roots.
Show that $p^2 - 4p - 32 > 0$

3. Given that the equation: $kx^2 + 8x + k = 0$
where k is a positive constant, has a repeated root, find the value of k.

4. The equation: $4x^2 - 3x - (q + 2) = 0$
where q is a constant, has no real roots. Find the set of possible values of q.

5. The equation: $x^2 + 5tx + 2t = 0$
where t is a constant, has real roots. Prove that: $t(25t - 8) \geq 0$

6. In a right-angled triangle, the two shorter sides have lengths $2x$ and $x + 1$ cm.
The length of the hypotenuse is $2x + 1$cm. Find the lengths of the sides of the triangle.

EXERCISE

2.5 Simultaneous Equations

Revision

For this section, you will need to know how to re-arrange and solve linear equations.

EXAMPLE 1

Make p the subject of the equation $n = 4p - 3$

First isolate the term in p: $4p = n + 3$

Then, divide both sides by 4: $p = \dfrac{n + 3}{4}$

EXAMPLE 2

Solve the equation $2(x + 6) = 15$

Expand brackets: $2x + 12 = 15$

$2x = 3$

$x = \dfrac{3}{2}$

EXAMPLE 3

Factorise the quadratic expression $x^2 - x - 12$

The two numbers that have a product of –12 and sum –1 are: –4 and +3.

So: $x^2 - x - 12 = (x + 3)(x - 4)$

EXAMPLE 4

Solve the simultaneous equations:

$3x + y = 1$ (1)

$2x + 4y = 7$ (2)

Multiply one or both of the equations so that the x or the y terms are the same in both:

Multiply equation (1) by 4: $12x + 4y = 4$

Rewrite equation (2): $2x + 4y = 7$

The y terms are now equal. Subtract the equations: $10x = -3$

$$x = -\frac{3}{10}$$

Substitute into equation (1): $-\frac{9}{10} + y = 1$

$$y = \frac{19}{10}$$

EXERCISE

REVISION EXERCISE 2G

1. Make y the subject of these equations:
   a) $4x - 2y = 1$ b) $2x - 5 - y = 0$ c) $4(x + 3y) = 3$
   d) $5(x + 1) - 3(x + y) = 12$

2. For each linear equation, solve to find the unknown:
   a) $2(a + 3) = 6$ b) $15 - 2(b + 1) = 3$ c) $7 + c = 8 - c$
   d) $6d = 5(3d + 18)$ e) $\frac{3}{2 + e} = 4$

3. Factorise the following quadratic expressions:
   a) $x^2 + 11x + 18$ b) $x^2 - 10x + 24$ c) $x^2 - 6x + 5$
   d) $x^2 + x - 12$ e) $x^2 - x - 42$

4. Solve each pair of simultaneous equations:
   a) $6y + 6x = 6$, $3y + 5x = 5$
   b) $6x + 7y = 3$, $2x + 4y = 6$
   c) $6x + 2y = 42$, $-3x + 6y = -21$
   d) $8x + 6y = 62$, $-4x + 4y = 4$

EXERCISE

Further Simultaneous Linear Equations

Until now, you have solved simultaneous equations involving two variables, such as those in question 4 of the revision exercise above.

You will sometimes encounter systems of linear equations involving three variables.

Essentially, the same methods are used as for two variables: substitution and elimination. We usually eliminate one variable using two of the equations, then eliminate the same variable from a different pair of equations. This leaves two equations in two unknowns, which can be solved using the techniques you have revised above.

EXAMPLE 1

At a toll booth on a motorway, different prices are charged for cars, trucks and motorbikes. During one hour, 48 cars, 12 trucks and 4 motorbikes passed through the toll. The amount of money collected was £132. During the second hour, 36 cars, 24 trucks and 6 motorbikes passed through. The amount of money collected was £141. During the third hour, £141 was collected from 54 cars, 6 trucks and 12 motorbikes. Find the cost for a car, a truck and a motorbike to pass through the toll booth.

Let us say it costs £x for a car at the toll, £y for a truck and £z for a motorbike. Then:

$$48x + 12y + 4z = 132 \qquad (1)$$

$$36x + 24y + 6z = 141 \qquad (2)$$

$$54x + 6y + 12z = 141 \qquad (3)$$

Dividing equation (1) by 4 gives: $12x + 3y + z = 33$ (4)

Dividing equation (2) by 3 gives: $12x + 8y + 2z = 47$ (5)

Dividing equation (3) by 3 gives: $18x + 2y + 4z = 47$ (6)

Subtracting (4) from (5) eliminates x to give: $5y + z = 14$ (7)

We can also eliminate x from (5) and (6):

$3 \times (5)$ gives: $36x + 24y + 6z = 141$ (8)

$2 \times (6)$ gives: $36x + 4y + 8z = 94$ (9)

Subtracting (9) from (8) gives: $20y - 2z = 47$ (10)

Now we have two equations (7) and (10) involving the two variables, y and z.

$4 \times (7)$ gives: $20y + 4z = 56$

Subtract (10) gives: $6z = 9$

$$z = 1.5$$

Substituting z into (7) gives: $5y = 12.5$

$$y = 2.5$$

Substituting y and z into (4) gives: $12x + 7.5 + 1.5 = 33$

$$x = 2$$

So the prices are: cars £2, trucks £2.50, motorbikes £1.50.

Sometimes a set of equations needs some work before you obtain the set of simultaneous equations to solve.

EXAMPLE 2

Solve these simultaneous equations:

$$4^x \times 8^y = 4\sqrt{2} \quad (1)$$

$$8x - 3y = \frac{5}{2} \quad (2)$$

We must manipulate equation (1) to obtain a linear equation:

$$4^x \times 8^y = 4\sqrt{2}$$

Rewrite everything as a power of two: $(2^2)^x \times (2^3)^y = (2^2)\left(2^{\frac{1}{2}}\right)$

Using the laws of indices: $2^{2x} \times 2^{3y} = 2^{\frac{5}{2}}$

Add the powers on the left-hand side: $2^{2x+3y} = 2^{\frac{5}{2}}$

Because the bases are equal, the powers must be equal: $2x + 3y = \frac{5}{2}$ (3)

Now we have two linear equations, (2) and (3).

Adding them gives: $10x = 5$

$$x = \frac{1}{2}$$

Substituting x into (3): $2\left(\frac{1}{2}\right) + 3y = \frac{5}{2}$

$$3y = \frac{5}{2} - 1$$

$$y = \frac{1}{2}$$

Hint: when finding the final variable, substitute the variables you have found into the equation that looks simplest.

EXERCISE

EXERCISE 2H

1. Solve each set of simultaneous equations:

a) $3x - 2y + z = 1$
$2x + 2y + z = 15$
$x + 4y + z = 21$

b) $3x + y + 2z = 0$
$6x - z = 11$
$x + 2y + z = -13$

c) $x + y + 2z = 4$
$2y - z = 4$
$5x + 2y - 5z = 80$

d) $-x - y + 2z = -2$
$12x + 2y - 10z = 9$
$2x + 3y + 4z = -18$

EXERCISE

2. At Frugal Supermarket it costs me £1.22 to buy 6 apples, 2 bananas and 1 carrot. The man behind me in the queue buys 2 apples, 1 banana and 4 carrots. His bill is 93p. Following him is an old lady buying 1 apple, 6 bananas and 3 carrots. She is charged £1.96. What do apples, bananas and carrots cost?

3. At the local cinema, a packet of popcorn, a cola and a ticket for a film costs £9. Last week, I went with some friends. We bought 3 cinema tickets, 3 packets of popcorn and two colas. The cost was £25.50. Today I bought 2 tickets, 1 box of popcorn to share and no drinks, which came to £13. Assuming the prices have not changed, how much are the ticket, the popcorn and the cola?

4. Solve the simultaneous equations:

a) $\dfrac{4^p}{2^q} = 16$

$5p - 3q = 9$

b) $\dfrac{1}{\sqrt{x+6}} = \dfrac{3}{\sqrt{y}}$

$2y + 3x = 3$

c) $5^{2a}\sqrt{5} = 125^{b+1} \times 5^{\frac{3}{2}}$

$a + 3b = 11$

d) $9^{1-x} \times 27^{1-x} = 3^y\sqrt{3}$

$1 - 10x = y$

e) $10^{2m-5}\left(\dfrac{1}{100^n}\right) = \dfrac{1}{10^{m+n}}$

$4m - 3n = 0$

Simultaneous Quadratic and Linear Equations

At GCSE you learnt that you could think about simultaneous equations graphically. For example, if you were trying to solve the simultaneous equations:

$$x + y = 5 \qquad 3x + 5y = 19$$

You could draw a graph of the two lines:

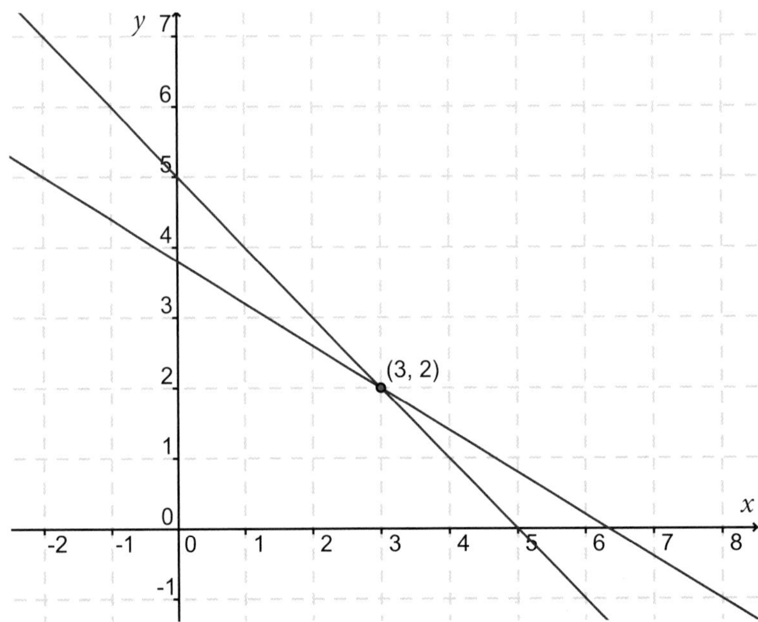

Because the lines intersect at the point (3, 2), the solution to the simultaneous equations is:

$x = 3, y = 2$

If the lines are parallel, there will not be a solution.

You can do a similar thing if one of the equations is a quadratic.

Sometimes there are two solutions, sometimes one and sometimes none as shown below.

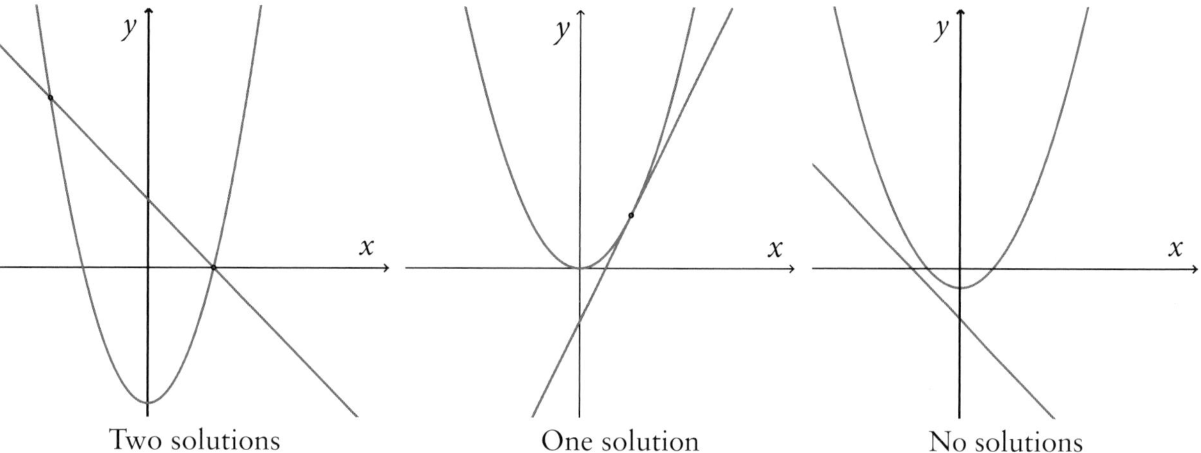

Two solutions One solution No solutions

The best way to solve simultaneous quadratic and linear equations is the **substitution method.**

EXAMPLE 1

Solve the simultaneous equations:

$y = x^2 - 4 \quad (1)$

$y = 2 - x \quad (2)$

Wherever y occurs in (1), substitute from equation (2)

$2 - x = x^2 - 4$

Simplify: $x^2 + x - 6 = 0$

Factorise: $(x + 3)(x - 2) = 0$

So: $x = -3$ or $x = 2$

When $x = -3$, $y = 5$

When $x = 2$, $y = 0$

EXAMPLE 2

Solve the simultaneous equations:

$x - 5y + 1 = 0 \quad (1)$

$x^2 - 5xy + y^2 = 15 \quad (2)$

This time, we substitute for x. Wherever x occurs in (2) we substitute from equation (1):

From (1): $x = 5y - 1 \quad (3)$

Substituting into (2) gives: $(5y - 1)^2 - 5(5y - 1)y + y^2 = 15$

Expand brackets: $25y^2 - 10y + 1 - 25y^2 + 5y + y^2 = 15$

Simplify: $y^2 - 5y - 14 = 0$

continued...

Example 2...

Factorise: $(y-7)(y+2)=0$

$y=7$ or $y=-2$

Using (3): When: $y=7, x=34$

When: $y=-2, x=-11$

You can also use this method to work out where a quadratic curve intersects a straight line on a graph.

EXAMPLE 3

By solving simultaneous equations, work out the intersection points of the straight line given by:

$$y+8x=0 \quad (1)$$

and the parabola given by:

$$y=x^2-9 \quad (2)$$

Substituting (2) into (1) gives: $x^2-9+8x=0$

Factorising gives: $(x-1)(x+9)=0$

$x=1$ or $x=-9$

So the intersection points are (1, –8), (–9, 72)

Note: If there are two solutions, always remember to pair your x and y values together correctly!

AMAZING, BUT TRUE

Not all quadratic equations are parabolas when plotted on a graph. The equation: $x^2-5xy+y^2=15$ gives a two-branch curve known as a **hyperbola,** as shown.

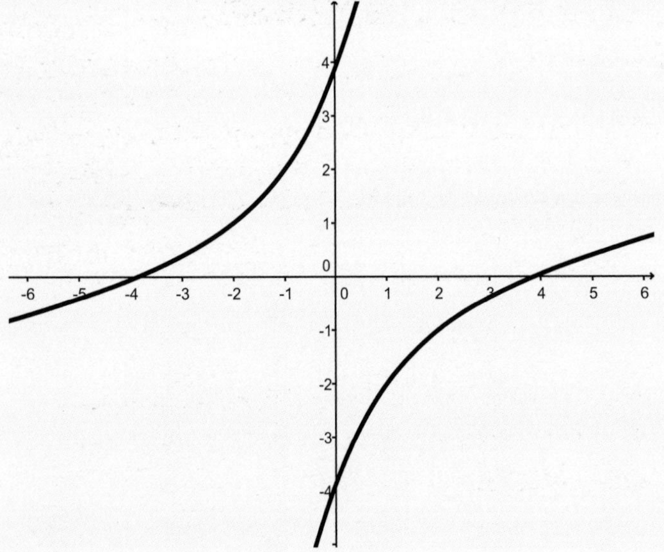

You can also get circles and ellipses. All four are from a family of curves known as **conic sections.**

Don't worry. Hyperbolas are not on the C1 specification.

EXERCISE

EXERCISE 2I

1. Solve each pair of simultaneous equations:

a) $x + y = 6$, $x^2 + 8y = 81$ b) $x + y = 4$, $x^2 + 4y = 48$ c) $x + y = 4$, $x^2 + 6y = 51$

d) $x + y = 2$, $x^2 + 4y = 29$ e) $x + y = 5$, $x^2 + 6y = 46$ f) $x + y = 5$, $x^2 + 4y = 32$

2. Solve the following pairs of simultaneous equations to find x and y:

a) $x - 3y + 1 = 0$, $x^2 - 3xy + y^2 = 11$ b) $x - 4y + 1 = 0$, $x^2 - 4xy + y^2 = 6$ c) $x - 3y + 1 = 0$, $x^2 - 3xy + y^2 = 19$

d) $x - 2y + 1 = 0$, $x^2 - 2xy + y^2 = 9$ e) $x - 4y + 1 = 0$, $x^2 - 4xy + y^2 = 22$ f) $x - 6y + 1 = 0$, $x^2 - 6xy + y^2 = 8$

3. Work out the intersection points of the following pairs of curves and straight lines:

a) $y = x^2 - 16$, $y + 6x = 0$ b) $y = x^2 - 25$, $y + 24x = 0$

4. Solve the simultaneous equations, giving your answers in the form $a \pm b\sqrt{3}$

a) $y = x - 4$, $2x^2 - xy = 8$ b) $y = x - 8$, $2x^2 - xy = 11$

EXERCISE

2.6 Solution of Linear and Quadratic Inequalities

IN THE REAL WORLD – MANUFACTURING

Simultaneous equations are used in industry, for the manufacture of many different products. For example, it may be important to maximise the profits on a particular type of breakfast cereal by reducing the amount of an expensive ingredient. But at the same time, it is important not to affect the flavour. There may be other important variables to consider as well, such as legal limits on particular ingredients. If each of these factors can be modelled by an equation, then we must solve them simultaneously to find a solution.

Revision

Solving an equation involves finding a particular value, or values, that satisfy that equation. Solving an **inequality** is different: you will find a set of values.

You did some work on solving linear inequalities at GCSE.

EXAMPLE 1 (REVISION)

Solve the following inequality and plot the set of values on a number line:

$$-3x - 3(x + 14) > 0$$

Expand brackets: $-3x - 3x - 42 > 0$

$$-6x - 42 > 0$$

$$-6x > 42$$

$$x < -7$$

(Remember: when you multiply or divide an inequality by a negative number, you reverse the inequality sign).

You also learned how to plot these answers on a number line, like this:

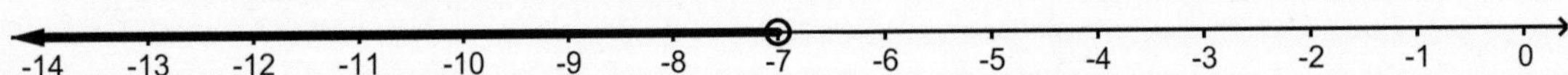

At the ends of these inequality lines, we use an open circle (as above) to indicate that the value is not included in the set (corresponding to a < or > sign), or a full circle to indicate that the value is included (e.g. if we were displaying the inequality $x \leq -7$). An arrow indicates that the set goes on indefinitely in that direction.

Solving Quadratic Inequalities

To solve a quadratic **inequality,** re-arrange the quadratic so that you could solve the associated **equation** $ax^2 + bx + c = 0$

You will also need to remember how to sketch a quadratic graph.

EXAMPLE 2

Solve the following inequality and plot the set of values on a number line:

$$x^2 + 2x > 8$$

Rearramge: $x^2 + 2x - 8 > 0$

So: $(x - 2)(x + 4) > 0$

Now sketch the graph of: $y = (x - 2)(x + 4)$

Consider the equation: $(x - 2)(x + 4) = 0$

This has the solutions: $x = 2$ or $x = -4$

We also know that the quadratic has a minimum point (not a maximum) because we have a positive x^2 term.

So the graph looks as shown on the right:

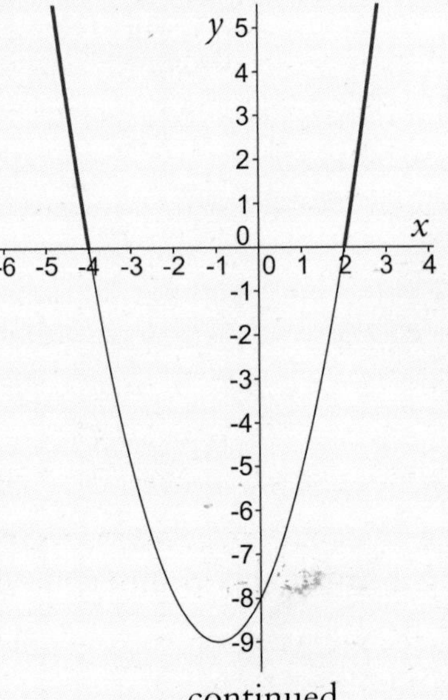

continued...

Example 2...

Now we can see that $(x-2)(x+4)>0$ is satisfied in the bolder regions of the curve.

The values of x are $x<-4$ or $x>2$

This composite set of values is shown as below:

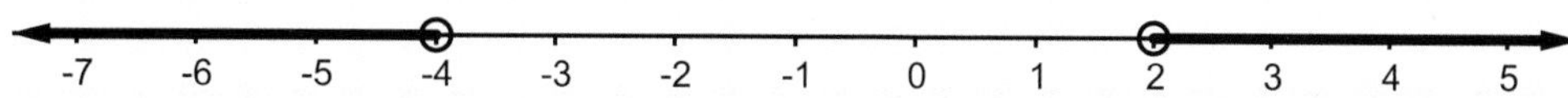

Sometimes you will be faced with simultaneous inequalities.

EXAMPLE 3

Find the values of x that satisfy both the following inequalities:

$$x^2+2x>8 \quad (1)$$

$$2x+1<3 \quad (2)$$

From Example 2 we know that inequality (1) is satisfied when $x<-4$ or $x>2$

(2) gives us: $x<1$

For both to be true, we must find where the two sets overlap.

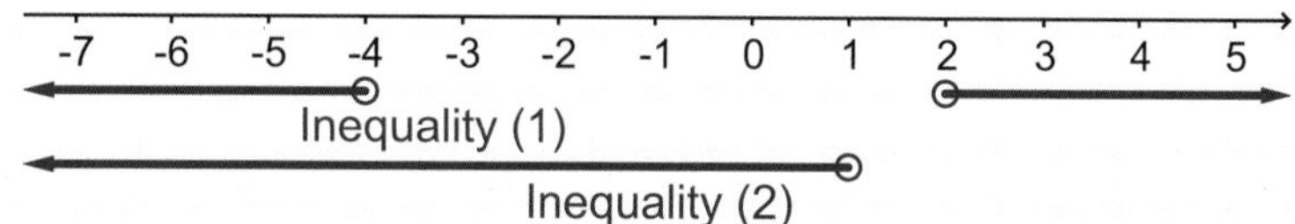

The set of values satisfying both inequalities is $x<-4$

EXAMPLE 4

Find the values of x that satisfy the inequality $-x^2-5x+6\geq 0$

Consider the graph of $y=-x^2-5x+6$. We must determine where the curve lies above the x-axis.

$y=-x^2-5x+6$
$y=-(x^2+5x-6)$
$y=-(x+6)(x-1)$

The curve crosses the x-axis at $x=-6$ and $x=1$.

It has a maximum point, since the coefficient of x^2 is negative.

Hence, a sketch of the curve is as opposite.

The curve is above the x-axis in the bold region, i.e. $-6\leq x\leq 1$

Note: We must use $\leq$ signs here, as specified in the original inequality.

(Check it: the values $x=-6$ and $x=1$ do satisfy the inequality.)

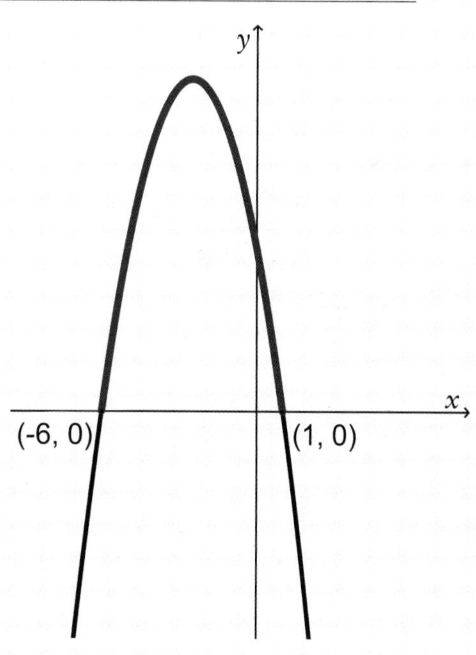

EXERCISE

EXERCISE 2J

1. Solve:

a) $7 + x \leq 14$ b) $x - 9 \leq 12$ c) $4x - 7 < x$ d) $1 - x \leq 6$

e) $\frac{3x}{2} - 1 \geq 1 - \frac{3x}{2}$ f) $6x - 1 < 65$ g) $12x + 7 > 8x + 3$ h) $6x - 1 < x$

i) $1 - x \leq x - 1$ j) $7x + 8 > 3x + 2$ k) $\frac{x}{2} > x + 3$ l) $6 - \frac{4x}{3} \leq \frac{21x}{5} + 2$

2. Find the set of values satisfying the following inequalities:

a) $2(t + 1) \geq 4(t - 1)$ b) $w - 4(3 - 2w) > 6$ c) $4p + 2(1 - p) \geq 2(2p + 1)$

d) $3v > 2(2v + 5)$ e) $z - 1 - 3(1 - z) < 0$ f) $3(u + 6) - 4u \leq 4(u - 1)$

3. By sketching an appropriate quadratic curve, find the set of values that satisfies each of the following inequalities:

a) $(x + 4)(x - 1) > 0$ b) $(x + 5)(x - 4) > 0$ c) $(x - 3)(x + 3) < 0$

d) $(2x - 3)(x - 4) > 0$ e) $-(x - 2)(x + 5) > 0$ f) $-(x - 1)(x + 4) < 0$

g) $(x - 2)(x + 5) < 0$ h) $-(x - 3)(x + 7) < 0$

4. Find the set of values that satisfy the following inequalities:

a) $x^2 - 2x - 24 \geq 0$ b) $x^2 - 3x - 10 > 0$ c) $x^2 + 2x - 3 < 0$ d) $x^2 - 5x - 24 > 0$

e) $x^2 + 3x - 88 < 0$ f) $x^2 + 2x - 99 > 0$ g) $x^2 - 3x - 10 > 0$ h) $x^2 - 6x - 16 \geq 0$

i) $x^2 + 3x - 4 < 0$ j) $x^2 + 2x - 8 > 0$ k) $x^2 - 4x - 12 > 0$ l) $x^2 + 6x - 16 < 0$

m) $x^2 + 3x - 154 < 0$ n) $x^2 - 5x - 36 \geq 0$

5. Find the values of x that satisfy the following inequalities:

a) $x^2 + 5x - 1 \geq 2x + 3$ b) $x^2 + 8x - 2 \leq 5x + 2$ c) $x^2 - 5x - 33 > -7x + 2$

d) $x^2 + 8x - 50 \geq 5x + 4$ e) $x^2 + 6x - 98 < 4x + 1$ f) $x^2 - 4x - 126 \geq -7x + 4$

g) $x^2 + 6x - 74 > 2x + 3$ h) $x^2 + 7x - 103 < 4x + 5$ i) $-x^2 + 6x + 2 > 2x - 3$

j) $-x^2 - x < -10x + 14$ k) $-2x^2 + 30 > -x^2 + 7x$

6. Using a number line to help, if necessary, find the set of values of x satisfying both inequalities:

a) $5x - 5 < 2x + 4$, $3x^2 - 15x + 12 < 0$
b) $7x - 10 < 3x + 4$, $-2x^2 + 12x - 10 > 0$
c) $8x - 9 \leq 3x + 4$, $2x^2 - 14x + 20 \leq 0$

d) $3x - 3 > x + 2$, $3x^2 - 18x + 15 > 0$
e) $5x - 5 \geq 3x + 3$, $-2x^2 + 11x - 5 < 0$
f) $9x - 7 > 4x + 2$, $x^2 - 5x + 4 \geq 0$

g) $5x - 8 \leq 3x + 4$, $3x^2 - 25x + 28 < 0$
h) $6x - 5 \geq 3x + 1$, $3x^2 - 17x + 10 > 0$
i) $5x - 7 \leq 3x + 3$, $-3x^2 + 20x - 12 \geq 0$

j) $6x - 7 < 4x + 4$, $3x^2 - 24x + 21 < 0$
k) $5x - 4 > 3x + 4$, $-3x^2 + 19x - 20 < 0$
l) $6x - 9 > 2x + 5$, $-3x^2 + 24x - 21 \leq 0$

EXERCISE

SUMMARY

You have now seen three techniques for solving a quadratic equation:

- **Factorising. Use this whenever possible.**
- **Completing the square.**
- **The quadratic formula.**

The second and third techniques can both be used in all cases, so unless you are specifically asked to use a particular technique, you can choose. However, it is good to be familiar with both methods.

To solve three simultaneous equations in three variables, eliminate one of the variables from two different pairs of equations. Then solve the remaining two equations in the remaining two variables.

To solve simultaneous equations where one is a quadratic, use the method of substitution.

When you solve any inequality, the solution is a range or set of values, not a single value.

Use the normal rules of algebra to re-arrange an inequality, but if you divide or multiply by a negative number, the inequality sign changes.

To solve a quadratic inequality, sketch a graph of the corresponding quadratic equation.

When solving simultaneous quadratic and linear inequalities, a number line is often useful, to see where the two sets overlap.

Chapter 3
Algebraic Manipulation

3.1 Introduction

IN THE REAL WORLD

The word algebra comes from the Arabic *al-jabr,* meaning restoration. The idea has been studied for thousands of years. The ancient Babylonians used algebra to calculate the square root of two, about 3000 years ago!

Keywords

Expanding: The process of removing the brackets

Factorising: Rewriting an expression as a product of its factors; the opposite of expanding brackets.

Terms: Each part of an algebraic expression, separated by + or – signs.

Like terms: Terms that contain the same variables, e.g. $4x$ and $2x$. However $4x$ and $4xy$ are not like terms.

Polynomial: A function of x, whose terms are ax^n for any values a and n, e.g. $4x^2 + 2x + 1$. (The last term has $a = 1$ and $n = 0$).

Before You Start

You should know how to:

Simplify algebraic expressions by collecting like terms;

EXAMPLE 1

Simplify: $q + 5p - 4q - (-3p) - pq$

---

1) Remember that $-(-3p)$ is $+3p$

2) Remember that you cannot mix your p or q terms with your pq term

So: $q + 5p - 4q - (-3p) - pq = 8p - 3q - pq$

Evaluate algebraic expressions;

EXAMPLE 2

Find the value of $x^2 + 3x$ given that $x = 5$

When $x = 5$

$$x^2 + 3x = 5^2 + 3(5) = 40$$

Expand brackets;

EXAMPLE 3

Expand: a) $-3x(2x + 4)$ b) $(4x - 1)(2x + 3)$

---

a) Remember that the minus sign affects all the terms inside the brackets:

$-3x(2x + 4) = -6x^2 - 12x$

b) Remember all four combinations and be careful with signs:

$$(4x - 1)(2x + 3) = 8x^2 + 12x - 2x - 3$$
$$= 8x^2 + 10x - 3$$

Factorise linear expressions;

EXAMPLE 4

Factorise: $-18x + 48y$

Note that each term has a factor of 6.

$-18x + 48y = 6(8y - 3x)$

Remember: you can always check your factorisation by expanding the brackets.

Factorise quadratic expressions;

EXAMPLE 5

Factorise: $x^2 - x - 6$

The coefficient of x^2 is 1.

The coefficient of x is –1.

The units term is –6.

We find two numbers that add up to –1 and multiply to make –6:

$x^2 - x - 6 = (x - 3)(x + 2)$

Again, you can check your factorisation by expanding brackets.

Recognise and use the Difference of Two Squares;

The general rule for Difference of Two Squares is:

$$a^2 - b^2 = (a - b)(a + b)$$

EXAMPLE 6

Solve: $9x^2 - 64 = 0$

$$(3x)^2 - 8^2 = 0$$
$$(3x - 8)(3x + 8) = 0$$
$$x = \frac{8}{3} \text{ or } x = -\frac{8}{3}$$

Perform long division without a calculator.

EXAMPLE 7

Calculate $702 \div 26$

$$\begin{array}{r} 27 \\ 26\overline{)702} \\ \underline{520} \\ 182 \\ \underline{182} \\ 0 \end{array}$$

The answer is 27 with no remainder.

REVISION EXERCISE 3A

1. Simplify:
   a) $a + 3a - b - 3b$ b) $2c - (-d) + c$ c) $2e - f + ef + f$
   d) $a^2 + b^2 - 5a + 6b - 2ab$ e) $a + 6b - 4b - 2a$ f) $d - (-7c) + (-2d) - c$
   g) $7e - 2f + 3f + ef$ h) $2g^2 + 3h^2 - 4g - 3h + 2gh$
2. Evaluate these expressions using the value of x given:
   a) If $x = 1$, find $3x - 7$ b) If $x = 2$, find $x^3 - 2x^2$
   c) If $x = 3$, find $3(1 - x)$ d) If $x = 4$, find $(x - 5)(x + 5)(x - 4)$
   e) $f(x) = x^2 - 2x - 7$. Find $f(1)$ f) If $x = 5$, find $x^2 - 2x + 1$
   g) If $x = 2$, find $2 + 2x^2$ h) If $x = 3$, find $3(1 - x)(2 - x)$
   i) If $x = 4$, find $(x - 4)(x^3 - 3x^2 + 21x - 17)$ j) $f(x) = 3x^2 + 2x - 7$. Find $f(1)$
3. Expand the brackets in the following expressions:
   a) $2v(1 + v)$ b) $-4(w^2 - 2)$ c) $y(3y + 1)$ d) $(4x + 3)(4x - 3)$
   e) $4v(2 + 3v)$ f) $-3(2w^2 - 1)$ g) $y(-2y + 6)$ h) $(4x + 4)(4x - 4)$
4. Factorise the following expressions:
   a) $-5y^2 - 25y$ b) $36p - 6p^3$ c) $26qr - 13r$ d) $-4s^5 + 5s^4$
   e) $-9y^2 - 24y$ f) $6p - p^2$ g) $16q - 8qr$ h) $3s^4 - 4s^3$
5. Factorise the following quadratic expressions:
   a) $x^2 + 5x + 4$ b) $x^2 + 20x + 100$ c) $x^2 - 12x + 27$ d) $x^2 - 15x + 54$
   e) $x^2 + 10x + 16$ f) $x^2 - 5x + 4$ g) $x^2 + 14x + 48$ h) $x^2 - 2x - 24$

EXERCISE

EXERCISE

EXERCISE

6. Use the difference of two squares to factorise the following:
   a) $x^2 - 4$ b) $16x^3 - 36x$ c) $x^2 - 9$ d) $9x^3 - 16x$
7. Calculate by long division:
   a) $1248 \div 24$ b) $9999 \div 99$ c) $2088 \div 32$ d) $2920 \div 71$
   e) $2208 \div 23$ f) $975 \div 39$ g) $5466 \div 65$ h) $3840 \div 85$

EXERCISE

What You Will Learn

In this chapter, you will learn how to:

- Divide by an algebraic fraction;
- Cancel algebraic terms;
- Put an algebraic expression over a common denominator;
- Perform algebraic division (similar to the long division above).

3.2 Algebraic Manipulation of Polynomials

All of the above skills (expanding brackets, collecting like terms and factorisation) will be put to use in this section. In addition, we will introduce further techniques, which you may or may not have met before.

Divide by an Algebraic Fraction

Remember that dividing by a fraction is easily achieved by turning the fraction upside down (finding the **reciprocal**) and multiplying instead of dividing.

EXAMPLE 1

Work out $16 \div \frac{2}{3}$

$$\begin{aligned} 16 \div \frac{2}{3} &= 16 \times \frac{3}{2} \\ &= \frac{48}{2} \\ &= 24 \end{aligned}$$

You can perform division by an algebraic fraction in the same way.

EXAMPLE 2

Simplify $\frac{1}{x} \div \frac{a+b}{c}$

$$\begin{aligned} &\frac{1}{x} \div \frac{a+b}{c} \\ &= \frac{1}{x} \times \frac{c}{a+b} \\ &= \frac{c}{x(a+b)} \end{aligned}$$

Cancel Algebraic Terms

You can also cancel algebraic terms in the same ways you have cancelled the terms in numerical fractions.

EXAMPLE 3

Simplify: $\frac{a^2 - b^2}{2} \times \frac{1}{a+b}$

$$\frac{a^2 - b^2}{2} \times \frac{1}{a+b}$$

$$= \frac{(a+b)(a-b)}{2} \times \frac{1}{a+b}$$

$$= \frac{a-b}{2} \times \frac{1}{1} \quad \text{(using the difference of two squares)}$$

$$= \frac{a-b}{2} \quad \text{(cancelling the two } (a+b) \text{ terms)}$$

Put an Algebraic Expression Over a Common Denominator

When algebra is involved, the common denominator can usually be found by multiplying the two denominators together.

EXAMPLE 4

Use a common denominator to simplify the following:

$$\frac{1}{x-1} + \frac{x}{x+3}$$

We use $(x - 1)(x + 3)$ as the common denominator.

Multiply top and bottom of first fraction by $x + 3$.

Multiply top and bottom of second fraction by $x - 1$.

Putting the two terms over this common denominator gives:

$$\frac{x+3}{(x-1)(x+3)} + \frac{x(x-1)}{(x-1)(x+3)}$$

$$= \frac{(x+3) + x(x-1)}{(x-1)(x+3)} = \frac{x^2+3}{(x-1)(x+3)}$$

EXERCISE

EXERCISE 3B

1. Factorise each expression, where possible, and simplify the fractions:

a) $\frac{x^2 - 14x + 45}{x - 9}$ b) $\frac{x^2 + 12x + 35}{x + 7}$ c) $\frac{x^2 + 6x - 7}{x - 1}$

d) $\frac{x^2 - 3x - 28}{x + 4}$ e) $\frac{x^2 + 5x + 6}{x + 3}$

EXERCISE

EXERCISE

2. Factorise and simplify:

a) $\frac{x^2 + 8x + 16}{x^2 + 5x + 4}$ b) $\frac{x^2 - 9x + 14}{x^2 - 8x + 7}$ c) $\frac{x^2 - 2x - 15}{x^2 + 4x + 3}$

d) $\frac{x^2 - 8x + 12}{x^2 - 3x - 18}$ e) $\frac{x^2 + 4x - 32}{x^2 + 6x - 16}$

3. Simplify:

a) $(x^2 + 3x - 4) \div \frac{x+4}{x+6}$ b) $(x^2 - 6x + 5) \div \frac{x-1}{x-8}$ c) $(x^2 - 4x + 3) \div \frac{x-3}{x+7}$

d) $(x^2 - 12x + 36) \div \frac{x-6}{x+9}$ e) $(x^2 + 3x - 54) \div \frac{x-6}{x-8}$

4. Put these expressions over a common denominator and simplify as far as possible:

a) $\frac{x}{x+1} + \frac{1}{x-1}$ b) $\frac{2}{3x-2} - \frac{4}{2x-3}$ c) $\frac{1}{(x^2+5x+6)} - \frac{2}{x+2}$

d) $\frac{4+2x}{(x-1)(x+2)} + \frac{3-x}{(x-1)(x-3)}$

EXERCISE

Simple Algebraic Division

Keywords

Degree: The highest power a polynomial contains. For example, a quadratic has degree 2.

Dividend: The polynomial being divided. The numerator.

Divisor: The polynomial being used to divide the dividend. The denominator.

Quotient: The answer.

Remainder: What is left over after division.

This technique is also known as **Polynomial Long Division.** It is very similar to the numerical long division you have already practised.

EXAMPLE 1

Work out: $\frac{x^3 + 3x^2 - 10x - 24}{x+4}$

Because this is a division, we set it out like this:

quotient

divisor → $x+4\overline{)x^3 + 3x^2 - 10x - 24}$

dividend

continued...

Example 1...

In the **divisor** $(x + 4)$, the **lead term** is x. What must we multiply x by to get x^3?

The answer is x^2. This must go above the second term in the answer line:

$$\begin{array}{r|l} & x^2 \\ \hline x+4 & x^3 + 3x^2 - 10x - 24 \end{array}$$

Now, multiply the divisor by this part of the answer, write the result on the next line down and subtract:

$$\begin{array}{r|l} & x^2 \\ \hline x+4 & x^3 + 3x^2 - 10x - 24 \\ & \underline{x^3 + 4x^2} \\ & \quad\;\; -x^2 \end{array}$$

At this point, we must bring down the term in the next column, –10x.

$$\begin{array}{r|l} & x^2 \\ \hline x+4 & x^3 + 3x^2 - 10x - 24 \\ & \underline{x^3 + 4x^2} \\ & \quad\;\; -x^2 - 10x \end{array}$$

Repeat the operation: what must we multiply the lead term x by, in order to get $-x^2$?

The answer is $-x$, so this goes in the next space in the answer line. Then multiply the divisor by the $-x$, write the result in the next line down, subtract and bring down the next term, –24:

$$\begin{array}{r|l} & x^2 \quad -x \\ \hline x+4 & x^3 + 3x^2 - 10x - 24 \\ & \underline{x^3 + 4x^2} \\ & \quad\;\; -x^2 - 10x \\ & \quad\;\; \underline{-x^2 - \;\,4x} \\ & \qquad\qquad -6x - 24 \end{array}$$

We perform the division for a third time: the lead term x goes into $-6x$ -6 times.

So -6 is the third term in our answer line. Again, multiply the divisor by this and write the result, $-6x - 24$, in the next line down. Performing the subtraction again gives 0:

$$\begin{array}{r|l} & x^2 \quad -x \quad\; -6 \\ \hline x+4 & x^3 + 3x^2 - 10x - 24 \\ & \underline{x^3 + 4x^2} \\ & \quad\;\; -x^2 - 10x \\ & \quad\;\; \underline{-x^2 - \;\,4x} \\ & \qquad\qquad -6x - 24 \\ & \qquad\qquad \underline{-6x - 24} \\ & \qquad\qquad\qquad\quad 0 \end{array}$$

The zero indicates that there is no remainder. So from this we can write down:

$$\frac{x^3 + 3x^2 - 10x - 24}{x + 4} = x^2 - x - 6$$

Because there is no remainder, we know that $(x + 4)$ is a factor of

$$x^3 + 3x^2 - 10x - 24$$

You can see that polynomial long division has a lot in common with numerical long division. Here are some rules to follow, to help you organise your work:

- You can use polynomial long division if the degree of the divisor is less than or equal to the degree of the dividend. In the above example, the divisor has degree 1; the dividend has degree 2.
- If the divisor has degree 1 (which usually means it has two terms), begin writing the quotient above the second term in the dividend. If the divisor has degree 2, begin writing the quotient above the third term in the dividend, etc.
- Sometimes, the dividend will not have a term in x^2, for example. If any terms are missing from the dividend, fill them in with zero terms, as shown in the next example:

EXAMPLE 2

Work out: $(x^3 - x + 5) \div (x - 1)$

Remember to include the $0x^2$ term in the dividend. Then proceed as before:

$$\begin{array}{r|l} & x^2 + x + 0 \\ x - 1 & x^3 + 0x^2 - x + 5 \\ & \underline{x^3 - x^2} \\ & \quad x^2 - x \\ & \quad \underline{x^2 - x} \\ & \qquad 0x + 5 \\ & \qquad \underline{0x - 0} \\ & \qquad\quad 5 \end{array}$$

The remainder is 5. From this we can say:

$$(x^3 - x + 5) \div (x - 1) = x^2 + x + \frac{5}{x - 1}$$

When writing out your answer like this, remember to put the remainder over the divisor. This is similar to saying:

$$11 \div 2 = 5\frac{1}{2}$$

EXERCISE

EXERCISE 3C

1. Use long division to rewrite these expressions:
   a) $(x^3 - x^2 - 2x) \div (x + 1)$
   b) $(x^3 + 2x + 3) \div (x + 1)$
   c) $(3x^3 + 2x^2 + 3x + 2) \div (3x + 2)$
   d) $(3x^3 + 4x^2 + 4x) \div (x + 1)$
   e) $(3x^3 - 2x + 2) \div (x + 2)$

2. Rewrite these expressions with a remainder:
   a) $(x^3 - x^2 - x + 1) \div (x + 1)$
   b) $(x^3 + 2x^2 - 3x + 1) \div (x + 2)$
   c) $(2x^3 + 3x^2 - 2x + 1) \div (x + 3)$
   d) $x^3 \div (x + 3)$
   e) $(3x^3 - 3x^2 - x - 4) \div (x + 3)$

3. Use long division to rewrite these expressions:
   a) $(x^4 + x^3 - x^2 + 1) \div (x + 1)$
   b) $(x^4 + x^3 + 3x^2 + 4x + 1) \div (x + 1)$
   c) $(2x^4 + 4x^3 - 4x^2 - 3x + 3) \div (x + 1)$
   d) $(2x^4 - 3x^3 + 3x + 1) \div (2x + 1)$
   e) $(2x^4 + 3x^3 - 4x^2 - 3x + 2) \div (x + 2)$
   f) $(3x^4 + 4x^3 - 3x^2 - 2x + 2) \div (x + 1)$

4. Using long division, rewrite these expressions with a remainder:
   a) $(x^4 + x^3 - 4x^2 - x + 1) \div (x + 2)$
   b) $(x^4 + x^3 + 3x^2 - 4x + 2) \div (x + 1)$
   c) $(x^4 + 3x^3 + 3x^2 + x + 2) \div (x + 3)$
   d) $(2x^4 - x^3 - 3x + 1) \div (x + 1)$
   e) $(3x^4 - 4x^3 - x^2 + 2) \div (x + 1)$

EXERCISE

3.3 The Remainder Theorem

The Remainder Theorem is a quick method to find the remainder following a polynomial division.

THE REMAINDER THEOREM

When any polynomial $f(x)$ is divided by $(ax - b)$, where a and b are real numbers, the remainder is $f\left(\frac{b}{a}\right)$.

(Similarly, when $f(x)$ is divided by $(ax + b)$, the remainder is $f\left(-\frac{b}{a}\right)$.)

PROOF OF THE REMAINDER THEOREM

(This is not in the course specification)

Consider the polynomial $f(x)$ and divide by $(ax - b)$. We are left with some function $Q(x)$ (the quotient) and a remainder r: $\frac{f(x)}{ax - b} = Q(x) + \frac{r}{ax - b}$

Multiplying throughout by $(ax - b)$ gives: $f(x) = (ax - b)Q(x) + r$

When $x = \frac{b}{a}$, $f\left(\frac{b}{a}\right) = \left[a\left(\frac{b}{a}\right) - b\right]Q(x) + r$

$$\Rightarrow f\left(\frac{b}{a}\right) = r$$

EXAMPLE 1

Find the remainder when $(x^2 + 7x + 4)$ is divided by $(x - 2)$.

Let $f(x) = (x^2 + 7x + 4)$.

As we are dividing by $(x - 2)$, we must evaluate $f(2)$:

$$\begin{aligned} f(2) &= 2^2 + 7(2) + 4 \\ &= 22 \end{aligned}$$

So dividing $(x^2 + 7x + 4)$ by $(x - 2)$ gives a remainder of 22.

Note: This method doesn't tell us anything about the quotient. It is, of course, possible to check your answer using long division.

EXAMPLE 2

Find the remainder when $f(x) = 8x^3 + 7x^2 - 3x - 4$ is divided by $(3x + 1)$.

According the remainder theorem, we must evaluate $f\left(-\frac{1}{3}\right)$.

$$\begin{aligned} f\left(-\frac{1}{3}\right) &= 8\left(-\frac{1}{3}\right)^3 + 7\left(-\frac{1}{3}\right)^2 - 3\left(-\frac{1}{3}\right) - 4 \\ &= -\frac{8}{27} + \frac{21}{27} + 1 - 4 \\ &= \frac{13}{27} - 3 \\ &= -\frac{68}{27} \end{aligned}$$

You will also find the remainder theorem useful when finding a missing constant in a polynomial function.

EXAMPLE 3

The function $f(x) = x^3 + ax^2 + 6x - 7$ has remainder -3 when divided by $(x - 2)$.

Find the value of a.

According to the remainder theorem, because the divisor is $(x - 2)$, we must consider $f(2)$.

$$\begin{aligned} (2)^3 + a(2)^2 + 6(2) - 7 &= -3 \\ 8 + 4a + 12 - 7 &= -3 \\ 13 + 4a &= -3 \\ 4a &= -16 \\ a &= -4 \end{aligned}$$

Sometimes you will combine these techniques. You will find an unknown constant, then use it to evaluate a remainder.

EXAMPLE 4

Given that $f(x) = 4x^3 + 3x^2 - 49x + c$ and that $f(x)$ has a factor $(x - 3)$:

a) Evaluate the constant c;

b) Factorise $f(x)$ completely;

c) Find the remainder when $f(x)$ is divided by $(2x - 3)$.

---

a) $f(x)$ has a factor $x - 3$. By the remainder theorem, this means that $f(3) = 0$.

$f(3) = 4\times3^3 + 3\times3^2 - 49\times3 + c$

$f(3) = 108 + 27 - 147 + c$

Because $f(x)$ has a factor $(x - 3)$,

$108 + 27 - 147 + c = 0$

$c = 12$

b) "Factorise completely" means factorise as fully as possible. Firstly, take out the factor of $x - 3$ we have already found:

$f(x) = (x - 3)(4x^2 + 15x - 4)$

The quadratic could be found by long division, which is left as an exercise for the reader. In this case, the function can now be written as the product of three linear terms:

$f(x) = (x - 3)(4x - 1)(x + 4)$

c) When $f(x)$ is divided by $(2x - 3)$, the remainder is given by $f\left(\frac{3}{2}\right)$:

$$f\left(\frac{3}{2}\right) = \left(\frac{3}{2} - 3\right)\left(4\left(\frac{3}{2}\right) - 1\right)\left(\frac{3}{2} + 4\right)$$

$$= \left(-\frac{3}{2}\right)(5)\left(\frac{11}{2}\right)$$

$$= -\frac{165}{4} \quad = -41\frac{1}{4}$$

EXERCISE 3D

EXERCISE

1. In each case, find the remainder when $f(x)$ is divided by the given linear function of x.
   a) $f(x) = 4x^3 + 4x^2 - 7x - 2$ divided by $(x + 2)$
   b) $f(x) = 3x^3 + 3x^2 - 6x - 2$ divided by $(x - 2)$
   c) $f(x) = 6x^3 + 5x^2 - 3x - 5$ divided by $(x + 1)$
   d) $f(x) = 7x^3 + 7x^2 - 4x - 1$ divided by $(x - 1)$
   e) $f(x) = 4x^3 + 2x^2 - 8x - 3$ divided by $(2x + 3)$
   f) $f(x) = 3x^3 + 5x^2 - 7x - 6$ divided by $(x + 2)$
   g) $f(x) = x^4 - 3x^3 - 2x^2 + 2x + 3$ divided by $(x + 1)$
   h) $f(x) = 2x^4 - 4x^3 - 5x^2 - 4$ divided by $(x - 2)$
   i) $f(x) = 3x^4 - 5x^2 - 5x - 4$ divided by $(x + 2)$
   j) $f(x) = 4x^4 - 4$ divided by $(x + 2)$

EXERCISE

EXERCISE

k) $f(x) = 2 + x^4$ divided by $(x - 2)$

l) $f(x) = -x + 3x^2 + 3x^3 + 4x^4$ divided by $(x + 1)$

m) $f(x) = 5x^4 - 3x^2 - 1$ divided by $(x - 1)$

n) $f(x) = -2 - x^2 + x^4$ divided by $(x - 2)$

2. Find the value of a given that $f(x) = x^3 + ax^2 + 10x - 11$

   has remainder –3 when divided by $x - 4$.

3. Given $f(x) = 4x^3 - 12x^2 - 4x + 12$,

   a) find the remainder when $f(x)$ is divided by $(x - 2)$.

   b) Given also that $(x + 1)$ is a factor of $f(x)$, factorise $f(x)$ completely.

4. Given that $f(x) = 3x^3 + 4x^2 - 13x + c$ and that $f(1) = 0$,

   a) find the value of c;

   b) factorise $f(x)$ completely;

   c) find the remainder when $f(x)$ is divided by $(4x - 2)$.

5. Given $f(x) = px^3 + 5x^2 + 11x + q$ and given that the remainder when $f(x)$ is divided by $(x - 1)$ is equal to the remainder when $f(x)$ is divided by $(2x + 1)$,

   a) find the value of p;

   b) Given also that $q = 3$, and p has the value found in part (a), find the value of the remainder.

6. Given $f(x) = 12x^3 + px^2 + qx + 6$ and given that $f(x)$ is exactly divisible by $(3x - 1)$, and also that when $f(x)$ is divided by $(x - 1)$ the remainder is –24,

   a) find the value of p and the value of q.

   b) Hence factorise $f(x)$ completely.

7. The function f is defined such that $f(x) = (x^2 + p)(5x + 74) + 222$

   where is p a constant.

   a) Write down the remainder when $f(x)$ is divided by $(5x + 74)$.

   Given that the remainder when $f(x)$ is divided by $(x - 6)$ is 3654,

   b) prove that $p = -3$;

   c) factorise $f(x)$ completely.

8. The function f is defined such that $f(n) = n^3 + pn^2 + 15n + 14$ where p is a constant.

   a) Given that $f(n)$ has a remainder of 5 when it is divided by $(n + 3)$, prove that $p = 7$.

   b) Show that $f(n)$ can be written in the form $f(n) = (n + 3)(n + s)(n + t) + 5$

   where s and t are integers to be found.

EXERCISE

3.4 The Factor Theorem

The Factor Theorem is a special case of the Remainder Theorem. It is a quick method for deciding whether $(x - a)$ is a factor of $f(x)$.

THE FACTOR THEOREM

If $(ax - b)$ is a factor of the polynomial $f(x)$, then $f\left(\frac{b}{a}\right) = 0$.

PROOF OF THE FACTOR THEOREM

(This is not in the course specification)

The factor theorem follows from the Remainder Theorem:

If $(ax - b)$ is a factor of the polynomial $f(x)$, then $(ax - b)$ divides $f(x)$ exactly and the remainder is zero.

Hence, by the remainder theorem, $f\left(\frac{b}{a}\right) = 0$

EXAMPLE 1

Show that $(x - 8)$ is a factor of

$f(x) = x^3 - 5x^2 - 18x - 48$

$$f(8) = (8)^3 - 5(8)^2 - 18(8) - 48$$
$$= 512 - 320 - 144 - 48$$
$$= 0$$

Hence, $(x - 8)$ is a factor of $f(x)$.

Note: Be careful with your signs!

If $f(a) = 0$, then $(x - \mathrm{a})$ is a factor.

If $f(-a) = 0$, then $(x + \mathrm{a})$ is a factor.

Sometimes, as in the Remainder Theorem, you will need to find a missing constant in the polynomial.

EXAMPLE 2

Find the value of a, given that $(x - 2)$ is a factor of $f(x)$,

where: $f(x) = x^3 + ax^2 + 9x - 10$

By the Factor Theorem, $f(2) = 0$

So $(2)^3 + a(2)^2 + 9(2) - 10 = 0$

$$8 + 4a + 18 - 10 = 0$$
$$16 + 4a = 0$$
$$a = -4$$

EXAMPLE 3

a) Show that $(x - 4)$ and $(x - 5)$ are factors of:

$f(x) = x^3 - 8x^2 + 11x + 20$

b) Factorise $f(x)$ completely.

---

a) $f(4) = (4)^3 - 8(4)^2 + 11(4) + 20$

$= 0$

Hence $(x - 4)$ is a factor of $f(x)$.

$f(5) = (5)^3 - 8(5)^2 + 11(5) + 20$

$= 0$

Hence $(x - 5)$ is a factor of $f(x)$.

b) $f(x) = (x - 4)(x - 5)(\ldots)$

$f(x) = (x - 4)(x - 5)(x + 1)$

This last step can be done by inspection to complete the final set of brackets:
- we must have $1x$ to give x^3 when multiplied out;
- we must have +1 to make the units +20 when multiplied out.

Alternatively, use long division to find the final linear factor.

If you know one linear factor of a cubic, there will be a quadratic factor that you can also find using long division. When you have found the quadratic, you might be able to factorise it to end up with three linear factors for the cubic. Of course, not all quadratics will factorise.

EXAMPLE 4

a) Show that $(x - 7)$ is a factor of $f(x) = x^3 - 10x^2 + 11x + 70$

b) Using long division, factorise $f(x)$ completely.

---

a) $f(7) = (7)^3 - 10(7)^2 + 11(7) + 70$

$= 0$

Hence $(x - 7)$ is a factor of $f(x)$.

b) Use long division to find the quadratic factor:

$$\begin{array}{r} x^2 \;\; -3x \;\; -10 \\ x-7\overline{)\, x^3 - 10x^2 + 11x + 70} \\ \underline{x^3 - 7x^2} \qquad\qquad\quad \\ -3x^2 + 11x \qquad \\ \underline{-3x^2 + 21x} \qquad \\ -10x + 70 \\ \underline{-10x + 70} \\ 0 \end{array}$$

Note: The remainder is zero because, as we have already discovered, $(x - 7)$ is a factor.

Hence:

$f(x) = (x - 7)(x^2 - 3x - 10)$

Now, factorise the quadratic:

$f(x) = (x - 7)(x - 5)(x + 2)$

Sometimes you may need to use trial and improvement to find one of the factors of a cubic, before going on to factorise it completely.

EXAMPLE 5

Factorise $f(x)$ completely, where:

$f(x) = x^3 - 5x^2 - 4x + 20$

Trial and improvement:

Guess $(x + 1)$ is a factor:

$$\begin{aligned} f(-1) &= (-1)^3 - 5(-1)^2 - 4(-1) + 20 \\ &= -1 - 5 + 4 + 20 \\ &= 18 \end{aligned}$$

Hence $(x + 1)$ is **not** a factor.

Guess $(x + 2)$ is a factor:

$$\begin{aligned} f(-2) &= (-2)^3 - 5(-2)^2 - 4(-2) + 20 \\ &= -8 - 20 + 8 + 20 \\ &= 0 \end{aligned}$$

Hence $(x + 2)$ is a factor.

Find the quadratic factor using long division:

$$\begin{array}{r} x^2 \quad -7x \quad +10 \\ x+2 \overline{\big) x^3 - 5x^2 - 4x + 20} \\ \underline{x^3 + 2x^2} \qquad\qquad \\ -7x^2 - 4x \qquad \\ \underline{-7x^2 - 14x} \qquad \\ 10x + 20 \\ \underline{10x + 20} \\ 0 \end{array}$$

Hence: $f(x) = (x + 2)(x^2 - 7x + 10)$

$= (x + 2)(x - 5)(x - 2)$

EXERCISE

EXERCISE 3E

1. For each of the following functions $f(x)$, decide whether or not the given linear expression is a factor.

a) $f(x) = x^3 + 5x^2 - 62x - 22$
$(x - 2)$

b) $f(x) = x^3 + 3x^2 - x - 18$
$(x - 2)$

EXERCISE

EXERCISE

c) $f(x) = x^3 - 2x^2 - 33x - 14$
$(x - 1)$

d) $f(x) = x^3 + 12x^2 + 39x - 59$
$(x + 1)$

e) $f(x) = x^3 + 4x^2 - 17x - 12$
$(x - 3)$

f) $f(x) = x^3 - 3x^2 - 6x - 20$
$(x - 5)$

g) $f(x) = x^3 + 11x^2 + 33x - 19$
$(x - 1)$

h) $f(x) = x^3 + 5x^2 - 35x - 4$
$(x - 4)$

i) $f(x) = x^3 - 6x^2 - 5x - 17$
$(x + 1)$

j) $f(x) = x^3 + 13x^2 + 44x - 14$
$(x - 2)$

k) $f(x) = x^3 + 5x^2 - 46x - 20$
$(x - 5)$

l) $f(x) = x^3 - 4x^2 - 14x - 49$
$(x - 3)$

2. Show that $(x - 8)$ and $(x - 9)$ are factors of $f(x) = x^3 - 13x^2 + 4x + 288$ and factorise $f(x)$ completely.

3. a) Using the factor theorem, show that $(x + 3)$ is a factor of:
$f(x) = x^3 - 2x^2 - 11x + 12$

b) Factorise $f(x)$ completely.

4. Given that $f(x) = 2x^3 + x^2 - 166x + 240$,

a) Use the factor theorem to show that $(x + 10)$ is a factor of $f(x)$.

b) Factorise $f(x)$ completely.

c) Write down all the solutions to the equation $2x^3 + x^2 - 166x + 240 = 0$

5. Find the value of a given that $(x - 2)$ is a factor of $f(x)$, where:
$f(x) = x^3 + ax^2 + 8x - 4$

6. Given that $(x - 3)$ is a factor of $f(x)$, where $f(x) = x^3 + px^2 + 9x - 9$, find the value of p.

7. Use the Factor Theorem to factorise $f(x)$ completely:

a) $f(x) = x^3 - x^2 - 16x + 16$

b) $f(x) = x^3 - 4x^2 - 3x + 18$

c) $f(x) = x^3 - 3x^2 - 9x + 27$

d) $f(x) = x^3 - 2x^2 - 9x + 18$

EXERCISE

SUMMARY

There are many ways in which an algebraic expression can be manipulated:

- You can divide an algebraic fraction by another by finding the reciprocal of the second fraction and multiplying.
- You can cancel algebraic terms if the same expression appears in numerator and denominator.
- You can use a common denominator when adding or subtracting expressions.

You can use **polynomial long division** to divide one polynomial by another, providing the degree of the divisor is less than or equal to the degree of the dividend.

If only the remainder is required, the **Remainder Theorem** is quicker than long division.

If you need to know whether a linear expression is a factor of a polynomial (i.e. the remainder is 0), the **Factor Theorem** can be used.

Review Exercise

Chapters 1 to 3

EXERCISE

1. Solve these equations for x:

   a) $(3x - 1)(4x - 9) = 0$ b) $(2x + 2)(3x + 5) = 0$ c) $4x(x + 8) = 0$

2. Expand the brackets to solve these quadratic equations for x:

   a) $x(x - 11) = 3(x - 15)$ b) $x(x - 12) = 4(x - 16)$ c) $x(x - 7) = 6(x - 6)$

3. Factorise these equations and hence solve for x. Leave your answers as fractions where appropriate.

   a) $8(-5x - 8) = 5x(-5x - 8)$ b) $-7(2x + 7) = -5x(2x + 7)$

   c) $4(-8x + 4) = -8x(-8x + 4)$

4. Use the difference of two squares to solve the following:

   a) $x^2 - 16 = 0$ b) $64x^2 - 25 = 0$ c) $\frac{x^2}{4} - 36 = 0$

5. Solve the following equations for by taking square roots:

   a) $(6x + 3)^2 = 25$ b) $\left(\frac{x}{3} + 13\right)^2 = 4$

6. Solve these equations by completing the square.

   a) $2x^2 + 32x + 5 = 9$ b) $2x^2 + 28x + 3 = 1$

   c) $3x^2 - 24x + 4 = 10$ d) $4x^2 - 16x + 2 = 10$

7. For each of the following quadratic curves, find the coordinates of

   i) the point of intersection with the y-axis

   ii) the turning point.

   a) $y = x^2 - 12x + 20$ b) $y = x^2 - 10x + 16$ c) $y = x^2 - 16x + 16$

   d) $y = -x^2 + 14x + 20$ e) $y = -x^2 - 8x + 12$ f) $y = -x^2 - 14x + 14$

8. Solve these equations using the quadratic formula. Give your answers in simplified surd form.

   a) $x^2 - 3x - 9 = 0$ b) $x^2 - x - 31 = 0$ c) $2x^2 + 2x - 3 = 0$

9. For each of the following equations, calculate the value of the discriminant. From this, decide whether the equation has two solutions, only one, or none at all. If there are solutions, calculate them, leaving your answer in surd form where appropriate.

   a) $x^2 + 2x - 4 = 0$ b) $3x^2 - 3x + 7 = 0$ c) $5x^2 - x - 2 = 0$

EXERCISE

10. Solve the following inequalities for x:

    a) $3 - x \geq -15$ b) $\frac{2x}{3} \geq 1 + \frac{4x}{5}$

11. Find the set of values that satisfy the following inequalities:

    a) $x^2 - 2x - 15 > 0$ b) $x^2 + 4x - 12 < 0$

12. Using a number line to help, if necessary, find the set of values of x satisfying both inequalities:

    a) $7x - 7 < 3x + 3$, $3x^2 - 13x + 4 \leq 0$ b) $8x - 10 < 3x + 2$, $2x^2 - 15x + 7 < 0$ c) $4x - 5 > 2x + 1$, $3x^2 - 14x + 8 \geq 0$

13. Put this expression over a common denominator and simplify as far as possible

    $$\frac{x+2}{(x+1)(3x+1)} + \frac{3-x}{(x-1)(3x+1)}$$

14. Use long division to rewrite these expressions:

    a) $\frac{x^2 + 4x - 1}{x - 2}$ b) $\frac{x^3 - 3x^2 + 1}{x - 1}$

15. Find the remainder when $f(x) = x^3 + 5x^2 + 4x + 1$ is divided by $(6x + 3)$.

16. For each of the following functions $f(x)$, decide whether or not the given linear expression is a factor.

    a) $f(x) = x^3 + 2x^2 - 13x - 6$, $(x - 3)$

    b) $f(x) = x^3 + 6x^2 + 16x - 21$, $(x + 3)$

    c) $f(x) = x^3 + 3x^2 - 22x - 24$, $(x - 4)$

17. a) Use the factor theorem to show that $(x + 7)$ is a factor of $f(x) = 2x^3 + x^2 - 71x + 140$

    b) Factorise $f(x)$ completely.

Chapter 4
Graphs and Curve Sketching

4.1 Introduction

At GCSE you learnt how to draw an accurate **plot** of a curve or straight line, usually from its equation and a table of (x, y) values.

At A-Level, you will often be asked to draw a **sketch** of a curve. A sketch does not have to be as accurate as a plot. But you will need to highlight certain key points, for example the general shape of the curve and where it crosses the axes.

Keywords

Cubic: An equation linking y and x in which there is a term in x^3.

Reciprocal: One over. For example, the reciprocal of 2 is $\frac{1}{2}$; the reciprocal of x is $\frac{1}{x}$.

Root: A solution. You can often find roots to $f(x) = 0$ by sketching a graph.

Asymptote: On a graph, a line that a curve approaches, but never touches.

Before You Start

You should know how to:

Factorise an expression.

Sketch the graph of a quadratic.

EXAMPLE 1

Factorise $x^3 + 3x^2 - 4x$

$$\begin{aligned} x^3 + 3x^2 - 4x &= x(x^2 + 3x - 4) \\ &= x(x + 4)(x - 1) \end{aligned}$$

EXAMPLE 2

Sketch the curve $y = x^2 - 6x + 8$

Firstly, because we have a positive coefficient of x^2, this curve has a minimum point. Factorising gives:

$y = (x - 4)(x - 2)$

To find out where the graph intersects the x-axis, we set $y = 0$:

$(x - 4)(x - 2) = 0$

$(x - 4) = 0$ or $(x - 2) = 0$

$x = 4$ or $x = 2$

To find out where the graph intersects the y-axis, we set $x = 0$:

When $x = 0$, $y = 8$.

We now have enough information to sketch the curve:

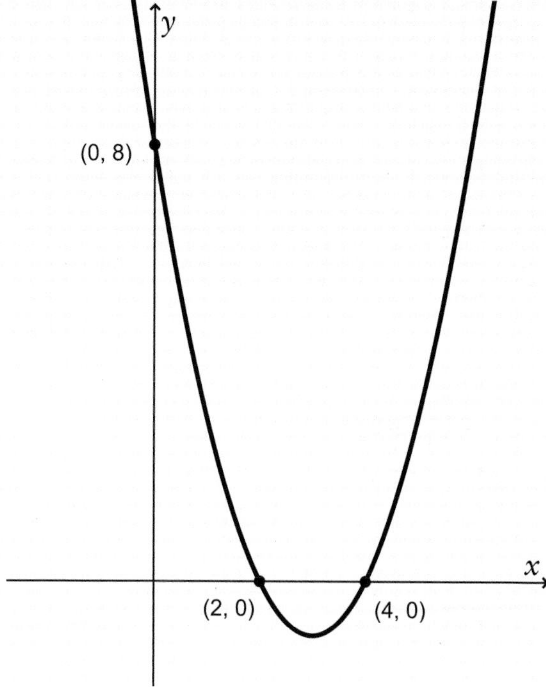

Remember that a sketch is exactly that! You do not need to draw a table of values or plot any (x, y) points exactly. You are not plotting a graph.

Instead, you will need to show the shape of the curve, and where it crosses the axes.

EXERCISE

REVISION EXERCISE 4A

1. Factorise the following expressions:

a) $x^3 + 5x^2 + 6x$　b) $9x^3 - 16x$　c) $9x^3 - 25x$

d) $x^3 - 4x^2 + 3x$　e) $x^3 - 3x^2 + 2x$

2. Sketch the following quadratic curves, indicating all important points, such as where the curves cross the axes:

a) $y = (x - 1)(x + 1)$　b) $y = x(x + 3)$　c) $y = x^2 - 2x - 3$

d) $y = -x^2 - 5x - 6$　e) $y = x^2 - 16$

EXERCISE

What You Will Learn

In this chapter you will learn how to:

- Sketch the graph of a cubic equation;
- Sketch a reciprocal curve;
- Solve equations using these graphs;
- Perform simple transformations on these graphs.

In Chapter 2, you learnt that Completing the Square is a useful technique for finding the maximum or minimum point of a parabola.

In Chapter 6, you will learn how to find the coordinates of the maximum or minimum points for all of the curves you are sketching.

These points are also known as the **turning points** or **stationary points.**

In this chapter, you will not mark these points on your sketches, but you will have to in an exam.

You will learn how to find the coordinates of stationary points in Chapter 6.

IN THE REAL WORLD – THE GHERKIN

Modern architecture is all about mathematics. A highly geometrically-shaped building like the Gherkin in London is often defined using a set of equations. A sketch of the building using these equations is a starting point for all modern architecture. There are many Computer Assisted Design software packages available to help in the task of designing a building. These help the architect not just with the physical appearance, but also with the airflow inside and around the building, the strength of the structure, ensuring there is enough light in and around the building, the location of doors and windows, etc.

4.2 Graphs of Functions: Sketching Cubic Curves

The general cubic equation is: $y = ax^3 + bx^2 + cx + d$

The shape of a cubic curve is typically one of these:

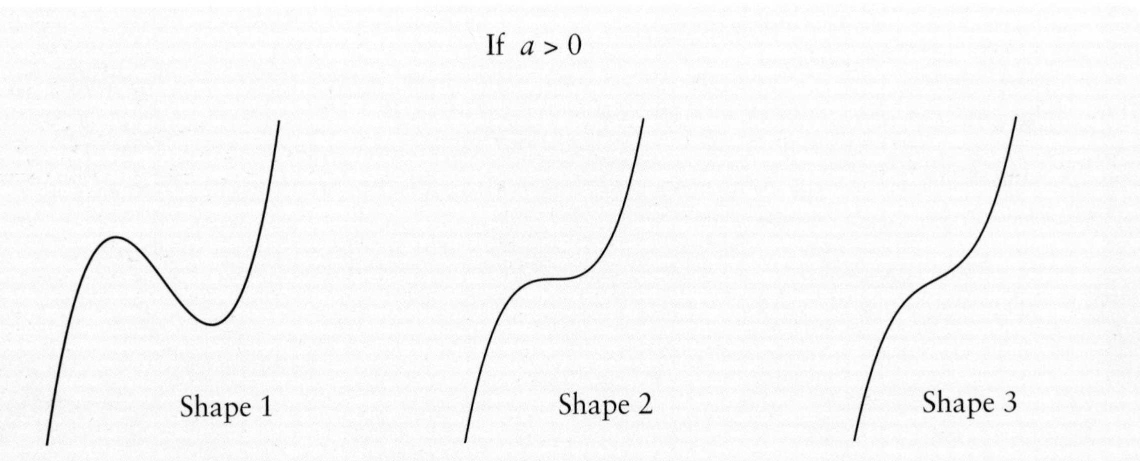

If $a < 0$

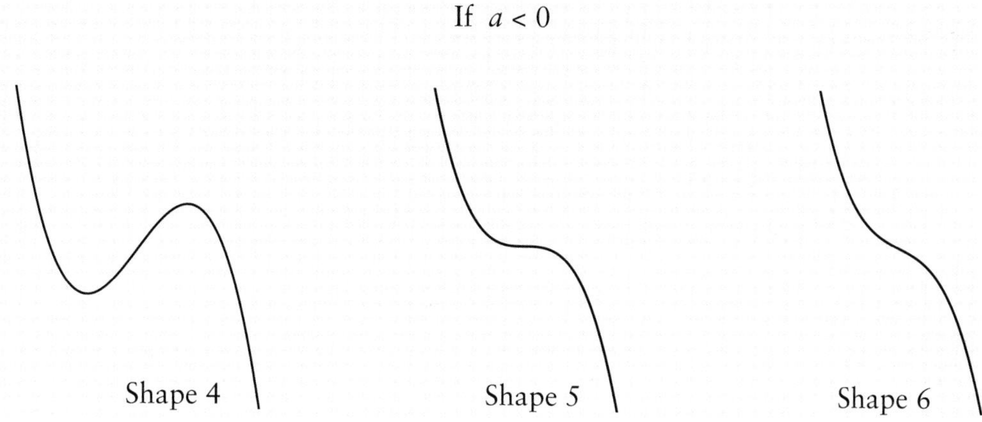

As with quadratic curves, it is possible to sketch a cubic curve without plotting exact points.

EXAMPLE 1

Sketch the graph of the cubic: $y = (x + 1)(x - 1)(x - 2)$

Expanding brackets, we obtain: $y = x^3 - 2x^2 - x + 2$

Firstly, note that the coefficient of the term x^3 is 1. (i.e. $a = 1$). This indicates that the curve takes one of the curve shapes 1 to 3 above, since $a > 0$.

Secondly, work out where the curve crosses the x-axis:

When $y = 0$: $(x + 1)(x - 1)(x - 2) = 0$

So either: $x = -1, x = 1$ or $x = 2$.

This curve crosses the x-axis in three places: (–1, 0), (1, 0) and (2, 0).

Because there are three crossing points, the curve must be similar to shape 1 above.

Finally, work out where the curve crosses the y-axis:

When: $x = 0$: $y = (0 + 1)(0 - 1)(0 - 2)$

So: $y = 2$

This curve crosses the y-axis at the point (0, 2).

We now have enough information to sketch the curve:

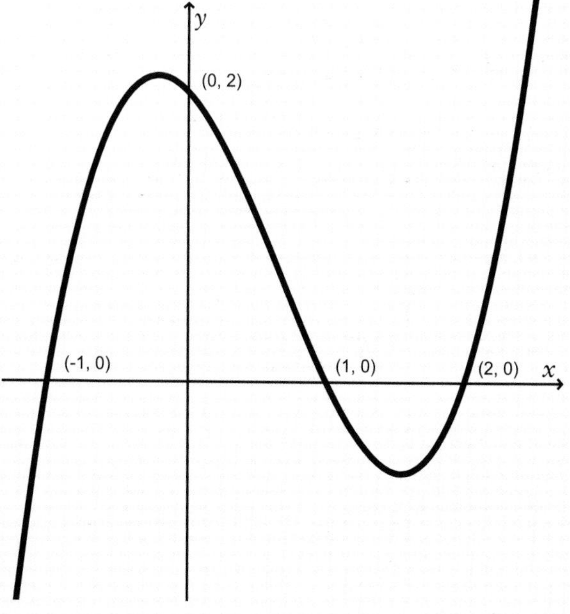

As discussed earlier, later in this book you will learn how to find the coordinates of the stationary points of a curve (one maximum and one minimum point in this case).

EXAMPLE 2

Sketch the graph defined by the equation:

$$y = -x(x-1)(x-2)$$

Tip: multiply out the two sets of brackets first:

$$y = -x^3 + 3x^2 - 2x$$

This time note that the curve is one of the curve shapes 4 to 6 above, since $a = -1$.

To find out where the curve crosses the y-axis:

When $x = 0$: $\quad y = -(0)(-1)(-2)$

$\qquad\qquad\qquad y = 0$

So the curve passes through (0, 0).

To find out where the curve crosses the x-axis:

When $y = 0$: $\quad x = 0, x = 1$ or $x = 2$

So the curve passes through (0, 0), (1, 0) and (2, 0).

Because there are three crossing points, the curve must be similar to shape 4 above.

We now have enough information to sketch the curve:

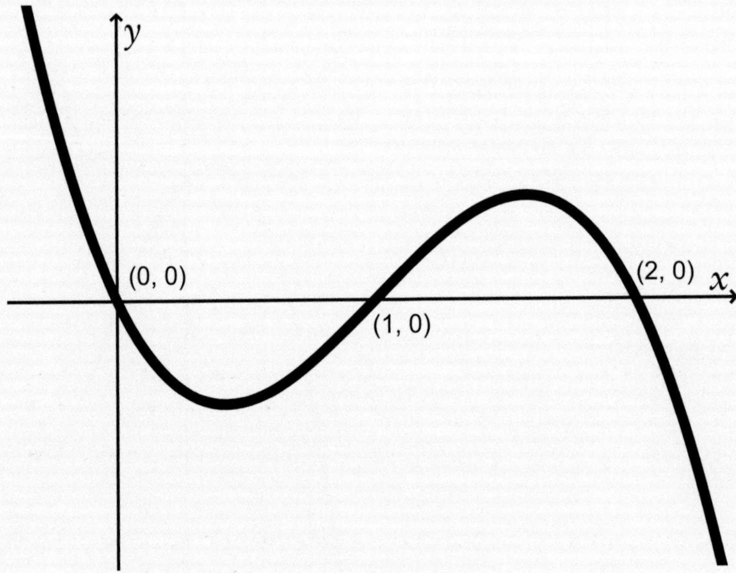

In the two examples above, we have looked at two cubics that both intersect the x-axis 3 times. This indicates that the solution to the equation $y = 0$ has three roots.

Here are some of the possibilities for the number of roots:

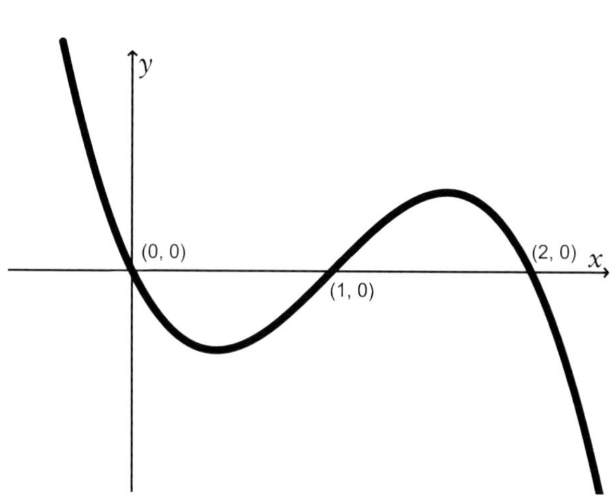

Three **unique roots.**
The example shown is:

$$y = -x^3 + 3x^2 - 2x$$

One **triple root.** The curve becomes flat on the x-axis. The example shown is:

$$y = -(x + 1)^3$$

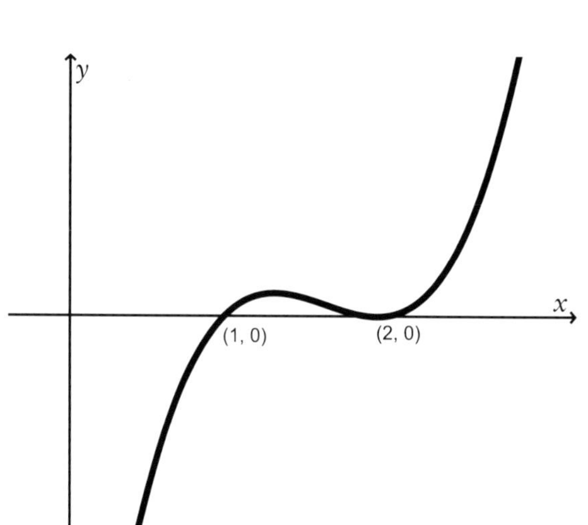

One **unique root** and one **repeated root.**
The example shown is:

$$y = (x - 1)(x - 2)^2$$

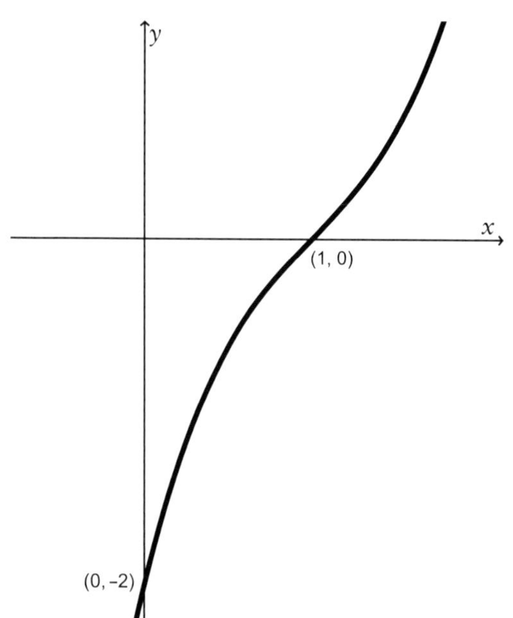

One **unique root.**
The example shown is:

$$y = x^3 - 3x^2 + 4x - 2$$

In the case of the **triple root,** notice that the curve is flat when it intersects the x-axis. This is a new type of stationary point, which is neither a maximum nor a minimum. We call it a **point of inflection.**

As with quadratics, it can be difficult or impossible to factorise some cubics. In the next example, you will learn a technique that can be used to estimate the number of roots of a cubic.

EXAMPLE 3

By sketching two suitable curves on the same diagram, estimate the number of roots of the equation:

$$y = x^3 - x - 3$$

First, note that it is not possible to factorise our function of x.

We are trying to solve:

$x^3 - x - 3 = 0$

This is equivalent to solving:

$x^3 = x + 3$

Now we can sketch the two curves:

$y = x^3$ and $y = x + 3$

Any intersection points will be the roots of our original equation.

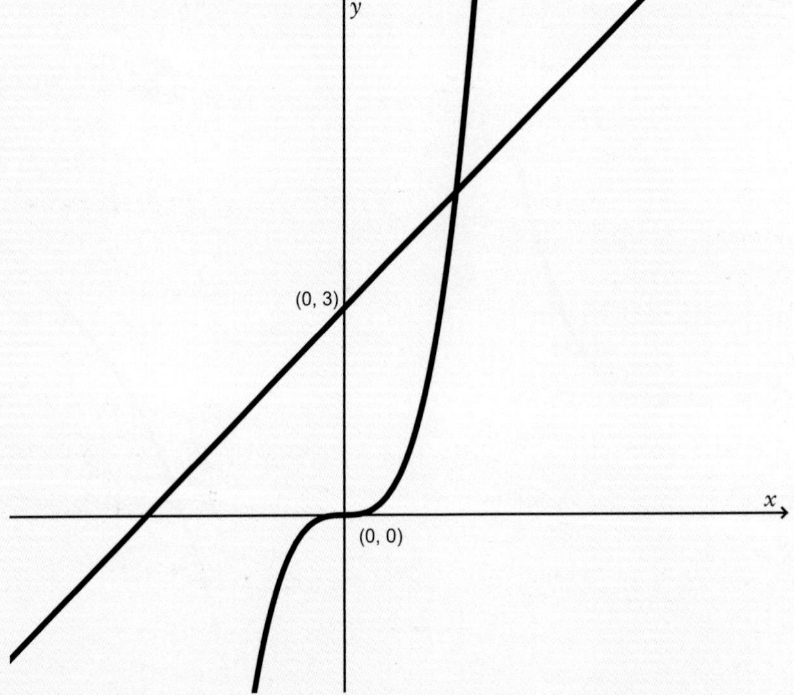

We can see that the two curves intersect once.
This means there is one root to the original equation $y = x^3 - x - 3$

Note: the question does not ask us to find or estimate the solution(s). It only asks how many there are.

Note the use of the word **curve** in this example.
Two **curves** were sketched, even though one is a straight line.
It may seem odd, but straight lines are all curves.

EXERCISE

EXERCISE 4B

1. State where each curve intersects both the y-axis and the x-axis.

a) $f(x) = (x + 4)(x - 3)(x + 1)$
b) $f(x) = -(x - 3)(x - 9)(x + 1)$
c) $f(x) = x(x - 3)(x + 2)$
d) $f(x) = -x(x - 9)(8 - x)$
e) $f(x) = (2x - 1)(x - 3)^2$
f) $f(x) = (2x + 1)x^2$
g) $f(x) = -x(x^2 - 25)$
h) $f(x) = (x + 3)^3$
i) $f(x) = (2x - 1)^3$
j) $f(x) = x^3 - 12x^2 + 36x$

2. Factorise and find the roots of each equation. Hence sketch the curves.

a) $y = x^3 - 18x^2 + 81x$
b) $y = x^3 - 30x^2 + 225x$

3. Factorise and find solutions to $f(x) = 0$. Hence sketch the curve $y = f(x)$.

a) $f(x) = x^3 + 5x^2 + 6x$
b) $f(x) = x^3 + 18x^2 + 80x$
c) $f(x) = -x^3 - 11x^2 - 10x$
d) $f(x) = x^3 + 13x^2 + 40x$
e) $f(x) = x^3 + 17x^2 + 70x$
f) $f(x) = 16x^3 - 25x$
g) $f(x) = 9x^3 - 16x$
h) $f(x) = -x^3 + 3x^2 - 2x$
i) $f(x) = x^3 - 5x^2 + 4x$
j) $f(x) = -x^3 + 12x^2 - 35x$

4. Given each function $f(x)$ below:
i) Express $f(x)$ in the form $x(ax^2 + bx + c)$ where a, b and are c constants.
ii) Hence factorise $f(x)$ completely.
iii) Sketch the curve $y = f(x)$.
iv) State the roots of the equation $f(x) = 0$.

a) $f(x) = (x^2 - 8x)(x - 4) + 3x$
b) $f(x) = (x^2 - 8x)(x - 3) + 4x$
c) $f(x) = -(x^2 - 9x)(x - 5) - 3x$

EXERCISE

4.3 Graphs of Functions: Sketching Reciprocal Curves

The general form of a reciprocal curve is: $y = \frac{k}{x}$ where k is an integer.

A sketch of a reciprocal graph looks like one of these two:

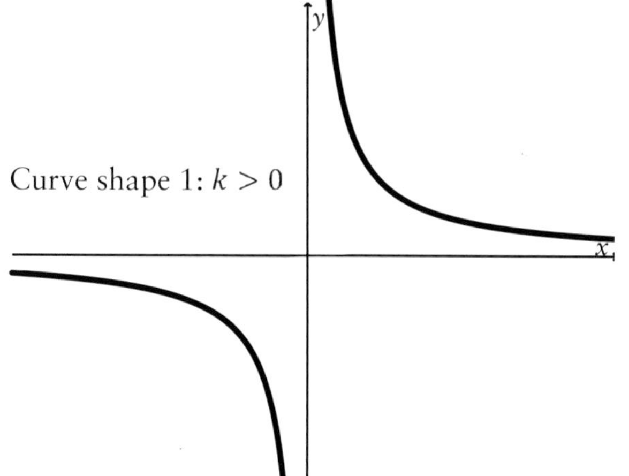

Curve shape 1: $k > 0$

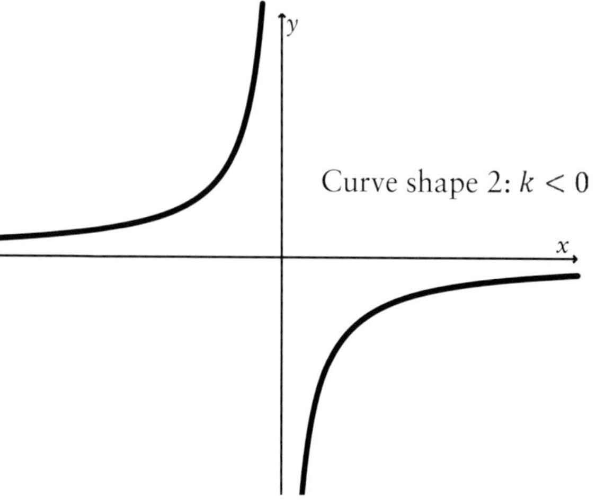

Curve shape 2: $k < 0$

You may not have seen curves that have two distinct branches, like this, before.
In the first case, you can see that y gets closer and closer to zero as x gets closer to infinity.

We say: y approaches 0 as x approaches infinity.

And we write: $y \to 0$ as $x \to \infty$

For curve shape 2: $y \to 0$ as $x \to -\infty$

The lines $x = 0$ and $y = 0$ are therefore **asymptotes** of both curves.

The curves approach these lines, but never touch them.

Looking at the equation of the curve, $y = \frac{k}{x}$, you can see that x can never take the value 0, because you cannot divide by 0. If you were sketching a reciprocal curve, you could use this technique to discover where the asymptotes lie. The line $x = 0$ must be one asymptote.

If you re-arranged the equation, you would also see that y cannot be 0, so the line $y = 0$ is the second asymptote.

EXAMPLE 1

Sketch the graph of: $y = \frac{2}{x}$

A table of values gives these points:

x	–4	–2	–1	–0.5	0.5	1	2	4
y	–0.5	–1	–2	–4	4	2	1	0.5

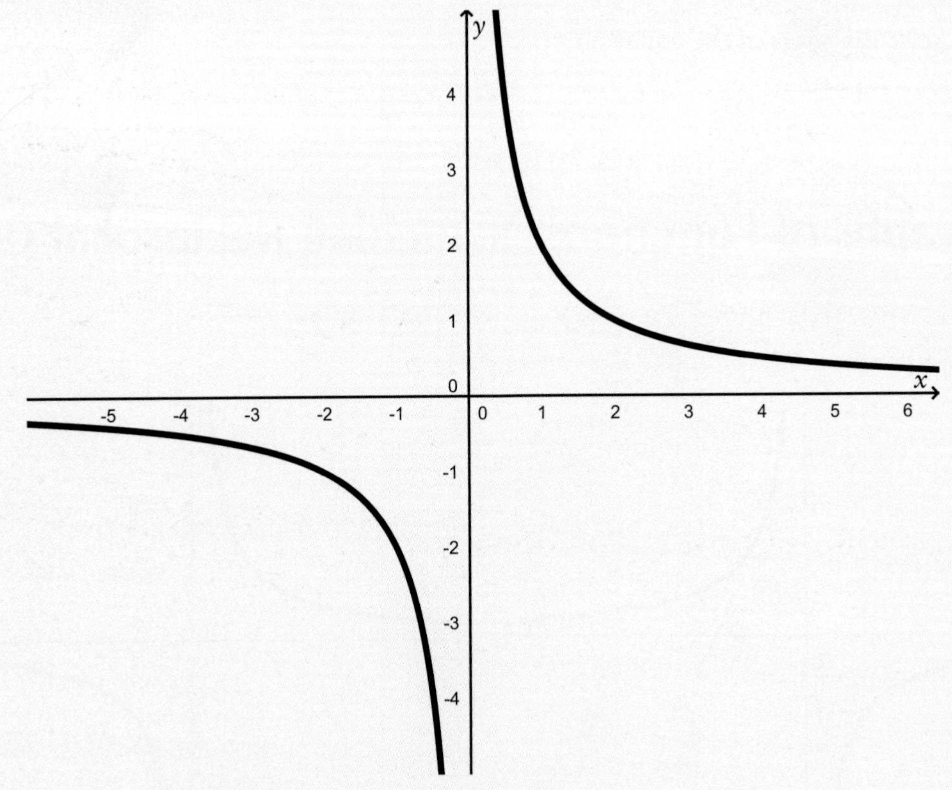

The lines $x = 0$ and $y = 0$ are asymptotes to the curve.

Now that you know the general shape of the reciprocal curve, you do not need to draw a table of values for every sketch.

EXAMPLE 2

Sketch the curves

$$y = -\frac{2}{x} \text{ and } y = -\frac{4}{x}$$

on the same diagram.

Recall that this type of reciprocal curve has asymptotes along $x = 0$ and $y = 0$.

We can also see that the second curve will always have y-values double those of the first curve.

Using this information, the sketch looks like this:

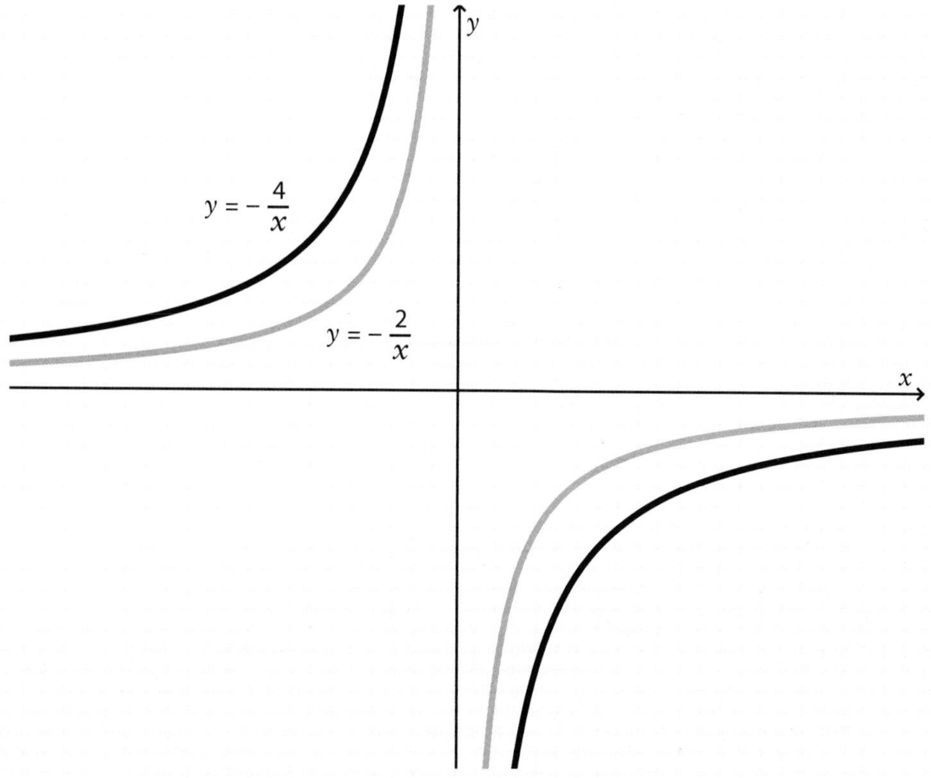

In general, the further k is from 0 (positive or negative), the further the curve lies from its asymptotes.

EXAMPLE 3

a) Write down the equations of the vertical and horizontal asymptotes of the curve:

$$y = \frac{6x+1}{2-3x}$$

b) Sketch the curve.

---

a) Looking at the denominator of the equation, x cannot take the value $\frac{2}{3}$.

Therefore, $x = \frac{2}{3}$ is the vertical asymptote.

As $x \to \infty$, $6x + 1 \to 6x$ and $2 - 3x \to -3x$

Therefore $y \to \frac{6}{-3} = -2$

Therefore, $y = -2$ is the horizontal asymptote.

To find the points of intersection with the axes:

When $x = 0$, $\quad y = \frac{1}{2}$.

Therefore crosses y-axis at $\left(0, \frac{1}{2}\right)$.

When $y = 0$, $\quad 6x + 1 = 0 \Rightarrow x = -\frac{1}{6}$.

Therefore crosses x-axis at $\left(-\frac{1}{6}, 0\right)$.

b) We can sketch the curve:

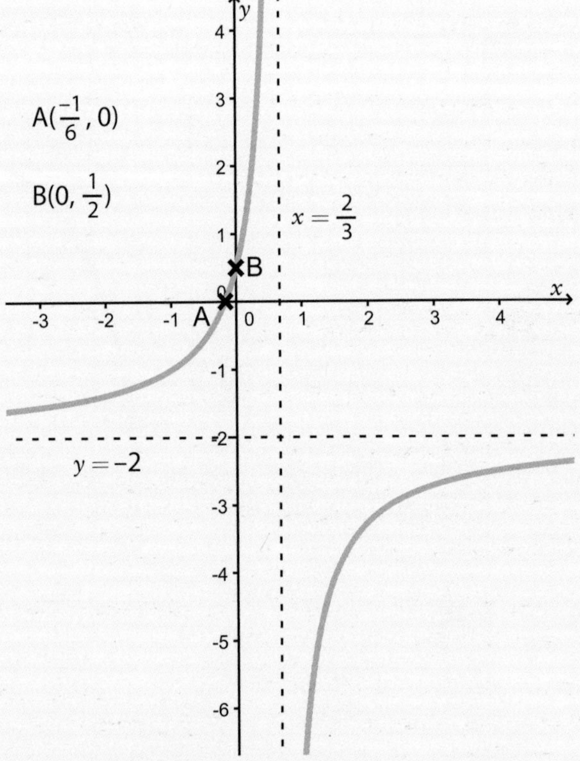

EXERCISE

EXERCISE 4C

1. Sketch each pair of curves on the same diagram:

   a) $y = \frac{1}{x}$ and $y = \frac{3}{x}$ b) $y = -\frac{2}{x}$ and $y = -\frac{6}{x}$

   c) $y = \frac{1}{2x}$ and $y = \frac{1}{4x}$ d) $y = -\frac{1}{2x}$ and $y = -\frac{1}{6x}$

2. a) Sketch the curve given by: $y = \frac{1}{x}$

   b) Using a table of values, or by comparing with your sketch from part a), sketch, on the same diagram, the curve given by: $y = \frac{1}{x^2}$

3. Consider the curve: $y = \frac{x}{x - 1}$

   a) What value can x not take? What is the equation of the vertical asymptote?

   b) Where does the curve cross the y-axis?

   c) What happens to y as x approaches infinity and minus infinity?

   d) Sketch the curve.

4. a) Write down the equations of the vertical and horizontal asymptotes for the curve $y = \frac{2 + x}{2 - 3x}$.

   b) Sketch the curve.

EXERCISE

Key Points

Reciprocal curves have two branches. If k is positive, these branches will lie in the first and third quadrants, if negative in the second and fourth.

The closer k is to zero (positive or negative), the closer the curve lies to the asymptotes.

Look at the equation to see which values x cannot take. These will be the vertical asymptotes to the curve. To find the horizontal asymptotes, consider the value that y approaches as x approaches plus and minus infinity.

4.4 Using Graphs to Solve Equations

Use of Intersection Points of Graphs to Solve Equations

In Chapter 2, you learnt how to solve simultaneous **quadratic and linear** equations algebraically. You also learnt that if you plot the curves corresponding to the two equations, the solution to the simultaneous equations is given by the intersection points. You had already learnt a similar technique at GCSE for two simultaneous **linear** equations.

This technique can be taken further. In general, any two simultaneous equations can be solved graphically by finding the intersection points.

More often, you will be asked to use this technique in reverse: you will be asked to solve two simultaneous equations algebraically. This will give you information about the intersection points of two curves you are sketching.

EXAMPLE 1

a) Sketch the graph of the curve $y = \frac{5}{x}$

On the same diagram, sketch the line $y = 2x + 3$

b) Find the coordinates of the points of intersection of the curve $y = \frac{5}{x}$ and the line $y = 2x + 3$

c) Find the range of values of x for which $2x + 3 > \frac{5}{x}$

---

a) Using the reciprocal curve sketching techniques learnt in the previous section, we can sketch the curve $y = \frac{5}{x}$.

We can also sketch the straight line $y = 2x + 3$, knowing that the y-intercept is 3 and the gradient 2:

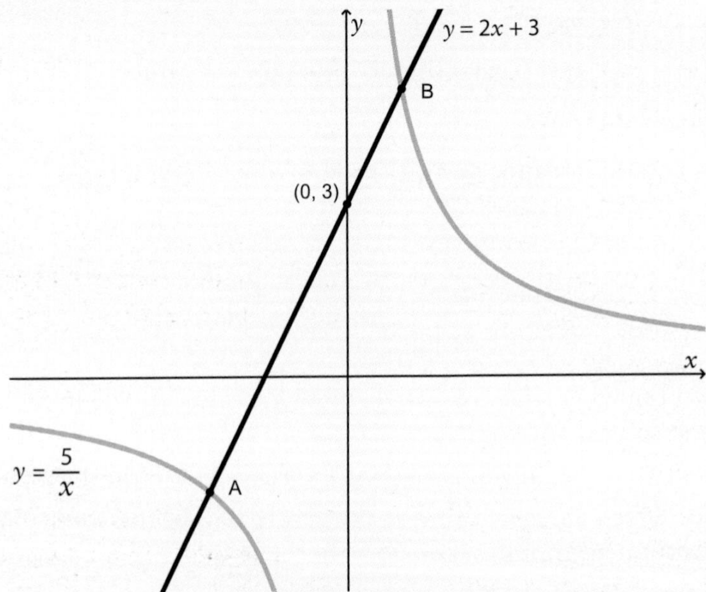

b) From our sketch, we can see that the two curves intersect at two points, labelled A and B. Note that, in this case, the straight line intersects the curve once on each branch of the curve. It is possible in some cases for a straight line to intersect the same branch twice. To find the coordinates of the two intersection points, we must solve the simultaneous equations:

$$y = \frac{5}{x} \quad \text{and} \quad y = 2x + 3$$

Using the substitution method to eliminate y:

$$\frac{5}{x} = 2x + 3$$

Multiplying throughout by x gives: $5 = 2x^2 + 3x$

Re-arranging leaves a quadratic equation: $2x^2 + 3x - 5 = 0$

Factorising: $(2x + 5)(x - 1) = 0$

$2x = -5$ or $x = 1$

So: $x = -\frac{5}{2}$ or $x = 1$.

To find y, substitute both values into one of our equations.
Choose the simplest one:

$$y = 2x + 3$$

When $x = -\frac{5}{2}, y = -2$

When $x = 1, y = 5$

So the coordinates of the two points of intersection are:

A(–2.5, –2) and B(1, 5).

Be careful to pair the x and y values together correctly!

c) From the sketch we can see that the straight line $y = 2x + 3$ lies above the curve $y = \frac{5}{x}$ between point A and the y-axis, then again to the right of point B.

Hence $2x + 3 > \frac{5}{x}$ when $-2.5 < x < 0$ or $x > 1$

If you are asked only to calculate the number of points of intersection, not their coordinates, try to re-arrange the equations into a single quadratic equation. As discussed in Chapter 2, calculating the **discriminant** $b^2 - 4ac$ will then give information about the number of solutions:

$b^2 - 4ac > 0$ Two real roots
$b^2 - 4ac = 0$ One real root
$b^2 - 4ac < 0$ No real roots

EXAMPLE 2

By calculating an appropriate discriminant, determine the number of intersection points of the curve $y = x^2 - 3x + 5$ and the straight line $y = -4x$.

Consider these as simultaneous equations. To find points of intersection, we would solve: $x^2 - 3x + 5 = -4x \Rightarrow x^2 + x + 5 = 0$

To find the number of points of intersection, we do not need to solve the equation, but only calculate the discriminant:

$b^2 - 4ac = 1^2 - 4(1)(5) = -19$

A negative discriminant means that there are no solutions to this quadratic. Hence there are no points of intersection.

EXERCISE 4D

1. Draw a sketch of each pair of curves on the same diagram, showing that there are two intersection points. Find the solutions to each pair of simultaneous equations.

   a) $y = -\frac{1}{x}$, $y = 2x - 3$ b) $y = -\frac{3}{x}$, $y = 2x + 7$

   c) $y = -\frac{4}{x}$, $y = 2x + 9$ d) $y = \frac{24}{x}$, $y = 4x + 10$

   e) $y = -\frac{15}{x}$, $y = 2x - 11$ f) $y = -\frac{52}{x}$, $y = 4x - 34$

2. Sketch the following pairs of curves on the same diagram. Find all the solutions to the simultaneous equations.

   a) $y = x^2 - 2x + 5$, $y = 7x - 15$ b) $y = x^2 - 4x + 8$, $y = 13x - 62$

3. a) Solve the simultaneous equations:

   $y + 4x = 6$ $4x^2 - 2x - y = 6$

   b) On the same diagram, sketch the two curves.

   c) Using your sketch, or otherwise, find the set of values of x for which:
   $4x^2 - 2x - 6 > 6 - 4x$

4. Two quadratic curves have equations given below. In each case:
   i) Eliminate y to obtain a single quadratic equation.
   ii) By calculating the **discriminant**, decide whether the curves have 0, 1 or 2 points of intersection.
   iii) Sketch the two curves on the same diagram, marking any points of intersection.

   a) $y = 2x^2 + 3$, $y = x^2 + 4$
   b) $y = 2x^2$, $y = 4x^2 + 4x + 2$
   c) $y = x^2 + 2x + 1$, $y = 2x^2 + 4$
   d) $y = -x^2$, $y = x^2 + 5x + 2$
   e) $y = -x^2 + 2x - 4$, $y = 2x^2 - 4x - 1$
   f) $y = -x^2 - 4x - 4$, $y = 4x^2$

5. Eliminate y to obtain a single equation and find any points of intersection of the two curves:

   $y = x^2 + 6x + 3$ $y = x^2 + 4x + 3$

   Sketch the two curves, marking this point of intersection.

6. Consider the two equations:

   $y = (x - 1)(x - 2)(x - 3)$ $y = 2x - 6$

   a) Solve the simultaneous equations.
   (Hint: eliminate y and then factorise the cubic.)

   b) Sketch the two curves on the same diagram. Using your solution to part a) you will be able to mark on the points of intersection.

EXERCISE

EXERCISE

EXERCISE

7. For each pair of equations:
   i) On the same axes sketch the two curves and give the coordinates of all the points where the curves cross the x-axis.
   ii) Use algebra to find the coordinates of the points where the graphs intersect.

   a) $y = x^2(x - 2)$ and $y = x(12 - x)$

   b) $y = x^2(x - 3)$ and $y = x(24 - x)$

EXERCISE

Key Points

You have learnt the shape of cubic curves and reciprocal curves.

You have learnt that simultaneous equations can be solved by plotting two curves on the same graph. The intersection points are the solutions.

You can use this method in reverse: solving simultaneous equations first can help you determine the intersection points of two curves.

4.5 Transformations

You will need to know what effect some transformations have on the shape of curves. These transformations are:
- translation parallel to the x- and y-axes and
- stretching parallel to the x- and y-axes.

Translations

Remember that to **translate** an object on the x-y plane means to move it without changing its shape or orientation.

Suppose you know the shape of the curve $y = f(x)$. Adding a constant will **translate** the curve parallel to the y-axis.

EXAMPLE 1

On the same diagram, sketch the graphs of:

a) $y = x^2$ b) $y = x^2 + 4$ c) $y = x^2 - 5$

---

a) Sketch the graph of $y = f(x)$ where: $f(x) = x^2$

We know that this quadratic gives a parabola, with a minimum point at (0,0).

b) We have performed the transformation: $y = f(x) + 4$

This represents a translation by 4 units, parallel to the y-axis.

c) We have performed the transformation: $y = f(x) - 5$

This represents a translation by 5 units downwards, parallel to the y-axis.

continued...

Example 1...

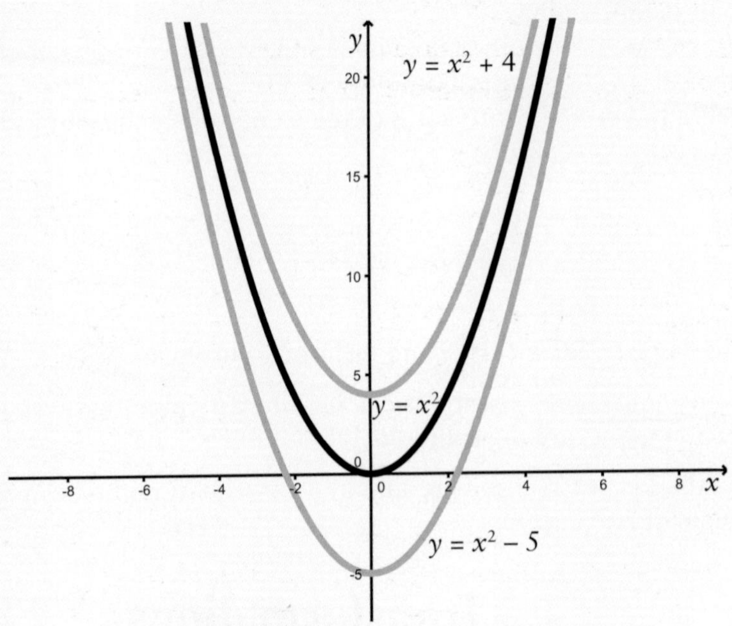

You will also be asked to translate a curve parallel to the x-axis. The curve $y = f(x)$ will be translated a units parallel to the x-axis by the transformation $y = f(x - a)$.

EXAMPLE 2

On the same diagram, sketch the graphs of:

a) $y = x^2$ b) $y = (x - 2)^2$ c) $y = (x + 3)^2$

---

a) Sketch the graph of $y = f(x)$ where: $f(x) = x^2$
We know that this quadratic gives a parabola, with a minimum point at (0,0).

b) We have performed the transformation: $y = f(x - 2)$
This represents a translation by 2 units in the **positive direction**, parallel to the x-axis.

c) We have performed the transformation: $y = f(x + 3)$
This represents a translation by 3 units in the **negative direction**, parallel to the x-axis.

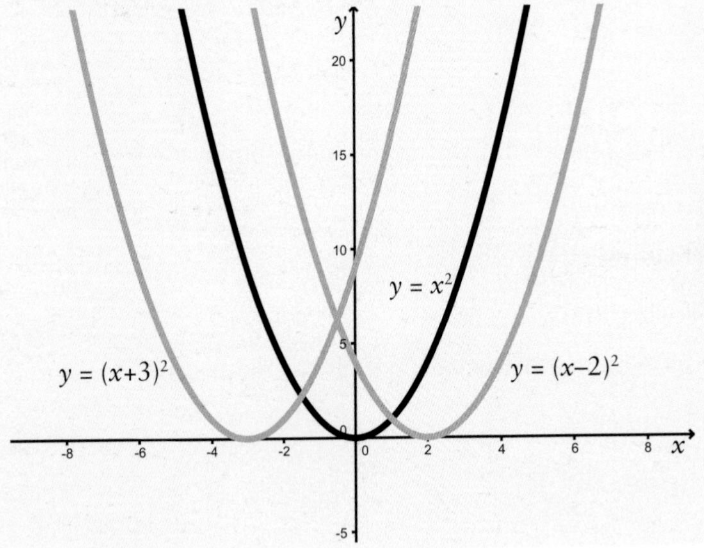

Note again that: $f(x + a)$ causes a translation in the **negative** x-direction, whereas $f(x - a)$ causes a translation in the **positive** x-direction.

Any curve can be translated in these two ways:

- add a constant to perform a translation parallel to the y-axis;
- replace x with $(x \pm a)$ to perform a translation parallel to the x-axis.

EXAMPLE 3

$$f(x) = \frac{3}{x}$$

a) Describe the transformation that has taken place from f to each of the following functions:

i) $g(x) = \frac{3}{x} + 3$

ii) $h(x) = \frac{3}{x+4}$

b) i) Sketch the curves $y = f(x)$ and $y = g(x)$ on the same diagram.

ii) Sketch the curves $y = f(x)$ and $y = h(x)$ on the same diagram.

---

a) i) Here, we have added a constant to $f(x)$:

$g(x) = f(x) + 3$

So this is a translation of 3 units parallel to the y-axis (3 units upwards).

ii) Here, we have replaced x by $x + 4$, so

$h(x) = f(x + 4)$

This is a translation of 4 units parallel to the x-axis (4 units to the left).

b) i) $g(x)$ is a translation of $f(x)$, three units in the positive y-direction. Note the horizontal asymptote lies at $y = 3$.

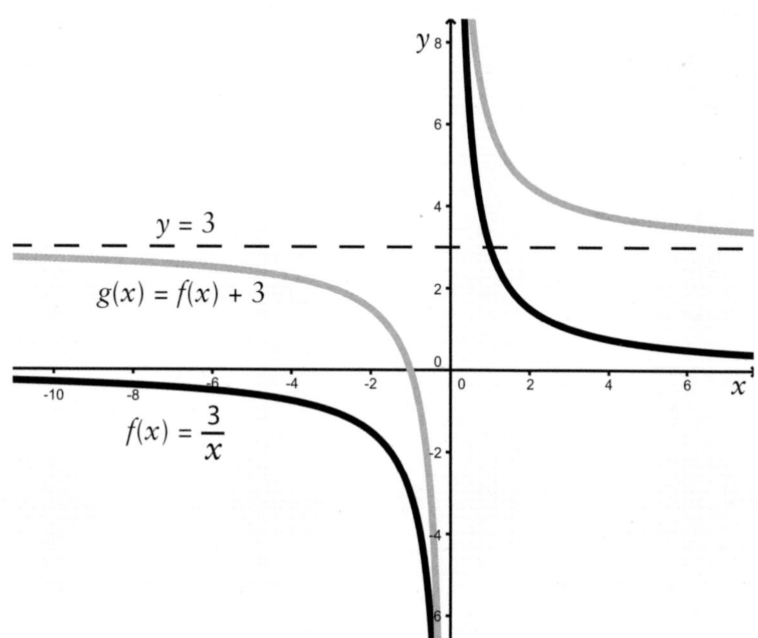

continued...

Example 3...

b) ii) $h(x)$ is a translation of $f(x)$, four units in the negative x-direction.

Note the vertical asymptote lies at $x = -4$.

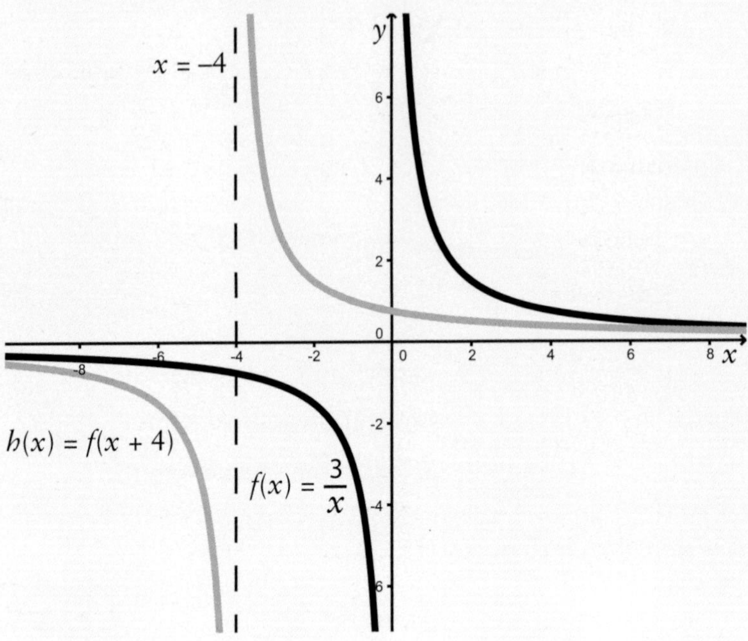

Translations can be combined.

EXAMPLE 4

$$f(x) = x^3$$

Sketch graphs of $f(x)$ and $f(x - 4) + 2$ on the same diagram.

There are two translations here:

- in the positive x-direction by 4 units, then
- in the positive y-direction by 2 units.

Note the turning point of the new function is at the point $(4, 2)$.

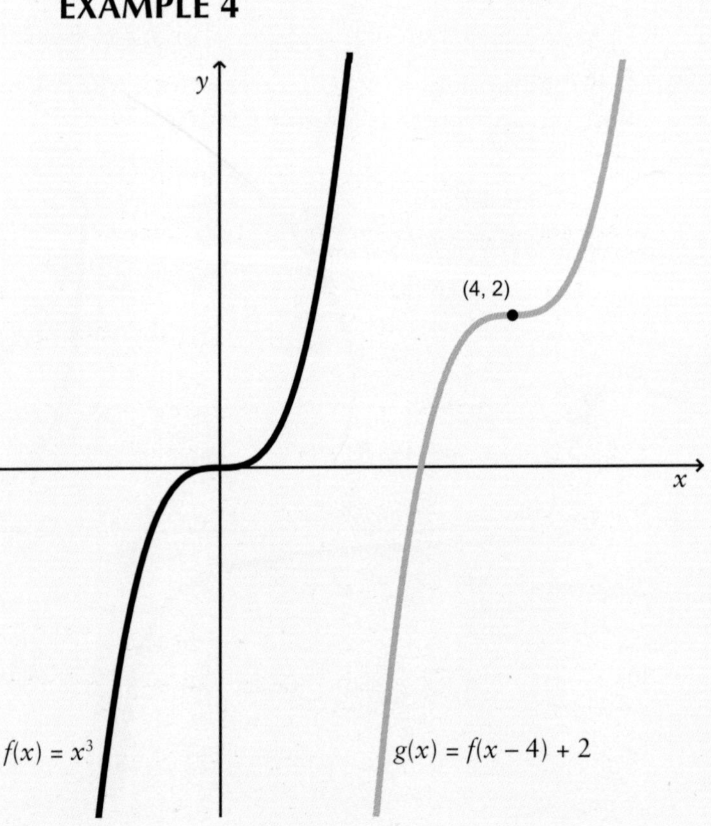

EXAMPLE 5

Given $f(x) = x^2$, write down the equation of the function $g(x)$ that represents:

a) a translation of $f(x)$ by 3 units in the positive x-direction;

b) a translation of $f(x)$ by 3 units in the positive y-direction.

---

a) $g(x) = f(x - 3)$
$= (x - 3)^2$

b) $g(x) = f(x) + 3$
$= x^2 + 3$

EXERCISE 4E

1. In each case, describe the translation that has taken place from f to g.

a) $f(x) = x^2;\ g(x) = (x + 1)^2$

b) $f(x) = x^2;\ g(x) = x^2 - 20$

c) $f(x) = \frac{5}{x};\ g(x) = \frac{5}{x + 2}$

d) $f(x) = \frac{5}{x};\ g(x) = \frac{5}{x} - 10$

e) $f(x) = \frac{5}{x + 1};\ g(x) = \frac{5}{x - 1}$

f) $f(x) = \frac{5}{x + 1};\ g(x) = 4 + \frac{5}{x + 1}$

g) $f(x) = (x - 2)^3;\ g(x) = x^3$

h) $f(x) = (x - 2)^3;\ g(x) = 1 + (x + 1)^3$

i) $f(x) = \frac{x}{2};\ g(x) = \frac{x + 2}{2}$

j) $f(x) = \frac{x}{2};\ g(x) = \frac{x}{2} + 1$

2. Write down an equation for $f(x) + a$ for the given function $f(x)$ and constant a.

a) $f(x) = 3x;\ a = 2$

b) $f(x) = x - 1;\ a = 1$

c) $f(x) = x^2 - 2x + 2;\ a = -4$

d) $f(x) = x^3;\ a = -1$

3. Write down an equation for $f(x + a)$ for the given function $f(x)$ and constant a.

a) $f(x) = 3x;\ a = 2$

b) $f(x) = x - 1;\ a = 1$

c) $f(x) = x^2 - 2x + 2;\ a = -4$

d) $f(x) = x^3;\ a = -1$

e) $f(x) = \frac{2}{x};\ a = -2$

f) $f(x) = x^2 + x;\ a = -1$

g) $f(x) = x^2(x - 1);\ a = 1$

4. For each function $f(x)$ in (a) to (d) below,

i) Sketch its graph.

ii) $g(x) = f(x) - 2$ and $h(x) = f(x + 2)$.
Write down the equations for the functions $g(x)$ and $h(x)$.

iii) On the same diagram sketch the graphs of $g(x)$ and $h(x)$.
Label each curve carefully.

iv) For each curve on your diagram, describe what transformation has taken place.

a) $f(x) = x^2$ b) $f(x) = 3x$ c) $f(x) = \frac{1}{x}$ d) $f(x) = (x - 2)^3$

EXERCISE

EXERCISE

EXERCISE

5. Sketch the graph of $f(x) = x(x-1)(x+2)$
   On the same diagram, sketch the graph of $y = f(x) + 3$
   Describe the transformation that has taken place.

6. a) Sketch the graph of $f(x) = -x(x-1)(x+1)$
   On the same diagram, sketch the graph of $y = f(x+2)$
   Mark clearly all the points where the two curves intersect the x-axis.
   b) Where do the two curves intersect each other?

7. Sketch the graph of the function: $f(x) = -\dfrac{5}{x}$

   On the same diagram, sketch the curve: $g(x) = f(x+2) + 5$
   Mark the asymptotes clearly.

8. Given: $f(x) = (x-1)^2 + 3$
   What transformation has taken place to obtain the function: $g(x) = x^2$?
   Sketch both curves on the same diagram.

9. a) Given: $f(x) = \dfrac{2-x}{x-1}$

   What is the equation of the function $g(x)$, which represents a translation of $f(x)$ by one unit in the negative x-direction and one unit in the positive y-direction? Simplify $g(x)$ as far as possible.
   b) Sketch the graphs of $y = f(x)$ and $y = g(x)$ on the same diagram, marking all asymptotes.

10. a) Sketch the graph of $y = f(x)$ where $f(x) = -x(x-2)$
    b) What is the equation of the function $g(x)$, if $g(x) = f(x+1) - 1$
    c) Describe the transformation that has taken place.
    d) Sketch $y = g(x)$ on the same diagram.

EXERCISE

Reflecting and Stretching

The graph of any function $f(x)$ is reflected in the x-axis by drawing the graph of $-f(x)$.

EXAMPLE 6

Given $f(x) = x^2$

write down the function $-f(x)$ and sketch its graph.

$$-f(x) = -x^2$$

The graph of $y = -f(x)$ is a reflection in the x-axis of the graph of $y = f(x)$:

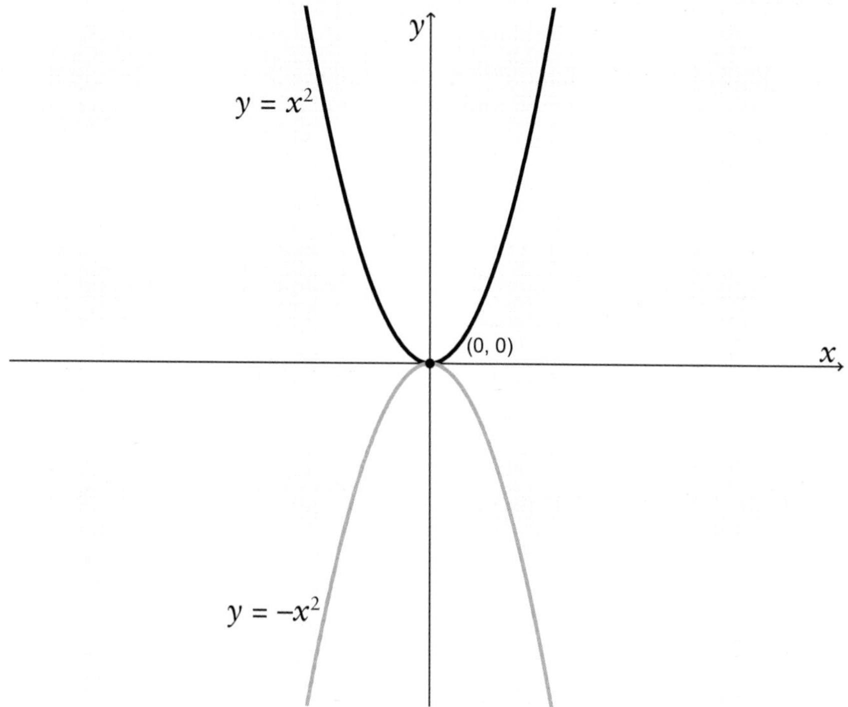

The graph of any function $f(x)$ is reflected in the y-axis by drawing the graph of $f(-x)$.

EXAMPLE 7

Given $f(x) = (1 + x)^3$

write down the function $f(-x)$ and sketch its graph.

To obtain $f(-x)$, replace x with $-x$: $f(-x) = (1 - x)^3$

To sketch the curve, reflect the graph of $y = f(x)$ in the y-axis.

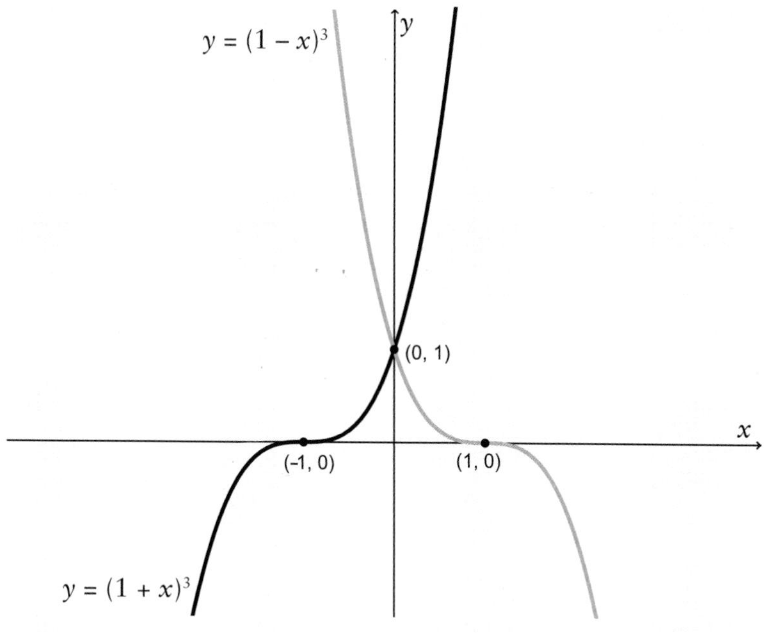

Multiplying a function by a constant represents a **stretch** of its graph parallel to the y-axis.

EXAMPLE 8

Given $f(x) = \dfrac{1}{x}$ and $a = 3$

sketch the graph of $y = af(x)$.

The graph of $y = af(x)$ is a stretch, scale factor 3, parallel to the y-axis, of the graph of $y = f(x)$.

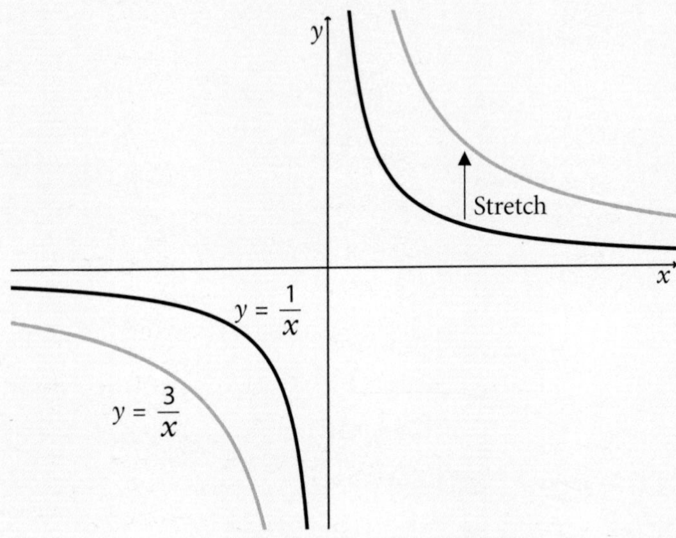

The graph of the function $f(ax)$ can be obtained by **stretching** the graph of $f(x)$ parallel to the x-axis, with a stretch factor of $\dfrac{1}{a}$.
You can also think of this as **shrinking** the graph, parallel to the x-axis, with a shrink factor of a.

EXAMPLE 9

Given $f(x) = x^2$ and $a = 2$,

write down the function $f(ax)$ and sketch its graph.

$$f(ax) = (2x)^2$$
$$= 4x^2$$

The graph of $f(ax)$ is a stretch, factor ½, (or a shrink, factor 2), parallel to the x-axis:

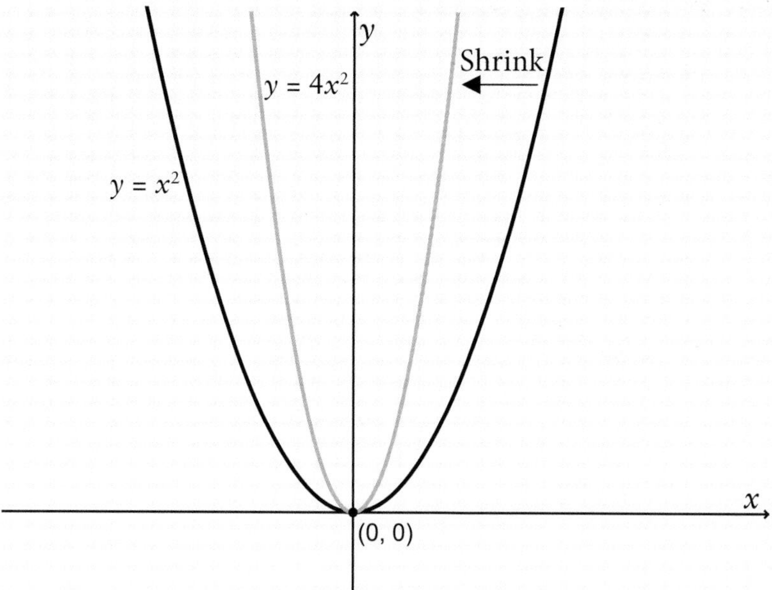

A stretch and a reflection can be combined. For example, the graph $y = -2f(x)$ would be a reflection of $y = f(x)$ in the x-axis, followed by a stretch in the y-direction, factor 2.

Sometimes you will need to perform a stretch in both x- and y-directions.

EXAMPLE 10

Given

$$f(x) = x(x - 1)^2$$

Sketch the graphs of $y = f(x), y = f(2x)$ and $y = 2f(x)$ on the same diagram.

Thinking about the curve $y = f(x)$, this has a root at $x = 0$ and a repeated root at $x = 1$. This means it crosses the x-axis at the origin, then touches the axis again with a stationary point at $x = 1$. Because the term in x^3 would be positive, we also know that the curve's general direction is bottom left to top right. This gives us enough information to sketch the curve.

Now consider $y = f(2x)$. This represents a stretch with scale factor ½ (i.e. a shrinking) of the original curve, parallel to the x-axis.

To find the equation of this curve, replace x with $2x$ in the original equation:

$$f(2x) = 2x(2x - 1)^2$$

Finally, consider $y = 2f(x)$.

This is a stretch with scale factor 2 parallel to the y-axis.

The equation is: $2f(x) = 2x(x - 1)^2$

Using our knowledge of stretch transformations, we can now sketch all three curves:

continued...

Example 10...

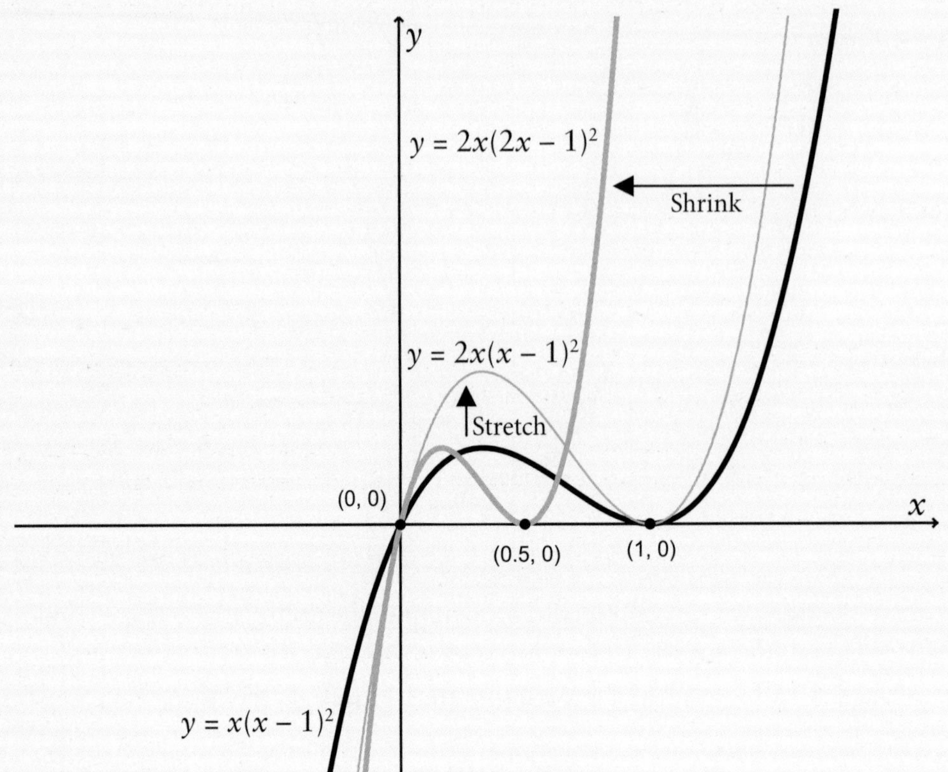

EXERCISE

EXERCISE 4F

1. For each of the following functions $f(x)$, find the corresponding functions $af(x)$ and $f(ax)$, where a is given.

   a) $f(x) = x^2;\ a = 2$
   b) $f(x) = x^3 + 1;\ a = 2$
   c) $f(x) = 2x;\ a = 3$
   d) $f(x) = \frac{2}{x};\ a = 5$
   e) $f(x) = x^2;\ a = -1$
   f) $f(x) = \frac{1}{x^2};\ a = -1$
   g) $f(x) = 3x^3;\ a = -1$
   h) $f(x) = 1 - x;\ a = -2$
   i) $f(x) = x(x-1)(x-2);\ a = 2$
   j) $f(x) = x^2(x-1);\ a = -2$

2. The function $f(x)$ is given by: $f(x) = \frac{1}{x}$

   a) On the same diagram, sketch the graphs of $y = f(x)$ and $y = af(x)$ where $a = 3$.

   b) On another diagram, sketch the graphs of $y = f(x)$ and $y = f(ax)$ where $a = -2$.

3. For each of the following functions $f(x)$, sketch the graphs of $y = f(x)$ and $y = af(x)$ on the same diagram. From your graphs, estimate the value of x where $f(x) = af(x)$.

   a) $f(x) = x^2;\ a = -2$
   b) $f(x) = x^3 + 1;\ a = -1$
   c) $f(x) = 2x + 1;\ a = 2$
   d) $f(x) = (x-1)(x+1);\ a = 2$
   e) $f(x) = x(x+2)^2 + 1;\ a = -1$

   (Hint: first think about the function $f(x) = x(x+2)^2$ and apply a translation of 1 unit in the positive y-direction.)

EXERCISE

EXERCISE

4. For each of the following functions $f(x)$, sketch the graphs of $y = f(x)$ and $y = f(ax)$ on the same diagram. From your graphs, estimate the value of x where $f(x) = f(ax)$.

a) $f(x) = x^2 + 1;\ a = 2$

b) $f(x) = x^2 - 1;\ a = \frac{1}{2}$

c) $f(x) = 2x^3;\ a = \frac{1}{2}$

d) $f(x) = x(x - 1);\ a = -1$

e) $f(x) = x(x + 2)^2;\ a = 2$

EXERCISE

Transforming Functions In General

You can use your knowledge of transformations to transform the graph of any function. Sometimes you will not be given its equation, only a sketch of the curve.

To do this, note the important features of the given sketch, e.g. where the curve crosses the axes and the position of the turning points. Work out where the corresponding features will be on the new curve, to help you create the new sketch.

EXAMPLE 11

The graph of the function $y = f(x)$ is shown below.

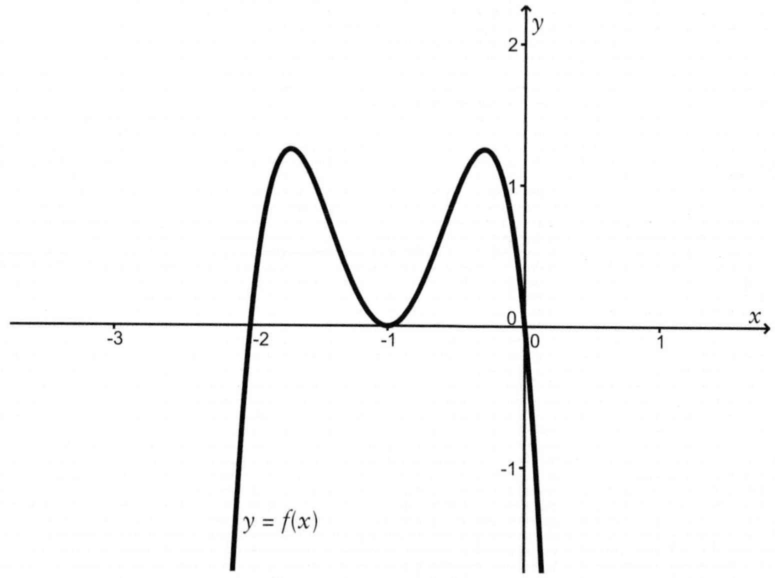

Draw sketches of the graphs of:

a) $y = f(x) + 2$ b) $y = 2f(x)$ c) $y = f(2x)$

d) $y = -f(x)$ e) $y = f(-x)$ f) $y = f(x + 2)$

First note the key features of the graph of $y = f(x)$:
It crosses the x-axis when $x = -2$ and 0.
It also touches the x-axis when $x = -1$ at a minimum point.
The origin is the only point where the curve crosses the y-axis.
The curve has a maximum between $x = -2$ and -1. The y value is just over 1.
There is another maximum between $x = -1$ and 0. The y value is just over 1.

continued...

Example 11...

a) $y = f(x) + 2$
This is a translation of 2 units in the positive y-direction.
The curve will cut the y-axis at $x = 2$.
The two maxima will remain between $x = -2$ and -1; $x = -1$ and 0.
The y values at these maxima is just over 3.

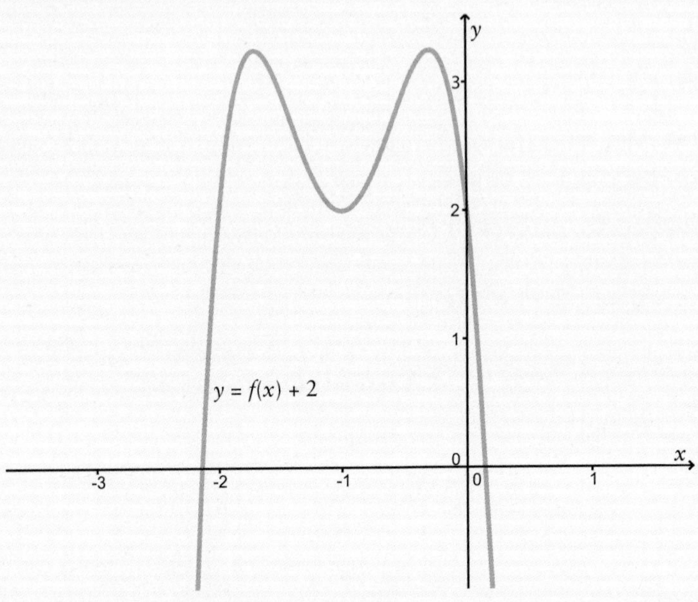

b) $y = 2f(x)$
This is a stretch, scale factor 2 in the y-direction.
The curve crosses the x-axis in the same places as $y = f(x)$.
The curve has a maximum between $x = -2$ and -1.
The y value is between 2 and 3.
There is another maximum between $x = -1$ and 0.
The y value is between 2 and 3.

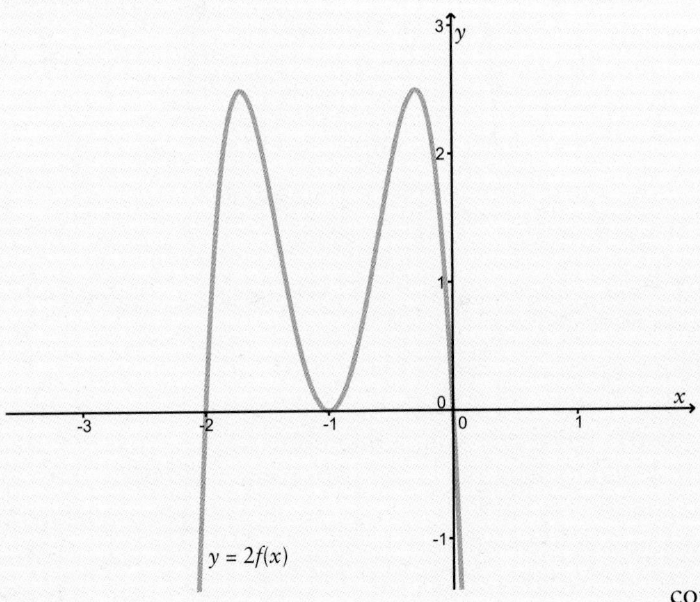

continued...

Example 11...

c) $y = f(2x)$
This is a stretch, scale factor ½ in the x-direction (i.e. a shrink, scale factor 2).
The curve crosses the x-axis at $x = -1$ and 0. It touches the x-axis at $x = -0.5$.
The curve has a maximum between $x = -1$ and -0.5. The y value is just over 1.
There is another maximum between $x = -0.5$ and 0. The y value is just over 1.

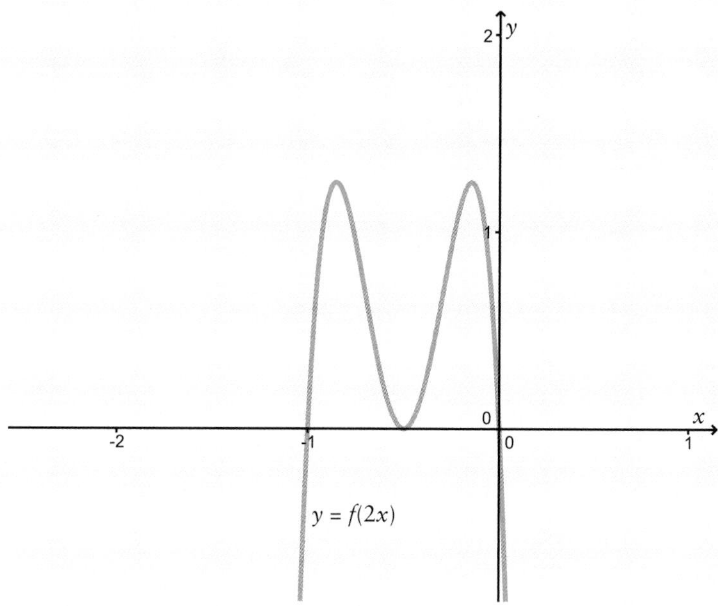

d) $y = -f(x)$
This is a reflection in the x-axis.
The curve crosses the x-axis at the same points as $y = f(x)$, with a maximum at $x = -1$.
The curve has a minimum between $x = -2$ and -1. The y value is just under -1.
There is another minimum between $x = -1$ and 0. The y value is just under -1.

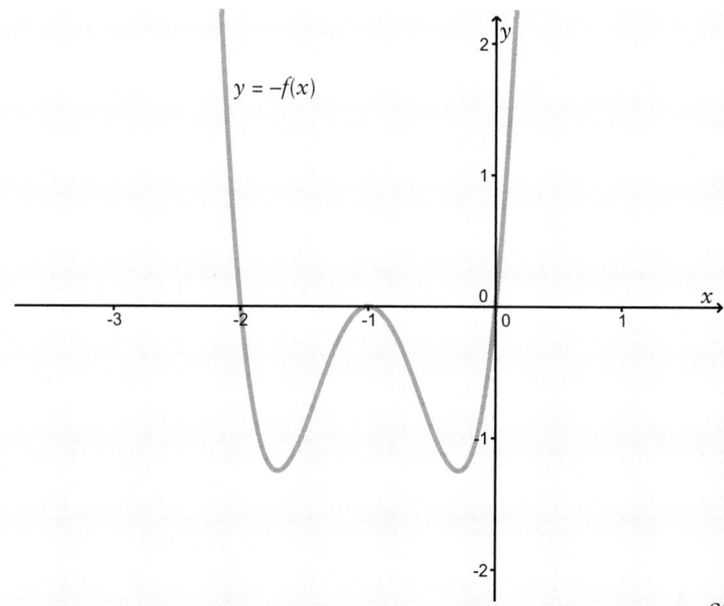

continued...

Example 11...

e) $y = f(-x)$
This is a reflection in the y-axis.
It crosses the x-axis when $x = 0$ and 2.
It also touches the x-axis when $x = 1$ at a minimum point.
The curve has a maximum between $x = 0$ and 1. The y value is just over 1.
There is another maximum between $x = 1$ and 2. The y value is just over 1.

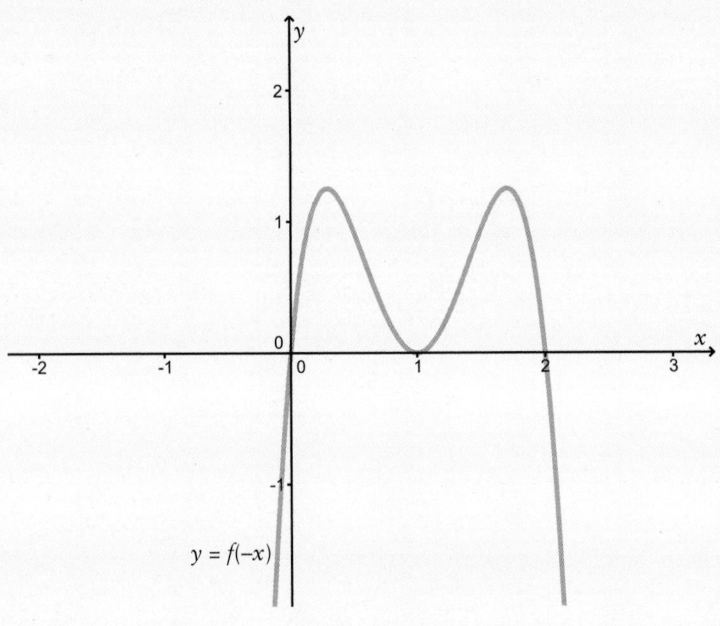

f) $y = f(x + 2)$
This is a translation by 2 units in the negative x-direction.
The curve crosses the x-axis when $x = -4$ and -2.
It also touches the x-axis when $x = -3$ at a minimum point.
The curve has a maximum between $x = -4$ and -3. The y value is just over 1.
There is another maximum between $x = -3$ and -2. The y value is just over 1.

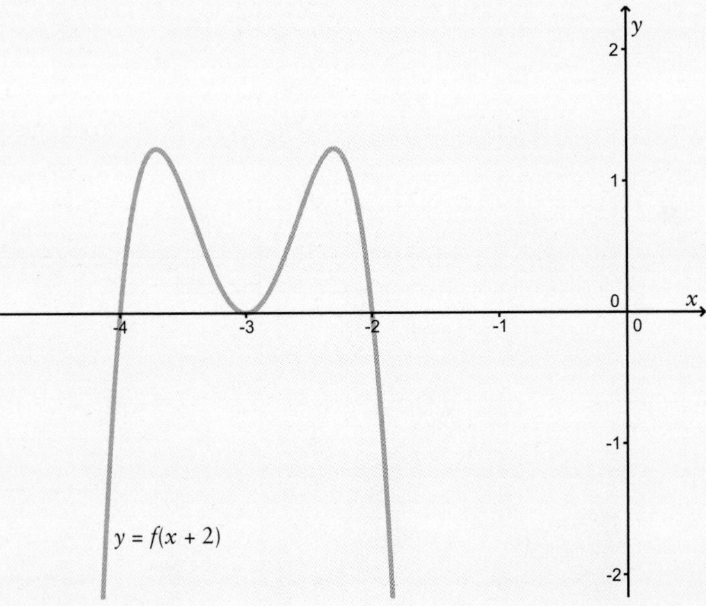

EXERCISE

EXERCISE 4G

1. Describe in words the following transformations on the graph $y = f(x)$.

   a) $y = -f(x)$ b) $y = 2f(x)$ c) $y = f(x) - 3$

   d) $y = f(2x)$ e) $y = f(x - 3)$ f) $y = f(-x)$

2. The diagram shows the curve with equation $y = f(x)$. On separate diagrams, sketch the following curves, taking care to mark the coordinates of the turning point in each case.

   a) $y = -f(x)$ b) $y = 2f(x)$ c) $y = f(x) - 3$

   d) $y = f(2x)$ e) $y = f(x - 3)$ f) $y = f(-x)$

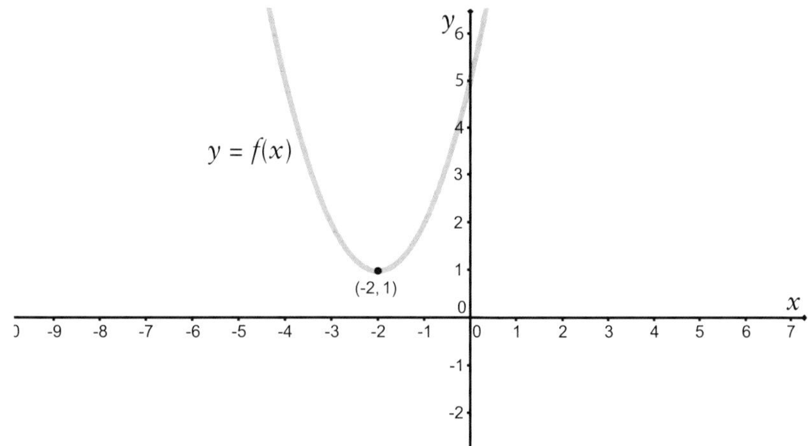

3. The diagram shows the curve with equation $y = f(x)$. On separate diagrams, sketch the following curves, taking care to mark the asymptotes in each case:

   a) $y = -f(x)$ b) $y = 2f(x)$ c) $y = f(x) - 3$

   d) $y = f(2x)$ e) $y = f(x - 3)$ f) $y = f(-x)$

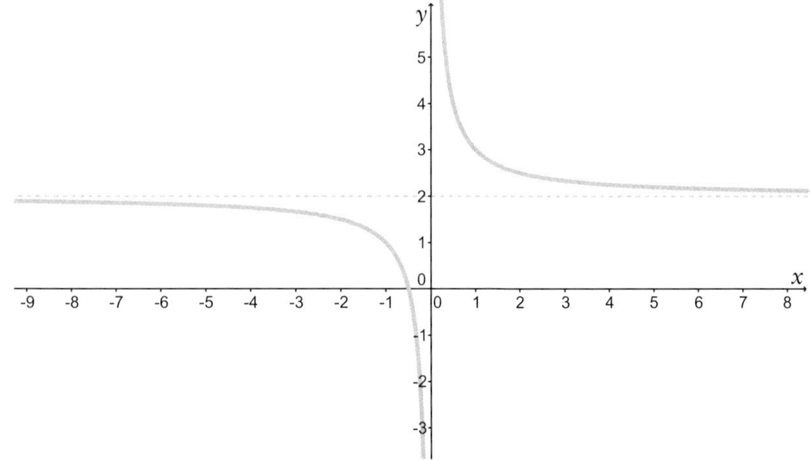

EXERCISE

EXERCISE

4. The sketch shows the function with equation $y = f(x)$.
   On separate diagrams, sketch the graphs of:

   a) $y = -f(x)$ b) $y = 2f(x)$ c) $y = f(x) - 2$

   d) $y = f(2x)$ e) $y = f(x - 2)$ f) $y = f(-x)$

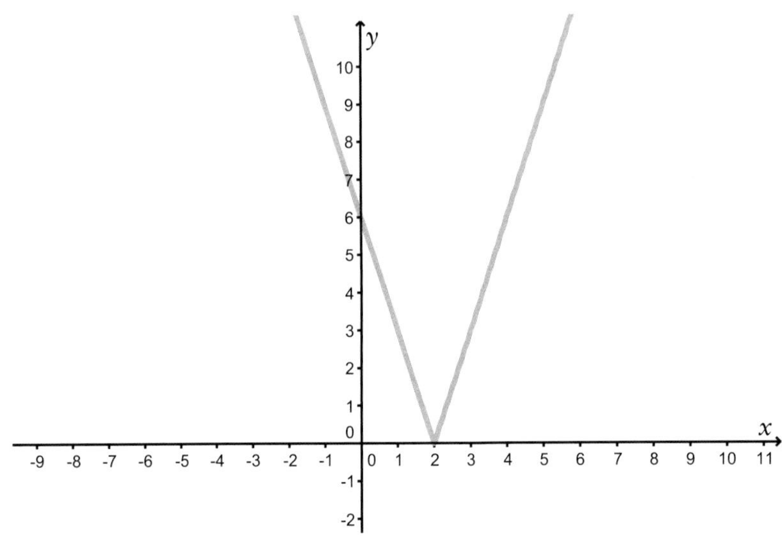

5. The diagram shows a sketch of the function $y = f(x)$. On separate diagrams, sketch the following graphs, taking care to mark the image of point A.

   a) $y = -f(x)$ b) $y = 2f(x)$ c) $y = f(x) + 2$

   d) $y = f(2x)$ e) $y = f(x + 2)$ f) $y = f(-x)$

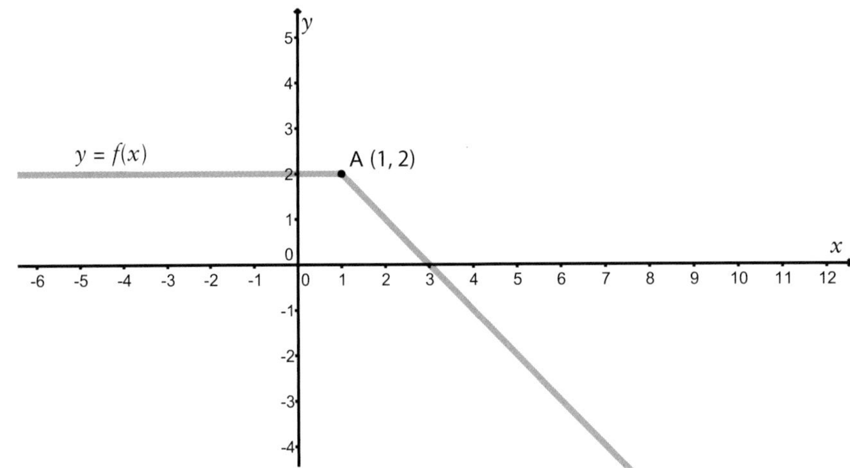

6. The diagram opposite shows a part of a curve with equation $y = f(x)$.
   On separate diagrams, sketch the curves of:

   a) $y = -f(x)$ b) $y = 2f(x)$ c) $y = f(x) + 2$

   d) $y = f(2x)$ e) $y = f(x + 2)$ f) $y = f(-x)$

EXERCISE

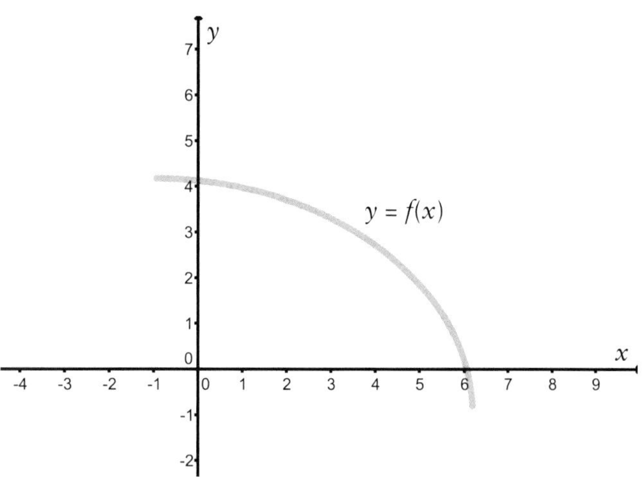

EXERCISE

SUMMARY

- The general cubic equation is: $y = ax^3 + bx^2 + cx + d$
- The shape of a cubic curve is typically one of these:

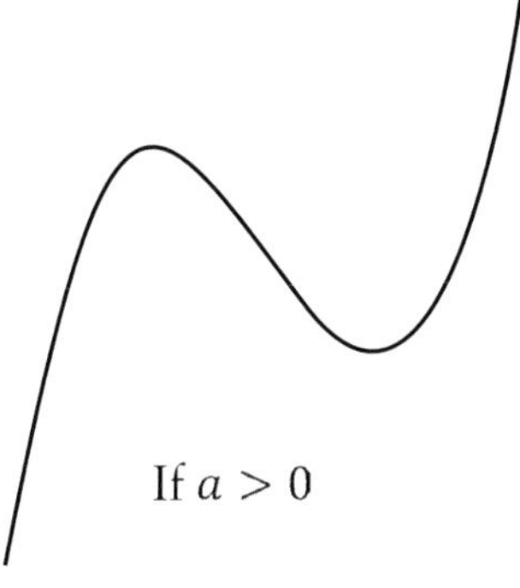

If $a > 0$

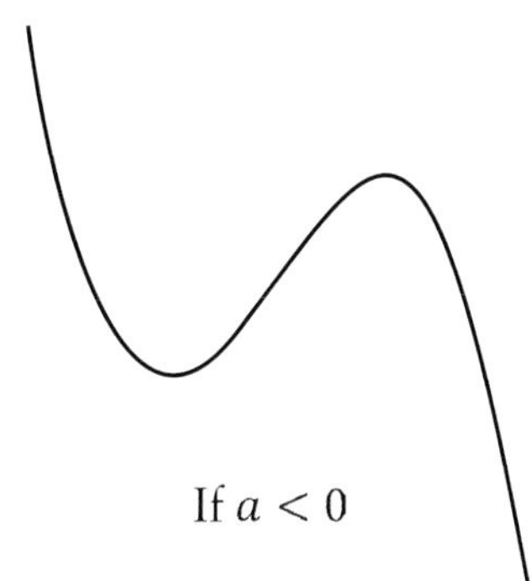

If $a < 0$

- The general equation of a reciprocal function is: $y = \frac{k}{x}$ where k is an integer.
- A sketch of a reciprocal curve looks like one of these two:

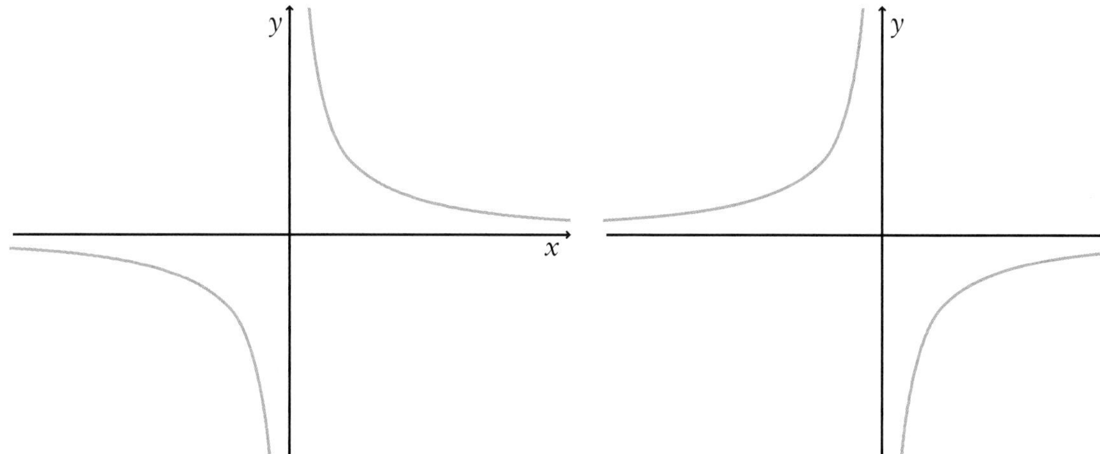

Curve shape 1: $k > 0$

Curve shape 2: If $k < 0$

SUMMARY...

- With reciprocal curves of the form $y = \dfrac{ax + b}{cx + d}$ calculate the value that x cannot take by setting the denominator equal to zero. This gives the equation of the horizontal asymptote.
- Consider the value of y as x approaches infinity. This gives the equation of the vertical asymptote.
- Solving simultaneous equations gives the intersection points of two curves.
- Similarly, sketching two curves can give you an idea how many solutions there are to the corresponding simultaneous equations and approximations to those solutions.
- There are various useful techniques when sketching the graph of any curve:
  - Remember the general shape.
  - Identify the points where the curve crosses the axes.
  - With quadratic curves, you can identify **turning points** by **completing the square**. Later you will learn a method to find the turning points of any curve.
- The graph of $y = f(x)$ is transformed according to the following rules:

$y = -f(x)$	Reflection in x-axis
$y = af(x)$	Stretch in y-direction, scale factor a
$y = f(x) - a$	Translation by a units in negative y-direction
$y = f(ax)$	Stretch in x-direction, scale factor $\frac{1}{a}$. (Shrink, scale factor a)
$y = f(x - a)$	Translation by a units in positive x-direction
$y = f(-x)$	Reflection in y-axis

Chapter 5

Equation of a Straight Line

5.1 Introduction

At GCSE you learnt how to draw a **plot** of a straight line, usually by writing up a table of values from the equation of the line.

In this chapter you will learn more about the equations of straight lines. You will also learn some properties of parallel and perpendicular lines.

Keywords

Linear: any relationship that can be plotted on a graph as a straight line is said to be **linear**, e.g. exchange rates, miles driven per litre of petrol, etc.

Gradient: the steepness of a line on a graph.

***y*-Intercept:** where a straight line crosses the y-axis.

Parallel: parallel lines do not cross. They have the same **gradient**.

Perpendicular: perpendicular lines cross each other at right angles.

Before You Start

You should know how to:

Recognise a linear equation.

Plot a straight line graph.

Identify the gradient and *y*-intercept from the equation of a straight line.

EXAMPLE 1a

$$y = 3x + 4$$

This is a linear equation. The powers of x and y are 1.

EXAMPLE 1b

$$y = 3x^2$$

This is **not** a linear equation. It contains a term in x^2.

EXAMPLE 1c

$$\frac{x-1}{2y+3} = 5$$

This is a linear equation. Re-arranging gives:

$$x - 1 = 10y + 15$$

The powers of x and y are 1.

EXAMPLE 1d

$$3 - xy = x + y$$

This is **not** a linear equation. It contains a term in xy.

EXAMPLE 2

Plot the straight line given by the equation $y = 2x - 3$.

First use a table of values to find some of the points on the line. Choose any x-values and work out the y-values from the equation.

x	0	1	2	3
y	−3	−1	1	3

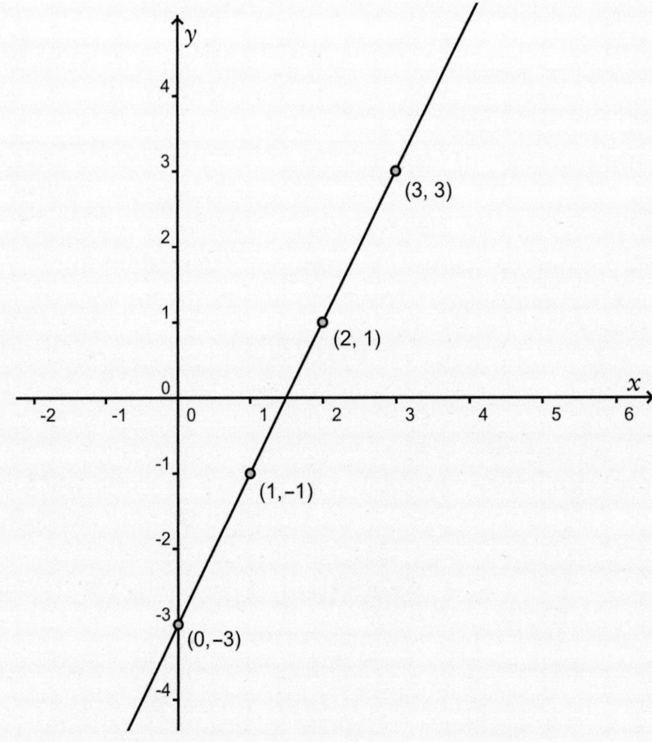

EXAMPLE 3

Without plotting a graph, state the gradient and the y-intercept of the straight line given by the equation $y = 2x - 3$

The gradient is 2 and the y-intercept is –3.

The gradient tells us the y-coordinate increases by 2 units every time the x-coordinate increases by 1.

The y-intercept tells us that the line crosses the y-axis at the point (0, 3).

EXERCISE

REVISION EXERCISE 5A

1. Which of these equations are linear equations?

   a) $4y + 3x = 1$ b) $y = 3x^2$ c) $2(x - 1) + 4(y + 1) = 0$

   d) $x + y + xy = 3$ e) $\dfrac{y - 1}{x + 1} = 1$ f) $x = 1$

2. By drawing up a suitable table of values, plot the following straight line graphs. State the gradient and the y-intercept for each.

   a) $y = x + 1$ b) $y = \dfrac{x}{2} + 1$

   c) $y = 2x + 1$ d) $y = -x - 1$

3. Without plotting the graphs, state the gradient and the y-intercept of the following straight lines:

   a) $y = 5x + 3$ b) $y = -2x - 3$

   c) $2y = 4x + 7$ d) $y + 1 = x$

EXERCISE

What You Will Learn

In this chapter you will learn:

- To find the gradient of a line between two points;
- To recognise a linear equation in various forms;
- To find the equation of a straight line;
- To identify the gradient and y-intercept from the equation of a straight line;
- To find the midpoint of a line segment;
- You will also learn some of the properties of parallel and perpendicular lines.

IN THE REAL WORLD

In 2005, scientists studying the amount of ice in the Arctic Ocean discovered an alarming trend: the ice was disappearing. When they plotted a graph of the total surface area of the ice measured each summer from 1997 to 2005, they spotted a **linear trend.** This meant that the total surface area of the ice was decreasing by roughly the same amount each year. Using this **straight line graph,** the scientists predicted that there would be no ice left in the Arctic Ocean by about 2040. Since then, the trend has become even more worrying. The latest measurements show that the decrease in ice cover is speeding up. A straight line graph may no longer be the best way to model the sea ice data. The latest predictions suggest that the Arctic Ocean could be ice-free during the summer by 2020, or sooner.

5.2 The Equation of a Straight Line

The Gradient

The gradient is a measure of the steepness of a straight line.

The gradient of a straight line connecting the points (x_1, y_1) and (x_2, y_2) is $m = \dfrac{y_2 - y_1}{x_2 - x_1}$

Some people find it helpful to remember: $m = \dfrac{rise}{run}$

In other words, the gradient is how much the straight line rises between the two points divided by the horizontal distance it crosses.

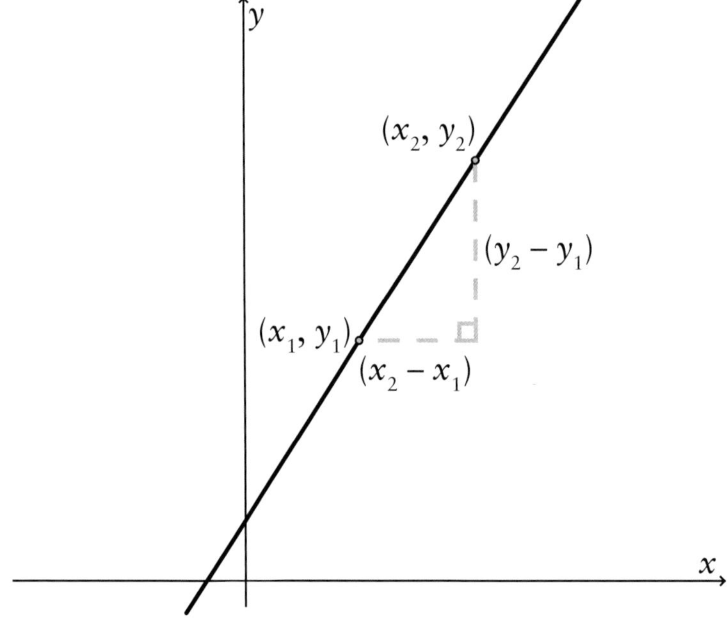

EXAMPLE 1

Find the gradient of the straight line connecting the points (2, 1) and (–4, –3).

$$m = \frac{y_2 - y_1}{x_2 - x_1}$$

$$m = \frac{-3 - 1}{-4 - 2}$$

$$m = \frac{2}{3}$$

At GCSE, you learnt that a straight line is often written in the form $y = mx + c$.

In this section you will learn about two other forms for the equation of a straight line.

The Equation $y - y_1 = m(x - x_1)$

If you know the coordinates of any point on the line (x_1, y_1) and the gradient m of the line, you can use $y - y_1 = m(x - x_1)$ to find the equation of the straight line.

EXAMPLE 1

Find the equation of the line that passes through the point (2, 0) with gradient 3.

State where the line crosses the y-axis.

$$y - y_1 = m(x - x_1)$$

We use $(x_1, y_1) = (2, 0)$ and $m = 3$

$$\therefore y - 0 = 3(x - 2)$$

$$\Rightarrow y = 3x - 6$$

The y-intercept is –6.

You can also use two points on the line to find the line's equation. Firstly, use the two points to find the line's gradient. The gradient of the line is given by:

$$m = \frac{rise}{run} = \frac{y_2 - y_1}{x_2 - x_1}$$

EXAMPLE 2

Find the equation of the line passing through the points (2, 3) and (4, 10).

We use $(x_1, y_1) = (2, 3)$ and $(x_2, y_2) = (4, 10)$.

$$m = \frac{y_2 - y_1}{x_2 - x_1}$$

$$= \frac{10 - 3}{4 - 2}$$

$$= \frac{7}{2}$$

continued...

Example 2...

$$y - y_1 = m(x - x_1)$$

We can use any point on the line for (x_1, y_1)

$$y - 3 = \frac{7}{2}(x - 2)$$

$$y = \frac{7}{2}x - 4$$

Note: Use improper fractions in the equations of straight lines, not mixed numbers.

EXERCISE

EXERCISE 5B

1. Find the gradient of the straight line passing through the following pairs of points:

   a) (–4, 0) and (–2, 2) b) (1, –2) and (–1, –1) c) (0, 2) and (5, –2)

   d) (–5, –4) and (1, 4) e) (0, –1) and (4, 0)

2. Find the equation of the straight line with the given gradient, passing through the given point:

   a) Gradient 2, Point (2, 1) b) Gradient 1, Point (–2, 2)

   c) Gradient 3, Point (–1, –1) d) Gradient ½ , Point (5, 0)

   e) Gradient –2, Point (0, 0) f) Gradient –1, Point (–1, –1)

3. Find the equation of the straight line passing through the two points given:

   a) A(0, 0), B(3, 3) b) A(2, 0), B(3,3) c) A(0, 2), B(3, 5)

   d) A(–2, 2), B(6, 6) e) A(0, 0), B(–2, 6) f) A(–2, 3), B(1, –3)

4. The points A and B have coordinates (4, 3) and (5, 12) respectively.
   Find, in the form $y = mx + c$, an equation for the straight line through A and B.

5. Write down the equation of a straight line that has gradient 4 and passes through the point (0, 3).

6. Write down the equation of a straight line that has gradient –1 and passes through the point (0, –1).

7. The line $y = mx + 2$ passes through the point A(1, 3).
   Find the value of m, the gradient of the line.

8. A straight line l has gradient 5 and passes through the point (11, 7). Find its equation.

9. A straight line l has gradient 7 and passes through the point (8, 3). Find its equation.

10. Find an equation for the straight line passing through A(6, 5) and B(5, 3).
    Give your answer in the form $y = mx + c$.

11. Find an equation for the straight line passing through A(–3, 4) and B(–6, –5).
    Give your answer in the form $y = mx + c$.

12. Find an equation for the straight line passing through A(7, 1) and B(7, –4).

13. The points A and B have coordinates (3, 1) and (5, 11) respectively. Find, in the form $y = mx + c$, an equation for the straight line through A and B.

14. The straight line $y = 5x - 1$ intersects the x-axis at the point C and the y-axis at the point D. Write down the coordinates of C and D.

EXERCISE

$ax + by + c = 0$

The form $ax + by + c = 0$ is known as the **general form** for the equation of a straight line, where a, b and c are constants and integers. You can write the equation of any straight line in this form.

EXAMPLE 1

A straight line is described by the equation $y = 5x + 3$

Write this equation in the form $ax + by + c = 0$

$$y = 5x + 3$$

Re-arrange to give: $5x - y + 3 = 0$

EXAMPLE 2

Write the following equation in the form $ax + by + c = 0$:

$$\frac{1}{x+1} = \frac{2}{2y-3}$$

Re-arrange to give: $2y - 3 = 2(x + 1)$

$$2x - 2y + 5 = 0$$

EXERCISE

EXERCISE 5C

1. Write the following equations in the form $ax + by + c = 0$:

a) $2y = 3x + 3$ b) $3y = 5$ c) $x - 1 = 0$

d) $2y = \frac{3}{2}(x - 1)$ e) $\frac{x}{5} = \frac{y}{4}$ f) $\frac{2x}{5y} = \frac{5}{2}$

g) $7(1 + y) = 2(2 - x)$ h) $\frac{1+x}{1+y} = \frac{3}{4}$ i) $\frac{2+3x}{3} = \frac{3+2y}{4}$

j) $\frac{2}{1+3x+2y} = \frac{4}{3-x-2y}$

2. Find where the line $4x + 3y - 12 = 0$ crosses
   a) the x-axis
   b) the y-axis

3. Find where the line $5x + 12y = 0$ crosses
   a) the x-axis
   b) the y-axis

4. Find the equation of the line with gradient –2 and y-intercept 3.

   Give your answer in the general form $ax + by + c = 0$.

5. Find the equation of the line with gradient $\frac{2}{3}$ and y-intercept $-\frac{3}{2}$.

   Give your answer in the general form $ax + by + c = 0$.

EXERCISE

EXERCISE

6. The point (1, 3) lies on the line with equation $ax + by - 6 = 0$. The line has a gradient of –3. What are the values of the integers a and b? Write down the equation of the line in its general form.
7. The two straight lines: $x + 2y - 12 = 0$ and $-2x + y - 1 = 0$ intersect each other at the point A.
   a) Find the coordinates of A.
   b) Sketch the two lines.
   (Hint: for this question you will need simultaneous equations.)

EXERCISE

5.3 Midpoint of a Line Segment

A straight line is infinitely long in both directions.
A **line segment** is a part of a straight line and has a finite length.

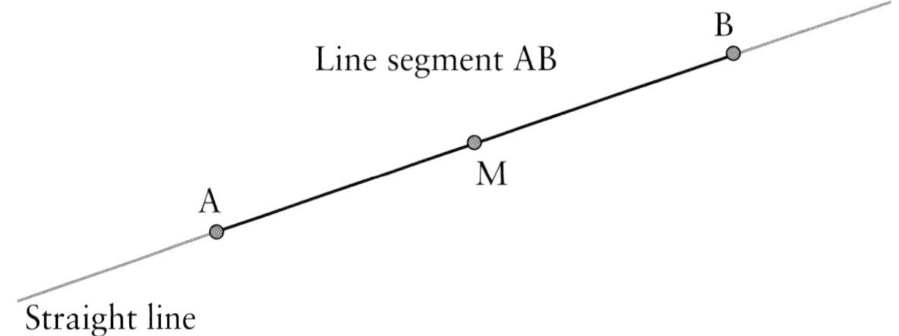

You may be asked to find the midpoint of a line segment, shown as point M in the diagram above.

The x-coordinate of the midpoint of a line segment is the average of the x-coordinates of the end points. The y-coordinate is the average of the two y-coordinates.

The midpoint of line segment $A(x_1, y_1)$ and $B(x_2, y_2)$ is $M(x_3, y_3)$, given by:

$$x_3 = \frac{x_1 + x_2}{2}$$

$$y_3 = \frac{y_1 + y_2}{2}$$

EXAMPLE 1

Find the midpoint M of the line segment between the points A(1, 8) and B(7, 10).

For the midpoint $M(x_3, y_3)$:

$$x_3 = \frac{x_1 + x_2}{2} = \frac{1 + 7}{2} = 4$$

$$y_3 = \frac{y_1 + y_2}{2} = \frac{8 + 10}{2} = 9$$

Therefore M has coordinates (4, 9).

EXAMPLE 2

Point M(3, 4) is the midpoint of the line segment AB.
Given the coordinates of point A are (5, 7), find the coordinates of B.

To find $B(x_2, y_2)$:

$$x_3 = \frac{x_1 + x_2}{2} \Rightarrow x_2 = 2x_3 - x_1$$

$$y_3 = \frac{y_1 + y_2}{2} \Rightarrow y_2 = 2y_3 - y_1$$

$$x_2 = 2 \times 3 - 5 = 1$$

$$y_2 = 2 \times 4 - 7 = 1$$

Therefore B has coordinates (1, 1).

EXERCISE 5D

1. Find the midpoints of the line segments joining points A and B.

   a) A(1, 3), B(9, 7)

   b) A(−1, 3), B(11, 5)

   c) A(−3, 3), B(1, −13)

   d) A(4, 2), B(19, 6)

   e) A(6, 1), B(−1, −10)

   f) $A(1 + \sqrt{2}, 0), B(3 - \sqrt{2}, 2)$

   g) $A\left(\frac{\sqrt{3} - 1}{2}, 4\right), B\left(\frac{1 - \sqrt{3}}{2}, 6\right)$

2. Find the exact coordinates of the midpoints of the following line segments.

   a) $A(1, 16), B(\pi, 6)$

   b) $A(3, 2\sqrt{2}), B(2, 2)$

3. M is the midpoint of the line segment AB. Given the coordinates of A and M, find the coordinates of B.

   a) A(2, 10), M(0, 8)

   b) A(0, 7), M(2, 7)

   c) A(8, −3), M(−9, 7)

   d) A(1, 10), M(−10, −7)

   e) $A(2\pi, -\pi), M(1 + \pi, \pi)$

4. The endpoints of a line segment are $A(4k + 1, -7)$ and $B(2k^2 + 1, 1)$, where k is an integer. The midpoint of the line segment is M.

   a) Find the y-coordinate of M.

   b) Show that the x-coordinate of M is $(k + 1)^2$.

   c) Given that the x-coordinate of M is 4, find the two possible values of k.

EXERCISE

EXERCISE

5.4 Parallel and Perpendicular Lines

Conditions for Two Straight Lines to be Parallel or Perpendicular to Each Other

Consider the two straight lines: $y = 3x + 4$

$$y = 3x - 10$$

These lines both have gradient 3, so they are parallel and do not intersect.

Two lines with the same gradient are parallel.

Now consider the two straight lines: $y = 2x + 4$

$$y = -\frac{1}{2}x - 5$$

When plotted you can see these two lines are at right angles to each other (perpendicular). These two straight lines have gradients 2 and –½.

Notice that $2 \times -\frac{1}{2} = -1$

Two straight lines are perpendicular if the product of their gradients is –1.

Using these two rules, it is possible to determine whether two straight lines are parallel, perpendicular or neither without plotting or sketching the lines.

EXAMPLE 1

Re-arrange the equations of these two straight lines to find out whether they are parallel, perpendicular or neither.

$$y + 3x - 6 = 0 \quad (1)$$

$$3y - x + 4 = 0 \quad (2)$$

From (1), $y = -3x + 6$

This line has gradient –3 and y-intercept 6.

From (2), $3y = x - 4$

$$y = \frac{1}{3}x - \frac{4}{3}$$

This line has gradient $\frac{1}{3}$ and y-intercept $-\frac{4}{3}$.

Now compare the gradients, –3 and $\frac{1}{3}$.

They are not the same, so the lines are not parallel.

However, $-3 \times \frac{1}{3} = -1$. So the lines are perpendicular.

EXAMPLE 2

These two straight lines are perpendicular:

$$px + 4y + r = 0 \quad (1)$$
$$-4x + y + 3 = 0 \quad (2)$$

Find the value of p.

From (1), $4y = -px - r$

$$y = -\frac{p}{4}x - \frac{r}{4}$$

The gradient of this line is $-\frac{p}{4}$

From (2), $y = 4x - 3$

The gradient of this line is 4.

We have been told the two lines are perpendicular. Therefore:

$$\left(-\frac{p}{4}\right) \times 4 = -1$$
$$-p = -1$$
$$p = 1$$

EXAMPLE 3

Consider the straight line $y = \frac{1}{2}x - 4$

This line runs parallel to another straight line, which passes through the points $(3, a)$ and $(a, 27)$. Find the value of a.

For the first straight line, the gradient is ½. Because the two lines are parallel, the gradient of the second line must also be ½.

We learnt earlier that, if we know two points on a straight line, (x_1, y_1) and (x_2, y_2), the gradient can be found using:

$$m = \frac{y_2 - y_1}{x_2 - x_1}$$

Two points on the second line are:

$(x_1, y_1) = (3, a)$
$(x_2, y_2) = (a, 27)$

Therefore, the gradient of the second line is $\frac{27 - a}{a - 3}$

Therefore $\frac{27 - a}{a - 3} = \frac{1}{2}$

$$54 - 2a = a - 3$$
$$3a = 57$$
$$a = 19$$

EXERCISE

EXERCISE 5E

1. By re-arranging both equations into the form $y = mx + c$, determine whether each pair of equations represents parallel lines, perpendicular lines or neither.

   a) $y = 2x;\ y = 2x + 3$
   b) $y = 3x + 4;\ y = \frac{1}{3}x - 2$
   c) $2y + 3x + 4 = 0;\ 4y + 6x - 1 = 0$
   d) $6y + 3x + 1 = 0;\ y = 2x$
   e) $2(3 - y) = 3(2 - x);\ y = \frac{2}{3}x + 1$
   f) $y = -x - 4;\ x = -y - 4$
   g) $2(1 - x) - 3(1 - 2y) = 2(1 + x) + 5(2 + 2y);\ 4x - y + 3 = 0$

2. Put these equations into pairs. There is one pair of parallel lines, one pair of perpendicular lines and one pair which are neither:

   a) $y = 3x + 4$
   b) $2y + 2x = 1$
   c) $y = -\frac{1}{3}x - 5$
   d) $y - 2x - 3 = 0$
   e) $x = -y$
   f) $y = \frac{1}{2}x + 3$

3. A straight line has the equation $y - px + 14 = 0$. It is parallel to a line with the equation $2y + 14x - p = 0$. Find the value of p.

4. A line L has the equation $7x + 2y + 5 = 0$.

   a) Write the equation in the form $y = mx + c$.

   b) Find the gradient of a line perpendicular to L.

5. The line with equation $6x + 2y - 9 = 0$ is parallel to the line with equation $y = ax - 8$. Find the value of a.

6. The line with equation $2x + 4y - 1 = 0$ is perpendicular to the line with equation $y = ax + 13$. Find the value of a.

7. The straight line L is parallel to the line $2y + 3x - 4 = 0$. L passes through the point (1, 3). Find the equation of the line L in its general form.

8. The straight line M is perpendicular to the line N, which has equation $3y + xc = 0$. M and N both pass through the point (3, 10).

   a) Find the value of c.

   b) Find the equation of the line M in its general form.

9. Find the equation of the straight line passing through the point (3, –1), which is perpendicular to the line with equation $3x - 2y - 7 = 0$.

10. The line L_1 passes through the point $A(a, 2a)$. It is parallel to another line L_2, which passes through the point $B(0, a)$. A third line L_3 passes through both A and B and is perpendicular to both L_1 and L_2.

    a) Find the gradient of L_3.

    b) Find the equation of L_1 in its general form, leaving the constant a in your answer.

EXERCISE

SUMMARY

- You can find the gradient of a line between two points (x_1, y_1) and (x_2, y_2) using the formula

  $$m = \frac{y_2 - y_1}{x_2 - x_1} \qquad (1)$$

- A linear equation can appear in various forms including

  $y = mx + c$

  $ax + by + c = 0$

  $y - y_1 = m(x - x_1)$

- If the gradient m and a point (x_1, y_1) on a straight line are known, you can find the equation of the line using

  $$y - y_1 = m(x - x_1) \qquad (2)$$

- If two points on a straight line are known, first calculate the gradient using (1), then use (2) to find the equation of the line.

- The form
  $ax + by + c = 0$
  is known as the general equation of a straight line.

- To identify the gradient and y-intercept of a straight line, first re-arrange the equation into the form
  $y = mx + c$

- The midpoint of line segment $A(x_1, y_1)$ and $B(x_2, y_2)$ is $M(x_3, y_3)$, given by:

  $$x_3 = \frac{x_1 + x_2}{2} \qquad y_3 = \frac{y_1 + y_2}{2}$$

- Parallel lines have equal gradients.
  Perpendicular lines have gradients that multiply to make –1.

Chapter 6
Differentiation

6.1 Introduction

What is Differentiation?

Differentiation is a technique used to find the **gradient** of a curve at any point. You can also think of it as finding a **rate of change**. For example, if you have a graph of velocity against time, differentiating will give you the rate of change of velocity, or acceleration. Differentiation is a part of the area of mathematics called **calculus**.

In Chapter 2 we discussed **quadratic** curves. You learnt about the method called **Completing the Square** to solve a quadratic equation. You were also shown that this technique could help you to find the **turning point** of a quadratic curve.

In this chapter you will learn a more advanced way to find the turning points of any curve using differentiation. Of course, this will help you when sketching curves. But there is much more to differentiation than that. You will use the techniques learnt here in a wide variety of mathematics and possibly beyond.

At first, these new techniques may seem strange. In fact, the calculus may be the most important part of mathematics you will ever learn!

Sections 6.2 and 6.3 of this chapter are included as background information for the reader. However, this material is **not included** in the A-Level specification and may be omitted.

Keywords

Calculus: The area of mathematics of which differentiation is a part.

Gradient: The steepness of a curve at any point.

Derivative/gradient function: A function that allows you to calculate the gradient at any point on a curve.

Differentiate: To find the gradient function.

Turning point/stationary point: A point on a curve where the gradient is zero.

Tangent: A straight line that touches a curve at a point, but does not cross it.

Normal: A straight line at right angles to a tangent.

Increasing: A function is increasing if its gradient is positive in a certain interval.

Decreasing: A function is decreasing if its gradient is negative in a certain interval.

Before You Start

You should know how to:

Manipulate indices.

Use the rules of algebraic manipulation.

Sketch curves (You will need this for the section Stationary Points: Maxima and Minima).

Solve inequalities (You will need this for the section Increasing and Decreasing Functions).

What You Will Learn

In this chapter you will learn how to:

- Find the gradient of the tangent to a curve at any point;
- Find the **derivative function;**
- Differentiate expressions involving x^n;
- Solve problems involving rates of change;
- Find **second order** derivatives;
- Find the equations of tangents and normals;
- Find the maximum and minimum points (turning or stationary points) of curves;
- Investigate whether functions are increasing or decreasing.

EXAMPLE 1

Write $(x^3)\sqrt{x}$ as x^n where n a fraction.

The square root is equivalent to the power of a half:

$$(x^3)\sqrt{x} = x^3x^{\frac{1}{2}}$$

Using the rules of indices, add the powers:

$$= x^{3+\frac{1}{2}}$$
$$= x^{\frac{7}{2}}$$

EXAMPLE 2

Write the following as the sum of two powers of x.

$$\frac{x^4 + x^2}{\sqrt{x}}$$

$$\frac{x^4 + x^2}{\sqrt{x}} = \frac{x^4}{\sqrt{x}} + \frac{x^2}{\sqrt{x}}$$
$$= x^4x^{-\frac{1}{2}} + x^2x^{-\frac{1}{2}}$$
$$= x^{\frac{7}{2}} + x^{\frac{3}{2}}$$

EXAMPLE 3

Simplify the following:

$(x^2 + 2x - 3) - (3x - 1)$

$$(x^2 + 2x - 3) - (3x - 1) = x^2 + 2x - 3 - 3x + 1$$
$$= x^2 - x - 2$$

EXAMPLE 4

Sketch the curve $y = (x - 1)^3 + 4$, marking the coordinates of the point at which the curve is flat and the point where the curve intersects the y-axis.

The curve is based on the cubic $y = x^3$.

It is translated by 1 unit in the positive x-direction and 4 units in the positive y-direction.

Recall the curve $y = x^3$ is flat at the origin.

Hence the point at which the curve $y = (x - 1)^3 + 4$ is flat is $(1, 4)$.

To find the coordinates of the point where the curve crosses the y-axis, set $x = 0$.

$$y = (x - 1)^3 + 4$$
$$= -1 + 4$$
$$= 3$$

We now have enough information to draw a sketch of the curve:

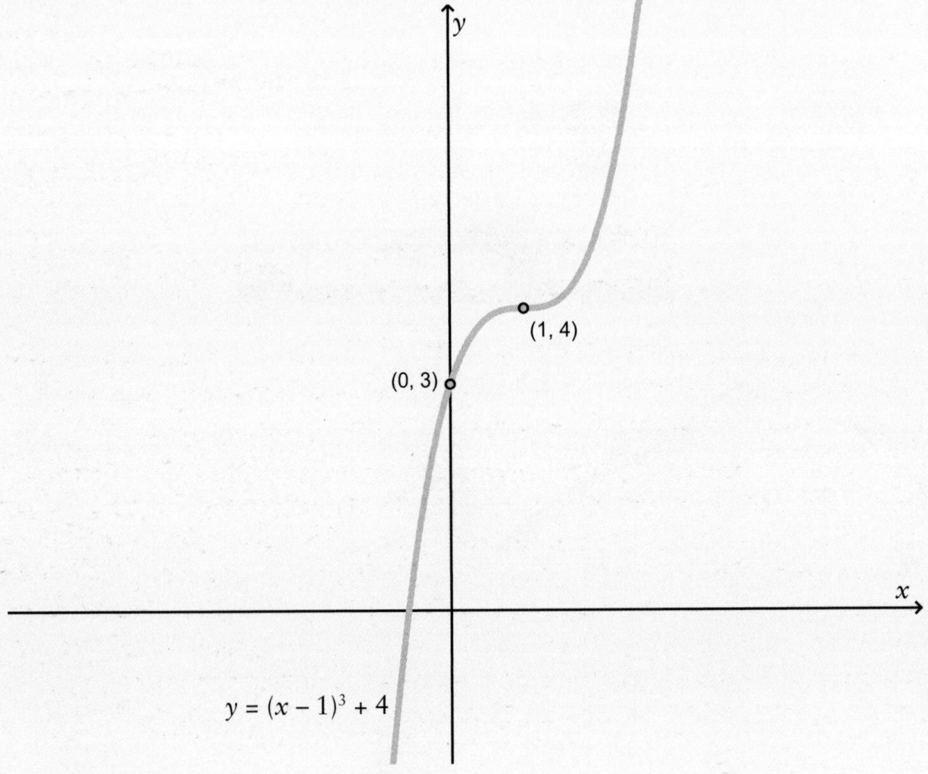

EXAMPLE 5

Find the range of values of x of that make $x(x + 9) < 0$.

Sketch the curve $y = x(x + 9)$.

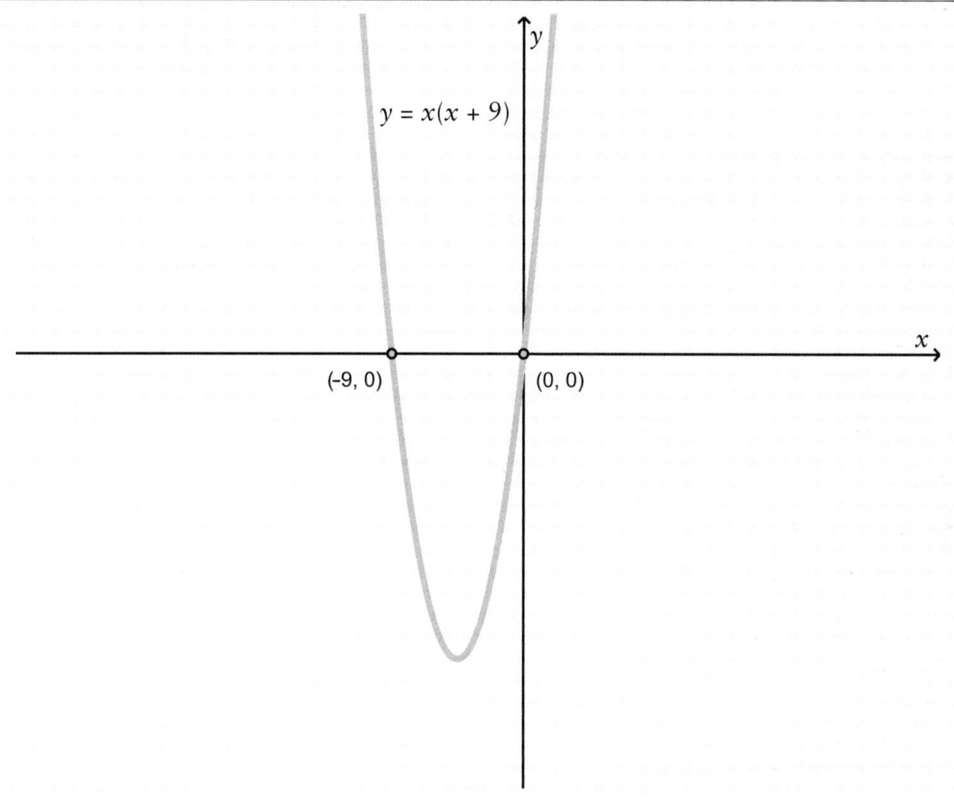

From this we can see that $x(x + 9) < 0$ when

$x > -9$ and $x < 0$.

We write $-9 < x < 0$.

IN THE REAL WORLD

Differentiation is calculating a **rate of change.** This includes calculating acceleration, which is the rate of change of velocity. Calculating acceleration is easy when it is constant, but when it is changing differentiation becomes essential.

Aircraft pilots are one group of people who need to have precise measurements of acceleration. They need to know their exact acceleration on the runway because without enough acceleration they would not be able to take off. Differentiation is used in many diverse areas. Geographers use differentiation to work out how quickly populations are changing; engineers use it to model flows within pipes; biologists to study changes in the populations of species; investment banks use derivative products in increasingly sophisticated ways. The calculus, discovered by Newton and Leibniz, is arguably the greatest mathematical innovation in all of human history.

EXERCISE

REVISION EXERCISE 6A

1. Find the simplest way to write the following algebraic expressions:

   a) $(2x - 1) - (3x - 1)$ b) $(x^2 + 4x - 3) - (2x + 1)$

   c) $(x - 1)^2 + (x + 1)^2$ d) $(1 - x) - (1 - x^2) + (1 - x^3)$

   e) $2x(1 - x) + 6x(x - 1)$

2. Write the following in the form of x^n:

   a) x^2x b) $\dfrac{x^2}{x^{1/2}}$ c) $\dfrac{\sqrt{x}}{x^3}$ d) $\dfrac{x^{-1/2}}{\sqrt{x}}$ e) $\dfrac{x^{1/2}}{\sqrt{x}}$

3. Write the following as sums of powers of x:

   a) $(1 - x)(1 + x^2)$ b) $\dfrac{x^{-1} + x^2}{x^3}$ c) $x(x - 1)(4x + 1)$

   d) $\dfrac{2x^2 + 5x^{-2}}{\sqrt{x}}$ e) $\dfrac{(1 + x)(1 - x)}{x^2}$

4. Sketch the following curves.

   a) $y = \dfrac{3}{x}$ b) $y = \dfrac{1}{x^2}$ c) $y = 2x^3$ d) $y = (x + 2)^3 - 5$

5. Find the values of x for which:

   a) $(x + 1)(x - 3) < 0$ b) $x(x + 9) > 0$

   c) $2x^2 + x - 1 > 0$ d) $2x^2 - 18 < 0$

EXERCISE

6.2 The Gradient of the Tangent to a Curve

The Derivative of *f(x)* as the Gradient of the Tangent to the Graph of $y = f(x)$ at a Point

This section is included as background information for the reader. However, this material is **not included** in the A-Level specification and may be omitted.

How would you work out the gradient of a curve at any point?

You know how to work out the gradient of a straight line, using the formula:

$$m = \frac{rise}{run} = \frac{y_1 - y_0}{x_1 - x_0}$$

You could draw a tangent to the curve at any point and use this method.

The tangent would have the same gradient as the curve. This is shown opposite.

However, there are problems with this method:
1. You need to plot the curve to find the gradient.
2. There may be inaccuracies in your measurements.

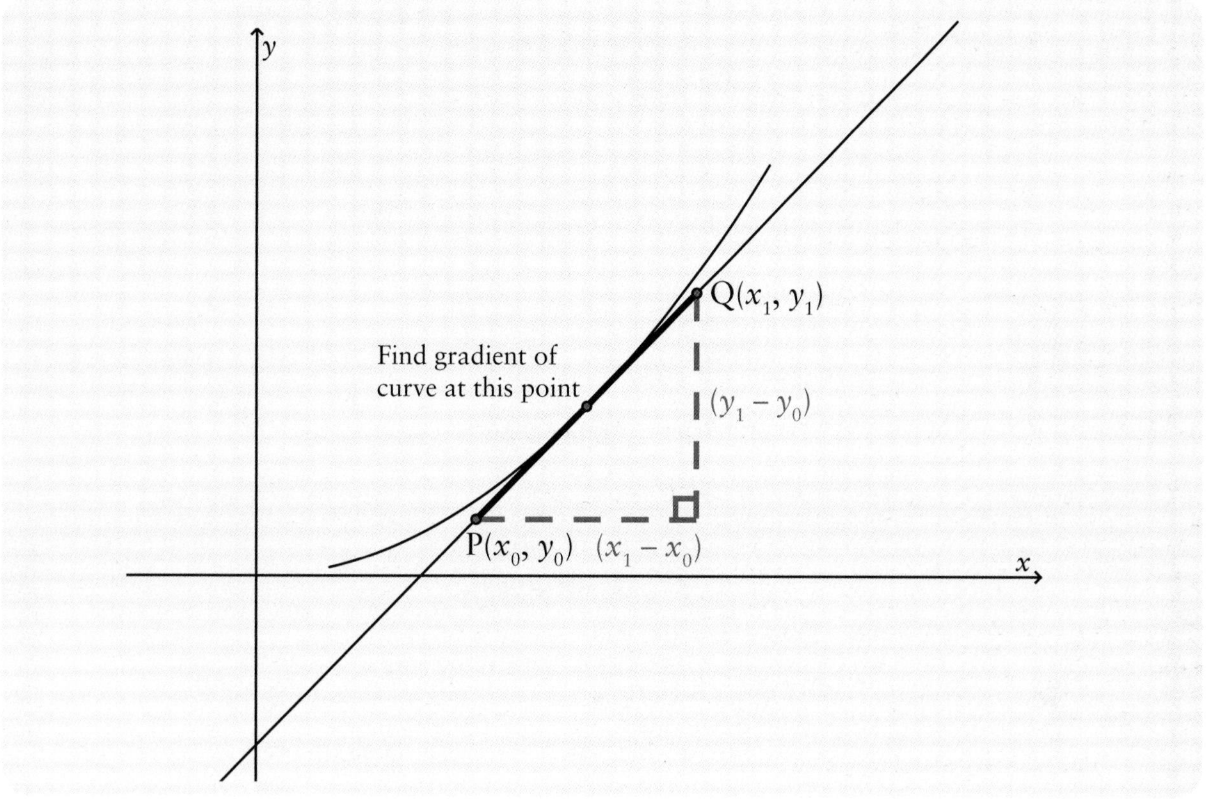

The Gradient of the Tangent as a Limit

In the previous section, we discussed finding the gradient of a curve by drawing a tangent to the curve. There are disadvantages with this method, so in this section we discuss another technique, which uses two points close together on the curve. A chord between these two points would have approximately the same gradient as the curve itself. Consider the two points P (x_0, y_0) and Q (x_1, y_1).

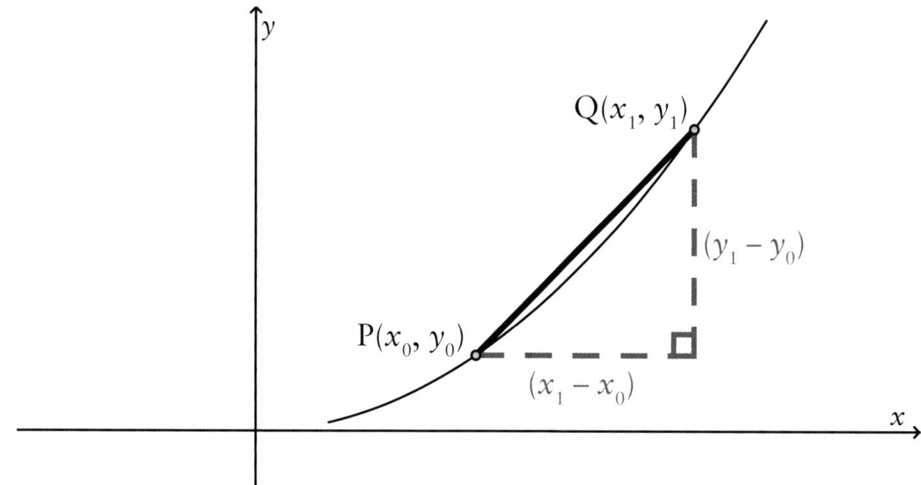

You can see that the gradient of the line PQ is:

$$m = \frac{rise}{run} = \frac{y_1 - y_0}{x_1 - x_0}$$

We can use this as an approximation of the gradient of the curve at P.
The approximation becomes better when the distance PQ becomes smaller:

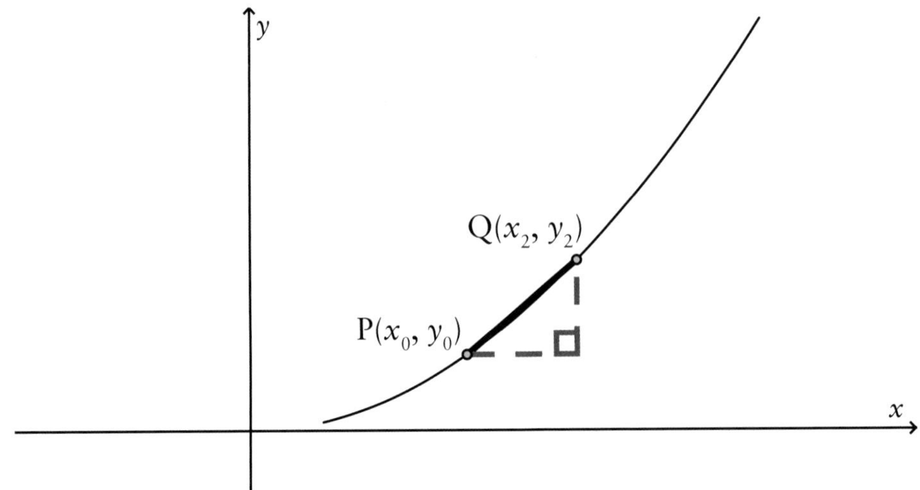

When Q moves to the point (x_2, y_2) you can see that the gradient of the chord PQ is a better approximation of the gradient of the curve.

The closer your two points P and Q, the better the approximation is going to be.

In general, as Q approaches P, the gradient of the chord PQ approaches the gradient of the curve.

This technique is known as the **Method of Small Increments.**
We can use it to estimate the gradient of a curve at a point.

EXAMPLE 1

Consider the curve $y = x^2$

By considering smaller and smaller chords, estimate the gradient at point P(1,1).

For the point Q, use the following values for x_1 and calculate the y-coordinate y_1.

$$x_1 = 2,\ 1.1,\ 1.01,\ 1.001$$

We draw up the following table, using the equation $y = x^2$ to calculate our y_1 values from the x_1 values given.

x_0	y_0	x_1	y_1	$m = \dfrac{y_1 - y_0}{x_1 - x_0}$
1	1	2	4	3
1	1	1.1	1.21	2.1
1	1	1.01	1.0201	2.01
1	1	1.001	1.002001	2.001

We can see that as our chord gets smaller, our estimate of the gradient m gets closer to 2.
We can therefore state that the gradient of the curve at (1, 1) is 2.

EXERCISE

EXERCISE 6B

You may use a calculator for this exercise.

1. By considering the gradient of a chord from the point P(1, 1) to the point Q, estimate the gradient of the curve $y = x^3$ at P. Use the following x-values for Q:

   $x_1 = 2, 1.1, 1.01, 1.001$

2. The curve C has equation $y = x^2 - 2x - 1$. Estimate the gradient of the curve at the point P(2, −1) by considering the gradient of the chord from P to Q, for each of the following values of the x-coordinate of Q:

   $x_1 = 3, 2.1, 2.01, 2.001$

EXERCISE

6.3 Differentiation From First Principles

In section 6.2 we estimated the gradient at a single point on a curve using a chord between two points, making those two points closer and closer together.

In this section, you will improve on this method. You will learn how to find the **derivative** or **gradient function**, which we write as $\frac{dy}{dx}$. The derivative will usually be a function of x.
It can be used to calculate the gradient at **any point** on the curve.

This section is included as background information for the reader. However, this material is **not included** in the A-Level specification and may be omitted.

EXAMPLE 1

Consider again the curve $y = x^2$

Find the derivative $\frac{dy}{dx}$ from first principles.

Consider a general point on this curve P (x, y).

Now consider a point on the curve close to P, Q $(x + \delta x, y + \delta y)$.

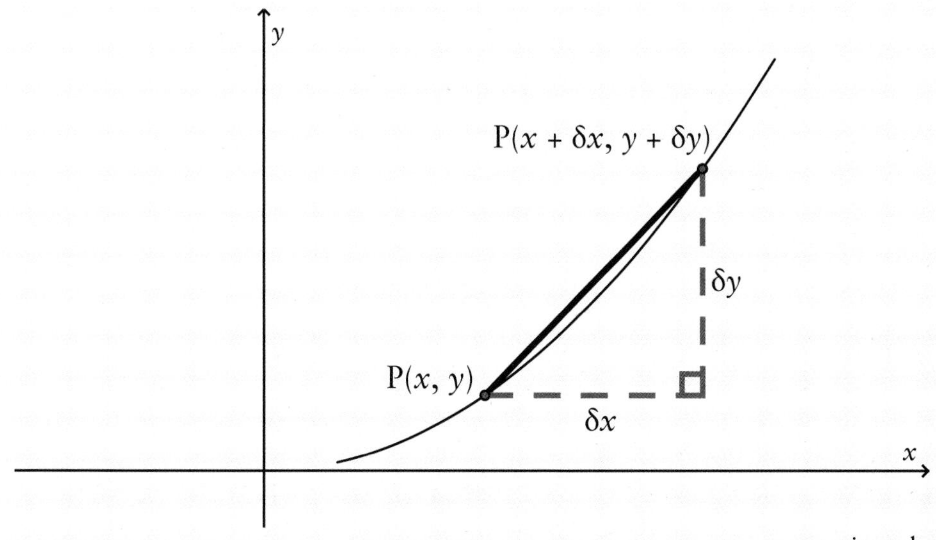

continued...

Example 1...

Note: The Greek letter δ (delta) is often used to denote a small increment or change. δx is a small change in x, so $x + \delta x$ is a number close to x.

Using the equation of the curve:

$$y = x^2 \quad (1)$$

and $y + \delta y = (x + \delta x)^2$

Expanding brackets gives: $y + \delta y = x^2 + 2x\delta x + \delta x^2$ (2)

(2) – (1) gives $\delta y = 2x\delta x + \delta x^2$

Dividing by δx gives $\frac{\delta y}{\delta x} = 2x + \delta x$.

As δx and δy approach zero (the points P and Q are getting closer together), we can discard the term δx. At the limit, we replace $\frac{\delta y}{\delta x}$ with $\frac{dy}{dx}$.

Hence $\frac{dy}{dx} = 2x$

This is the gradient function.
We can use it to calculate the gradient of the curve $y = x^2$ at any point.

For example when $x = 1$, $\frac{dy}{dx} = 2$;

when $x = 5$, $\frac{dy}{dx} = 10$.

Note: You may sometimes see this notation: $\frac{dy}{dx} = \lim_{x \to 0} \frac{\delta y}{\delta x}$

This means: the derivative $\frac{dy}{dx}$ is the limiting value of $\frac{\delta y}{\delta x}$ as x approaches zero.

EXAMPLE 2

Find the derivative of the function $y = 4 - x^2$ from first principles.

Consider the point $P(x, y)$ and a point on the curve close to P, $Q(x + \delta x, y + \delta y)$.

$$y = 4 - x^2 \quad (1)$$

and $y + \delta y = 4 - (x + \delta x)^2$

Expanding brackets gives: $y + \delta y = 4 - (x^2 + 2x\delta x + \delta x^2)$ (2)

(2) – (1) gives $\delta y = -2x\delta x - \delta x^2$

Dividing by δx gives $\frac{\delta y}{\delta x} = -2x + \delta x$.

As δx and δy approach zero, we can discard the term δx. At the limit, we replace $\frac{\delta y}{\delta x}$ with $\frac{dy}{dx}$.

Hence $\frac{dy}{dx} = -2x$.

EXAMPLE 3

Find the derivative of the function $y = 5 - 2x$ from first principles.

Consider the point P(x, y) and a point on the curve close to P, Q $(x + \delta x, y + \delta y)$.

$y = 5 - 2x \quad (1)$

and $y + \delta y = 5 - 2(x + \delta x)$

Expanding brackets gives: $y + \delta y = 5 - 2x - 2\delta x \quad (2)$

(2) – (1) gives $\delta y = -2\delta x$

Dividing by δx gives $\frac{\delta y}{\delta x} = -2$

As δx and δy approach zero, we replace $\frac{\delta y}{\delta x}$ with $\frac{dy}{dx}$.

Hence $\frac{dy}{dx} = -2$

EXERCISE 6C

1. For each of the following curves, by first finding expressions for δy and $\frac{\delta y}{\delta x}$, find $\frac{dy}{dx}$.

   a) $y = x + 2$ b) $y = x^2 + 2$ c) $y = 5x$

   d) $y = 5 - 3x$ e) $y = x(x - 1)$

2. Differentiate each of the following:

   a) $y = 2 - x^2$ b) $y = 2 + 3x$ c) $y = 2x^2 + 5x$

   d) $y = 3x(1 - x)$ e) $y = 2x(x + 1)$

3. Find the derivative $\frac{dy}{dx}$ for each function. Hence calculate the gradient of each curve at the point given.

   a) $y = x^2 + 10$ at point (1, 11) b) $y = (x - 1)(x + 2)$ at point (0, –2)

   c) $y = 3x^2 + 2x + 1$ at point (1, 6) d) (Difficult) $y = x^3$ at point (1, 1)

   e) (Difficult) $y = x^3 + 3x^2$ at point (1, 4)

EXERCISE

EXERCISE

6.4 Differentiation of Powers of x

Notation

Note that there is an alternative notation for the derivative or gradient function.

If we have defined a function, for example $f(x) = 3x^2$

then we can write the derivative as: $f'(x) = 6x$

$f'(x)$ and $\frac{dy}{dx}$ mean **the same thing** and are both notations for the derivative.

We would most often use $\frac{dy}{dx}$ if the original equation involves y.

We would use $f'(x)$ if the original equation is defined in terms of $f(x)$.

Throughout the rest of this chapter you may see both notations being used.

Differentiation of x^n

Consider the following results:

$$y = x^2 \Rightarrow \frac{dy}{dx} = 2x \qquad y = x^3 \Rightarrow \frac{dy}{dx} = 3x^2 \qquad y = x^4 \Rightarrow \frac{dy}{dx} = 4x^3$$

You may have spotted a pattern when considering these derivatives. The general rule is:

$$y = x^n \Rightarrow \frac{dy}{dx} = nx^{n-1}$$

Also, note that a multiplying constant will not affect the differentiation:

$$y = ax^n \Rightarrow \frac{dy}{dx} = anx^{n-1}$$

For the C1 module, you will not be asked to find a derivative from first principles. Instead, you will often use the rules above.

EXAMPLE 1

Find the derivative of $y = 4x$.

$$y = 4x^1$$

Multiply by the power and reduce the power by 1: $\frac{dy}{dx} = 1 \times 4x^{1-1}$

$$\frac{dy}{dx} = 4x^0$$

$$\frac{dy}{dx} = 4$$

This result was expected. We already know that the straight line $y = 4x$ has a gradient of 4.

EXAMPLE 2

Find $\frac{dy}{dx}$ when $y = 4$

$y = 4x^0$

Multiply by the power and reduce the power by 1:

$$\frac{dy}{dx} = 0 \times 4x^{-1}$$

$$\frac{dy}{dx} = 0$$

This result was also expected.
We know that any horizontal line,
such as $y = 4$ has a gradient of 0.

Note: Differentiating a constant will always give 0.

EXAMPLE 3

A curve has equation $y = 3x^{\frac{2}{3}}$.

a) Find $\frac{dy}{dx}$

b) Find the gradient of the curve at the point (8, 12).

a) $y = 3x^{\frac{2}{3}}$

Multiply by the power and reduce the power by 1:

$$\frac{dy}{dx} = \frac{2}{3} \times 3x^{-\frac{1}{3}}$$

$$\frac{dy}{dx} = 2x^{-1/3}$$

or

$$\frac{dy}{dx} = \frac{2}{\sqrt[3]{x}}$$

b) When $x = 8$

$$\frac{dy}{dx} = \frac{2}{\sqrt[3]{8}}$$

$$\frac{dy}{dx} = \frac{2}{2}$$

$$\frac{dy}{dx} = 1$$

EXERCISE 6D

1. Find the derivative $\frac{dy}{dx}$ for each of the following equations.

a) $y = 3x^2$ b) $y = 2x$ c) $y = -7x$ d) $y = 2x^5$

e) $y = \frac{3}{7}x^7$ f) $y = -2x^3$ g) $y = -\frac{5x}{4}$ h) $y = \frac{1}{3}x^{-3}$

2. By rewriting these equations in the form $y = ax^n$, differentiate to find $\frac{dy}{dx}$.

a) $y = \frac{1}{x}$ b) $y = \sqrt{x}$ c) $y = \frac{1}{\sqrt{x}}$ d) $y = x\sqrt{x}$

e) $y = \frac{1}{x\sqrt{x}}$ f) $y = -\frac{2}{x^2}$ g) $y = \frac{2}{3x\sqrt{x}}$ h) $y = -\frac{3}{\sqrt[3]{x}}$

3. Find the gradient of each curve at the point given:

a) $y = 3x$; $(-1, -3)$ b) $y = x^2$; $(2, 4)$ c) $y = \frac{1}{x}$; $(2, 0.5)$

d) $y = \sqrt{x}$; $(4, 2)$ e) $y = \frac{4}{\sqrt{x}}$; $(4, 2)$ f) $y = -\frac{4}{x^2}$; $(2, -1)$

g) $y = \frac{5}{3x\sqrt{x}}$; $\left(4, \frac{5}{24}\right)$ h) $y = \frac{24}{\sqrt[3]{x}}$; $(8, 12)$

4. Consider $y = x^2$.
   a) What is the derivative $\frac{dy}{dx}$?
   b) What happens to $\frac{dy}{dx}$ when x approaches infinity?
   (Hint: try putting some very large values of x into your expression for $\frac{dy}{dx}$.)
   c) What happens to $\frac{dy}{dx}$ when x approaches negative infinity?

5. Consider $y = x^3$.
   a) What is the derivative $\frac{dy}{dx}$?
   b) What happens to $\frac{dy}{dx}$ when x approaches infinity?
   c) What happens to $\frac{dy}{dx}$ when x approaches negative infinity?
   d) How does your answer to part c differ from your answer to question 4 part c? How do these results relate to the graphs of the two curves?

6. Match the following functions with their derivatives:

Functions:	$\frac{1}{3}x^3$	$(x + 1)(x - 2)$	$3x^3$	$\frac{5}{x^2}$	$5x^2$
Derivatives:	$9x^2$	x^2	$-\frac{10}{x^3}$	$10x$	$2x - 1$

EXERCISE

EXERCISE

Differentiation of Sums and Differences

When differentiating a sum of powers of x, we simply differentiate each term in turn.

$$\text{If } y = f(x) + g(x), \text{ then } \frac{dy}{dx} = f'(x) + g'(x).$$

EXAMPLE 1

Find $\frac{dy}{dx}$ when $y = x^2 + 3x + 1$

Differentiating x^2 gives $2x$.

Differentiating $3x$ gives 3.

Differentiating 1 gives 0.

$$\frac{dy}{dx} = 2x + 3$$

Remember: differentiating a constant gives zero.

Multiply out brackets before differentiating:

EXAMPLE 2

$f(x) = (x + 3)(x - 2)$

Find $f'(x)$.

Expanding brackets: $f(x) = x^2 + x - 6$

$f'(x) = 2x + 1$

Sometimes you will need to differentiate with respect to a variable other than x.

EXAMPLE 3

a) $y = 4t^3 + 3t^4$ Find $\frac{dy}{dt}$.

b) Find $f'(\theta)$ when $f(\theta) = \theta^2 - \theta^3$.

---

a) Differentiate with respect to t:

$$\frac{dy}{dt} = 12t^2 + 12t^3$$

b) Differentiate with respect to θ:

$f'(\theta) = 2\theta - 3\theta^2$

EXERCISE 6E

1. Differentiate the following with respect to x:

   a) $y = 3x^2 + 4x$ b) $y = 3x^4 - x$ c) $y = \frac{1}{x} + \frac{4}{x^2}$

   d) $y = \frac{x}{3} + \frac{x^2}{4}$ e) $y = (x-3)(x-1)$ f) $y = x^2(x+3)$

   g) $y = x^2(x^2 - x + 1)$ h) $y = (1 + x^2)(x^2 - 1)$ i) $y = \sqrt{x} + 3x$

   j) $y = \frac{1 - \sqrt{x}}{x}$ k) $y = \sqrt{x}(2x - 1)$ l) $y = \frac{1}{\sqrt{x}}(1 - x^2)$

2. Differentiate the following equations with respect to the variable in the right-hand side of the equation:

   a) $y = 4t^2 + 3t$ b) $P = v^2 - \frac{1}{v}$ c) $v = 3 + 10t$

   d) $s = t + 5t^2$ e) $p = \frac{1}{q}(q - 1)$ f) $W = \sqrt{x}(x^2 - 1)$

   g) $A = (1 - s)(2s - 1)$ h) $z = \frac{\theta^4 - \theta^2}{\theta^3}$ i) $m = (n^2 + 1)(3n - 2)$

   j) $A = \pi r^2$ (Note: π is a constant)

3. Find $f'(x)$ given $f(x)$ in each case:

   a) $f(x) = 1 - 2x^2$ b) $f(x) = \frac{1 - x}{x}$ c) $f(x) = \frac{4x^4 - x^3}{x^2}$

   d) $f(x) = \frac{x^2 + 2}{x}$ e) $f(x) = \frac{(x-2)^2}{x}$ f) $f(x) = \frac{1 - \sqrt{x}}{\sqrt{x}}$

   g) $f(x) = (x - 2)(2x - 1)$ h) $f(x) = x(2x^2 - x)$ i) $f(x) = \sqrt{x} + x\sqrt{x} + x$

   j) $f(x) = \frac{px^2 + qx}{r}$ (Note: p, q and r are constants.)

4. Given $f(x) = 3x + 2$ and $g(x) = x^2$:

   a) Find $f'(x)$ b) Find $g'(x)$

   c) Find $f'(x)g'(x)$ d) Find $\frac{f'(x)}{g'(x)}$

   e) Work out $h(x)$ where $h(x) = f(x)g(x)$ f) Find $h'(x)$

   g) Does $h'(x) = f'(x)g'(x)$? h) Work out $j(x)$ where $j(x) = \frac{f(x)}{g(x)}$

   i) Find $j'(x)$ j) Does $j'(x) = \frac{f'(x)}{g'(x)}$?

EXERCISE

EXERCISE

6.5 Differentiation as a Rate of Change

In previous sections, you have learnt how to work out the derivative for various functions. You learnt that the derivative measures the gradient of the curve, when one variable is plotted against another.

However, there is another interpretation of the derivative: the rate at which one variable is changing with respect to the other.

EXAMPLE 1

Consider a circle, which is increasing in size.
What is the rate of change of the area when the radius is:

a) 1 cm b) 2 cm c) 3 cm ?

The formula for the area of a circle is $A = \pi r^2$.

Differentiate with respect to r: $\frac{\mathrm{d}A}{\mathrm{d}r} = 2\pi r$ (remember, π is just a constant).

a) When $r = 1$, $\frac{\mathrm{d}A}{\mathrm{d}r} = 2\pi \approx 6$

b) When $r = 2$, $\frac{\mathrm{d}A}{\mathrm{d}r} = 4\pi \approx 12$

c) When $r = 3$, $\frac{\mathrm{d}A}{\mathrm{d}r} = 6\pi \approx 18$

In other words, the area changes at a smaller rate when the radius is small, and a higher rate as the radius increases. When the radius is 3 cm, the area increases by about 18 cm^2 every time the radius increases by 1 cm.

EXAMPLE 2

A box in the shape of a cube increases in size.

a) If each side of the cube has length x cm, and the volume of the box is V cm^3, write down an equation linking the volume and side length.

b) Differentiate to find an equation for the rate of change of the volume with respect to the side length.

c) What is the rate of change of the volume when the side length is 1 cm?

d) What is the rate of change of the volume when the side length is 2 cm?

---

a) $V = x^3$

b) $\frac{\mathrm{d}V}{\mathrm{d}x} = 3x^2$

continued...

Example 2...

c) When $x = 1, \dfrac{dV}{dx} = 3$

d) When $x = 2, \dfrac{dV}{dx} = 12$

In other words:

when the cube has side length 1 cm, the volume is increasing at a rate of 3 cm^3 per 1 cm increase in side length;

when the cube has side length 2 cm, the volume is increasing at a rate of 12 cm^3 per 1 cm increase in side length.

EXAMPLE 3

The velocity of a ball is governed by the equation:

$$v = \frac{12}{t} + 6t$$

where t is the time between 1 and 3 seconds.

a) Acceleration is the rate of change of velocity with respect to time. Differentiate v to find an equation for the acceleration of the ball.

b) When $t = 1$, is the ball accelerating or decelerating?

c) When $t = 2$, is the ball accelerating or decelerating?

---

a) $\dfrac{dv}{dt} = -\dfrac{12}{t^2} + 6$

b) When $t = 1, \dfrac{dv}{dt} = -\dfrac{12}{1^2} + 6 = -6$

The acceleration is negative, so the ball is decelerating.

c) When $t = 2, \dfrac{dv}{dt} = -\dfrac{12}{2^2} + 6 = 3$

The acceleration is positive, so the ball is accelerating.

EXERCISE

EXERCISE 6F

1. Find the rate of change of the variable on the left with respect to the variable on the right-hand side of the equation:

a) $y = 2x^2$

b) $F = p^4 + \dfrac{1}{p}$

c) $A = \dfrac{5}{2}r^2 + \dfrac{7}{2}r$

d) $b = \dfrac{\sqrt{c} + c}{c^2}$

e) $x = \dfrac{5}{y^2}$

EXERCISE

EXERCISE

2. Find the rate of change of y with respect to x when y takes the value given:

   a) $y = 2x;\ x = 1$ b) $y = 3x^2;\ x = 2$ c) $y = \frac{1}{3}x^3;\ x = 3$

   d) $y = 2\sqrt{x};\ x = 4$ e) $y = \frac{3}{4}x^4 + \frac{2}{3}x^3 + \frac{3}{2}x^2 - 2x;\ x = -1$

3. The volume of water flowing in a pipe is related to the pressure by the formula $V = 3p^2 + \frac{4}{p}$ (where V is measured in m^3s^{-1} and p in bars). Find the rate of change of the volume when the pressure is 2 bars.

4. The surface area of a cylinder is given by the formula $A = 2\pi r^2 + 2\pi rh$, where r is the radius and h is the height.

   a) Eliminate h from this equation by considering the case when the height is equal to the radius (i.e. $h = r$).

   b) The cylinder increases in size, but the height remains equal to the radius. Differentiate your answer to part a) to find the rate of change of A with respect to the radius r.

   c) How fast is the area changing per centimetre increase in the radius when the radius is 2 cm? Leave π in your answer.

5. A tourist drops a coin from a tall building. The distance (in metres) it has fallen is given by the equation $x = 24t + 5t^2$, where t is the time (in seconds). Find the velocity of the coin after 10 seconds. (Hint: velocity is the rate of change of distance with respect to time.)

6. The formula $c = 2s + \sqrt[3]{s}$ links two of the variables in an experiment.

   a) Find the rate of change of c with respect to s.

   b) (Difficult) What is the value of s when the rate of change of c with respect to s is $\frac{10}{3}$.

EXERCISE

6.6 Gradients of Tangents and Normals

In section 6.2 we saw that the gradient of a curve at a point is equal to the gradient of the tangent at the same point.

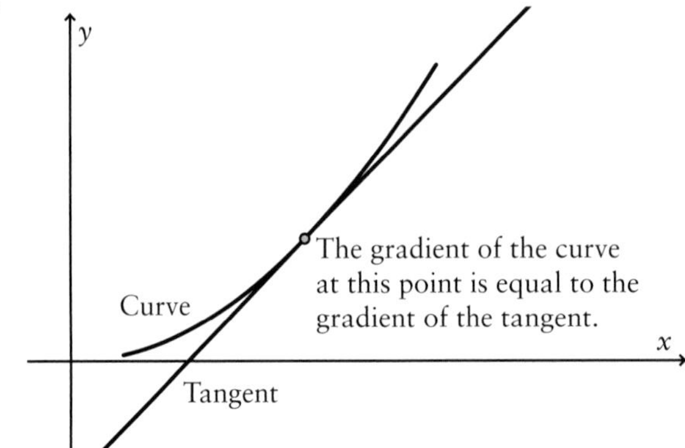

Previously, we discussed measuring the gradient of the tangent and using this to find the gradient of the curve at the point. However, we can also do the reverse: find the gradient of the tangent using the gradient of the curve, which we will work out using differentiation.

EXAMPLE 1

Find the gradient of the tangent at the point (2, 4) on the curve $y = x^2$.

A sketch of the curve and the tangent looks like the graph shown on the right:

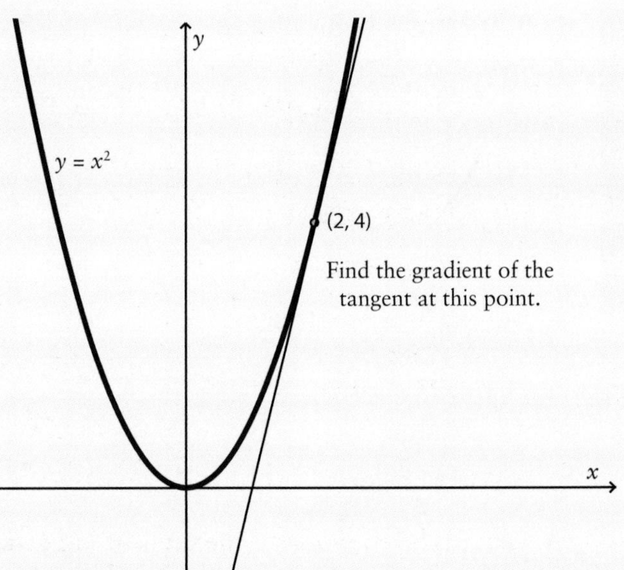

Equation of curve: $y = x^2$

Differentiate to find gradient function:

$$\frac{dy}{dx} = 2x$$

At point (2, 4) $x = 2$, so $\frac{dy}{dx} = 4$.

Since the gradient of the tangent equals the gradient of the curve at this point, the gradient of the tangent is also 4.

EXAMPLE 2

Find the **equation** of the tangent to the curve $y = x^3 - 4x$ at the point (1, –3).

We can sketch the curve by factorising its equation: $y = x(x^2 - 4)$

Using the difference of two squares: $y = x(x - 2)(x + 2)$.

This curve crosses the x-axis where $x = 0$, 2 and –2.

Remembering our work on cubics, the term in x^3 is positive, so this begins in the bottom left and ends in the top right quadrant of the graph.

continued...

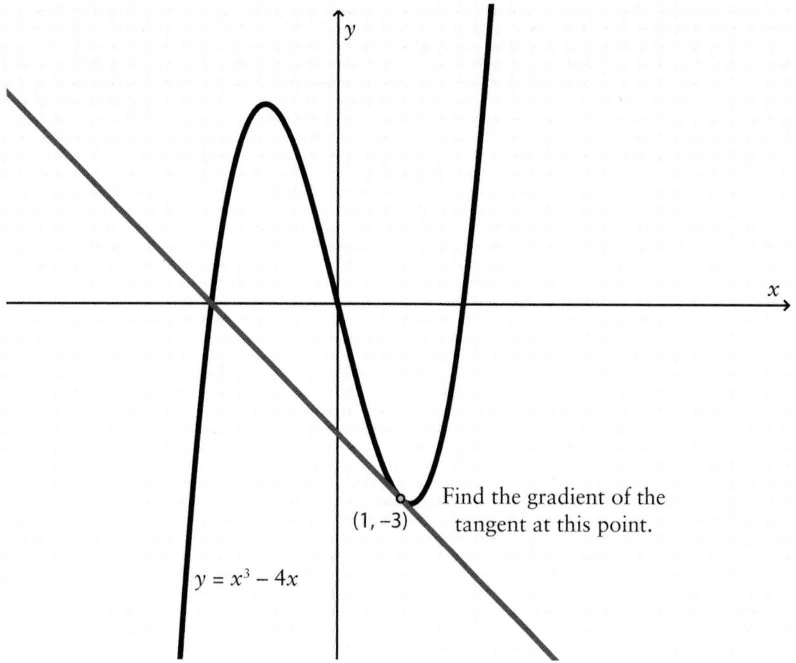

Equation of curve: $y = x^3 - 4x$

Differentiate to find gradient function: $\dfrac{\mathrm{d}y}{\mathrm{d}x} = 3x^2 - 4$

At point (1, –3) $x = 1$, so $\dfrac{\mathrm{d}y}{\mathrm{d}x} = 3(1)^2 - 4 = -1$

Since the gradient of the tangent equals the gradient of the curve at this point, the gradient of the tangent is also –1.

However, this question asks for the **equation** of the tangent. We use the equation of a straight line: $y - y_1 = m(x - x_1)$

We know the gradient $m = -1$ and a point on the line (1, –3). Therefore: $y - (-3) = -1(x - 1)$

$$y + 3 = -x + 1$$

Hence the equation of the tangent is: $y = -x - 2$

The equation of the tangent indicates that the gradient is –1 and the y-intercept is –2. This agrees with our sketch.

The **normal** to a curve is the straight line at right angles to the tangent at a point on the curve.

The normal also cuts the curve at right angles as shown:

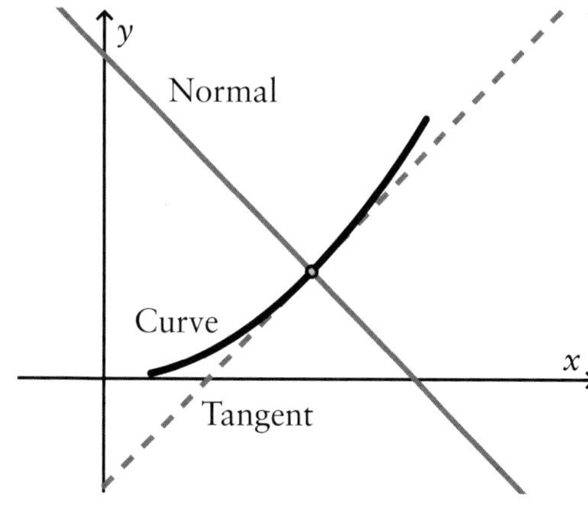

Now, remember from Chapter 5:

Two straight lines are perpendicular if the product of their gradients is –1.

Hence, using the gradient of the tangent, it is also possible to find the gradient of the normal to the curve.

If we call the gradient of the tangent m_1 and the gradient of the normal m_2, then:

$$m_1 m_2 = -1$$

$$m_2 = -\frac{1}{m_1}$$

We could also find the **equation** of the normal.

EXAMPLE 3

Find the equation of the normal to the curve $y = x^2 - 4x + 1$ at the point (3, –2).

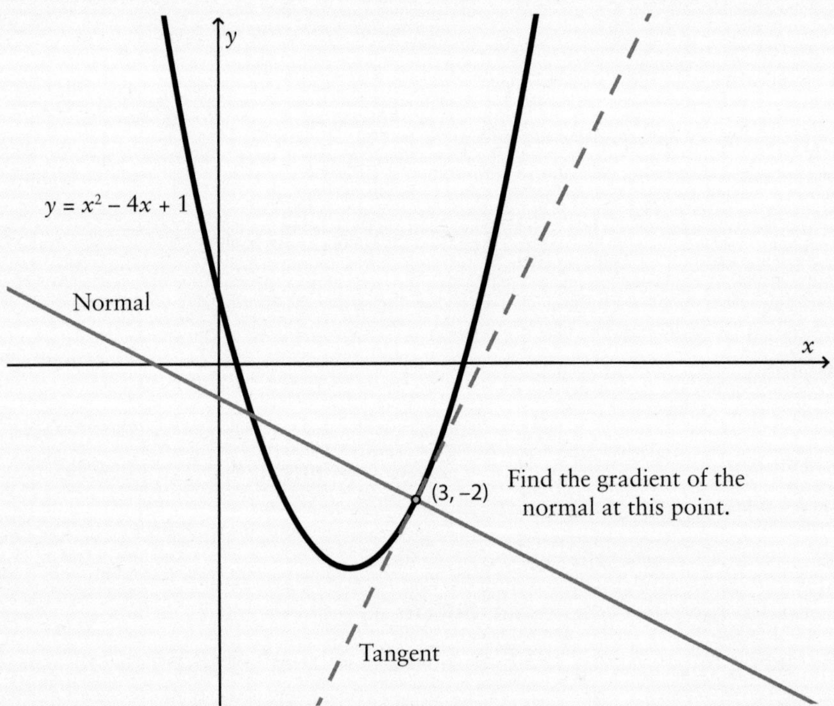

Equation of curve: $y = x^2 - 4x + 1$

Differentiate to find gradient function: $\frac{dy}{dx} = 2x - 4$

At point (3, –2) $x = 3$, so $\frac{dy}{dx} = 2(3) - 4 = 2$

So the gradient of the tangent is $m_1 = 2$.

Using $m_2 = -\frac{1}{m_1}$ to find the gradient of the normal, we find $m_2 = -\frac{1}{2}$.

This question asks for the **equation** of the normal. From the equation of a straight line: $y - y_1 = m(x - x_1)$

continued...

We know the gradient is $-\frac{1}{2}$ and a point on the line is (3, –2).

Therefore: $y-(-2) = -\frac{1}{2}(x-3)$

$$y+2 = -\frac{1}{2}x+\frac{3}{2}$$

$$y = -\frac{1}{2}x-\frac{1}{2}$$

Hence the equation of the normal in its general form is: $x + 2y + 1 = 0$.

Note: a sketch is not essential to answer this type of question. It may, however, help you to visualise the problem.

EXERCISE 6G

1. Consider the curve $y = x^2$.
   a) Find the gradient function $\frac{dy}{dx}$.
   b) Find the gradient of the curve at the point (1, 1).
   c) Find the equation of the tangent to the curve at this point.
2. Find the equation of the tangent to the curve $y = x^4 - 4x^2 + 3$ where $x = 2$.
3. Find the equation of the tangent at the point $x = 4$ on the curve $y = x^3 - 7x^2 + 5$.
4. Find, in general form, the equation of the normal at the point $x = 2$ on the curve $y = x^4 - 4x^2 + 4$.
5. The curve C has equation $y = x^3 - 3x + \frac{3}{x}$. The points A and B both lie on C and have coordinates (1, –3) and (–1, 3) respectively.
   a) Show that the gradient of C at A is equal to the gradient of C at B.
   b) Find the equation for the normal to C at A in its general form.
6. The curve C has equation $y = 4x^2 + \frac{5-x}{x}$. The point P on C has x-coordinate 1.
   a) Show that the value of $\frac{dy}{dx}$ at P is 3. (Hint: Rewrite the equation for C. Split the fraction part into two separate fractions.)
   b) Find an equation of the tangent to C at P.
7. The curve C is given by the equation $y = x^4(4x^6 + 4x^3)$. Calculate the gradient of the tangent at the point $x = 1$ on C.
8. The curve C has equation $y = (x-2)(x^2-16)$. The curve cuts the x-axis at the points P(2, 0), Q and R.
   a) Write down the x-coordinates of Q and R.
   b) Show that $\frac{dy}{dx} = 3x^2 - 4x - 16$.
   c) Show that $y = -9x + 36$ is an equation of the tangent to C at the point (–1, 45).

EXERCISE

EXERCISE

You can also use information about the gradient to find out the coordinates of a point on a curve.

EXAMPLE 4

Find the coordinates of the point on the curve $y = x^2 + 4x - 2$ where the gradient of the curve is 2.

Equation of curve: $y = x^2 + 4x - 2$

Differentiate to find gradient function: $\frac{dy}{dx} = 2x + 4$

We need to know where the gradient is 2, so we must solve:

$2x + 4 = 2$

$x = -1$

Substitute $x = -1$ into equation of curve $y = x^2 + 4x - 2$:

$y = -5$

So the coordinates of the point are $(-1, -5)$.

EXERCISE 6H

1. Find the coordinates of the point on the curve $y = x^2$ where the gradient of the curve is –2.
2. Consider the curve $y = -\frac{1}{x^2}$.
   a) Differentiate to find $\frac{dy}{dx}$.
   b) Find the coordinates of the point where the gradient of the curve is ¼.
3. The curve C has equation $y = 2\sqrt{x}$. What are the coordinates of the points where:
   a) $\frac{dy}{dx} = \frac{1}{2}$ b) $\frac{dy}{dx} = \frac{1}{3}$
4. If $y = 6x + 2x^3$,
   a) find $\frac{dy}{dx}$.
   b) Hence find the coordinates of the points where the gradient of the curve is 12.
5. At a point P on the curve $y = 4x^2 - 16x$ the tangent to the curve is parallel to the x-axis. What are the coordinates of the point P?
6. There are two points P and Q on the curve $y = x(x^2 - 51)$ where the gradient of the curve is –3. What are the x-coordinates of P and Q?
7. What are the coordinates of the two points at which the gradient of the curve $y = \frac{1}{x}$ is –4?
8. There are two points on the curve $y = \frac{1}{3}x^3 - 4x^2 + 2$ at which the gradient is –12. What are the coordinates of those points?

EXERCISE

EXERCISE

EXERCISE

9. A curve C has equation $y = 4x^3 - 42x^2 + 125x + 12$.

   a) Find $\frac{dy}{dx}$ in terms of x.

   b) The points P and Q lie on C. The gradient of C at both P and Q is 5. The x-coordinate of P is 2. Find the x-coordinate of Q.

   c) Find an equation for the tangent to C at P, giving your answer in the form $y = mx + c$.

10. The velocity of a stone falling off a cliff reaches 30 ms^{-1} as it hits the sea. Given that its distance from the cliff-top is given by the formula $s = 5t^2$, find the height of the cliff. (Hint: velocity is the rate of change of distance with respect to time.)

11. The Cheshire Cat's face slowly disappears, leaving only its smile, which then also disappears. The amount of face remaining is governed by the equation $F = 5(9 - \sqrt{t})$, where F is the area of face in cm^2 and t is the time in seconds.

   a) How big is the Cheshire Cat's face in cm^2 initially?

   b) Find the time at which the rate of change of facial area is $-\frac{1}{2}$ $\text{cm}^2\ \text{s}^{-1}$.

   c) How long does it take for the entire face to disappear?

EXERCISE

6.7 Stationary Points: Maxima and Minima

A **stationary point** (or **turning point**) of a curve is where the curve has a gradient 0, i.e. the curve is flat at this point. Here are some examples of stationary points:

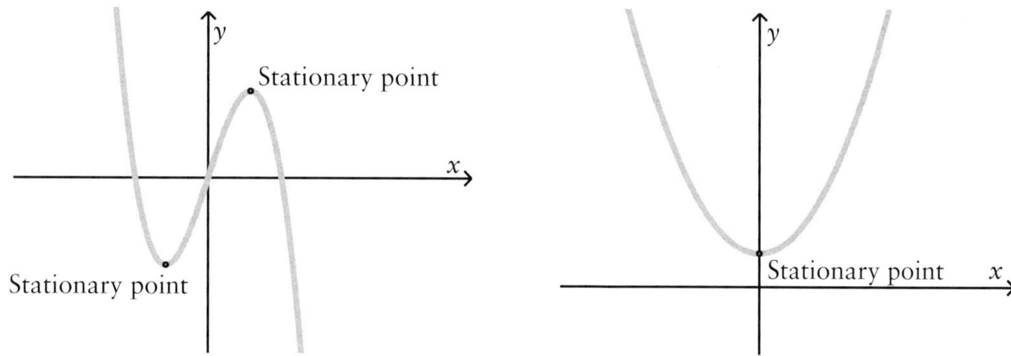

We can work out the position of a stationary point by finding the gradient function $\frac{dy}{dx}$ and setting it equal to zero.

EXAMPLE 1

Find the coordinates of the stationary point of the curve $y = x^2 - 4x + 5$.

$$\frac{dy}{dx} = 2x - 4$$

At stationary points, the gradient is zero, so:

$$2x - 4 = 0$$

$$x = 2$$

When $x = 2$, , $y = 1$ so the coordinates of the stationary point are (2, 1).

(Note: you could also have used Completing the Square to solve this.)

EXAMPLE 2

The curve $f(x) = (x + a)(x + 1)$ has a turning point where $x = 4$.
Find the value of a.

$f(x) = (x + a)(x + 1)$

$f(x) = x^2 + (a + 1)x + a$

$f'(x) = 2x + (a + 1)$

At turning point $f'(x) = 0$ and $x = 4$

$2(4) + (a + 1) = 0$

$a = -9$

You should be familiar with three types of stationary point: a **maximum point**, a **minimum point** and a **point of inflection**. The meanings of these terms are best demonstrated with diagrams:

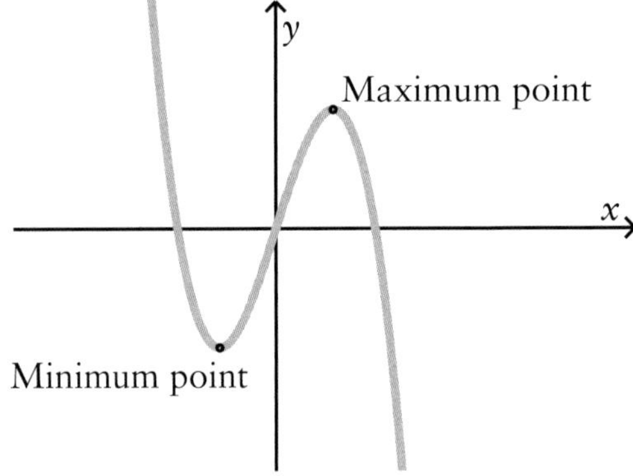

At a maximum point, the y-value reaches a local maximum; at a minimum point a local minimum. A **point of inflection** is the type of stationary point you often see in cubic curves:

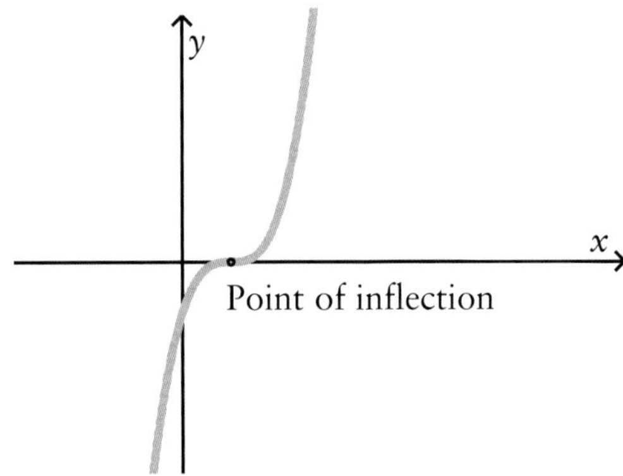

At a point of inflection, the gradient of the curve is zero, but it is neither a local maximum, nor a local minimum.

- At all stationary points $\frac{dy}{dx} = 0$

You can also see that:

- At a maximum point, the gradient changes from positive to negative.
- At a minimum point, the gradient changes from negative to positive.
- The sign of the gradient is either positive on both sides of a point of inflection, or negative on both sides.

EXERCISE

EXERCISE 6I

1. Find the coordinates of the stationary points of the following curves:
   a) $y = x^2 + 2$ b) $y = x^2 + 4x$ c) $y = -x^2 + 8x$
   d) $y = x^3 - 3x + 3$ e) $y = x(x + 5)$ f) $y = 2x^2 - 20x$
   g) $y = 2x^2 - 8x + 6$ h) $y = -2x^2 + 20x + 1$ i) $y = 2x^3 - 15x^2 + 36x - 91$
   j) $y = x(x + 1)(x - 1)$ k) $y = (x - 1)^3 - 1$
2. Find the coordinates of the turning points of the curve $y = 2x^3 - 24x^2 + 72x - 61$.
3. The curve C has equation $y = 2 + 9x^2 - 4x^3$.
   a) Find $\frac{dy}{dx}$.
   b) Find the coordinates of the two stationary points of the curve.
4. The curve C has equation $f(x) = \frac{(x^2 - 4)^2}{x^3}, x \neq 0$
   a) Show that $f(x) = x - 8x^{-1} + 16x^{-3}, x \neq 0$.
   b) Hence differentiate $f(x)$.
   c) Verify that the graph of $y = f(x)$ has turning points at $x = \pm 2$.
5. The function $f(x)$ is defined as $f(x) = x^{2/3}(20 - x)$.
   a) Find the derivative function $f'(x)$.
   b) Find the coordinates of the stationary point of $y = f(x)$.
6. The curve $y = 3x^2 + kx$ has a turning point at $x = 3$. Find the value of k.
7. The curve with equation $y = px^2 - qx$ (where p and q are constants) has a stationary point at (4, –48).
   a) Differentiate to find $\frac{dy}{dx}$.
   b) Find the values of p and q. (Hint: you will need to solve two simultaneous equations: one from the original equation, one from your answer to part a.)
8. The curve $y = x^3 + bx^2 + cx + 2$ has a point of inflection at the point (–1, 1). What are the values of the constants b and c?

EXERCISE

6.8 Increasing and Decreasing Functions

An **increasing function** is a function whose gradient is positive for all values of x.

A **decreasing function** is one whose gradient is negative.

For example, the function $f(x) = 2x$ is an increasing function. It represents a straight line with a positive gradient for all values of x.

A function can also be increasing or decreasing for a certain range of x values.

For example, if $f(x) = x^2$, then:

- the graph of $y = f(x)$ is decreasing when $x < 0$;
- the graph of $y = f(x)$ is increasing when $x > 0$.

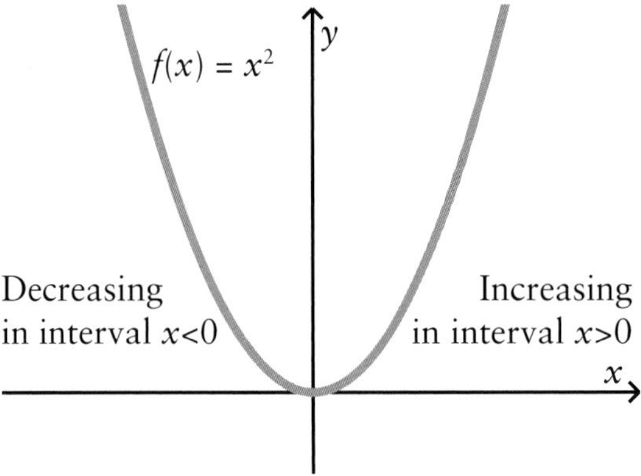

Formally:

- The function $f(x)$ is increasing if $f(x_2) > f(x_1)$ when $x_2 > x_1$ for all values of x in the given interval.

Similarly:

- The function $f(x)$ is decreasing if $f(x_2) < f(x_1)$ when $x_2 > x_1$ for all values of x in the given interval.

You may also hear the expressions **monotonic increasing function** and **monotonic decreasing function.** These expressions have the same meanings as increasing and decreasing functions.

EXAMPLE 1

Consider the function $f(x) = x^3 - 3x^2 + 4$.

Is the function increasing, decreasing or stationary when

a) $x = 1$ b) $x = 2$ c) $x = 4$?

Differentiate: $f'(x) = 3x^2 - 6x$

a) When $x = 1$, $f'(x) = 3(1)^2 - 6(1)$

$= -3$

Negative gradient: the function is decreasing when $x = 1$.

b) When $x = 2$, $f'(x) = 3(2)^2 - 6(2)$

$= 0$

Zero gradient: there is a stationary point when $x = 2$

c) When $x = 4$, $f'(x) = 3(4)^2 - 6(4)$

$= 24$

Positive gradient: the function is increasing when $x = 4$.

You can use information about whether a function is increasing or decreasing to decide whether stationary points are minima or maxima. A minimum point has a negative gradient to the left of it and a positive gradient to the right. A maximum point has a positive gradient to the left of it and a negative gradient to the right.

We describe a stationary point by referring to its **nature**. For example, the nature of the stationary point on the curve $f(x) = x^2$ is **minimum**. The nature of the stationary point on the curve $f(x) = -x^2$ is **maximum**. The nature of the stationary point in the cubic $f(x) = x^3$ is a **point of inflection.**

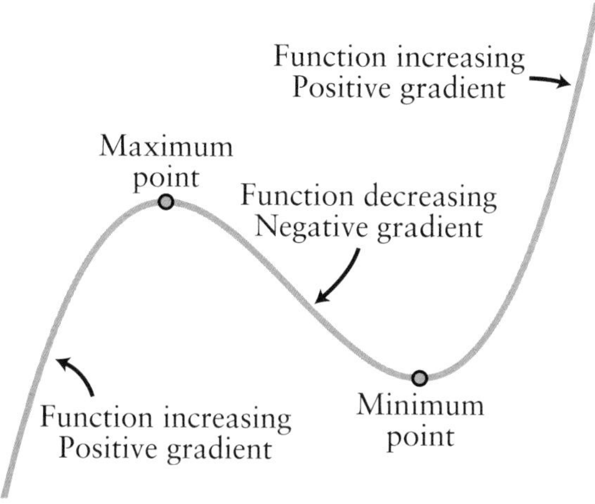

In summary:

Type of stationary point	Gradient	Behaviour
Maximum	0	Increasing to decreasing
Minimum	0	Decreasing to increasing
Point of inflection	0	Decreasing to decreasing OR Increasing to increasing

EXAMPLE 2

Consider the function $f(x) = \frac{3x}{2} - \frac{x^3}{8}$

a) Find the coordinates of the two stationary points on the curve $y = f(x)$.

b) By investigating the gradient of the curve either side of each stationary point, determine their nature.

---

a) $f(x) = \frac{3x}{2} - \frac{x^3}{8}$ so $f'(x) = \frac{3}{2} - \frac{3x^2}{8}$

At stationary points:

$$\frac{3}{2} - \frac{3x^2}{8} = 0$$

$$\frac{3}{2} = \frac{3x^2}{8}$$

$$x^2 = 4$$

$$x = \pm 2$$

So the two stationary points are (–2, –2) and (2, 2).

continued...

Example 2...

b) Consider the gradient of the curve.

$$f'(x) = \frac{3}{2} - \frac{3x^2}{8}$$

$$= \frac{3}{2}\left(1 - \frac{x^2}{4}\right)$$

When $x < -2$, $f'(x) < 0$ (function is decreasing);

When $-2 < x < 2$, $f'(x) > 0$ (function is increasing);

When $x > 2$, $f'(x) < 0$ (function is decreasing).

The stationary point at (–2, –2) lies between decreasing and increasing regions, hence it is a minimum point.

The stationary point at (2, 2) lies between increasing and decreasing regions, hence it is a maximum point.

Hence we can sketch the graph:

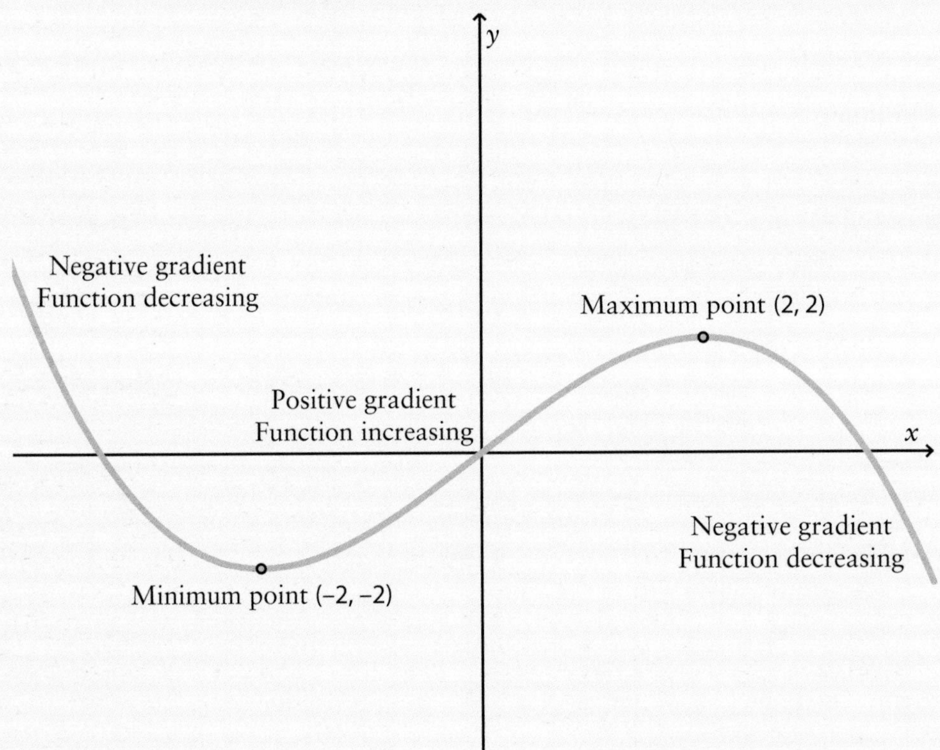

EXERCISE

EXERCISE 6J

1. Find the gradient of each curve at the point specified. State whether the curve is increasing or decreasing at that point.

a) $y = 3x^2;\ x = 2$

b) $y = 3x^2;\ x = -2$

c) $y = (x - 3)(x + 2);\ x = 2$

d) $y = (x - 3)(x + 2);\ x = -1$

e) $y = 3 - 2x - x^2;\ x = 0$

f) $y = 3 - 2x - x^2;\ x = -5$

EXERCISE

EXERCISE

g) $y = 3x;\ x = 2$ h) $y = x^3 + 2x;\ x = -1$

i) $y = -\dfrac{x}{2};\ x = 2$ j) $y = -\dfrac{1}{x};\ x = -1$

k) $y = \sqrt{x} + 1;\ x = 1$ l) $y = \dfrac{\sqrt{x} + 1}{x^{3/2}};\ x = 1$

2. Find the range of values of x for which each function is increasing or decreasing:

a) $f(x) = x^2 + 2x$ b) $f(x) = x^3 - 3x + 1$

c) $f(x) = 7x$ d) $f(x) = -2x + 1$

e) $f(x) = (x - 2)(x + 3)$ f) $f(x) = \dfrac{1}{x}, x \neq 0$

g) $f(x) = \dfrac{1}{\sqrt{x}}, x > 0$ h) $f(x) = x(x - 1)$

i) $f(x) = x^{3/2} - 3x, x > 0$ j) $f(x) = \dfrac{1}{x^2}, x \neq 0$

3. Show that the function $f(x) = 5x^3 + 2x + 5$ is always increasing.

4. Show that the function $f(x) = 1 - 3x - 3x^3$ is always decreasing.

5. Is the function $f(x) = 1 - 6x - 4x^3$ always increasing, always decreasing or neither?

6. The equation of a curve is $y = 8 + 8x^2 - 2x^3$. Find the set of values of x for which the curve is increasing.

7. A curve has the equation $y = 2x^3 - 15x^2 + 24x - 43$.

a) Find the coordinates of the two turning points of the curve.

b) By investigating whether the curve is increasing or decreasing either side of the turning points, determine their nature.

8. Show that the curve $y = 3x^2 - 6x + 10$ has a stationary point at (1, 7).
By investigating the gradient of the curve in appropriate regions, determine the nature of this stationary point.

9. A curve has the equation $y = 3 + 9x^2 - 9x^3$. Find the coordinates of the two turning points of the curve and determine their nature.

10. A curve has the equation $y = 2x^4 - 4x^3$.

a) Find $\dfrac{dy}{dx}$.

b) Find the x-coordinates of the stationary points of the curve and determine their nature.

EXERCISE

6.9 Second Order Derivatives

Differentiation of $\frac{dy}{dx}$ gives the **second derivative**. We write the second derivative as $\frac{d^2y}{dx^2}$.

In function notation, we write $f'(x)$ for the first derivative and $f''(x)$ for the second.

EXAMPLE 1

a) Find the first and second derivatives of $y = 2x^3 - 5x^2 + 4x - 3$.

b) Given $f(x) = \frac{1}{x} - \frac{1}{x^2}$, find the second derivative.

---

a) $$\frac{dy}{dx} = 6x^2 - 10x + 4$$

$$\frac{d^2y}{dx^2} = 12x - 10$$

b) $$f(x) = x^{-1} - x^{-2}$$

$$f'(x) = -x^{-2} + 2x^{-3}$$

$$f''(x) = 2x^{-3} - 6x^{-4}$$

The second derivative is useful to determine the nature of stationary points:

- If the second derivative is positive at a stationary point, the stationary point is a minimum.
- If the second derivative is negative at a stationary point, the stationary point is a maximum.
- If the second derivative is zero at a stationary point, the stationary point may be a maximum, a minimum or a point of inflection.

EXAMPLE 2

a) Find the coordinates of the stationary points of the curve

$$y = \frac{1}{3}x^3 - 2x^2 + 3x + 1$$

b) By finding the second derivative, determine the nature of the stationary points.

c) Sketch the curve, marking clearly the stationary points and the coordinates of the point at which the curve intercepts the y-axis.

---

a) Differentiate:

$$\frac{dy}{dx} = x^2 - 4x + 3$$

$$= (x - 1)(x - 3)$$

At stationary points: $(x - 1)(x - 3) = 0$

There are stationary points at $x = 1$ and $x = 3$.

continued...

When $x = 1, y = \frac{7}{3}$; when $x = 3, y = 1$

Stationary points are: $\left(1, \frac{7}{3}\right), (3, 1)$

b) Differentiate again:

$$\frac{d^2y}{dx^2} = 2x - 4$$

When $x = 1$

$$\frac{d^2y}{dx^2} = 2(1) - 4 = -2$$

$\frac{d^2y}{dx^2} < 0$, hence the stationary point at $x = 1$ is a maximum.

When $x = 3$

$$\frac{d^2y}{dx^2} = 2(3) - 4 = 2$$

$\frac{d^2y}{dx^2} > 0$ hence the stationary point at $x = 3$ is a minimum.

c) When $x = 0, y = 1$. Hence the curve intercepts the y-axis at (0, 1).

Recall from Chapter 4, because the term in x^3 is positive, the general direction of the curve is bottom left to top right. With the locations and nature of the two stationary points, we now have enough information to sketch the curve:

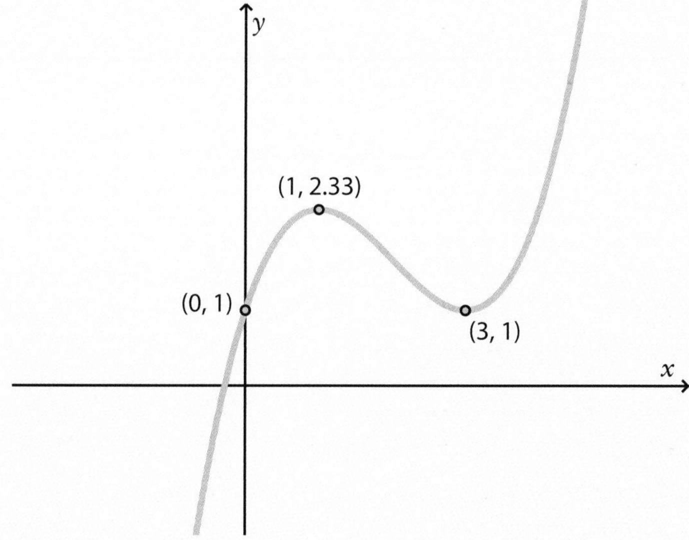

EXERCISE 6K

EXERCISE

1. Find the first and second derivatives of each of these functions.

a) $f(x) = 2x^2 + 1$
b) $f(x) = \frac{1}{4}x^4 + \frac{1}{3}x^3$
c) $f(x) = x + \frac{1}{x}$
d) $f(x) = \frac{x}{2}$
e) $f(x) = 3\sqrt{x}$
f) $f(x) = \frac{3}{\sqrt{x}}$
g) $f(x) = 2x^6 - 2x^{-6}$
h) $f(x) = (2x + 1)(1 - x)$
i) $f(x) = x(1 - x^2)$

EXERCISE

j) $f(x) = \frac{1}{x}(x + x^2)$

2. Find the first and second derivatives of these curves when $x = -1$:

a) $y = \frac{1}{2}x^2$ b) $y = 2x^3 - 2x$ c) $y = 5x$

d) $y = \frac{1}{2x}$ e) $y = (3x + 1)(2x + 1)$

3. Find the first and second derivatives of these curves when $x = 1$:

a) $y = x(1 - x + x^2)$ b) $y = 3\sqrt{x}$ c) $y = 3\sqrt{x} + \frac{3}{\sqrt{x}}$

d) $y = \frac{4 - 2\sqrt{x}}{\sqrt{x}}$ e) $y = \frac{5}{2}cx - \frac{3}{4}$, where c is a constant

4. Find the coordinates and nature of the stationary points of the curve: $y = 2x^3 - 24x^2 + 72x - 63$

5. Find the coordinates and nature of the stationary point on the curve with equation: $y = 4x^2 - 24x$

6. Show that the curve with equation $y = 7x^2 - 14x + 3$ has a minimum stationary point at (1, –4).

7. Find $\frac{dy}{dx}$ where $y = -4x^2 - \frac{1}{x}$. Hence find the coordinates of the stationary point of the curve $y = -4x^2 - \frac{1}{x}$ and determine its nature.

8. The curve C has equation $y = 2x^3 - 5x^2 - 4x + 3$.

a) Find $\frac{dy}{dx}$.

b) Using the result from part a, find the x-coordinates of the stationary points of C.

c) Find $\frac{d^2y}{dx^2}$.

d) Hence or otherwise, determine the nature of the stationary points of C.

9. Given $f(x) = 3 + 9x^2 - 3x^3$, find the coordinates of the two stationary points on the curve $y = f(x)$ and determine the nature of these stationary points.

10. The curve with equation $y = (4x + 2)(x^2 - k)$, where k is a constant, has a stationary point where $x = 1$.

a) Determine the value of k.

b) Find the x-coordinates of the stationary points and determine the nature of each.

11. Given $f(x) = \frac{(x^2 - 6)^2}{x^3}, x \neq 0$,

a) Show that $f(x) = x - 12x^{-1} + 36x^{-3}$.

b) Hence or otherwise differentiate $f(x)$ with respect to x.

c) Verify that the graph of $y = f(x)$ has stationary points at $x = \pm\sqrt{6}$

d) Determine the nature of the stationary point at $x = \sqrt{6}$.

EXERCISE

6.10 Practical Applications

There are many practical applications of calculus, in many diverse areas. In this section you will learn how to use your knowledge of stationary points to solve real-life problems.

Imagine plotting a graph of a car's speed v against time t. If we knew the equation for the speed of a car, we could differentiate to obtain $\frac{dv}{dt}$, which represents the gradient of the curve. The gradient of the curve becomes zero when v reaches its maximum or its minimum.

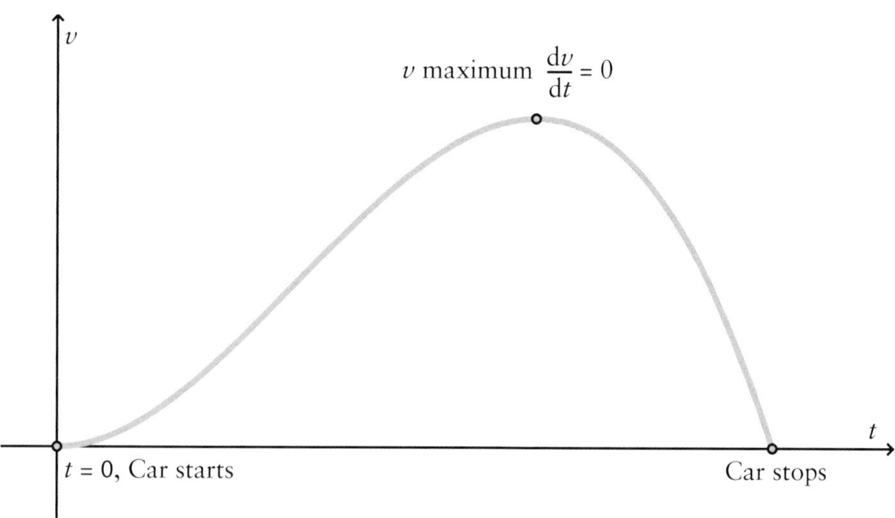

We use the fact that the gradient is zero at maxima and minima in all the problems in this section.

EXAMPLE 1

A farmer has 800 metres of fencing and plans to make a rectangular enclosure for his animals. Show that, to give his animals the greatest amount of space, the enclosure should be square.

Let the length of the enclosure be x and the width y.

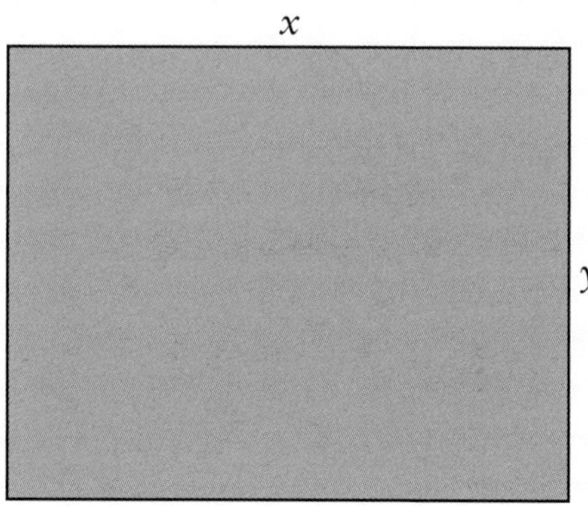

The area A is given by $A = xy$ (1)

If the amount of fencing available is 800 m, then

$2x + 2y = 800$
$x + y = 400$
$y = 400 - x$ (2)

continued...

Example 1... Substituting (2) into (1) gives: $A = x(400 - x)$

$A = 400x - x^2$

Differentiate:

$\frac{dA}{dx} = 400 - 2x$

The area is at a maximum when $\frac{dA}{dx} = 0$.

$400 - 2x = 0$

$x = 200$

Substituting into (2): $y = 200$

The length and width of the enclosure should both be 200m, so the enclosure will be square.

We have used the fact that $\frac{dA}{dx} = 0$ to find the value of x at which A reaches its maximum value.

However, we have not sketched the graph of A against x.

How do we know that A is a maximum, not a minimum?

To complete this question, we must differentiate again: $\frac{d^2A}{dx^2} = -2$

$\frac{d^2A}{dx^2}$ is negative, which shows that the stationary point is a maximum.

EXAMPLE 2

I think of a number, subtract 2, square, and add 1.
What is the smallest possible answer?

Let my number be x. Let the result be y.

We are looking for the smallest possible value for y.

$y = (x - 2)^2 + 1$

$y = x^2 - 4x + 5$

$\frac{dy}{dx} = 2x - 4 \quad (1)$

y reaches a minimum when $\frac{dy}{dx} = 0$

$2x - 4 = 0$

$x = 2$

This represents the number I originally thought of.

$y = (x - 2)^2 + 1$

$y = 1$

The smallest possible answer is 1.
How do we know this is a minimum, not a maximum?

Differentiate (1): $\frac{d^2y}{dx^2} = 2$

The positive value means we have found a minimum value of y.

EXERCISE 6L

1. A stone is thrown into the air and after t seconds its distance s metres above the ground is given by the equation $s = 30t - 5t^2$.

   a) Using calculus, find the time taken for the stone to reach its maximum height.

   b) What is the maximum height?

2. In a laboratory, a particle is accelerated such that its acceleration a ms^{-2} after t seconds is governed by the equation $a = 3t(2 - t)$

   a) After how many seconds does the particle reach its maximum acceleration?

   b) What is the maximum acceleration?

3. If I add a positive real number to its reciprocal, what is the smallest possible answer I could get?

4. A lorry is driven from London to Birmingham at a steady speed of v kilometres per hour. The total cost of the journey £C is given by

   $$C = \frac{1000}{v} + \frac{2v}{5}$$

   a) Find the value of v for which C is a minimum.

   b) Find $\frac{d^2C}{dv^2}$ and hence verify that C is a minimum for this value.

   c) Calculate the minimum total cost of the journey.5. In a wind tunnel, the wind speed is set to v ms^{-1}. For $v > 0.5$, the force exerted on a model building, F Newtons, is modelled by

   $$F = \frac{2}{v} + \frac{v^2}{125}$$

   a) Show by calculus that there is a value of v for which F has a stationary value, and find this value of v.

   b) Find the second derivative of F to show that this value of v gives a minimum value of F.

   c) Find the minimum value of F.

6. A beaker containing water is made in the shape of a cylinder with a hemispherical lid. The cylinder has radius r cm and height h cm.

   a) Given that the volume of the cylinder is 300 cm^3, find h in terms of r.

   b) Show that the surface area A of the beaker is given by:

   $$A = 3\pi r^2 + \frac{600}{r}$$

   c) The beaker's manufacturer wants to minimise the amount of plastic used. Find the value of r that achieves this, giving an exact answer involving π.

7. A running track is built in the shape of a rectangle with a semicircle on either end, as shown. The length of the rectangle is l and the radius of each semicircle is r. The perimeter of the track must be 400 m.

EXERCISE

a) Find an expression for l in terms of r.

b) Find an expression for the area of the rectangle, A, in terms of r (eliminating l).

c) The planning committee wish to ensure the rectangular area is maximised. Find the radius r that ensures A is a maximum. Leave π in your answer.

d) By finding $\frac{d^2A}{dr^2}$, verify that you have found a maximum.

e) Investigation: Somebody on the planning committee suggests the *entire* enclosed area should be maximised. What value would r take then? Again leave π in your answer. What value would l take? What shape would the track be?8. A glass box is to be made with a square base and an open top. The box must have a volume of 500 m^3. The length and width of the base are x metres and the height is h metres.

a) Find h in terms of x.

b) Show that the total surface area A of the box is given by $A = x^2 + \frac{2000}{x}$.

c) Glass for the box costs £10 per square metre. Find the dimensions of the box that minimise the amount of glass used and calculate the cost of the glass using these dimensions.

9. A factory makes matchboxes. The pieces of card used measure 3 cm by 2 cm. Squares of side x cm are cut from each corner of the sheet and the remainder is folded along the dotted lines to make an open tray for the matchbox, as shown.

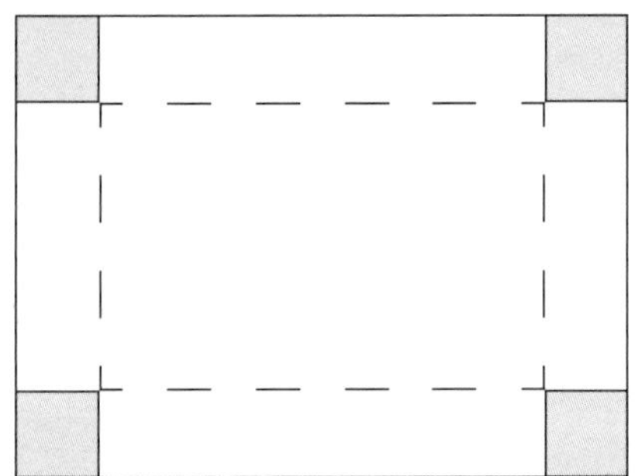

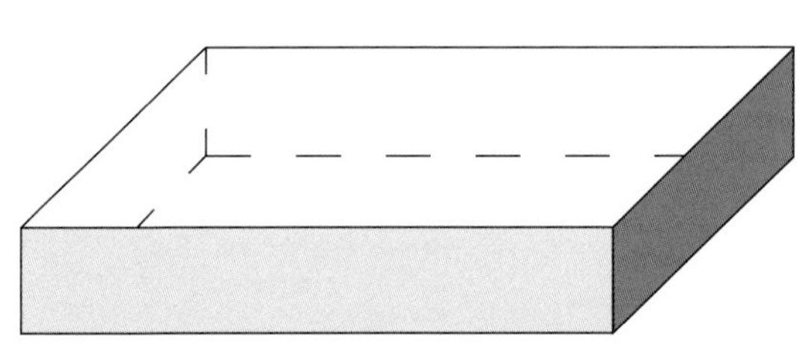

a) Show that the volume V of the tray is given by $V = 6x - 10x^2 + 4x^3$

b) Thinking about the lengths of the sides of the piece of card, state the range of possible values for x.

c) Find the value of x for which V is a maximum, leaving your answer in surd form.

d) By considering the second derivative of V, show that the value of x you have found does give the maximum value of V.

10. The diagram shows the plan of a garden in the shape of a rectangle joined to a semicircle.

The length of the rectangular part is $10x$ m and the width is y m. The diameter of the semicircular part is $10x$ m. The perimeter of the garden is 20 m.

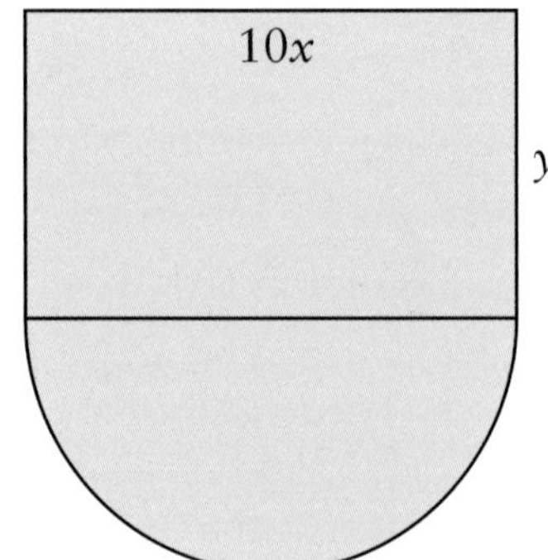

EXERCISE

EXERCISE

EXERCISE

a) Show that the area, A, of the garden is given by $A = 100x - \left(50 + \frac{25\pi}{2}\right)x^2$

b) Use calculus to show that the value of x at which A has a stationary value is given by $x = \frac{4}{4+\pi}$.

c) Use the second derivative of A to prove that the value of x you found in part b gives the maximum value of A.

d) Calculate the maximum area of the garden, leaving your answer in terms of π.

EXERCISE

SUMMARY

Differentiation is a technique used to find the **gradient** of a curve at any point. You can also think of it as finding a **rate of change**.

$f'(x)$ and $\frac{dy}{dx}$ are both notations for the **gradient function** or **derivative**.

To differentiate a power of x, the general rule is:

$$y = ax^n \Rightarrow \frac{dy}{dx} = anx^{n-1}$$

For sums and differences, differentiate each term in turn:

If $y = f(x) + g(x)$, then $\frac{dy}{dx} = f'(x) + g'(x)$.

Having used $\frac{dy}{dx}$ to find the gradient of a curve at a point, you can then find the equation of tangents and normal to curves.

The gradient function can also be used to determine whether a function is increasing or decreasing in a particular range.

You can find the position of **stationary points** or turning points on the curve by setting $\frac{dy}{dx} = 0$.

To determine whether a stationary point is a maximum or a minimum, you must find the **second derivative** $\frac{d^2y}{dx^2}$:

- If $\frac{d^2y}{dx^2} > 0$ at a stationary point, the stationary point is a minimum.
- If $\frac{d^2y}{dx^2} < 0$ at a stationary point, the stationary point is a maximum.
- If $\frac{d^2y}{dx^2} = 0$ at a stationary point, the stationary point may be a maximum, a minimum or a point of inflection.

Review Exercise

Chapters 4 to 6

EXERCISE

1. Factorise and find the roots of the equation $f(x) = x^3 - 5x^2 + 6x$

2. a) Factorise and find the roots of the equation $y = x^3 - 12x^2 + 36x$

   b) Hence sketch the curve $y = x^3 - 12x^2 + 36x$

3. a) Given $f(x) = (x^2 - 6x)(x - 1) + 4x$ express $f(x)$ in the form $x(ax^2 + bx + c)$ where a, b and c are constants.

   b) Hence factorise $f(x)$ completely.

   c) Sketch the curve $y = f(x)$.

   d) State the roots of the equation $f(x) = 0$.

4. Consider the two curves defined by: $y = x^2(x - 3)$; $y = x(8 - x)$
   For this pair of equations:

   a) On the same axes sketch the two curves and give the coordinates of all the points where the curves cross the x-axis.

   b) Use algebra to find the coordinates of the points where the graphs intersect.

5. Sketch this pair of curves on the same diagram:

   $y = -\frac{2}{x}$; $y = -\frac{1}{8x}$

6. a) Draw a sketch of the following pair of curves on the same diagram, showing that there are two intersection points.

   $y = -\frac{28}{x}$; $y = 2x - 15$

   b) Find, using algebra, the solutions to the simultaneous equations:

   $y = -\frac{28}{x}$; $y = 2x - 15$

7. a) Solve the simultaneous equations
   $y + 3x = 4$
   $2x^2 - x - y = 20$

EXERCISE

b) On the same diagram, sketch the two curves, showing the points of intersection of the two curves and the points of intersection with the coordinate axes.

c) Using your sketch, or otherwise, find the set of values of x for which $2x^2 - x - 20 > 4 - 3x$

8. Two quadratic curves are defined by the equations

$y = -2x^2 + 4x - 2$

$y = x^2 - 2x + 1$

a) Eliminate y to obtain a single quadratic equation and simplify as far as possible.

b) By calculating the **discriminant** of the quadratic obtained in part a), decide whether the curves have 0, 1 or 2 points of intersection.

c) Sketch the two curves on the same diagram, marking any points of intersection.

9. In each case, describe the translation that has taken place from function f to function g:

a) $f(x) = x^2;\ g(x) = (x - 2)^2$

b) $f(x) = \frac{2}{x};\ g(x) = \frac{2}{x - 3}$

c) $f(x) = x^3 - 1;\ g(x) = (x + 1)^3 + 1$

10. A function is defined such that $f(x) = (x + 2)^2 - 4$

a) Find what transformation takes place to obtain the function $g(x) = x^2$

b) Sketch both curves on the same diagram.

11. The diagram shows a sketch of the function $y = f(x)$

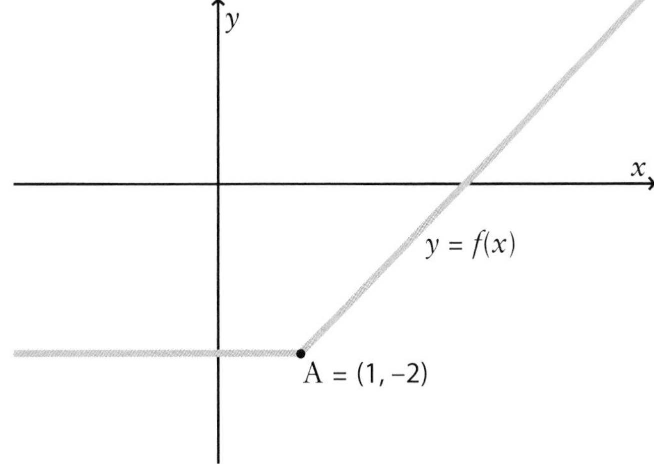

On separate diagrams, sketch the following graphs, taking care to mark the image of point A.

a) $y = -f(x)$

b) $y = 2f(x)$

c) $y = f(x + 2)$

EXERCISE

EXERCISE

12. Which of these equations are linear equations?

$3y - 2x = 5$

$y = \frac{1}{x}$

$3(1 - x) - 4(x - 5) = 2y$

$3x(2 + x) - 4x(x + 1) = 2y$

13. Find the gradient of the straight line passing through the points (3, –4) and (–3, –2).

14. Find the equation of the straight line with the given gradient, passing through the given point:

a) Gradient 4, Point (–1, –2)

b) Gradient –2, Point (5, 0)

15. Find the equation of the straight line passing through the two points given:

a) A(6,0), B(4, –2)

b) A(1, 1), B(2, –1)

16. The points A and B have coordinates (1, 4) and (6, –6) respectively. Find, in the form $y = mx + c$, an equation for the straight line through A and B.

17. Write the following equations in the form $ax + by + c = 0$

a) $\frac{x}{3} + \frac{y}{2} = 10$

b) $\frac{2}{5 + 3x} = \frac{6}{3 + y}$

18. Find where the line $5x - 4y + 20 = 0$ crosses

a) the x-axis

b) the y-axis

19. The point (3, 6) lies on the line L with equation $ax + by - 21 = 0$.

The line has a gradient of $-\frac{1}{3}$.

a) What are the values of the integers a and b?

b) Write down the equation of the line in its general form.

c) The straight line $dx + ey - 1 = 0$ is perpendicular to L and also passes through the point (3, 6). Find the values of d and e and write down the equation of the line in its general form.

d) Sketch the two lines on the same diagram.

20. The line with equation $-9x + 3y - 1 = 0$ is parallel to the line with equation $y = ax - 8$. Find the value of a.

EXERCISE

21. The line L_1 passes through the point $P(p, 3p)$. It is parallel to another line L_2, which passes through the point $Q(0, p)$. A third line L_3 passes through both P and Q and is perpendicular to both L_1 and L_2.

    a) Find the gradient of L_3.

    b) Find the equation of L_1 in its general form, leaving the constant p in your answer.

22. Differentiate the following with respect to x:

    a) $y = 5x^2 - 3x + 1$ b) $y = \frac{1}{2}x(x + 1)$ c) $y = \sqrt{x}(x - 1)$

23. Find the gradient of the curve at the point given:

    a) $y = \frac{2}{x}$, (2, 1) b) $y = -\frac{1}{\sqrt{x}}$, (1, 1) c) $y = \frac{2}{5x\sqrt{x}}$, $(1, \frac{2}{5})$

24. Differentiate the following equations with respect to the variable in the right-hand side of the equation:

    a) $v = 20t - 5t^2$ b) $A = \frac{1}{3}\pi r(r - 1) + 2\pi r^2$ c) $z = (\theta^4 - 1)(\theta^2 + 1)$

25. Find $f'(x)$ given $f(x)$ in each case:

    a) $f(x) = \frac{4}{x}$ b) $f(x) = \frac{(x + 3)^2}{x}$ c) $f(x) = \sqrt{x}(1 + \sqrt{x})$

26. The volume of water flowing in a pipe is related to the pressure by the formula $V = 2p^3 - \frac{4}{p}$ (where V is measured in m^3s^{-1} and p in bars). Find the rate of change of the volume when the pressure is 2 bars.

27. The formula $b = 3q - \frac{2}{\sqrt{q}}$ links the number of bacteria to the quantity of nutrients supplied in a laboratory experiment.

    a) Find the rate of change of b with respect to q.

    b) (Difficult) What is the value of q when the rate of change of b with respect to q is 11.

28. The curve C is given by the equation $y = x^3(3x^2 + 2x)$. Calculate the gradient of the tangent at the point $x = 1$ on C.

29. The curve C has equation $y = x^3 - 3x + \frac{4}{x}$. The points A and B both lie on C and have coordinates (2, 4) and (–2, –4) respectively.

    a) Show that the gradient of C at A is equal to the gradient of C at B.

    b) Find the equation for the normal to C at A in its general form.

EXERCISE

30. The curve C has equation $y = \frac{4}{\sqrt{x}}$ What are the coordinates of the points where

a) $\frac{dy}{dx} = -2$ b) $\frac{dy}{dx} = -16$

31. There are two points on the curve $y = \frac{1}{3}x^3 - 2x^2 - 8$ at which the gradient is 5. What are the x-coordinates of those points?

32. Find the coordinates of the stationary points of the following curves:

a) $y = 2x^2 - 10x$ b) $y = x(x-3)^2$

33. Find the coordinates of the turning point on the curve with equation: $y = 8x^2 - 24x$

34. The curve C has equation $f(x) = \frac{(x^2-2)^2}{x^3}, x \neq 0$.

a) Show that $f(x) = x - \frac{4}{x} + \frac{4}{x^3}, x \neq 0$.

b) Hence differentiate $f(x)$.

c) Verify that the graph of $y = f(x)$ has turning points at $x = \pm\sqrt{2}$.

35. The curve with equation $y = px^2 - qx$ (where p and q are constants) has a stationary point at $(-1, 4)$.

a) Differentiate to find $\frac{dy}{dx}$.

b) Find the values of p and q. (Hint: you will need to solve two simultaneous equations: one from the original equation, one from your answer to part a.)

36. The curve $y = x^3 + bx^2 + cx + 7$ has a point of inflection at the point $(-2, -1)$. What are the values of the constants b and c?

37. Find the range of values of x for which each function is increasing or decreasing:

a) $f(x) = (x-3)(x+4)$

b) $f(x) = x^{5/3} - 5x$

38. A curve has the equation $y = 3x^4 - 8x^3$.

a) Find $\frac{dy}{dx}$.

b) Find the coordinates of the stationary points of the curve and determine their nature.

39. Find the first and second derivatives of each of these functions:

a) $f(x) = \frac{x^2}{2}$ b) $f(x) = x\sqrt{x}\left(x + \frac{1}{\sqrt{x}}\right)$

EXERCISE

40. Find the first and second derivatives of these curves when $x = \sqrt{2}$:

    a) $y = 3x^5 - 4x^3$ b) $y = (2x + 1)(3x - 1)$

41. Find the first and second derivatives of these curves when $x = c$, where c is a constant:

    a) $y = cx^2 + c^2x$ b) $y = \frac{c}{x} - \frac{x}{c}$

42. Find the x-coordinates and nature of the turning points of

    $y = 2x^3 - 27x^2 + 48x - 40$

43. The curve with equation $y = (6x + 3)(x^2 - k)$, where k is a constant, has a stationary point where $x = 1$.

    a) Determine the value of k.

    b) Find the coordinates of the stationary points and determine the nature of each.

44. A stone is thrown into the air and after t seconds its distance s metres above the ground is given by the equation $s = 36t - 9t^2$

    a) Using calculus, find the time taken for the stone to reach its maximum height.

    b) What is the maximum height?

45. In an architect's computer model of a bridge, the force on the bridge depends on the velocity of a car driving over it. For velocity v ms^{-1} greater than 1, the force, F kiloNewtons, is modelled by:

    $$F = \frac{40}{v} + \frac{v^2}{50}$$

    a) Show by calculus that there is a value of v for which F has a stationary value, and find this value of v.

    b) Find the second derivative of F to show that this value of v gives a minimum value of F.

    c) Find the minimum value of F.

46. Given $y = 8\sqrt{x}$, show that $2x\left(\frac{dy}{dx}\right)^2 - y\frac{dy}{dx} = 0$

Chapter 7

Coordinate Geometry

7.1 Introduction

Keywords

Circumference: Distance around a circle

Chord: Line segment between two points on a circle

Diameter: Chord passing through the centre of a circle

Radius: Half a diameter, from centre to circumference

Tangent: Line touching circle at only one point

Bisect: Cut in half

Perpendicular: At 90°

Perpendicular bisector: A line that cuts another line exactly in half at 90°

Before You Start

You should know how to:

Find the equation of a line joining two points;

Complete the square;

Determine the number of roots of a quadratic equation.

EXAMPLE 1

Find the equation of the line joining the points (1, 3) and (–5, 4).

$(x_1, y_1) = (1, 3)$ and $(x_2, y_2) = (-5, 4)$

The gradient of the line segment is given by:

$$m = \frac{y_2 - y_1}{x_2 - x_1}$$

$$m = \frac{4 - 3}{-5 - 1}$$

$$m = -\frac{1}{6}$$

The equation of a straight line passing through point (x_1, y_1) is:

$$y - y_1 = m(x - x_1)$$

$$y - 3 = -\frac{1}{6}(x - 1)$$

$$x + 6y - 19 = 0$$

EXAMPLE 2

Complete the square to solve for x

$$x^2 - 4x + 3 = 0$$

$$x^2 - 4x + 3 = 0$$

Half the coefficient of x is 2: $(x - 2)^2 - 4 + 3 = 0$

Collect the number terms on the right: $(x - 2)^2 = 1$

Square root: $x - 2 = \pm 1$

$$x = 3 \text{ or } x = 1$$

EXAMPLE 3

How many roots exist to the equation:

$$2x^2 + 7x - 9 = 0\ ?$$

$$2x^2 + 7x - 9 = 0$$

Find the discriminant: $b^2 - 4ac = 7^2 - 4(2)(9)$

$$= 49 - 72$$

$$< 0$$

Therefore, there are no roots to this equation.

Note: the question did not ask for the roots themselves, just the number of them.

What You Will Learn

In this chapter you will learn how to:

- Apply circle theorems to problems in coordinate geometry;
- Find the equation of a circle;
- Find the number of intersection points of a line and circle and find their coordinates

IN THE REAL WORLD – THE SOLAR SYSTEM

The planets orbit the sun in elliptical (oval–shaped) orbits. Most of the planets, however, have orbits that are almost circular. This gives astronomers the chance to make quick calculations about the approximate positions of the planets.

By solving equations involving circles and straight lines, it is even possible to estimate whether asteroids and meteors are likely to pose any significant danger.

A collision with an asteroid of 50 metre diameter could have the same effect as a nuclear bomb! This seems to have happened over Siberia in 1908. An even larger impact probably wiped out the dinosaurs 65 million years ago.

EXERCISE

REVISION EXERCISE 7A

1. Find the equation of the straight line joining the points:
   a) (1, 1) and (–1, –1)
   b) (10, 3) and (0, 6)
   c) (–2, –1) and (4, 1)
   d) (12, 2) and (–12, 4)
   e) (6, 7) and (–7, –6)

2. Complete the square for the following functions:
   a) $f(x) = x^2 + 4x$
   b) $f(x) = x^2 + 8x + 6$
   c) $f(x) = -x^2 - 10x + 6$

3. Solve the following for x by completing the square:
   a) $x^2 + 6x = -8$
   b) $-x^2 - 4x = -5$
   c) $x^2 + 2x - 17 = 0$

4. By calculating the discriminant, find the number of roots of the following quadratic equations:
   a) $x^2 + x - 1 = 0$
   b) $x^2 + 5x + 25 = 0$
   c) $x^2 - 8x + 16 = 0$
   d) $-x^2 - 2x = 3$
   e) $(x - 1)^2 = -1$

EXERCISE

7.2 Circle Theorems

Angle in a Semicircle is a Right Angle

You may remember from your GCSE that an angle at the circumference of a semicircle is always a right angle:

In this diagram, angle A is 90° because the chord BC is a diameter of the circle.

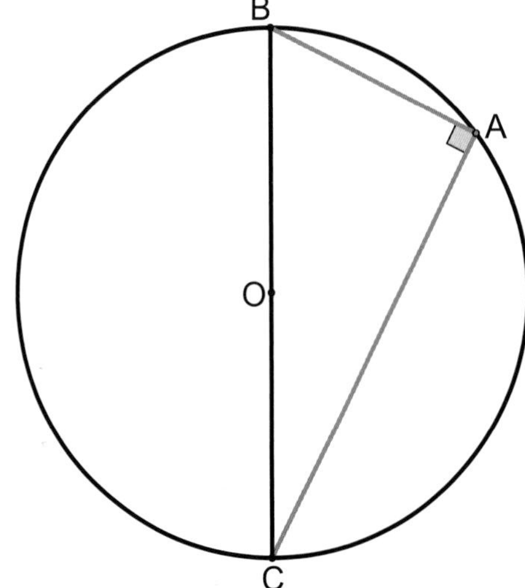

You may sometimes hear the word **subtended.** Angle A is subtended by the diameter BC.

EXAMPLE 1

The circle C, shown, has centre (0, 0).
Point Y has coordinates (–5, 0) and Z (5, 0).
Angle XZY = 70°. What is the size of angle XYZ?

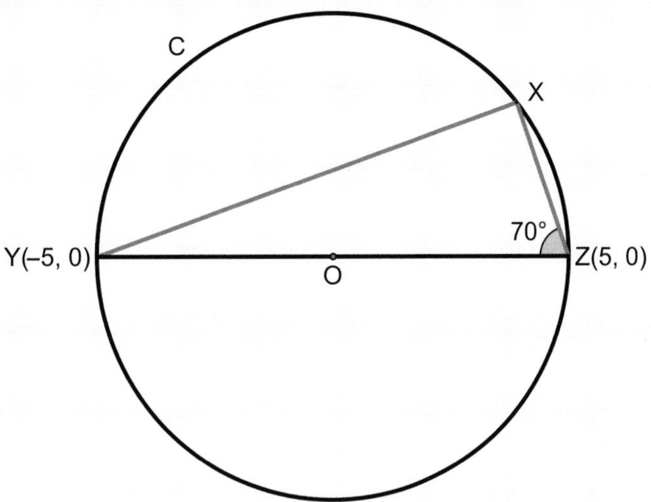

Chord YZ passes through the centre, O, so is a diameter.

Hence XYZ is a triangle in a semi–circle. Therefore angle YXZ is 90°.

Angles in the triangle add up to 180°, so angle XYZ is 20°.

EXAMPLE 2

Points X(–2, –2), Y(2p, 2p+10) and Z(4, 2) lie on the circumference of the circle shown, with centre A.

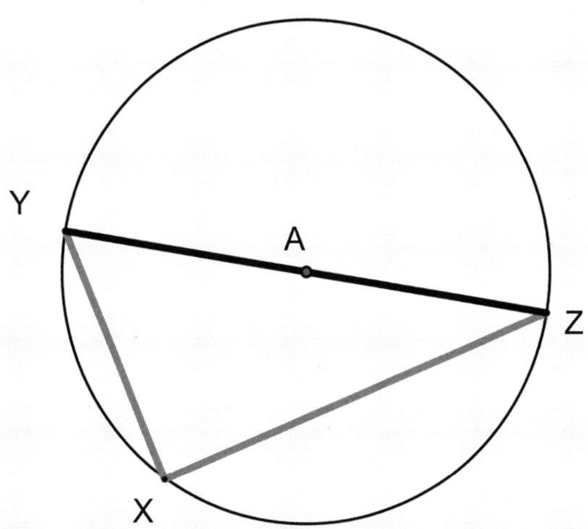

a) Find the gradient of the chord XZ.

b) Using your answer to part a), find the gradient of the chord XY.

c) Find the value of p.

---

a) Gradient $m = \dfrac{-2-2}{-2-4}$

$= \dfrac{2}{3}$

b) YZ is a diameter, so angle YXZ is 90°.

This means XY and XZ are perpendicular.

For perpendicular lines, the product of the two gradients is –1.

So gradient of XY $= -1/\dfrac{2}{3}$

$= -\dfrac{3}{2}$

c) Gradient of XY $= -\dfrac{3}{2}$

Rise over run: $\dfrac{2p + 10 - (-2)}{2p - (-2)} = -\dfrac{3}{2}$

$\dfrac{2p + 12}{2p + 2} = -\dfrac{3}{2}$

Cross–multiply: $4p + 24 = -6p - 6$

$10p = -30$

$p = -3$

Perpendicular From Centre to a Chord

The perpendicular from the centre of a circle to a chord will always bisect the chord.

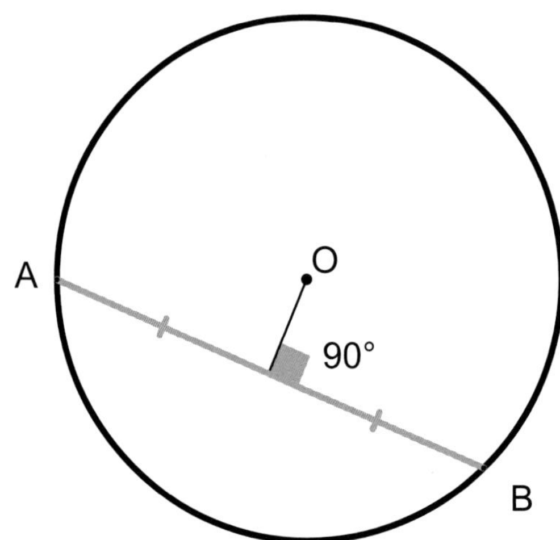

EXAMPLE 3

In the circle shown, the chord AB cuts the radius OD at 90° at point C.

The coordinates of points B and C are (4, 2) and (3, 3) respectively.

What are the coordinates of A?

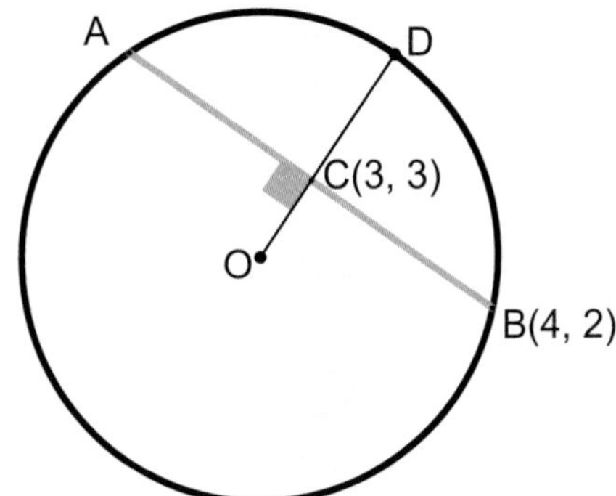

Using the theorem that the perpendicular from the centre to a chord always bisects the chord, C must be the midpoint of AB.

The average of the x-coordinates of A and B gives the x-coordinate of C. Then repeat for the y-coordinates.

Therefore, if the coordinates of A are (x, y).

$$\frac{x+4}{2} = 3 \text{ and } \frac{y+2}{2} = 3$$

$$x = 2, y = 4$$

The coordinates of A are (2, 4).

EXAMPLE 4

Find the equation of the perpendicular bisector of the chord AB, where A is (10, 5) and B is (4, 8).

Gradient of chord AB $= \frac{8-5}{4-10} = -\frac{1}{2}$

Therefore the gradient of the perpendicular bisector is 2.

Midpoint M of AB is $\left(\frac{4+10}{2}, \frac{5+8}{2}\right)$

Therefore the coordinates of M are $\left(7, \frac{13}{2}\right)$

Equation of line: $y - y_1 = m(x - x_1)$

$$y - \frac{13}{2} = 2(x - 7)$$

$$4x - 2y - 15 = 0$$

Perpendicularity of Radius and Tangent

A tangent to a circle meets a radius of the circle at 90°.

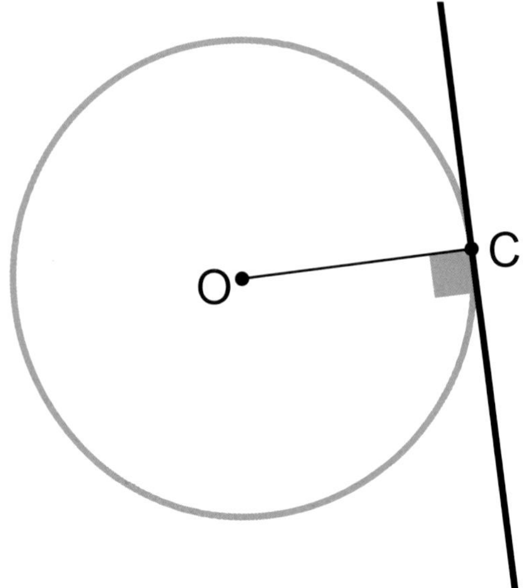

EXAMPLE 5

A tangent and radius to the circle C meet at the point (4, 3). The gradient of the tangent is $-\frac{4}{3}$. What is the gradient of this radius?

Tangent and radius are perpendicular, therefore the gradient of the radius is $\frac{3}{4}$

EXAMPLE 6

A tangent and radius to the circle C meet at the point (1, 4). The gradient of the radius is $-\frac{1}{5}$. What is the equation of the tangent?

Tangent and radius are perpendicular, therefore the gradient of the tangent is 5.

Equation of tangent: $y - y_1 = m(x - x_1)$

$$y - 4 = 5(x - 1)$$

$$y = 5x - 1$$

EXERCISE

EXERCISE 7B

1. The end points A and B of a chord within a circle are given. Find the coordinates of the midpoint P of AB.
   a) A(4, –5), B(4, –1) b) A(3, 4), B(–1, –6) c) A(5, –8), B(1, 4)
   d) A(7, 0), B(2, 11) e) A(1, –2), B(9, –5)

2. A diameter of a circle has end points A and B. Given the coordinates of A and the centre O, find the coordinates of B.
   a) A(–3, 5), O(–5, 9) b) A(–5, –6), O(10, –6) c) A(–8, –4), O(–4, 8)
   d) A(4, 4), O(4, 8) e) A(–8, 1), O(–1, –7)

3. Find the gradient of the tangent to each circle, given the coordinates of the centre O and the point C where the tangent meets a radius:
   a) O (0, 0), C (2, 1) b) O (10, –1), C (0, –2) c) O (3, 6), C (2, 5)
   d) O (–2, 7), C (6, 1) e) O (4, 5), C (5, 5)

4. Find the equation of the perpendicular bisector to each chord, given the coordinates of the two end points of the chord:
   a) A (–2, 7), B (6, 1) b) A (–5, 2), B (–2, 7) c) A (15, 15), B(10, 20)
   d) A (3, –4), B (1, –4) e) A (2, 1), B (1, 2)

5. In the circle C, with the centre given, the angle A is subtended by the chord BC. State whether or not angle A is a right angle.
   a) B(–8, 4), C(4, –8), Centre (–2, –2) b) B(7, –5), C(–7, 7), Centre (0, 1)
   c) B(–3, 6), C(6, –10), Centre (0.5, –2) d) B(–6, –7), C(–6, –2), Centre (–6, –4.5)
   e) B(–2, 9), C(–8, –2), Centre (–5, –3.5)

6. The line $y = 2x - 4$ is a tangent to the circle C, touching C at the point P(3, 2). The point Q is the centre of C.
   a) Find an equation for the straight line through P and Q.
   b) Given that Q lies on the line $y = 1$, show that the x-coordinate of Q is 5.

7. A circle passes through the points (10, 10), (16, 10) and (10, 20).
   a) Find the coordinates of the centre of the circle.
   b) Find the exact radius of the circle.

8. The points A and B lie on a circle with centre P. The point A has coordinates (3, –2) and the mid–point M of AB has coordinates (4, 2). The line L_1 passes through the points M and P.

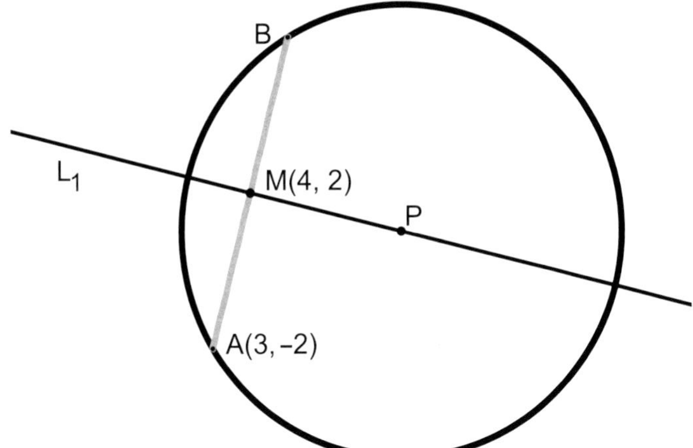

EXERCISE

a) Find an equation for L_1.
b) Given that the x-coordinate of P is 8, use your answer to part (a) to show that the y-coordinate of P is 1.

9. The circle shown has centre M, with AB as a diameter. A, B and C all lie on the circle and have coordinates A $(1, 2 + 4\sqrt{2})$), B(q, –2q) and C $(3, 2 + 2\sqrt{2})$.

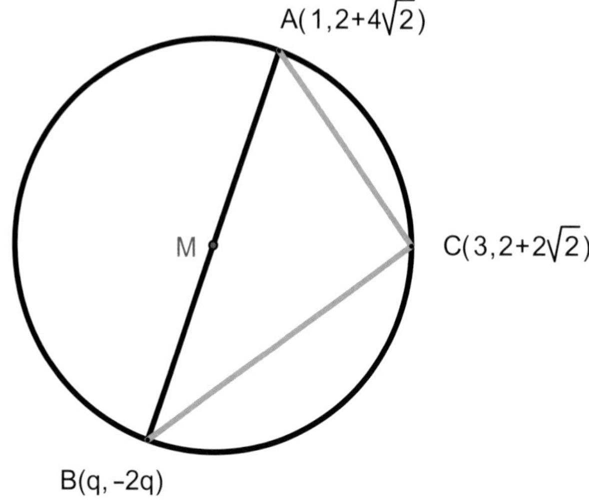

a) Find the **exact** gradient of AC.
b) Hence find the exact gradient of BC.
c) Find the value of q.

10. A radio transmitter located at C can send signals to three spies X, Y and Z as long as they are within a 13 km radius. Each spy is now located somewhere on the 13 km circle, with spy X being the furthest north. When drawn on a map, spy X is located at (18, 10). The distance between X and Y is $\sqrt{26}$ km and the gradient of the line between them is –5.
a) What are the coordinates of spy Y?

Given that the spies X and Z are directly opposite each other on the 13 km circle:
b) Find the gradient of the line between Y and Z.

Z has x-coordinate –6.
c) Find the y-coordinate of Z .
d) Find the coordinates of the transmitter.
e) What direction would somebody have to travel from the transmitter to reach spy Y?

7.3 The Equation of a Circle

The general equation of a circle is: $(x - a)^2 + (y - b)^2 = r^2$
where (a, b) are the coordinates of the centre and r is its radius.

Proof of the Equation of a Circle

Consider a circle with radius r, centre (a, b). Consider a general point P(x, y) on the circle. Construct a right–angled triangle between C and P as shown:

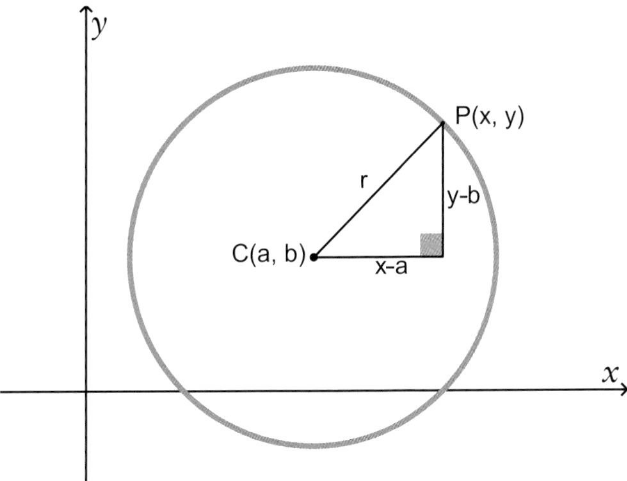

Using Pythagoras' Theorem:

$$(x-a)^2 + (y-b)^2 = r^2$$

Centre and Radius

Given the equation of a circle, you can find its centre and its radius.

EXAMPLE 1

Find the centre and radius of the circle C with equation

$$(x-7)^2 + (y-4)^2 = 25$$

Comparing the equation of C with the general equation of a circle:

$$(x-a)^2 + (y-b)^2 = r^2$$

we can see that the centre is (7, 4) and the radius is 5.

So, given the centre and radius of a circle, you can find its equation.

EXAMPLE 2

The circle C has centre (10, –5) and radius 3. Find its equation.

We use the general equation of a circle:

$$(x-a)^2 + (y-b)^2 = r^2$$

$$(a, b) = (10, -5) \text{ and } r = 3$$

Therefore the equation of C is: $(x-10)^2 + (y+5)^2 = 9$

There is a second form of the equation of a circle, which is obtained by expanding the brackets:

$$x^2 + y^2 + 2gx + 2fy + c = 0$$

Sometimes you will need to solve problems using this equation, by rewriting the equation in the standard form. You will do this by **completing the square**.

EXAMPLE 3

The equation of a circle is $x^2 + y^2 + 2x - 4y + 1 = 0$.
Find its centre and radius.

Complete the square for both x and y:

$$(x + 1)^2 - 1 + (y - 2)^2 - 4 + 1 = 0$$

Re-arrange: $(x + 1)^2 + (y - 2)^2 = 4$

Hence, the circle has centre $(-1, 2)$ and radius 2.

Points of Intersection

You will often have to solve problems involving the intersection points of circles and straight lines. There are three possible outcomes:

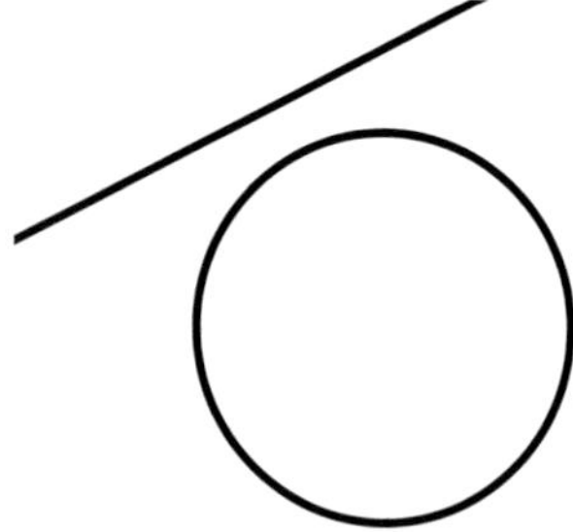

No points of intersection

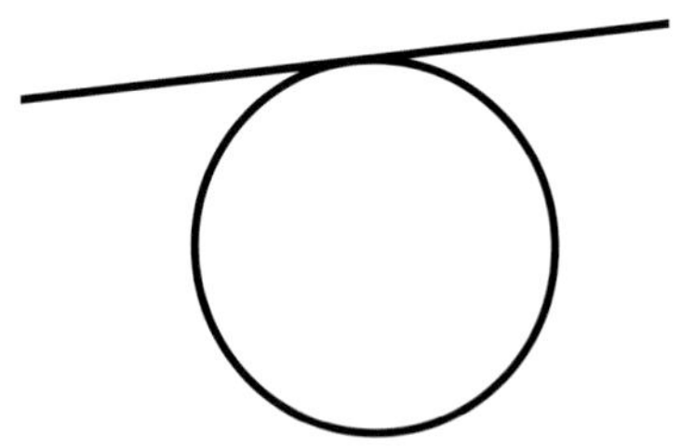

One point of intersection (the line is a tangent to the circle)

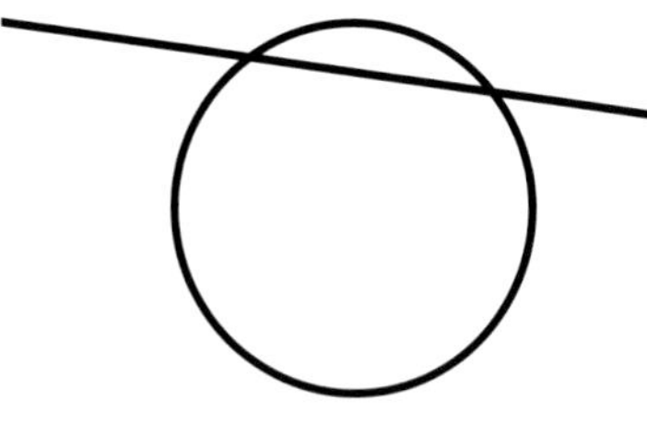

Two points of intersection

You can find the points of intersection by solving the equations of the line and circle simultaneously.

EXAMPLE 4

Find the points of intersection of the circle C with equation $(x - 3)^2 + (y - 2)^2 = 25$ and the straight line $y = x$.

$$(x - 3)^2 + (y - 2)^2 = 25 \quad (1)$$

$$y = x \quad (2)$$

Substitute (2) into (1):

$$(x - 3)^2 + (x - 2)^2 = 25$$

Expand: $x^2 - 6x + 9 + x^2 - 4x + 4 = 25$

Re-arrange: $2x^2 - 10x - 12 = 0$

Divide both sides by 2: $x^2 - 5x - 6 = 0$

Factorise: $(x - 6)(x + 1) = 0$

$$x = 6 \quad \text{or} \quad x = -1$$

Using (2), when $x = 6, y = 6$ When $x = -1, y = -1$

Hence the points of intersection are $(6, 6)$ and $(-1, -1)$.

By showing there is only one point of intersection, you can prove that a line is a tangent to a circle.

EXAMPLE 5

Show that the line $x - 2y - 8 = 0$ is a tangent to the circle C with equation $(x - 3)^2 + (y + 5)^2 = 5$

$x - 2y - 8 = 0$ (1)

$(x - 3)^2 + (y + 5)^2 = 5$ (2)

Re-arrange (1): $y = \frac{x}{2} - 4$

Substitute in (2): $(x - 3)^2 + \left(\frac{x}{2} + 1\right)^2 = 5$

Expand: $x^2 - 6x + 9 + \frac{x^2}{4} + x + 1 = 5$

Re-arrange: $\frac{5x^2}{4} - 5x + 5 = 0$

$$x^2 - 4x + 4 = 0$$

$$(x - 2)^2 = 0$$

There is only one solution: $x = 2$, which indicates that the line and circle intersect at only one point.

When $x = 2, y = -3$, so the point of intersection is (2, –3).

You should remember that, when solving a quadratic equation, the number of solutions is governed by the value of the value of the discriminant $b^2 - 4ac$

Discriminant > 0	two solutions
Discriminant = 0	one solution
Discriminant < 0	no solutions

Sometimes, we are asked only to find the number of intersection points, not their coordinates.

EXAMPLE 2

Find the **number** of points of intersection between the straight line

$y = 4x - 1$ (1)

and the circle with equation

$(x - 3)^2 + (y + 6)^2 = 17$ (2)

Substitute (1) into (2):

$$(x - 3)^2 + (4x + 5)^2 = 17$$

Expand: $x^2 - 6x + 9 + 16x^2 + 40x + 25 = 17$

Re-arrange: $17x^2 + 34x + 17 = 0$

$$x^2 + 2x + 1 = 0$$

To find the number of solutions, calculate the discriminant:

$b^2 - 4ac = 2^2 - 4(1)(1)$

$= 0$

Hence there is only one solution. The line is a tangent to the circle.

EXERCISE

EXERCISE 7C

1. Determine whether the point A, with coordinates given, lies on the circle C whose equation is also given:
   a) A(1, 9), C: $(x + 5)^2 + (y - 9)^2 = 36$ b) A(1, 3), C: $(x - 10)^2 + (y + 7)^2 = 4$
   c) A(–4, –9), C: $(x + 7)^2 + (y - 8)^2 = 64$ d) A(–1, –5), C:$(x + 8)^2 + (y + 5)^2 = 49$
   e) A(–7, 6), C: $(x - 5)^2 + (y - 10)^2 = 81$ f) A(–9, 7), C: $(x + 5)^2 + (y - 10)^2 = 25$
   g) A(0, –2), C: $(x + 4)^2 + (y - 8)^2 = 100$ h) A(–6, –7), C: $(x + 2)^2 + (y + 4)^2 = 25$
   i) A(10, –1), C: $(x - 10)^2 + (y + 9)^2 = 64$ j) A(5, –2), C: $(x - 7)^2 + (y - 2)^2 = 100$

2. The point A, with coordinates given, lies on the circle C, whose equation is also given. Find the value of a.
   a) A(2, –4), C: $(x - 4)^2 + (y + 4)^2 = a$ b) A(4, –10), C: $(x + 4)^2 + (y + 10)^2 = a$
   c) A(–2, –8), C: $(x - 6)^2 + (y + 2)^2 = a$ d) A(–8, –6), C: $(x + 6)^2 + (y + 8)^2 = a$
   e) A(5, –1), C: $(x - 3)^2 + (y + 2)^2 = a$ f) A(–5, 0), C: $(x + 7)^2 + y^2 = a$
   g) A(–5, –5), C: $(x + 2)^2 + (y + 6)^2 = a$ h) A(0, 7), C: $(x - 1)^2 + (y - 8)^2 = a$
   i) A(–6, 8), C: $(x + 8)^2 + (y - 6)^2 = a$ j) A(–5, 0), C: $(x + 7)^2 + (y + 4)^2 = a$

3. Find the equation of the circle with centre C, which passes through the point A:
   a) C(–5, 7), A(–5, –1) b) C(8, 7), A(8, 3) c) C(–2, –1), A(–8, –9)
   d) C(10, 5), A(9, 1) e) C(9, 3), A(8, 4) f) C(–2, 2), A(1, 1)
   g) C(–5, 2), A(–6, 0) h) C(8, 0), A(10, 2) i) C(5, –2), A(3, –5)
   j) C(–1, 9), A(–5, 7)

4. The chord AB is a diameter of circle C. Given the coordinates of A and B, find the equation of C:
   a) A(10, –8), B(10, –2) b) A(6, 5), B(2, –1) c) A(–2, –2), B(0, –4)
   d) A(6, –1), B(10, –5) e) A(–3, 7), B(–11, 3) f) A(2, 8), B(–2, 6)
   g) A(–1, 0), B(5, –6) h) A(5, 5), B(7, –1) i) A(5, –4), B(3, –12)
   j) A(–2, 0), B(2, 6)

5. Find the **number** of points of intersection between the circle and the straight line, whose equations are given:
   a) $(x - 1)^2 + (y - 3)^2 = 4;\ y = -x + 2$ b) $x^2 + (y + 6)^2 = 12;\ y = -x - 5$
   c) $(x - 9)^2 + y^2 = 2;\ y = x + 3$ d) $(x - 3)^2 + (y - 1)^2 = 20;\ y = 2x + 5$
   e) $(x - 7)^2 + y^2 = 13;\ y = x + 6$ f) $(x + 1)^2 + (y + 5)^2 = 2;\ y = -2x - 7$
   g) $(x - 10)^2 + (y + 10)^2 = 20;\ y = -2x$ h) $x^2 + y^2 + 6x - 12y + 25 = 0;\ y = -3x$
   i) $x^2 + y^2 - 8x - 2y + 4 = 0;\ y = 2x + 3$ j) $x^2 + y^2 - 8x - 18y + 95 = 0;\ y = x + 7$

EXERCISE

EXERCISE

6. The straight line $y = ax - 6$ touches the circle with equation $(x - 7)^2 + (y - 3)^2 = 2$ at only one point. Find the two possible values of a.

7. The circle C has centre (5, 13) and touches the x–axis.
a) Find an equation of C in terms of x and y.
b) Find an equation of the tangent to C at the point (10, 1) giving your answer in the form: $ay + bx + c = 0$ where a, b, and c are integers to be found.

8. The circle C has equation $x^2 + y^2 - 4x - 8y + 4 = 0$
a) By completing the square for x and y, find the coordinates of the centre and the radius of C.
b) Find an equation for each of the two tangents to C that pass through the origin O.

9. The Cartesian equation of the circle C is: $x^2 + y^2 - 8x - 6y + 16 = 0$
a) Find the coordinates of the centre of C and its radius.
b) Find, in Cartesian form, an equation for each tangent to C which passes through the origin O.

10. The circle $(x - 2)^2 + y^2 = 18$ and the straight line $y = x - 2$ intersect at the points A and B.
a) Find the coordinates of A and B.
b) Show that the chord AB is a diameter of the circle.

EXERCISE

SUMMARY

You need to understand and use the following circle theorems:

1. The angle in a semicircle is always a right angle.

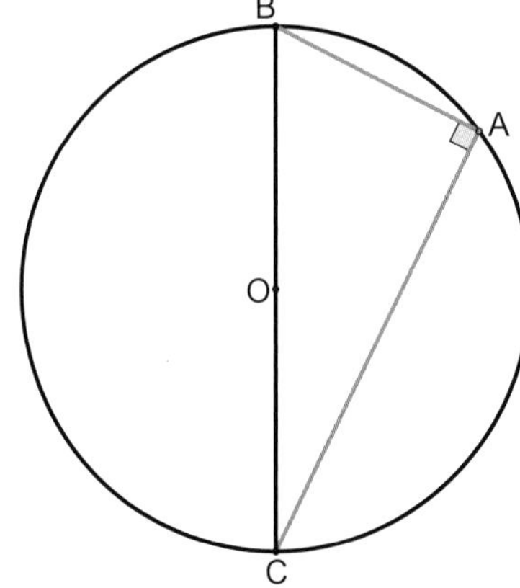

2. The perpendicular from the centre of a circle to a chord bisects the chord.

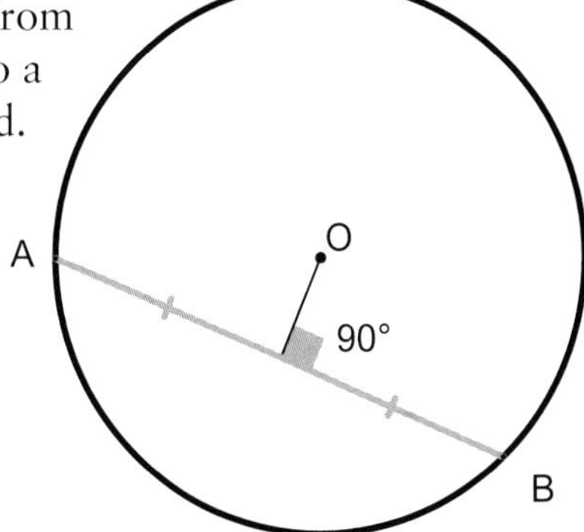

3. The tangent to a circle is perpendicular to the radius it touches.

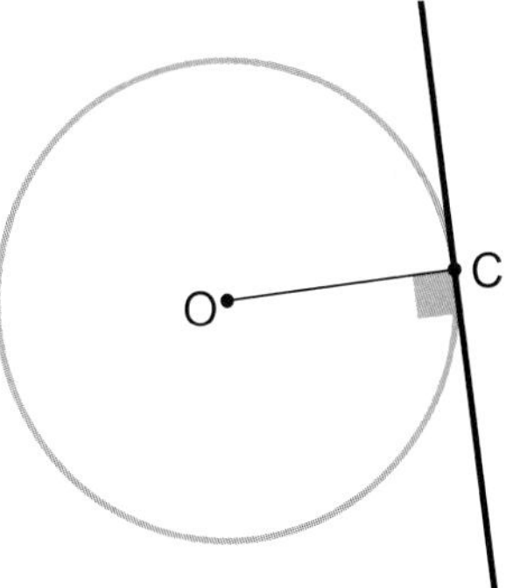

The second and third theorems are often useful when working out the gradient or equation of a line.

The general equation of a circle is:

$(x-a)^2 + (y-b)^2 = r^2$

where (a,b) are the coordinates of the centre and r is its radius.

This is sometimes written as:

$x^2 + y^2 + 2gx + 2fy + c = 0$

You will use the first form most often, especially when finding the centre and radius of a circle.

You can find the points of intersection of a circle with a straight line by solving the equations of the line and circle simultaneously.

A line is a tangent to a circle if there is only one point of intersection.

Chapter 8

Sequences and Series

8.1 Introduction

Keywords

Sequence: A list of numbers, generated by some rule.

Series: The summation of a sequence of numbers.

Term: One of the numbers in a sequence or series.

Recurrence formula or **recurrence relationship** or **recursion relationship:** A formula for a sequence, in which each term is defined as some function of the previous terms.

Oscillate: A sequence oscillates if its terms alternately go up and down.

Converge: A sequence converges if the terms get closer and closer to a particular value. A series converges if there is a non–infinite value for the sum.

Diverge: A sequence or series diverges if it doesn't converge.

Arithmetic series: A series in which the **difference** between each pair of terms is constant.

Geometric Series: A series in which the **ratio** of each pair of terms is constant.

Before You Start

You should know how to:

Solve linear equations;

Solve quadratic equations;

Solve simultaneous equations in 2 and 3 variables;

Find the nth term of a sequence.

EXAMPLE 1

Solve the equation to find x:

$$4x - 1 = 3(2x - 2)$$

Expand brackets: $4x - 1 = 6x - 6$

Re-arrange: $2x = 5$

$$x = \frac{5}{2}$$

EXAMPLE 2

Solve the following equation to find x:

$x^2 - 4x - 21 = 0$

Two numbers whose sum is –4 and product is –21 are 3 and –7:

$(x - 7)(x + 3) = 0$

Either $x - 7 = 0$ or $x + 3 = 0$

So $x = 7$ or $x = -3$

EXAMPLE 3

Solve the following simultaneous equations for a and b:

$2a - 3b = -17(1)$

$3a - 2b = -8 \quad (2)$

Multiply (1) by 3: $6a - 9b = -51 \quad (3)$

Multiply (2) by 2: $6a - 4b = -16 \quad (4)$

Subtract (3) from (4): $5b = 35$

$b = 7$

Substitute into (1): $2a - 3(7) = -17$

$2a = 4$

$a = 2$

EXAMPLE 4

Find the nth term of the following sequence:

2, 6, 10, 14, … (1)

The **common difference** is 4. This means that the nth term contains $4n$.

The sequence whose n^{th} term is $4n$ is:

4, 8, 12, 16, …

To get the nth term of (1), therefore, we adjust by subtracting 2:

$4n - 2$

Check this formula:

When $n = 1$, the formula gives $4(1) - 2 = 2$

When $n = 2$, the formula gives $4(2) - 2 = 6$

When $n = 3$, the formula gives $4(3) - 2 = 10$

The formula $4n - 2$ is giving the correct results.

EXERCISE

REVISION EXERCISE 8A

1. Solve the following linear equations:
   a) $2x - 3 = 1$ b) $6(w + 1) = -18$ c) $z = 4(2z + 3)$
   d) $2(y - 1) = 3(2y + 1)$ e) $\frac{1}{v+2} = \frac{3}{4v+5}$
2. Solve the following quadratic equations:
   a) $x^2 + 6x - 7 = 0$ b) $(x + 10)(x - 8) = 0$ c) $x^2 - 6x = -8$
   d) $x^2 = 2x - 1$ e) $(1 - x)^2 = 3x + 1$
3. Solve the following sets of simultaneous equations:
   a) $-5x + 5y = -25$, $5x - 2y = 40$
   b) $6x - 4y = 64$, $-4x - 2y = -38$
   c) $x - 10y = 71$, $x - 8y = 55$
   d) $-9x + 4y = 14$, $-6x + 9y = 3$
   e) $-2x + y = 3$, $8x - 10y = 30$
   f) $-4x - 7y - 3z = 19$, $-6x - 2y + z = -8$, $-2x - 2y + 7z = -12$
4. Find the nth term of the following sequences:
   a) 1, 4, 7, 10, ...   b) 5, 7, 9, 11, ...   c) –3, 1, 5, 9, ...
   d) –5, –15, –25, –35, ...   e) 17, –3, –23, –43, ...

EXERCISE

What You Will Learn

In this chapter you will learn to:

- Use recurrence relations to form sequences;
- Recognise an arithmetic progression, use the formulae for the general term and the sum;
- Recognise a geometric progression, use the formulae for the general term and the sum;
- Understand sigma notation;
- Understand and use the binomial expansion.

IN THE REAL WORLD – THE NAUTILUS

Mathematical sequences crop up in surprising places, particularly in nature. The nautilus is a shellfish and one of the oldest known animals on Earth. It has been in existence for half a billion years. One of the reasons for the survival of this species over such a long time is the ingenious design of the creature's shell. The shell grows in a spiral shape and is divided into chambers, with the fish living in the newest, largest chamber. All the older chambers are used for buoyancy. The nautilus can raise or lower itself in the water by adjusting the amount of air in these chambers, and this technique enables it to reach waters where the temperature is suitable and there is sufficient food. Each time the nautilus grows a new chamber, it is larger than the last. Comparing the size of each chamber with the last, a remarkably consistent mathematical sequence is formed, called a geometric progression.

8.2 Definitions

A **sequence** is a list of numbers that follows some rule. Each number in the list is called a **term**.

A **series** is the summation of all the terms in a sequence.

For example, a sequence could be: $1, \frac{1}{2}, \frac{1}{4}, \frac{1}{8}, \ldots$

The corresponding series would be: $1 + \frac{1}{2} + \frac{1}{4} + \frac{1}{8} + \cdots$

Sequences and series do not have to be infinite. For example, a sequence with only 5 terms is:

17, 15, 13, 11, 9

8.3 Sequences Given By a Formula

You have already revised finding the nth term for a sequence. We often denote this as u_n.

Sometimes you will be given the formula, and asked to find particular terms.

EXAMPLE 1

Find the second, third and fourth terms u_2, u_3, and u_4, for the sequence:

$$u_n = -4n + 6$$

When $n = 2$, the formula gives: $u_2 = -4(2) + 6$

$= -2$

When $n = 3$: $u_3 = -4(3) + 6$

$= -6$

When $n = 4$: $u_4 = -4(4) + 6$

$= -10$

EXAMPLE 2

Find u_2 and u_8 where:

$$u_n = -(n+2)^2$$

$$u_2 = -(2+2)^2$$

$$= -16$$

$$u_8 = -(8+2)^2$$

$$= -100$$

EXAMPLE 3

The nth term of a sequence is given by the formula:

$$u_n = (n-1)(n-5)$$

Which terms of the sequence give the result $u_n = -3$?

$$(n-1)(n-5) = -3$$

Expand brackets: $n^2 - 6n + 5 = -3$

Re-arrange: $n^2 - 6n + 8 = 0$

Factorise: $(n-2)(n-4) = 0$

$$n = 2 \text{ or } n = 4$$

Check the answers:

When $n = 2$, $u_n = (2-1)(2-5) = (1)(-3) = -3$

When $n = 4$, $u_n = (4-1)(4-5) = (3)(-1) = -3$

The second and fourth terms of the sequence are both –3.

Sometimes n may take an algebraic value.

EXAMPLE 4

A sequence is defined by the formula: $u_n = n^2$

Find the term in the sequence when $n = 3k + 1$

$$u_{3k+1} = (3k+1)^2$$
$$= 9k^2 + 6k + 1$$

You may be asked to find specific constants in the formula for a sequence. Where more than one constant is required, this involves solving simultaneous equations.

EXAMPLE 5

The terms of a sequence are given by the formula: $u_n = 2pn + qn^2$
where p and q are constants. Find p and q given that: $u_3 = 48$ and $u_4 = 72$

$u_3 = 48$ so $2p(3) + q(3)^2 = 48$

$$6p + 9q = 48$$

Divide by 3: $2p + 3q = 16$ (1)

$u_4 = 72$ so $2p(4) + q(4)^2 = 72$

$$8p + 16q = 72$$

Divide by 8: $p + 2q = 9$

$$p = 9 - 2q \quad (2)$$

Substitute (2) into (1):

$$2(9-2q) + 3q = 16$$
$$18 - q = 16$$
$$q = 2$$

Substitute into (2): $p = 9 - 2(2) = 5$ $\qquad p = 5, q = 2$

Some sequences **oscillate**. An oscillating sequence is one whose terms alternately go up and down.

EXAMPLE 6

A sequence is defined by the formula:

$$u_n = 2(-1)^n$$

Find the first 4 terms.

When $n = 1$, $u_n = 2(-1)^1 = -2$

When $n = 2$, $u_n = 2(-1)^2 = 2$

When $n = 3$, $u_n = 2(-1)^3 = -2$

When $n = 4$, $u_n = 2(-1)^4 = 2$

EXERCISE

EXERCISE 8B

1. Find the first 4 terms of each sequence:
   a) $u_n = 2n - 3$ b) $u_n = 10 - 3n^2$ c) $u_n = (n-2)^2$
   d) $u_n = n^2 + 3n - 6$ e) $u_n = (n-3)(n+2)$ f) $u_n = n^3 + 1$
   g) $u_n = (1 - n^2)(1 - n)$ h) $u_n = 2pn^2 + qn$ where $p = 2, q = 3$
   i) $u_n = (-1)^n(1 + n)$ j) $u_n = \dfrac{2 + 3n}{3 + 2n}$
2. Find which term of the sequence gives the following values:
   a) $u_n = 4n + 1,\ u_n = 45$ b) $u_n = 9 - 3n^2,\ u_n = -39$
   c) $u_n = (2n + 1)^2,\ u_n = 49$ d) $u_n = n^2 - 3n + 3,\ u_n = 13$
   e) $u_n = (n - 1)(n + 4),\ u_n = 50$ f) $u_n = 8 - n^3,\ u_n = 0$
   g) $u_n = (n^2 + 1)(n - 3),\ u_n = 0$
   h) $u_n = (p + q)n + pqn^2$ where $p = 1,\ q = 2,\ u_n = 14$
   i) $u_n = n(-1)^n,\ u_n = 10$ j) $u_n = \dfrac{1 + 2n}{3 + 4n},\ u_n = \dfrac{7}{15}$
3. A sequence has the general term $u_n = an - 7$. Given that the fourth term of the sequence is 9, find the value of a.
4. The term of a sequence is defined by the formula: $u_n = a(2n - b)$
   Given that the fourth term is 9 and the fifth term is 15, find the values of a and b.
5. The nth term of a sequence is defined by the formula: $u_n = \dfrac{n - 1}{an - b}$ where a and b are constants.
   Given $u_3 = \dfrac{2}{9}$ and $u_4 = \dfrac{3}{13}$, find the values of a and b.
6. The first three terms of a sequence are 6, 12 and 20. The sequence is defined by the formula $u_n = an^2 + bn + c$
   Given a, b, and c are all positive constants, find their values.

EXERCISE

EXERCISE

7. A sequence is defined by the formula: $u_n = n^2 - 4n + 8$
Show that all the terms of the sequence are positive. (Hint: complete the square.)

8. Find the smallest term in the sequence defined by the formula: $u_n = n^2 - 6n + 4$
(Hint: complete the square.)

9. a) Show that all the terms of the sequence $u_n = 4n - 7$ are odd numbers.
b) Give a formula for a sequence in which all the terms are even numbers.

10. The first, second and third terms of a sequence are –1, 4 and 9. Find a formula that would give these terms.

11. A sequence is defined by the formula: $u_n = n(n-1)$.
Given $n = 3k - 2$, a second sequence can be formed.
a) Find a formula for this new sequence.
b) Show that all the terms in this second sequence are multiples of 3.

EXERCISE

8.4 Recurrence Relationships

Recurrence relationships for a sequence often take the form $u_{n+1} = f(u_n)$.
That is, each term is some function of the previous term.

EXAMPLE 1

A sequence is defined by the recurrence formula:

$$u_n = u_{n-1} + 3$$

Given $u_1 = 7$, find the first 4 terms.

$$u_1 = 7$$
$$u_2 = u_1 + 3 = 10$$
$$u_3 = u_2 + 3 = 13$$
$$u_4 = u_3 + 3 = 16$$

Sometimes you may be asked to find the formula for the recurrence relationship. Sometimes this may involve trial and improvement.

EXAMPLE 2

Find the recurrence formula for the following sequence:

1, 3, 7, 15, 31, ...

Since the first two terms are 1 and 3, we try $u_{n+1} = 3u_n$

This does not work because the third term would be 9.

Try: $u_{n+1} = u_n + 2$

This does not work either, since the third term would be 5.

Try $u_{n+1} = 2u_n + 1$

This gives the correct sequence:

1, 3, 7, 15, 31, ...

Sometimes, finding the recurrence formula may involve solving simultaneous equations.

EXAMPLE 3

A recurrence relationship is defined by the formula:

$$u_{n+1} = au_n + b$$

Given the first three terms are 3, 4 and 6, find the values of a and b.

$$u_1 = 3$$

Using the recurrence formula: $u_2 = a(3) + b = 4$ (1)

Using the recurrence formula: $u_3 = a(4) + b = 6$ (2)

Rewrite (1): $3a + b = 4$

Rewrite (2): $4a + b = 6$

Subtract (1) from (2): $a = 2$

Using (1): $3(2) + b = 4$

$b = -2$

The recurrence formula is:

$$u_{n+1} = 2u_n - 2$$

EXERCISE 8C

1. Write down the first 4 terms of each of these sequences:

a) $u_{n+1} = u_n - 4,\ u_1 = 1$

b) $u_{n+1} = (u_n)^2 - 2,\ u_1 = 1$

c) $u_{n+1} = (u_n - 1)^2,\ u_1 = 3$

d) $u_{n+1} = \frac{1}{4}u_n + 1,\ u_1 = 2$

e) $u_{n+1} = \frac{2u_n}{3},\ u_1 = 27$

f) $u_{n+1} = u_n(u_n - 1) + 1,\ u_1 = 3$

g) $u_{n+1} = \frac{u_n}{1 + u_n},\ u_1 = 3$

h) $u_{n+1} = 2u_n - 1,\ u_1 = \frac{1}{4}$

i) $u_{n+1} = -2u_n + \frac{1}{2},\ u_1 = -\frac{3}{4}$

j) $u_{n+1} = (-1)^{u_n},\ u_1 = 2$

2. Write a recurrence relationship linking u_{n+1} to u_n for each sequence:

a) 2, 5, 8, 11, ...

b) –5, –10, –15, –20, ...

c) 37, 37, 37, 37, ...

d) 2, –2, 2, –2, 2, ...

e) 2, 4, 2, 4, 2, ...

f) 2, 4, 8, 16, ...

g) $1, \frac{1}{2}, \frac{1}{4}, \frac{1}{8}, \frac{1}{16}, \ldots$

h) 256, 16, 4, 2, ...

i) 2, 4, 16, 256, ...

j) 1, 2, 6, 22, 86, ...

3. Write down the first 5 terms of the sequence defined by the recurrence formula:

$$u_{n+1} = \frac{1 + 2u_n}{3 + 4u_n}$$

where $u_1 = 1$, giving your answers to 2 decimal places.

4. The sequence of positive numbers u_1, u_2, u_3 is given by $u_{n+1} = (u_n - 3)^2,\ u_1 = 4$

a) Find u_2, u_3 and u_4.

b) Write down the value of u_{50}.

EXERCISE

EXERCISE

EXERCISE

5. A sequence is defined by the recurrence relationship: $u_{n+1} = ku_n - 2k$ where k is a integer. Given $u_1 = 1$ and $u_3 = -15$, find the two possible values of k.

6. A sequence is generated by the recurrence formula: $u_{n+1} = \frac{d}{u_n} + 1$ where d is a constant. Given $u_1 = 2$ and $u_3u_2 = \frac{11}{3}$, find the value of d.

7. The recursion formula $u_{n+1} = au_n + bu_n^2$ is used to generate the sequence of numbers $u_1 = 1, u_2 = -2, u_3 = 16, \ldots$
Find the values of the constants a and b.

8. The sequence $u_1, u_2, u_3, \ldots u_n$ is defined by the recurrence relation

$u_{n+1} = pu_n + 9, u_1 = 5$

where p is a constant. Given that $u_3 = 11$, show that one possible value of p is 0.2 and find the other value of p.

9. A sequence is defined by the recurrence relation $u_{n+1} = \sqrt{\frac{u_n}{3} + \frac{a}{u_n}}, n = 1,2,3$
where a is a constant.
   a) Given that $a = 19$ and $u_1 = 3$, find the values of u_2, u_3 and u_4 giving your answers to 2 decimal places.
   b) Given instead that $u_1 = u_2 = 3$, calculate the value of a.
   c) Given this value of a, write down the value of u_5.

10. A recursion formula is used to generate a sequence: $u_{n+1} = (-1)^n u_n + q$ where $u_1 = 1$.
   a) Show that $u_4 = 1 - q$.
   b) Given that $u_4 = -5u_5$, find the value of q.

EXERCISE

8.5 Behaviour of Sequences

A sequence is said to **converge** if the terms get closer and closer to some value.
If each term is a constant multiple of the next, there is a simple test for convergence:

If a sequence is defined by the formula: $u_{n+1} = ku_n$ then the sequence converges if $-1 < k < 1$.

EXAMPLE 1

A sequence is defined by the recurrence relationship:

$$u_{n+1} = \frac{u_n}{2}, \qquad u_1 = 1$$

a) Find the first 3 terms and u_{15}.
b) Does the sequence converge?

---

a) The terms of this sequence are:

$u_1 = 1, u_2 = 0.5, u_3 = 0.25, \ldots$

$u_{15} = \left(\frac{1}{2}\right)^{14} = 6.1 \times 10^{-5}$

continued...

Example 1...

b) This sequence is of the form $u_{n+1} = ku_n$ where $k = \frac{1}{2}$

Since $|k| < 1$, the sequence converges.

If we know a sequence converges, it is possible to use the recurrence formula to find the value at which the sequence converges. As a sequence converges to a particular value, eventually each term will be the same as the next. Or:

$$\text{As } n \longrightarrow \infty,\ u_{n+1} \rightarrow u_n.$$

Hence, we can replace both u_{n+1} and u_n in the formula with u and solve the equation.

EXAMPLE 2

A sequence is defined by the recurrence relationship:

$$u_{n+1} = 1 + \frac{1}{u_n}, \qquad u_1 = 1$$

Given that the sequence does converge, find the value to which the terms converge.

To find the value at which the sequence converges, replace both u_{n+1} and u_n in the formula with u:

$$u = 1 + \frac{1}{u}$$

Multiply both sides by u and re-arrange: $u^2 - u - 1 = 0$

Using the quadratic formula: $u = \frac{1 \pm \sqrt{5}}{2}$

Since the initial value is 1, and each term is larger than the last, the convergent value must be greater than 1.

Hence the convergent value is $\frac{1 + \sqrt{5}}{2}$

If the sequence does not converge, it **diverges**.

EXAMPLE 3

A sequence is defined by the recurrence relationship:

$$u_{n+1} = \frac{4u_n}{3}, \qquad u_1 = 1$$

a) Find the first 3 terms of the sequence.
b) Does the sequence converge or diverge?

---

a) The terms of this sequence are:

$$u_1 = 1,\ u_2 = \frac{4}{3},\ u_3 = \frac{16}{9}, \ldots$$

b) This sequence is of the form $u_{n+1} = ku_n$

where $k = \frac{4}{3}$.

Since $|k| > 1$, the sequence diverges.

It is possible for both convergent and divergent sequences to oscillate. An oscillating sequence is one in which successive terms are alternately higher then lower than the last.

EXAMPLE 4

By calculating the first 5 terms in each case, state whether the following sequences are convergent or divergent and whether or not they oscillate.

a) $u_{n+1} = -\frac{7}{5}u_n + 1, u_1 = 0$

b) $u_{n+1} = \frac{6}{1+u_n}, u_1 = 3$

---

a) The terms are:

0, 1, –0.4, 1.56, –1.184

The sequence oscillates and diverges.

b) The terms are:

3, 1.5, 2.4, 1.76, 2.17 (the last two to 2 d.p.)

The sequence oscillates and converges.

EXERCISE

EXERCISE 8D

1. A sequence is defined recursively by the formula: $u_{n+1} = \frac{3}{4}u_n, \quad u_1 = 1$
   a) Find u_2, u_3 and u_4.
   b) State whether this sequence converges or diverges.

2. A sequence is defined by the recurrence formula: $u_{n+1} = 3au_n, \quad u_1 = 1$, where a is a constant.
   a) Find the first four terms of the sequence in terms of a.
   b) Find the range of values of a for which this is a convergent sequence.

3. By finding the first 4 terms, determine whether the sequence defined by the recurrence formula $u_{n+1} = 1 + u_n^2$, $u_1 = 1$ converges or diverges.

4. a) Find the first 5 terms of the sequence defined by the recurrence formula:
   $u_{n+1} = \frac{3}{2+u_n}, u_1 = 3$
   b) Hence state whether the sequence converges or diverges, and whether or not it oscillates.

5. A sequence is defined by the recurrence formula: $u_{n+1} = \frac{u_n}{5} + 2, u_1 = 1$

   By forming and solving an equation, show that the sequence converges to a value c and find the exact value of c.

6. The terms of a sequence are given by the recurrence relationship:
   $u_{n+1} = 1 + u_n, \quad u_1 = 1$
   Does the sequence converge or diverge?

EXERCISE

EXERCISE

7. A sequence is generated using the recurrence formula: $u_{n+1} = 1 + \frac{u_n}{2}, u_1 = 3$

   Do the terms of the sequence converge to a particular value or diverge? If the sequence converges, find the value.

8. The terms of a sequence are generated using the formula: $u_{n+1} = -\frac{7}{10}u_n + 1, u_1 = 1$

   a) Find the first 5 terms of the sequence, to two decimal places where necessary.
   b) Is the sequence oscillating?
   c) The sequence converges to a limit c. By forming and solving an equation, find c.

9. Find the range of values of p for which the sequence: $u_{n+1} = (1 - p)u_n$ is a convergent sequence.

10. A sequence has the recurrence formula $u_{n+1} = \frac{a-1}{a+1}u_n$ where a is a constant.

    Find the range of values of a that ensure this is a convergent sequence.

EXERCISE

Investigation – Chaos in Populations

Note: You may find it useful to set this task up as a spreadsheet.

In the natural world, the population of a group of animals can sometimes be modelled from year to year using a simple recurrence relationship:

$$p_{n+1} = r\frac{p_n}{p_m}(p_m - p_n)$$

p_m is the maximum population the local environment can sustain. r is called a breeding factor. r takes low values, such as 1.2, for species that do not breed very quickly (for example giant pandas) and high values, such as 4, for species that breed very quickly (for example rabbits).

Let us assume that in a particular population of snakes, $r = 2.5$. For the snakes we will assume the initial population $p_0 = 20$, and the maximum $p_m = 100$. We can work out next year's population:

$$p_1 = r\left(\frac{p_0}{p_m}\right)(p_m - p_0)$$

$$= 2.5\left(\frac{20}{100}\right)(100 - 20)$$

$$= 40$$

In the second year,

$$p_2 = 2.5\left(\frac{40}{100}\right)(100 - 40)$$

$$= 60$$

a) Check out what happens to the population of snakes over the next few years.

b) If the breeding factor for a species is very low, for example 0.8, what happens to the population after a few years? Assume again that the population starts at 20 and the maximum is 100.

c) For a group of wild mice, $r = 3.7$. Can you work out the population for the first 10 years? Again assume $p_m = 100$.

Your answers should demonstrate some of the different types of behaviour we see within animal populations: stability, extinction and unpredictability or chaos.

8.6 Arithmetic Progressions

An arithmetic progression is a special type of sequence. The difference between a term and the previous one remains constant.

An example of an arithmetic progression is: 5,7,9,11, ...

In this case, the **common difference** is 2.

8.7 Arithmetic Series

An arithmetic series is a special kind of series. Just like the arithmetic progression, an arithmetic series is a series in which there is a common difference between successive terms.

An example of an arithmetic series is: $1 + \frac{3}{2} + 2 + \frac{5}{2} + 3 + \cdots$

In this case, the common difference is $\frac{1}{2}$

Recurrence formulae are sometimes used to give the terms of a series, just as they are for sequences. A recurrence formula for the terms of an arithmetic series is: $u_{n+1} = u_n + d$ where d is a constant.

The first term of an arithmetic series is denoted a.

Hence, the first three terms are:

$$\begin{aligned} u_1 &= a \\ u_2 &= a + d \\ u_3 &= a + 2d \end{aligned}$$

From this, the general term of an arithmetic series is: $u_n = a + (n - 1)d$

The formula for the general term is useful in solving many different types of problem.

EXAMPLE 1

Find the 50th term in the arithmetic series:

4+6+8+10+ ...

Find the first term and common difference: $a = 4$ and $d = 2$.

To find the 50th term, use:

$$\begin{aligned} u_n &= a + (n - 1)d \\ u_{50} &= 4 + (50 - 1)2 \\ &= 102 \end{aligned}$$

It is possible to find the number of terms in an arithmetic series.

EXAMPLE 2

Find the number of terms in the series:

$$47 + 40 + 33 + 26 + \cdots - 58 - 65$$

$$u_n = a + (n-1)d$$

$$-65 = 47 + (n-1)(-7)$$

$$n - 1 = \frac{-65 - 47}{-7}$$

$$= 16$$

Hence $n = 17$

You can also find the first term of an arithmetic series.

EXAMPLE 3

The final term of an arithmetic series is 76. Given that the common difference is 5 and there are 22 terms, find the first term.

$$u_n = a + (n-1)d$$

$$76 = a + (21)(5)$$

$$a = 76 - 105$$

$$a = -29$$

You can find where in a series the terms become larger or smaller than a certain value.

EXAMPLE 4

An arithmetic series is given by the recursion formula:

$$u_{n+1} = 6 + u_n, \qquad u_1 = -30$$

Which term is the first that is greater than 100?

$$u_n > 100$$

$$\Rightarrow a + (n-1)d > 100$$

$$-30 + (n-1)6 > 100$$

$$n - 1 > \frac{130}{6}$$

$$n > 22.67 \text{ (2 d.p.)}$$

The 23rd term is greater than 100.

EXERCISE

EXERCISE 8E

1. Which of these are arithmetic series?

a) $1 + 2 + 3 + 4 + \cdots$

b) $30 + 28 + 26 + 24 + \ldots$

c) $10^1 + 10^2 + 10^3 + 10^4 + \ldots$

d) $\frac{1}{2} + \frac{1}{3} + \frac{1}{4} + \frac{1}{5} + \ldots$

e) $\frac{1}{3} + \frac{2}{3} + 1 + \frac{4}{3} + \frac{5}{3} + \cdots$

f) $(1 + \sqrt{2}) + (3 + 2\sqrt{2}) + (5 + 3\sqrt{2}) + (7 + 4\sqrt{2}) + \ldots$

EXERCISE

EXERCISE

g) $100 + -100 + -300 + -500 + \ldots$ h) $\frac{1}{3} + \frac{2}{4} + \frac{3}{5} + \frac{4}{6} + \frac{5}{7} + \cdots$

i) $(2z + 1) + (2.5z + 3) + (3z + 5) + (3.5z + 7) + (4z + 9) \ldots$

j) $16f + 8f + 4f + 2f + f + \ldots$

2. Find the number of terms in the sequence: $1, 7, 13, 19, \ldots, 49$.

3. For each of the following arithmetic series, find the 10th and 50th terms.
a) $5 + 11 + 17 + 23 + 29 + \ldots$ b) $-1 + 2 + 5 + 8 + 11 \ldots$
c) $4.7 + 2.7 + 0.7 + -1.3 + -3.3 \ldots$ d) $-2.2 + -1.45 + -0.7 + 0.05 + 0.8 \ldots$
e) $5p + 7p + 9p + 11p + 13p \ldots$ f) $\frac{11}{3} + \frac{13}{3} + \frac{15}{3} + \frac{17}{3} + \frac{19}{3} \ldots$

g) $(3y + 1) + (y + 3) + (-y + 5) + (-3y + 7) + (-5y + 9) \ldots$

h) $2 \times 10^4 + 2.5 \times 10^4 + 3 \times 10^4 + 3.5 \times 10^4 + 4 \times 10^4 \ldots$

i) $(7 - 7\sqrt{2}) + (6 - 6\sqrt{2}) + (5 - 5\sqrt{2}) + (4 - 4\sqrt{2}) + (3 - 3\sqrt{2}) \ldots$

j) 1001, 1002.5, 1004, 1005.5, 1007.

4. The first three terms of an arithmetic sequence are: $p, 6p - 8, 3p + 8$
a) Show that $p = 3$.
b) Find the value of the 50th term of this sequence.

5. Three consecutive terms of an arithmetic sequence are $(7x - 7)$, $(x - 3)$ and $(3 - x)$. Find the next term.

6. The first three terms of an arithmetic sequence are: $k, 4k - 9, 3k + 6$
a) Show that $k = 6$
b) Find the value of the 60th term of this sequence.

7. On Zoe's 11th birthday she started to receive an annual allowance. The first annual allowance was £500 and on each following birthday the allowance was increased by £200.
a) Show that, immediately after her 12th birthday, the total of the allowances that Zoe had received was £1200.
b) Find the amount of Zoe's annual allowance on her 18th birthday.

8. In the first year after opening, a car showroom sold 210 cars. A model for future trading assumes that sales will increase by x cars per month for the next 37 months, so that $(210 + x)$ will be sold in the second month, $(210 + 2x)$ in the third month, and so on. Using this model with $x = 6$, calculate the number of cars sold in the 38th month.

EXERCISE

8.8 Sum of an Arithmetic Series

How would you add the terms in an arithmetic series to find the sum?

IN THE REAL WORLD

There is a well–known story, which may or may not be true, about the mathematician Karl Friedrich Gauss when he was at primary school. His teacher asked the class to add the numbers 1 to 100, thinking this would keep them busy until the end of the lesson. About 30 seconds later Gauss gave him the answer. How did he do it?

Gauss rearranged the numbers to add them like this:

$$(1 + 100) + (2 + 99) + (3 + 98) + \cdots + (50 + 51) \ = ?$$

Notice that every pair of numbers adds up to 101. There are 50 pairs of numbers, so the answer is $50 \times 101 = 5050$.

You can see how Gauss's method would work for any number of integers. It leads us to a formula that can be used to find the sum of any arithmetic series.

PROOF OF THE FORMULA FOR THE SUM OF AN ARITHMETIC SERIES

You should learn this proof and the formula.

Consider the series whose first term is a and common difference is d.

Let the sum of the first n terms be S_n. Then:

$$S_n = a + [a + d] + [a + 2d] + \cdots + [a + (n - 2)d] + [a + (n - 1)d] \quad (1)$$

Simply reversing the order of the terms, we can also write:

$$S_n = [a + (n - 1)d] + [a + (n - 2)d] + \cdots + [a + 2d] + [a + d] + a \quad (2)$$

Add equations (1) and (2):

$$2S_n = [2a + (n - 1)d] + [2a + (n - 1)d] + \cdots + [2a + (n - 1)d] + [2a + (n - 1)d]$$

In this series, there are n terms, which are all the same. So:

$$2S_n = n[2a + (n - 1)d]$$

$$S_n = \frac{n}{2}[2a + (n - 1)d]$$

You will use the notation S_n a lot. For example, S_{100} is the sum of the first 100 terms, S_{19} the sum of the first 19 terms, etc.

EXAMPLE 1

What is the sum of the first 31 terms of arithmetic series:

$$5 + 8 + 11 + 14 + \cdots$$

Always begin by writing down what we know:

$a = 5$, $d = 3$ and $n = 31$.

$$S_n = \frac{n}{2}[2a + (n-1)d]$$

$$S_{31} = \frac{31}{2}[2(5) + (31-1)3]$$

$$S_{31} = 15.5 \times (10 + 90)$$

$$S_{31} = 1550$$

EXAMPLE 2

Find the sum of the series:

$$20 + 18 + 16 + \cdots + -90$$

We know: $a = 20$ and $d = -2$.
We need to know how many terms there are.

$$u_n = a + (n-1)d$$

$$-90 = 20 + (n-1)(-2)$$

$$(n-1) = \frac{-110}{-2}$$

$$n = 56$$

Now apply the formula:

$$S_n = \frac{n}{2}[2a + (n-1)d]$$

$$S_{56} = \frac{56}{2}[2(20) + 55(-2)]$$

$$S_{56} = 28(40 - 110)$$

$$S_{56} = -1960$$

EXAMPLE 3

A girl saves money over a period of 100 weeks. She saves 7p in Week 1, 12p in Week 2, 17p in Week 3, and so on until Week 100. Her weekly savings form an arithmetic series.
(a) Find the amount she saves in Week 100.
(b) Calculate her total savings over the complete 100 week period.

---

continued...

Example 3... a) $a = 7, d = 5, n = 100$

For week 100, $u_n = a + (n - 1)d$

$= 7 + 99(5)$

$= 502$ pence

b) $S_n = \frac{n}{2}[2a + (n - 1)d]$

$S_{100} = 50[2(7) + (99)5]$

$= £254.50$

There is a formula for the sum of the first n natural numbers, which is worth remembering.

EXAMPLE 4

Prove that the sum of the first n natural numbers is given by the formula

$$S_n = \frac{n}{2}(1 + n)$$

The series: $1 + 2 + 3 + \cdots + n$

The first term $a = 1$ and common difference $d = 1$.

The general formula for the sum of an arithmetic series is: $S_n = \frac{n}{2}[2a + (n - 1)d]$

Substitute for a and d: $S_n = \frac{n}{2}[2(1) + (n - 1)(1)]$

$$S_n = \frac{n}{2}[2 + (n - 1)]$$

$$S_n = \frac{n}{2}(1 + n)$$

EXERCISE 8F

1. Find the sum of the following series to the specified number of terms:
   - a) $2 + 4 + 6 + 8 + 10 \ldots$ (10 terms)
   - b) $10 + 8 + 6 + 4 + 2 \ldots$ (11 terms)
   - c) $0.5 + 1.5 + 2.5 + 3.5 + 4.5 \ldots$ (12 terms)
   - d) $-10 + -15 + -20 + -25 + -30 \ldots$ (10 terms)
   - e) $\frac{17}{3} + \frac{18}{3} + \frac{19}{3} + \frac{20}{3} + \frac{21}{3} + \ldots$ (9 terms)
   - f) $10^4 + (2 \times 10^4) + (3 \times 10^4) + (4 \times 10^4) + \ldots$ (10 terms)
   - g) $-5 + 5i, -4 + 4i, -3 + 3i, -2 + 2i, -1 + 1i \ldots$ (11 terms)
   - h) $3\sqrt{5} + 5\sqrt{5} + 7\sqrt{5} + 9\sqrt{5} + 11\sqrt{5} + \cdots$ (20 terms)
   - i) $(1 + x) + 1 + (1 - x) + (1 - 2x) + (1 - 3x) \ldots$ (11 terms)
   - j) $\frac{1}{4} + \frac{21}{4} + \frac{41}{4} + \frac{61}{4} + \frac{81}{4} \ldots$ (8 terms)

EXERCISE

EXERCISE

2. Sum the arithmetic series with first term 6, common difference 7 and 13 terms.

3. Find the sum of the integers from 1 to 2000 which are not divisible by 5.

4. A company makes a profit of £49000 in the year 2011. A model for future performance assumes that yearly profits will increase in an arithmetic sequence with common difference d. This model predicts total profits of £612500 for the 5 years 2011 to 2015 inclusive.
   a) Find the value of d.
   b) Using your value of d find the predicted profit for the year 2018.

5. A man repays a loan over a period of n months. His monthly repayments form an arithmetic sequence. He repays £129 in the first month, £127 in the second month, £125 in the third month, and so on. He makes his final repayment in the nth month, where $n > 16$.
   a) Find the amount the man repays in month number 16.
   Over the n months, he repays a total of £4000.
   b) Form an equation in n, and show that your equation may be written as $n^2 - 130n + 4000 = 0$.
   c) Solve the equation in part (b) to find two solutions.
   d) State, with a reason, which of these solutions to the equation is not a sensible solution to the repayment problem.

6. A marathon runner prepares for a race by completing a practice run on each of 9 consecutive days. On each day after the first run, she runs further than she did on the previous day. The lengths of her 9 practice runs form an arithmetic sequence with first term a km and common difference d km. She runs 16.4 km on the 9th day, and she runs a total of 118.8 km over the 9 day period. Find the value of a and the value of d.

7. On the first day of Christmas, my true love sent to me a partridge in a pear tree. On the second day of Christmas, my true love sent to me two turtle doves and a partridge in a pear tree. i.e. my true love has sent 1 present on day 1, 3 presents on day 2, etc. Calculate how many presents I receive on the 5th day of Christmas assuming my true love hasn't run out of money.

8. Consider the arithmetic series: $3 + 5 + 7 + \cdots$
   a) Using the general formula for the nth term, find and simplify a formula for the nth term of this series, leaving n in your answer.
   b) Using the general formula for the sum to n terms, find and simplify a formula for the sum to n terms of this series, again in terms of n.

9. There is an alternative formula for the sum to n terms of an arithmetic series: $S_n = \frac{n}{2}(a + l)$ where l is the last term. Can you prove this formula?

EXERCISE

8.9 Sigma notation

Sigma notation provides a more concise way to write series.
Sigma (written Σ) is a Greek letter and in mathematics is always used to represent a sum.
For example

$$\sum_{r=1}^{r=n} r = 1 + 2 + 3 + \cdots + n$$

The subscript and superscript $r = 1$ and $r = n$ mean that these are the first and last values. The r following the sigma sign will be replaced by every value in this range, and all the resulting values will be summed.

Sometimes the subscript and/or superscript will simply be a number. In this case, assume the variable r is being substituted.

EXAMPLE 1

Evaluate $\sum_{r=1}^{4} (2r + 1)$

Substitute the values 1, 2, 3 and 4 into $(2r + 1)$ and sum:

$$\sum_{r=1}^{4} (2r + 1) = 3 + 5 + 7 + 9$$

$$= 24$$

Be aware that r may not start from 1.

EXAMPLE 2

Evaluate $\sum_{r=2}^{5} r^2$

Substitute the values 2, 3, 4 and 5 into r^2 and sum:

$$\sum_{r=2}^{5} r^2 = 4 + 9 + 16 + 25$$

$$= 54$$

The upper or lower limit of the summation may be a general term.

EXAMPLE 3

Evaluate $\sum_{r=2}^{n} r^{-1}$

Substitute the values 2, 3, 4, ... , n into r^{-1} and sum:

$$\sum_{r=2}^{n} r^{-1} = \frac{1}{2} + \frac{1}{3} + \frac{1}{4} + \cdots + \frac{1}{n}$$

You may be asked to write a series in sigma notation.

EXAMPLE 4

Use sigma notation to denote the following arithmetic series:

$$7 + 9 + 11 + \cdots + 23$$

Revise how to make a formula for the general term of a **sequence,** discussed in Section 8.1. Now apply this method to finding the general term of an arithmetic series.

$a = 7$ and $d = 2$

This indicates that the general term is $2r + 5$. This will be our expression to be summed over. Find the number of terms:

$$u_n = a + (n - 1)d$$

$$23 = 7 + (n - 1)(2)$$

$$(n - 1) = \frac{16}{2}$$

$$n = 9$$

Therefore:

$$7 + 9 + 11 + \cdots + 23 = \sum_{1}^{9} (2r + 5)$$

Check: If you use sigma notation to denote a series, always check your answer by evaluating some of the terms:

$$\sum_{1}^{9} (2r + 5) = (2(1) + 5) + (2(2) + 5) + (2(3) + 5) + \cdots + (2(9) + 5)$$

$$= 7 + 9 + 11 + \cdots + 23$$

Our answer appears to be correct.

EXERCISE

EXERCISE 8G

1. Write down the arithmetic series corresponding to the following:

a) $\sum_{1}^{4} (r + 1)$ b) $\sum_{3}^{7} \left(\frac{r}{2}\right)$ c) $\sum_{1}^{5} \left(\frac{r}{10}\right)$ d) $\sum_{-3}^{3} (-r)$

e) $\sum_{0}^{4} (20 - 5r)$ f) $\sum_{97}^{100} (100r)$ g) $\sum_{0}^{3} \left(\frac{r}{4}\right)$ h) $\sum_{3}^{4} (5r + 1)$

i) $\sum_{5}^{8} \left(\frac{r}{2} - 1\right)$ j) $\sum_{1}^{5} (1)$

EXERCISE

EXERCISE

2. Find the formula for the general term of each series. Use this to write the series in sigma notation, beginning at $r = 1$.
   a) $3 + 4 + 5 + 6$
   b) $10 + 13 + 16 + \cdots + 28$
   c) $-5 + -7 + -9 + \cdots$ (20 terms)
   d) $1000 + 998 + 996 + \cdots$ (10 terms)
   e) $15 + 8 + 1 + -6 + -13 + -20$
   f) $21 + 41 + 61 + \cdots$ (10 terms)
   g) $\frac{5}{2} + \frac{7}{2} + \frac{9}{2} + \frac{11}{2} + \frac{13}{2}$
   h) $3a + 5a + 7a + \cdots$ (b terms)
   i) $5\sqrt{3} + 7\sqrt{3} + 9\sqrt{3} + 11\sqrt{3} + \cdots$ (13 terms)
   j) $t^2 + 2t^2 + 3t^2 + \cdots$ (6 terms)
3. Find the following sums as simply as possible:
   a) $\sum_{1}^{5}(5r)$ b) $\sum_{2}^{6}(3r+1)$ c) $\sum_{r=0}^{4}(3+rx)$ d) $\sum_{1}^{8}\left(\frac{r}{3}+1\right)$ e) $\sum_{r=1}^{10}\left(\frac{3r-1}{2}\right)$

   f) $\sum_{1}^{20}(0.05r+1)$ g) $\sum_{r=-5}^{5}(2r+y)$ h) $\sum_{1}^{15}\left(\frac{3r}{4}+2\right)$ i) $\sum_{1}^{100}(-2r-98)$ j) $\sum_{-4}^{0}\left(\frac{r}{2}+2\right)$
4. Prove that $\sum_{1}^{n}(6r-1) = n(3n+2)$
5. For some value of n, $\sum_{1}^{n}(-2r-5) = -160$

   Form and solve a quadratic equation to find the value of n.
6. Consider the arithmetic series: $\sum_{1}^{n}(8-2r)$
   a) Write out the first 5 terms of the series.
   b) Using the general formula for the sum to n terms, show that the sum to n terms of this series is given by: $S_n = 7n - n^2$
   c) Using the general formula for the nth term, show that the nth term of this series is given by: $u_n = 8 - 2n$
   d) By equating your answers to part (a) and part (b), form and solve a quadratic equation to find where in the series the sum is equal to the individual term.

8.10 Geometric Progressions

Another special type of **sequence** is a geometric progression. In a geometric progression, the ratio between successive terms is constant. For example: 2, 6, 18, 54, ...

In this geometric progression, the **common ratio** is 3.

8.11 Geometric Series

A second special type of **series** is the geometric series. Like the geometric progression, a geometric series is a series in which there is a common ratio between successive terms.

An example of a geometric series is: $1 + \frac{1}{2} + \frac{1}{4} + \frac{1}{8} + \cdots$

In this case, the common ratio is $\frac{1}{2}$

A recurrence formula for the terms of a geometric series is: $u_{n+1} = u_n r$

where r, the common ratio, is a constant.

The first term of a geometric series is denoted a.

Hence, the first three terms are: $u_1 = a$

$u_2 = ar$

$u_3 = ar^2$

From this, the general term of an arithmetic series is: $u_n = ar^{n-1}$

The formula for the general term is useful in solving many different types of problem.

EXAMPLE 1

Find the general term for the geometric series:

$$7 + 14 + 28 + 56 + \cdots$$

$a = 7$ and $r = 2$

Hence the general term is:

$$\begin{aligned} u_n &= ar^{n-1} \\ &= 7 \times 2^{n-1} \end{aligned}$$

If r is negative, the geometric series oscillates.
If $|r|$ is less than one, each term in the geometric series is smaller in magnitude than the last.

EXAMPLE 2

Find the general term for each of these geometric series:

$$1 - 2 + 4 - 8 + 16 - \cdots$$

$$3 + 1 + \frac{1}{3} + \frac{1}{9} + \cdots$$

---

a) $a = 1$ and $r = -2$

General term:

$$\begin{aligned} u_n &= ar^{n-1} \\ &= (1)(-2)^{n-1} \\ &= (-2)^{n-1} \end{aligned}$$

b) $a = 3$ and $r = \frac{1}{3}$

$$\begin{aligned} u_n &= ar^{n-1} \\ &= 3\left(\frac{1}{3}\right)^{n-1} \end{aligned}$$

Remember that a sequence is simply a list of numbers, whereas a series is the sum of that list.

Geometric sequences and series are both used in many real-life situations. Geometric sequences, for example, are particularly useful when calculating the interest to be paid on a loan or a savings account.

EXAMPLE 3

Oliver took out a loan of £2000 to buy his car. The interest added to the loan is 5% of the outstanding amount every year. If Oliver does not pay back any of the loan,

a) How much will he owe after 1 year?
b) How much will he owe after 5 years?

Initially Oliver owes £2000. This is the first term in the sequence.

a) After one year, the amount owing is: £2000 $\times$ 1.05 = £2100 (2nd term)

b) After 2 years: £2000 $\times$ $(1.05)^2$ = £2205 (3rd term)

The general term is $u_n = ar^{n-1}$

We are interested in the 6th term of the sequence. (**Careful: not the 5th term!**)

$u_6 = 2000 \times (1.05)^5$

$= £2552.56$

Sometimes a geometric progression will involve algebraic expressions.

EXAMPLE 4

The first three terms of a geometric progression are:

$p - 2, 2p$ and $3p + 20$

Find the two possible values of p.

If this is a geometric progression, then the ratio between successive terms remains constant, i.e.

$$\frac{2p}{p-2} = \frac{3p+20}{2p}$$

Cross-multiply: $4p^2 = (3p + 20)(p - 2)$

Expand brackets: $4p^2 = 3p^2 + 14p - 40$

Re-arrange: $p^2 - 14p + 40 = 0$

Factorise: $(p - 4)(p - 10) = 0$

$p = 4$ or $p = 10$.

EXERCISE

EXERCISE 8H

1. Which of these are geometric progressions?

a) $1, 2, 3, 4, \ldots$

b) $-5, 10, -20, 40, \ldots$

c) $32, 30, 28, 26, \ldots$

d) $10^1, 10^2, 10^3, 10^4, \ldots$

e) $\frac{1}{2}, \frac{1}{3}, \frac{1}{4}, \frac{1}{5}, \ldots$

f) $1, \sqrt{2}, 3, 2\sqrt{2}, 5, 3\sqrt{2}, 7, 4\sqrt{2}, \ldots$

g) $1, \sqrt{2}, 2, 2\sqrt{2}, 4, \ldots$

h) $100, -100, -300, -500, \ldots$

i) $100, 1, 0.01, 0.0001, \ldots$

j) $\frac{1}{3}, \frac{2}{4}, \frac{3}{5}, \frac{4}{6}, \frac{5}{7}, \ldots$

k) $16f, 8f, 4f, 2f, f, \ldots$

EXERCISE

EXERCISE

2. Write down the first 5 terms of the following geometric progressions.
   a) First term 1, common ratio 3
   b) First term –4, common ratio 2
   c) First term –2, common ratio –2
   d) First term 64, common ratio $\frac{1}{2}$
   e) First term 10^3, common ratio 10
   f) First term 32, common ratio 1.5
   g) First term 2, common ratio $\sqrt{2}$
   h) First term $\frac{1}{2}$, common ratio $\frac{1}{2}$
   i) First term a, common ratio b
   j) First term y, common ratio $\frac{1}{y}$
3. A company makes a profit of £55000 in the year 2011. A model for future performance assumes that yearly profits will increase in a geometric sequence with common ratio 1.05. Using this model find the predicted profit for the year 2021. Give your answer to 3 significant figures.
4. The second and fourth terms of a geometric series are 2 and 0.32 respectively. Given that all the terms in the series are positive, find the common ratio and the first term.
5. Find the 5th term of the sequence 1, 10, 100, ...
6. Find the 6th term of the sequence 6, 36, 216, ...
7. A sequence of positive integers, $u_1, u_2, u_3, ...$ is given by: $u_{n+1} = 5u_n$, $u_1 = 7$
   a) Write down the first 4 terms of this sequence.
   b) Give u_n in terms of n.
8. The terms of a geometric progression are $(x + 1)$, $(x + 2)$ and $(x + 5)$. Find the value of x and hence find the three terms.
9. A ball is dropped from a height of h metres. Every time the ball bounces, it reaches a certain constant fraction f of its previous height, where $f < 1$.
   a) Show that the sequence of heights forms a geometric progression.
   b) If the height reached after the second bounce (the third term in the progression) is 0.32 metres and the height after the fourth bounce (the fifth term) is 0.0512 m, find the value of f.
   c) Find the initial height of the ball.

EXERCISE

8.12 The Sum of a Finite Geometric Series

There are two formulae for the sum of a geometric series. In this section we look at a **finite geometric series**, for example: $1 + 2 + 4 + 8 + 16$

PROOF OF THE FORMULA FOR THE SUM OF A FINITE GEOMETRIC SERIES

You should learn this proof and the formula.

Consider the series whose first term is a and common ratio is r.

The series has n terms and the sum is S_n. Then: $S_n = a + ar + ar^2 + \cdots + ar^{n-1}$ (1)

Multiplying both sides by r, we can also write: $rS_n = ar + ar^2 + ar^3 + \cdots + ar^n$ (2)

Now subtract (2) from (1).

Most of the terms cancel out, leaving: $S_n - rS_n = a - ar^n$

continued...

Factorise both sides: $S_n(1 - r) = a(1 - r^n)$

$$S_n = \frac{a(1 - r^n)}{1 - r}$$

Sometimes you may see the formula in this form:

$$S_n = \frac{a(r^n - 1)}{r - 1}$$

This is easier to use when $r > 1$.

EXAMPLE 1

Find the sum of the first 5 powers of 2.

The series is: $2 + 4 + 8 + 16 + 32$

First term $a = 2$, common ratio $r = 2$ and number of terms $n = 5$

$$S_n = \frac{a(r^n - 1)}{r - 1}$$

$$S_n = \frac{2(2^5 - 1)}{2 - 1}$$

$$= 62$$

EXAMPLE 2

Mr Wise puts £100 into his savings account every year on the first of January. The rate of interest paid is 4% per year. Form a geometric series for the amount at the end of 3 years. By considering the amount in the savings account at the end of each year, calculate how much Mr Wise has saved after 3 years.

Balance at end of first year: $1.04 \times 100 = 104$

At the start of the second year, Mr Wise deposits another £100.

Balance at start of second year: $100 + 104$

Balance at end of second year: $(1.04)(100 + 104) = 104 + (104)(1.04)$

At the start of the third year, Mr Wise deposits another £100.

Balance at start of third year: $100 + (104) + (104)(1.04)$

Balance at end of third year: $1.04 \times \big(100 + (104) + (104)(1.04)\big)$

$$= 104 + (104)(1.04) + (104)(1.04)^2$$

We have a geometric series with first term $a = 104$ and common ratio $r = 1.04$. There are three terms, so $n = 3$.

To find the total: $S_n = \dfrac{a(r^n - 1)}{r - 1}$

$$S_3 = \frac{104(1.04^3 - 1)}{1.04 - 1}$$

$= £324.65$ (to the nearest penny).

Sigma notation can be used with geometric series, as with arithmetic series.

EXAMPLE 3

Expand, then evaluate:

$$\sum_{r=1}^{4} 3^r$$

To expand the series, replace r with each value from 1 to 4:

$$\sum_{r=1}^{4} 3^r = 3^1 + 3^2 + 3^3 + 3^4$$

This is a geometric series, with first term $a = 3$, 4 terms and common ratio $r = 3$.

$$S_n = \frac{a(r^n - 1)}{r - 1}$$

$$S_4 = \frac{3(3^4 - 1)}{3 - 1}$$

$$= 120$$

EXERCISE

EXERCISE 8I

1. Find the sum of each geometric series:

a) $1 + 3 + 9 + 27 + \cdots$ (5 terms)

b) $\frac{1}{2} + \frac{1}{4} + \frac{1}{8} + \cdots$ (6 terms)

c) $1 + -2 + 4 + -8 + \cdots$ (5 terms)

d) $\frac{3}{4} + \frac{3}{16} + \frac{3}{64} + \cdots$ (5 terms)

e) $30 + 5 + \frac{5}{6} + \frac{5}{36} + \cdots$ (6 terms)

f) $100 + 150 + 225 + \cdots$ (10 terms)

g) $1 + 1.1 + 1.21 + 1.331 + \cdots$ (7 terms)

h) $1 + (0.8) + (0.8)^2 + (0.8)^3 + \cdots$ (7 terms)

i) $10 + 1 + 0.1 + 0.01 + \cdots$ (6 terms)

j) $\sqrt{2} + (\sqrt{2})^2 + (\sqrt{2})^3 + (\sqrt{2})^4$

k) $1 + -1 + 1 + -1 + \cdots$ (9 terms)

2. Evaluate:

a) $\sum_{1}^{5} 3^r$

b) $\sum_{1}^{10} \left(\frac{1}{2}\right)^r$

c) $\sum_{0}^{4} (\sqrt{2})^r$ (as a surd)

d) $\sum_{1}^{6} \frac{1}{2}(2)^r$

e) $\sum_{-3}^{3} 3^r$

f) $\sum_{0}^{5} (-2)^r$

g) $\sum_{1}^{4} 4^{r-1}$

h) $\sum_{0}^{4} \left(\frac{1}{\sqrt{2}}\right)^r$ (as a surd)

i) $\sum_{0}^{3} 2^{2r}$

j) $\sum_{1}^{10} 2^{1-r}$

EXERCISE

EXERCISE

3. A ball is dropped from a height of 2 metres, then bounces 4 times, each time reaching $\frac{3}{4}$ of its previous height. How far does the ball travel before it is caught at the top of its trajectory after the fourth bounce?

4. Find: $\sum_{1}^{8} 200(3)^r$

5. The first and second terms of a geometric series G are 18 and 9 respectively. Find, to 3 significant figures, the sum of the first 16 terms of G.

6. Find the sum of the first 5 terms of the series: $1 + 6 + 36 + \cdots$

7. A banker receives a Christmas bonus of £11000 in the year 2011. The banker's contract promises a 4% increase in bonus every year, the first increase being given in 2012.
   a) Find, to the nearest £100, the banker's bonus in the year 2014.

   The banker will receive a bonus each year from 2011 until he retires at the end of 2027.
   b) Find, to the nearest £1000, the total amount of bonus he will receive in the period from 2011 until he retires at the end of 2027.

8. The sum of a geometric series with four terms is an integer. Given that the common ratio is $\frac{1}{2}$, find one possible value for the first term.

9. The first term of a geometric series is a and the second term is b.
   a) What are the third and fourth terms?
   b) What is the 10th term?

10. The second term of a geometric series is 6 and the third term is $3(x + 1)$. Given the sum of the first 3 terms is 21,
    a) Find the two possible values of x.
    b) Find the two possibilities for the first three terms of the series.

EXERCISE

8.13 The Sum of an Infinite Geometric Series

In this section, we will discuss summing an infinite number of terms of a geometric series.

We discussed **convergent sequences** in Section 8.5. You learnt how to tell whether the terms in a sequence converge towards a particular value, or whether the terms diverge.

Geometric series can also be convergent or divergent. A convergent series is a series in which the **sum to infinity** (the sum of all the terms) is a finite number. We use the notation S_∞ to denote the sum to infinity.

Consider the geometric series: $1 + \frac{11}{10} + \frac{121}{100} + \frac{1331}{1000} \ldots$

For this series, a = 1 and $r = \frac{11}{10}$.
The series could also be written with its terms as decimals: $1 + 1.1 + 1.21 + 1.331 + \cdots$

It is clear that the terms are increasing in size. It is not possible to find a sum to infinity. The series is divergent.

Consider a second geometric series: $1 + \frac{9}{10} + \frac{81}{100} + \frac{729}{1000} + \cdots$

For this series, a = 1 and $r = \frac{9}{10}$.

The terms in this series are getting smaller and smaller. The sum changes less and less with each added term. This series converges to a particular value, which is 10.

A geometric series is convergent if and only if $|r| < 1$

PROOF OF THE FORMULA FOR THE SUM OF AN INFINITE GEOMETRIC SERIES

You should learn this proof and the formula.

Consider the infinite geometric series, whose first term is a and common ratio is r. The series has n terms and the sum is S_n. Then:

$$S_n = a + ar + ar^2 + \cdots$$

For all geometric series

$$S_n = \frac{a(1 - r^n)}{1 - r}$$

If the series is convergent, $|r| < 1$. As $n \to \infty$, $r^n \to 0$

Therefore for convergent geometric series,

$$S_\infty = \frac{a(1 - 0)}{1 - r}$$

$$S_\infty = \frac{a}{1 - r}$$

EXAMPLE 1

Find the sum to infinity of the geometric series:

$$\sum_{1}^{\infty} 2^{1-r}$$

The series is: $1 + \frac{1}{2} + \frac{1}{4} + \cdots$

$a = 1$ and $r = \frac{1}{2}$

$$S_\infty = \frac{a}{1 - r}$$

$$= \frac{1}{1/2}$$

$$= 2$$

You may be given the sum to infinity and asked to find other properties of the series.

EXAMPLE 2

A geometric series has its first term equal to its common ratio. The sum to infinity of this series is 11. Find the exact value of the common ratio of this series.

We have been told a = r and $S_\infty = 11$

$$S_\infty = \frac{a}{1-r}$$

Substitute the information we know: $11 = \frac{r}{1-r}$

$$11(1-r) = r$$

$$12r = 11$$

$$r = \frac{11}{12}$$

EXERCISE 8J

1. Find the sum to infinity of the following geometric series:

a) $\frac{1}{2} + \frac{1}{4} + \frac{1}{8} + \cdots$

b) $1 + (0.8) + (0.8)^2 + (0.8)^3 + \cdots$

c) $10 + 1 + 0.1 + 0.01 + \cdots$

d) $-4 + -2 + -1 + -0.5 + \cdots$

e) $100 + 50 + 25 + 12.5 + \cdots$

f) $1 + \frac{1}{\sqrt{2}} + \frac{1}{(\sqrt{2})^2} + \frac{1}{(\sqrt{2})^3} + \cdots$ (as a surd)

g) $6.4 + 1.6 + 0.4 + 0.1 + \cdots$

h) $8 + \ -4 + \ 2 + \ -1 + \ \ldots$

i) $1 + \frac{1}{\pi^2} + \frac{1}{\pi^4} + \frac{1}{\pi^6} + \cdots$

j) $6x + 1 + \frac{1}{6x} + \cdots$ (where $\left|\frac{1}{6x}\right| < 1$)

2. Evaluate:

a) $\sum_1^\infty 2^{3-2r}$

b) $\sum_1^\infty \left(\frac{1}{2}\right)^r$

c) $\sum_1^\infty \left(\frac{1}{\sqrt{3}}\right)^r$ (as a surd)

d) $\sum_1^\infty \left(\frac{1}{3}\right)^{r-1}$

e) $\sum_1^\infty a^r$ (where $|a| < 1$)

f) $\sum_1^\infty 2^{1-r}$

g) $\sum_1^\infty 2\left(\frac{7}{8}\right)^r$

h) $\sum_1^\infty \left(\frac{x}{x+1}\right)^r$ (where $x \neq -1$)

i) $\sum_1^\infty 9\left(\frac{1}{4}\right)^r$

j) $\sum_1^\infty 10(10)^{-r}$

3. Find the sum to infinity of the geometric series 5, 0.5, 0.05, ...

4. The sum to infinity of a geometric series is 6 times the first term. Find the common ratio.

EXERCISE

EXERCISE

EXERCISE

5. The second and fourth terms of a geometric series are 4.5 and 3.645 respectively. Given that all the terms in the series are positive, find:
   a) the common ratio and the first term.
   b) the sum to infinity of the series.

6. The first term of a geometric series is 140. The sum to infinity is 700.
   a) Show that the common ratio r is 0.8.
   b) Find, to 2 decimal places, the difference between the 6th and 7th terms.
   c) Calculate the sum of the first 8 terms.

7. Find the sum to infinity of the geometric series: $\frac{5}{6}+\frac{5}{18}+\frac{5}{54}+\cdots$

8. A geometric series has first term a and common ratio r. The second term is –4 and the sum to infinity is –25.
   a) Show that: $25r^2 - 25r + 4 = 0$
   b) Find the two possible values of r.
   c) Find the corresponding values of a.

9. The first and second terms of a geometric series G are 120 and 12 respectively.
   a) Find, to 3 significant figures, the sum of the first 19 terms of G.
   b) Find the sum to infinity of G.

10. A geometric series has first term 1400 and its sum to infinity is 800.
   a) Show that the common ratio of the series is $-\frac{3}{4}$.
   b) Find, to 3 decimal places, the difference between the 9th and 10th terms.
   c) Write down an expression for the sum of the first n terms of the series.
   d) Given that n is odd, prove that the sum of the first n terms of the series is $800(1 + 0.75^n)$.

EXERCISE

8.14 Binomial Expansion

Factorials and Combinatorials

Before we discuss the binomial expansion, we need to introduce some new mathematical notation.

The **factorial** of a number n is the product of all the positive integers up to n.

We denote factorials with an exclamation mark.
It is important to remember that, by definition, $0! = 1$.

EXAMPLE 1

Find 5!

$$\begin{aligned} 5! &= 5 \times 4 \times 3 \times 2 \times 1 \\ &= 120 \end{aligned}$$

When dividing factorials, there is often a lot of cancelling.

EXAMPLE 2

Find:

$$\frac{7!}{3!}$$

$$\frac{7!}{3!} = \frac{7 \times 6 \times 5 \times 4 \times 3 \times 2 \times 1}{3 \times 2 \times 1}$$

Note: $3 \times 2 \times 1$ cancels out, so:

$$\frac{7!}{3!} = 7 \times 6 \times 5 \times 4$$

$$= 840$$

The second new piece of notation is **combinatorial** notation.

You will see a combinatorial written as either ${}^{n}C_r$ or $\binom{n}{r}$.

The definition is as follows:

$${}^{n}C_r = \frac{n!}{(n-r)!\,r!}$$

This calculation gives the number of ways you could choose r objects from a total of n. (The order you choose the objects does not matter.) For this reason, we often read ${}^{n}C_r$ as "n choose r".

EXAMPLE 3

Out of a class of 15 pupils, a PE teacher must choose 11 of them to play for the school team. How many different ways could she choose the team?

$${}^{15}C_{11} = \frac{15!}{(15-11)!\,11!}$$

$$= \frac{15 \times 14 \times 13 \times 12 \times 11 \times 10 \times 9 \times 8 \times 7 \times 6 \times 5 \times 4 \times 3 \times 2 \times 1}{(4 \times 3 \times 2 \times 1)(11 \times 10 \times 9 \times 8 \times 7 \times 6 \times 5 \times 4 \times 3 \times 2 \times 1)}$$

Note the last 11 integers cancel out.

$$= \frac{15 \times 14 \times 13 \times 12}{4 \times 3 \times 2 \times 1}$$

We can do some more cancelling, since we have 12 in the numerator and 4×3 in the denominator.

$$= \frac{15 \times 14 \times 13}{2 \times 1}$$

Finally, cancel a factor of 2:

$$= 15 \times 7 \times 13$$

$$= 1365$$

There should be an ^nC_r button on your calculator.

Note: n must be greater than or equal to r. If not, $(n - r)$ is negative. The factorial of a negative number is not defined. Try something like $^6C_8$ on your calculator.

EXAMPLE 4

Evaluate:

(a) $^5C_2$

(b) $\binom{10}{9}$

(a) $$^5C_2 = \frac{5!}{3!\,2!} = \frac{5 \times 4 \times 3 \times 2 \times 1}{(3 \times 2 \times 1)(2 \times 1)} = \frac{5 \times 4 \times 3}{3 \times 2 \times 1} = \frac{5 \times 4}{2 \times 1} = 10$$

(b) $$\binom{10}{9} = \frac{10!}{1!\,9!} = \frac{10}{1} = 10$$ **Note:** the 9! cancels out.

This means there are 10 ways to choose 9 items from a collection of 10. This seems to be correct. The 10 different ways are to leave each one out in turn.

EXERCISE

EXERCISE 8K

1. Calculate:

a) $2!$ b) $\frac{8!}{4!}$ c) $\frac{3!}{5!}$ d) $2! \times 3! \times 5!$ e) $\frac{6!}{2!\,4!}$

f) $1! + 3! + 5!$ g) $0! + 1!$ h) $\frac{1!}{0!\,1!}$ i) $\frac{100!}{99!}$ j) $\frac{6!\,8!}{5!\,7!}$

2. Evaluate:

a) $\binom{8}{7}$ b) $\binom{5}{2}$ c) $\binom{10}{2}$ d) $\binom{8}{3}$ e) $\binom{7}{3}$

f) $^{100}C_1$ g) $^8C_4$ h) $^5C_0$ i) $^6C_3$ j) $^{20}C_{20}$

EXERCISE

The Binomial Expansion

Consider the following:

$$(1+x)^0 = 1$$
$$(1+x)^1 = 1 + x$$
$$(1+x)^2 = 1 + 2x + x^2$$
$$(1+x)^3 = 1 + 3x + 3x^2 + x^3$$
$$(1+x)^4 = 1 + 4x + 6x^2 + 4x^3 + x^4$$

It takes a long time to expand out brackets, particularly with large integer powers. The **binomial expansion** provides a shortcut.

All of the expansions above are examples of the binomial expansion (so called because there are two terms inside the brackets).

Looking at the coefficients only, an interesting pattern emerges:

$$\begin{array}{ccccccccc} & & & & 1 & & & & \\ & & & 1 & & 1 & & & \\ & & 1 & & 2 & & 1 & & \\ & 1 & & 3 & & 3 & & 1 & \\ 1 & & 4 & & 6 & & 4 & & 1 \end{array}$$

Each number is the sum of the two numbers above it. This pattern is known as **Pascal's Triangle**. It contains many interesting sequences of numbers.

The numbers in Pascal's Triangle are also the numbers obtained from $\binom{n}{r}$, if n is the row number and r the column (both starting from 0):

$$\begin{array}{ccccccccc} & & & & \binom{0}{0} & & & & \\ & & & \binom{1}{0} & & \binom{1}{1} & & & \\ & & \binom{2}{0} & & \binom{2}{1} & & \binom{2}{2} & & \\ & \binom{3}{0} & & \binom{3}{1} & & \binom{3}{2} & & \binom{3}{3} & \\ \binom{4}{0} & & \binom{4}{1} & & \binom{4}{2} & & \binom{4}{3} & & \binom{4}{4} \end{array}$$

Using Pascal's triangle, we could work out all the coefficients in any expansion of $(1+x)^n$. However, this method is only practical for small values of n, e.g. up to 4.

With higher values, we would need more rows in Pascal's Triangle, and working out the coefficients would take too long.

EXAMPLE 1

Work out the binomial expansion of $(1+x)^3$

We look at the fourth row of Pascal's Triangle to get the coefficients.

$$(1+x)^3 = \binom{3}{0}(1) + \binom{3}{1}x + \binom{3}{2}x^2 + \binom{3}{3}x^3$$
$$= 1 + 3x + 3x^2 + x^3$$

In general,

$$(1+x)^n = \binom{n}{0} + \binom{n}{1}x + \binom{n}{2}x^2 + \cdots + \binom{n}{n-1}x^{n-1} + \binom{n}{n}x^n$$

There is another way to write the binomial expansion, using factorials.

$$(1+x)^n = 1 + nx + \frac{n(n-1)}{2!}x^2 + \frac{n(n-1)(n-2)}{3!}x^3 + \cdots + \frac{n(n-1)}{2!}x^{n-2} + nx^{n-1} + x^n$$

It is important to remember at least one of these formulae.

EXAMPLE 2

Write down the binomial expansion for $(1+y)^4$

Using the factorial form of the binomial expansion:

$$(1+y)^4 = 1 + 4y + \frac{4(3)}{2!}y^2 + \frac{4(3)(2)}{3!}y^3 + y^4$$
$$= 1 + 4y + 6y^2 + 4y^3 + y^4$$

You must take care when the second term is something other than x.

EXAMPLE 3

Expand $(1+3x)^3$

$$(1+3x)^3 = 1 + (3)(3x) + \frac{(3)(2)}{2!}(3x)^2 + (3x)^3$$
$$= 1 + 3(3x) + 3(3x)^2 + (3x)^3$$
$$= 1 + 9x + 27x^2 + 27x^3$$

In another common type of question, the first term is not 1. There are two methods for handling this. The first involves factorising.

EXAMPLE 4

Find the binomial expansion for $(2+z)^4$

$$(2+z)^4 = 2^4\left(1+\frac{z}{2}\right)^4$$

Note: when 2 is taken outside the bracket, it becomes 2^4. You must **also remember** to divide the second term by 2, or whatever factor has been taken out.

Now you can apply the binomial expansion formula.
Leave 2^4 outside the brackets until the end.

$$= 2^4\left[1 + (4)\left(\frac{z}{2}\right) + \frac{(4)(3)}{2!}\left(\frac{z}{2}\right)^2 + \frac{(4)(3)(2)}{3!}\left(\frac{z}{2}\right)^3 + \left(\frac{z}{2}\right)^4\right]$$

$$= 16\left[1 + 4\left(\frac{z}{2}\right) + 6\left(\frac{z}{2}\right)^2 + 4\left(\frac{z}{2}\right)^3 + \left(\frac{z}{2}\right)^4\right]$$

continued...

Example 4... $= 16\left[1 + 2z + \frac{3z^2}{2} + \frac{z^3}{2} + \frac{z^4}{16}\right]$

$= 16 + 32z + 24z^2 + 8z^3 + z^4$

The second technique for the expansion of $(a + bx)^n$ is to remember another formula:

$$(a + bx)^n = \binom{n}{0}a^n + \binom{n}{1}bxa^{n-1} + \binom{n}{2}(bx)^2a^{n-2} + \cdots + \binom{n}{n}(bx)^n$$

It is important to learn one or both of these methods.

EXAMPLE 4 – ALTERNATIVE METHOD

Find the binomial expansion for $(2 + z)^4$

$$(2 + z)^4 = \binom{4}{0}2^4 + \binom{4}{1}z \times 2^3 + \binom{4}{2}z^2 \times 2^2 + \binom{4}{3}z^3 \times 2 + \binom{4}{4}z^4$$

$$= 16 + 32z + 24z^2 + 8z^3 + z^4$$

You may be asked for only one term of the expansion, for example the term in x^3.

EXAMPLE 5

Find the term that is independent of x in the expansion of:

$$\left(x + \frac{6}{x}\right)^4$$

$$(a + bx)^n = \binom{n}{0}a^n + \binom{n}{1}bxa^{n-1} + \binom{n}{2}(bx)^2a^{n-2} + \cdots + \binom{n}{n}(bx)^n$$

$a = x$ and $bx = \frac{6}{x}$

We are interested in the third term of the expansion.

Third term: $\binom{4}{2}\left(\frac{6}{x}\right)^2(x)^2 = 6 \times 36$ (The x^2 cancels out)

$= 216$

Note: if x is small (i.e. less than 1), the terms to higher powers will not be very important to the sum. Some questions will, therefore, ask you to find only the first few terms in the expansion.

Once you have found an expansion, you may be asked to use it to find a value.

EXAMPLE 6

a) Find the first 4 terms in the binomial expansion of $(1 - x^2)^8$

b) Use your answer to part a) to estimate the value of 0.99^8

---

a) Be careful with the minus sign here.

$(1 - x^2)^8 = \left(1 + (-x^2)\right)^8$

continued...

Example 6...

Now we can apply the binomial expansion.

$$(1 - x^2)^8 = 1 + 8(-x^2) + \frac{8(7)}{2!}(-x^2)^2 + \frac{8(7)(6)}{3!}(-x^2)^3 + \cdots$$
$$= 1 - 8x^2 + 28x^4 - 56x^6 + \cdots \quad (1)$$

b) Substitute $x = 0.1$ into (1):

$0.99^8 \approx 1 - 8(0.1)^2 + 28(0.1)^4 - 56(0.1)^6$

Note: this is an estimate because we have only taken the first four terms.

$= 0.922744$

EXERCISE 8L

1. Find the first four terms in the binomial expansion of the following:

a) $(1 + x)^6$ b) $(1 + 2x)^4$ c) $(1 - x)^4$ d) $\left(1 + \frac{x}{2}\right)^3$ e) $(1 - 2x)^5$

f) $(1 + x)^{10}$ g) $(1 + 5x)^3$ h) $\left(1 - \frac{x}{10}\right)^3$ i) $(1 + 10x)^4$ j) $\left(1 - \frac{19x}{27}\right)^6$

2. Find the first 3 terms of the binomial expansion of:

a) $(2 + x)^7$ b) $(2 + 2x)^3$ c) $\left(10 - \frac{x}{10}\right)^3$ d) $\left(1 - \frac{1}{x}\right)^3$ e) $(4 + 3x)^4$

f) $(2 + x^2)^4$ g) $\left(x + \frac{1}{x}\right)^4$ h) $\left(\sqrt{2} + \frac{x}{\sqrt{2}}\right)^4$ i) $(5 + 2x)^4$ j) $\left(\frac{1}{a} + a^2x\right)^3$

(coefficients to 3 s.f.)

3. a) Expand $\left(1 + \frac{x}{2}\right)^6$ in ascending powers of x as far as the term in x^3, simplifying each term.
   b) Hence find 1.05^6, correct to 3 decimal places.

4. a) Write down the first 4 terms of the binomial expansion, in ascending powers of x, of $(1 + ax)^n$ where $n > 2$.
   Given that in this expansion the coefficient of x is 14 and the coefficient of x^2 is 93.1
   b) Calculate the value of n and the value of a.
   c) Find the coefficient of x^3.

5. a) Find the first 3 terms, in ascending powers of x, of the binomial expansion of: $(1 + px)^9$ where p is a positive constant.
   b) Given that, in this expansion the coefficients of x and x^2 are $-q$ and $4q$ respectively, find the value of p and the value of q.

6. The expansion of $(4 + px)^6$ in ascending powers of x, as far as the term in x^2 is $4096 + Ax + 60x^2$. Given that $p > 0$, find the value of p and the value of A.

7. Find the term that is independent of x in the expansion of: $\left(x + \frac{4}{x}\right)^6$

8. Neglecting terms in x^4 and higher, find an approximation in ascending powers of x for: $(1 - x)(1 + 3x)^5$

EXERCISE EXERCISE

EXERCISE

9. a) Using the binomial expansion find an approximation for $(1 - x)^n$ up to and including a term in x^3, in the form $1 + ax + bx^2 + cx^3$, where a, b, and c are expressions in terms of n.
   b) Given $2a + b - 3c = 0$, find n.

10.
   a) Find the binomial expansion for $(1 - 2x)^4$ up to and including the term in x^3.
   b) Use your answer to part a) to find an approximation for 0.99^4 to 3 decimal places.

EXERCISE

SUMMARY

A **sequence** is a list of numbers, generated by a rule.

The **general term** of a sequence is denoted u_n.

Sequences can be generated by a formula involving n, or by a **recurrence relation** involving the previous term.

An **arithmetic progression** is a sequence in which successive terms differ by a constant, called the **common difference.**

The recurrence relation for an arithmetic progression is $u_{n+1} = u_n + d$, where d is the common difference.

A **geometric progression** is a sequence in which the ratio of successive terms is constant.

The recurrence relation for a geometric progression is $u_{n+1} = u_n r$.

A **series** is the sum of the terms of a sequence.

An **arithmetic series** $a + (a + d) + (a + 2d) + \ldots$ has general term $u_n = a + (n - 1)d$, where a is the first term, d is the common difference and n is the number of terms.

The sum to n terms of an arithmetic series is given by $S_n = \frac{n}{2}[a + (n-1)d]$

A **geometric series** $a + ar + ar^2 + \ldots$ has general term ar^{n-1}. The first term is a and the common ratio is r.

The sum to n terms of a geometric series is given by $S_n = \frac{a(1-r^n)}{1-r}$.

An infinite geometric series converges if $|r| < 1$.

The sum to infinity of a convergent geometric series is given by $S_n = \frac{a}{1-r}$.

Sigma notation can be used to denote the sum of both arithmetic and geometric series.

The **binomial expansion** provides a way to expand brackets quickly:

$$(1 + x)^n = \binom{n}{0} + \binom{n}{1}x + \binom{n}{2}x^2 + \cdots + \binom{n}{n-1}x^{n-1} + \binom{n}{n}x^n$$

Chapter 9

Trigonometry

9.1 Introduction

Keywords

Radian: A unit of measurement for angles.

Arc: A part of the circumference of a circle.

Sector: The area enclosed by an arc and two radii of a circle.

Segment: The area between a chord and the circumference of a circle.

Trigonometric ratio: Any of the trigonometry functions acting on an angle, for example $sin\,30°$.

Before You Start

You should know how to:

- Solve quadratic equations;
- Change the subject of an equation;
- Use bearings.

EXAMPLE 1

Find the values of x that satisfy:

$$x^2 - 3x - 5 = 0$$

Use the quadratic formula:

$$x = \frac{-b \pm \sqrt{b^2 - 4ac}}{2a}$$

$$x = \frac{3 \pm \sqrt{(-3)^2 - 4(1)(-5)}}{2}$$

$$x = \frac{3 \pm \sqrt{9 + 20}}{2}$$

$$x = \frac{3 \pm \sqrt{29}}{2}$$

EXAMPLE 2

Make x the subject of the equation:

$$x - 1 = 3y(2 - x)$$

$$x - 1 = 3y(2 - x)$$

Expand brackets: $x - 1 = 6y - 3xy$

Take all the terms in x to one side: $x + 3xy = 1 + 6y$

Factorise left hand side: $x(1 + 3y) = 1 + 6y$

Divide by $(1 + 3y)$: $x = \dfrac{1 + 6y}{1 + 3y}$

EXAMPLE 3

A car leaves Appleville, travels due west for 40 km to Bramley, then 40 km due north to Crispin. What is the bearing of the car's final position from its starting point?

Note 1: Begin the bearing measurement from the north line, and go round clockwise.

Note 2: if your bearing is less than 100°, it must still have 3 digits, e.g. 045°.

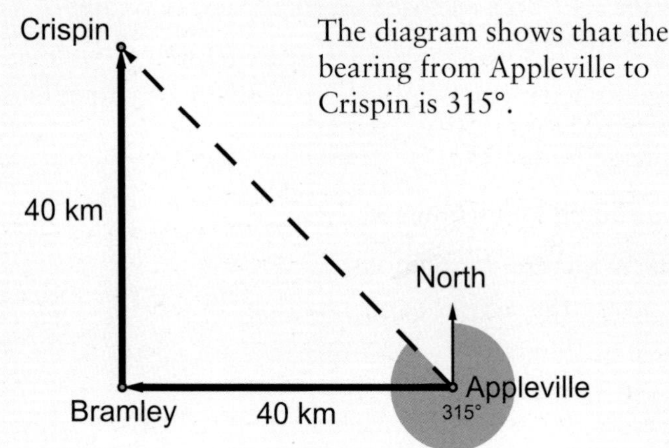

The diagram shows that the bearing from Appleville to Crispin is 315°.

EXERCISE

REVISION EXERCISE 9A

1. Solve these quadratic equations:
   a) $(4x - 5)^2 = 36$
   b) $3x^2 - 24x + 7 = 10$
   c) $4x^2 - 2x - 1 = 0$
   d) $x^2 = 3x + 29$
2. Make x the subject of these equations:
   a) $1 + 3x = 3(1 - x)$
   b) $2x + p = 3p(x - 1)$
   c) $xy = \dfrac{2(1 + y)}{x}$
   d) $\dfrac{(x + c)}{d} = \dfrac{2(x + e)}{f}$
3. What is the bearing of point B from point A?
   a) A(0, 0), B(2, 2)
   b) A(3, 0), B(3, –6)
   c) A(4, 4), B(1, 1)
   d) A(0, –100), B(–100, 0)

EXERCISE

What You Will Learn

In this chapter you will learn:

- how to use the sine and cosine rules;
- how to use radians;
- how to calculate some properties of a circle, such as arc length and the area of a sector;
- some trigonometric identities;
- some of the characteristics of trigonometric graphs;
- perform some transformations on those graphs;
- how to solve trigonometric equations.

IN THE REAL WORLD – VOYAGERS I & II

In 1977, NASA launched two small space probes, Voyager I and Voyager II. Their trajectories had been carefully planned to bring them close to the outer planets of our Solar System. For the first time, these worlds would be photographed and studied at close proximity.

The software in the two on–board computers has been updated many times since the launch. But trigonometry plays a key part in many aspects of the missions from the initial launch to setting the craft on the correct course and using the gravity of the giant planets to increase the velocity. How to take a clear photograph when travelling at many thousands of metres per second is another interesting mathematical challenge.

Throughout the 1980s, the two Voyager spacecraft provided breath–taking pictures of Jupiter, Saturn, Uranus, Neptune and many of their moons. Jupiter's Great Red Spot, a hurricane system large enough to swallow the Earth, that has been raging for over 300 years, was pictured in detail. Enormous volcanoes were discovered on Jupiter's moon Io. Scientists were amazed at the success of these two tiny spacecraft.

Along with three other space probes now leaving the Solar System, the two Voyagers are now the furthest man–made objects from Earth, but they continue to send back important information about their surroundings.

On board are pictures and data about planet Earth and human civilisation, in case the machines ever come into contact with intelligent extra–terrestrial beings.

9.2 Sine and Cosine Rules

Revision

At GCSE, you learnt how to calculate a missing side or a missing angle in a right–angled triangle, using the three formulae:

$$\sin\theta = \frac{opposite}{hypotenuse} \qquad \cos\theta = \frac{adjacent}{hypotenuse} \qquad \tan\theta = \frac{opposite}{adjacent}$$

The sine rule and cosine rule are useful for finding lengths or angles in triangles that **do not have any right angles**. Remember: if a triangle has right angles, you should use the formulae for sine, cosine and tangent that you learnt at GCSE.

The Sine Rule

The sine rule links two angles and two sides opposite those angles.

Consider the triangle below. The angles are A, B and C, none of which are right angles. The side lengths are a, b and c.

(Note that angle A is opposite the side with length a, etc. This is a very common way to label triangles.)

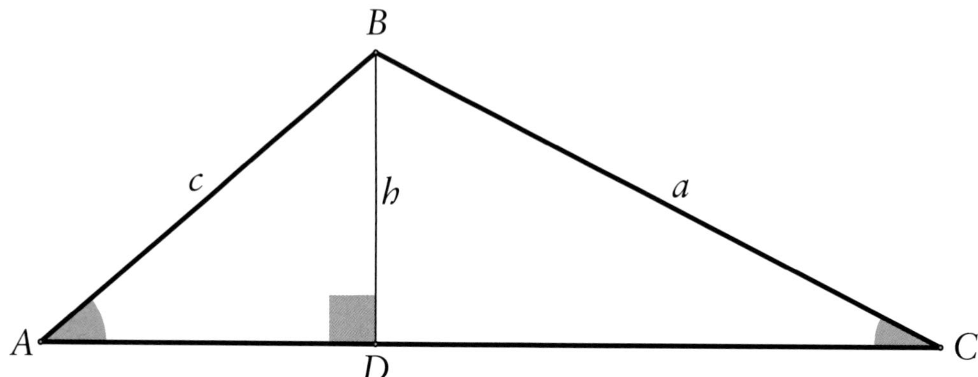

Suppose we know the side length c and we know the two angles A and C. The sine rule allows us to calculate the side length a:

$$\frac{a}{\sin A} = \frac{c}{\sin C}$$

We can say the same for angle B and side b, so the complete version of the sine rule is:

$$\frac{a}{\sin A} = \frac{b}{\sin B} = \frac{c}{\sin C} \quad \text{or} \quad \frac{\sin A}{a} = \frac{\sin B}{b} = \frac{\sin C}{c}$$

The second version of the sine rule above is useful when calculating an angle.

PROOF OF THE SINE RULE

You do not need to learn this proof.
In the diagram above, consider triangle ABD.

$$\sin A = \frac{h}{c}$$

Re-arrange: $h = c \sin A$ (1)

Now consider triangle BCD.

$$\sin C = \frac{h}{a}$$

Re-arrange: $h = a \sin C$ (2)

Substitute (2) into (1):

$$a \sin C = c \sin A$$

Re-arrange:

$$\frac{a}{\sin A} = \frac{c}{\sin C}$$

The same could be done with angle B and the side with length b.

EXAMPLE 1

In ΔABC, the angle A is 35°, the angle B is 40° and the side length a is 5 cm. Calculate the side length b.

It is a good idea to draw a sketch of the triangle:

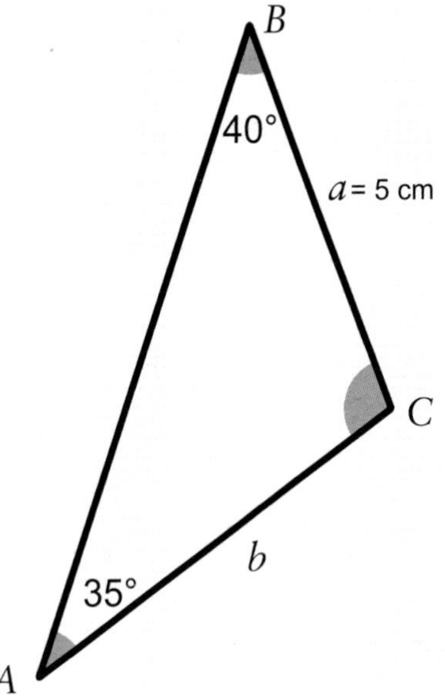

Then use the sine rule:

$$\frac{a}{\sin A} = \frac{b}{\sin B}$$

$$b = \frac{a}{\sin A} \times \sin B$$

$$= \frac{5}{\sin 35} \times \sin 40$$

$$= 5.60 \text{ cm } (3 \text{ s.f.})$$

Important: Remember to use full decimal values in your calculations. Only round values in the final answer.

EXAMPLE 2

In ΔABC, the angle A is 52°, the side length a is 5 cm and the side length c is 6 cm. Calculate the acute angle C.

We use the second form of the sine rule, since we are calculating an angle:

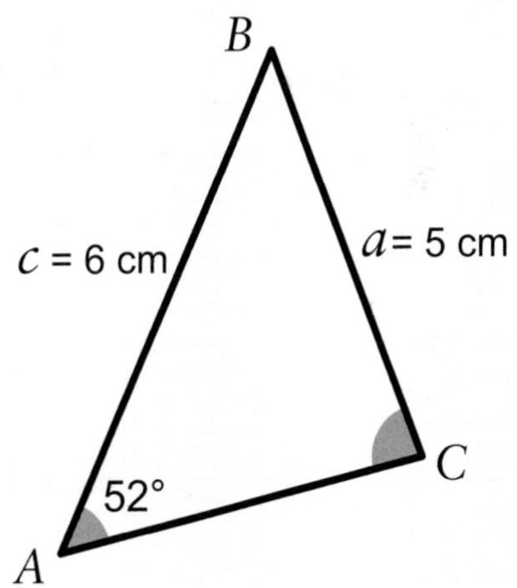

$$\frac{\sin C}{c} = \frac{\sin A}{a}$$

Re-arrange: $\sin C = c \times \dfrac{\sin A}{a}$

$$\sin C = 6 \times \frac{\sin 52°}{5}$$

$$\sin C = 0.9456 \ldots$$

$$C = 71.0°$$

Unless you are told otherwise, round angles to 1 decimal place and lengths to 3 significant figures.

Beware! When calculating an angle using the sine rule, it is possible there will be two solutions. This is known as the **ambiguous case**.

EXAMPLE 3

Calculate the angle B in triangle ABC, given that angle $A = 50°$, side $a = 10$ cm and $b = 12$ cm.

Sketch the triangle:

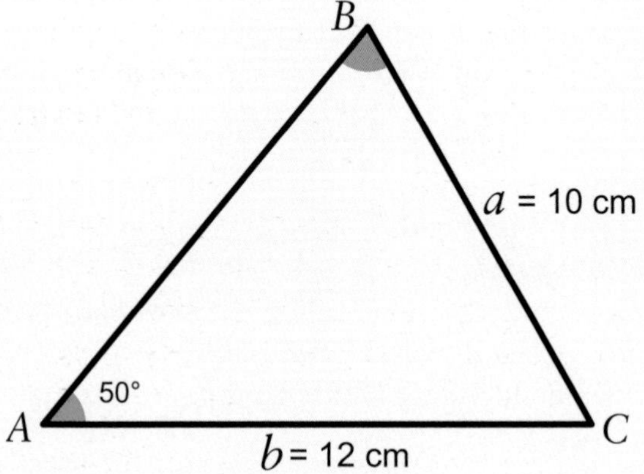

Then use the sine rule:

$$\frac{\sin B}{b} = \frac{\sin A}{a}$$

$$\sin B = b \times \frac{\sin A}{a}$$

$$\sin B = 0.919 \ldots$$

$$B = 66.8°$$

If there is a second solution, it will always be found by subtracting the first solution from 180°.

$$B_2 = 180 - 66.8$$
$$= 113.2°$$

We can check that both these solutions are possible by calculating C.
Use the fact that angles in a triangle add up to 180°.

First solution: $C = 180 - (50 + 66.8)$
$= 63.2°$

Second solution: $C = 180 - (50 + 113.2)$
$= 16.8°$

Both these angles are between 0 and 180°, so they create possible triangles.

If your second value for B resulted in a negative value of C, for example, it would show that this was not a possibility.

The two possible triangles ABC and AB_2C are shown below:

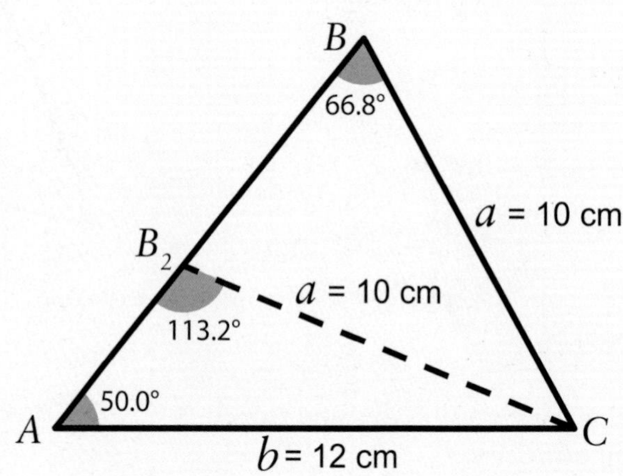

EXERCISE 9B

1. Find the missing length b in these triangles:
   a) Angles $A = 123°$, $B = 10°$, side length $a = 5$ cm.
   b) Angles $A = 84°$, $B = 76°$, side length $a = 10$ cm.
   c) Angles $A = 61°$, $B = 47°$, side length $a = 3$ cm.
   d) Angles $A = 121°$, $B = 45°$, side length $a = 13$ cm.

2. Find the missing angle in each triangle:
   a) Angle $A = 36°$, side lengths $a = 14$ cm, $b = 2$ cm. Find B.
   b) Angle $C = 123°$, side lengths $c = 8$ cm, $b = 7$ cm. Find B.
   c) Angle $A = 44°$, side lengths $a = 12$ cm, $c = 9$ cm. Find C.
   d) Angle $A = 163°$, side lengths $a = 14$ cm, $b = 5$ cm. Find B.
   e) Angle $B = 55°$, side lengths $b = 5$ cm, $c = 3$ cm. Find C.

3. Find the two possible values for the specified angle in these triangles (the ambiguous case). Find also the value of the third angle in both cases.
   a) Angle $B = 32°$, side lengths $b = 9$ cm, $a = 13$ cm. Find A.
   b) Angle $A = 22°$, side lengths $a = 7$ cm, $b = 14$ cm. Find B.
   c) Angle $B = 38°$, side lengths $b = 13$ cm, $c = 17$ cm. Find C.
   d) Angle $C = 57°$, side lengths $c = 6$ cm, $a = 7$ cm. Find A.
   e) Angle $A = 53°$, side lengths $a = 12$ cm, $c = 13$ cm. Find C.

4. In the triangle ABC, $AB = 6$ cm, $AC = 4$ cm, angle $ABC = 17.2°$ and angle $ACB = x°$.
   a) Use the sine rule to find the value of $\sin x$, giving your answer to 3 decimal places.
   b) Given that there are two possible values of x, find these values, giving your answers to 1 decimal place.

5. A ship at point S has a bearing of 120° from lighthouse L and a bearing of 040° from coastguard C. Given that the lighthouse is situated due north of the coastguard, and that the distance from the ship to the lighthouse is 17 km find
   a) The angle, when viewed from the ship, between the coastguard and lighthouse;
   b) The distance between the coastguard and the lighthouse.

6. In the diagram, AB and CD are parallel lines. Calculate the lengths of AC and AD.

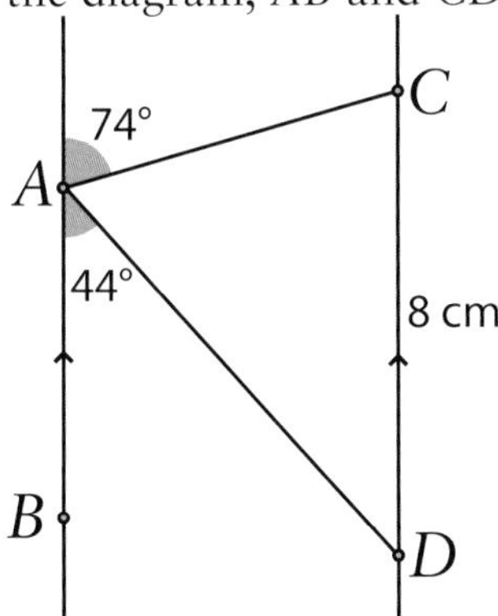

EXERCISE

7. The diagram shows the side elevation of a stadium. It is symmetrical about a vertical line through point F. The steel supports AC and BC measure 40 m and 100 m respectively. Angle CAF is 72° and CFD measures 99°. Find the size of the two angles CBF and BCF.

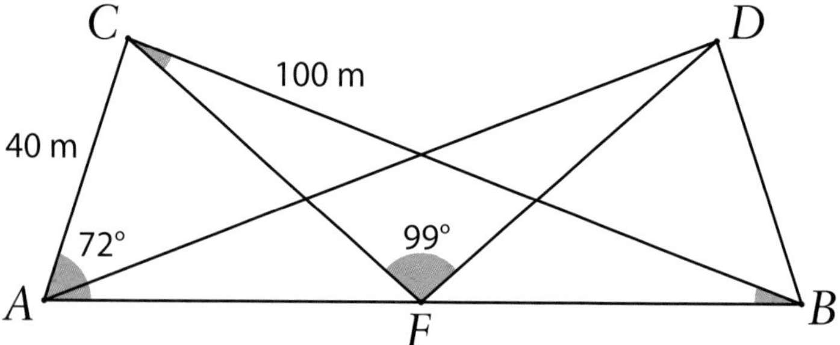

EXERCISE

The Cosine Rule

The **cosine rule** links three sides and one angle:

To find a side length:	or to find an angle:
$a^2 = b^2 + c^2 - 2bc\cos A$	$\cos A = \dfrac{b^2 + c^2 - a^2}{2bc}$

As usual, the angle A is the angle opposite side a. The cosine rule looks complicated at first, but it is easy to remember if you think of it as an extension of Pythagoras' Theorem.

PROOF OF THE COSINE RULE

You do not need to learn this proof.

Consider the triangle below, with vertices A, B and C and sides a, b and c.

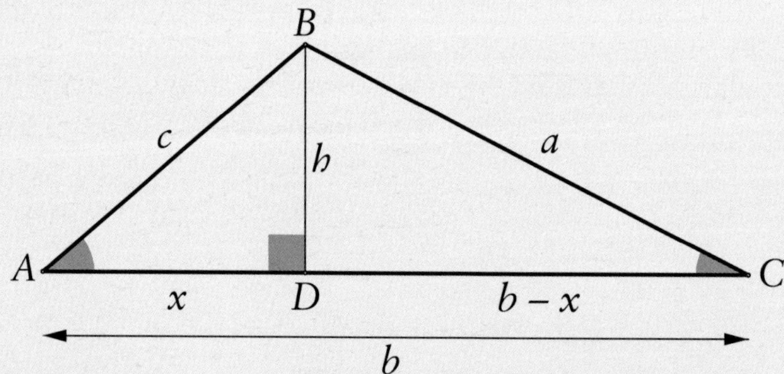

The vertical height h has been added to the diagram, and the base b has been divided into two sections measuring x and $(b - x)$.

Using the formula for cosine in ΔABD:

$$\cos A = \frac{x}{c}$$

Re-arrange: $x = c\cos A$ (1)

continued...

Pythagoras' Theorem in ΔBCD and ΔABD:

$$a^2 = h^2 + (b - x)^2 \quad (2)$$

$$c^2 = h^2 + x^2 \quad (3)$$

Subtract (2) – (3):

$$a^2 - c^2 = (b - x)^2 - x^2$$

Expand brackets and simplify:

$$a^2 - c^2 = b^2 - 2bx$$

Substitute for x from (1)

$$a^2 - c^2 = b^2 - 2bc \cos A$$

$$a^2 = b^2 + c^2 - 2bc \cos A$$

If you know three sides of a triangle, you can use the cosine rule to work out any angle.

EXAMPLE 1

The diagram shows triangle ABC, in which sides $a = 5\ cm$, $b = 6\ cm$ and $c = 7\ cm$. Find the size of angle A.

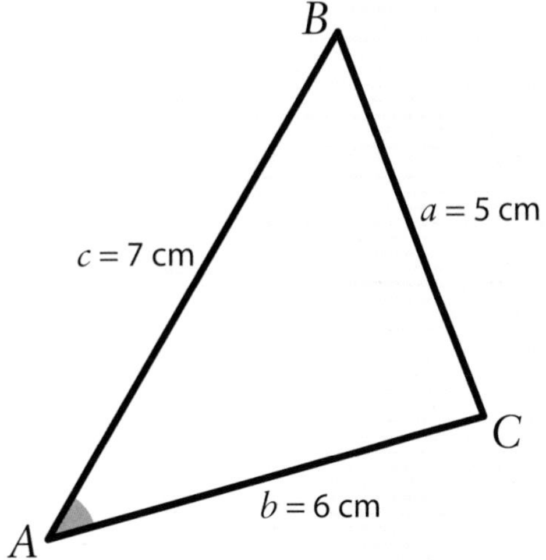

$$\cos A = \frac{b^2 + c^2 - a^2}{2bc}$$

$$= \frac{6^2 + 7^2 - 5^2}{2(6)(7)}$$

$$= 0.714\ldots$$

$$A = 44.4° \quad \text{(1d.p.)}$$

If you know two of the sides and **the angle between them**, you can calculate the missing side.

EXAMPLE 2

In ΔABC, $c = 12\ cm$, $b = 16\ cm$ and $A = 46°$. Calculate side a.

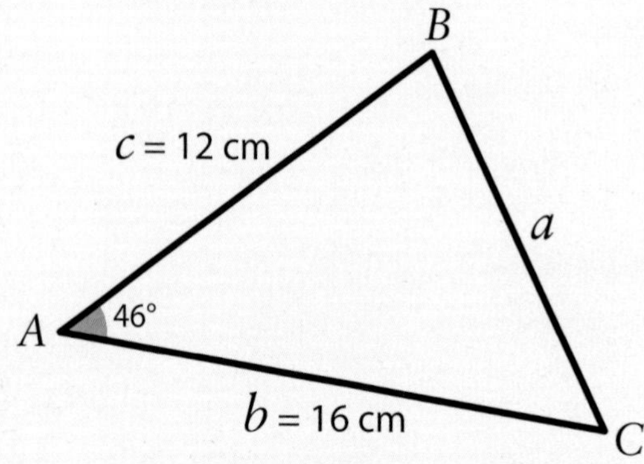

$$a^2 = b^2 + c^2 - 2bc\cos A$$

$$= 16^2 + 12^2 - 2(16)(12)\cos 46$$

$$a^2 = 133.25\ ...$$

$$a = 11.5\,\text{cm (3 s.f.)}$$

In all questions involving the cosine rule, there is a lot of calculator work. Remember: do not round any of the numbers in your working until you get to the final answer. If you round the numbers in your working, your final answer may not be accurate.

If you know two of the sides and one of the other angles (not the angle between the two known sides), you will need to use a combination of the sine and cosine rules.

EXAMPLE 3

The straight road between points A and B is 3.8km long.
The straight road between A and C is 6km long.
Given angle ABC is 104°, find the length of the straight road between B and C.

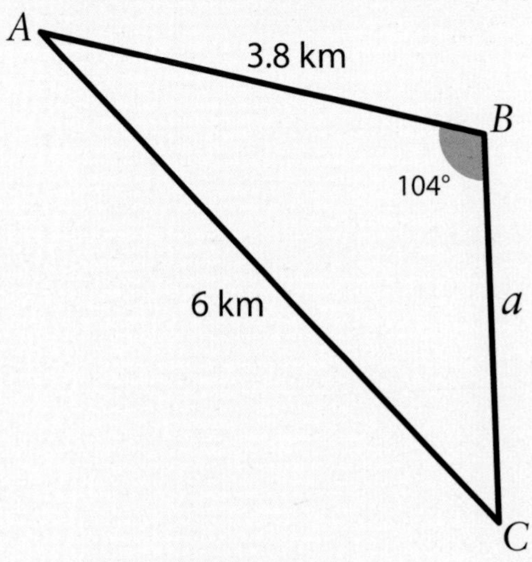

continued...

Example 3...

We cannot use the cosine rule directly to find a because we do not know angle A. First use the sine rule to find angle C:

$$\frac{\sin C}{c} = \frac{\sin B}{b}$$

$$\sin C = 3.8 \times \frac{\sin 104}{6}$$

$$= 0.61 \ldots$$

$$C = 37.9 \ldots \quad \text{Don't do any rounding yet!}$$

Now we can calculate angle A:

$$A = 180 - (B + C)$$

$$= 180 - (104 + 37.9 \ldots)$$

$$= 38.08 \ldots \quad \text{Still don't round this number!}$$

Finally use the cosine rule:

$$a^2 = b^2 + c^2 - 2bc \cos A$$

$$= 6^2 + 3.8^2 - 2(6)(3.8) \cos(38.8 \ldots)$$

$$= 14.55 \ldots$$

$$a = 3.81\ km \quad (3\ \text{s.f.})$$

Sometimes you will be asked to 'solve the triangle'. This means finding all of the missing sides and angles. You may also be required to re-label a diagram to use the cosine rule formula.

EXAMPLE 4

A humanoid stares out into space from planet Zog. On a bearing of 335° he sees planet Xig and on a bearing of 029° he sees planet Yug. He knows Xig and Yug are 74 and 90 million kilometres away respectively. Solve the triangle. (Assume for this question that the three planets all lie within the same horizontal plane.)

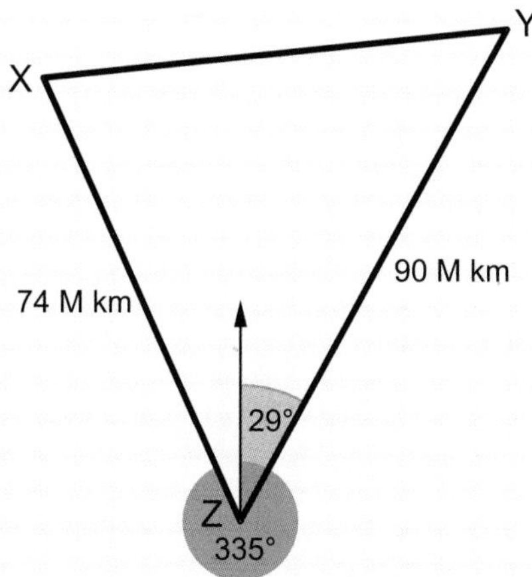

Firstly, angle $XZY = (360 - 335) + 29$

$= 54°$

Then, re-label the diagram.

continued...

Example 4...

Re-label the diagram:

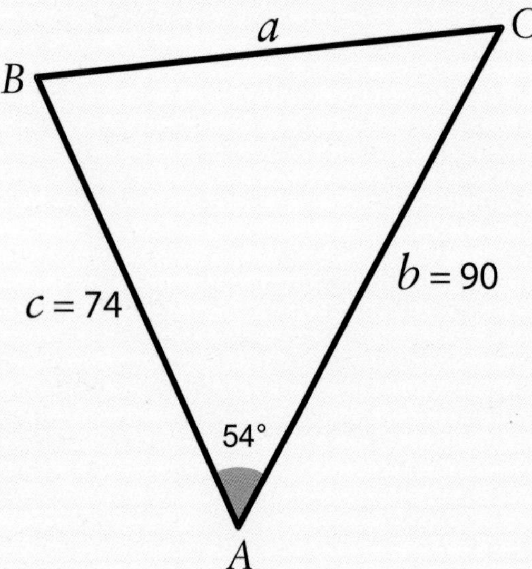

Now use the cosine rule:

$$a^2 = b^2 + c^2 - 2bc\cos A$$

$$= 90^2 + 74^2 - 2(90)(74)\cos 54$$

$$= 5746.7\ldots$$

$$a = 75.8 \ \ (3 \text{ s.f.})$$

The planets Xig and Yug are 75.8 million kilometres apart.
Use the sine rule to find angle B:

$$\frac{\sin B}{b} = \frac{\sin A}{a}$$

$$\sin B = 90 \times \frac{\sin 54}{75.8\ldots}$$

Be careful to use the full decimal value for *a* in this calculation, not your rounded answer!

$$\sin B = 0.960\ldots$$

$$B = 73.8° \ (1 \text{ d.p.})$$

Finally find angle C:

$$C = 180 - (54 + 73.8\ldots)$$

$$= 52.2° \ \ (1 \text{ d.p.})$$

We should give all our answers in terms of the original letters:

$$XY = 75.8 \ \text{ million km } (3 \text{ s.f.})$$

$$X = 73.8°, Y = 52.2° \ \ (\text{both to 1 d.p.})$$

EXERCISE

EXERCISE 9C

1. Find the lengths of the missing sides in the following triangles to 3 significant figures.
   a) $b = 11$ cm, $c = 8$ cm, $A = 33°$
   b) $b = 7$ cm, $c = 5$ cm, $A = 75°$
   c) $c = 6$ km, $a = 2$ km, $B = 33°$
   d) $a = 12$ cm, $b = 9$ cm, $C = 64°$
   e) $a = 11$ mm, $b = 6$ mm, $C = 36°$

2. Find the size of the angle specified in these triangles, to one decimal place.
   a) $a = 6$, $b = 9$, $c = 8$ cm. Find A.
   b) $x = 10$, $y = 7$, $z = 10$ cm. Find Y.
   c) $p = 9$, $q = 11$, $r = 5$ m. Find P.
   d) $a = 4$, $b = 5$, $c = 6$ mm. Find C.
   e) $a = 5$, $b = 7$, $c = 7$ cm. Find B.

EXERCISE

EXERCISE

3. Solve the following triangles, giving all your answers to 1 decimal place:
   a) $a = 14$ cm, $b = 12$ cm, $c = 7$ cm
   b) $a = 0.02$ mm, $b = 0.04$ mm, $c = 0.03$ mm
   c) $b = 13$ cm, $c = 14$ cm, $A = 43°$
   d) $c = 12$ feet, $a = 13$ feet, $B = 142°$
   e) $c = 7$ km, $a = 7$ km, $C = 68°$
   f) $a = 1.1$ cm, $b = 0.8$ cm, $A = 37°$

4. Is it possible to solve the following triangle? Explain your answer.
   $A = 55°$, $B = 45°$, $C = 80°$

5. Is it possible to solve the following triangle? Explain your answer.
   $a = 1.3$, $b = 0.2$, $c = 0.4\ cm$

6. A park is laid out in the shape of a trapezium, with gates at each corner, as shown. The distance between gates A and B is $2\sqrt{29}$ m, between B and C 24 m, between C and D $\sqrt{149}$ m and between D and A 35 m.

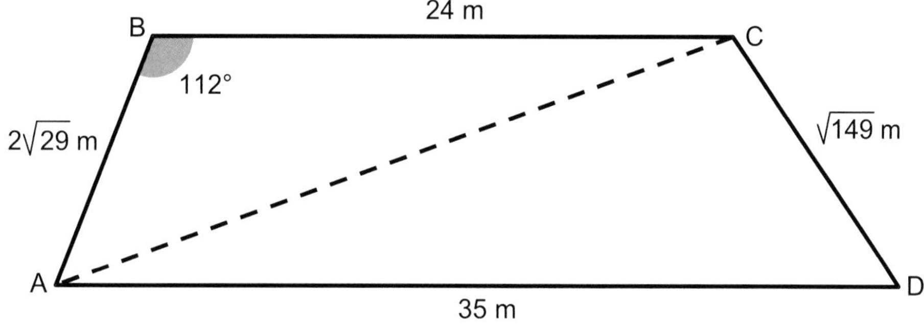

   a) Calculate the length of the path shown between gates A and C.
   b) Calculate the size of the angle ADC.

7. A lifeguard notices a man in trouble in the middle of a swimming pool. The pool is in the shape of a parallelogram, with the longest side 25 m and the shortest 10 m. The smallest corner angle of this quadrilateral is 60°. If the lifeguard is sitting at the corner measuring 120°, how far is he from the man?

8. An unmanned space probe takes a photograph of two moons of a planet, managing to get them both in the same picture. The probe is at point A and has reliable data that the moon Charion is 50,000 km away and the moon Ballisto is 80,000 km away. On–board sensors estimate the angle between the two moons to be 65°. Scientists analysing the photograph and data need to calculate the distance between the two moons. What is this distance?

EXERCISE

Area of a Triangle

Until now, you have used the formula $A = \frac{1}{2}base \times height$ to work out the area of a triangle.

Using trigonometry, the area of a triangle can also be found using the formula $A = \frac{1}{2}ab\ sinC$ where a and b are adjacent sides and C is the angle between them.

This formula is useful where the perpendicular height is not known.

PROOF OF $A = \frac{1}{2}ab\ sinC$

You do not need to learn this proof.

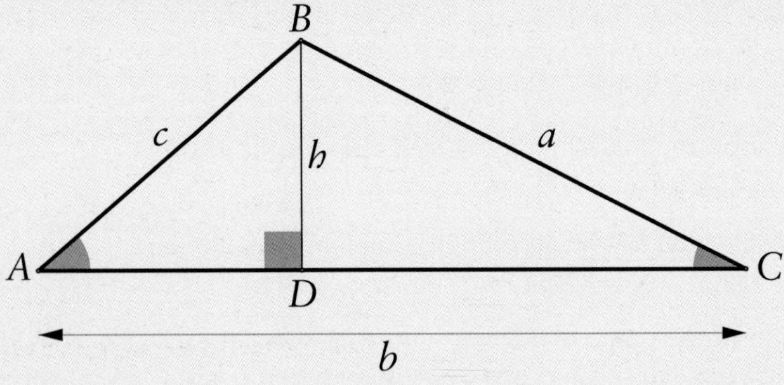

$$Area = \frac{1}{2}b \times h \quad (1)$$

Using ΔBCD: $\quad sin\ C = \frac{h}{a}$

Re-arrange: $\quad h = a\ sin\ C \quad (2)$

Substitute in (1): $\quad Area = \frac{1}{2}ab\ sin\ C$

You can show similar results using any two adjacent sides and the angle between them, so:

$$Area\ of\ triangle = \frac{1}{2}ab\ sin\ C = \frac{1}{2}bc\ sin\ A = \frac{1}{2}ac\ sin\ B$$

EXAMPLE 1

Find the area of the triangle in which $a = 7\ cm$, $b = 2\ cm$ and $C = 84°$.

Firstly, if you have not been given a diagram, it is always helpful to draw a sketch of the triangle.

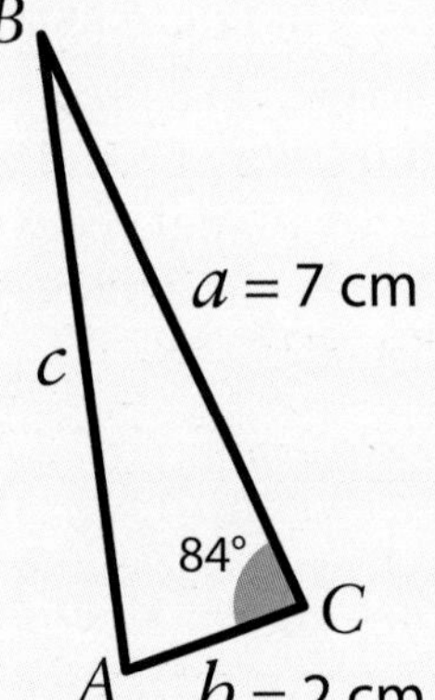

Then calculate the area.

$$A = \frac{1}{2}ab\ sinC$$

$$= \frac{1}{2}(7)(2)\ sin\ 84$$

$$= 6.96\ cm^2$$

Sometimes you will need to calculate the angle, before using the area formula.

EXAMPLE 2

Calculate the area of triangle ABC below.

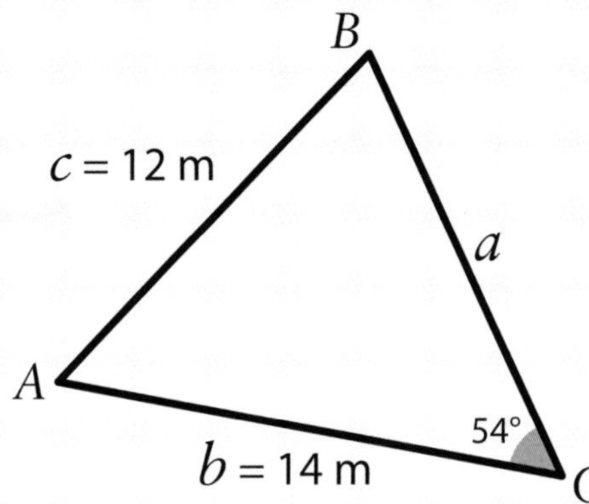

Here, we know two of the sides, but not the angle between them. Use the sine rule to find angle B:

$$\frac{\sin B}{b} = \frac{\sin C}{c}$$

$$\sin B = 14 \times \frac{\sin 54}{12}$$

$$= 0.94 \ldots$$

$$B = 70.7 \ldots° \quad \text{(No rounding yet!)}$$

Next, find angle A:

$$A = 180 - (B + C)$$

$$= 180 - (70.7 \ldots + 54)$$

$$= 55.29 \ldots°$$

Now use the area formula:

$$Area = \frac{1}{2} bc \sin A$$

$$= \frac{1}{2}(14)(12)\sin(55.29 \ldots)$$

$$= 69.1\ m^2 \quad \text{(3 s.f.)}$$

EXERCISE 9D

For this exercise, you may use these facts: $\sin 60° = \frac{\sqrt{3}}{2}$, $\sin 45° = \frac{1}{\sqrt{2}}$, $\sin 30° = \frac{1}{2}$

1. Calculate the area of the following triangles to 3 significant figures.
   a) $a = 5\ cm, b = 6\ cm, C = 59°$
   b) $a = 600\ m, b = 400\ m, C = 85°$
   c) $x = 1.2\ km, y = 4.6\ km, Z = 25°$
   d) $a = 1.2\ cm, b = 4.6\ cm, B = 25°$
   e) $c = 10\ m, a = 4\ m, B = 16°$
   f) $p = 9\ cm, q = 9\ cm, Q = 68°$

2. Find the length of the side b to 3 significant figures in each of these triangles.
   a) $a = 11\ cm, Area = 18\ cm^2, C = 120°$
   b) $a = 6\ cm, Area = 42\ m^2, C = 75°$
   c) $a = 30\ mm, Area = 46\ mm^2, C = 30°$
   d) $a = 10\ km, Area = 49\ km^2, C = 18°$

3. Find the acute angle C in the following triangles ABC. You are given the lengths of two sides and the triangle's area. Give your answers to 1 decimal place.
   a) $a = 20\ cm, b = 6\ cm, Area = 27\ cm^2$
   b) $a = 6\ cm, b = 9\ cm, Area = 25\ cm^2$
   c) $a = 3\ cm, b = 23\ cm, Area = 34\ cm^2$
   d) $a = 16\ cm, b = 5\ cm, Area = 11\ cm^2$

4. Find the area of the triangle PQR in which $PQ = 4\ cm$, $QR = 5\ cm$ and angle $Q = 30°$.

5. A man runs around the perimeter of a forest, which is triangular in shape. He knows the area of the forest is 25 km^2, and the product of the two shorter sides is 56 km^2. Find the size of the largest angle in the triangle, given that it is acute.

6. Two sides of a triangle measure $(x + 5)\ cm$ and $(x + 11)\ cm$. If the angle between these two sides is 60° and the area of the triangle is $10\sqrt{3}\ cm^2$, find x.

EXERCISE

EXERCISE

EXERCISE

7. A child's drawing of a house is made up of an equilateral triangle on top of a square. If the base of the drawing is 5 cm long, calculate the total area of the drawing. Give your answer as a surd.

8. In the trapezium shown, $BC = p$, $AC = q$ and $AD = r$. Angle $ACB = \theta$.

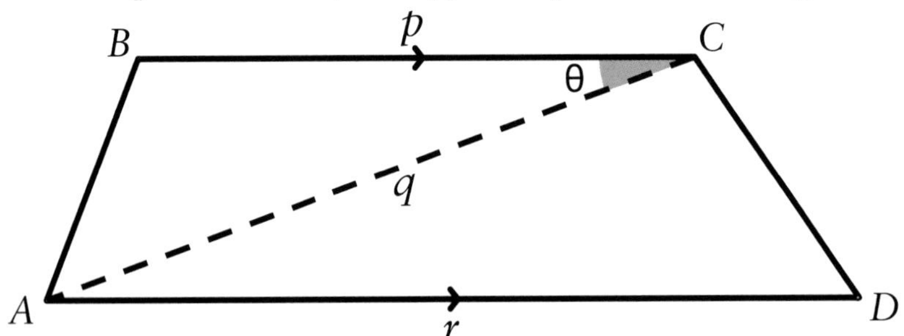

a) Write down an expression using $sin\,\theta$ for the area of triangle ABC.

b) Write down an expression using $sin\,\theta$ for the area of triangle ACD.

c) Given that the area ΔABC of is $\frac{3}{4}$ of the area of ΔACD, show that $4BC = 3AD$.

EXERCISE

9.3 Radian Measure

Until now, you have measured angles in degrees. In this chapter and your further work, you will increasingly use a different unit of measure for angles: **radians**.

One radian is approximately 57°. To be more precise:

$$1\,radian = \left(\frac{180}{\pi}\right)^{\circ} \quad \text{or} \quad \pi\,radians = 180^{\circ}$$

You might also find it useful to remember:

$$1^{\circ} = \frac{\pi}{180}radians$$

From this, you can see that there are 2π radians in a circle. You should learn and remember this.

EXAMPLE 1

Convert:

a) 360° to radians

b) 4π radians to degrees

c) $\frac{\pi}{2}$ radians to degrees

d) 45° to radians

---

a) $180^{\circ} = \pi$ radians so $360^{\circ} = 2\pi$ radians

b) $2\pi\,radians = 360^{\circ}$ so $4\pi\,radians = 720^{\circ}$

c) $2\pi\,radians = 360^{\circ}$ so $\frac{\pi}{2}radians = 90^{\circ}$

d) From part c), $90^{\circ} = \frac{\pi}{2}radians$ so $45^{\circ} = \frac{\pi}{4}radians$

You will encounter the Greek letter θ (pronounced "theta") frequently in this chapter. It is often used as an angle variable, just as is x often used for numbers.

Length of an Arc of a Circle

There is an important relationship between the length of an **arc** of a circle and the angle **subtended** by that arc at the circle's centre.

If s is the length of an arc, r is the radius and θ is the angle in radians, then:

$s = r\theta$

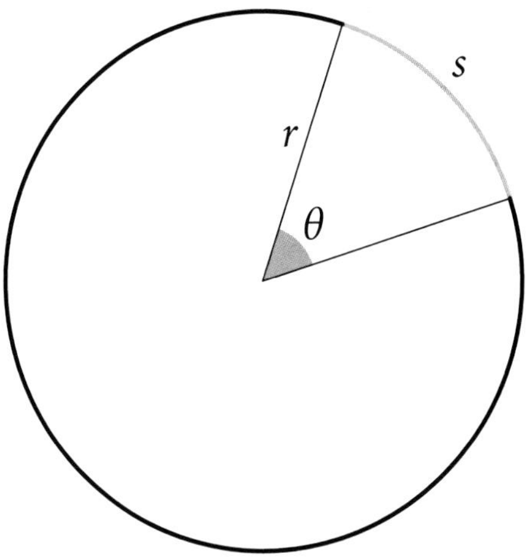

PROOF OF ARC LENGTH FORMULA

You do not need to learn this.

Work out the fraction of the circle occupied by the arc and the angle.

Arc: $\dfrac{s}{2\pi r}$

Angle: $\dfrac{\theta}{360°}$ or $\dfrac{\theta}{2\pi}$ in radians

These fractions must be equal.

Therefore: $\dfrac{s}{2\pi r} = \dfrac{\theta}{2\pi}$

or $s = r\theta$

EXAMPLE 1

An arc subtends an angle of 30° at the centre of a circle of radius 15 cm. Calculate the length of the arc to 3 significant figures.

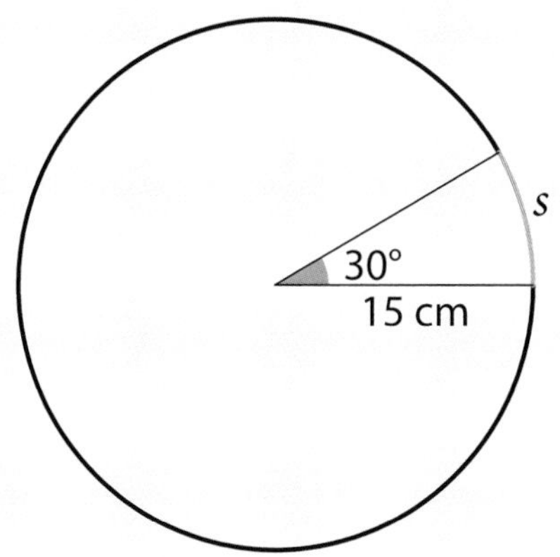

The angle must be converted to radians:

$1° = \dfrac{\pi}{180} \textit{radians}$ so $30° = \dfrac{\pi}{6} \textit{radians}$

$s = r\theta$

$s = 15 \times \dfrac{\pi}{6}$

$= 7.85$ cm (3 s.f.)

EXAMPLE 2

Calculate the perimeter of this icon used in a computer game. It is based on a circle of radius 5 cm. The angle subtended by the missing region is 50°.

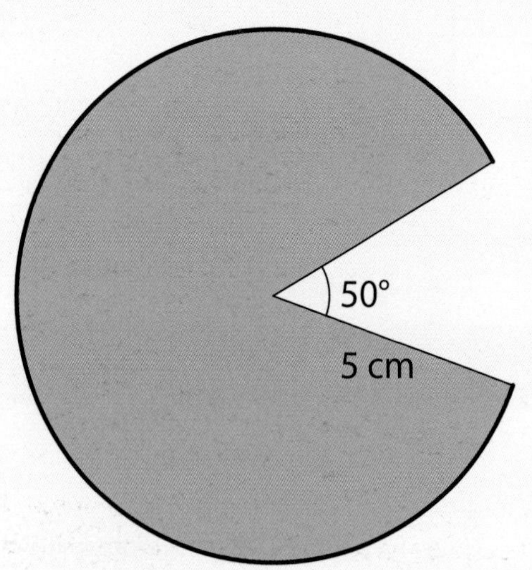

Angle subtended by major arc is:

$360 - 50 = 310°$

$= 5.41 \ldots$ radians

Remember to keep the whole decimal value for the next calculation!

Arc length: $s = r\theta$

$= 5 \times 5.41$

$= 27.05$ cm

The entire perimeter comprises the major arc and two radii.

So: perimeter $= 27.05 + 5 + 5$

$= 37.1$ cm (3 s.f.)

Area of a Sector of a Circle

There is also a formula for the area of a **sector** of a circle: $A = \frac{1}{2}r^2\theta$

PROOF OF SECTOR AREA FORMULA

You do not need to learn this.

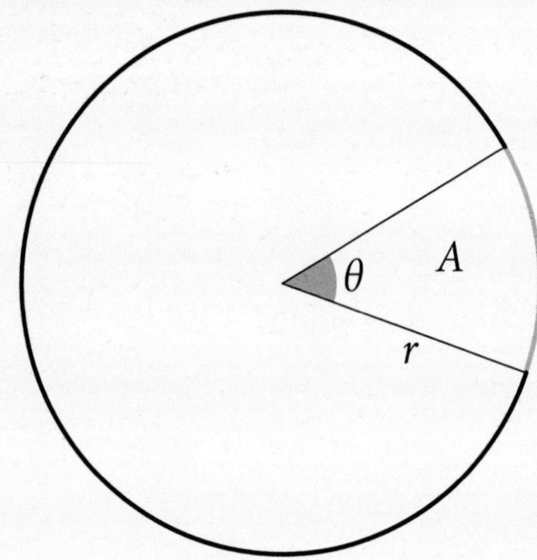

Work out the fraction of the circle occupied by the sector:

$\frac{\theta}{360°}$ or $\frac{\theta}{2\pi}$ in radians

Area of whole circle:

πr^2

Therefore area of sector:

$A = \pi r^2 \times \frac{\theta}{2\pi}$ or $A = \frac{1}{2}r^2\theta$

EXAMPLE 1

A circle has radius 10 cm. Find the exact area of a minor sector of this circle subtending an angle of 60°.

Calculate θ in radians: $\theta = 60 \times \frac{\pi}{180} = \frac{\pi}{3}$

Then calculate the area: $A = \frac{1}{2}r^2\theta$

$$A = \frac{1}{2}10^2\left(\frac{\pi}{3}\right)$$

$$= \frac{50\pi}{3}$$

Area of a Segment of a Circle

You can also calculate the area of a segment of a circle using the formula: $A = \frac{1}{2}r^2(\theta - \sin\theta)$

Again, the angle θ must be measured in radians.

PROOF OF SEGMENT AREA FORMULA

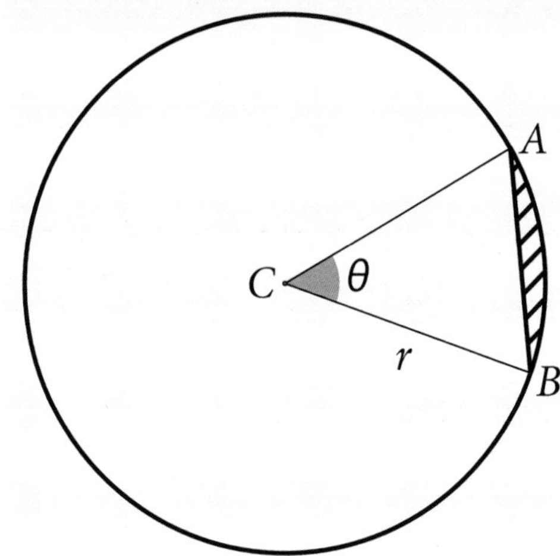

From the diagram, you can see that the area of a segment of the circle (shown hatched) is the area of the sector ABC minus the area of the triangle ABC.

Area of sector ABC: $A = \frac{1}{2}r^2\theta$

Area of triangle ABC: $= \frac{1}{2}ab\sin\theta$

$$= \frac{1}{2}r^2\sin\theta$$

Area of segment ABC = Area of sector – Area of triangle

$$= \frac{1}{2}r^2\theta - \frac{1}{2}r^2\sin\theta$$

$$= \frac{1}{2}r^2(\theta - \sin\theta)$$

EXAMPLE 2

A circle centre C has radius 5 cm. Chord *AB* subtends an angle of 49.5° at the circle's centre. Calculate the area of the segment bounded by the arc and chord between points *A* and *B*.

First convert the angle to radians:

Angle: $= 49.5° = 49.5 \times \frac{\pi}{180}$ *radians*

$= 0.864$ **Don't round this value.**

Area of segment $= \frac{1}{2}r^2(\theta - \sin\theta)$

$= \frac{1}{2}5^2(0.864 \ldots - \sin(0.864 \ldots))$

$= 1.29 \text{ cm}^2$

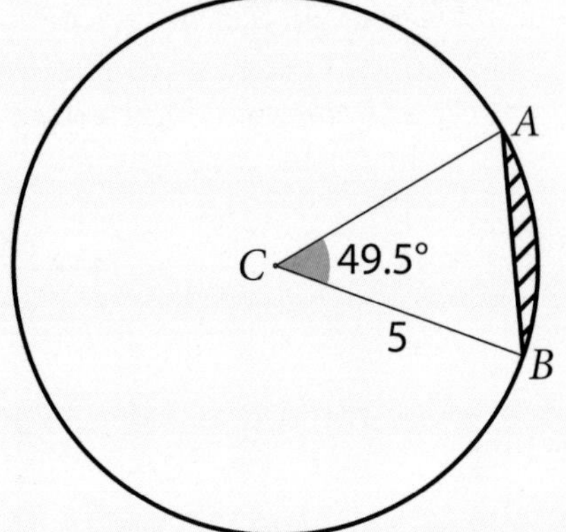

EXERCISE 9E

1. Convert the following angles from degrees to radians, leaving your answer in exact form.

a) 30° b) 45° c) 60° d) –60° e) 135°

f) –90° g) 20° h) –360° i) 540° j) 3600°

2. Convert the following angles from radians to degrees.

a) $\frac{2\pi}{3}$ b) $\frac{4\pi}{3}$ c) $\frac{\pi}{18}$ d) $\frac{\pi}{180}$ e) $-\frac{\pi}{30}$

f) $\frac{5\pi}{2}$ g) $\frac{3\pi}{20}$ h) $\frac{5\pi}{4}$ i) 0 j) $\frac{4\pi}{9}$

3. Find the following angles in radians, giving your answers to 3 significant figures where appropriate.

a) 720° b) 33° c) 28° d) 182° e) 329°

f) 179° g) 68° h) 595° i) –89° j) –235°

4. Find the following angles in degrees, giving exact answers.

a) 4π b) 9π c) $\frac{9\pi}{2}$ d) $\frac{\pi}{6}$ e) $\frac{5\pi}{6}$

f) $-\frac{\pi}{4}$ g) -5π h) 1 i) 6 j) –2.5

5. Work out the following on your calculator. Remember to use degrees and radians modes where appropriate.

a) $\cos 60°$ b) $\cos -60°$ c) $\sin 60°$ d) $\sin -60°$ e) $\cos \frac{3\pi}{2}$

f) $\cos 45°$ g) $\sin 45°$ h) $\tan 45°$ i) $\tan \pi$ j) $\tan -\pi$

EXERCISE

EXERCISE

EXERCISE

6. Find the lengths of the arcs of each circle, giving your answers to 3 significant figures.
   a) Radius 1 cm, angle π *radians.*
   b) Radius 2 m, angle $\frac{3\pi}{2}$ *radians*
   c) Radius 4 cm, angle 60°
   d) Radius 100 m, angle 120°
   e) Radius 5 mm, angle 90°

7. Find the areas of the following circle sectors, correct to 3 significant figures. Be careful to convert from degrees to radians if necessary.
   a) Radius 4 cm, angle subtended 60°
   b) Radius 10 cm, angle subtended $\frac{\pi}{2}$
   c) Radius 1 cm, angle subtended $\frac{\pi}{4}$
   d) Radius 0.2 m, angle subtended 24°
   e) Radius 9 km, angle subtended 30°

8. The area of a sector of a circle is 12 m^2 and the angle subtended by this sector at the centre is 45°. Find the radius of the circle.

9. Find the perimeter of the sector of a circle if the radius of the circle is 20 m and the angle subtended by the sector at the centre of the circle is 20°. Give your answer to 1 decimal place.

10. The area of a segment of a circle is 30 cm^2. The angle subtended by this segment at the centre of the circle is 25°.
    a) Find the radius of the circle.
    b) Using the cosine rule, find the length of the chord subtending the angle.

11. The solid lines on the diagram are the outline of a Christmas decoration *ABC*. *AB* and *AC* are straight lines, with *AB* = *AC* = 9 mm. The curve *BC* is an arc of a circle, centre O, where *OB* = *OC* = 9 mm and *O* is in the same plane as *ABC*. The angle *BAC* is 0.5 radians.

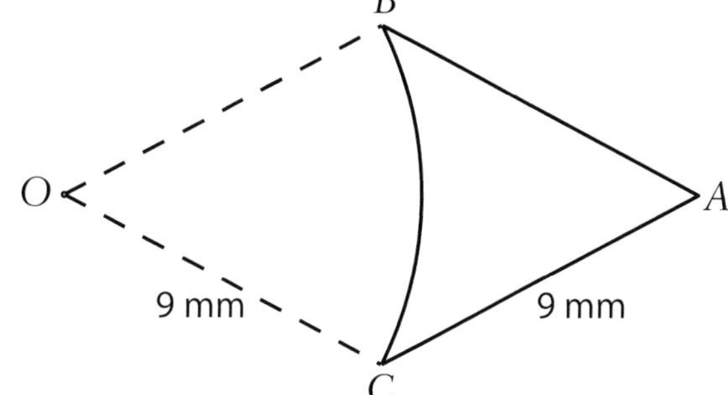

    Giving your answers to 3 significant figures:
    a) Find the perimeter of the decoration.
    b) Find the area of the decoration.

12. In the diagram *OAB* is a sector of a circle radius 6 m. The chord *AB* is 4 m long.

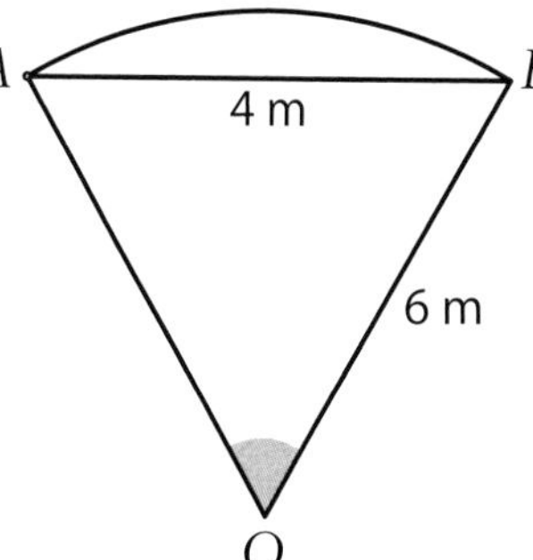

    a) Using the cosine rule, show that $\cos AOB = \frac{7}{9}$.
    b) Hence find the angle *AOB* in radians, giving your answer to 3 decimal places.
    c) Calculate the area of the sector *AOB* to 3 significant figures.
    d) Hence calculate the area of the segment bounded by the chord *AB* and the arc *AB*.

EXERCISE

13. The diagram shows the outline of a company logo. It is in the shape of a sector ABC of a circle with centre A and radius AB. The triangle ABC is equilateral and has perpendicular height $h = 3\ cm$.
a) Find, in surd form, the length of AB.

b) Find, in terms of π, the area of the logo.
c) Prove that the perimeter of the logo is: $\dfrac{2\sqrt{3}}{3}(\pi + 6)\ cm$

14. A man takes three bites out of a triangular slice of pizza, as shown in the diagram. Each of the man's bites has radius 2 cm.

If the lengths of the sides of the triangle were 5, 12 and 14 cm, before the bites were taken, what area of pizza is left?

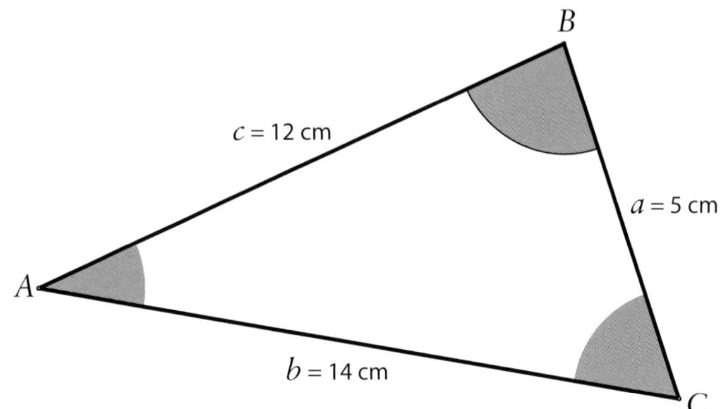

15. The diagram shows an earring, made of a sector of a circle ABC, with a circle P removed. Circle P just touches the radii AB and AC and the arc BC. AB and AC both measure 12 cm; angle BAC is $\dfrac{\pi}{3}$ radians.
a) Find the exact area of sector ABC.
b) Find the radius of circle P.
c) Find, in cm^2, the area of metal required to make the earring.

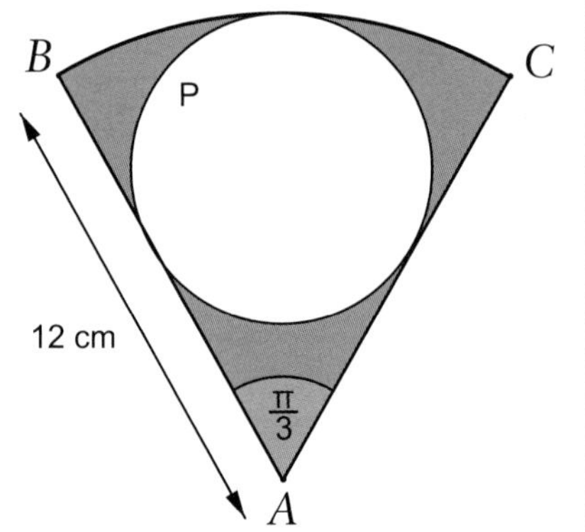

9.4 The CAST diagram

Until now, we have mainly looked at angles between 0 and 90°.

The **CAST diagram** helps you to find the sine, cosine and tangent of angles outside this range. It is often used between 0° and 360° or between –180°and 180°.

The angle 0° is aligned with the x-axis. From this reference line, all angles are measured anticlockwise, for example the angle θ shown in the diagram is 30°. An angle of 180° is aligned with the negative x-axis and 360° is in the same position as 0°.

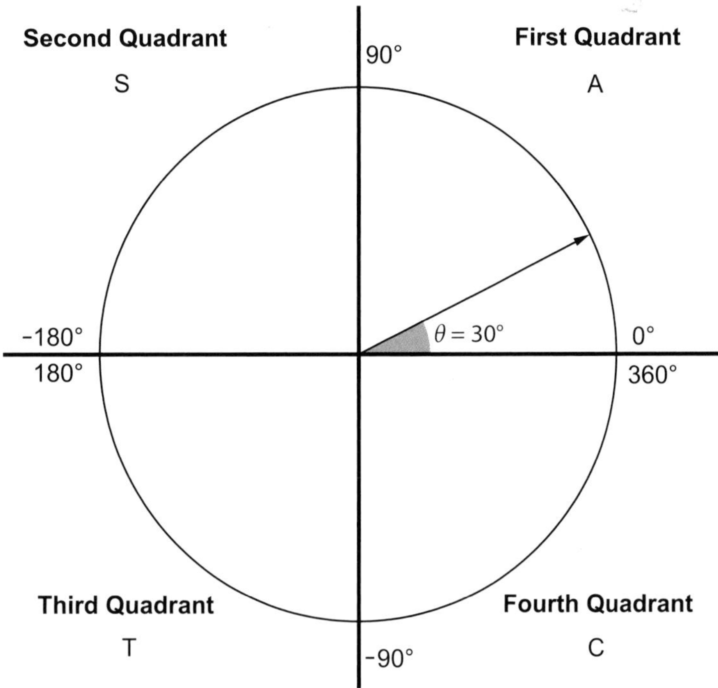

The diagram takes its name CAST from the four quadrants. In the C (fourth) quadrant, the cosine of angles is positive. In the A quadrant, all functions (sine, cosine and tangent) of the angles are positive. In the S quadrant only the sine is positive; in the T quadrant, only tan is positive. This information is summarised in this table:

	θ	Positive	Negative
First quadrant (A)	0 – 90°	All	
Second quadrant (S)	90 – 180°	$\sin\theta$	$\cos\theta, \tan\theta$
Third quadrant (T)	180 – 270°	$\tan\theta$	$\sin\theta, \cos\theta$
Fourth quadrant (C)	270 – 360°	$\cos\theta$	$\sin\theta, \tan\theta$

EXAMPLE 1

Using the CAST diagram, state whether the sine of the following angles are positive or negative.

a) 40° b) 120° c) 190° d) 335°

---

a) 40° lies within the first quadrant, so sin 40° is positive.

b) 120° lies within the second quadrant, so sin 120° is positive.

c) 190° lies within the third quadrant, so sin 190° is negative.

d) 335° lies within the fourth quadrant, so sin 335° is negative.

Check these results on your calculator.

Given the sine, cosine or tangent of any angle within quadrant 1, you can use symmetry within the CAST diagram to find the sine, cosine and tangent of certain angles within quadrants 2, 3 and 4. These angles can be found by a reflection of the acute angle in the x and y–axes, or by a rotation through 180°.

EXAMPLE 2

Draw the angles 150°, 210° and 330° on the CAST diagram. **State the equivalent acute angles made with the x-axis.** Given $sin\, 30° = \frac{1}{2}$, find:

a) $sin\, 150°$ b) $sin\, 210°$ c) $sin\, 330°$

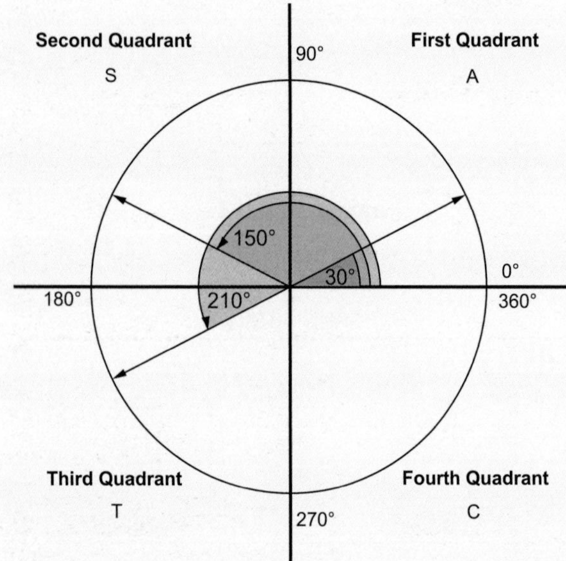

Each of these three angles makes an equivalent acute angle of 30° with the x-axis.

Firstly, note that 150° is a reflection of 30° in the 90° line.

210° is a rotation of 30° through 180°.

The angle 330° has not been marked on the diagram. This is left as an exercise. 330° is a reflection of 30° in the 0° line.

This means we can work out sine, cosine and tangent of these angles using sine, cosine and tangent of 30°.

a) 150° lies in the second quadrant, so sine is positive: $sin\, 30° = \frac{1}{2} \Rightarrow sin\, 150° = \frac{1}{2}$

b) 210° lies in the third quadrant, so sine is negative: $sin\, 30° = \frac{1}{2} \Rightarrow sin\, 210° = -\frac{1}{2}$

c) 330° lies in the fourth quadrant, so sine is negative: $sin\, 30° = \frac{1}{2} \Rightarrow sin\, 330° = -\frac{1}{2}$

Check these results on your calculator.

In its usual form, the CAST diagram is labelled from 0° to 360°. If you are considering other angles, the diagram can be relabelled, for example from –180° to 180°.

You will often work out the first angle on your calculator, then use this to find other solutions.

EXAMPLE 3

Given $cos\,\theta = \frac{\sqrt{2}}{2}$, where θ is an acute angle:

a) find θ (in degrees) using your calculator.

Use the CAST diagram to find:

b) $cos(-45°)$ c) $cos(-135°)$

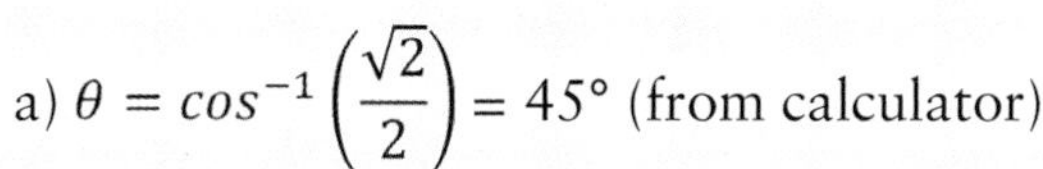

a) $\theta = cos^{-1}\left(\frac{\sqrt{2}}{2}\right) = 45°$ (from calculator)

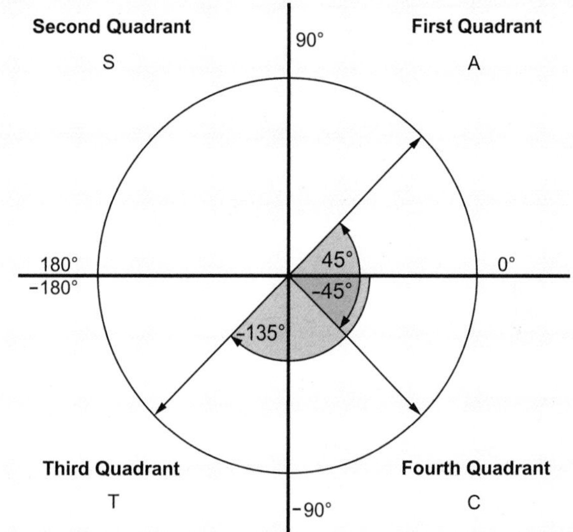

Now draw the CAST diagram. Note that:

–45° is a reflection of 45° in the 0° line.

–135° is a rotation of 45° through 180°.

This means we can work out sine, cosine and tangent of these angles using sine, cosine and tangent of 45°.

b) –45° lies in the fourth quadrant, so cosine is positive:

$$cos\,45° = \frac{\sqrt{2}}{2} \Rightarrow cos\,-45° = \frac{\sqrt{2}}{2}$$

c) –135° lies in the third quadrant, so cosine is negative:

$$cos\,45° = \frac{\sqrt{2}}{2} \Rightarrow cos\,-135° = -\frac{\sqrt{2}}{2}$$

Check these results on your calculator.

You will also need to use the CAST diagram with angles measured in radians.

EXAMPLE 4

Given $tan\,\theta = \frac{\sqrt{3}}{3}$, where θ is an acute angle in radians,

a) find θ on your calculator.

Use the CAST diagram to find

b) $tan\frac{5\pi}{6}$ c) $tan-\frac{\pi}{6}$

---

continued...

Example 4...

a) $\theta = tan^{-1}\left(\frac{\sqrt{3}}{3}\right) = \frac{\pi}{6}$ (from calculator)

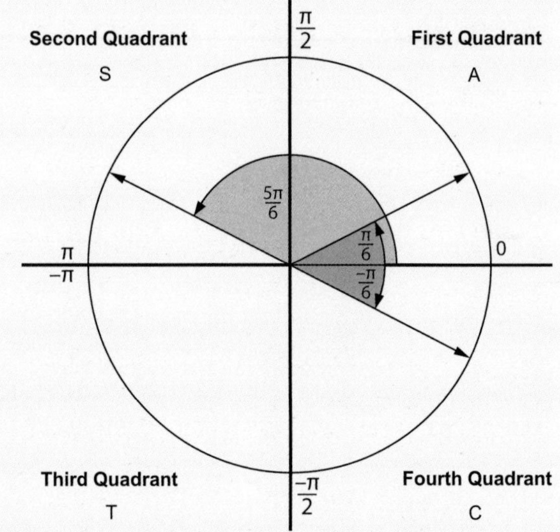

Now draw the CAST diagram. Note that:

$-\frac{\pi}{6}$ is a reflection of $\frac{\pi}{6}$ in the 0 line.

$\frac{5\pi}{6}$ is a reflection of $\frac{\pi}{6}$ in the $\frac{\pi}{2}$ line.

This means we can work out sine, cosine and tangent of these angles using sine, cosine and tangent of $\frac{\pi}{6}$.

b) $-\frac{\pi}{6}$ lies in the fourth quadrant, so tangent is negative.

$$tan\frac{\pi}{6} = \frac{\sqrt{3}}{3} \Rightarrow tan\left(-\frac{\pi}{6}\right) = -\frac{\sqrt{3}}{3}$$

c) $\frac{5\pi}{6}$ lies in the second quadrant, so tangent is negative.

$$tan\frac{\pi}{6} = \frac{\sqrt{3}}{3} \Rightarrow tan\frac{5\pi}{6} = -\frac{\sqrt{3}}{3}$$

Check these results on your calculator.

Here, the results are summarised for all the functions. You do not need to remember these results, but you do need to know how to work them out for specific angles, as in the examples above.

In degrees	In radians
$sin(180° - \theta) = sin\,\theta$	$sin(\pi - \theta) = sin\,\theta$
$sin(180° + \theta) = -\,sin\,\theta$	$sin(\pi + \theta) = -\,sin\,\theta$
$sin(360° - \theta) = -\,sin\,\theta$	$sin(2\pi - \theta) = -\,sin\,\theta$
$cos(180° - \theta) = -\,cos\,\theta$	$cos(\pi - \theta) = -\,cos\,\theta$
$cos(180° + \theta) = -\,cos\,\theta$	$cos(\pi + \theta) = -\,cos\,\theta$
$cos(360° - \theta) = cos\,\theta$	$cos(2\pi - \theta) = cos\,\theta$
$tan(180° - \theta) = -\,tan\,\theta$	$tan(\pi - \theta) = -\,tan\,\theta$
$tan(180° + \theta) = tan\,\theta$	$tan(\pi + \theta) = tan\,\theta$
$tan(360° - \theta) = -\,tan\,\theta$	$tan(2\pi - \theta) = -\,tan\,\theta$

The CAST diagram can even be used with very big or small angles. For example, we could relabel the diagram from 360° to 720°, or from –720° to –360°. Any angle that is a multiple of 360° (–720°, –360°, 0°, 360°, 720°, etc.) will always take the place of the 0° line.

These two diagrams show these two ranges, with some example angles:

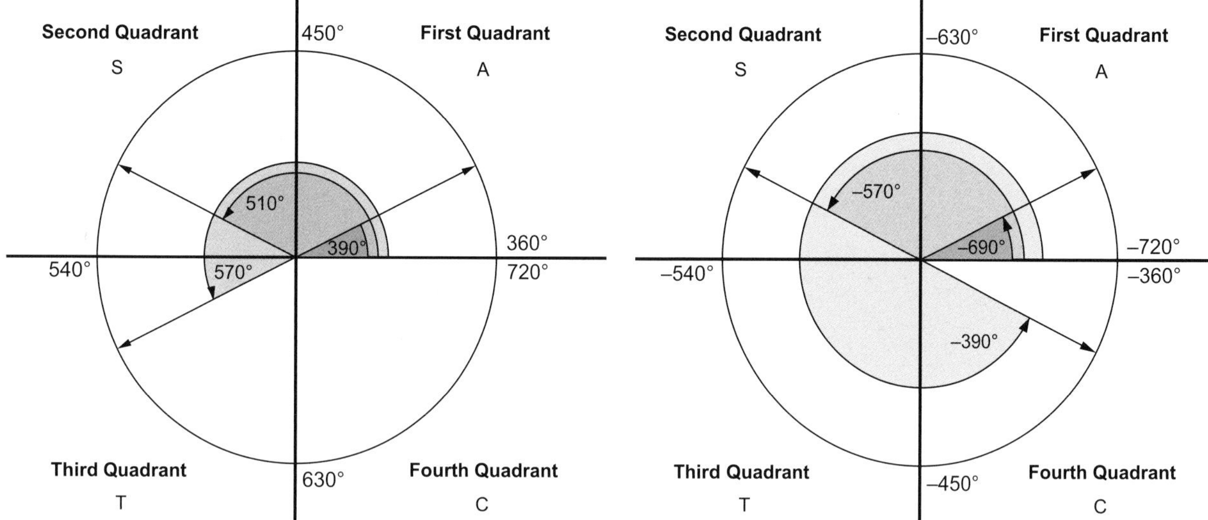

EXERCISE 9F

1. Sketch the following angles on the same CAST diagram, showing clearly which quadrant they are in:
   a) 30° b) 45° c) 100° d) 210° e) 260° f) 320°

2. Sketch the following angles in radians on the same CAST diagram, showing clearly which quadrant they are in:
   a) $\frac{\pi}{4}$ b) $\frac{\pi}{3}$ c) $\frac{3\pi}{4}$ d) $\frac{5\pi}{4}$ e) $\frac{11\pi}{8}$ f) $\frac{7\pi}{4}$

3. By using a CAST diagram, determine the sign (i.e. positive or negative) of each of the following trigonometric ratios.
   a) $sin\,54\,°$ b) $cos\,46\,°$ c) $tan\,120\,°$ d) $cos\,150\,°$ e) $sin\,100\,°$
   f) $sin\left(\frac{5\pi}{4}\right)$ g) $cos\left(\frac{\pi}{4}\right)$ h) $tan\left(\frac{13\pi}{8}\right)$ i) $sin\left(\frac{15\pi}{8}\right)$ j) $cos\,305\,°$

4. If θ is an acute angle, simplify the following:
   a) $sin(180° + \theta)$ b) $sin(180° - \theta)$ c) $cos(180° + \theta)$
   d) $sin(360° - \theta)$ e) $cos(360° - \theta)$ f) $sin(360° + \theta)$
   g) $cos(360° + \theta)$ h) $tan(360° + \theta)$ i) $sin(\pi - \theta)$
   j) $cos(2\pi - \theta)$

5. If θ is an acute angle, simplify the following expressions:
   a) $sin(180 - \theta) + sin(180 + \theta)$ b) $cos(180 - \theta) + cos(180 + \theta)$
   c) $tan(180 - \theta) + tan(180 + \theta)$ d) $sin(180 - \theta) - sin(360 - \theta)$
   e) $cos(\pi - x) + cos(2\pi - x)$ f) $tan(180 - \theta)\,tan(180 + \theta)$
   g) $sin(360 - \theta)\,sin(180 + \theta)$ h) $2\,cos(2\pi + x) + 3\,cos(\pi + x)$

6. Rewrite the following using acute angles:
   a) $sin\,365\,°$ b) $cos\,380\,°$ c) $tan\,449\,°$
   d) $tan(-10°)$ e) $cos(-170°)$ f) $sin(-350°)$
   g) $tan(2\pi + 1)$ h) $sin(-10\pi + x)$ where $0 < x < \frac{\pi}{2}$
   i) $sin(85°) + sin(95°)$ j) $cos(-180° - x)$ where $0° < x < 90°$

9.5 The Graphs of the Sine, Cosine and Tangent Functions

Keywords

Period of a function: the distance between repeating parts of its curve.

Asymptote: a straight line that a curve approaches, but never touches.

Symmetries and Periodicities

You should be familiar with the key features of the sine, cosine and tangent graphs.

The Sine Curve

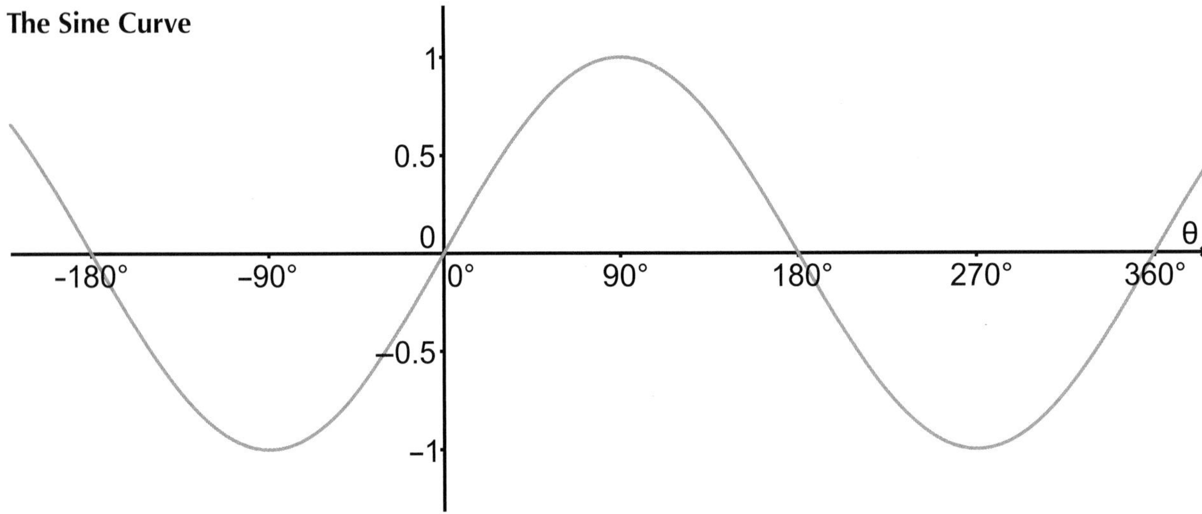

- The curve $y = sin\,\theta$ passes through the origin.
- It reaches a maximum value of 1 when $\theta = 90°$ (or $\frac{\pi}{2}$ radians) and a minimum value of –1 when $\theta = 270°$ (or $\frac{3\pi}{2}$ radians).
- It has a period of 360° (or 2π radians), meaning the curve has maxima at $\theta = \cdots - 270°, 90°, 450°, \ldots$ and minima at $\theta = \cdots - 90°, 270°, 630°, \ldots$
- $y = 0$ when $\theta = \cdots - 360°, -180°, 0°, 180°, 360°, \ldots$
- Because of this periodicity, $sin(\theta - 360°) = sin\,\theta = sin(\theta + 360°)$
- The sine curve has symmetry about the line $\theta = 90°$, meaning that: $sin(90° + \theta) = sin(90° - \theta)$

The Cosine Curve

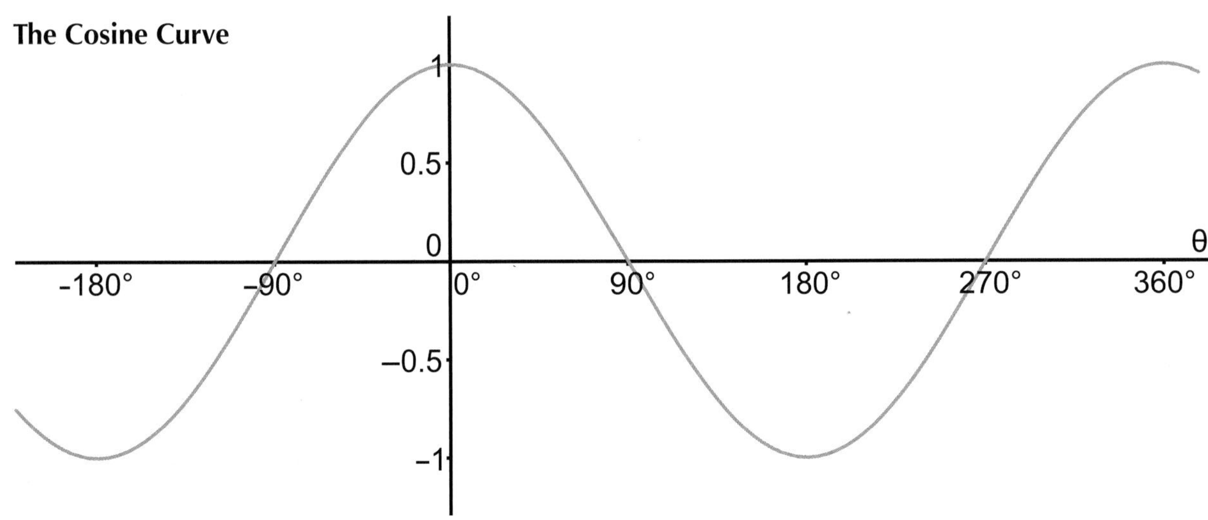

- The curve $y = cos\,\theta$ has a maximum value of 1 when $\theta = 0°$ (or 0 radians) and a minimum value of –1 when $\theta = 180°$ (or π radians).
- It has a period of 360° (or 2π radians), meaning the curve has maxima at $\theta = \cdots - 360°, 0°, 360°, \ldots$ and minima at $\theta = \cdots - 540°, -180°, 180°, 540°, \ldots$
- $y = 0$ when $\theta = \cdots - 270°, -90°, 90°, 270°, \ldots$
- Because of this periodicity, $cos(\theta - 360°) = cos\,\theta = cos(\theta + 360°)$
- The cosine curve has symmetry about the line $\theta = 0°$, meaning that: $cos\,\theta = cos(-\theta)$

The Tangent Curve

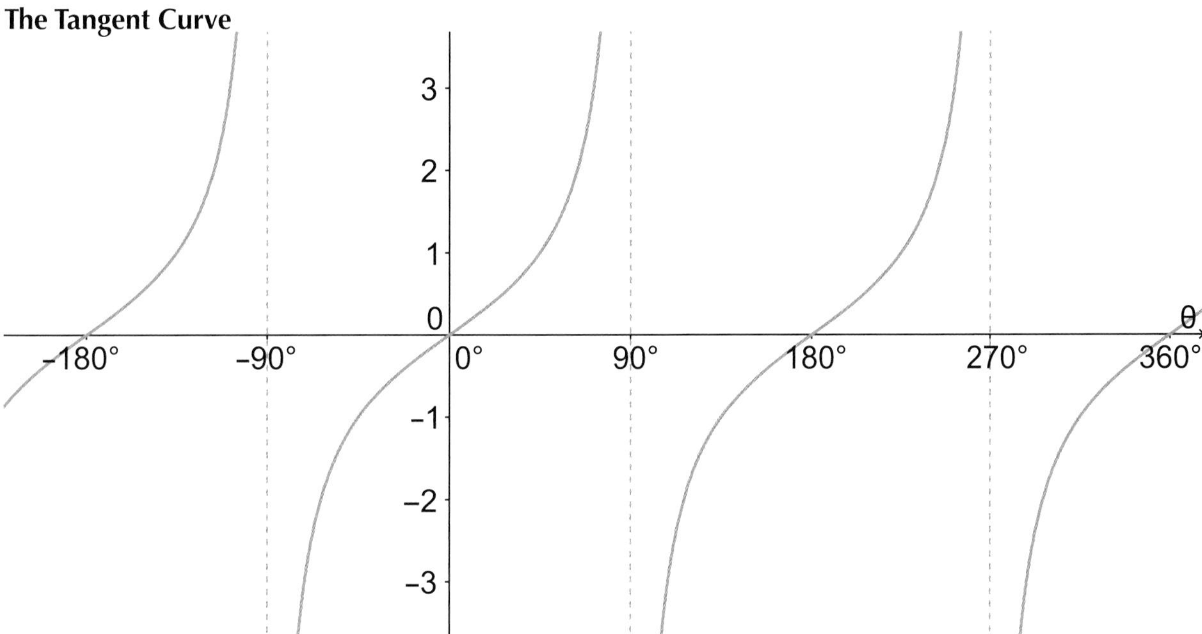

- The curve $y = tan\,\theta$ has a period of 180° or π radians.
- $y = 0$ when $\theta = \cdots - 180°, 0°, 180°, \ldots$
- There are no maxima or minima. Instead, the curve approaches asymptotes at $\theta = \cdots -270°, -90°, 90°, 270°, \ldots$
- We write $y \to \infty$ as $x \to 90°$.
- Because of the periodicity, $tan(\theta - 180°) = tan\,\theta = tan(\theta + 180°)$.
- The tangent curve does not have any lines of symmetry.

Special Triangles

When finding trigonometric ratios, you may find it useful to consider two right-angled triangles. They are known as special triangles.

The first special triangle is drawn with two equal sides of 1 unit and an angle of 45°. By Pythagoras' Theorem, this means the hypotenuse is $\sqrt{2}$.

From this triangle, it can be seen that: $sin\,45° = \frac{1}{\sqrt{2}} = \frac{\sqrt{2}}{2}$

$$cos\,45° = \frac{1}{\sqrt{2}} = \frac{\sqrt{2}}{2}$$

$$tan\,45° = \frac{1}{1} = 1$$

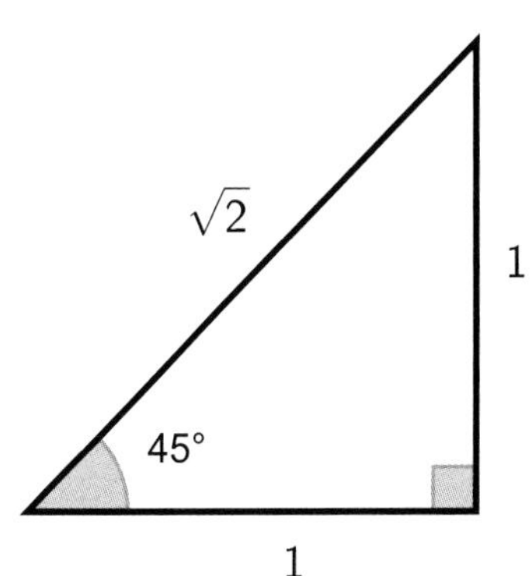

The second special triangle is half of an equilateral triangle of side length 2. The two shorter sides are 1 and $\sqrt{3}$ units. From this triangle, it can be seen that:

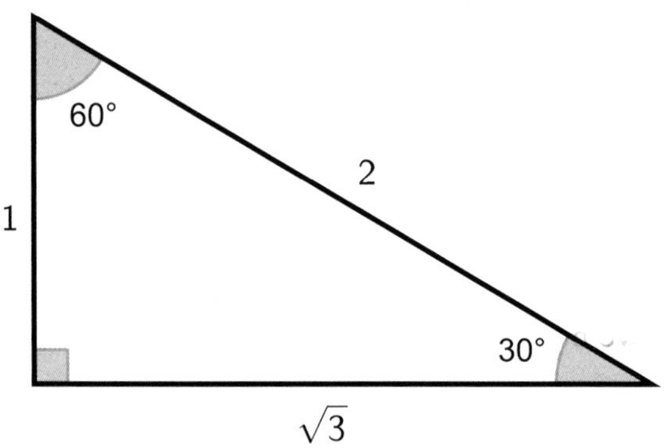

$$\sin 60° = \frac{\sqrt{3}}{2} \qquad \sin 30° = \frac{1}{2}$$

$$\cos 60° = \frac{1}{2} \qquad \cos 30° = \frac{\sqrt{3}}{2}$$

$$\tan 60° = \frac{\sqrt{3}}{1} = \sqrt{3} \qquad \tan 30° = \frac{1}{\sqrt{3}} = \frac{\sqrt{3}}{3}$$

Some Important Results

You should learn some of the key values from the sine, cosine and tangent graphs. These are summarised here:

	0° or 0 radians	30° or $\frac{\pi}{6}$	45° or $\frac{\pi}{4}$	60° or $\frac{\pi}{3}$	90° or $\frac{\pi}{2}$
$\sin\theta$	0	$\frac{1}{2}$	$\frac{\sqrt{2}}{2}$	$\frac{\sqrt{3}}{2}$	1
$\cos\theta$	1	$\frac{\sqrt{3}}{2}$	$\frac{\sqrt{2}}{2}$	$\frac{1}{2}$	0
$\tan\theta$	0	$\frac{\sqrt{3}}{3}$	1	$\sqrt{3}$	$\pm\infty$

You learnt about surds earlier in this book. Surds appear a lot in trigonometry, especially $\sqrt{2}$ and $\sqrt{3}$. These exact values for certain acute angles will help you to find the exact values for many other trigonometric ratios.

EXAMPLE 1

Given $\cos 45° = \frac{\sqrt{2}}{2}$ use the CAST diagram to find the exact value of cos 315°

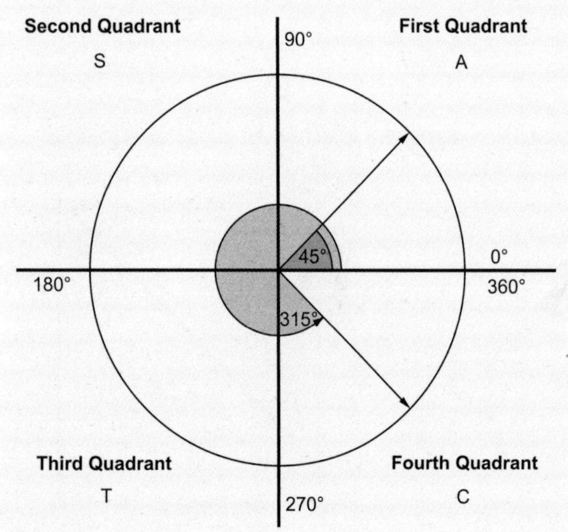

Note that 315° is a reflection of 45° in the 0° line.

This means we can work out the cosine of 315° using the cosine of 45°.

Cosine is positive in the fourth quadrant, so:

$$\cos 315° = \frac{\sqrt{2}}{2}$$

If you are given one trigonometric ratio and asked to find another, a sketch of a right–angled triangle is often useful.

EXAMPLE 2

Given $\sin x = \frac{2}{\sqrt{6}}$, where x is an acute angle, find the exact values of $\cos x$ and $\tan x$

We have been given the opposite and hypotenuse sides in a right-angled triangle:

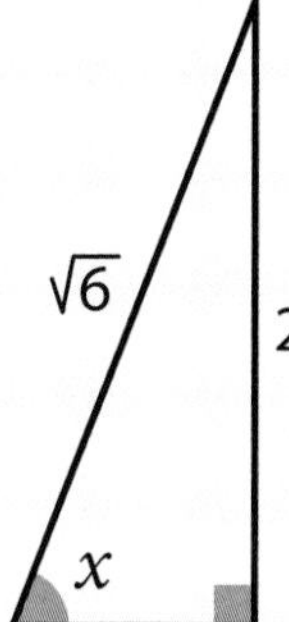

We can calculate a using **Pythagoras' Theorem:**

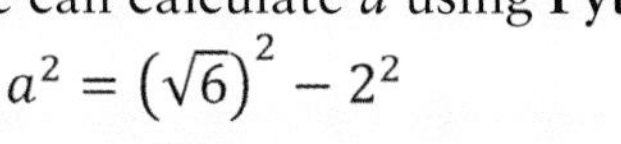

$$a^2 = \left(\sqrt{6}\right)^2 - 2^2$$

$$a = \sqrt{2}$$

Now we can look at the triangle again to work out $\cos x$ and $\tan x$.

$$\cos x = \frac{adjacent}{hypotenuse}$$

$$= \frac{\sqrt{2}}{\sqrt{6}} = \frac{1}{\sqrt{3}}$$

$$\tan x = \frac{opposite}{adjacent}$$

$$= \frac{2}{\sqrt{2}} = \sqrt{2}$$

Note: the question asks for exact values. This means leaving the answers as surds.
Note also: this question does not ask you to find the angle itself.

If you are asked for trigonometric ratios of an obtuse angle first consider the related acute angle.

EXAMPLE 3

Given that x is obtuse and $\cos x = -\frac{3}{5}$, find $\sin x$ and $\tan x$.

---

x is obtuse, so the angle lies in the second quadrant. $\cos x$ is always negative in the second quadrant. The associated acute angle y lies in the first quadrant and $\cos y$ is positive, i.e. $\cos y = \frac{3}{5}$. So we can draw the triangle.

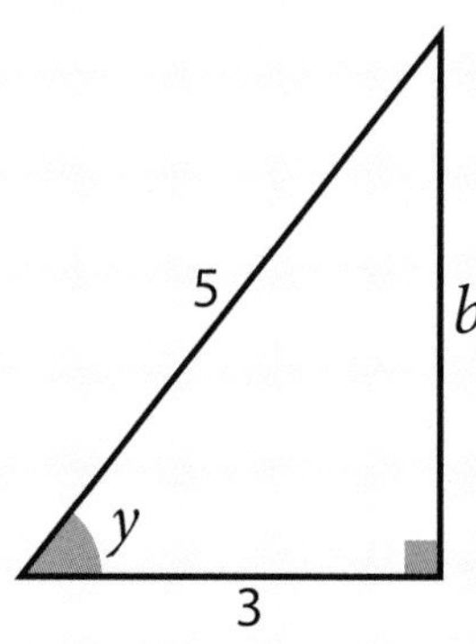

Next, calculate b using **Pythagoras' Theorem:**

$$b^2 = 5^2 - 3^2$$

$$b = 4$$

Look at the triangle to work out $\cos y$ and $\tan y$ for the acute angle y.

$$\sin y = \frac{opposite}{hypotenuse}$$

$$= \frac{4}{5}$$

$$\tan y = \frac{opposite}{adjacent}$$

$$= \frac{4}{3}$$

continued...

Example 3...

Since the angle x is obtuse, we know it lies in the second quadrant, where sine is always positive. Therefore:

$$\sin x = \frac{4}{5}$$

The tan function is always negative in the second quadrant, therefore:

$$\tan x = -\frac{4}{3}$$

(The angle is 126.8°, but you are not required to find this.)

If you have to find trigonometric ratios for reflex angles, use the same technique: consider first the associated acute angle.

When finding an angle, you will often have to find all the possible solutions within a given range.

EXAMPLE 4

$$\cos x = \frac{\sqrt{3}}{2}$$

Find all the possible values of x in the range $-2\pi < x \leq 2\pi$

We know that one solution is $x = \frac{\pi}{6}$, within the first quadrant.

The cosine function is also positive in the fourth quadrant. Our next solution is therefore

$$x = 2\pi - \frac{\pi}{6}$$
$$= \frac{11\pi}{6}$$

All other solutions can be found by adding or subtracting 2π. Adding 2π to our first two answers would give us solutions that are not within the desired range.

However, we can obtain two more solutions by subtracting 2π.

$$x = \frac{\pi}{6} - 2\pi = -\frac{11\pi}{6}$$
$$x = \frac{11\pi}{6} - 2\pi = -\frac{\pi}{6}$$

The complete set of solutions is: $-\frac{11\pi}{6}, -\frac{\pi}{6}, \frac{\pi}{6}, \frac{11\pi}{6}$

EXERCISE

EXERCISE 9G

1. Sketch the graph of $y = \sin x$, where x is in radians and $0 < x < 2\pi$.
2. Sketch the graph of $y = \cos x$, where x is in radians and $0 < x < 2\pi$.
3. Sketch the graph of $y = \tan x$, where x is in radians and $0 < x < 2\pi$.
4. Using the graph of $y = \sin x$, state how many solutions there are for $0° \leq x \leq 360°$ to the equations:

   a) $\sin x = \frac{1}{2}$ b) $\sin x = 0$ c) $\sin x = 2$ d) $\sin x = 1$

EXERCISE

5. Using the graph of $y = \cos x$, where x is in radians, state how many solutions there are for $-\pi \leq x \leq \pi$ to the equations:

   a) $\cos x = -\frac{1}{2}$ b) $\cos x = 0$ c) $\cos x = -2$ d) $\cos x = -1$

6. Using the graph of $y = \tan x$, state how many solutions there are for $0° \leq x \leq 360°$ to the equations:

   a) $\tan x = -\frac{1}{2}$ b) $\tan x = 0$ c) $\tan x = 2$ d) $\tan x = -1$

7. Using the CAST diagram, find the following:

   a) Given $\sin 60° = \frac{\sqrt{3}}{2}$, find $\sin 120°$ b) Given $\cos 45° = \frac{\sqrt{2}}{2}$, find $\cos 135°$

   c) Given $\tan 45° = 1$, find $\tan 225°$ d) Given $\tan\frac{\pi}{6} = \frac{\sqrt{3}}{3}$, find $\tan\frac{5\pi}{6}$

   e) Given $\cos\frac{\pi}{3} = \frac{1}{2}$, find $\cos\frac{4\pi}{3}$ f) Given $\sin\frac{\pi}{4} = \frac{\sqrt{2}}{2}$, find $\sin\frac{7\pi}{4}$

8. Find the following trigonometric ratios using the information given and Pythagoras' Theorem:

   a) Given $\cos x = \frac{3}{7}$, and x is acute, find $\sin x$ and $\tan x$.

   b) Given $\tan x = \frac{4}{\sqrt{3}}$, and x is acute, find $\cos x$ and $\sin x$.

   c) Given $\sin x = \frac{10}{11}$, and x is acute, find $\cos x$ and $\tan x$.

   d) Given $\cos x = \sqrt{\frac{3}{7}}$, and x is acute, find $\sin x$ and $\tan x$.

   e) Given $\tan x = \frac{\sqrt{3}+1}{\sqrt{3}-1}$, and x is acute, find $\cos x$ and $\sin x$.

   f) Given $\cos x = \frac{\sqrt{5}}{3}$, and x is acute, find $\sin x$ and $\tan x$.

   g) Given $\tan x = 1$, and x is acute, find $\cos x$ and $\sin x$.

   h) Given $\cos x = -\frac{1}{3}$ and x is obtuse, find $\sin x$ and $\tan x$.

   i) Given $\sin x = \frac{3}{8}$ and x is obtuse, find $\cos x$ and $\tan x$.

   j) Given $\tan x = -\frac{1}{6}$ and x is obtuse, find $\cos x$ and $\sin x$.

   k) Given $\tan x = \frac{2}{5}$ and x is reflex, find $\cos x$ and $\sin x$.

9. Find all the values of x satisfying the following within the range specified.

   a) $\tan x = \sqrt{3}$, $0° \leq x < 360°$ b) $\cos x = -\frac{\sqrt{3}}{2}$, $0° \leq x < 360°$

   c) $\sin x = \frac{1}{2}$, $-180° \leq x < 180°$ d) $\tan x = 1$, $-180° \leq x < 180°$

   e) $\cos x = -\frac{1}{\sqrt{2}}$, $-180° \leq x < 180°$ f) $\sin x = \frac{\sqrt{3}}{2}$, $0 \leq x < 2\pi$

continued...

EXERCISE

g) $\cos x = \frac{1}{\sqrt{2}}, 0 \le x < 2\pi$

h) $\sin x = \frac{1}{2}, 0 \le x < 4\pi$

i) $\tan x = -\frac{1}{\sqrt{3}}, -2\pi \le x < 2\pi$

j) $\sin x = -2, 0 \le x < 4\pi$

9.6 Transformations of Trigonometric Graphs

Revision

In the C1 module, you learnt about transformations of curves.

Translations

To translate an object is to move it without changing its shape.

Any curve can be translated in these two ways:
- add a constant to perform a translation parallel to the y-axis;
- replace x with $(x \pm a)$ to perform a translation parallel to the x-axis.

These translations can be combined to perform a translation in both directions at once.

Reflecting and Stretching

The graph $y = -f(x)$ of is a reflection in the x-axis of $y = f(x)$.

The graph $y = f(-x)$ of is a reflection in the y-axis of $y = f(x)$.

The graph of $y = af(x)$ is a stretch parallel to the y-axis of $y = f(x)$.

The graph of $y = f(ax)$ is a stretch of the graph of $y = f(x)$ parallel to the x-axis, with a stretch factor of $\frac{1}{a}$, or a shrinking of the graph of $f(x)$ with a shrink factor of a.

All of these transformations can be applied to the trigonometric functions.

EXAMPLE 1

Plot the graph of $y = \cos(x + 30°)$

When compared with $y = \cos x$, we have replaced x with $(x + 30°)$. This is a translation by 30° parallel to the x-axis, in the negative direction.

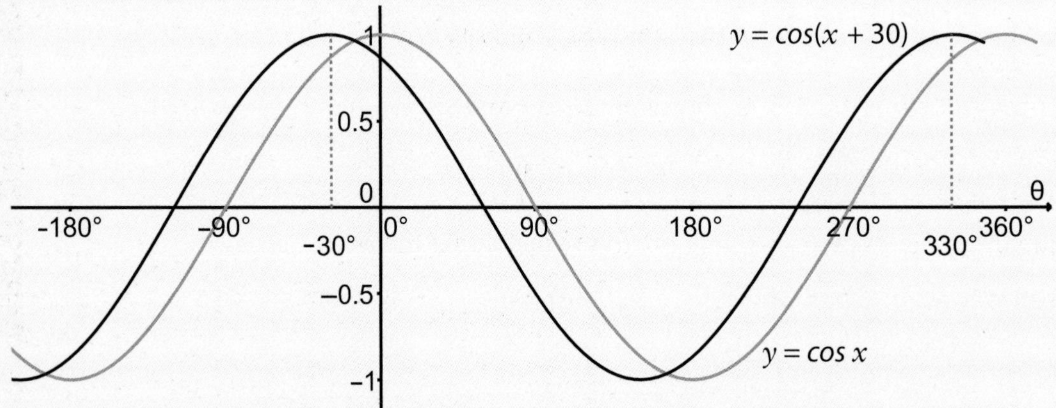

The graph of $y = \cos(x + 30°)$ has maxima at (–30°, 1) and (330°, 1).

It has a minimum at (150°, –1)

EXAMPLE 2

Plot the graph of $y = 3sin\ 2x$

When compared with $y = sin x$, this is a stretch, scale factor ½, in the x direction, followed by a stretch, scale factor 3, in the y direction.

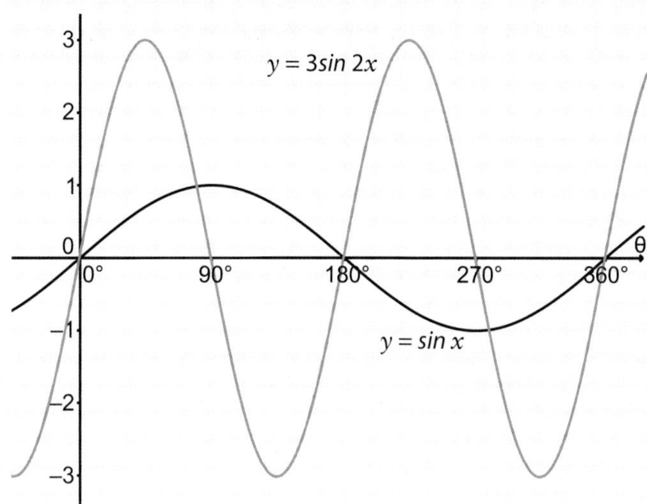

The graph of $y = 3sin\ 2x$ has a maximum at (45°, 3) and a minimum at (135°, –3).

The period of $y = 3sin\ 2x$ is 180°

EXERCISE 9H

1. Sketch each pair of curves on the same diagram for $0° \le x \le 360°$
   a) $y = sin\,x,\ y = 1 + sin\,x$ b) $y = cos\,x,\ y = -1 + cos\,x$
   c) $y = tan\,x,\ y = 1 + tan\,x$ d) $y = sin\,x,\ y = sin(x + 45°)$
   e) $y = cos\,x,\ y = cos(x - 30°)$ f) $y = tan\,x,\ y = tan(x + 90°)$

2. Sketch each pair of curves on the same diagram for $0 \le x \le 2\pi$
   a) $y = sin\,x,\ y = -1 + sin\,x$ b) $y = cos\,x,\ y = cos\,x - 2$
   c) $y = tan\,x,\ y = tan\,x - 1$ d) $y = sin\,x,\ y = sin\left(x + \frac{\pi}{3}\right)$
   e) $y = cos\,x,\ y = cos\left(x - \frac{\pi}{4}\right)$ f) $y = tan\,x,\ y = tan\left(x + \frac{\pi}{6}\right)$

3. Sketch each pair of curves on the same diagram for $0° \le x \le 360°$
   a) $y = sin\,x,\ y = -sin\,x$ b) $y = cos\,x,\ y = -cos\,x$
   c) $y = tan\,x,\ y = -tan\,x$

4. Sketch each pair of curves on the same diagram for $0° \le x \le 360°$ and write down the period of each.
   a) $y = cos\,x,\ y = cos\ 2x$ b) $y = sin\,x,\ y = sin\frac{x}{2}$
   c) $y = tan\,x,\ y = tan\ 2x$ d) $y = cos\,x,\ y = cos\ 3x$

EXERCISE EXERCISE

5. Sketch the following pairs of curves on the same diagram.
   a) $y = \sin x$, $y = -\sin(x + 30°)$ for $0° \leq x \leq 360°$
   b) $y = \cos x$, $y = 2\cos(x - 60°)$ for $0° \leq x \leq 360°$
   c) $y = \tan x$, $y = 2\tan(-x)$ for $0° \leq x \leq 180°$
   d) $y = \sin x$, $y = 2\sin(2x)$ for $0 \leq x \leq 2\pi$
   e) $y = \cos x$, $y = 2\cos\left(\frac{x}{2}\right)$ for $0 \leq x \leq 2\pi$
   f) $y = \tan x$, $y = -\frac{1}{2}\tan(-x)$ for $0° \leq x \leq 180°$

6. Write down the equations for the functions sketched here.

(a)

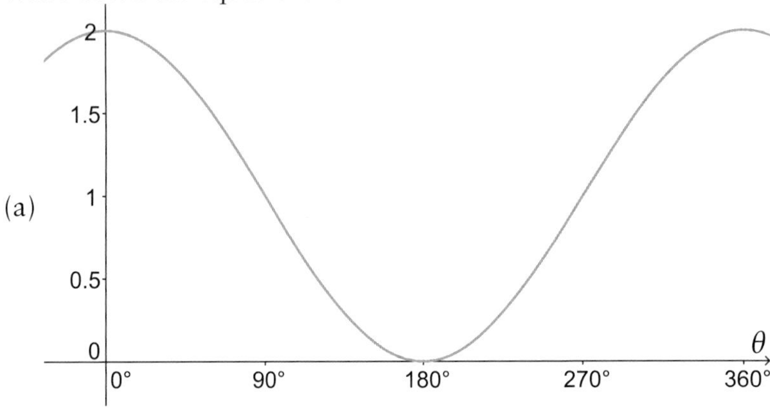

(b)

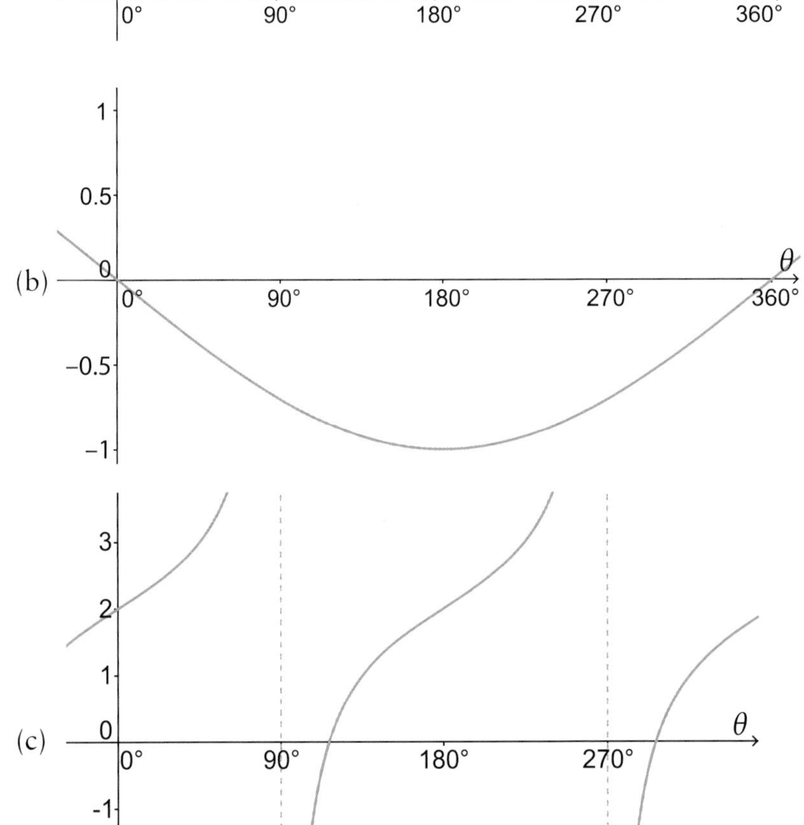

(c)

3
2
1
0
θ
0°
90°
180°
270°
-1
-2
-3

EXERCISE

EXERCISE

(d)

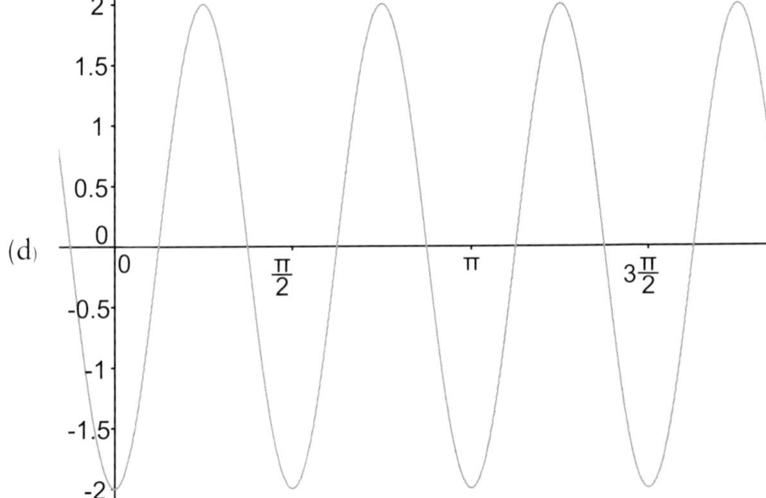

7. Plot the four graphs of:
$y = cos\, x$, $y = -\sin(x - 90°)$, $y = sin(x + 90°)$, $y = -cos(x + 180°)$
on the same diagram.

What do you notice?

9.7 Trigonometry Identities

Notation

Throughout this section, you will come across the symbol ≡. This is the identity symbol. It indicates that something is always true, not just for some particular values of x or θ.

An important result to remember is:

$$tan\,\theta \equiv \frac{sin\,\theta}{cos\,\theta}$$

PROOF

You do not need to learn this proof, but you will use the result more than any other trigonometric identity.

$$\frac{sin\,\theta}{cos\,\theta} = \frac{opposite}{hypotenuse} \div \frac{adjacent}{hypotenuse}$$

$$= \frac{opposite}{hypotenuse} \times \frac{hypotenuse}{adjacent}$$

$$= \frac{opposite}{adjacent}$$

$$= tan\,\theta$$

$$\therefore tan\,\theta \equiv \frac{sin\,\theta}{cos\,\theta}$$

You will also need to remember:

$$\sin^2\theta + \cos^2\theta \equiv 1$$

PROOF

You do not need to learn this proof, but you will use the result very frequently.

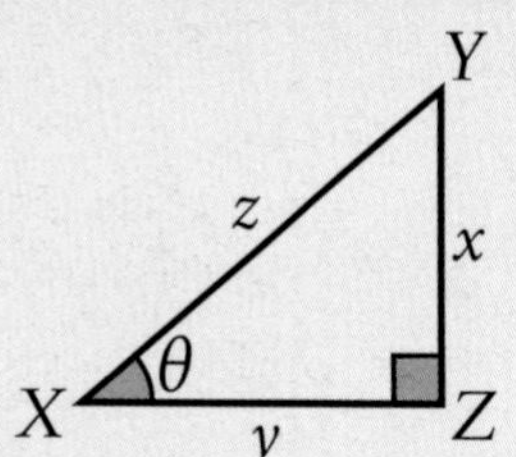

$$\sin^2\theta + \cos^2\theta = \frac{x^2}{z^2} + \frac{y^2}{z^2}$$

$$= \frac{x^2 + y^2}{z^2}$$

Using Pythagoras' Theorem:

$$x^2 + y^2 = z^2$$

$$\therefore \sin^2\theta + \cos^2\theta = \frac{z^2}{z^2}$$

$$\therefore \sin^2\theta + \cos^2\theta \equiv 1$$

The two results above can be used to simplify many other trigonometric expressions and to prove many identities.

EXAMPLE 1

Simplify $\cos x + \sqrt{1 - \sin^2 x}$

Use $\sin^2 x + \cos^2 x = 1$

Re-arranging gives: $1 - \sin^2 x = \cos^2 x$

$$\therefore \cos x + \sqrt{1 - \sin^2 x} = \cos x + \sqrt{\cos^2 x}$$

$$= \cos x + \cos x$$

$$= 2\cos x$$

When proving an identity, take the expression on one side of the equals sign, then work on it one step at a time until you reach the expression on the other side. We use the abbreviations *LHS* for left–hand side and for *RHS* right–hand side.

EXAMPLE 2

Prove the identity $\tan x \cos x \sin x \equiv \sin^2 x$

$LHS = \dfrac{\sin x}{\cos x}\cos x \sin x$ (using $\tan x = \dfrac{\sin x}{\cos x}$)

$= \sin x \sin x$ (cancelling $\cos x$)

$= \sin^2 x$

$= RHS$

$\therefore \tan x \cos x \sin x \equiv \sin^2 x$

EXAMPLE 3

Prove the identity $tan\,x + \frac{1}{tan\,x} \equiv \frac{1}{sin\,x} + \frac{1}{cos\,x}$

$$LHS = \frac{sin\,x}{cos\,x} + \frac{cos\,x}{sin\,x} \qquad \text{(using } tan\,x = \frac{sin\,x}{cos\,x}\text{)}$$
$$= \frac{sin\,x + cos\,x}{sin\,x\,cos\,x}$$
$$= \frac{sin\,x}{sin\,x\,cos\,x} + \frac{cos\,x}{sin\,x\,cos\,x}$$
$$= \frac{1}{cos\,x} + \frac{1}{sin\,x}$$
$$= RHS$$
$$\therefore tan\,x + \frac{1}{tan\,x} \equiv \frac{1}{sin\,x} + \frac{1}{cos\,x}$$

EXERCISE 9I

1. Simplify the following trigonometric expressions:

a) $\frac{cos\,x}{sin\,x}$

b) $sin^2\,3x + cos^2\,3x$

c) $\sqrt{tan^2\,x\,cos^2\,x}$

d) $\frac{1 - sin^2\,A}{cos^2\,A} - \frac{1 - cos^2\,A}{sin^2\,A}$

e) $sin^2\,A + 2\,cos^2\,A$

f) $(cos\,x + sin\,x)^2 + (cos\,x - sin\,x)^2$

g) $1 + \frac{1}{tan^2\,x}$

h) $(tan\,A\,cos\,A)^2 + \left(\frac{sin\,A}{tan\,A}\right)^2$

i) $(sin\,x - 1)(sin\,x + 1)(cos\,x - 1)(cos\,x + 1)$

j) $\frac{sin\,\theta}{\frac{1}{sin\,\theta} - sin\,\theta}$

2. Prove the following identities:

a) $\frac{1 - cos^2\,x}{tan\,x} \equiv sin\,x\,cos\,x$

b) $(cos\,A - sin\,A)^2 \equiv 1 - 2\,sin\,A\,cos\,A$

c) $2\,sin^2\,\theta + 14\,cos^2\,\theta - 2 \equiv 12\,cos^2\,\theta$

d) $sin^2\,x\,(1 - sin^2\,x)\left(1 + \frac{1}{tan^2\,x}\right) \equiv cos^2\,x$

e) $\frac{\sqrt{1 - cos^2\,x}}{cos\,x} \equiv tan\,x$

f) $\frac{-\,sin\,x + 2\,cos\,x}{cos\,x} \equiv 2 - tan\,x$

g) $\frac{\sqrt{1 - sin^2\,x}}{cos\,x} \equiv 1$

h) $tan\,B + \frac{1}{tan\,B} \equiv \frac{1}{sin\,B\,cos\,B}$

i) $\frac{sin\,\theta}{cos\,\theta\,tan\,\theta} + \frac{6}{tan\,\theta} - \frac{6\,sin^2\,\theta}{tan\,\theta} \equiv \frac{6\,cos^2\,\theta}{tan\,\theta} + 1$

j) $tan\,x \equiv \sqrt{sin^2\,x\,tan^2\,x + sin^2\,x}$

3. $x = t\,cos\,\theta$ and $y = t\,sin\,\theta$. Find a simplified expression for $\sqrt{x^2 + y^2}$.

EXERCISE

9.8 Solution of Trigonometric Equations

You will often be asked to solve a trigonometric equation, for example find all solutions to:

$3 - 3cos\theta - sin^2\theta = 0$ for $-\pi < \theta < \pi$

Because of the periodic nature of the trigonometric functions, there will usually be more than one solution. Typically, you will find the first solution on your calculator, often an acute angle. This is called the **principal value**. Then you will use the CAST diagram, or a sketch of the trigonometric graph to find the remaining solutions within the range specified, e.g. between 0° and 360°.

In the C2 module, questions are usually one of the following types:

1. Simple equations with multiple solutions, e.g. $sin\,x = \frac{1}{2}$
2. Equations involving multiple angles, e.g. $cos(3x - 45°) = \frac{\sqrt{3}}{2}$
3. Equations requiring $tan\,x = \frac{sin\,x}{cos\,x}$
4. Quadratics involving just one trig function, e.g. $tan^2\,x - 2\,tan\,x + 1 = 0$
5. Quadratics requiring the identity $sin^2\,x + cos^2\,x \equiv 1$

The 'Cheat Sheet' for solving trigonometric equations is at the end of this chapter.

EXAMPLE 1

Solve the equation $cos\,x = \frac{\sqrt{3}}{2}$ for $-360° \leq x \leq 360°$

From the calculator: $x = cos^{-1}\left(\frac{\sqrt{3}}{2}\right)$

Note: Some calculators have buttons marked arcsin, arccos and arctan, instead of sin^{-1}, cos^{-1} and tan^{-1}. Usually you will press SHIFT-sin, SHIFT-cos, etc.

From the calculator, $x = 30°$. This solution is an acute angle.

Now use the CAST diagram to find the other answers in the range specified. Cosine is positive in quadrants 1 and 4. Therefore, a second solution can be found by reflecting $x = 30°$ in the x-axis.

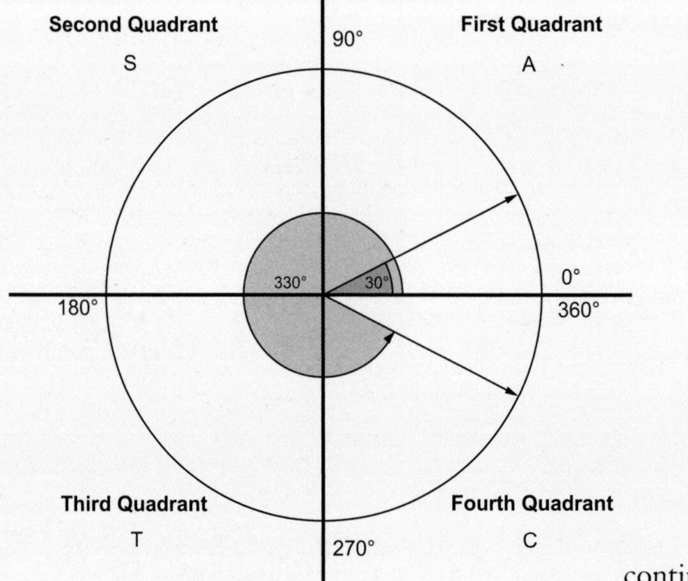

continued...

Example 1...

So $x = 330°$ is a second solution.

The sine curve has period 360°. Therefore, any subsequent solutions can be found by adding or subtracting 360° from these two solutions, bearing in mind that the specified range is $-360° \leq x \leq 360°$.

$30° + 360° = 390°$ – not in the specified range.

$330° + 360° = 690°$ – not in the specified range.

$30° - 360° = -330°$ – within the specified range.

$330° - 360° = -30°$ – within the specified range.

Subtracting 360° again would take us outside the range.

Therefore, our four solutions are –330°, –30°, 30°, 330°.

(Check your answers on your calculator!)

You will often have to find the solutions to trigonometric equations involving multiple angles. For these problems, use a substitution.

EXAMPLE 2

Find all solutions to $tan\, 2\theta = \sqrt{3}$ within the range $-180° \leq \theta \leq 180°$

Use the substitution $x = 2\theta$. Then $tan\, x = \sqrt{3}$.

From the calculator, $x = 60°$. This is an acute angle.

Using the CAST diagram, we can find a second solution. The tangent function is positive in the first and third quadrants. We find the second solution by rotating the first through 180°:

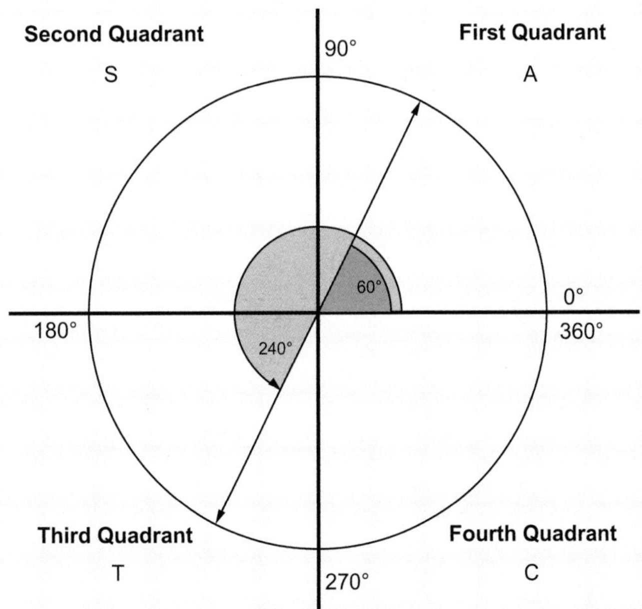

continued...

Example 2...

$x = 240°$ is a possible solution.

The tangent function has period 180°, so further solutions can be found by adding or subtracting 180° from these two solutions:

$x = \cdots - 480°, -300°, -120°, 60°, 240°, 420°, \ldots$

Now $x = 2\theta \Rightarrow \theta = \frac{x}{2}$

So solutions for θ are found by halving our answers for x:

$\theta = \cdots - 240°, -150°, -60°, 30°, 120°, 210°, \ldots$

Within the range $-180° \leq \theta \leq 180°$, $\theta = -150°, -60°, 30°, 120°$

Check your answers on your calculator.

You can solve equations where the angle is a sum or a difference in a similar way.

EXAMPLE 3

Find all solutions to $sin\left(x + \frac{\pi}{3}\right) = \frac{1}{2}$ for $-\pi \leq x \leq \pi$

Here the angle x is measured in radians.

Use a substitution $\theta = x + \frac{\pi}{3}$. Now we must solve $sin\,\theta = \frac{1}{2}$

From the calculator, one solution is $\theta = \frac{\pi}{6}$, which is an acute angle.

Since sine is positive in the first and second quadrants, a second solution for θ can be found by reflecting the first solution in the y-axis.

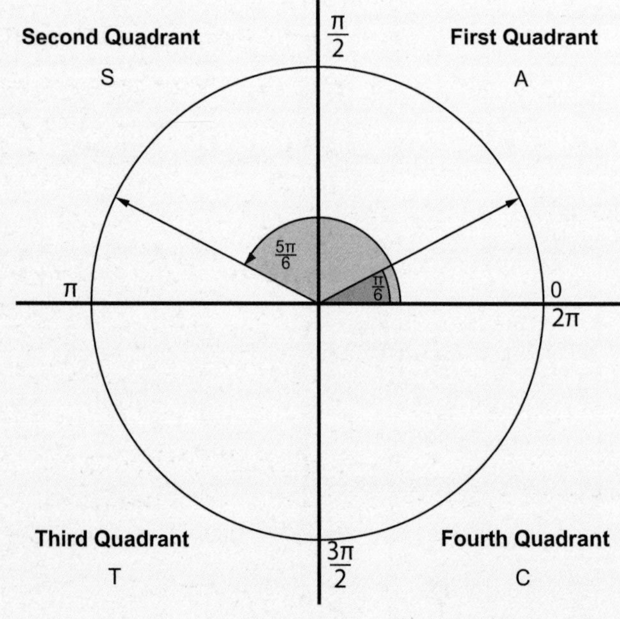

$\theta = \frac{\pi}{6}, \frac{5\pi}{6}$

Since the sine function has a period of 2π radians, subsequent solutions can be found by adding or subtracting 2π from the two solutions already found:

$\theta = \cdots - \frac{11\pi}{6}, -\frac{7\pi}{6}, \frac{\pi}{6}, \frac{5\pi}{6}, \frac{13\pi}{6}, \frac{17\pi}{6}, \ldots$

Now: $\theta = x + \frac{\pi}{3} \Rightarrow x = \theta - \frac{\pi}{3}$

So: $x = \cdots - \frac{13\pi}{6}, -\frac{3\pi}{2}, -\frac{\pi}{6}, \frac{\pi}{2}, \frac{11\pi}{6}, \frac{5\pi}{2}, \ldots$

Since the specified range is $-\pi \leq x \leq \pi$, there are only two solutions:

$x = -\frac{\pi}{6}, \frac{\pi}{2}$

Note: Do not fall into the trap of replacing $sin\left(x+\frac{\pi}{3}\right)$ with $sin\,x + sin\left(\frac{\pi}{3}\right)$.
These two expressions are not equal. To use mathematical language, the sine function is not distributive. Neither are the other trigonometry functions.

You will use a similar technique when the trigonometric ratio is squared, or raised to some other power.

EXAMPLE 4

Solve $4\,tan^2 x = 1$ for $-\pi \leq x \leq \pi$.

$$4\,tan^2 x = 1$$

$$\Rightarrow tan^2 x = \frac{1}{4}$$

$$\Rightarrow tan\,x = \pm\frac{1}{2}$$

Consider first $tan\,x = \frac{1}{2}$ The calculator gives $x = 0.464\ radians$, which is an acute angle.
Using the CAST diagram, we obtain a second solution $x = 3.605\ radians$, but this is outside the specified range.

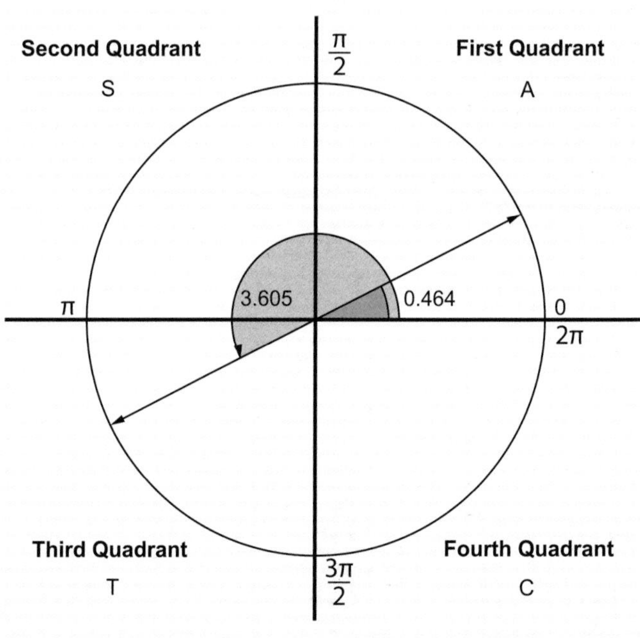

The tangent function has period π radians, so we add and subtract π to find subsequent solutions:

$0.464 - \pi = -2.678\ radians.$

This is the only other solution within the specified range.

Next, consider $tan\,x = -\frac{1}{2}$.
The calculator gives $x = -0.464\ radians.$

Since this solution lies in the fourth quadrant, the tan function is negative. Using the CAST diagram, we obtain a second solution in the second quadrant, where tan is also negative.

continued...

Example 4...

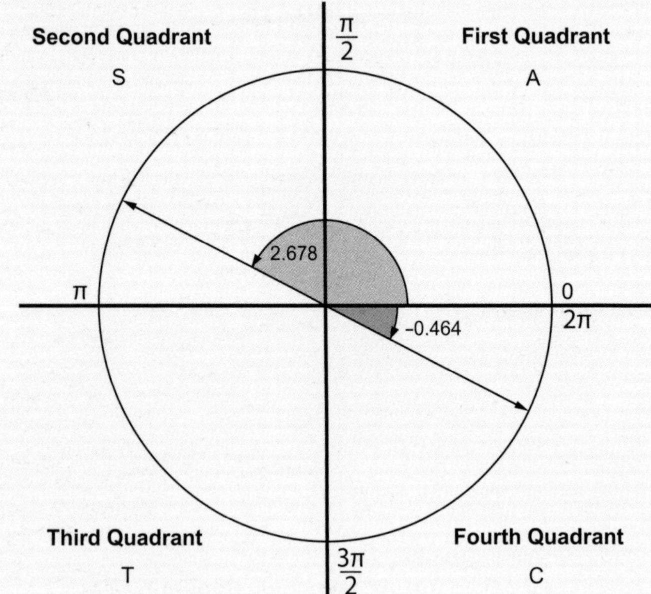

$x = 2.678\ radians.$

This is within the specified range.

Adding and subtracting π from these two solutions does not give us any additional solutions within the range.

Combining the solutions, we have:

$x = -2.68, -0.46, 0.46, 2.68\ radians$ (2 d.p.)

You will often have to re-arrange a trigonometric equation before solving it. Use the usual rules of algebra, treating $sin\,\theta$, for example, as the unknown.

EXAMPLE 5

Find solutions to the equation $sin^2 x = \dfrac{3 - 5\,sin\,x}{2}$ where $0° \leq x \leq 360°$

$$sin^2 x = \frac{3 - 5\,sin\,x}{2}$$

Re-arrange: $2\,sin^2 x = 3 - 5\,sin\,x$

$2\,sin^2 x + 5\,sin\,x - 3 = 0$

Now we have a quadratic equation, with $sin\,x$ as the unknown.

Factorising: $(2\,sin\,x - 1)(sin\,x + 3) = 0$

$$sin\,x = \frac{1}{2} \text{ or } sin\,x = -3$$

There are no solutions to $sin\,x = -3$, since the sine function gives answers between 0 and 1. Consider the sine graph to convince yourself of this!

We solve $sin\,x = \frac{1}{2}$ in the usual way.

The first answer is obtained from the calculator: $x = 30°$.

Subsequent answers can be obtained from the CAST diagram:

continued...

Example 5...

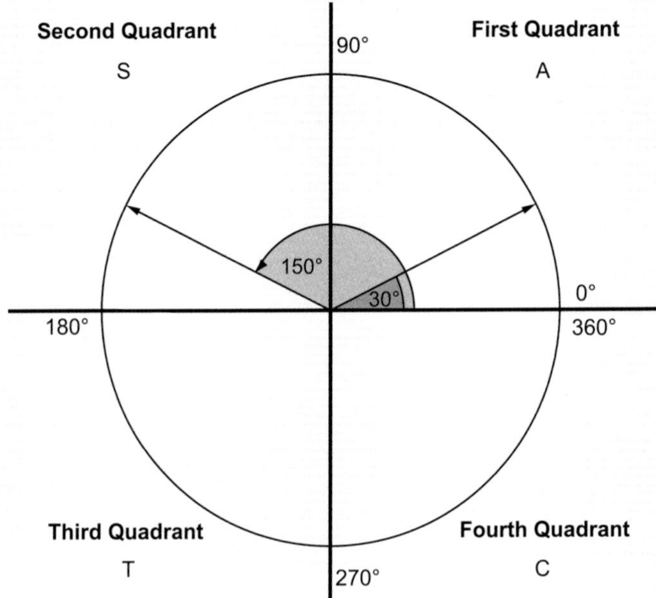

The sine function is positive in the second quadrant, so the second solution is 150°.

Sine has period 360°, but adding and subtracting 360° to our two solutions does not give any additional results within the specified range.

Therefore $x = 30°, 150°$.

You may need to use the quadratic formula if you cannot factorise a quadratic.

EXAMPLE 6

Find solutions to: $4(tan^2\,\theta - tan\,\theta) = 1$ in the range $-\pi \leq \theta \leq \pi$.
Give your answers to 3 significant figures.

$$4(tan^2\,\theta - tan\,\theta) = 1$$

Re-arrange: $4\,tan^2\,\theta - 4\,tan\,\theta - 1 = 0$

Using the formula: $$tan\,\theta = \frac{4 \pm \sqrt{16 - 4(4)(-1)}}{8}$$

$$tan\,\theta = \frac{4 \pm \sqrt{32}}{8}$$

$$tan\,\theta = \frac{1 \pm \sqrt{2}}{2}$$

First consider $tan\,\theta = \dfrac{1 + \sqrt{2}}{2}$

From the calculator, $\theta = 0.8790\,...$

Use the CAST diagram in the usual way to obtain $\theta = -2.263, 0.8790$. Adding and subtracting π gives no more solutions within the specified range.

Then consider $tan\,\theta = \dfrac{1 - \sqrt{2}}{2}$

From the calculator, $\theta = -0.2042\,....$

Use the CAST diagram again to obtain $\theta = -0.2071, 2.937$. Adding and subtracting π gives no more solutions within the specified range.

Therefore: $\theta = -2.26, -0.204, 0.879, 2.94$ (3 s.f.)

When re-arranging your equation, you will often make use of your trigonometry identities.

EXAMPLE 7

Find all the values of θ in the range $0° \leq \theta \leq 360°$ satisfying $4\, sin\, \theta\, tan\, \theta = 15$

$$4\, sin\, \theta\, tan\, \theta = 15$$

$$4\, sin\, \theta \left(\frac{sin\, \theta}{cos\, \theta}\right) = 15$$

$$\Rightarrow \frac{4\, sin^2\, \theta}{cos\, \theta} = 15$$

$$\Rightarrow 4(1 - cos^2\, \theta) = 15\, cos\, \theta$$

$$\Rightarrow 4\, cos^2\, \theta + 15\, cos\, \theta - 4 = 0$$

$$\Rightarrow (4\, cos\, \theta - 1)(cos\, \theta + 4) = 0$$

$$\Rightarrow cos\, \theta = \frac{1}{4}$$

$$\theta = 75.5°, 284° \text{ (3 s.f.)}$$

GOTCHA!

When re-arranging a trigonometric equation, be careful when dividing by a trigonometric function. Consider this example:

$sin\, x\, cos\, x = sin\, x$

Dividing both sides of the equation by $sin\, x$ may seem sensible. But this approach will result in losing solutions to the equation. Instead, you should re-arrange:

$sin\, x\, cos\, x - sin\, x = 0$

and factorise:

$sin\, x\, (cos\, x - 1) = 0$

To obtain all solutions, we must solve $sin\, x = 0$ or $cos\, x - 1 = 0$. If you had cancelled $sin\, x$ as your first step, you would have lost all the solutions resulting from $sin\, x = 0$.

EXERCISE

EXERCISE 9J

1. Solve these equations, giving all solutions between 0° and 360°, correct to 3 significant figures where appropriate.

a) $sin\, x = \frac{\sqrt{3}}{2}$ b) $cos\, x = -\frac{1}{2}$ c) $cos\, \theta = -0.43$

d) $tan\, \theta = 2$ e) $cos\, A = 0.25$ f) $sin\, y = \frac{\sqrt{5}}{5}$

g) $tan\, x = 0.2$ h) $cos\, A = 0.77$ i) $cos\, x = 0.99$

j) $tan\, t = \frac{11}{7}$ k) $cos\, \theta = \frac{1}{3}$ l) $\sin z = \frac{1 - \sqrt{3}}{2}$

m) $cos\, y = \sqrt{2} - 1$ n) $\cos \theta = -0.6$ o) $sin\, x = 0.15$

EXERCISE

EXERCISE

2. Solve the following trigonometric equations giving angles in the range $0 < x < 2\pi$ to 2 decimal places.
   a) $sin\,x = 0.82$ b) $cos\,x = 0.77$ c) $cos\,x = -0.49$
   d) $sin\,x = -0.23$ e) $tan\,x = -0.94$

3. Solve these equations, giving all solutions between 0° and 180°, correct to 3 significant figures where appropriate.
   a) $tan\,2\theta = 2$ b) $sin\,2x = 0.8$ c) $cos\,2x = -0.5$
   d) $sin\,3x = \frac{\sqrt{2}}{2}$ e) $tan\,3\theta = 30$ f) $sin\left(\frac{x}{2}\right) = \frac{3}{4}$
   g) $cos\left(\frac{x}{3}\right) = -\frac{\sqrt{3}}{2}$ h) $cos(4y) = \frac{1}{2}$ i) $tan\left(\frac{x}{3}\right) = -1$
   j) $sin\left(\frac{A}{2}\right) = 0.6$

4. Solve these equations, giving all solutions between 0° and 360° or 0 and 2π as appropriate. Give your answers to 3 significant figures where appropriate.
   a) $tan(x - 45°) = \sqrt{3}$ b) $tan\left(x + \frac{\pi}{3}\right) = 1$
   c) $cos(x - 90°) = \frac{1}{\sqrt{2}}$ d) $1 + sin(x - 30°) = \frac{1}{2}$
   e) $tan(x + 20°) = \frac{1}{\sqrt{2}}$ f) $tan(2x) = 1$ (x in radians)
   g) $sin(3x - 30°) = \frac{1}{2}$ h) $cos(2x - 120°) + 1 = 1$
   i) $tan(10° - 2x) = \frac{\sqrt{3}}{3}$ j) $cos\left(2x + \frac{\pi}{6}\right) = -\frac{1}{2}$

5. Solve these equations, giving all solutions between 0° and 360° or 0 and 2π as appropriate. Give your answers to 3 significant figures where appropriate.
   a) $cos^2\,\theta = \frac{3}{4}$ (θ in degrees) b) $sin^2\,x = \frac{1}{9}$ (x in degrees)
   c) $tan^2\,y = 3$ (y in degrees) d) $10\,cos^2\,x - \frac{5}{2} = 0$ (x in radians)
   e) $2\,cos^2\,x + cos\,x = 0$ (x in radians) f) $sin\,x(cos\,x + sin\,x) = 0$ (x in radians)

6. Solve the following quadratics by re-arranging, if necessary, then factorising. Give your answers in degrees, to 3 significant figures where appropriate, between 0° and 360°.
   a) $sin^2\,x + sin\,x - 2 = 0$ b) $2\,cos^2\,\theta + cos\,\theta - 1 = 0$
   c) $tan^2\,t - tan\,t - 6 = 0$ d) $tan^2\,x - 3\,tan\,x = 4$
   e) $6\,sin^2\,y - 16\,cos\,y = 0$ f) $sin^2\,x = 1 + cos\,x$
   g) $3\,cos^2\,\theta - 2\,cos\,\theta - 1 = sin^2\,\theta$ h) $cos^2\,x - 3(1 + sin\,x) = 0$

7. Use the quadratic formula to solve the following. Give your answers in degrees, to 3 significant figures where appropriate, between 0° and 360°.
   a) $2\,tan^2\,x - tan\,x - 3 = 0$ b) $sin^2\,x - 5\,sin\,x - 2 = 0$
   c) $2\,cos^2\,x + 3\,cos\,x - 4 = 0$ d) $7\,cos^2\,x - 2\,cos\,x - 4 = 0$

8. Use the quadratic formula to solve the following. Give your answers in radians, to 3 significant figures where appropriate, between $-\pi$ and π.
   a) $sin^2\,\theta + 2\,sin\,\theta - 2 = 0$ b) $cos^2\,x - 4\,cos\,x = -1$
   c) $2\,tan^2\,y - 2\,tan\,y - 3 = 0$ d) $2sin^2\,x + sin\,x = 2$
   e) $2\,tan\,\theta = \sqrt{3}(tan\,\theta - 1)(tan\,\theta + 1)$

EXERCISE

9. Solve the equation: $\sin x = \cos x$ where $0 < x < 2\pi$

10. Given that: $5\sin 2\theta = \cos 2\theta$ find the values of θ, to two decimal places, in the interval $0° \leq \theta \leq 360°$.

11. Show that the equation: $14\cos^2\theta = 12 + 12\sin\theta$ may be written as a quadratic equation in $\sin\theta$. Hence solve the equation, giving all values of θ such that $0° \leq \theta \leq 360°$.

12. Find all the values of θ in the range $0° \leq \theta \leq 360°$ satisfying: $5\sin\theta\tan\theta = 24$

EXERCISE

SUMMARY

With the cosine and sine rules, you can work out missing sides and angles in triangles that do not have any right angles.

The **sine rule** links two angles and two sides. Therefore, if you know two angles and a side, you can work out the missing side. Or if you know two sides and an angle, you can calculate the missing angle.

The **cosine rule** links three sides and one angle. Therefore, if you know three sides of a triangle, you can work out any angle. If you know two of the sides and one angle, you can calculate the missing side.

Radians are used more often than degrees to measure angles at A–level, but you will still use both. To convert between degrees and radians, use: $\pi \text{ radians} = 180°$

Always use radians when calculating:

- the area of a triangle using $A = \frac{1}{2}ab\sin C$
- the length of an arc using $s = r\theta$
- the area of a sector $A = \frac{1}{2}r^2\theta$
- the area of a segment $A = \frac{1}{2}r^2(\theta - \sin\theta)$

You should remember the key points of the sine, cosine and tangent graphs.

You can perform transformations (translations, reflections and stretches) of these curves in the same way as you performed these transformations on other curves in the C1 module.

The CAST diagram can help you to find solutions to trigonometric equations, after you have found the **principal value** on a calculator.

Solving Trigonometry Equations - 'Cheat Sheet'

Type	How to spot it	Method	Example
1. Equations involving multiple angles	Instead of $\sin x$, $\cos x$ or $\tan x$ these equations have something more complicated in place of x, for example $\cos 2x$ or $\sin(3x-15°)$.	1. You may optionally use a substitution, e.g. $y = 3x - 15°$. 2. Use $\sin^{-1}$, $\cos^{-1}$ or $\tan^{-1}$ on your calculator to get principal value. 3. Use the CAST diagram to find successive values. Go round twice if the equation involves $2x$, three times for $3x$ etc. 4. Rearrange or substitute back to get values of x.	Q. Solve $\sin(2x-15°)=\frac{1}{2}$ for $0 \le x \le 360°$ A. Principal value is 30°. Going round CAST diagram twice gives us: $2x - 15° = 30°, 150°, 390°, 510°$ $x = 22.5°, 82.5°, 202.5°, 262.5°$.
2. Equations requiring $\tan x = \frac{\sin x}{\cos x}$	These equations involve $\sin x$ AND $\cos x$, but not $\sin^2 x$ or $\cos^2 x$.	1. Divide the whole equation by $\cos x$. 2. Rearrange into the form $\tan x = constant$ 3. Use $\tan^{-1}$ on your calculator to get the principal value. 4. Use the CAST diagram to obtain all values in the required range.	Q. Solve $3\sin x + \cos x = 0$ for $0 \le x \le 360°$. A. Dividing by $\cos x$ and rearranging gives us $\tan x = -\frac{1}{3}$. Principal value is $-18.4°$. From CAST diagram, solutions within the range are $161.6°, 341.6°$.
3. Quadratics involving just one trig function	These have a squared trig function, e.g. $\sin^2 x$, but only involve one of the three trig functions, not a mixture.	1. Rearrange equation so that all the terms are on one side, equal to zero. 2. Factorise the equation. It may be helpful to use a substitution, e.g. $y = \sin x$. 3. Find up to 2 solutions to the quadratic in the normal way. 4. If a substitution has been used, don't forget to substitute back.	Q. Solve $\sin^2 x = 2 - \sin x$ for $0 \le x \le 360°$. A. Re-arrange to give: $\sin^2 x + \sin x - 2 = 0$ Let $y = \sin x$, then $y^2 + y - 2 = 0$. Factorise: $(y-1)(y+2) = 0$ $y = 1$ or $y = -2$ No solutions for $\sin x = -2$. Solving $\sin x = 1$ gives only one solution: $x = 90°$.
4. Quadratics requiring the identity $\sin^2 x + \cos^2 x \equiv 1$	These equations involve either: $\sin^2 x$ and $\cos x$ OR $\cos^2 x$ and $\sin x$.	If equation has $\sin^2 x$, replace with $1 - \cos^2 x$. If equation has $\cos^2 x$, replace with $1 - \sin^2 x$. Re-arrange and solve quadratic as in case 3, above.	Q. Solve $-\cos^2 x = 1 - \sin x$ for $0 \le x \le 360°$. A. Replace $\cos^2 x = 1 - \sin^2 x$ and re-arrange giving: $\sin^2 x + \sin x - 2 = 0$ Proceed as in 3, above.

Review Exercise

Chapters 7 to 9

EXERCISE

1. Find the **number** of points of intersection between the circle and the straight line, whose equations are given:
   a) $(x-6)^2 + (y-5)^2 = 12$, $y = 3x - 2$
   b) $(x+2)^2 + (y+5)^2 = 3$, $x - y - 1 = 0$
   c) $x^2 + y^2 + 12x + 20 = 0$, $y = -x - 7$
   d) $x^2 + y^2 - 2x - 12y + 35 = 0$, $y = -x + 9$
2. Determine whether the point A, with coordinates given, lies on the circle C whose equation is also given:
   a) A(–2, –6), C: $(x-1)^2 + (y+3)^2 = 16$
   b) A(–9, 9), C: $(x+10)^2 + (y-9)^2 = 1$
3. The point A, with coordinates given, lies on the circle C, whose equation is also given. Find the value of a.
   a) A(6, –8), C: $(x-8)^2 + (y+7)^2 = a$
   b) A(–10, 9), C: $(x+9)^2 + (y-10)^2 = a$
4. Find the equation of the circle with centre C, which passes through the point A:
   a) C(–3, 3), A(–6, 3)
   b) C(0, –1), A(4, 1)
5. The chord AB is a diameter of circle C. Given the coordinates of A and B, find the equation of C:
   a) A(–4, –4), B(–6, 2)
   b) A(3, –7), B(–1, –9)
6. The circle $(x+2)^2 + (y+4)^2 = 32$ and the straight line $y = x - 2$ intersect at the points A and B.
   a) Find the coordinates of A and B.
   b) Show that the chord AB is a diameter of the circle.
7. Find the first 4 terms of each sequence:
   a) $u_n = 1 + n^2$
   b) $u_n = 6 - 5n$
8. Find which term of the sequence gives the following values:
   a) $u_n = -1 - 5n$, $u_n = -21$
   b) $u_n = n^2 + 2n - 4$, $u_n = 44$
9. The second term of a sequence is 6 and the fourth term is 12. Given that the formula for the sequence is: $u_n = an^2 + b$ find the values of the constants a and b.
10. Write down the first 4 terms of each of these sequences:
    a) $u_{n+1} = 3u_n + 4$, $u_1 = 1$
    b) $u_{n+1} = \frac{3u_n}{4} + 4$, $u_1 = 80$
11. Write a recurrence relationship linking u_{n+1} to u_n for each sequence:
    a) 6, 4, 2, 0, –2, ...
    b) 1, 4, 10, 22, 46, ...

EXERCISE

12. Peter gets more and more Christmas cards each year. Every Christmas, he counts the number of cards he receives. The number of cards seems to form the sequence a_1, a_2, a_3, where $a_1 = 7$. $a_{n+1} = 3a_n - 3, n \geq 1$
a) Find the value of a_2 and the value of a_3.
b) Assuming this trend continues, calculate the total number of cards Peter will have received after 5 years.

13. The terms of a sequence are generated using the formula: $u_{n+1} = -\frac{4}{7}u_n - 1, u_1 = 1$
a) Find the first 5 terms of the sequence, to two decimal places where necessary.
b) Is the sequence oscillating?
c) The sequence converges to a limit c. By forming and solving an equation, find c.

14. Which of these are arithmetic series?
a) $16 + 20 + 24 + 28 + \ldots$
b) $-0.25 + 0.25 + 0.75 + 1.25 + 1.75 \ldots$

15. For each of the following arithmetic series, find the 10th and 50th terms.
a) $20 + 17 + 14 + 11 + 8 \ldots$
b) $\frac{5}{2} + 2 + \frac{3}{2} + 1 + \frac{1}{2} \ldots$

16. Find the sum of the following series to the specified number of terms:
a) $100 + 75 + 50 + 25 + 0 \ldots$ (13 terms)
b) $(3 + 3\sqrt{3}) + (3 + 2\sqrt{3}) + (3 + \sqrt{3}) + 3 + (3 - \sqrt{3}) \ldots$ (7 terms)

17. Write down the arithmetic series corresponding to the following:
a) $\sum_{2}^{6} (4 - 2r)$
b) $\sum_{-3}^{3} 2r + 3$

18. Find the formula for the general term of each series. Use this to write the series in sigma notation, beginning at $r = 1$.
a) $3 + 1 + -1 + -3$
b) $x + (1 + x) + (2 + x) + \cdots + (10 + x)$

19. Find the following sums as simply as possible:
a) $\sum_{1}^{5} (30 - 6r)$
b) $\sum_{r=1}^{20} \left(\frac{r}{3} + \frac{x}{2}\right)$

20. Which of these are geometric progressions?
a) $(a + x), (a + x)^2, (a + x)^3, (a + x)^4, \ldots$
b) $\frac{1}{3}, \frac{2}{3}, 1, \frac{4}{3}, \frac{5}{3}, \ldots$

21. The second and fourth terms of a geometric series are 1.8 and 0.072 respectively. Given that all the terms in the series are positive, find the common ratio and the first term.

22. Find the sum of each geometric series:
a) $\frac{5}{3} + \frac{5}{9} + \frac{5}{27} + \cdots$ (6 terms)
b) $4 + -2 + 1 + -\frac{1}{2} + \frac{1}{4} + \cdots$ (10 terms)

23. Evaluate:
a) $\sum_{1}^{5} (3 \times 2^r)$
b) $\sum_{0}^{3} (3)^{\frac{r}{2}}$ (as a surd)

24. Find the sum to infinity of the following geometric series:
a) $0.9 + 0.3 + 0.1 + \cdots$
b) $5 + \frac{5}{6} + \frac{5}{36} + \cdots$

EXERCISE

25. Evaluate:

a) $\sum_{1}^{\infty} \frac{1}{2}\left(\frac{1}{2}\right)^{r}$ b) $\sum_{1}^{\infty} (-2)^{1-r}$

26. The sum to infinity of a geometric series is 11 times the first term. Find the common ratio.

27. Calculate:

a) $2! \times 3!$ b) $\frac{19!}{20!}$ c) $\binom{8}{6}$ d) ${}^{100}C_{99}$

28. Find the first four terms in the binomial expansion of the following:

a) $(1 - 3x)^3$ b) $\left(1 - \frac{x}{3}\right)^4$

29. Find the first 3 terms of the binomial expansion of:

a) $(4 + 5x)^6$ b) $\left(\frac{1}{2} - x\right)^4$

30. Find the side length b in the triangle ABC with angles $A = 76°$ and $B = 46°$. One side a has length 5 cm.

31. Find the angle C in the triangle ABC, if angle $A = 82°$ and two of the sides have lengths $a = 17$ cm and $c = 5$ cm.

32. In triangle ABC, angle $A = 34°$, side lengths $a = 5$ cm, $b = 6$ cm. Find the two possible values (the ambiguous case) for angle B. Find also the value of the third angle in C both cases.

33. Find the length of the side a in the following triangle to 3 significant figures.
$b = 8\,m,\quad c = 8\,m,\quad A = 78°$

34. Find the size of angle B in this triangle, to one decimal place.
$a = 10,\quad b = 11,\quad c = 12\,cm$

35. Solve the following triangles, giving all your answers to 1 decimal place:
a) $a = 10\,cm,\quad b = 7\,cm,\quad c = 7\,cm$
b) $b = 5\,mm,\quad c = 3\,mm,\quad A = 149°$
c) $a = 15\,cm,\quad b = 2\,cm,\quad A = 111°$

36. Calculate the area of the following triangles to 3 significant figures.
a) $b = 9\,cm,\quad c = 16\,cm,\quad A = 37°$
b) $d = 7\,cm,\quad e = 12\,cm,\quad E = 60°$

37. Find the length of the side b to 3 significant figures in the triangle ABC, where $a = 16\,cm$, the area is $43\,cm^2$ and angle $C = 56°$.

38. Find the acute angle C in the triangle ABC, where $a = 5\,cm$, $b = 20\,cm$ and the area is $29\,cm^2$. Give your answer to 1 decimal place.

39. Convert the following angles from degrees to radians, leaving your answer in exact form: a) 90° b) 36°

40. Convert the following angles from radians to degrees: a) 4π b) $\frac{\pi}{30}$

41. Find the following angles in radians, giving your answers to 3 significant figures where appropriate: a) 49° b) 409°

EXERCISE

42. Work out the following on your calculator. Remember to use degrees and radians modes where appropriate.

a) $cos\,120\,°$ b) $sin\frac{3\pi}{2}$

43. Find the perimeter of the sector of a circle if the radius of the circle is 15 cm and the angle subtended by the sector at the centre of the circle is 17.5°. Give your answer to 1 decimal place.

44. By using a CAST diagram, determine the sign (i.e. positive or negative) of each of the following trigonometric ratios.

a) $tan\left(\frac{3\pi}{4}\right)$ b) $sin\,215\,°$

45. If θ is an acute angle, simplify the following:

a) $tan(180° + \theta)$ b) $sin(2\pi - \theta)$

46. Rewrite the following using acute angles:

a) $tan\left(\frac{11\pi}{4}\right)$ b) $cos(640°)$

47. Find the following trigonometric ratios using the information given:

a) Given $sin\,x = \frac{2}{5}$, and x is acute, find $cos\,x$ and $tan\,x$.

b) Given $cos\,x = -\frac{8}{9}$ and x is obtuse, find $sin\,x$ and $tan\,x$.

48. Find all the values of x satisfying the following within the range specified.

a) $cos\,x = \frac{1}{2},\ 0° \le x < 180°$ b) $tan\,x = \frac{\sqrt{3}}{3},\ 0 \le x < 4\pi$

49. Simplify the following trigonometric expressions:

a) $(1 + cos\,\theta)^2 + sin^2\,\theta$ b) $tan^2\,x\,sin^2\,x\,cos^2\,x$

50. Prove the following identities:

a) $1 + tan^2\,x \equiv \frac{1}{cos^2\,x}$ b) $1 + tan\,\theta + tan^2\,\theta \equiv \frac{(1 + cos\,\theta\,sin\,\theta)}{cos^2\,\theta}$

51. Solve these equations, giving all solution between 0° and 360°, correct to 3 significant figures where appropriate.

a) $tan\,x = -\sqrt{3}$ b) $sin\,x = \frac{2}{7}$

52. Solve these equations, giving all solutions between 0° and 180°, correct to 3 significant figures where appropriate.

a) $cos\,3x = 0.4$ b) $sin\left(\frac{x}{3}\right) = 1 - \sqrt{2}$

53. Solve these equations, giving all solutions between 0° and 360° or 0 and 2π as appropriate. Give your answers to 3 significant figures where appropriate.

a) $sin\left(x - \frac{\pi}{3}\right) = \frac{1}{2}$ b) $cos(x - 180°) - 1 = -\frac{1}{4}$

54. Use the quadratic formula to solve the following. Give your answers in radians, to 3 significant figures where appropriate, between $-\pi$ and π.

a) $cos^2\,x + 2\,cos\,x - 2 = 0$ b) $2\,tan^2\,x + tan\,x = 5$

55. Find all the values of θ in the range $0° \le \theta \le 360°$ satisfying: $3\,sin\,\theta\,tan\,\theta = 8$

EXERCISE

Chapter 10

Logarithms

10.1 Introduction

Keywords

Exponential: A relationship in which the growth rate is proportional to the current value

Logarithm: The logarithm of a number is the power to which a base must be raised in order to make the number. For example, the logarithm of 1000, base 10, is 3.

Before You Start

You should know how to:

Solve quadratic equations;

Manipulate indices;

Sketch curves and recognise asymptotes.

EXAMPLE 1

Solve $x^2 - 7x + 10 = 0$

$$x^2 - 7x + 10 = 0$$

$$(x - 5)(x - 2) = 0$$

$$x = 5 \text{ or } x = 2$$

EXAMPLE 2

Simplify $(3x^2)^3 \times (2x^3)^2$

$$(3x^2)^3 \times (2x^3)^2$$

$$= 27x^6 \times 4x^6$$

$$= 108x^{12}$$

EXAMPLE 3

Find x, where $2^6 = 4^x$

$$2^6 = 4^x$$
$$\Rightarrow 2^6 = (2^2)^x$$
$$\Rightarrow 2^6 = 2^{2x}$$
$$\Rightarrow 6 = 2x$$
$$x = 3$$

What You Will Learn

In this chapter you will learn how to:

- Understand and sketch exponential curves;
- Use the laws of logarithms;
- Solve equations involving logarithms.

IN THE REAL WORLD – MALTHUS

Thomas Malthus was an English scholar and clergyman of the 19th century. He became well–known through his writings on population growth and the ability of society and the world to cope. Malthus believed that populations tend to grow in an exponential way (which you will learn about in this chapter). Because of this growth, he argued, sooner or later the population will be overcome by famine and disease.

Malthus's ideas were controversial at the time. Other scholars believed that society could continue improving indefinitely: that slowly, through new technology and innovation, society will become ever more perfect. Of course, since the time of Malthus the world's population has increased beyond what he would have considered possible. Many people think this is evidence Malthus has been proved wrong.

Was he? The world may now be at a critical point in its history, when the ingenuity of man to cope with an ever–growing population will be tested as never before. If we can succeed, we could prove Malthus wrong again.

EXERCISE

REVISION EXERCISE 10A

1. Simplify the following:

   a) $x^2 \times x^3$ b) $y^7 \div y^4$ c) $(z^2)^5 \times z^3$ d) $p^{-1} \times p^{-2}$ e) $\left(q^{\frac{3}{2}}\right)^2 \div q^{-2}$

2. Find x, where:

   a) $100^5 = 10000^x$ b) $2^8 = 4^x$ c) $4^x = \dfrac{1}{64}$

EXERCISE

3. Solve the following equations for x:
   a) $x(x+3)=0$ b) $x^2+3x-4=0$ c) $2x^2+5x-3=0$
   d) $x^3+x^2-6x=0$ e) $3x^2+5x-2=0$

4. Sketch the following curves and state the equations of any asymptotes.
   a) $y=\dfrac{1}{x}$ b) $y=\dfrac{2}{x}$ c) $y=\dfrac{1}{x^2}$ d) $y=\dfrac{1}{x}+1$

EXERCISE

10.2 $y = a^x$ and its Graph

The general equation of an exponential graph is $y = a^x$

EXAMPLE 1

By drawing up tables of values, plot the two graphs of $y = 2^x$ and $y = 2^{-x}$ on the same diagram. Use $-5 \le x \le 5$

x	–5	4	3	2	–1	0	1	2	3	4	5
2^x	0.03125	0.0625	0.125	0.25	0.5	1	2	4	8	16	32
2^{-x}	32	16	8	4	2	1	0.5	0.25	0.125	0.0625	0.03125

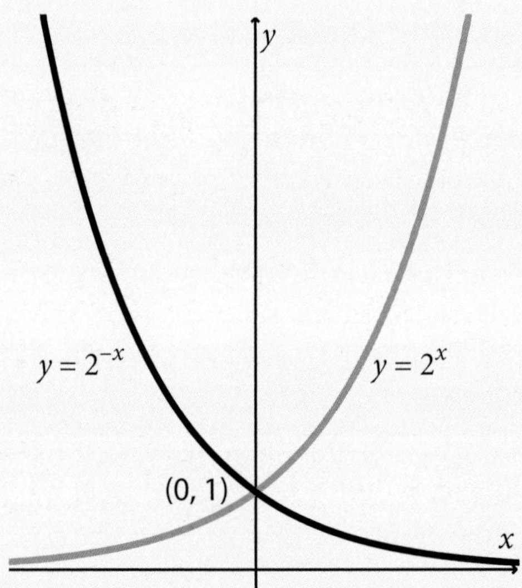

Key Points of the Graph of $y=a^x$

From Example 1, you can see many of the key points of exponential curves.

- The x-axis is an asymptote; $y = a^x$ approaches this asymptote for small values of x.
- The greater the value of a, the steeper the curve.
- For positive values of x, the curve $y = a^x$ rises more and more steeply.
- The curves cross the y-axis at (0, 1).
- $y = a^x$ is a reflection in the y-axis of $y = a^{-x}$.

There is a special exponential curve

$$y = e^x$$

You will study this in the C3 module.

Transformations of $y = a^x$

You can perform transformations of the graph of $y = a^x$ using the rules you learnt in the C1 module.

Translation

The curve $y = a^x + b$ represents a translation of the curve $y = a^x$ by b units in the positive y–direction.
The curve $y = a^{(x-b)}$ = represents a translation of the curve $y = a^x$ by b units in the positive x–direction.

Reflection

You have already seen that the curve $y = a^{-x}$ represents a reflection of the curve $y = a^x$ in the y-axis.
The curve $y = -a^x$ represents a reflection of the curve $y = a^x$ in the x-axis.

Stretching

The curve $y = ba^x$ represents a stretch of the curve $y = a^x$ by a factor of b, parallel to the y-axis.
The curve $y = a^{bx}$ represents a stretch of the curve $y = a^x$ by a factor of $\frac{1}{b}$, parallel to the x-axis.

EXAMPLE 2

Sketch the curve $y = \left(\frac{5}{2}\right)^x + 3$.

Mark clearly where the curve cuts the y-axis and the equation of the asymptote.

This is a translation of the curve $y = \left(\frac{5}{2}\right)^x$, by 3 units in the positive y–direction.

The point of intersection with the y-axis is (0, 4).

The equation of the asymptote is $y = 3$.

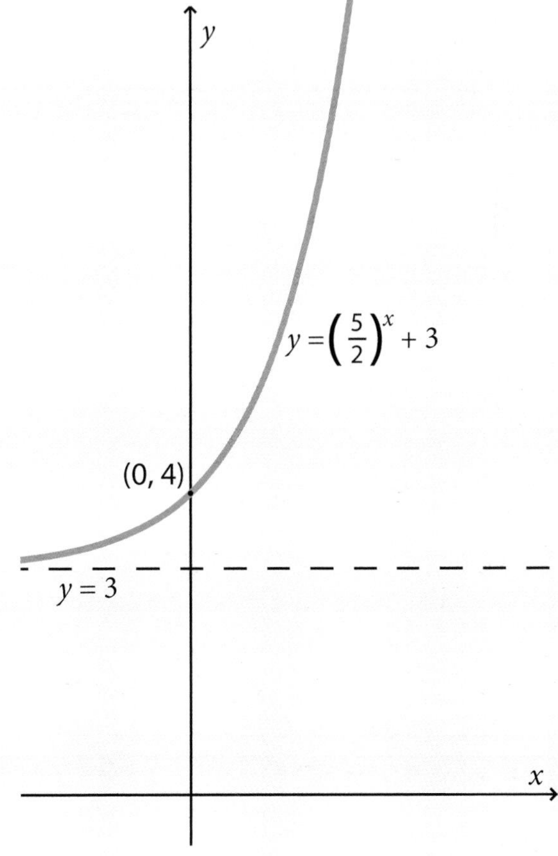

EXAMPLE 3

Sketch the curve $y = 2(2^{3x})$

When compared with $y = 2^x$ this represents:

a) a shrink, factor 3, parallel to the x-axis

b) a stretch, factor 2, parallel to the y-axis.

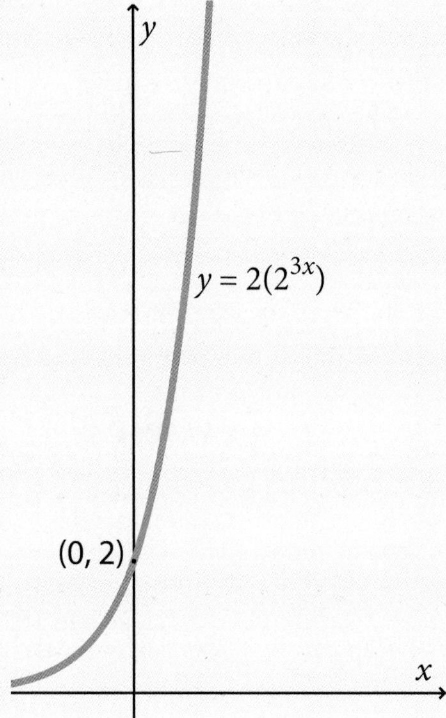

EXERCISE

EXERCISE 10B

1. Plot these curves on the same diagram. Use $-5 \leq x \leq 5$.

   a) $y = 3^{-x}$ b) $y = 2^{-x}$ c) $y = 2^x$ d) $y = 3^x$

2. a) Show, using the rules of indices, that $\left(\frac{1}{4}\right)^x = 4^{-x}$.

   b) Hence plot the curve $y = \left(\frac{1}{4}\right)^x$. Plot the curve $y = 4^x$ on the same diagram.

3. a) Plot the graphs of $y = 3^x$ and $y = x + 3$ on the same diagram. Use $0 \leq x \leq 3$.

   b) Show that there is one solution in this range to the equation $3^x = x + 3$. Estimate this value of x.

   c) By extending your graph to the range $3^x = x + 3$, show that there is a second solution. Estimate this value of x.

4. a) Show, using the rules of indices, that $2^{2x} = 4^x$.

   b) Hence plot the curve $y = 2^{2x}$. Plot the curve $y = 4^{-x}$ on the same diagram.

EXERCISE

EXERCISE

5. On separate diagrams, sketch the graphs of the following curves. Sketch also the curve $y = 3^x$ on each diagram. Mark clearly where each curve crosses the y-axis.
   a) $y = 3^{2x}$ b) $y = 3^{x/2}$ c) $y = 2(3^x)$

6. On separate diagrams, sketch the graphs of the following curves. Sketch also the curve $y = 2^x$ on each diagram. Mark clearly where each curve crosses the y-axis.
   a) $y = 2^{-x}$ b) $y = -2^x$ c) $y = -2^{-x}$

7. On separate diagrams, sketch the graphs of the following curves. Sketch also the curve $y = 2^x$ on each diagram. Mark clearly where each curve crosses the y-axis and the equations of any asymptotes.
   a) $y = 2^x - 1$ b) $y = 1 - 2^x$ c) $y = 2^{x+1}$ d) $y = 1 - 2^{x-1}$

8. Consider the following table of values. For lines a, b and c, write down an equation that could have given these results.

x	−2	−1	0	1	2
a) $y =?$	$\frac{1}{9}$	$\frac{1}{3}$	1	3	9
b) $y =?$	$-\frac{1}{9}$	$-\frac{1}{3}$	−1	−3	−9
c) $y =?$	$\frac{8}{9}$	$\frac{2}{3}$	0	−2	−8

EXERCISE

10.3 Logarithms

Consider the exponential equation $y = a^x$.
How could we re-arrange this to make x the subject?
For this, we need some new notation. We say that x is the **logarithm** of y, base a.
As an equation, we write: $x = log_a\, y$

It is important to remember the relationship between exponentials and logarithms:

$$y = a^x \Leftrightarrow x = log_a\, y$$

$\Leftrightarrow$ means 'if and only if'. If one statement is true, so is the other.

EXAMPLE 1

Given $1000 = 10^3$, write an equivalent statement using logarithms.

$$1000 = 10^3 \Leftrightarrow log_{10}\, 1000 = 3$$

EXAMPLE 2

Write equivalent statements using logarithms for: a) $2^6 = 64$ b) $3^5 = 243$

---

a) $2^6 = 64 \Leftrightarrow log_2\, 64 = 6$

b) $3^5 = 243 \Leftrightarrow log_3\, 243 = 5$

EXAMPLE 3

Write equivalent statements using exponential equations for:

a) $log_3 9 = 2$

b) $log_5 125 = 3$

c) $log_{10} 1000000 = 6$

---

a) $3^2 = 9$

b) $5^3 = 125$

c) $10^6 = 1000000$

In general,

$$log_a a = 1$$
$$log_a 1 = 0$$

On your calculator, you may have three buttons to calculate logarithms:

[*log*] [*log*■ ■] [*ln*]

The first of these buttons performs logarithms base 10. With the second button, you can enter the base. The third button will be covered when we look at **natural logarithms** in the C3 module. If you are not given the base of a logarithm, you can assume it is base 10.

EXAMPLE 4

Use your calculator to work out:

a) $log_{10} 100$ b) $log_4 64$ c) $log_6 6$ d) $log\ 10$ e) $log_6 216$

---

a) On your calculator, enter:

[*log*] 100

Answer: 2

b) On your calculator, enter:

[*log*■ ■] 4 64

Answer: 3

By the same method:

c) $log_6 6 = 1$ d) $log\ 10 = 1$ e) $log_6 216 = 3$

If an equation contains an unknown power, you can take logs to solve the equation.

EXAMPLE 5

Solve to find x: $10^x = 200$

$$10^x = 200$$
$$\Rightarrow x = log_{10} 200$$
$$x = 2.30 \text{ (3 s.f.)}$$

You will learn more about solving equations involving logs in section 10.6.

EXERCISE

EXERCISE 10C

1. Without a calculator, find the value of:
   a) $log_{10} 1$ b) $log_6 216$ c) $log\ 10000$ d) $log_3 27$ e) $log_8 64$
   f) $log_2 \frac{1}{16}$ g) $log_{10} 0.01$ h) $log_3 3\sqrt{3}$ i) $log_8 2$ j) $log_9 3$
2. Use your calculator to work out the following. Give your answers to 3 significant figures.
   a) $log\ 450$ b) $log_8 65$ c) $log_5 2$
   d) $log_{10} 8$ e) $log_3 10$ f) $log_9 4$
3. Write equivalent statements using logarithms:
   a) $100 = 10^2$ b) $5^{-3} = 0.008$ c) $\frac{1}{4} = 4^{-1}$
   d) $9^0 = 1$ e) $2^2 = 4$ f) $8^1 = 8$
   g) $6^5 = 7776$ h) $7^{10} = 282475249$ i) $10^7 = 10000000$
   j) $5^3 = 125$
4. Write equivalent statements using exponential equations:
   a) $log_7 7 = 1$ b) $log_4 1 = 0$ c) $log_2 128 = 7$
   d) $log_2 \frac{1}{16} = -4$ e) $log_6 \left(\frac{1}{6}\right) = -1$ f) $log_8 64 = 2$
   g) $log_4 64 = 3$ h) $log_7 2401 = 4$ i) $log_5 625 = 4$
   j) $log_3 \left(\frac{1}{59049}\right) = -10$ k) $log_2 8\sqrt{2} = \frac{7}{2}$
5. Find the base a in the following equations:
   a) $log_a 9 = 2$ b) $log_a 9 = 1$ c) $log_a 64 = 6$
   d) $log_a 16 = 2$ e) $log_a 256 = 4$ f) $log_a \left(\frac{1}{8}\right) = -3$
   g) $log_a 0.01 = -2$ h) $log_a \left(\frac{1}{4}\right) = -2$ i) $log_a 256 = 8$
   j) $log_a \left(\frac{1}{1000000}\right) = -6$
6. By forming a log equation, solve the following equations to find x. Give your answers to 3 significant figures where appropriate.
   a) $3^x = 27$ b) $6^x = \frac{1}{6}$ c) $10^x = 1000000000$
   d) $4^x = \frac{1}{2}$ e) $5^x = 1$ f) $9^x = 12$
   g) $2^x = 97$ h) $10^x = 72$ i) $7^x = 78$
   j) $8^x = 32$
7. Do you think it makes any sense to talk about logarithms base 1? Explain your answer.

EXERCISE

10.4 Laws of Logarithms

There are three important laws of logarithms that you should learn.

Addition Law: $log_a x + log_a y = log_a(xy)$

Subtraction Law: $\therefore log_a x - log_a y = log_a\left(\frac{x}{y}\right)$

Power Law: $k\, log_a x = log_a x^k$

Note: when using the addition and subtraction laws, the two bases must be equal.

You do not need to learn the following proofs, but you should be very familiar with the results.

PROOF OF LAW 1 (ADDITION LAW)

Let $p = log_a x \Rightarrow x = a^p$ (1)

and let $q = log_a y \Rightarrow y = a^q$ (2)

(1) × (2) gives: $xy = a^{p+q}$ (using the rules of indices)

$\Rightarrow p + q = log_a(xy)$ (3)

(1) + (2) gives: $log_a x + log_a y = p + q$

$= log_a(xy)$ from (3)

$\therefore log_a x + log_a y = log_a(xy)$

PROOF OF LAW 2 (SUBTRACTION LAW)

Again let $p = log_a x \Rightarrow x = a^p$ (1)

and let $q = log_a y \Rightarrow y = a^q$ (2)

(1) ÷ (2) gives: $\frac{x}{y} = a^{p-q}$ (using the rules of indices)

$\Rightarrow p - q = log_a\left(\frac{x}{y}\right)$ (3)

(1) – (2) gives: $log_a x - log_a y = p - q$

$= log_a\left(\frac{x}{y}\right)$ from (3)

$\therefore log_a x - log_a y = log_a\left(\frac{x}{y}\right)$

PROOF OF LAW 3 (POWER LAW)

Let $p = log_a x \Rightarrow x = a^p$ (1)

Raise both sides to the power n:

$x^n = (a^p)^n = a^{pn}$ from the laws of indices.

$\Rightarrow log_a(x^n) = pn$

$\Rightarrow log_a(x^n) = n\, log_a x$

EXAMPLE 1

Write $log_3 4 + log_3 5$ as a single logarithm.

$$\begin{aligned} log_3 4 + log_3 5 &= log_3(4 \times 5) \text{ (using the addition law)} \\ &= log_3 20 \end{aligned}$$

EXAMPLE 2

Write $log\,12 + log\,5 - log\,30$ as a single logarithm.

$$\begin{aligned} log\,12 + log\,5 - log\,30 &= log(12 \times 5) - log\,30 \text{ (using the addition law)} \\ &= log\,60 - log\,30 \\ &= log\,2 \text{ (using the subtraction law)} \end{aligned}$$

EXAMPLE 3

Prove that $log_a\left(\frac{1}{x}\right) = -\,log_a x$

From the Power Law: $k\,log_a x = log_a x^k$

When: $k = -1$, $-\,log_a x = log_a x^{-1}$

i.e. $log_a\left(\frac{1}{x}\right) = -\,log_a x$

EXAMPLE 4

Simplify: a) $2\,log_5 3 + log_5 10$ b) $7\,log\,a + 6\,log\,b - 4\,log\,c$

---

a) $$\begin{aligned} 2\,log_5 3 + log_5 10 &= log_5 3^2 + log_5 10 \\ &= log_5 9 + log_5 10 \\ &= log_5 90 \end{aligned}$$

b) $$\begin{aligned} 7\,log\,a + 6\,log\,b - 4\,log\,c &= log\,a^7 + log\,b^6 - log\,c^4 \\ &= log\,a^7 b^6 - log\,c^4 \\ &= log\left(\frac{a^7 b^6}{c^4}\right) \end{aligned}$$

EXAMPLE 5

Simplify the expression $2\,log_5 8$ by writing it in terms of $log_5 2$ only.

$$\begin{aligned} 2\,log_5 8 &= 2\,log_5(2^3) \\ &= 2 \times 3\,log_5 2 \\ &= 6\,log_5 2 \end{aligned}$$

EXAMPLE 6

Write the expression $log\left(\frac{b^3c^2}{a^{1/4}}\right)$ in terms of $log\, a$, $log\, b$ and $log\, c$.

$$log\left(\frac{b^3c^2}{a^{1/4}}\right) = log\, b^3 + log\, c^2 - log\, a^{1/4}$$

$$= 3\,log\, b + 2\,log\, c - \frac{1}{4}log\, a$$

EXERCISE

EXERCISE 10D

1. Simplify the following using the Power Law.
   a) $log_2 1000$ b) $log_3 243$ c) $log_3 16$ d) $log_7 27$ e) $log_4\left(\frac{1}{1024}\right)$
   f) $log\, 125$ g) $2\,log_4 100$ h) $4\,log_2 81$ i) $log_4\left(\frac{1}{10}\right)$ j) $log_{10}\left(\frac{1}{8}\right)$
2. If possible, simplify the following using the Addition Law.
   a) $log_a 30 + log_a 2$ b) $log_9 23 + log_5 3$ c) $log_2 15 + log_2 6$
   d) $log_3 10 + log_3 17$ e) $log_5 13 + log_{13} 5$ f) $log_p 12 + log_p 3$
   g) $log\, 20 + log\, 5$ h) $log_6 9 + log_6 4$
3. If possible, simplify the following using the Subtraction Law.
   a) $log_a 30 - log_a 2$ b) $log_8 2 - log_7 3$ c) $log_2 18 - log_2 6$
   d) $log_3 70 - log_3 7$ e) $log_4 13 - log_5 13$ f) $log_q 36 - log_q 3$
   g) $log\, 20 - log\, 5$ h) $log_6 11 - log_6 4$
4. Simplify:
   a) $log_2 7 + 2\,log_2 3$ b) $2\,log_5 2 + log_5 20$ c) $2\,log\sqrt{3} - 2\,log\sqrt{2}$
   d) $log\sqrt{50} + log\sqrt{2}$ e) $2\,log_3 6 + log_3 2$ f) $3\,log_2 2 + 2\,log_2 3 - log_2 18$
   g) $\frac{1}{2}log_5 64 + log_5\left(\frac{125}{8}\right)$ h) $5\,log\, a + 2\,log\, b - 4\,log\, c$
5. Write the following in terms of $log\, a$, $log\, b$ and $log\, c$:
   a) $log\, abc$ b) $log\left(\frac{ab}{c}\right)$ c) $log(a^2bc)$
   d) $log(a^2\sqrt{bc})$ e) $log\left(\frac{a^{1/3}}{b^{1/2}}\right)$ f $log_5(5ab)$
   g) $log_2\left(\frac{a^2}{32c^2}\right)$ h) $log_3(27b^3)$
6. Simplify:
   a) $6\,log\, x + 2\,log\, y$ b) $3\,log\, p - 3\,log\, q$ c) $7\,log\, a + 6\,log\, b - 4\,log\, c$
7. Given that $log_2 x = a$, find, in terms of a, the simplest form of:
   a) $log_2(8x)$ b) $log_2\left(\frac{x^2}{2}\right)$
8. Given that $p = log_q 256$, express in terms of p:
   a) $log_q 4$ b) $log_q(64q)$
9. a) Write down the value of $log_2 8$.
   b) Express: $4\,log_a 3 + log_a 11$ as a single logarithm with base a.

EXERCISE

EXERCISE

10. Prove that the value of x that satisfies: $2\,log_2 x + log_2(x-1) = 1 + log_2(12x+18)$ is a solution of the equation $x^3 - x^2 - 24x - 36 = 0$.

11. By drawing up a suitable table of values, plot the graph of $y = log_{10} x$. (Hints: you do not need a negative x-axis, since the logarithm of a negative number is not defined. Choose several values of x between 0 and 1 and a few greater than 1.)

    Do you have any observations about your graph?

EXERCISE

10.5 The Change of Base Rule

You can change the base of a logarithmic expression. The change of base rule is:

$$log_a x = \frac{log_b x}{log_b a}$$

Notice that if we choose $x = b$,

$$log_a b = \frac{log_b b}{log_b a}$$

Then, since $log_b b = 1$:

$$log_a b = \frac{1}{log_b a}$$

You should remember the Change of Base Rule, but you do not need to learn the proof.

PROOF OF THE CHANGE OF BASE RULE

Let $\quad p = log_a x \Rightarrow x = a^p$

Take log (base b) of both sides: $log_b x = log_b a^p$

$\Rightarrow log_b x = p\, log_b a$ (using the Power Law)

$$\Rightarrow p = \frac{log_b x}{log_b a}$$

$$log_a x = \frac{log_b x}{log_b a}$$

EXAMPLE 1

Change the base from 7 to 10 in the following expression:

$log_7 q$

$$log_7 q = \frac{log_{10} q}{log_{10} 7}$$

The Change of Base Rule is particularly useful if your calculator does not have the button $\boxed{log_{\blacksquare}\,\blacksquare}$. You can change the logarithm to base 10 and use the $\boxed{log}$ button.

EXAMPLE 2

Work out $log_5 65$ on your calculator by changing to base 10.

$$log_5 65 = \frac{log_{10} 65}{log_{10} 5}$$

$$= \frac{1.8129\ ...}{0.6990\ ...}$$

Do not round your numbers until after the division.

$$= 2.59$$

EXERCISE

EXERCISE 10E

1. Find the following logarithms using the change of base rule to change to base 10. Give your answers to 3 significant figures.

   a) $log_7 8$ b) $log_3 2$ c) $log_2 6$ d) $log_8 10$ e) $log_5\left(\frac{1}{9}\right)$

   f) $log_4\left(\frac{1}{2}\right)$ g) $log_8\left(\frac{1}{6}\right)$ h) $log_{100} 10$ i) $log_8\left(\frac{1}{2}\right)$ j) $log_4\left(\frac{1}{10}\right)$

2. Using the fact that $log_a b = \frac{1}{log_b a}$ find the value of the following expressions:

   a) $log_{100} 10$ b) $log_{125} 5$ c) $log_{0.5} 2$ d) $log_{49} 7$

3. Prove that: $log_p \sqrt{2} = \frac{1}{log_2 p^2}$

EXERCISE

10.6 Solving Log Equations

The Solution of Equations of the Form $a^x = b$

This section will show you to solve equations in which the unknown is an index, such as $a^x = b$. You can take logs of both sides of an equation. The Power Law of logs can then be used to obtain a standard equation in the unknown.

EXAMPLE 1

Solve the equation: $2^x = 20$

Take logs of both sides: $log\ 2^x = log\ 20$

Use the power law on the left hand side: $x\ log\ 2 = log\ 20$

$$x = \frac{log\ 20}{log\ 2}$$

$$= 4.32 \text{ (3 s.f.)}$$

Check your answer! As when solving any equation, it is a good idea to check your answer by substituting the answer into the original equation. In this case the left–hand side does give a value of 20.

Both sides of the equation may involve the unknown as an index.

EXAMPLE 2

Solve for x: $5^x = 6^{x-1}$

Take logs: $\log 5^x = \log 6^{x-1}$

Use the Power Law on both sides: $x \log 5 = (x - 1) \log 6$

Expand the RHS: $x \log 5 = x \log 6 - \log 6$

$\log 5$ and $\log 6$ are constants.

You can treat these as you would treat any other constants in an equation.

Collect terms involving x: $x \log 6 - x \log 5 = \log 6$

$$x(\log 6 - \log 5) = \log 6$$

$$x = \frac{\log 6}{(\log 6 - \log 5)}$$

Be careful, as always, to use the unrounded values in all working. Only round the final answer.

$$= \frac{0.77815\ldots}{0.07918\ldots}$$

$$= 9.83 \ \ (3 \text{ s.f.})$$

Another common type of question is a log equation in which you must raise both sides to a power. This is the inverse of taking logs, which means it is a good way to eliminate logs from the equation.

EXAMPLE 3

Solve for x: $\log_5 x - \log_5(2x - 3) = 2$

Using the Subtraction Law: $\log_5\left(\frac{x}{2x-3}\right) = 2$

Raise both sides to power 5: $\frac{x}{2x-3} = 25$

$$x = 25(2x - 3)$$

$$x = 50x - 75$$

$$49x = 75$$

$$x = \frac{75}{49}$$

If you are asked to solve an equation involving both a^{2x} and a^x, you will have to solve a quadratic equation, remembering that $a^{2x} = (a^x)^2$. It is often best to use a substitution to solve this type of problem.

EXAMPLE 4

Solve $3^{2x} - 5(3^x) + 4 = 0$

Let $y = 3^x$

Then $y^2 = (3^x)^2 = 3^{2x}$

Then we must solve: $y^2 - 5y + 4 = 0$

$$(y - 1)(y - 4) = 0$$

$$y = 1 \text{ or } y = 4$$

continued...

Example 4... Substitute back for x: $3^x = 1$ or $3^x = 4$

Take logs: $log\, 3^x = log\, 1$ or $log\, 3^x = log\, 4$

Use the Power Law: $x\, log\, 3 = 0$ or $x\, log\, 3 = log\, 4$

$x = 0$ or $x = \frac{log\, 4}{log\, 3}$

$x = 0$ or $x = 1.26$ (3 s.f.)

You may need the Change of Base Rule when solving equations involving more than one logarithmic base.

EXAMPLE 5

Solve: $log_5\, x + 3\, log_x\, 5 = -4$

Use the special case of the Change of Base rule: $log_x\, 5 = \frac{1}{log_5\, x}$

$$log_5\, x + \frac{3}{log_5\, x} = -4$$

Now use the substitution $y = log_5\, x$

$$y + \frac{3}{y} = -4$$

$$y^2 + 3 + 4y = 0$$

$$(y+3)(y+1) = 0$$

$y = -3$ or $y = -1$

$log_5\, x = -3$ or $log_5\, x = -1$

$x = 5^{-3}$ or $x = 5^{-1}$

$x = \frac{1}{125}$ or $x = \frac{1}{5}$

or as decimals: $x = 0.008$ or $x = 0.2$

EXERCISE 10F

1. Take logs of each side of the equation and use the Power Law to solve these equations. Give your answers to 3 significant figures where appropriate.

   a) $4^x = 15$ b) $2^x = 15$ c) $4^x = 8$ d) $3^x = 11$ e) $2^x = \frac{1}{2}$

   f) $9^x = 0.6$ g) $8^x = 21$ h) $5^x = 19$ i) $2 = 2^x$ j) $\frac{1}{100} = 0.5^x$

2. Take logs of each side of the equation and use the Power Law to solve these equations. Give your answers to 3 decimal places where appropriate.

   a) $4^{x+4} = 7^x$ b) $3^{x+2} = 7^x$ c) $6^{x-4} = 2^{7x}$ d) $4^{x-4} = 6^{3x}$ e) $3^{x-4} = 5^{6x}$

   f) $5^{x-2} = 4^{4x}$ g) $7^{x-3} = 3^{6x}$ h) $2^{x+3} = 5^x$ i) $7^{x-4} = 6^{7x}$ j) $3^{x-2} = 6^{7x}$

3. Solve $log_4(14x + 3) - log_4\, x = 2$.

4. Given that $log_2\, x = a$, find, in terms of a, the simplest form of:

   a) $log_2(32x)$ b) $log_2\left(\frac{x^2}{2}\right)$

EXERCISE EXERCISE

EXERCISE

c) Hence, or otherwise, solve $log_2(32x) - log_2\left(\frac{x^2}{2}\right) = \frac{1}{2}$ giving your answer in the simplest surd form.

5. Solve the equation $8^{x+2} = 2^{x+10}$
 a) By taking logs of both sides.
 b) Using the laws of indices.
 Which method do you prefer? Is it always possible to solve equations like this using both methods?

6. a) Using the substitution $u = 3^x$, show that the equation: $9^x - 3^{x+1} - 180 = 0$ can be written in the form $u^2 - 3u - 180 = 0$
 b) Hence solve $9^x - 3^{x+1} - 180 = 0$ giving your answers to 2 decimal places.

7. Solve the equation $2\,log_4 x - log_4 3x = 1$

8. Solve the following using the change of base rule:
 a) $log_6 x + 1 = 2\,log_x 6$
 b) $log_2 x - 6\,log_x 2 = 1$
 c) $log\,x + 2 = 15\,log_x 10$
 d) $6\,log_x 3 - 2\,log_3 x = 1$

9. Solve for x: $log_2(x^2 + 13x + 42) - log_2(x^2 + 6x) = 3$

10. A savings scheme pays interest at a rate of 2% per year. Hence, after x years, the total value of an initial £1 investment is £y, where $y = 1.02^x$. Using logarithms, find the number of years it takes to double the total value of any initial investment.

10.7 SUMMARY

You should learn the shape of the exponential curve $y = a^x$ and be familiar with its key points:

- The x-axis is an asymptote; the curve approaches this asymptote for small values of x.
- The greater the value of a, the steeper the curve.
- For positive values of x, the curve $y = a^x$ rises more and more steeply.
- The curves cross the y-axis at (0, 1).
- $y = a^{-x}$ is a reflection in the y-axis of $y = a^x$.

You can apply the usual transformations to the curve $y = a^x$: translation in both x and y-directions, reflections in both x and y-directions, stretching in both x and y-directions.

Logarithms are the inverse of the exponential function. $y = a^x \Leftrightarrow x = log_a y$

You should know how to use your calculator to calculate logs to any base.

There are three important laws for combining logarithms:

Addition Law: $log_a x + log_a y = log_a(xy)$

Subtraction Law: $log_a x - log_a y = log_a\left(\frac{x}{y}\right)$

Power Law: $k\,log_a x = log_a x^k$

You should also be familiar with the Change of Base Rule: $log_a x = \frac{log_b x}{log_b a}$

You can use logarithms to solve equations with the unknown as the power, for example $3^x = 2^{1/x}$

Chapter 11

Integration

11.1 Introduction

What is Integration?

In the C1 module you learned about differentiation. You learned that differentiation gives a way to measure the gradient of a curve at any point. This gradient can also be considered a rate of change. You differentiate velocity, for example, to obtain acceleration, which is the rate of change of velocity.

Integration can also be considered in two different ways. Firstly, it is the reverse of differentiation. If you know the gradient function of a curve, integration will tell you the equation of the curve itself. Secondly, you can use integration to measure the area under a curve. If you progress to the C4 module, you will also use integration to calculate volumes.

Together, differentiation and integration form the branch of mathematics known as **calculus**, possibly the greatest innovation in the history of mathematics.

Keywords

Calculus: The area of mathematics of which integration is a part.

Gradient: The steepness of a curve at any point.

Derivative/gradient function: A function that allows you to calculate the gradient at any point on a curve.

Differentiation: A technique used to find the gradient function.

Integration / Indefinite integration: The reverse of differentiation; finding a function given its gradient function.

Definite integration: A technique used to find the area under a curve.

Numerical integration: A collection of techniques used to approximate integration.

Before You Start

You should know how to:

Expand brackets;
Manipulate indices;
Differentiate polynomials, e.g. $x^2 + 2x + 1$

What You Will Learn

In this chapter you will learn how to:

- Perform integration, the reverse of differentiation;
- Find the equation of a curve from its gradient function;
- Find the area under a curve using definite integration;
- Perform some types of numerical integration.

IN THE REAL WORLD – FLUID DYNAMICS

The world's atmosphere is turbulent and chaotic and this is one reason weather forecasting is so difficult. Predicting the motion of the Earth's atmosphere is one example of a **fluid dynamics** problem.

Many fluid dynamics problems can be described by a set of equations called the Navier-Stokes equations. They can be used to model ocean currents, water flow in a pipe and the airflow around an aircraft wing.

The Navier–Stokes equations are **differential equations**, which means they link derivatives (e.g. $\frac{dv}{dt}$) to other quantities. To obtain solutions for velocity, they must be **integrated.** This is what gives the Navier–Stokes equations great interest in a mathematical sense. Somewhat surprisingly, given their wide range of practical uses, mathematicians have not yet proven that solutions always exist. In weather forecasting, for example, the solutions must be approximated using a technique called **numerical integration.**

The Clay Mathematics Institute has declared the Navier–Stokes equations one of the seven most important open problems in mathematics and has offered a \$1 million prize for a solution. Any solution would not only revolutionise the modelling of the Earth's atmosphere; it would have huge consequences for many areas of physics, engineering and mathematics.

By the time you have finished studying this chapter, you will understand some of the techniques involved in integration and numerical integration. If you later study the C4 module, you will learn more about differential equations.

EXAMPLE 1

Expand the brackets: $(x + 1)(x - 3)$

$$\begin{aligned}(x+1)(x-3) &= x^2 - 3x + x - 3\\ &= x^2 - 2x - 3\end{aligned}$$

EXAMPLE 2

Simplify: $a\left(a^{\frac{3}{2}}\right)^2$

$$\begin{aligned}a\left(a^{\frac{3}{2}}\right)^2 &= a(a^3) \quad \text{(because } (a^b)^c = a^{bc}\text{)}\\ &= a^4 \text{ (add powers when multiplying).}\end{aligned}$$

EXAMPLE 3

Differentiate the following to find $\frac{dy}{dx}$: $y = 2x^2 - \frac{x}{2} + 3$

$$y = 2x^2 - \frac{x}{2} + 3$$
$$\frac{dy}{dx} = 4x - \frac{1}{2}$$

EXERCISE

REVISION EXERCISE 11A

1. Expand out the brackets in the following expressions.
   a) $x(x+1)$ b) $x^2(x^2+2x-1)$ c) $(x-1)(x-3)$
   d) $(2x+1)(3x-2)$ e) $(x^2-1)(x^2+1)$ f) $(x+2)^3$
2. Simplify the following expressions.
   a) $a^2 \times a^3$ b) $b^2 \div b^3$ c) $\frac{c^4}{c \div c^3}$ d) $\frac{(d^2)^4}{d^{-1}}$
3. Write the following in index form.
   a) $(\sqrt{e})^3$ b) $\frac{1}{\sqrt{f}}$ c) $g(\sqrt[3]{g})$ d) $\frac{h^3}{(\sqrt{h})^4}$
4. Differentiate the following with respect to x.
   a) $y = x^2 + 1$ b) $y = -x^3 + 4x^2 - 2x$ c) $y = \frac{1}{x^2} - \frac{1}{x}$
   d) $y = \sqrt{x}(2x^2 - 1)$ e) $y = (x-2)^2$

EXERCISE

11.2 Indefinite Integration of x^n

Consider: $y = x^2 + 1$

We can obtain the gradient function by differentiating: $\frac{dy}{dx} = 2x$

We could have obtained the same gradient function from many different functions:

$$y = x^2 + 2$$
$$y = x^2 - 1\text{, etc.}$$

The reverse of differentiation is called **integration** or, to be more precise, **indefinite integration.**

Many different functions give the same gradient function when differentiated. So when we integrate there are many possible answers. If: $\frac{dy}{dx} = 2x$

then: $y = x^2 + c$

where c can be any constant.

We call c the **constant of integration.** It is important to remember the constant of integration whenever you perform indefinite integration.

EXAMPLE 1

If $\frac{dy}{dx} = 4x$, find y.

Increase the power of x by 1 and divide by the new power:

$$y = \frac{4x^2}{2} + c$$

$$y = 2x^2 + c$$

Check your answer by differentiating y.

Remember that the power of x generally goes down by 1 when differentiating. Because integration is the reverse process, the power rises by 1 when integrating. Also, the entire term is divided by the new power.

$$\text{If } \frac{dy}{dx} = ax^n \text{ then } y = \frac{a}{n+1}x^{n+1} + c$$

These rules apply when the power of x is positive, negative and fractional.

EXAMPLE 2

Find y where:

a) $\frac{dy}{dx} = 3x$ b) $\frac{dy}{dx} = -6x^5$ c) $\frac{dy}{dx} = 3x^{-2}$ d) $\frac{dy}{dx} = 5x^{\frac{3}{2}}$ e) $\frac{dy}{dx} = 3x\sqrt{x}$

---

a) $\frac{dy}{dx} = 3x$ $\Rightarrow y = \frac{3x^2}{2} + c$ $\Rightarrow y = \frac{3}{2}x^2 + c$

b) $\frac{dy}{dx} = -6x^5$ $\Rightarrow y = -\frac{6x^6}{6} + c$ $\Rightarrow y = -x^6 + c$

c) $\frac{dy}{dx} = 3x^{-2}$ $\Rightarrow y = \frac{3x^{-1}}{-1} + c$ $\Rightarrow y = -3x^{-1} + c$

d) $\frac{dy}{dx} = 5x^{\frac{3}{2}}$ Increase the power by 1 and divide by the new power:

$y = \frac{5x^{\frac{5}{2}}}{5/2} + c$ $y = 2x^{\frac{5}{2}} + c$

e) You often have to re-arrange an expression before you can integrate it.

$\frac{dy}{dx} = 3x\sqrt{x} = 3x^{\frac{3}{2}}$ $y = \frac{3x^{\frac{5}{2}}}{5/2} + c$ $y = \frac{6}{5}x^{\frac{5}{2}} + c$

EXERCISE 11B

EXERCISE

1. Integrate the following to find y.

a) $\frac{dy}{dx} = 6x$ b) $\frac{dy}{dx} = x^6$ c) $\frac{dy}{dx} = 2x$ d) $\frac{dy}{dx} = -x^2$ e) $\frac{dy}{dx} = -4x^3$ f) $\frac{dy}{dx} = 6x^5$

g) $\frac{dy}{dx} = 3x^2$ h) $\frac{dy}{dx} = 50x^{99}$ i) $\frac{dy}{dx} = 10x^7$ j) $\frac{dy}{dx} = 12x^3$ k) $\frac{dy}{dx} = -9x^2$

EXERCISE

2. Integrate the following to find y.

a) $\frac{dy}{dx} = 3x^{-4}$ b) $\frac{dy}{dx} = -2x^{-2}$ c) $\frac{dy}{dx} = \frac{1}{3}x^{-4}$

d) $\frac{dy}{dx} = \frac{4}{3}x^{\frac{1}{3}}$ e) $\frac{dy}{dx} = ax^{-2}$ (where a is a constant)

f) $\frac{dy}{dx} = 7x^{-15}$ g) $\frac{dy}{dx} = 7x^{\frac{5}{2}}$

h) $\frac{dy}{dx} = -\frac{11}{5}x^{-\frac{16}{5}}$ i) $\frac{dy}{dx} = -9x^{-9/8}$

3. Simplify and integrate the following.

a) $\frac{dy}{dx} = \sqrt{x}$ b) $\frac{dy}{dx} = \left(\sqrt{x}\right)^3$ c) $\frac{dy}{dx} = \left(\frac{1}{x}\right)^3$

d) $\frac{dy}{dx} = (-x)^2$ e) $\frac{dy}{dx} = (-1)^4x$ f) $\frac{dy}{dx} = \frac{1}{\sqrt{x}}$

g) $\frac{dy}{dx} = (2x)^4$ h) $\frac{dy}{dx} = \left(\frac{1}{\sqrt{x}}\right)^4$ i) $\frac{dy}{dx} = \left(\frac{1}{x}\right)^4\left(\frac{x}{2}\right)^4$

j) $\frac{dy}{dx} = \frac{\left(\sqrt{x}\right)^4(x^3)^{-2}}{\left(x\sqrt{x}\right)^2}$

4. Stretch yourself!

Sketch three curves that, when differentiated, have the gradient function $\frac{dy}{dx} = 2x$

EXERCISE

11.3 Notation

The integral of a function $f(x)$ is usually represented using this notation:

$$\int f(x)\, dx$$

This should be read as 'the integral of $f(x)$ with respect to x'.

The general result from the previous section can be rewritten using this notation:

$$\int ax^n\, dx = \frac{a}{n+1}x^{n+1} + c$$

for $n \neq -1$. (You will learn how to integrate x^{-1} if you later study the C3 module.)

In Chapter 6, you learnt that $f'(x)$ and $\frac{dy}{dx}$ mean the same thing and are both notations for the derivative.

Therefore, we can write:

$$\int f'(x)\, dx = f(x)\, dx$$

EXAMPLE 1

Find $\int \frac{x^3}{4}\, dx$

This is another way of saying:

Find y if $\frac{dy}{dx} = \frac{x^3}{4}$

We proceed in the usual way: raise the power of x by 1, then divide the whole term by the new power. Finally, do not forget the constant of integration.

$$\int \frac{x^3}{4}\, dx = \left(\frac{x^4}{4}\right)/4 + c$$

$$= \frac{x^4}{16} + c$$

It is important to remember dx when writing an integral. This tells us we are integrating **with respect to** the variable x, i.e. it is the power of x that will increase by one. At this stage, there will only be one variable, but including dx will ensure good habits for later. You may be asked to integrate with respect to other variables.

EXAMPLE 2

Integrate to find an equation for s: $s = \int 4t\, dt$

We are integrating with respect to t.

Increase the power of t by 1, then divide by the new power.
Finally add a constant of integration.

$$s = 2t^2 + c$$

Remember to simplify surds and rewrite using index notation before integrating.

EXAMPLE 3

Find $\int 5x\sqrt{x}\, dx$

Rewrite using indices. You are adding the powers in this case.

$$\int 5x\sqrt{x}\, dx = \int 5x^{\frac{3}{2}}\, dx$$

Increase the power by one: $\frac{3}{2} \to \frac{5}{2}$

Divide by the new power:

$$= \frac{5x^{\frac{5}{2}}}{5/2}$$

But $5 \div \frac{5}{2} = 2$. And don't forget the constant!

$$= 2x^{\frac{5}{2}} + c$$

When integrating a constant, think of it multiplying the variable to the power 0. The solution then contains the variable to the power 1.

EXAMPLE 4

Find $\int 3\,dx$

$$\int 3\,dx = \int 3x^0\,dx$$

We are integrating with respect to x. The power of x goes up from 0 to 1. Dividing by the new power, 1, leaves the 3 unchanged.

$$= 3x + c$$

EXERCISE 11C

1. Find the following integrals.

a) $\int 4x\,dx$ b) $\int x^5\,dx$ c) $\int -x^3\,dx$ d) $\int -3x^2\,dx$ e) $\int 5\,dx$

f) $\int 3x^3\,dx$ g) $\int 100x^{49}\,dx$ h) $\int 10x^5\,dx$ i) $\int -12x^5\,dx$ j) $\int 9x^5\,dx$

2. Integrate the following.

a) $\int 4x^{-5}\,dx$ b) $\int -4t^{-2}\,dt$ c) $\int -\frac{1}{4}x^{-5}\,dx$ d) $\int \frac{5}{8}y^{\frac{1}{4}}\,dy$

e) $\int bx^{-3}\,dx$ (where b is a constant)

3. Integrate the right-hand side of the following equations.

a) $y = \int -\frac{9}{4}z^{-\frac{13}{4}}\,dz$ b) $y = \int -8x^{-17}\,dx$

c) $r = \int 6\theta^{\frac{7}{2}}\,d\theta$ d) $s = \int -x^{-11/10}\,dx$

4. Simplify and integrate the following.

a) $\int \sqrt{y}\,dy$ b) $\int -\left(\frac{1}{\sqrt{x}}\right)^6\,dx$

c) $\int \left(\frac{1}{s}\right)^3\left(\frac{s}{2}\right)^3\,ds$ d) $\int (-x)^4\,dx$

5. Integrate the right-hand side of the following equations.

a) $y = \int (-1)^2\,dp$ b) $z = \int \left(\sqrt{x}\right)^5\,dx$ c) $p = \int \left(\frac{2}{z}\right)^4\,dz$

d) $y = \int \frac{4}{\sqrt{x}}\,dx$ e) $s = \int (2t)^2\,dt$ f) $I = \int \frac{\left(\sqrt{x}\right)^6(x^2)^{-2}}{\left(x\sqrt{x}\right)^4}\,dx$

11.4 Sums and Differences

You can integrate sums and differences by integrating each term in turn. The general result is:

$$\int (f(x) + g(x))\,dx = \int f(x)\,dx + \int g(x)\,dx$$

EXAMPLE 1

Find y where: $y = \int (x^2 + x^3)\,dx$

The brackets make it clear that $(x^2 + x^3)$ is being integrated, not just x^2.

Integrate each term:

$$y = \frac{1}{3}x^3 + \frac{1}{4}x^4 + c$$

Strictly speaking, both terms give constants when integrated.
We combine them into a single constant, c.

You may need to expand brackets and re-arrange in other ways before integrating.

EXAMPLE 2

Expand the brackets and integrate: $\int \left(x^2 + \frac{1}{x}\right)^2 dx$

$$\begin{aligned}\int \left(x^2 + \frac{1}{x}\right)^2 dx &= \int \left(x^4 + 2(x^2)\left(\frac{1}{x}\right) + \left(\frac{1}{x}\right)^2\right) dx \\ &= \int (x^4 + 2x + x^{-2})\,dx \\ &= \frac{1}{5}x^5 + x^2 - x^{-1} + c\end{aligned}$$

EXAMPLE 3

Find: $\int \left(\left(\sqrt{x}\right)^3 + \frac{1}{\sqrt{x}}\right) dx$

Rewrite using index notation:

$$\begin{aligned}\int \left(\left(\sqrt{x}\right)^3 + \frac{1}{\sqrt{x}}\right) dx &= \int \left(x^{\frac{3}{2}} + x^{-\frac{1}{2}}\right) dx \\ &= \frac{2}{5}x^{\frac{5}{2}} + 2x^{\frac{1}{2}} + c\end{aligned}$$

EXAMPLE 4

Find: $\int (ax^2 + bx + c)\,dx$

$$\int (ax^2 + bx + c)\,dx = \frac{a}{3}x^3 + \frac{b}{2}x^2 + cx + d$$

We call the constant d here because c is already being used.

EXERCISE 11D

1. Find the following integrals.

a) $\int \left(3 + 4x^{\frac{3}{4}}\right) dx$ b) $\int \left(4 + 3\sqrt{x}\right) dx$ c) $\int (8x^2 + 7x)\, dx$

d) $\int (2x^4 + 3x)\, dx$ e) $\int (6x^3 + 4x)\, dx$ f) $\int \left(4 + \frac{3}{x^2}\right) dx$

g) $\int x(4 - x)\, dx$ h) $\int x(9 - x)\, dx$ i) $\int \left(x^{-7} + 4\sqrt{x}\right) dx$

j) $\int \left(x^{-4} + 6\sqrt{x}\right) dx$ k) $\int (3x^3 + 5x)\, dx$ l) $\int (8x - x^2 - 8)\, dx$

2. Given $f(x)$, find: $\int f(x)\, dx$

a) $f'(x) = 4x^3 + 3x^2 + 6$ b) $f'(x) = 16x^3 + 6x^2 + 5$

c) $f'(x) = 12x^3 + 6x^2 + 7$ d) $f'(x) = \frac{x}{2} + \frac{3}{x^2}$ e) $f'(x) = \frac{x}{3} + \frac{4}{x^2}$

f) $f'(x) = x^2 - 8x + 3$ g) $f'(x) = x^3 - 24x^2 + 144x$

h) $f'(x) = x^3 - 7x^2 + 15x + 3$ i) $f'(x) = x^2 - 4x + 3$

j) $f'(x) = x^2 + 7x + 19$

3. Expand the brackets to find:

a) $\int 4(2x^4 + x)\, dx$ b) $\int (x + 2)^2\, dx$ c) $\int (x^2 - 2)^2\, dx$

d) $\int \left(4\sqrt{x} + 9\right)^2 dx$ e) $\int (2 - x)^2\, dx$ f) $\int \left(1 - \frac{1}{x^2}\right)^2 dx$

g) $\int (1 - x)(1 + 2x)\, dx$ h) $\int x(2x^2 + 3x)\, dx$ i) $\int \frac{1}{x^4}(2x + 1)^2\, dx$

j) $\int x(x^2 + 2x + 1)^2\, dx$

4. If k is a constant, find:

a) $\int (k + 2)^2\, dx$ b) $\int (k + 2x)^2\, dx$ c) $\int (kx + 2)^2\, dx$ d) $\int (kx + 2x)^2\, dx$

5. Re-arrange or simplify to find the following integrals.

a) $\int \frac{(x^2 + 1)}{x^2} dx$ b) $\int \frac{(\sqrt{t} - 2t)}{t} dt$ c) $\int \frac{(\sqrt{z} + 3z)}{\sqrt{z}} dz$

d) $\int x\left(\frac{\sqrt{x} + 1}{2x^3}\right) dx$ e) $\int \frac{x^2 - 4}{x^3(x + 2)} dx$ f) $\int \frac{\theta - 1}{\theta\sqrt{\theta}} d\theta$

g) $\int \frac{1 + s}{\sqrt[3]{s}\sqrt{s}} ds$

6. Given: $\frac{dy}{dx} = 7 + \frac{2}{x^2}$ use integration to find y in terms of x.

7. Given: $\int 2(p + 3x)^2\, dx = 6x^3 - 24x^2 + 32x + c$ what is the value of p?

EXERCISE

EXERCISE

11.5 Finding the Constant of Integration

As mentioned in the Section 11.2, a constant of integration will always appear in the solution to an indefinite integration. This is because there are an infinite number of curves that have the same gradient function.

$$y = x^2 + 1 \Rightarrow \frac{dy}{dx} = 2x$$

$$y = x^2 \Rightarrow \frac{dy}{dx} = 2x$$

$$y = x^2 - 4 \Rightarrow \frac{dy}{dx} = 2x \quad \text{etc}$$

In each case $\int 2x\,dx = x^2 + c$

The family of curves $y = x^2 + c$ are all translations of each other parallel to the y-axis:

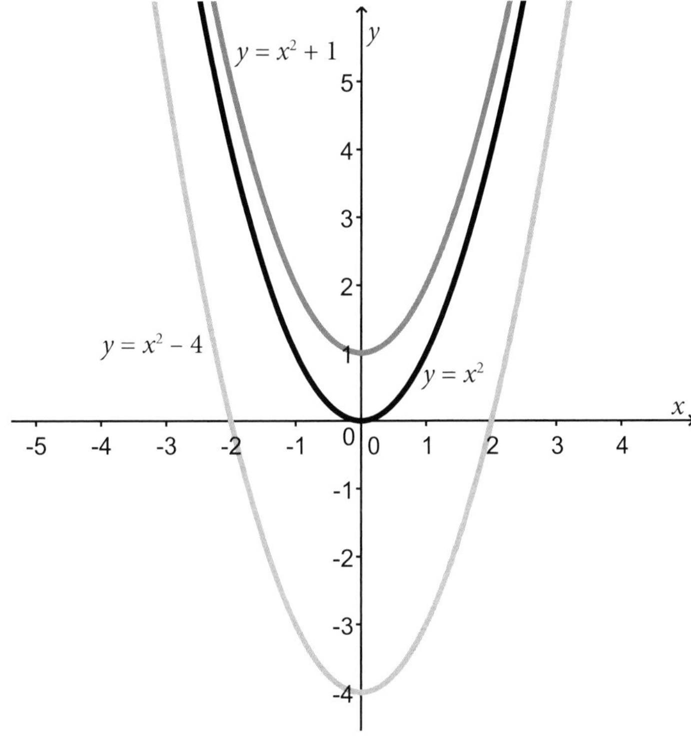

If we have been told a point on the curve, we can work out the constant of integration and the correct equation of the curve.

EXAMPLE 1

The gradient function of a curve is given by: $\frac{dy}{dx} = 6 + \frac{2}{x^2}$

a) Use integration to find y in terms of x.

b) Given also that the point (2, 7) lies on the curve, find the value of y at $x = 3$.

---

a) $y = \int \left(6 + \frac{2}{x^2}\right) dx$

$y = \int (6 + 2x^{-2})\,dx$

$y = 6x - 2x^{-1} + c$

continued...

Example 1... b) $y = 7$ when $x = 2$, therefore: $7 = 12 - 1 + c$

$$c = -4$$

So when $x = 3$: $y = 6x - 2x^{-1} + c$

$$y = 18 - \frac{2}{3} - 4$$

$$y = \frac{40}{3}$$

EXAMPLE 2

$$y = \int 2x\, dx$$

Find y in terms of x given that $x = 1$ when $y = 3$.

$$y = \int 2x\, dx$$

$$y = x^2 + c$$

When $x = 1$, $y = 3$, therefore: $3 = 1^2 + c$

$$c = 2$$

Therefore: $y = x^2 + 2$

EXERCISE

EXERCISE 11E

1. Given the gradient function $\frac{dy}{dx}$ of a curve and a point on the curve, find y in terms of x.

a) $\frac{dy}{dx} = 3x, \left(1, -\frac{3}{2}\right)$ b) $\frac{dy}{dx} = x^2 + 4, \left(1, \frac{16}{3}\right)$ c) $\frac{dy}{dx} = \frac{1}{x^2}, (1, 0)$

d) $\frac{dy}{dx} = x^3 + 1, (0, 1)$ e) $\frac{dy}{dx} = 2x^3 - \frac{3}{2}x^2 + x, (1, 2)$

f) $\frac{dy}{dx} = \frac{x-1}{x^3}, \left(1, -\frac{1}{2}\right)$ g) $\frac{dy}{dx} = \sqrt{x}, (1, 1)$ h) $\frac{dy}{dx} = 2x^2 + \sqrt{x}, (1, 2)$

i) $\frac{dy}{dx} = x^2 + 6x + 1, (-2, 8)$ j) $\frac{dy}{dx} = \frac{1}{x^2} + x^{-\frac{5}{2}}, \left(2, -\frac{2}{5}\right)$

2. Given that: $\frac{dy}{dx} = 5 + \frac{3}{x^2}$

a) Use integration to find y in terms of x.

b) Given also that $y = 5$ when $x = 2$, find the value of y at $x = 3$.

3. The gradient function of a curve is given by: $\frac{dy}{dx} = 4x^4 + 6x$

Given that $y = 8$ when $x = 0$, integrate to find y as a function of x.

4. Integrate to find y, given that: $\frac{dy}{dx} = 4x^2 + 7x$ and that $y = 6$ when $x = 1$.

5. The gradient function of a curve is given by: $\frac{dy}{dx} = ax + b$.
Given that the curve passes through the points (0, 2), (1, 3) and (2, 2), find a, b and the constant of integration. Hence state the equation of the curve.

EXERCISE

EXERCISE

6. The second derivative of a function can be written as $\frac{d^2y}{dx^2}$ or $f''(x)$.
It is obtained by differentiating a function twice. In reverse, you can integrate the second derivative twice to obtain the original function. Remember to include a constant of integration each time you integrate.
a) Given $\frac{d^2y}{dx^2} = 4x$ and given that $\frac{dy}{dx} = 1$ when $x = 1$, find $\frac{dy}{dx}$ in terms of x.
b) Given that $y = 10$ when $x = 3$, find y in terms of x.

EXERCISE

11.6 Definite Integration

Indefinite integration, introduced in the previous sections, gives you an integral as a function of x.

You can find the **numerical** value of an integral using a technique called **definite integration**. In the following sections, we will use this technique to find areas enclosed by curves.

Definite integrals are written with an upper and a lower limit, for example: $\int_1^3 x^3 \, dx$

These limits are values x of used to find exact values of the integral. The integral between the limits is evaluated by subtracting the value of the integral at the lower limit from the value at the upper limit.

Sometimes you may see the words 'upper bound' and 'lower bound'.
These mean the same as 'upper limit' and 'lower limit'.

You do not need a constant of integration when performing definite integration. Write the result of the integration inside square brackets, keeping the limits. In the next step, substitute the limits and subtract.

EXAMPLE 1

Find: $\int_1^3 x^3 \, dx$

Put the result of the integration in square brackets with the limits:

$$\int_1^3 x^3 \, dx = \left[\frac{1}{4}x^4\right]_1^3$$

Replace the square brackets with two sets of round brackets. In place of x, substitute in the limits. Subtract the result at the lower limit from the result at the upper limit.

$$= \left(\frac{1}{4}(3)^4\right) - \left(\frac{1}{4}(1)^4\right)$$

$$= \frac{81}{4} - \frac{1}{4}$$

$$= 20$$

EXAMPLE 2

Find: $\int_3^5 (x-1)\,dx$

$$\int_3^5 (x-1)\,dx = \left[\frac{1}{2}x^2 - x\right]_3^5$$
$$= \left(\frac{1}{2}(5)^2 - 5\right) - \left(\frac{1}{2}(3)^2 - 3\right)$$
$$= \left(\frac{25}{2} - 5\right) - \left(\frac{9}{2} - 3\right)$$

Be careful with the signs, especially in the second set of brackets.

$$= \frac{15}{2} - \frac{3}{2}$$
$$= 6$$

The general result is:

$$\int_a^b f'(x)\,dx = f(b) - f(a)$$

where $f'(x)$ is the gradient function of $f(x)$.

11.7 Area Defined by a Curve and the x-axis

You can use definite integration to find the area between a curve and either of the coordinate axes. Most often, you will be asked to find the area between a curve and the x-axis.

EXAMPLE 1

Find the area A under the curve $y = x^2$ between $x = 2$ and $x = 4$.

A sketch is not essential, but you may find it useful:

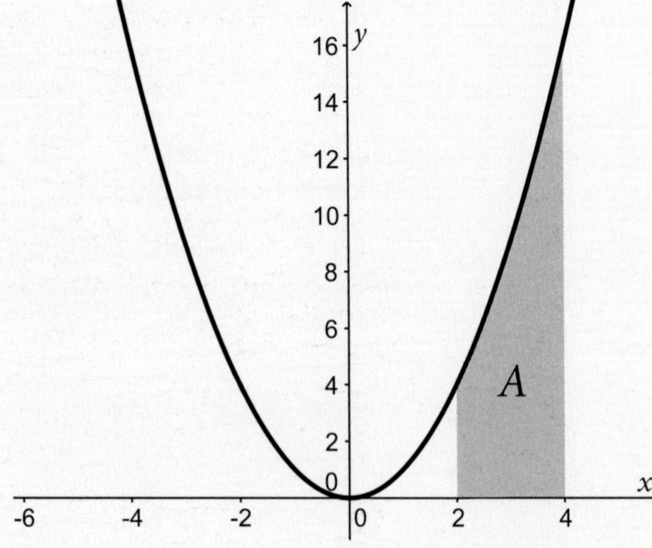

$$A = \int_2^4 x^2\,dx$$
$$= \left[\frac{1}{3}x^3\right]_2^4$$
$$= \left(\frac{1}{3}(4)^3\right) - \left(\frac{1}{3}(2)^3\right)$$
$$= \frac{64}{3} - \frac{8}{3}$$
$$= \frac{56}{3}$$

Note: There are no units. You may write "square units", but you will not be penalised for omitting this.

Sometimes you will be required to work out the upper and lower limits. In these cases, you must find where the curve intersects the x-axis.

EXAMPLE 2

Find the area enclosed by the curve $y = x(4 - x)$ and the x-axis.

Firstly, sketch the curve to find out where it intersects the x-axis.

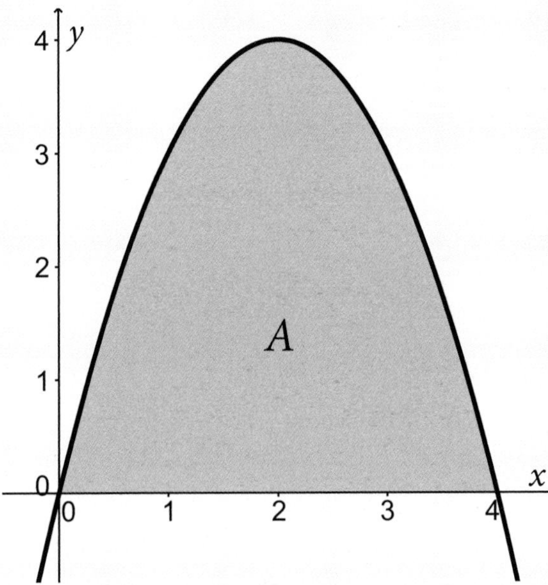

The sketch shows that the curve crosses the x-axis at (0, 0) and (4, 0). Our upper and lower limits are therefore $x = 4$ and $x = 0$.

$$A = \int_0^4 x(4 - x)\,dx$$

$$= \left[2x^2 - \frac{1}{3}x^3\right]_0^4$$

$$= \left(2(4)^2 - \frac{1}{3}(4)^3\right) - \left(2(0)^2 - \frac{1}{3}(0)^3\right)$$

$$= \left(32 - \frac{64}{3}\right) - (0 - 0)$$

$$= \frac{32}{3}$$

Note: As in most of the A-Level topics, answers are usually left as improper fractions rather than mixed numbers or decimals.

If the curve lies below the x-axis, the result from the definite integration will be negative. When finding an area, you should report the positive value.

EXAMPLE 3

Find the area enclosed by the curve $y = (x - 1)^3$, the x-axis and the y-axis.

Firstly, sketch the curve to find our limits. Remember that $y = (x - 1)^3$ is a translation by 1 unit in the positive x-direction of the curve $y = x^3$.

The curve intersects the x-axis at (1, 0), so the upper limit for the integration is $x = 1$.

To the left, the area is enclosed by the y-axis, so the lower limit is $x = 0$.

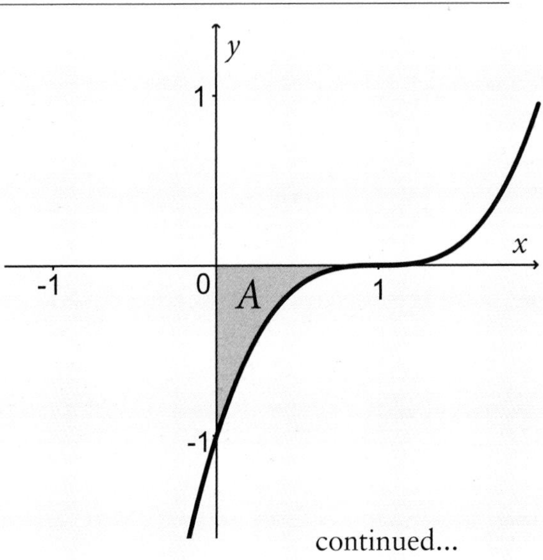

continued...

Example 3...

$$\int_0^1 (x-1)^3\,dx = \int_0^1 (x^3 - 3x^2 + 3x - 1)\,dx$$

$$= \left[\frac{x^4}{4} - x^3 + \frac{3x^2}{2} - x\right]_0^1$$

$$= \left(\frac{1^4}{4} - 1^3 + \frac{3(1)^2}{2} - 1\right) - \left(\frac{0^4}{4} - 0^3 + \frac{3(0)^2}{2} - 0\right)$$

$$= \left(\frac{1}{4} - 1 + \frac{3}{2} - 1\right) - 0$$

$$= -\frac{1}{4}$$

The integration gives a negative result because the area lies below the x-axis. When reporting the area, we must give the positive value.

$$A = \frac{1}{4}$$

Sometimes, a part of the curve lies above and a part below the x-axis. In these cases, you must consider each part separately. The result from one part will be negative. When finding the total area, make both answers positive and add them.

EXAMPLE 4

Find the total enclosed by the curve $y = x(x-2)$, the line $x = 3$ and the x-axis.

In order to sketch the curve, note that it is a translation of $y = x^2$, one unit in the positive x-direction and one unit in the negative y-direction.

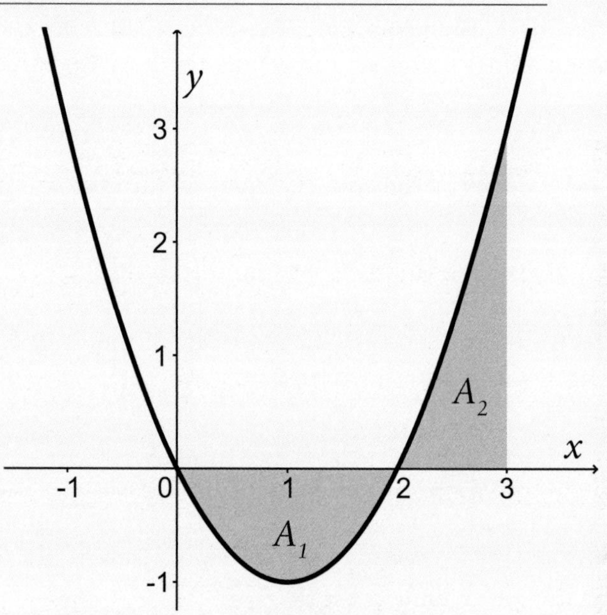

We can see that the curve intersects the x-axis at (0, 0) and (2, 0).

Between $x = 0$ and $x = 2$, the curve lies below the x-axis.

Between $x = 2$ and $x = 3$, the curve lies above the x-axis.

We must consider these two areas separately.

continued...

Example 4...

To find A_1:

$$\int_0^2 x(x-2)\,dx = \int_0^2 (x^2-2x)\,dx$$
$$= \left[\frac{1}{3}x^3 - x^2\right]_0^2$$
$$= \left(\frac{1}{3}2^3 - 2^2\right) - \left(\frac{1}{3}0^3 - 0^2\right)$$
$$= -\frac{4}{3}$$

Area $A_1 = \frac{4}{3}$

To find A_2:

$$\int_2^3 x(x-2)\,dx = \int_2^3 (x^2-2x)\,dx$$
$$= \left[\frac{1}{3}x^3 - x^2\right]_2^3$$
$$= \left(\frac{1}{3}3^3 - 3^2\right) - \left(\frac{1}{3}2^3 - 2^2\right)$$
$$= 0 - \left(-\frac{4}{3}\right)$$

Area $A_2 = \frac{4}{3}$

Thus the total area is $A_1 + A_2 = \frac{8}{3}$

EXERCISE 11F

EXERCISE

1. Evaluate the following. Give your answers to 3 significant figures where appropriate.

a) $\int_0^3 x(4-x)\,dx$ b) $\int_0^7 x(8-x)\,dx$ c) $\int_4^6 (x^{-3} + 10\sqrt{x})\,dx$

d) $\int_1^4 (8x^3 + 6x^2 + 4)\,dx$ e) $\int_1^2 (12x^3 + 9x^2 + 2)\,dx$ f) $\int_2^9 (5x^3 + 4x)\,dx$

g) $\int_1^5 (8x^3 + 7x)\,dx$ h) $\int_1^4 6\sqrt{x}\,dx$ i) $\int_0^4 (3\sqrt{x} + x)\,dx$

j) $\int_1^2 x^2\left(1 - \frac{1}{x^4}\right)dx$

2. Evaluate the following definite integrals. Give your answer in the form $a + b\sqrt{c}$ where a and b are integers.

a) $\int_1^8 \frac{2}{\sqrt{x}}dx$ b) $\int_1^{27} \frac{3}{\sqrt{x}}dx$ c) $\int_1^{125} \frac{6}{\sqrt{x}}dx$

3. The curve C is defined by the equation: $y = x^3 - 24x^2 + 144x$ as shown.

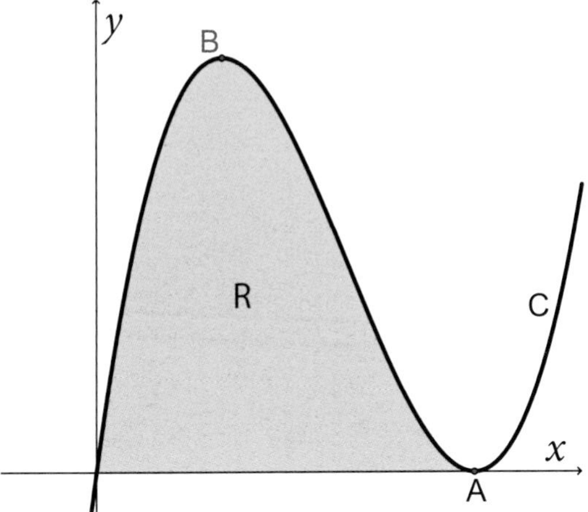

EXERCISE

C touches the x-axis at A and has a maximum turning point at B.

a) Show that the equation of the curve may be written as $y = x(x - 12)^2$

b) and hence write down the coordinates of A.

c) Find the coordinates of B.

d) The shaded region R is bounded by the curve and the x-axis. Find the area of R.

4. The diagram shows a sketch of $y = x^2 - 5x + 4$ with areas A and B. Find the areas A and B and the total shaded area.

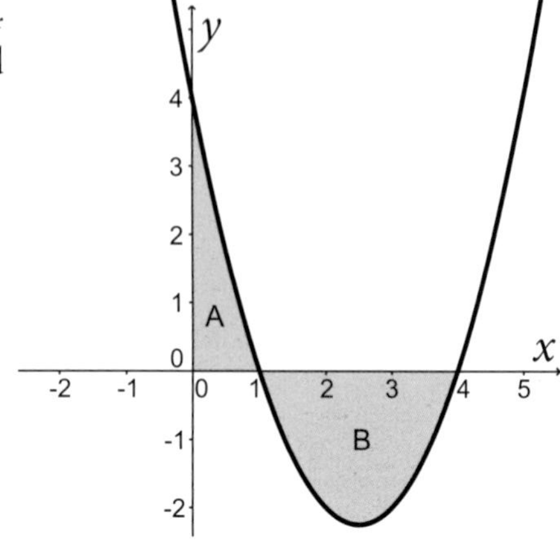

5. The diagram shows a sketch of part of the curve C with equation $y = x(x - 3)(x - 6)$ Use calculus to find the total area of the finite region shown, bounded by the lines $x = 0$ and $x = 5$, curve C and the x-axis.

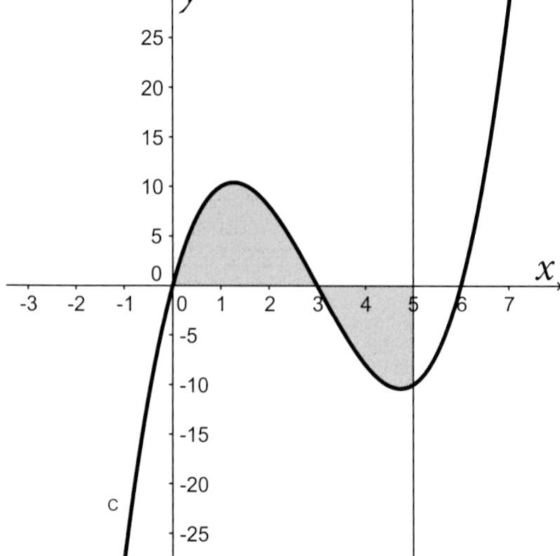

6. The diagram shows the logo of an Olympic ski jump venue. The design is modelled on a curve with equation: $y = 2x^3 - 6x^2 + 5x + 2$

The units on both axes are centimetres. Calculate how much material is required to make the shaded part of the logo.

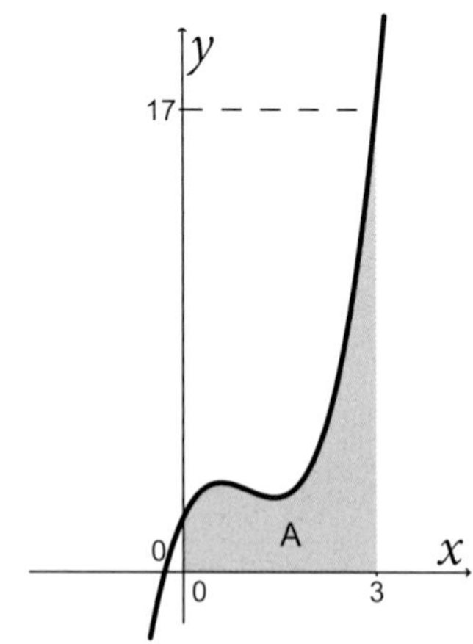

EXERCISE

EXERCISE

EXERCISE

7. The diagram shows a part of the curve: $y = 2x^3 - 4x^2$

a) Find the value of a, the x-coordinate of the point where the curve crosses the x-axis.

b) Given that the two shaded regions are equal in area, find the value of b.

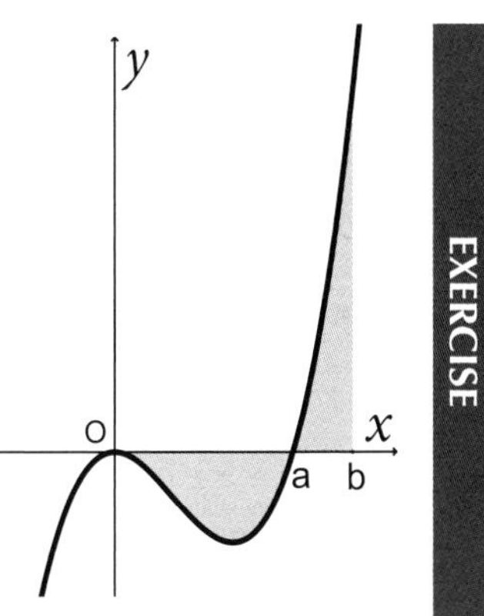

EXERCISE

11.8 Area Defined by a Curve and the y-axis

You can also use integration to find the area between a curve and the y-axis.

In this case, you must find x as a function of y, then integrate x with respect to y. The limits will refer to y-values. That is:

$$A = \int_a^b x\,dy$$

EXAMPLE 1

Calculate the area A shown in the diagram, bounded by the curve $y = x^2$, the y-axis and the straight lines $y = 2$ and $y = 4$.

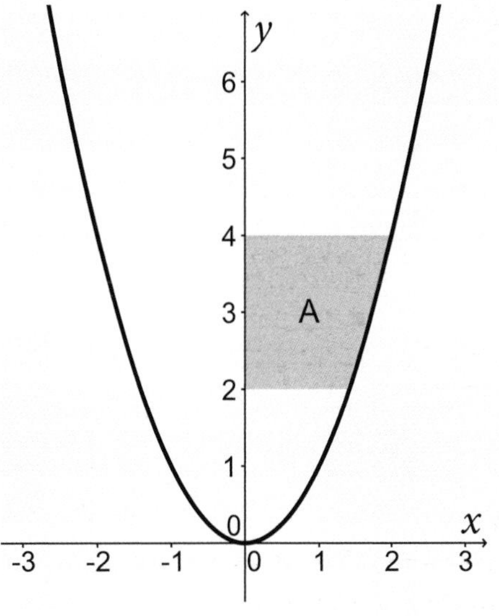

Re-arrange the equation of the curve to obtain x as a function of y:

$$y = x^2 \Rightarrow x = y^{\frac{1}{2}}$$

Now integrate with respect to y between the limits on the y-axis:

$$A = \int_2^4 y^{\frac{1}{2}}\,dy$$

$$= \left[\frac{2}{3}y^{\frac{3}{2}}\right]_2^4$$

$$= \left(\frac{2}{3}(4)^{\frac{3}{2}}\right) - \left(\frac{2}{3}(2)^{\frac{3}{2}}\right)$$

$$= 3.45 \text{ (3 s.f.)}$$

Note: The answer to the integration will be negative if the area under consideration lies to the left of the y-axis. As before, if you are required to give an area, you must report the positive value.

11.9 Area Between Two Curves

It is also possible to find the area between a curve and a straight line, or between two curves. If a diagram is not given, a sketch is essential in these cases.

The area is found by integrating the difference between the two functions.

$$A = \int_a^b (f(x) - g(x))\, dx$$

EXAMPLE 1

Find the area between the curve $y = x^2$ and the straight line $y = x$.

In this question no diagram is given, so we draw a sketch of the two functions and the area enclosed.

To find out the intersection points, we solve:

$$x^2 = x$$
$$x(x-1) = 0$$
$$x = 0 \text{ or } x = 1$$

When $x = 0$, $y = 0$. When $x = 1$, $y = 1$.

So the intersection points are (0, 0) and (1, 1).

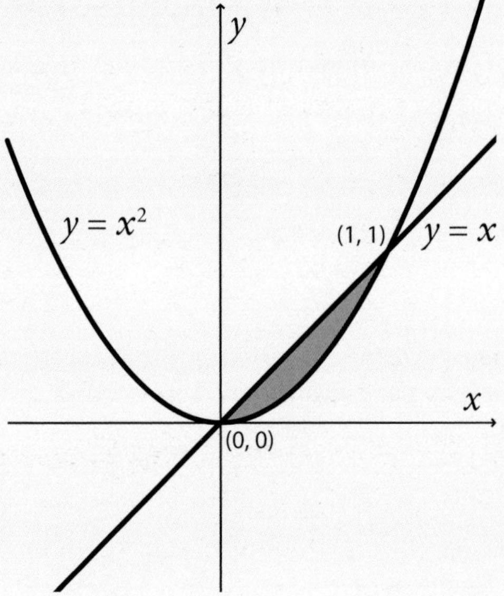

Note: It is important to subtract the function with the lower values in the range from the function with the higher values. If your subtraction is the other way round, your answer will be negative.

From the diagram we can see that the function $y = x^2$ is less than $y = x$ between $x = 0$ and $x = 1$. We must subtract x^2 from x and integrate.

$$A = \int_0^1 (x - x^2)\, dx$$
$$= \left[\frac{x^2}{2} - \frac{x^3}{3}\right]_0^1$$
$$= \left(\frac{1^2}{2} - \frac{1^3}{3}\right) - \left(\frac{0^2}{2} - \frac{0^3}{3}\right)$$
$$= \frac{1}{6}$$

EXERCISE 11G

1. Ollie is standing at point O, at the bottom of a hill with equation: $y = \frac{x}{3}$

   His friend Becky is standing on the hill at point B. Ollie throws a snowball at Becky and the snowball flies through the air with equation: $y = 4x - x^2$

   The snowball makes a direct hit.

   All distances are measured in metres.

   a) Calculate Becky's exact position, i.e. the coordinates of point B.

   b) Find the area of R, the region bounded by the slope and the trajectory of the snowball.

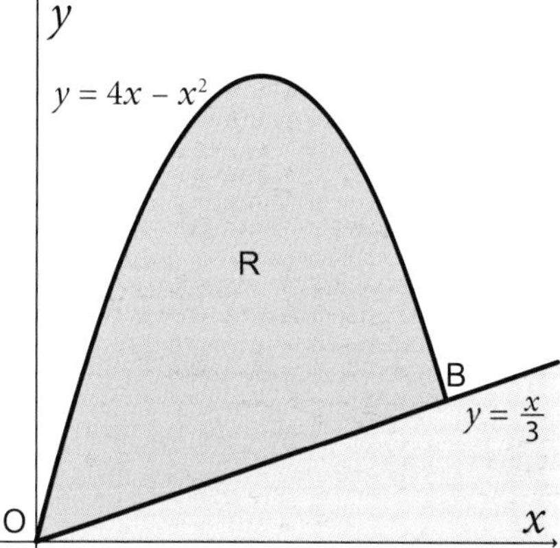

2. The curve C shown represents the graph of $y = \frac{x^2}{4}$

   The points A and B on the curve C have x-coordinates 2 and 4 respectively.

   a) Write down the y-coordinates of A and B.

   The finite region R is enclosed by C, the y-axis and the lines through A and B parallel to the x-axis.

   b) Express x in terms of y.

   c) Use integration to find the area of R.

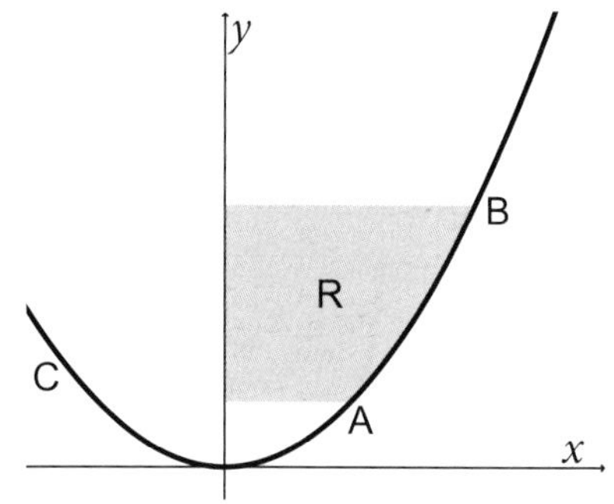

3. The diagram shows a sketch of part of the curve C with equation $y = x^3 - 7x^2 + 15x + 4$

   The point P, on C, has x-coordinate 1 and the point Q is the minimum turning point of C.

   a) Find $\frac{dy}{dx}$

   b) Find the coordinates of Q.

   c) Show that PQ is parallel to the x-axis.

   d) Calculate the area, shown shaded, bounded by C and the line PQ.

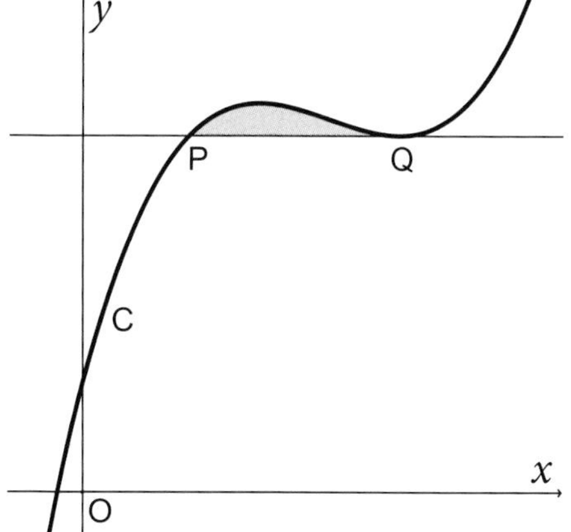

EXERCISE

EXERCISE

4. The diagram shows the curves $y = x^2 - 3$ and $y = 4 - x^2$ and the area A enclosed between them.

   a) Show that the x-coordinates of points B and C are $\pm\sqrt{\frac{7}{2}}$.

   b) Find the area A to 3 significant figures.

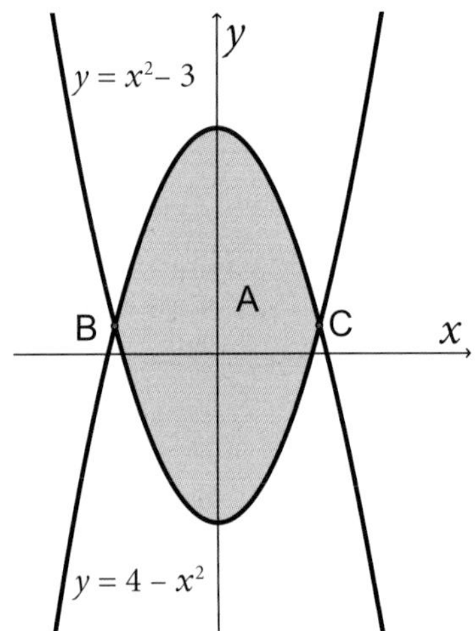

5. The line with equation: $y = 5x + 17$ and the curve with equation $y = x^2 + 8x + 7$ intersect at the points A and B, as shown.

   a) Find the coordinates of the points A and B.

   The shaded region S is bounded by the line and the curve.

   b) Use calculus to find the area of S.

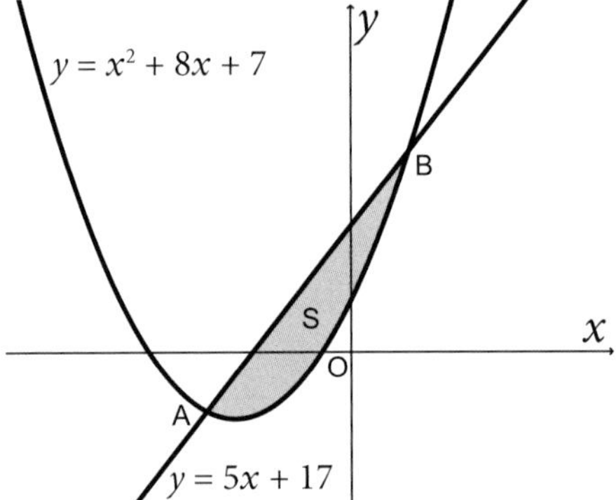

6. The curve given by $y = x^3 - 7x^2 + 16x$ has a maximum point at A and a minimum at B, as shown.

   a) Use calculus to find the x-coordinates of A and B.

   The line through B parallel to the y-axis meets the x-axis at the point N. The region R is bounded by the curve, the x-axis and the line from A to N.

   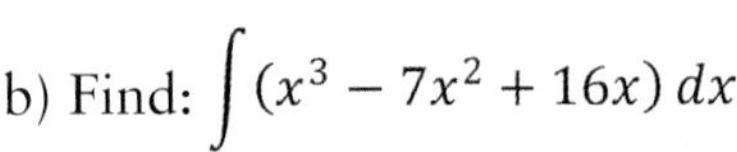

   b) Find: $\int (x^3 - 7x^2 + 16x)\, dx$

   c) Hence calculate the area of R.

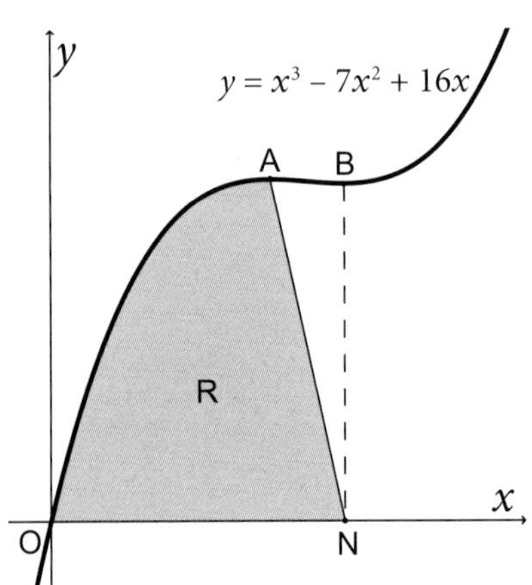

EXERCISE

7. The diagram shows the curves $f(x) = x^2$ and $g(x) = x^3$.

   The two curves intersect at points A(0, 0) and B.

   a) Find the coordinates of B.

   b) Using integration, find the shaded area between the curves.

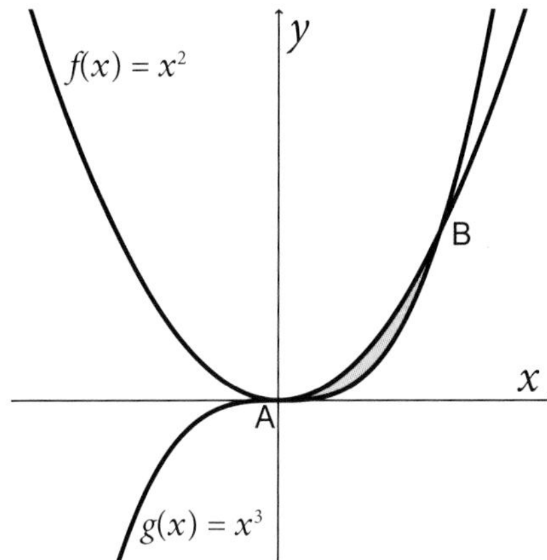

8. The diagram shows the curve $f(x) = x^3$

   The point A has coordinates (1, 0) and $B\left(2^{\frac{1}{3}}, 0\right)$.

   The points C and D lie on the curve and have the same x-coordinates as A and B respectively.

   a) Find the y-coordinates of points C and D.

   b) Show that the area A_1 is $\frac{3}{4}\left(2^{\frac{4}{3}} - 1\right)$.

   c) Find the exact value of the area A_2.

   d) Find the ratio $A_1 : A_2$.

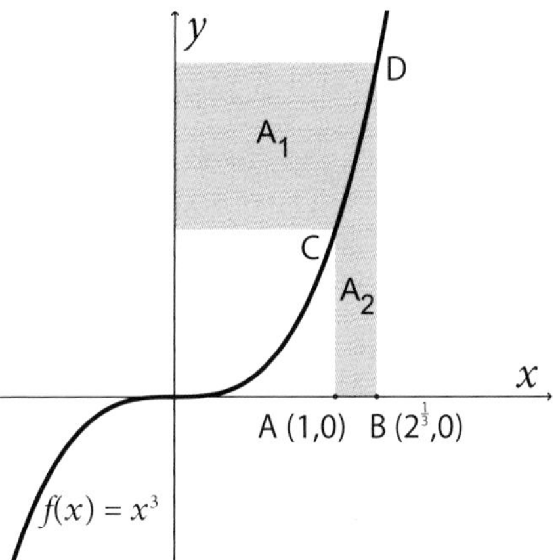

EXERCISE

11.10 The Trapezium Rule

Sometimes you may need to find the area under a curve, but it is not possible to integrate the function.

There are various techniques to find an approximation of the area under a curve. In this section we introduce the trapezium rule. The area is divided into strips or intervals, with each strip the shape of a trapezium, as shown in the diagram. The combined area of the trapezia is approximately equal to the area under the curve.

This diagram shows how we would approximate the integral $\int_a^b f(x)\,dx$ using 5 strips.

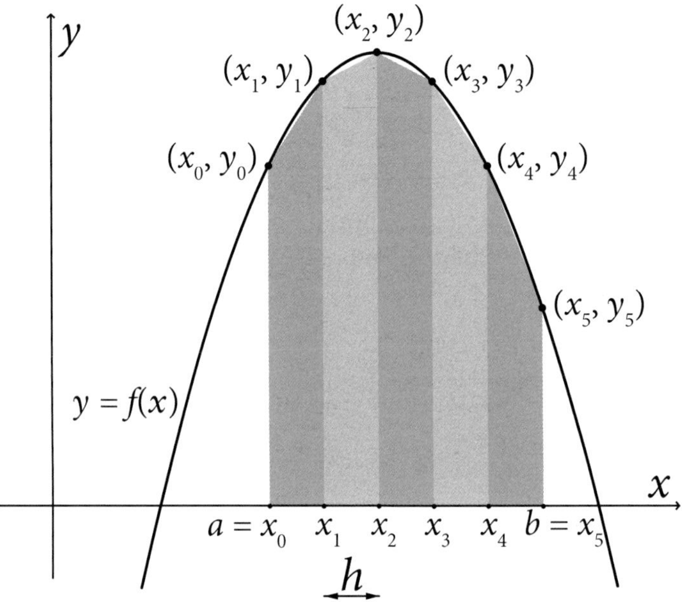

The Trapezium Rule can be written as:

$$\int_a^b f(x)\,dx \approx \frac{1}{2}h[y_0 + 2(y_1 + \cdots + y_{n-1}) + y_n]$$

where $y_0, \ldots, y_n$ are the ordinates (y-values) and h is the width of each strip.

$$h = \frac{b-a}{n} \text{ where } n \text{ is the number of strips.}$$

Notice that, in the example above, there are 5 strips (or intervals), but 6 ordinates. A question may specify the number of strips or the number of ordinates. The number of ordinates is always one more than the number of strips.

PROOF OF THE TRAPEZIUM RULE

You do not need to learn this proof.

The area of a trapezium is $\frac{1}{2}(a+b)h$ where a and b are the lengths of the parallel sides and h is the distance between them.

- The area of the first trapezium is $\frac{1}{2}(y_1 + y_0)h$
- The area of the second trapezium is $\frac{1}{2}(y_2 + y_1)h$

...

- The area of the last trapezium is $\frac{1}{2}(y_n + y_{n-1})h$

So $A \approx \frac{1}{2}(y_0 + y_1)h + \frac{1}{2}(y_1 + y_2)h + \cdots + \frac{1}{2}(y_{n-2} + y_{n-1})h + \frac{1}{2}(y_{n-1} + y_n)h$

continued...

Factorising, by taking $\frac{1}{2}h$ outside brackets:

$$A \approx \frac{1}{2}h[(y_0 + y_1) + (y_1 + y_2) + \cdots + (y_{n-2} + y_{n-1}) + (y_{n-1} + y_n)]$$

Notice that y_0 and y_n only appear once in the summation. All other y-values appear twice. So:

$$A \approx \frac{1}{2}h[y_0 + 2(y_1 + \cdots + y_{n-1}) + y_n]$$

EXAMPLE 1

Use the trapezium rule with 5 strips to estimate: $\int_1^6 \frac{x}{1+x^2}\,dx$. Use 4 decimal places where appropriate in your working and give your answer to 3 significant figures.

$a = 1$ and $b = 6$

The width of each strip h is found using: $h = \frac{b-a}{n}$

$$= \frac{6-1}{5} = 1$$

Five strips means 6 ordinates. The x values to use are 1, 2, 3, 4, 5 and 6.
We calculate the ordinates:

x	1	2	3	4	5	6
$y = \frac{x}{1+x^2}$	0.5	0.4	0.3	0.23529	0.19231	0.16216

$$A \approx \frac{1}{2}h[y_0 + 2(y_1 + \cdots + y_{n-1}) + y_n]$$

$$A \approx \frac{1}{2}(1)[0.5 + 2(0.4 + 0.3 + 0.23529 + 0.19231) + 0.16216]$$

$$A \approx 1.458683$$

$$A \approx 1.46 \text{ (3 s.f.)}$$

(The true area, using calculus, is 1.45889 to 6 s.f.)

Generally, the greater the number of strips, the better the approximation.

EXERCISE

EXERCISE 11H

1. a) Find an approximation to the area bounded by the x-axis, $y = 3x^2$, $x = 4$ and $x = 7$ using 3 intervals (i.e. 4 ordinates).
   b) Find the exact area.

2. The diagram shows a part of the curve $y = \frac{x}{(1+x)^2}$.

EXERCISE

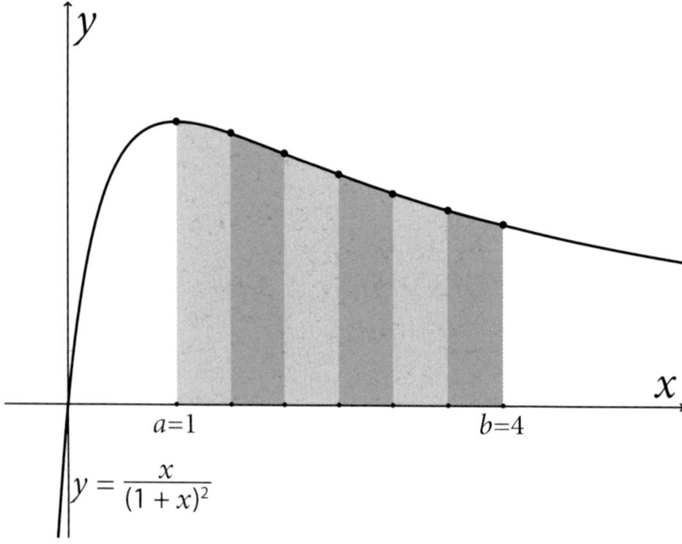

a) Complete the table below, to find the y-values associated with the x-values given. Give your answers to 5 decimal places where appropriate.

x	1	1.5	2	2.5	3	3.5	4
$y = \frac{x}{(1+x)^2}$							

b) Using the trapezium rule with 6 strips, find an approximation to: $\int_1^4 \frac{x}{(1+x)^2}\,dx$

3. Using the trapezium rule with 4 strips, find an approximation for the area under the curve $y = \frac{1}{1+x}$ between $x = 1$ and $x = 5$.

4. Find an approximation for $\int_0^3 2^x\,dx$. Use the trapezium rule with 7 ordinates.

5. The diagram shows a part of the curve $y = \sqrt{5x + 25}$.

a) Use the trapezium rule with 6 ordinates to approximate the following integral, giving your answer to 3 significant figures.
$\int_{-5}^{0} \sqrt{5x + 25}\,dx$

b) Re-arrange $y = \sqrt{5x + 25}$ to make x the subject of the equation.

c) Integrate x with respect to y between appropriate limits to find the exact area between the curve and the axes.

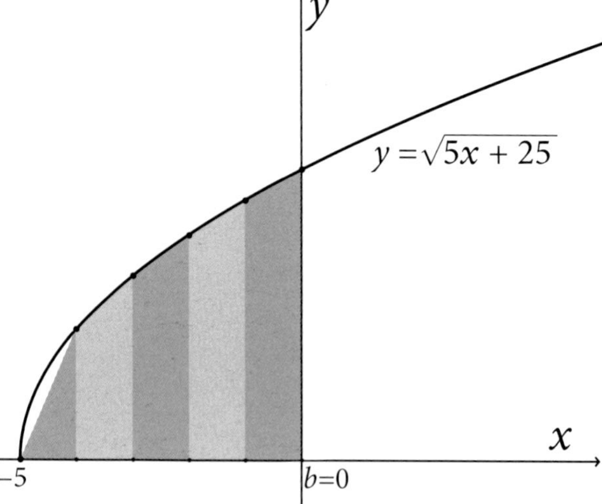

6. a) Complete the following table of values for $y = x(2 - x)$.

x	0	0.5	1	1.5	2
$y = x(2 - x)$	0		1		

b) Using your table of values, or otherwise, sketch the curve $y = x(2 - x)$ for $0 \leq x \leq 2$.

c) Use the trapezium rule with 4 strips to approximate: $\int_0^2 x(2 - x)\,dx$

d) Draw a new table using 9 values: 0, 0.25, 0.5, ..., 1.75 and 2. Calculate the y values and complete the table.

e) Use the trapezium rule with 8 strips to approximate: $\int_0^2 x(2 - x)\,dx$

f) By expanding the brackets and integrating, find the exact value of $\int_0^2 x(2 - x)\,dx$

g) Calculate the percentage errors:
   i) When using 4 strips using your answers to parts c) and f).
   ii) When using 8 strips using your answers to parts e) and f).

7. The speed, $v\ ms^{-1}$, of a rocket at time t seconds is given by:
$v = \sqrt{1.7^t - 1}, \qquad 0 \leq t \leq 24$

The following table shows the speed of the rocket at 4 second intervals.

t	0	4	8	12	16	20	24
v	0	2.71	8.29	-	69.75	-	-

a) Complete the table, giving the values of v to 2 decimal places.

The distance, s metres, travelled by the rocket in 24 seconds is given by:

$$s = \int_0^{24} \sqrt{1.7^t - 1}\,dt$$

b) Use the trapezium rule, with all the values from your table, to estimate the value of s.

8. The trapezium rule, with the table below, is used to estimate the area between the curve $y = \sqrt{(x^3 + 2)}$, the lines $x = 3$ and $x = 7$ and the x-axis.

x	3	4	5	6	7
y	5.385	8.124	11.269	-	-

a) Calculate, to 3 decimal places, the values of y for $x = 6$ and $x = 7$.
b) Use the values from the table and your answers to part a) to find an estimate, to 2 decimal places, for this area.

9. The diagram shows a part of a circle of radius 1.
The circle has the equation $y = \sqrt{1 - x^2}$

EXERCISE

EXERCISE

a) Use the trapezium rule with 10 strips (shown) to approximate $\int_0^1 \sqrt{1-x^2}\,dx$. Give your answer to 4 significant figures.

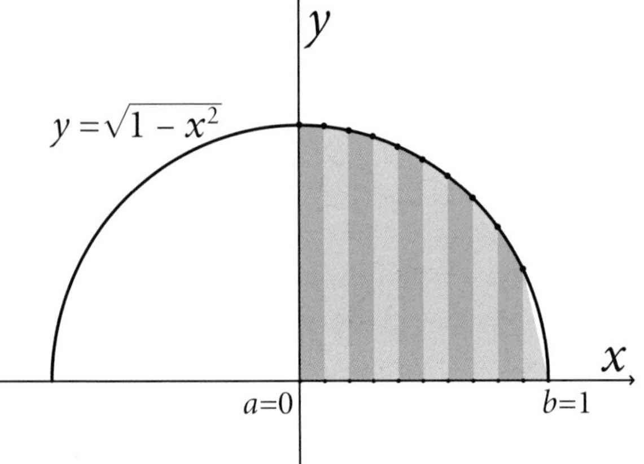

b) How could you use your answer to part a) to approximate the area of the whole circle? Find this approximation to 4 significant figures.

c) What is the exact area of the circle?

10. The diagrams show a **concave** curve and a **convex** curve. If you used the trapezium rule to find an approximation of the area beneath each curve, which approximation would be greater than the true value, which one less than it?

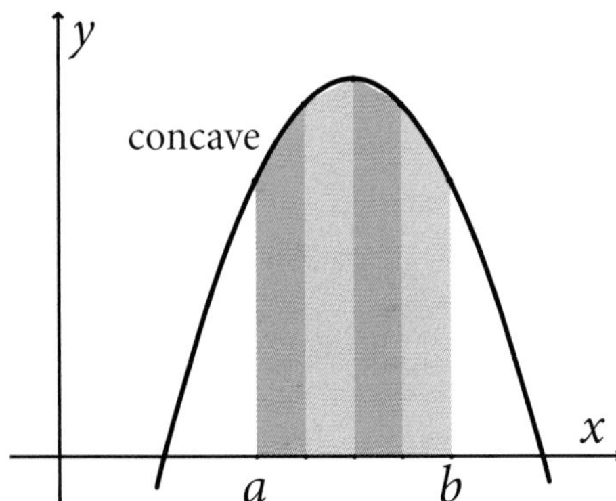

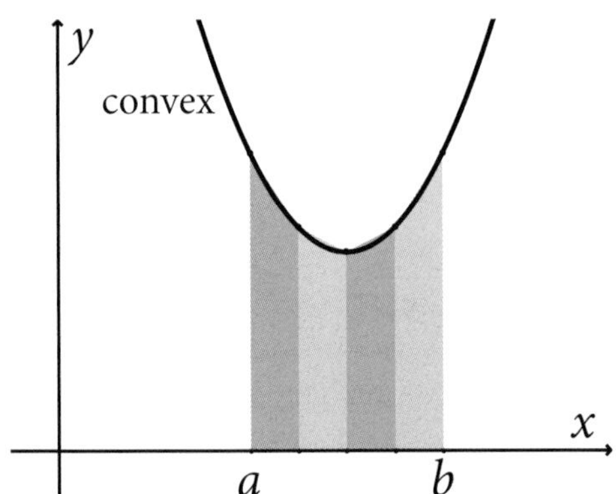

EXERCISE

SUMMARY

Indefinite integration is the reverse of differentiation. If you know the gradient function of a curve, integration will tell you the equation of the curve itself.

To integrate a function that is a power of x, raise the power by one and divide by the new power.

Sums and differences can be integrated by integrating each term in turn.

If you are told the coordinates of a point on the curve, you can calculate the constant of integration.

Definite integration is a way to find a numerical value of an integral. It can be used to measure the area between a curve and either of the coordinate axes. You can also calculate the area between two curves.

The trapezium rule can be used to approximate the area under a curve. This is an example of numerical integration.

Review Exercise

Chapters 10 and 11

EXERCISE

1. On separate diagrams, sketch the graphs of the following curves. Sketch also the curve $y = 4^x$ on each diagram. Mark clearly where each curve crosses the y-axis.
   a) $y = 4^{-x}$ b) $y = 1 + 4^{-x}$ c) $y = -4^{-x}$
   d) $y = 1 - 4^{-x}$ e) $y = 4^{2x}$ f) $y = 4^{-2x}$

2. Without a calculator, find the value of:
   a) $log_4 16$ b) $\log_3 \frac{1}{27}$

3. Write equivalent statements using logarithms:
   a) $2^4 = 16$ b) $3^{-4} = \frac{1}{81}$

4. Write equivalent statements using exponential equations:
   a) $log_2 1024 = 10$ b) $log_4 0.0625 = -2$

5. Find the base a in the following equations:
   a) $log_a 36 = 2$ b) $log_a \left(\frac{1}{6}\right) = -1$

6. By forming a log equation, solve the following equations to find x. Give your answers to 3 significant figures where appropriate.
   a) $7^x = 49$ b) $3^x = 64$

7. a) Write down the value of $log_4 64$.
   b) Express: $3\, log_a 2 + log_a 12$ as a single logarithm with base a.

8. Prove that the value of x that satisfies: $2\, log_2 x + log_2(x - 1) = 1 + log_2(35x + 100)$ is a solution of the equation $x^3 - x^2 - 70x - 200 = 0$

9. Simplify the following using the Power Law.
   a) $log_2 36$ b) $log_7 \left(\frac{1}{49}\right)$

10. Simplify
    a) $5\, log\, x + 5\, log\, y$ b) $3\, log\, p - 6\, log\, q$ c) $5\, log\, a + 7\, log\, b - 4\, log\, c$

11. Find the following logarithms using the change of base rule to change to base 10. Give your answers to 3 significant figures.
    a) $log_5 7$ b) $log_2 \left(\frac{1}{10}\right)$

continued

EXERCISE

EXERCISE

12. Take logs of each side of the equation and use the Power Law to solve these equations. Give your answers to 3 significant figures where appropriate.
 a) $2^x = 12$ b) $0.06 = 3^x$

13. Take logs of each side of the equation and use the Power Law to solve these equations. Give your answers to 3 decimal places where appropriate.
 a) $8^{x-3} = 2^{6x}$ b) $3^{x+4} = 4^x$

14. Given that $log_2 x = a$, find, in terms of a, the simplest form of:
 a) $log_2(16x)$ b) $log_2\left(\frac{x^4}{2}\right)$
 c) Hence, or otherwise, solve $log_2(16x) - log_2\left(\frac{x^4}{2}\right) = \frac{1}{2}$ giving your answer in the simplest surd form.

15. a) Using the substitution $u = 2^x$, show that the equation: $4^x - 2^{x+1} - 15 = 0$ can be written in the form $u^2 - 2u - 15 = 0$
 b) Hence solve: $4^x - 2^{x+1} - 15 = 0$ giving your answers to 2 decimal places.

16. Integrate the following to find y.
 a) $y = \int \frac{1}{2}x^7\, dx$ b) $y = \int -\frac{2}{5}x\, dx$

17. Integrate the following to find y.
 a) $y = \int \frac{1}{2}t^{-\frac{3}{2}}\, dt$ b) $y = \int 7x^{-8}\, dx$

18. Simplify the right-hand side of the following equations and integrate.
 a) $z = \int \left(\frac{1}{t}\right)^{-1} dt$ b) $p = \int \left(\frac{x}{\sqrt{x}}\right)^2 dx$

19. Integrate the following:
 a) $\int \left(8 + \frac{2}{x^2}\right) dx$ b) $\int \left(x^{-6} + 2\sqrt{x}\right) dx$

20. Expand the brackets to find:
 a) $\int 3(3x^3 + x)\, dx$ b) $\int x(x-1)^2\, dx$

21. Given the gradient function $\frac{dy}{dx}$ of a curve and a point on the curve, find y in terms of x for:
 a) $\frac{dy}{dx} = x^2 - 2x, (3, 2)$ b) $\frac{dy}{dx} = \frac{x+2}{\sqrt{x}}, \left(4, \frac{46}{3}\right)$

22. Integrate to find y, given that: $\frac{dy}{dx} = 6x^3 + 4x$ and that $y = 3$ when $x = 1$.

23. Evaluate the following. Give your answers to 3 significant figures where appropriate.
 a) $\int_0^2 x(9 - x)\, dx$ b) $\int_2^3 \left(x^{-2} + 4\sqrt{x}\right) dx$

continued

EXERCISE

24. The diagram shows the line with equation $y = 10 - x$ and the curve $y = x^2 - 3x + 2$.

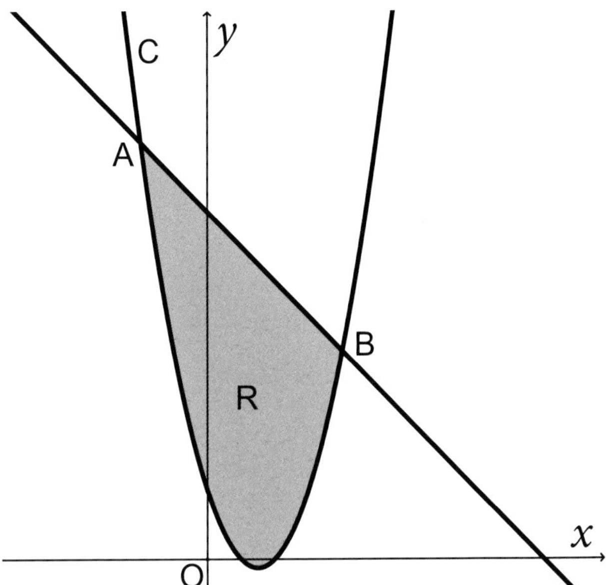

The line and the curve intersect at the points A and B, and O is the origin.
a) Calculate the coordinates of A and B.

The shaded region R is bounded by the line and the curve.
b) Calculate the area of R.

25. Using the trapezium rule with 5 strips, find an approximation for $\int_0^1 \frac{4}{1+x^2}\,dx$ giving your answer to 3 significant figures.

EXERCISE

Answers

CHAPTER 1. INDICES AND SURDS

Exercise 1A (Revision)

1. a) 16, 144, 225, 400
   b) 27, 125, 1000
   c) 4, 2
   d) 4, 8, 64, 512
2. a) $x^2 - 9 = (x - 3)(x + 3)$
   b) $a^2 - b^2 = (a - b)(a + b)$
   c) $1 - c^2 = (1 - c)(1 + c)$
   d) $(d + 10)(d - 10) = d^2 - 100$
   e) $e^2f^2 - (gh)^2 = (ef - gh)(ef + gh)$

Exercise 1B

1. a) 256 b) 81 c) 256
   d) 196 e) 17 f) 145
   g) 61 h) 81 i) $\frac{8}{27}$
   j) 0.0016
2. a) 7^2 b) 10^2 c) 10^{-2}
   d) 11^2 e) 10^{-3} f) $\left(\frac{3}{7}\right)^2$
   g) $(0.3)^2$ h) 10^{-5} i) 0.4^2

Exercise 1C

1. a) x^6 b) $8x^{-1}$ c) $3p$
   d) $12r$ e) $4s^5$ f) $27a^5$
   g) $9b^4$ h) $12c^6$ i) $12r^3$
   j) $32d^5$

Exercise 1D

1. a) 16 b) 243 c) 64
   d) 1024 e) 32 f) 81
   g) 256 h) 243
2. a) $2x^{\frac{1}{2}}$ b) $-\frac{1}{2x}$
3. a) $\frac{1}{25}$ b) 4^{-5} or $\frac{1}{1024}$
   c) g^{-6} d) t^2 e) 1
   f) 1 g) $\frac{1}{4}$ h) 8
   i) f^3 j) 16 k) b

Exercise 1E

1. a) $g = \frac{9}{2}$ b) $t = \frac{15}{2}$
   c) $f = -\frac{1}{4}$ d) $y = \frac{21}{2}$
   e) $k = -\frac{11}{2}$ f) $d = -\frac{7}{2}$
   g) $w = \frac{13}{2}$ h) $q = \frac{15}{8}$
   i) $z = \frac{7}{2}$ j) $g = -\frac{12}{5}$

Exercise 1F

1. $15\sqrt{2}$
2. $6\sqrt{5}$
3. $27 - 10\sqrt{2}$
4. $41 - 12\sqrt{5}$
5. $3\sqrt{2}$
6. $7\sqrt{5}$
7. $9 + 6\sqrt{2}$
8. $7 + 3\sqrt{5}$
9. a) $44 - 24\sqrt{2}$ b) $9 + 4\sqrt{2}$
   c) $\frac{5}{17} + \frac{2}{17}\sqrt{2}$ d) $3 - 2\sqrt{2}$
10. a) $76 - 42\sqrt{3}$ b) $\frac{2}{3} + \frac{1}{3}\sqrt{3}$
11. a) 14 b) 47 c) 13
    d) 33 e) 4 f) 3
    g) 43 h) 42 i) 57
    j) 8
12. a) $6 - 2\sqrt{6}$ b) $15 - 5\sqrt{5}$
    c) $12 - 6\sqrt{2}$ d) $28 - 14\sqrt{2}$

CHAPTER 2. QUADRATIC FUNCTIONS

Revision Exercise 2A

1. a) $2\sqrt{5}$ b) $4\sqrt{5}$ c) $6\sqrt{2}$
   d) 4 e) $\frac{-2 - \sqrt{6}}{2}$
2. a) $x^2 - x - 2$
   b) $4x^2 - 4x - 3$
   c) $3x^2 - 4x + 1$
   d) $1 - x^2$
   e) $-10p^2 - 9p + 9$

Exercise 2B

1. a) $x = -3$ or $x = -9$
   b) $x = -3$ or $x = -11$
   c) $x = -10$ or $x = -2$
   d) $x = -5$
   e) $x = -4$ or $x = -6$
   f) $x = 1$ or $x = -3$
   g) $x = 1$ or $x = -7$
   h) $x = 6$ or $x = -7$
   i) $x = 5$ or $x = 2$
   j) $x = -7$ or $x = -9$
2. a) $x = 3, x = 4$
   b) $x = \frac{5}{2}, x = -\frac{5}{2}$
   c) $x = 0, x = 4$
   d) $x = 0, x = 1$
   e) $x = -6, x = 4$
   f) $x = 3$
   g) $x = 1, x = -1$
   h) $x = 1$
   i) $x = -\frac{1}{2}, x = \frac{7}{2}$
   j) $x = 0, x = 91$
   k) $x = -6, x = -8$
   l) $x = -1$
   m) $x = -1, x = 1$
   n) $x = -1$
   o) $x = \frac{1}{4}, x = -\frac{1}{8}$
3. a) $x = 4$
   b) $x = 2, x = 9$
   c) $x = 6$
   d) $x = 5, x = -2$
   e) $x = 7, x = 8$
   f) $x = 10, x = -6$
   g) $x = 8, x = 10$
   h) $x = 1, x = 9$
   i) $x = -8, x = -9$
   j) $x = 3, x = 10$
   k) $x = 6$
   l) $x = 2$
4. a) $x = -1, x = 2$
   b) $x = \frac{5}{2}, x = \frac{2}{3}$
   c) $x = -2, x = 6$
   d) $x = -\frac{4}{9}, x = -\frac{1}{2}$
   e) $x = -\frac{8}{5}, x = -\frac{1}{2}$
   f) $x = \frac{7}{3}, x = -\frac{3}{7}$

g) $x = -\frac{8}{3}, x = -5$

h) $x = \frac{4}{7}, x = 1$

i) $x = -\frac{3}{8}, x = \frac{5}{7}$

j) $x = 1, x = -\frac{1}{2}$

k) $x = 3, x = -\frac{9}{5}$

l) $x = \frac{1}{3}, x = \frac{7}{6}$

m) $x = \frac{2}{3}, x = \frac{7}{5}$

n) $x = \frac{7}{2}, x = -\frac{6}{7}$

o) $x = \frac{3}{2}, x = \frac{3}{8}$

5. a) $x = \frac{1}{2}, -3$ b) $n = \frac{3}{2}, 4$
   c) $z = \frac{3}{2}, 8$ d) $p = \frac{1}{3}, 1$

6. a) $x = -7, 7$ b) $y = -9.9$
   c) $p = -2, 2$ d) $z = -\frac{7}{3}, \frac{7}{3}$
   e) $q = -3, 3$ f) $b = -\frac{3}{5}, \frac{3}{5}$
   g) $c = -\frac{4}{5}, \frac{4}{5}$ h) $x = -\frac{1}{8}, \frac{1}{8}$
   i) $y = -\frac{1}{2}, \frac{1}{2}$ j) $z = -\frac{1}{2}, \frac{1}{2}$
   k) $m = -\frac{7}{5}, \frac{7}{5}$ l) $n = -\frac{4}{7}, \frac{4}{7}$
   m) $x = -6, 6$ n) $y = -24, 24$
   o) $z = -30, 30$ p) $p = -48, 48$
   q) $q = -36, 36$ r) $r = -15, 15$
   s) $s = -56, 56$ t) $t = -21, 21$

Exercise 2C

1. a) $-2, -3$ b) $\frac{13}{5}, -\frac{7}{5}$
   c) $\frac{22}{7}, \frac{2}{7}$ d) $-\frac{1}{8}, -\frac{15}{8}$
   e) $-\frac{8}{5}, -2$ f) $\frac{17}{6}, \frac{3}{2}$
   g) 4, 20 h) 50, 80
   i) –12, –108 j) 0, 20
   k) 30, 36 l) –66, –78
   m) 35, 55 n) –33, 15
   o) 0, 72

2. a) $-3 \pm \sqrt{13}$ b) $-2 \pm \frac{\sqrt{13}}{2}$
   c) $-1 \pm \sqrt{5}$ d) $-3 \pm \sqrt{10}$
   e) $2 \pm \sqrt{5}$ f) $-5 \pm \sqrt{24}$
   g) $-1 \pm \sqrt{3}$ h) $2 \pm \sqrt{20}$
   i) $-2 \pm \sqrt{5}$

Exercise 2D

1. a) (0, 20), (1, 19)
   b) (0, 16), (2, 12)
   c) (0, 12), (5, –13)
   d) (0, 20), (4, 4)
   e) (0, 16), (3, 7)
   f) (0, 16), (–5, –9)
   g) (0, 16), (9, –65)
   h) (0, 12), (–3, 3)
   i) (0, 20), (7, –29)
   j) (0, 16), (–8, –48)
   k) (0, 16), (–6, –20)

2. a) (0, 8), (5, 33)
   b) (0, 16), (–3, 25)
   c) (0, 16), (–4, 32)
   d) (0, 16), (5, 41)
   e) (0, 8), (6,44)
   f) (0, 12), (–7, 61)
   g) (0, 20), (–8, 84)
   h) (0, 20), (9, 101)
   i) (0, 12), (–2, 16)
   j) (0, 14), (–3, 23)
   k) (0, 10), (9, 91)
   l) (0, 14), (7, 63)
   m) (0, 6), (–6, 42)
   n) (0, 8), (7, 57)
   o) (0, 14), (8, 78)

Exercise 2E

1. a) $\frac{-1+\sqrt{5}}{2}, \frac{-1-\sqrt{5}}{2}$
   b) $\frac{-5+3\sqrt{5}}{2}, \frac{-5-3\sqrt{5}}{2}$
   c) $\frac{1+3\sqrt{5}}{2}, \frac{1-3\sqrt{5}}{2}$
   d) $\frac{-1+5\sqrt{5}}{2}, \frac{-1-5\sqrt{5}}{2}$
   e) $\frac{1+\sqrt{5}}{2}, \frac{1-\sqrt{5}}{2}$
   f) $\frac{2+\sqrt{2}}{2}, \frac{2-\sqrt{2}}{2}$
   g) $\frac{-3+3\sqrt{5}}{2}, \frac{-3-3\sqrt{5}}{2}$
   h) $\frac{-2+\sqrt{7}}{3}, \frac{-2-\sqrt{7}}{3}$
   i) $-1+\sqrt{7}, -1-\sqrt{7}$
   j) $\frac{-2+\sqrt{2}}{2}, \frac{-2-\sqrt{2}}{2}$

2. a) $-2+\sqrt{3}, -2-\sqrt{3}$
   b) $\frac{-5+\sqrt{33}}{4}, \frac{-5-\sqrt{33}}{4}$
   c) $\frac{1+\sqrt{13}}{6}, \frac{1-\sqrt{13}}{6}$
   d) $\frac{-2+\sqrt{14}}{2}, \frac{-2-\sqrt{14}}{2}$
   e) $\frac{-1+\sqrt{2}}{2}, \frac{-1-\sqrt{2}}{2}$
   f) $\frac{-2+\sqrt{10}}{3}, \frac{-2-\sqrt{10}}{3}$
   g) $\frac{1+\sqrt{3}}{2}, \frac{1-\sqrt{3}}{2}$
   h) $\frac{3+\sqrt{57}}{6}, \frac{3-\sqrt{57}}{6}$
   i) $2+2\sqrt{2}, 2-2\sqrt{2}$
   j) $\frac{-2+\sqrt{13}}{3}, \frac{-2-\sqrt{13}}{3}$

Exercise 2F

1. a) $-1+\sqrt{3}, -1-\sqrt{3}$
   b) No solutions
   c) $\frac{-1+\sqrt{5}}{4}, \frac{-1-\sqrt{5}}{4}$
   d) No solutions
   e) No solutions
   f) No solutions
   g) $\frac{-1+\sqrt{33}}{8}, \frac{-1-\sqrt{33}}{8}$
   h) No solutions
   i) 2
   j) $\frac{1+\sqrt{5}}{2}, \frac{1-\sqrt{5}}{2}$
   k) $-1+\sqrt{5}, -1-\sqrt{5}$
   l) No solutions
   m) No solutions
   n) $\frac{1+\sqrt{6}}{5}, \frac{1-\sqrt{6}}{5}$

3. $k = 4$

4. $q < -\frac{41}{16}$

6. 3, 4, 5 cm

Revision Exercise 2G

1. a) $y = \frac{4x-1}{2}$ b) $y = 2x - 5$
   c) $y = \frac{3-4x}{12}$ d) $y = \frac{2x-7}{3}$

2. a) $a = 0$ b) $b = 5$
   c) $c = \frac{1}{2}$ d) $d = -10$
   e) $e = -\frac{5}{4}$

3. a) $(x+2)(x+9)$
   b) $(x-4)(x-6)$
   c) $(x-1)(x-5)$
   d) $(x+4)(x-3)$
   e) $(x-7)(x+6)$

4. a) $x = 1, y = 0$
   b) $x = -3, y = 3$
   c) $x = 7, y = 0$
   d) $x = 4, y = 5$

Exercise 2H

1. a) $x = 2, y = 4, z = 3$
   b) $x = 2, y = -8, z = 1$
   c) $x = 12, y = 0, z = -4$
   d) $x = -1, y = -2, z = -2.5$

2. Apples 10p, Bananas 25p, Carrots 12p.

3. Ticket £5.50, popcorn £2, cola £1.50
4. a) $p = 3, q = 2$
   b) $x = -5, y = 9$
   c) $a = 5, b = 2$
   d) $x = -\frac{7}{10}, y = 8$
   e) $m = 3, n = 4$

Exercise 2I

1. a) $x = 11, y = -5$
   $x = -3, y = 9$
   b) $x = 8, y = -4$
   $x = -4, y = 8$
   c) $x = 9, y = -5$
   $x = -3, y = 7$
   d) $x = 7, y = -5$
   $x = -3, y = 5$
   e) $x = 8, y = -3$
   $x = -2, y = 7$
   f) $x = 6, y = -1$
   $x = -2, y = 7$
2. a) $x = 14, y = 5$
   $x = -7, y = -2$
   b) $x = 19, y = 5$
   $x = -5, y = -1$
   c) $x = 17, y = 6$
   $x = -10, y = -3$
   d) $x = 7, y = 4$
   $x = -5, y = -2$
   e) $x = 27, y = 7$
   $x = -13, y = -3$
   f) $x = 41, y = 7$
   $x = -7, y = -1$
3. a) (2, –12), (–8, 48)
   b) (1, –24), (–25, 600)
4. a) $x = -2 + 2\sqrt{3}, y = -6 + 2\sqrt{3}$;
   $x = -2 - 2\sqrt{3}, y = -6 - 2\sqrt{3}$
   b) $x = -4 + 3\sqrt{3}, y = -12 + 3\sqrt{3}$;
   $x = -4 - 3\sqrt{3}, y = -12 - 3\sqrt{3}$

Exercise 2J

1. a) $x \le 7$ b) $x \le 21$ c) $x < \frac{7}{3}$
   d) $x \ge -5$ e) $x \ge \frac{2}{3}$ f) $x < 11$
   g) $x > -1$ h) $x < \frac{1}{5}$ i) $x \ge 1$
   j) $x > -\frac{3}{2}$ k) $x < -6$ l) $x \ge \frac{60}{83}$
2. a) $t \le 3$ b) $w > 2$ c) $p \le 0$
   d) $v < -10$ e) $z < 1$ f) $u \ge \frac{22}{5}$
3. a) $x < -4$ or $x > 1$
   b) $x < -5$ or $x > 4$
   c) $-3 < x < 3$
   d) $x < \frac{3}{2}$ or $x > 4$
   e) $-5 < x < 2$
   f) $x < -4$ or $x > 1$
   g) $-5 < x < 2$
   h) $x < -7$ or $x > 3$
4. a) $x \ge 6$ or $x \le -4$
   b) $x > 5$ or $x < -2$
   c) $-3 < x < 1$
   d) $x > 8$ or $x < -3$
   e) $-11 < x < 8$
   f) $x < -11$ or $x > 9$
   g) $x > 5$ or $x < -2$
   h) $x \ge 8$ or $x \le -2$
   i) $-4 < x < 1$
   j) $x < -4$ or $x > 2$
   k) $x > 6$ or $x < -2$
   l) $-8 < x < 2$
   m) $-14 < x < 11$
   n) $x \ge 9$ or $x \le -4$
5. a) $x \le -4$ or $x \ge 1$
   b) $-4 \le x \le 1$
   c) $x < -7$ or $x > 5$
   d) $x \le -9$ or $x \ge 6$
   e) $-11 < x < 9$
   f) $x \le -13$ or $x \ge 10$
   g) $x < -11$ or $x > 7$
   h) $-12 < x < 9$
   i) $-1 < x < 5$
   j) $x < 2$ or $x > 7$
   k) $-10 < x < 3$
6. a) $1 < x < 3$
   b) $1 < x < \frac{7}{2}$
   c) $2 \le x \le \frac{13}{5}$
   d) $x > 5$
   e) $x > 5$
   f) $x > 4$
   g) $\frac{4}{3} < x \le 6$
   h) $x > 5$
   i) $\frac{2}{3} \le x \le 5$
   j) $1 < x < \frac{11}{2}$
   k) $x > 5$
   l) $x \ge 7$

CHAPTER 3. ALGEBRAIC MANIPULATION

Exercise 3A

1. a) $4a - 4b$ b) $3c + d$
   c) $2e + ef$
   d) $a^2 + b^2 - 5a + 6b - 2ab$ (cannot be simplified)
   e) $2b - a$ f) $6c - d$
   g) $7e + f + ef$
   h) $2g^2 + 3h^2 - 4g - 3h + 2gh$ (cannot be simplified)
2. a) –4 b) 0 c) –6
   d) 0 e) –8 f) 16
   g) 10 h) 6 i) 0
   j) –2
3. a) $2v + 2v^2$ b) $-4w^2 + 8$
   c) $3y^2 + y$ d) $16x^2 - 9$
   e) $8v + 12v^2$ f) $-6w^2 + 3$
   g) $-2y^2 + 6y$ h) $16x^2 - 16$
4. a) $-5y(y + 5)$ b) $6p(6 - p^2)$
   c) $13r(2q - 1)$ d) $s^4(5 - 4s)$
   e) $-3y(3y + 8)$ f) $p(6 - p)$
   g) $8q(2 - r)$ h) $s^3(3s - 4)$
5. a) $(x + 1)(x + 4)$
   b) $(x + 10)(x + 10)$ or $(x + 10)^2$
   c) $(x - 3)(x - 9)$
   d) $(x - 9)(x - 6)$
   e) $(x + 8)(x + 2)$
   f) $(x - 1)(x - 4)$
   g) $(x + 6)(x + 8)$
   h) $(x - 6)(x + 4)$
6. a) $(x + 2)(x - 2)$
   b) $x(4x + 6)(4x - 6)$
   c) $(x + 3)(x - 3)$
   d) $x(3x + 4)(3x - 4)$
7. a) 52
   b) 101
   c) 65 remainder 8
   d) 41 remainder 9
   e) 96
   f) 25
   g) 84 remainder 6
   h) 45 remainder 15

Exercise 3B

1. a) $x - 5$ b) $x + 5$ c) $x + 7$
   d) $x - 7$ e) $x + 2$
2. a) $\frac{x + 4}{x + 1}$ b) $\frac{x - 2}{x - 1}$ c) $\frac{x - 5}{x + 1}$
   d) $\frac{x - 2}{x + 3}$ e) $\frac{x - 4}{x - 2}$
3. a) $(x - 1)(x + 6)$
   b) $(x - 5)(x - 8)$
   c) $(x - 1)(x + 7)$
   d) $(x - 6)(x + 9)$
   e) $(x + 9)(x - 8)$
4. a) $\frac{x^2 + 1}{(x + 1)(x - 1)}$
   b) $\frac{2 - 8x}{(3x - 2)(2x - 3)}$
   c) $\frac{-5 - 2x}{(x + 2)(x + 3)}$
   d) $\frac{1}{x - 1}$

Exercise 3C

1. a) $x^2 - 2x$
   b) $x^2 - x + 3$
   c) $x^2 + 1$

d) $3x^2 + x + 3 - \frac{3}{x+1}$
e) $3x^2 - 6x + 10 - \frac{18}{x+2}$

2. a) $x^2 - 2x + 1$
b) $x^2 - 3 + \frac{7}{x+2}$
c) $2x^2 - 3x + 7 - \frac{20}{x+3}$
d) $x^2 - 3x + 9 - \frac{27}{x+3}$
e) $3x^2 - 12x + 35 - \frac{109}{x+3}$

3. a) $x^3 - x + 1$
b) $x^3 + 3x + 1$
c) $2x^3 + 2x^2 - 6x + 3$
d) $x^3 - 2x^2 + x + 1$
e) $2x^3 - x^2 - 2x + 1$
f) $3x^3 + x^2 - 4x + 2$

4. a) $x^3 - x^2 - 2x + 3 - \frac{5}{x+2}$
b) $x^3 + 3x - 7 + \frac{9}{x+1}$
c) $x^3 + 3x - 8 + \frac{26}{x+3}$
d) $2x^3 - 3x^2 + 3x - 6 + \frac{7}{x+1}$
e) $3x^3 - 7x^2 + 6x - 6 + \frac{8}{x+1}$

Exercise 3D

1. a) –4	b) 22	c) –3
d) 9	e) 0	f) 4
g) 3	h) –24	i) 34
j) 60	k) 18	l) 5
m) 1	n) 10	

2. –6

3. a) –12
b) $f(x) = 4(x+1)(x-1)(x-3)$

4. a) 6
b)
c) $\frac{7}{8}$

5. a) –18
b) 1

6. a) $q = -8, p = -34$
b) $f(x) = 2(3x-1)(2x+1)(x-3)$

7. a) 222
c) $f(x) = x(5x-1)(x+15)$

8. b) $f(n) = (n+3)(n+3)(n+1) + 5$

Exercise 3E

1. a) is not a factor, remainder –118
b) is a factor
c) is not a factor, remainder –48
d) is not a factor, remainder –87
e) is a factor
f) is a factor
g) is not a factor, remainder 26
h) s not a factor, remainder 35
i) is not a factor, remainder –19
j) is not a factor, remainder 134
k) is a factor
l) is not a factor, remainder –100

2. $f(x) = (x-8)(x-9)(x+4)$

3. b) $f(x) = (x+3)(x-4)(x-1)$

4. b) $f(x) = (x+10)(2x-3)(x-8)$
c) $x = -10, 1.5, 8$

5. $a = -5$

6. $p = -5$

7. a) $f(x) = (x+4)(x-4)(x-1)$
b) $f(x) = (x+2)(x-3)(x-3)$
c) $f(x) = (x+3)(x-3)(x-3)$
d) $f(x) = (x+3)(x-3)(x-2)$

REVIEW EXERCISE CHAPTERS 1–3

1. a) $\frac{1}{3}, \frac{9}{4}$	b) $-1, -\frac{5}{3}$	c) 0, –8
2. a) 5, 9	b) 8	c) 4, 9
3. a) $-\frac{8}{5}, \frac{8}{5}$	b) $\frac{7}{5}, -\frac{7}{2}$	c) $\frac{1}{2}, -\frac{1}{2}$

4. a) $x = -4, 4$
b) $x = -\frac{5}{8}, \frac{5}{8}$
c) $x = -12, 12$

5. a) $\frac{1}{3}, -\frac{4}{3}$ b) $-33, -45$

6. a) $-8 \pm \sqrt{66}$ b) $-7 \pm 4\sqrt{3}$
c) $4 \pm 3\sqrt{2}$ d) $2 \pm \sqrt{6}$

7. a) (0, 20), (6, –16)
b) (0, 16), (5, –9)
c) (0, 16), (8, –48)
d) (0, 20), (7, 69)
e) (0, 12), (–4, 28)
f) (0, 14), (–7, 63)

8. a) $\frac{3+3\sqrt{5}}{2}, \frac{3-3\sqrt{5}}{2}$
b) $\frac{1+5\sqrt{5}}{2}, \frac{1-5\sqrt{5}}{2}$
c) $\frac{-1+\sqrt{7}}{2}, \frac{-1-\sqrt{7}}{2}$

9. a) $-1+\sqrt{5}, -1-\sqrt{5}$
b) No solutions
c) $\frac{1+\sqrt{41}}{10}, \frac{1-\sqrt{41}}{10}$

10. a) $x \leq 18$
b) $x \leq -\frac{15}{2}$

11. a) $x > 5$ or $x < -3$
b) $-6 < x < 2$

12. a) $\frac{1}{3} \leq x < 2.5$
b) $\frac{1}{2} < x < \frac{12}{5}$
c) $x \geq 4$

13. $\frac{1}{(x+1)(x-1)}$

14. a) $x + 6 + \frac{11}{x-2}$
b) $x^2 - 2x - 2 - \frac{1}{x-1}$

15. $\frac{1}{8}$

16. a) is a factor
b) is not a factor, remainder –42
c) is a factor

17. b) $(x+7)(2x-5)(x-4)$

CHAPTER 4. GRAPHS AND CURVE SKETCHING

Revision Exercise 4A

1. a) $x(x+2)(x+3)$
b) $x(3x+4)(3x-4)$
c) $x(3x+5)(3x-5)$
d) $x(x-1)(x-3)$
e) $x(x-1)(x-2)$

2. a)

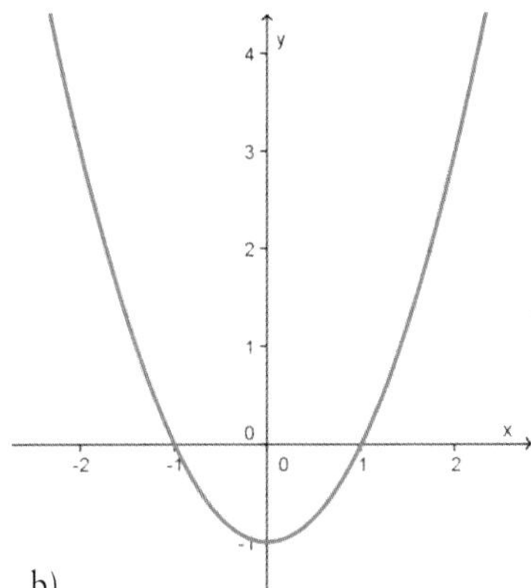

b)

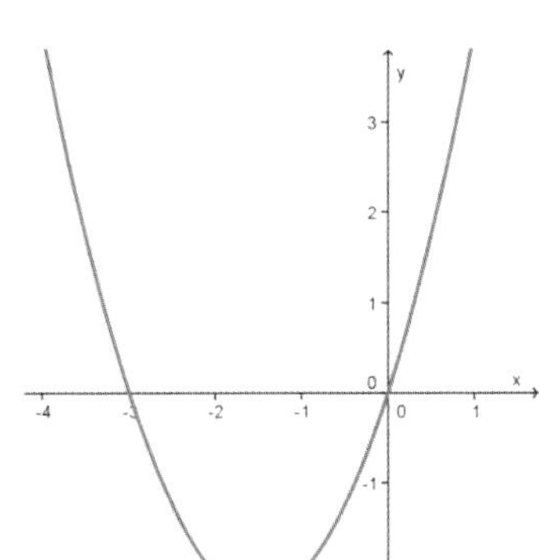

2. c)

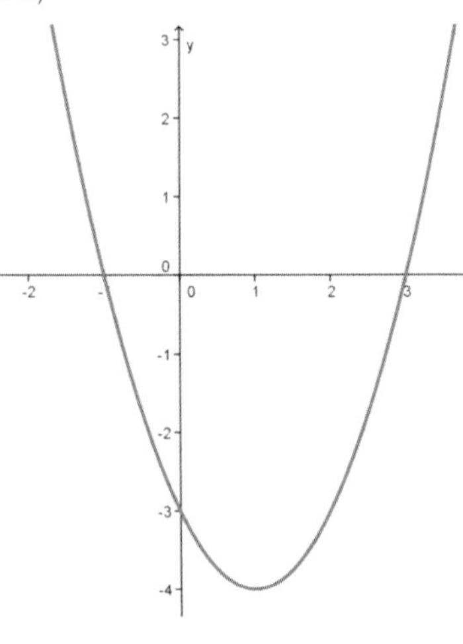

d)

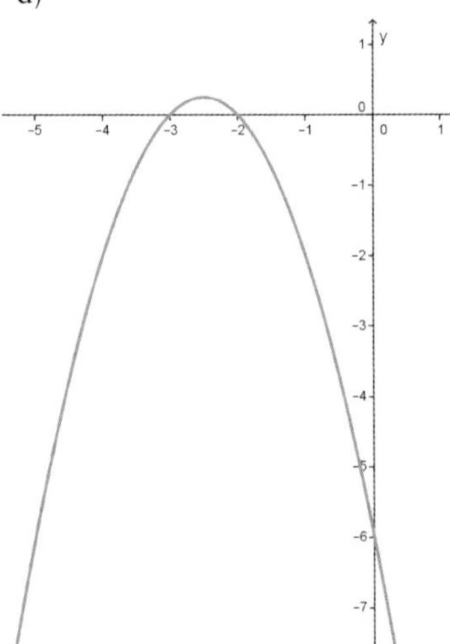

e)

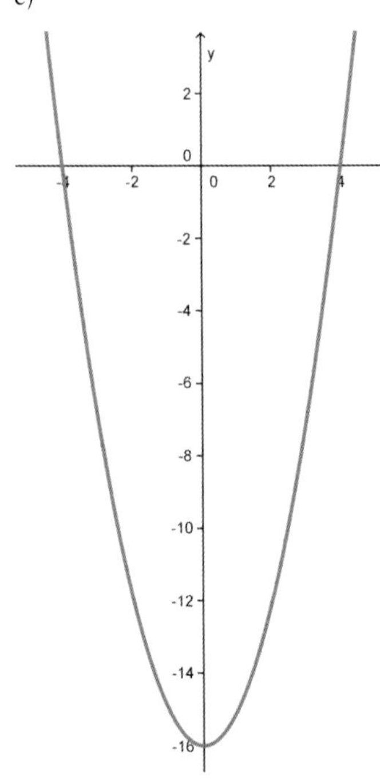

Exercise 4B

1. a) (0,–12); (–4,0), (3,0),(–1,0)
   b) (0,–27); (3,0), (9,0),(–1,0)
   c) (0,0); (0,0), (3,0),(–2,0)
   d) (0,0); (0,0), (9,0),(8,0)
   e) (0,–9); (0.5,0), (3,0)
   f) (0,0); (0,0), (–0.5,0)
   g) (0,0); (0,0), (5,0),(–5,0)
   h) (0,27); (–3,0)
   i) (0,–1); (0.5,0)
   j) (0,0); (0,0), (6,0)

2. a) $y = x(x-9)^2 \quad x = 0, 9$
   (repeated root)

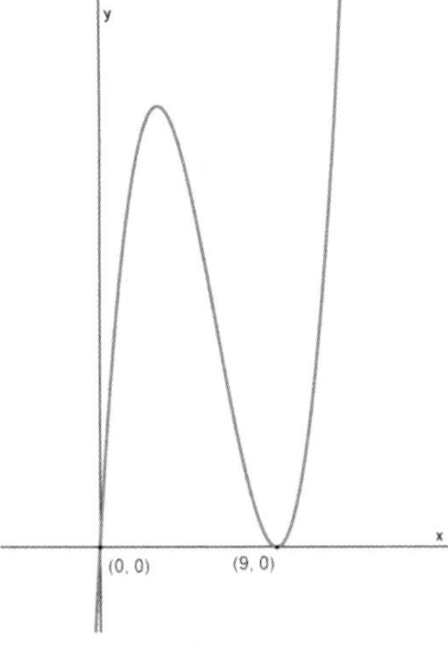

   b) $y = x(x-15)^2 \quad x = 0, 15$
   (repeated root)

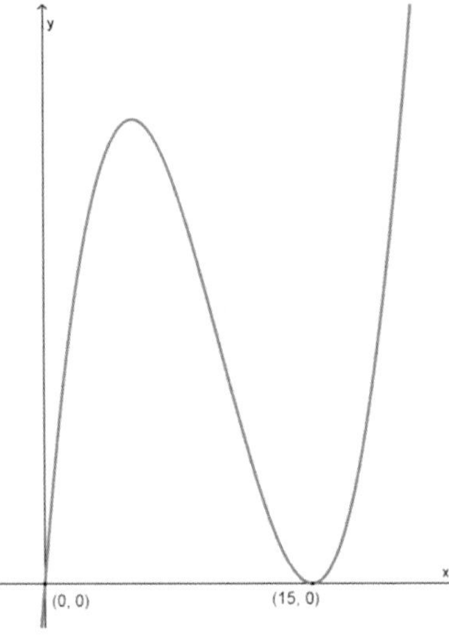

3. a) $f(x) = x(x+3)(x+2)$
   $x = 0, -3, -2$

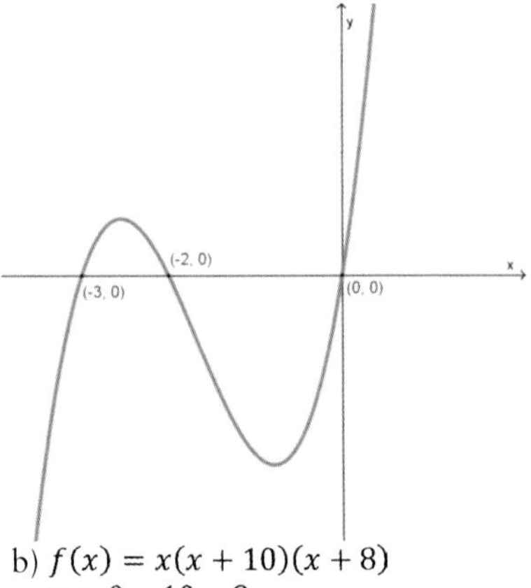

   b) $f(x) = x(x+10)(x+8)$
   $x = 0, -10, -8$

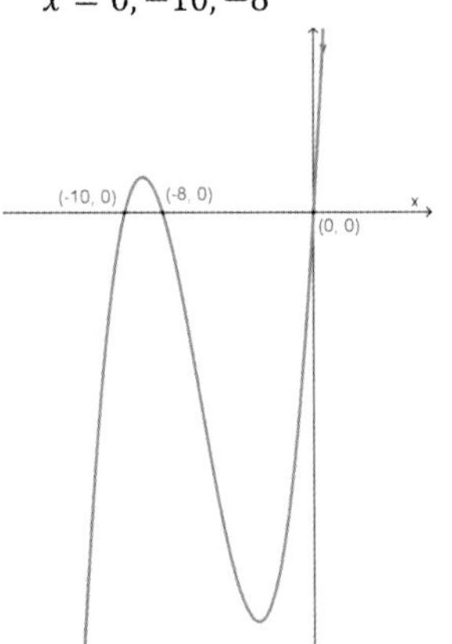

   c) $f(x) = -x(x+1)(x+10)$
   $x = 0, -1, -10$

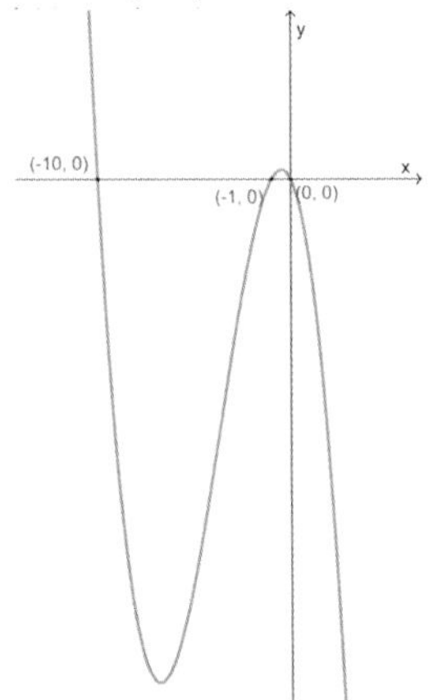

   d) $f(x) = x(x+8)(x+5)$
   $x = 0, -8, -5$

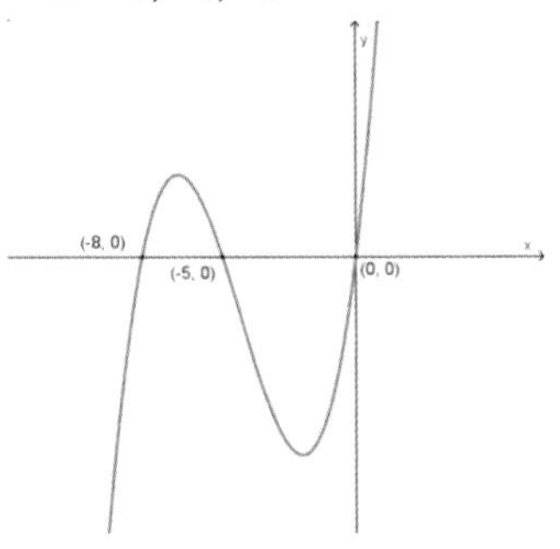

3. e) $f(x) = x(x+7)(x+10)$
$x = 0, -7, -10$

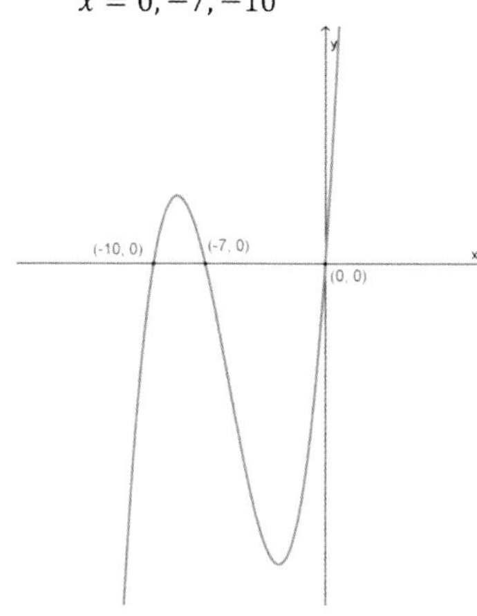

f) $f(x) = x(4x+5)(4x-5)$
$x = 0, -\frac{5}{4}, \frac{5}{4}$

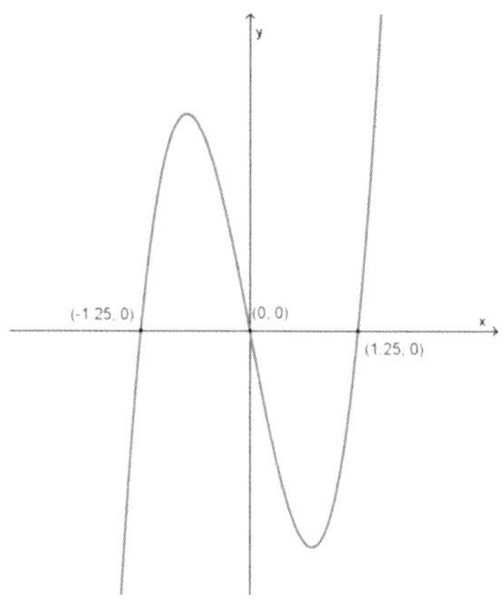

g) $f(x) = x(3x+4)(3x-4)$
$x = 0, -\frac{4}{3}, \frac{4}{3}$

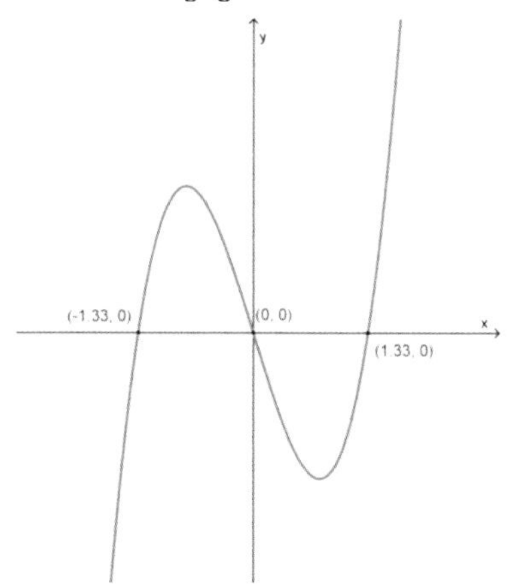

3. h) $f(x) = -x(x-1)(x-2)$
$x = 0, 1, 2$

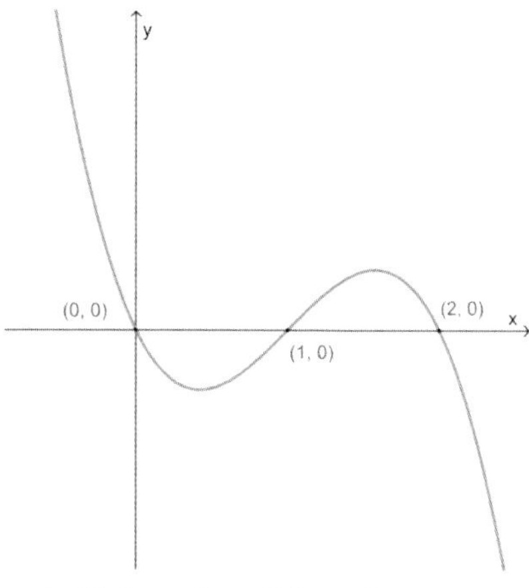

i) $f(x) = x(x-4)(x-1)$
$x = 0, 4, 1$

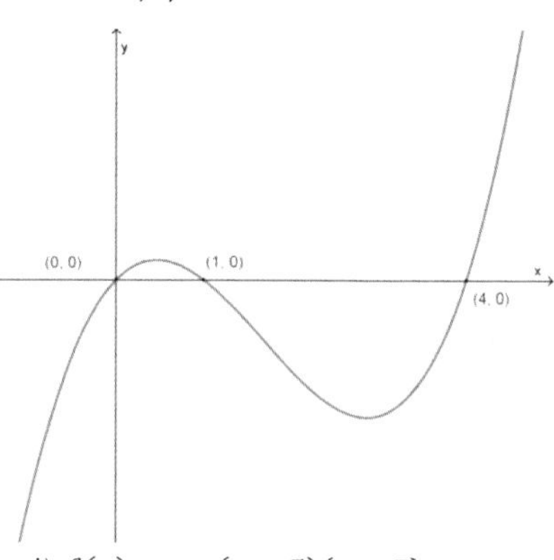

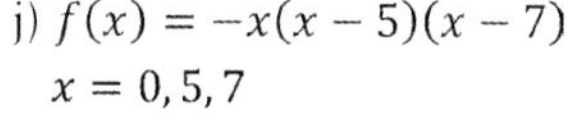

j) $f(x) = -x(x-5)(x-7)$
$x = 0, 5, 7$

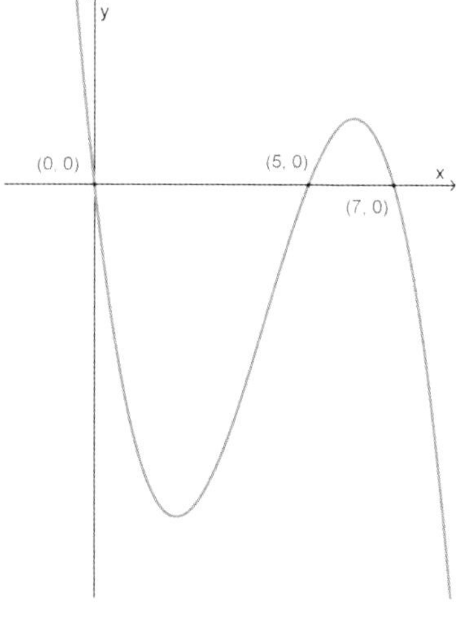

4. a) $f(x) = x(x-7)(x-5)$ $x = 0, 7, 5$

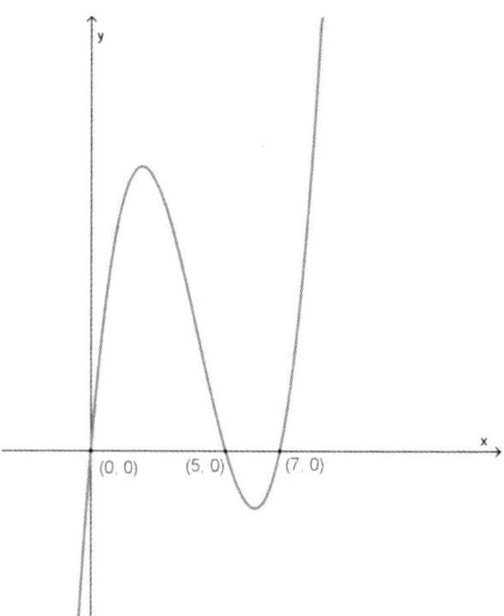

b) $f(x) = x(x-7)(x-4)$ $x = 0, 7, 4$

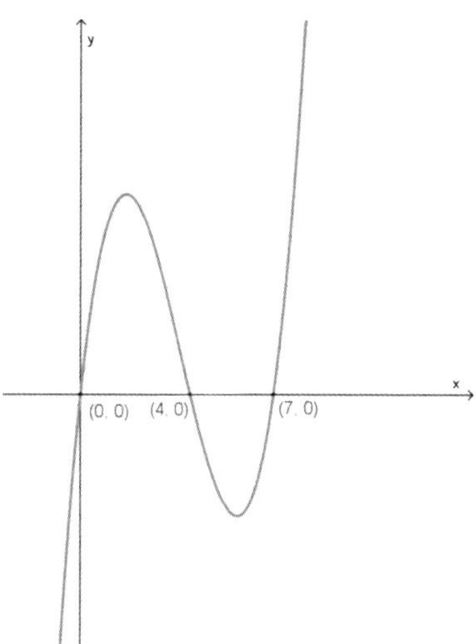

c) $f(x) = -x(x-8)(x-6)$ $x = 0, 8, 6$

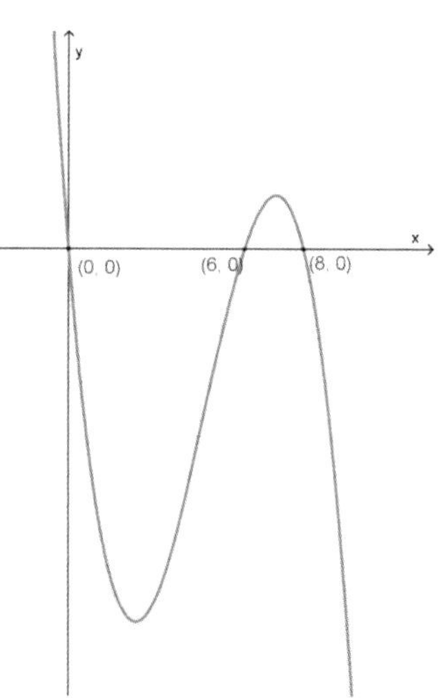

Exercise 4C

1. a)

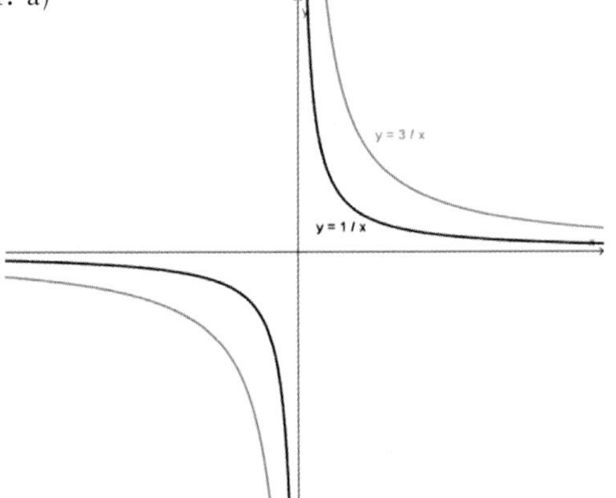

b)

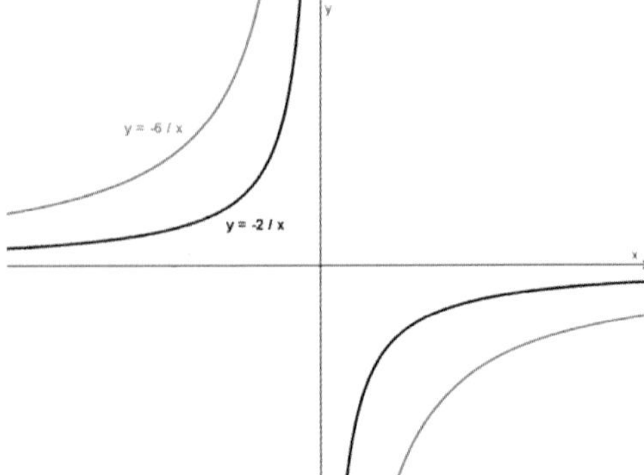

c)

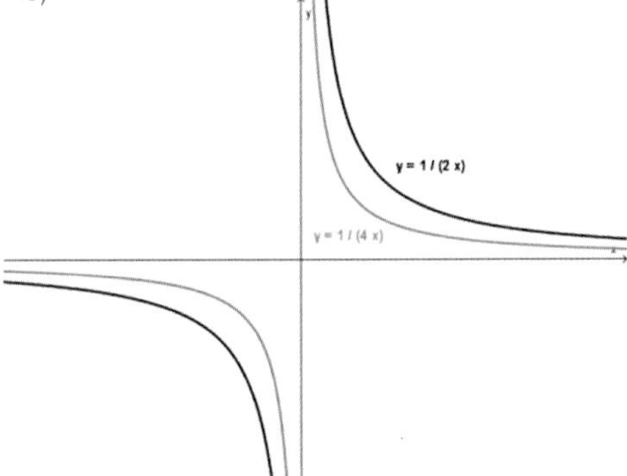

d)

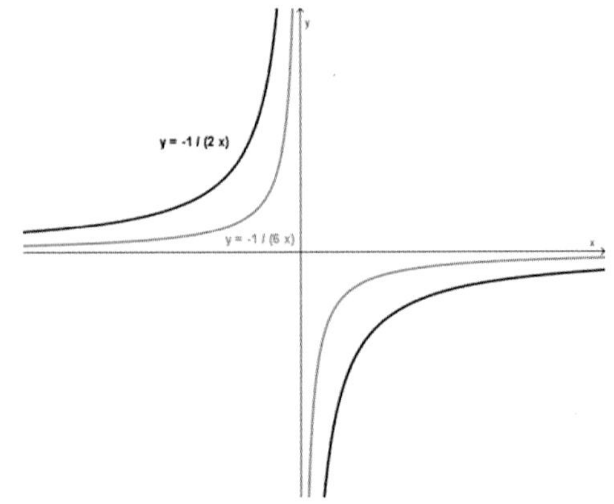

2.

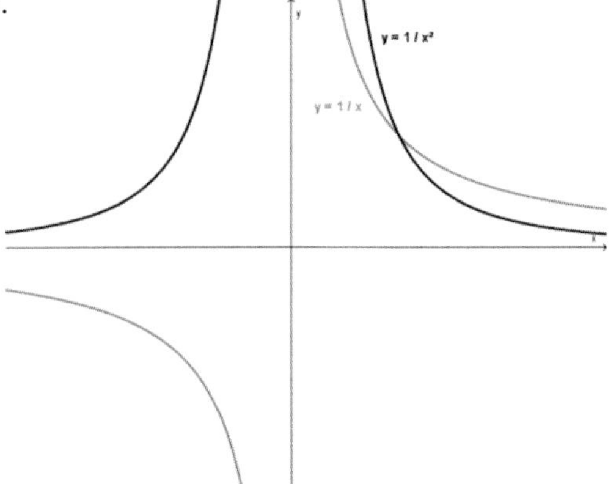

3. a) 1; $x = 1$ b) (0,0) c) y approaches 1

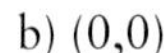

d)

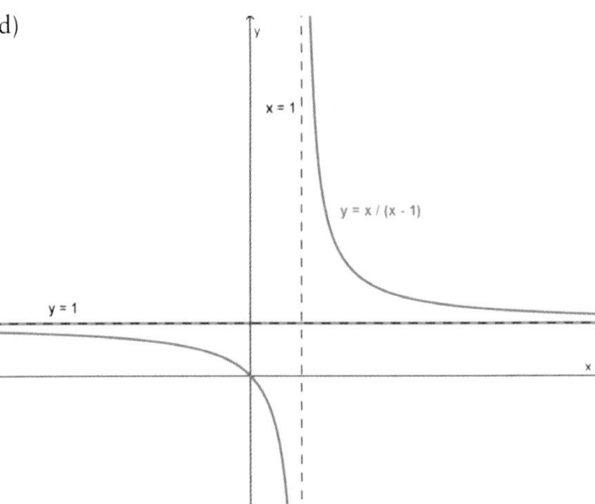

4. a) $x = \frac{2}{3}, y = -\frac{1}{3}$

b)

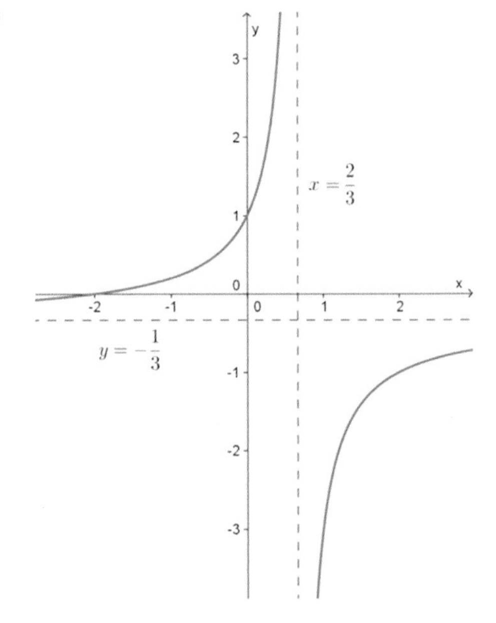

Exercise 4D

1. a)

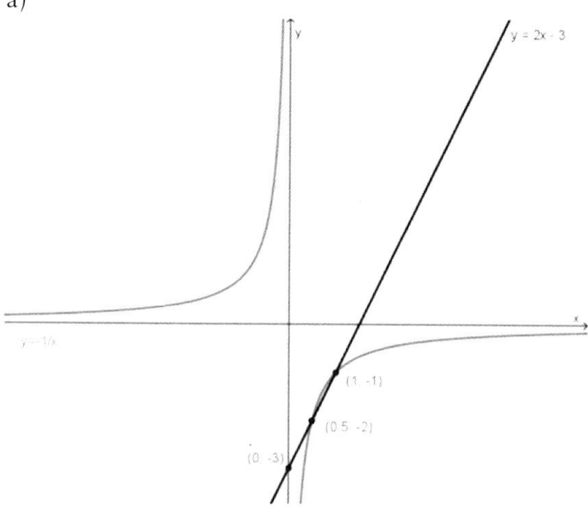

$x = 0.5, y = -2; x = 1, y = -1$

b)

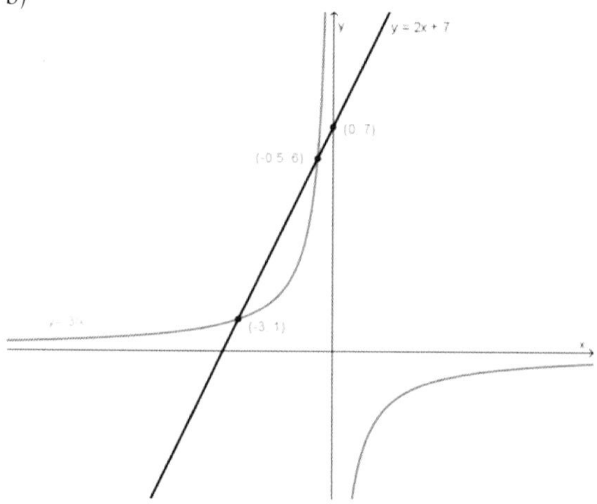

$x = -3, y = 1; \; x = -0.5, y = 6$

c)

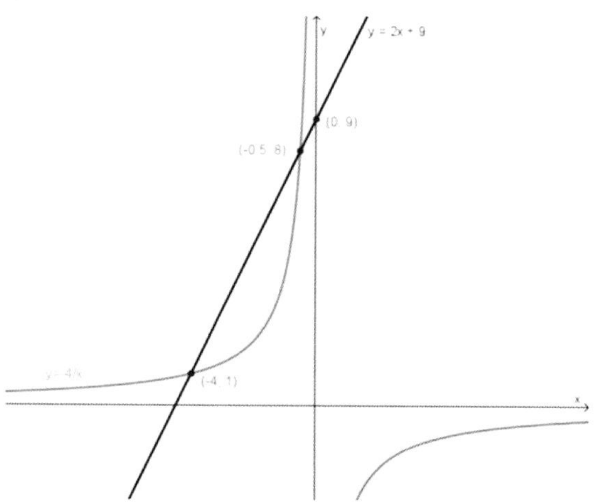

$x = -0.5, y = 8; \; x = -4, y = 1$

1. d)

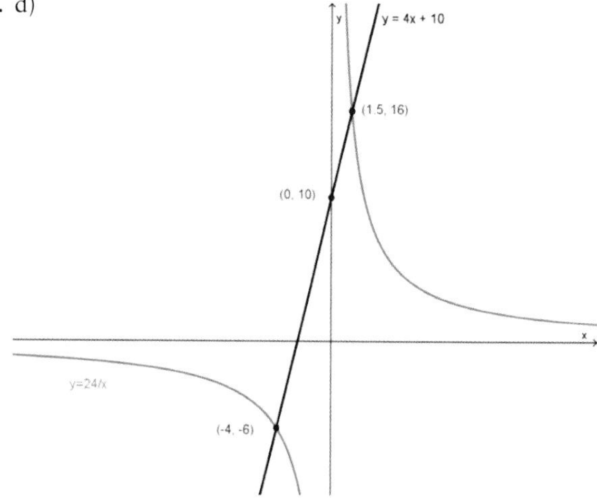

$x = 1.5, y = 16; \; x = -4, y = -6$

e)

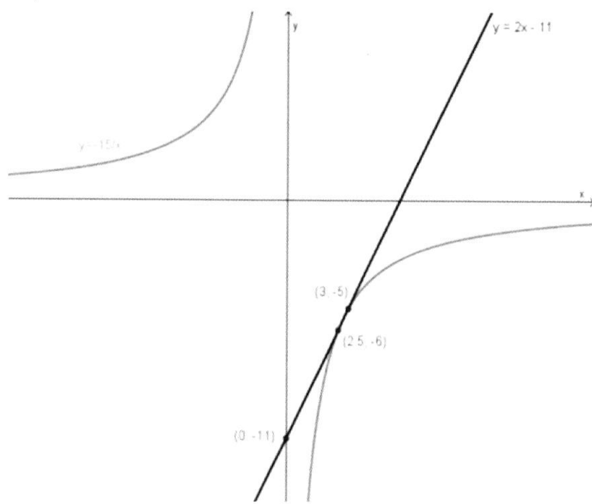

$x = 2.5, y = -6; \; x = 3, y = -5$

f)

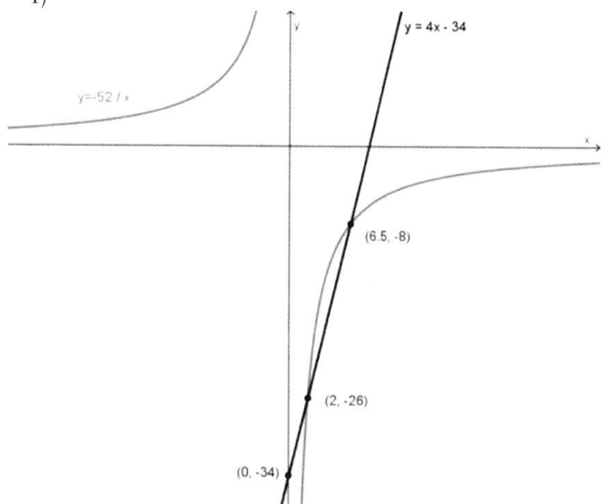

$x = 6.5, y = -8; \; x = 2, y = -26$

2. a)

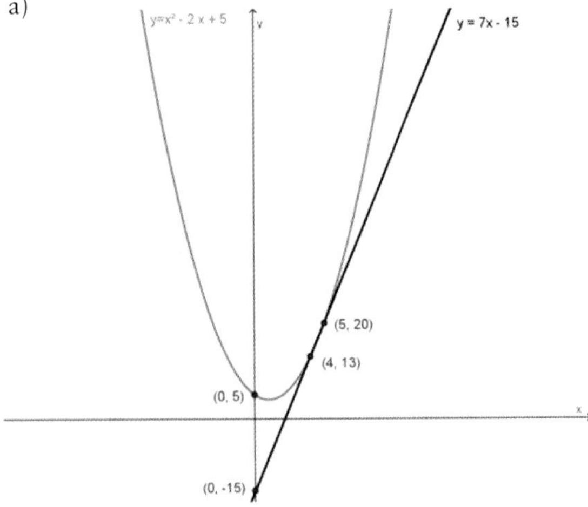

$x = 5, y = 20;\ x = 4, y = 13$

b)

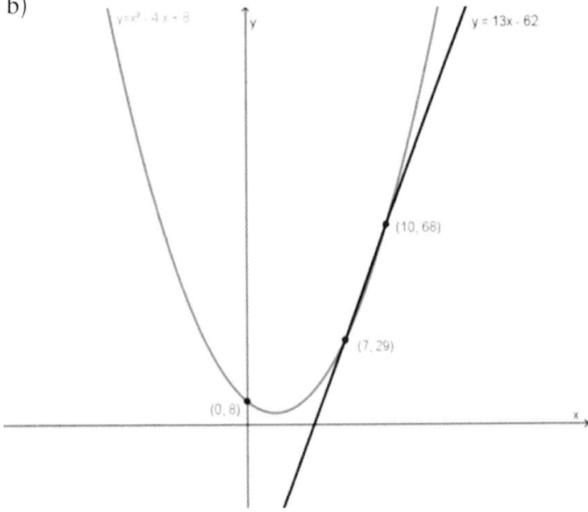

$x = 7, y = 29;\ x = 10, y = 68$

3. a) $x = 1.5, y = 0;\ x = -2, y = 14$

b)

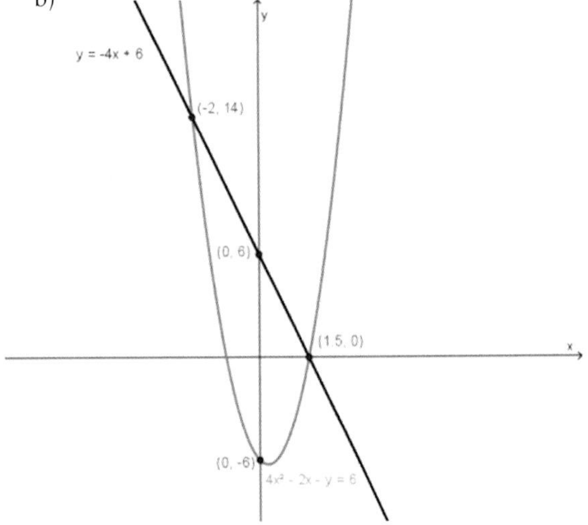

c) $x > 1.5$ or $x < -2$

4. a) $x^2 - 1 = 0$

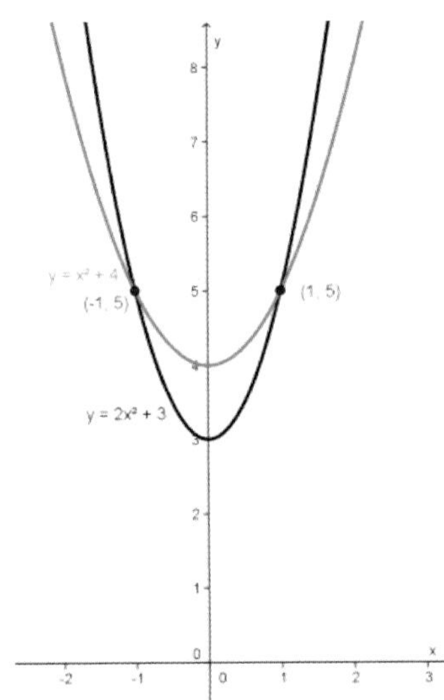

Two points of intersection (1, 5), (–1, 5)

b) $x^2 + 2x + 1 = 0$

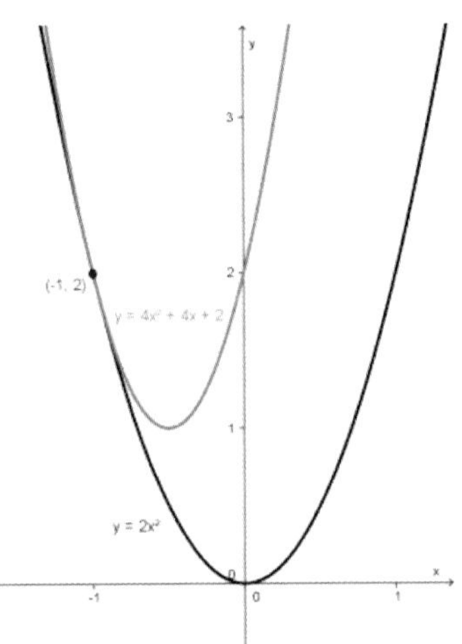

One point of intersection (–1, 2)

c) $x^2 - 2x + 3 = 0$

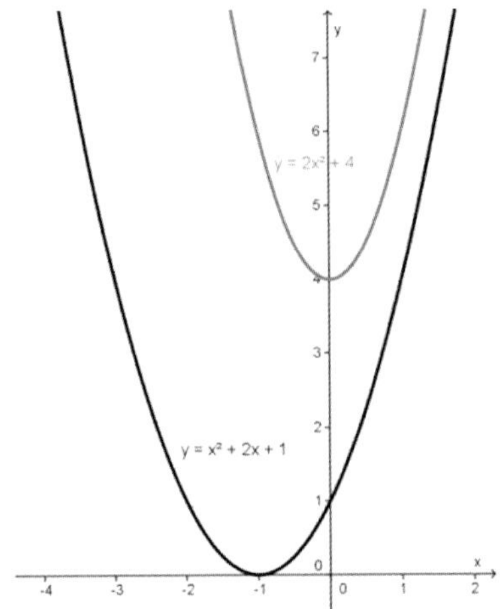

Zero points of intersection

4. d) $2x^2 + 5x + 2 = 0$

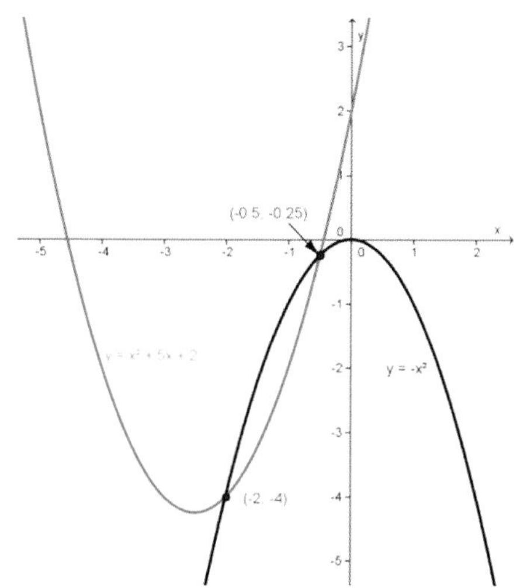

Two points of intersection (–0.5, –0.25), (–2, –4)

e) $x^2 - 2x + 1 = 0$

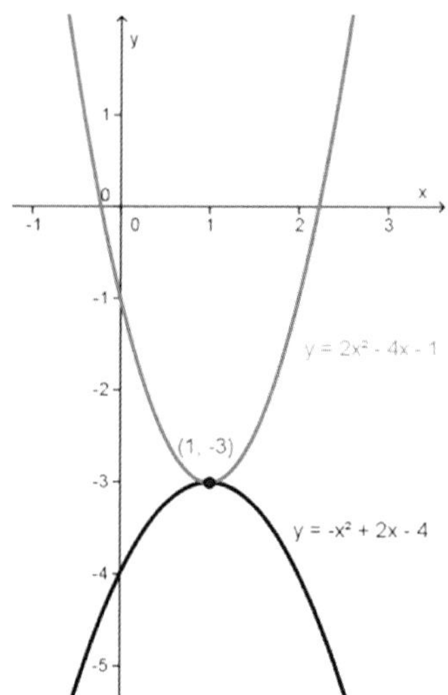

One point of intersection (1, –3)

f) $5x^2 + 4x + 4 = 0$

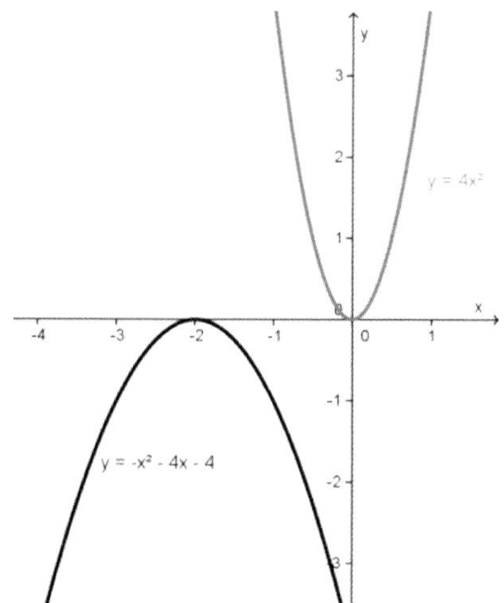

Zero points of intersection

5. $x = 0$

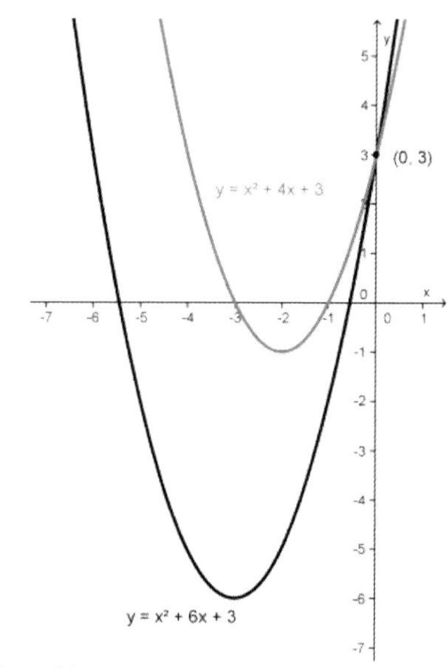

One point of intersection (0, 3)

6. a) $x = 0, 3$ (repeated root).

b)

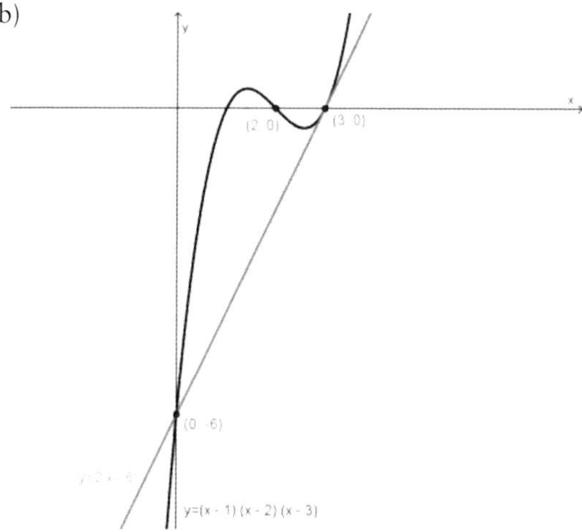

7. a)

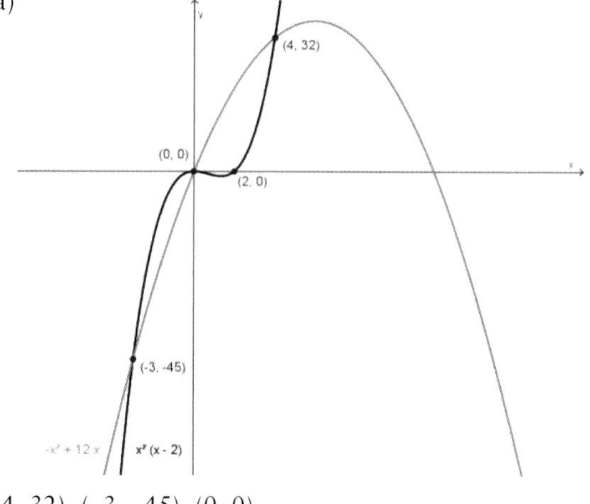

(4, 32), (–3, –45), (0, 0)

7. b)

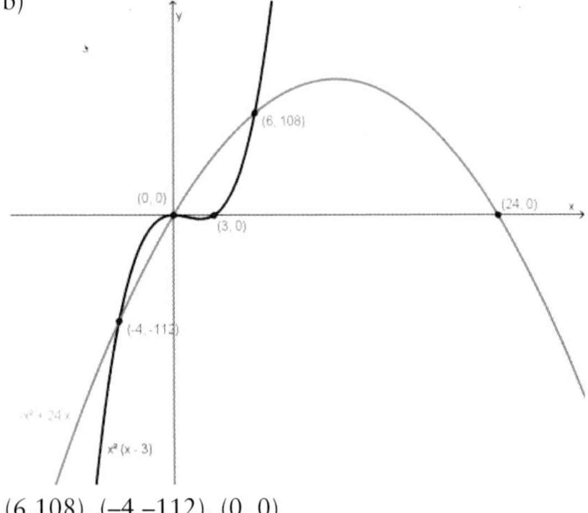

(6,108), (–4,–112), (0, 0)

Exercise 4E

1. a) 1 unit in negative x-direction
   b) 20 units in negative y-direction
   c) 2 units in negative x-direction
   d) 10 units in negative y-direction
   e) 2 units in positive x-direction
   f) 4 units in positive y-direction
   g) 2 units in negative x-direction
   h) 3 units in negative x-direction, 1 unit in positive y-direction
   i) 2 units in negative x-direction
   j) 1 unit in positive y-direction
   Note: the functions given in parts i) and j) are identical.
2. a) $f(x) + a = 3x + 2$
   b) $f(x) + a = x$
   c) $f(x) + a = x^2 - 2x - 2$
   d) $f(x) + a = x^3 - 1$
3. a) $f(x + a) = 3(x + 2)$
   b) $f(x + a) = x$
   c) $f(x + a) = (x - 4)^2 - 2(x - 4) + 2$
   d) $f(x + a) = (x - 1)^3$
   e) $f(x + a) = \dfrac{2}{x - 2}$
   f) $f(x + a) = (x - 1)^2 + (x - 1)$
   g) $f(x + a) = x(x + 1)^2$
4. a) $g(x) = x^2 - 2 \qquad h(x) = (x + 2)^2$

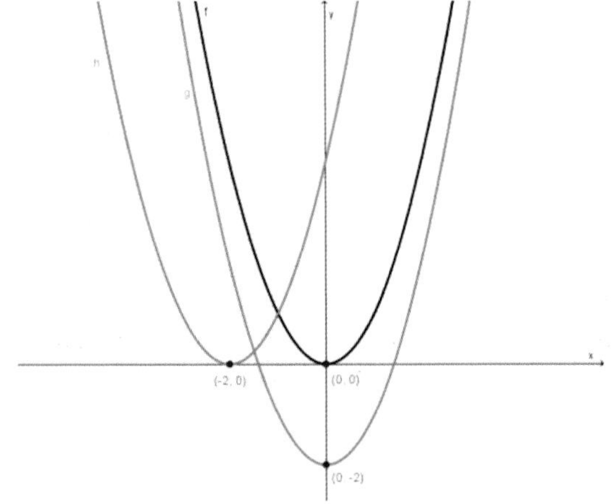

4. b) $g(x) = 3x - 2 \;\; h(x) = 3(x + 2)$

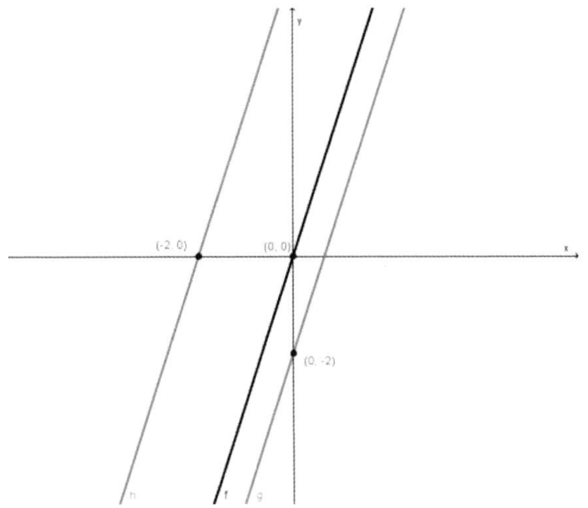

c) $g(x) = \dfrac{1}{x} - 2 \qquad h(x) = \dfrac{1}{x + 2}$

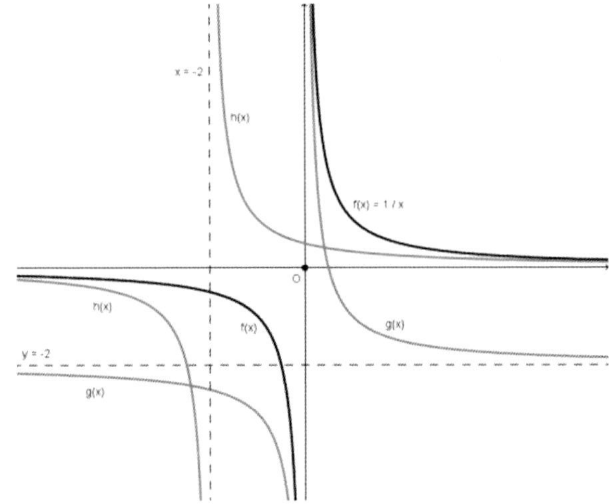

d) $g(x) = (x - 2)^3 - 2 \;\; h(x) = x^3$

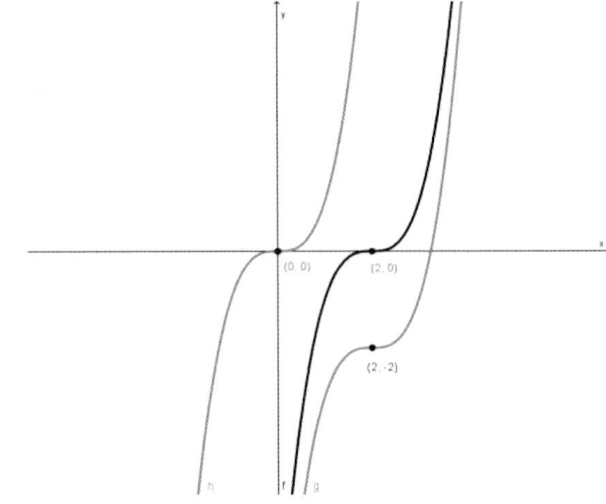

In each case, $g(x)$ is a translation two units in negative y-direction; $h(x)$ is a translation two units in negative x-direction.

5.

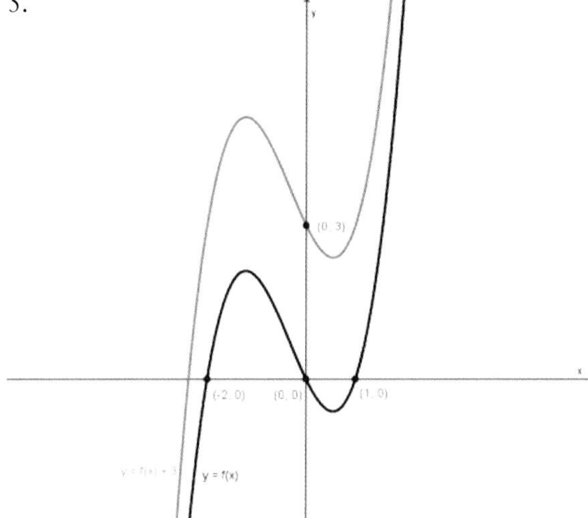

Translation, 3 units in positive y-direction.

6. a)

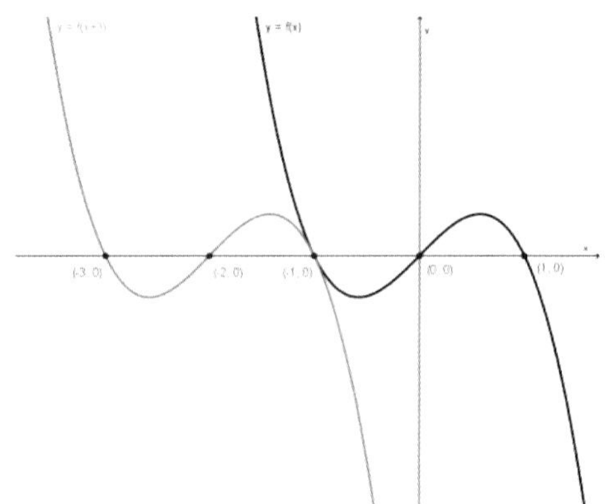

b) $(-1, 0)$

7.

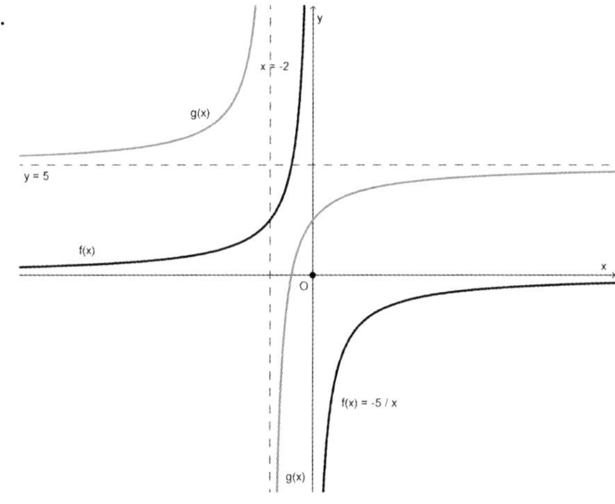

8. Translation 1 unit in negative x-direction, 3 units in negative y-direction.

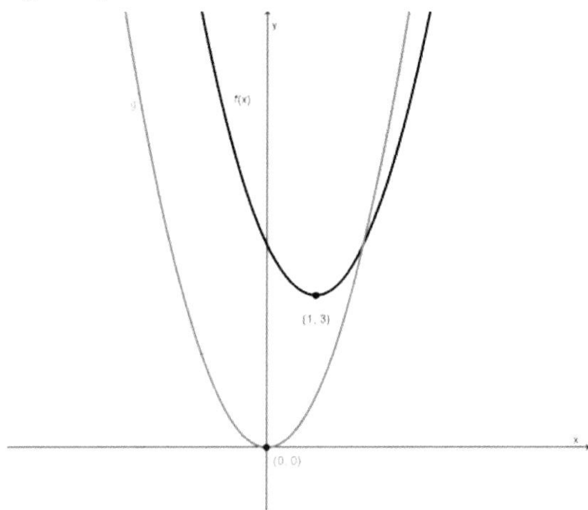

9. a) $g(x) = \dfrac{1}{x}$

b)

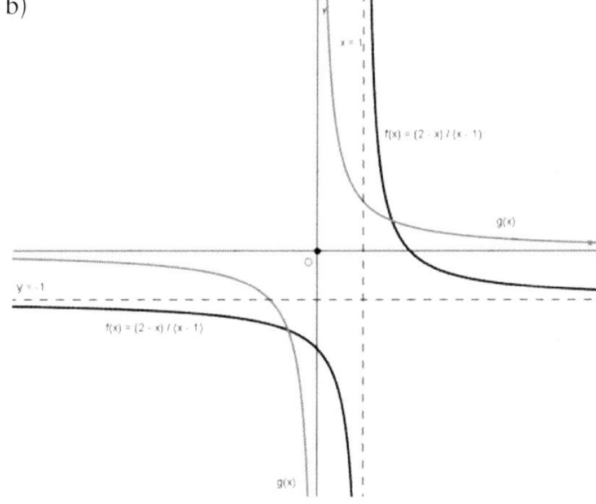

10. a)

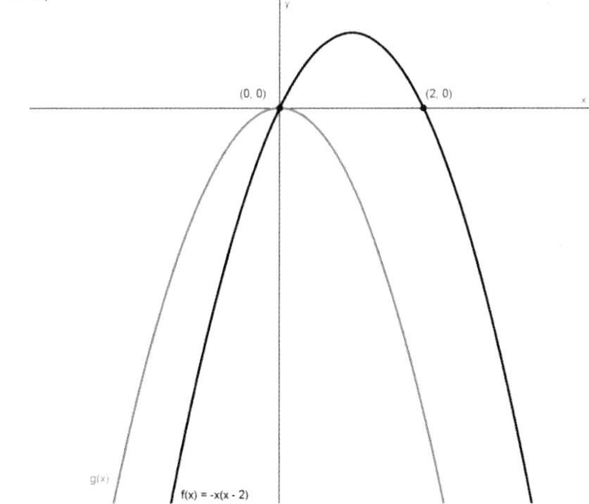

b) $g(x) = -x^2$

c) Translation by 1 unit in the negative x-direction, 1 unit in the negative y-direction.

Exercise 4F

1. a) $af(x) = 2x^2$; $f(ax) = 4x^2$
   b) $af(x) = 2x^3 + 2$; $f(ax) = 8x^3 + 1$
   c) $af(x) = 6x$; $f(ax) = 6x$
   d) $af(x) = \frac{10}{x}$; $f(ax) = \frac{2}{5x}$
   e) $af(x) = -x^2$; $f(ax) = x^2$
   f) $af(x) = -\frac{1}{x^2}$; $f(ax) = \frac{1}{x^2}$
   g) $af(x) = -3x^3$; $f(ax) = -3x^3$
   h) $af(x) = 2(x-1)$; $f(ax) = 1 + 2x$
   i) $af(x) = 2x(x-1)(x-2)$; $f(ax) = 4x(2x-1)(x-1)$
   j) $af(x) = -2x^2(x-1)$; $f(ax) = -4x^2(2x+1)$

2. a)

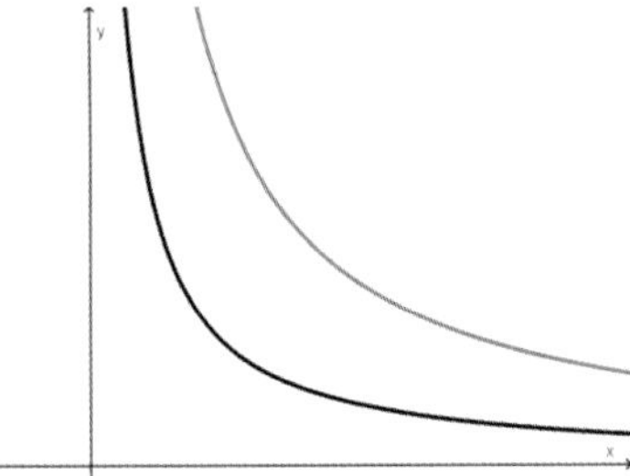

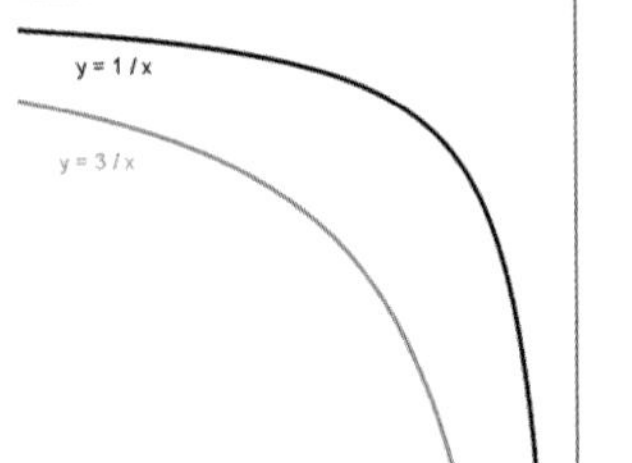

b)

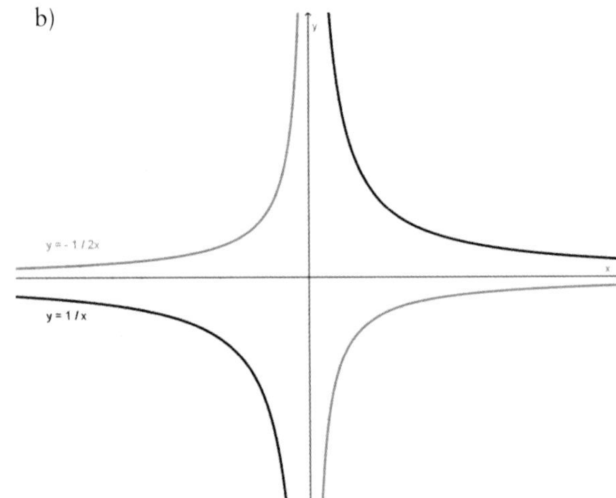

3. a)

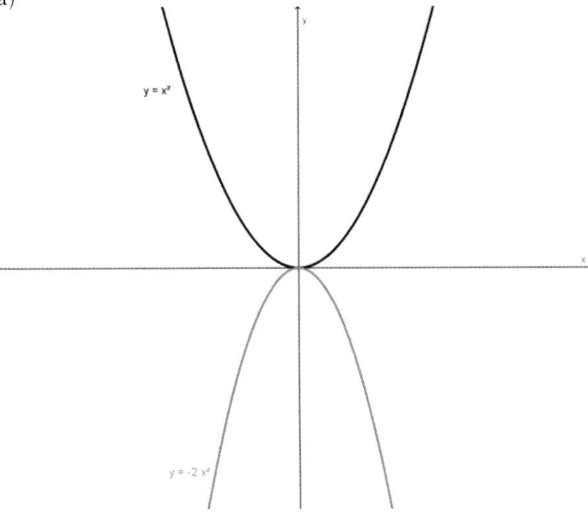

$x = 0$

b)

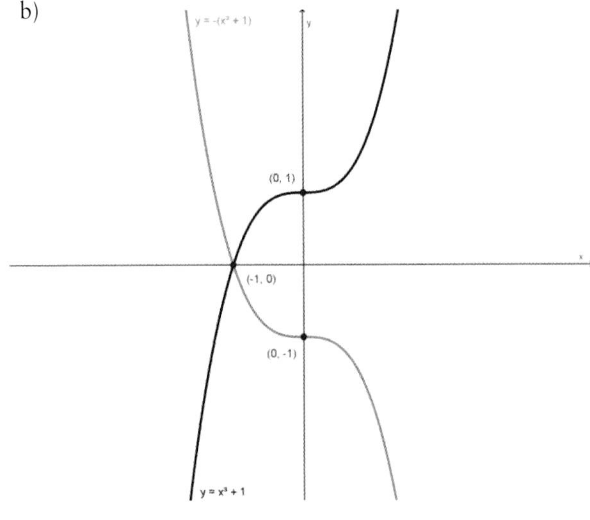

$x = -1$

c)

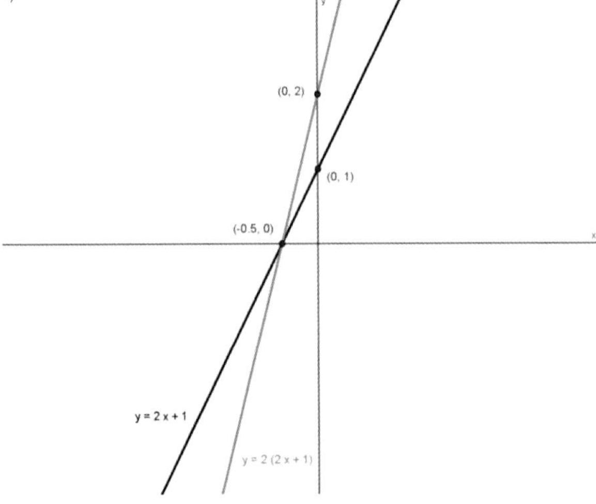

$x = -\frac{1}{2}$

3. d)

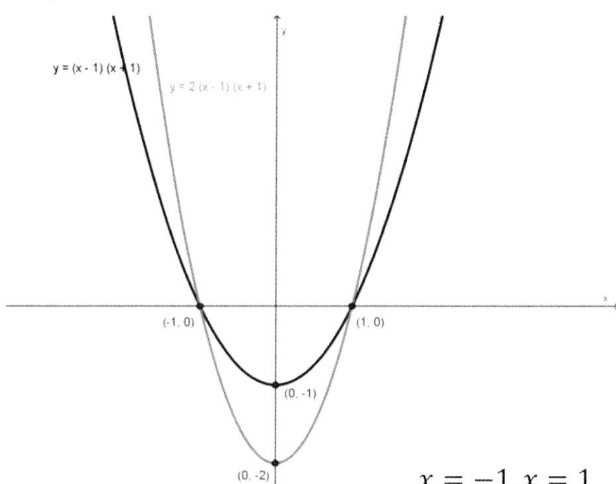

$x = -1, x = 1$

e)

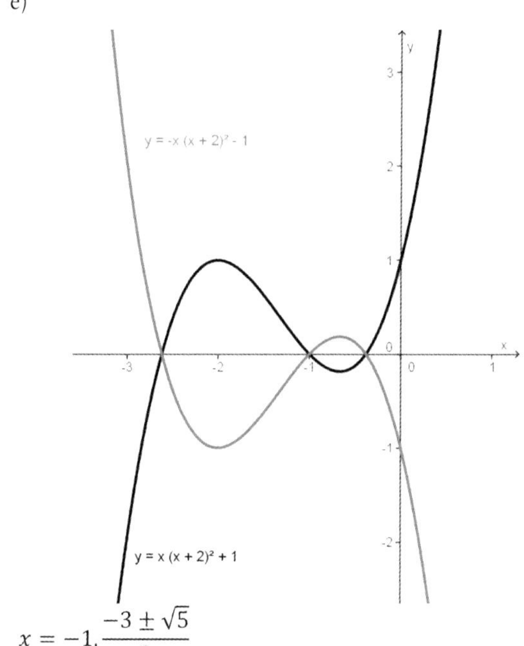

$x = -1, \frac{-3 \pm \sqrt{5}}{2}$

4. a)

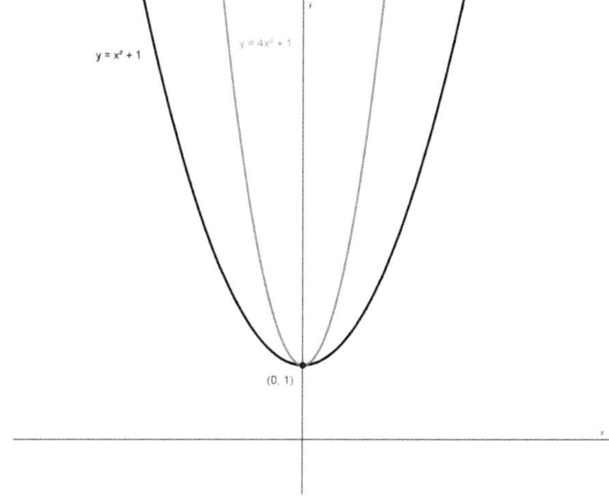

$x = 0$

4. b)

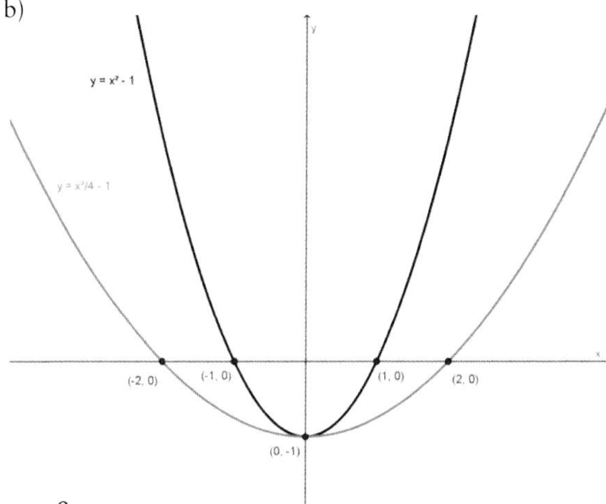

$x = 0$

c)

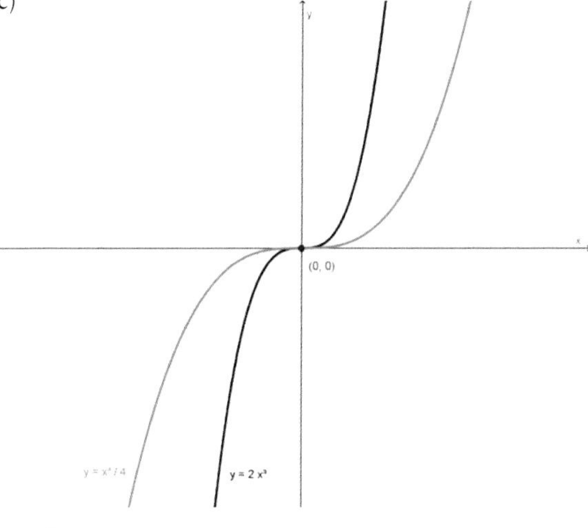

$x = 0$

d)

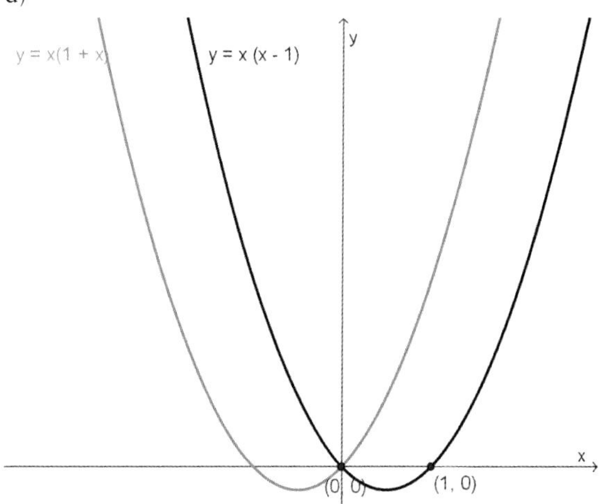

$x = 0$

4. e)

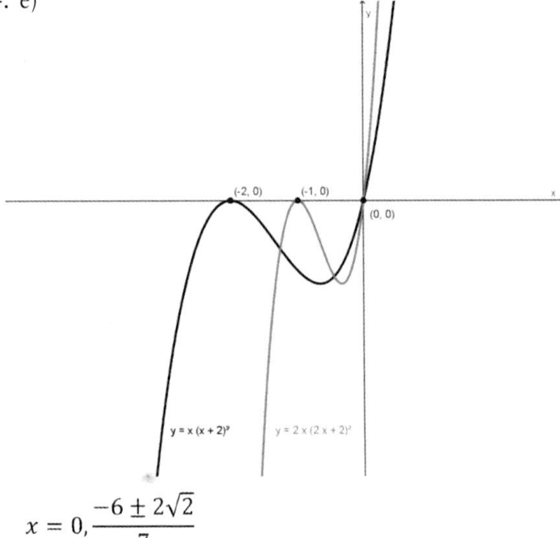

$x = 0, \dfrac{-6 \pm 2\sqrt{2}}{7}$

Exercise 4G

1. a) Reflection in x–axis
   b) Stretch in y-direction, scale factor 2
   c) Translation by 3 units in negative y-direction
   d) Stretch in x-direction, scale factor ½
   (Shrink, scale factor 2)
   e) Translation by 3 units in positive x-direction
   f) Reflection in y–axis

2. a)

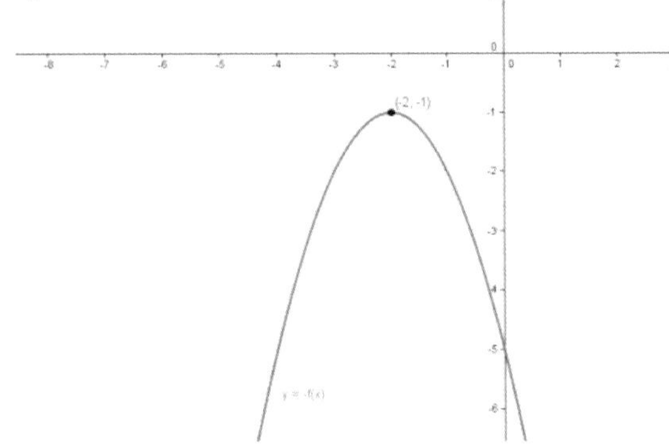

b)

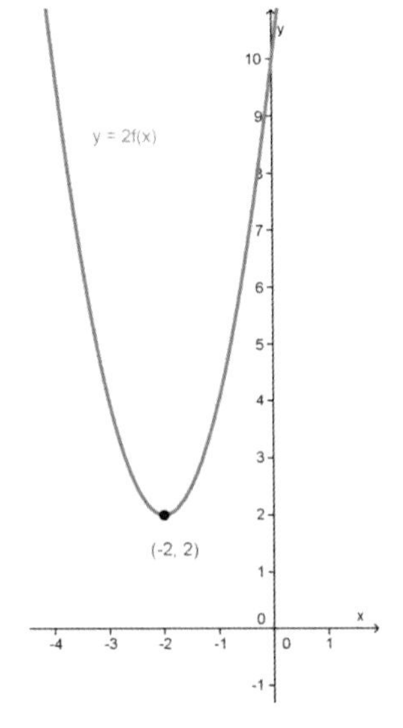

2. c)

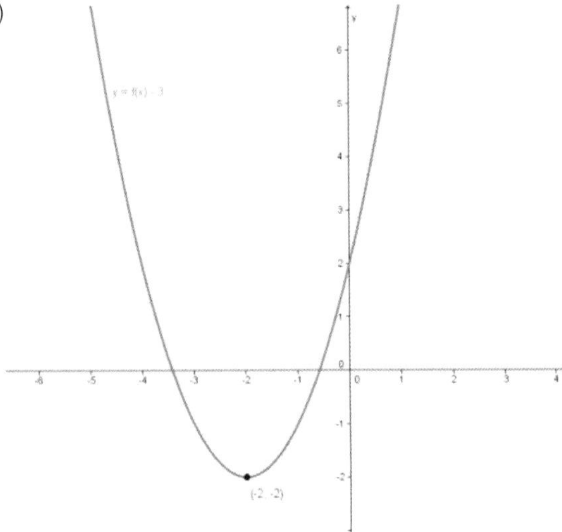

d)

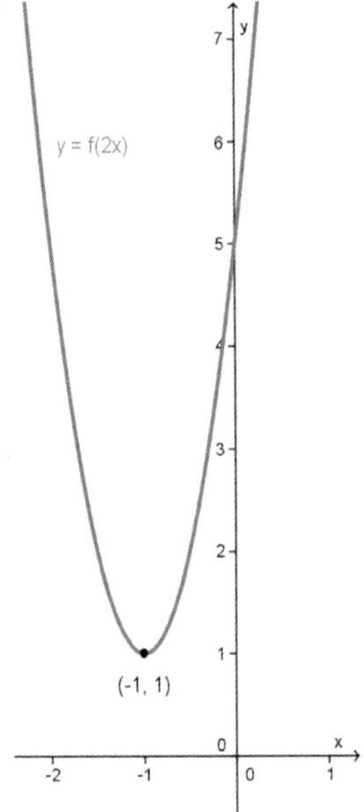

e)

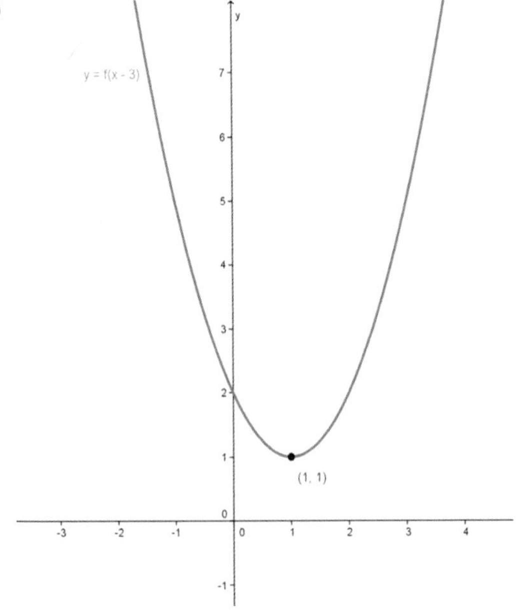

2. f)

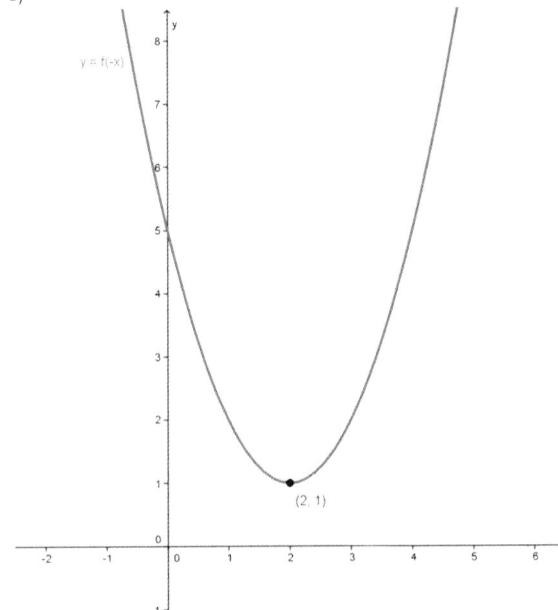

3. a)

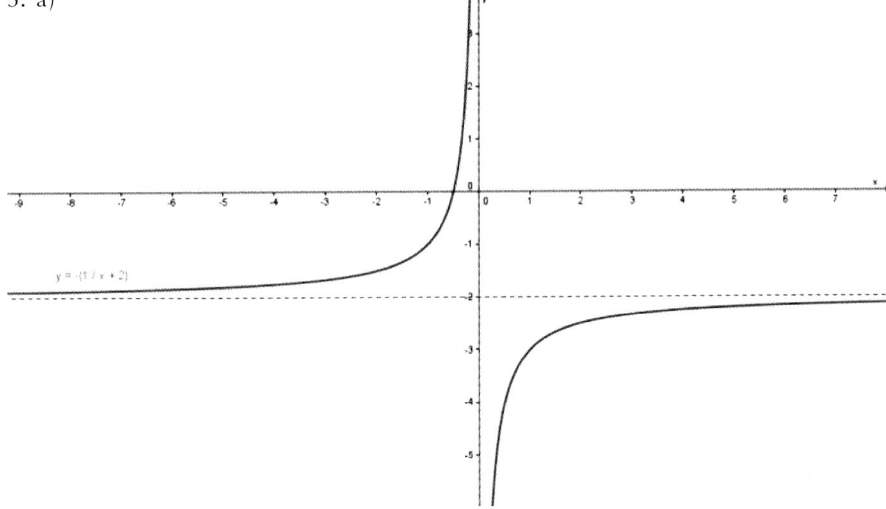

b)

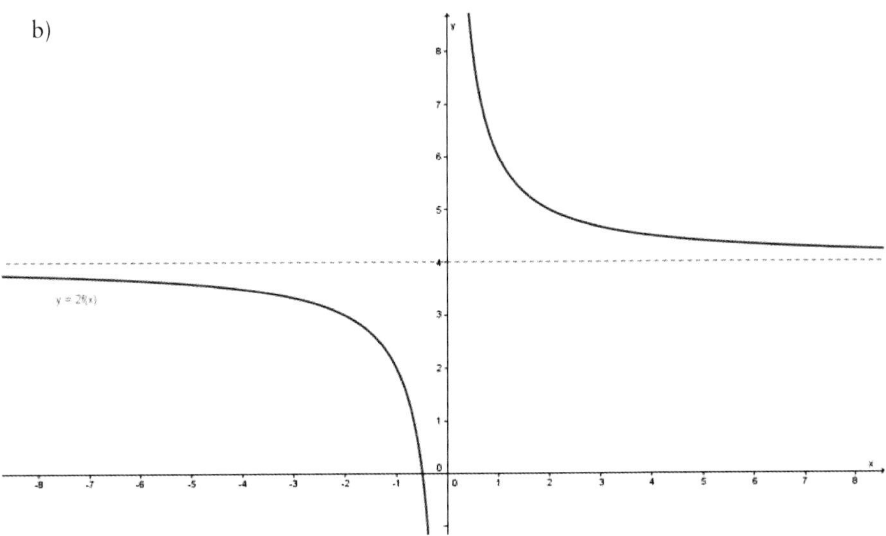

3. c)

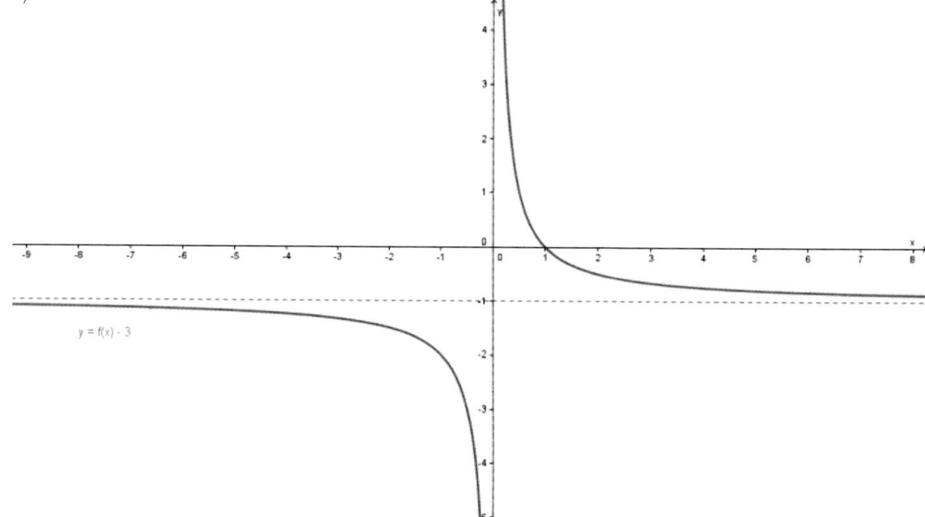

d)

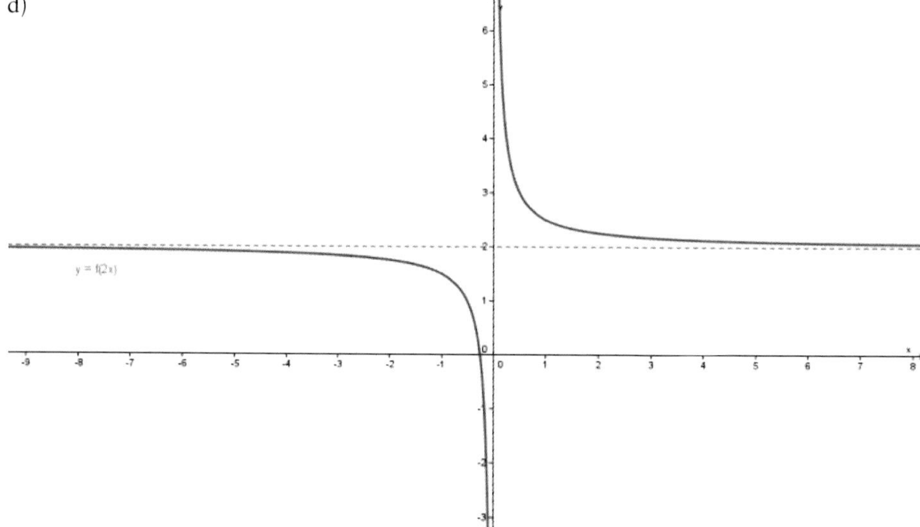

e)

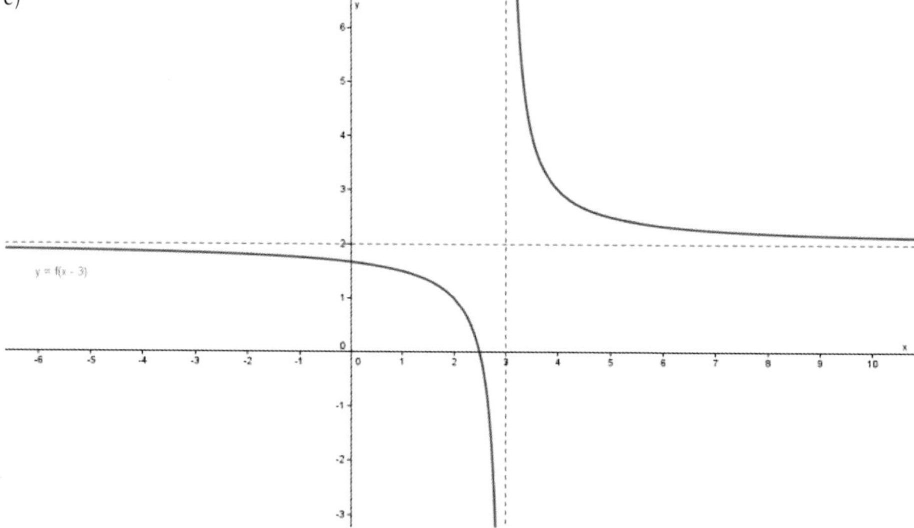

3. f)

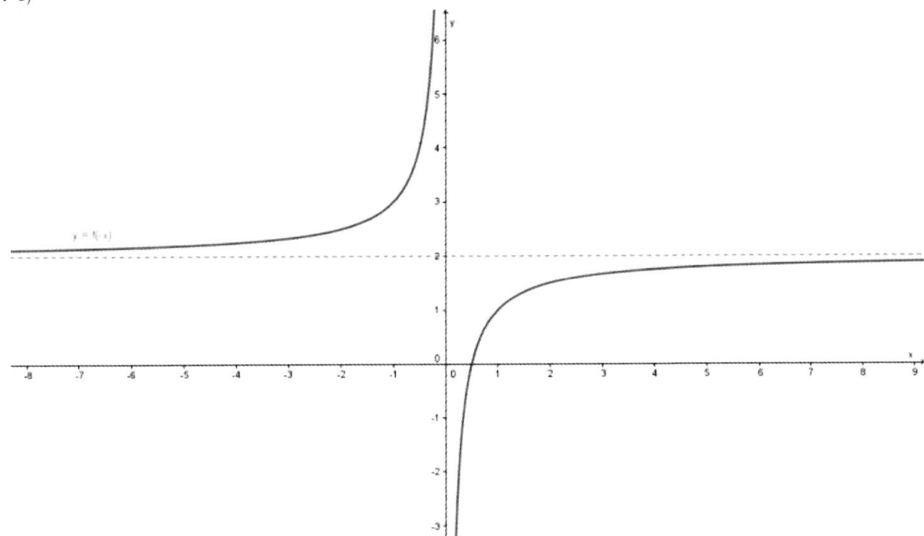

4. a)

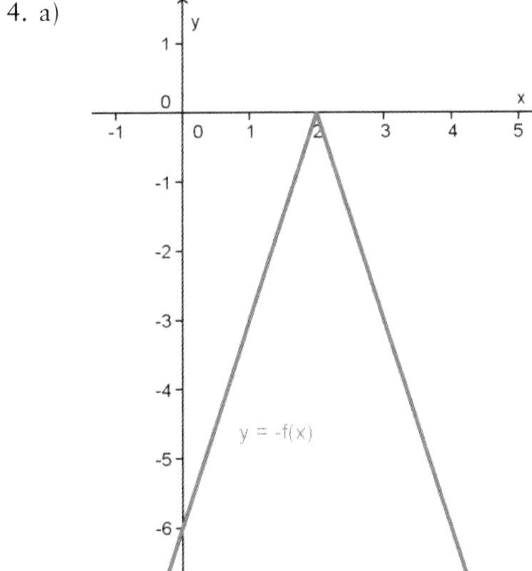

4. c)

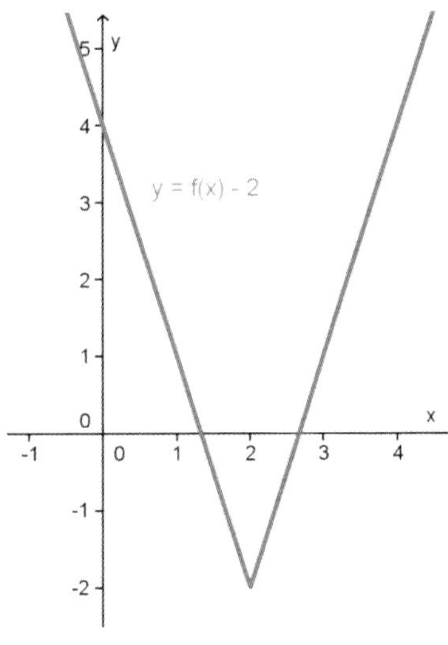

b)

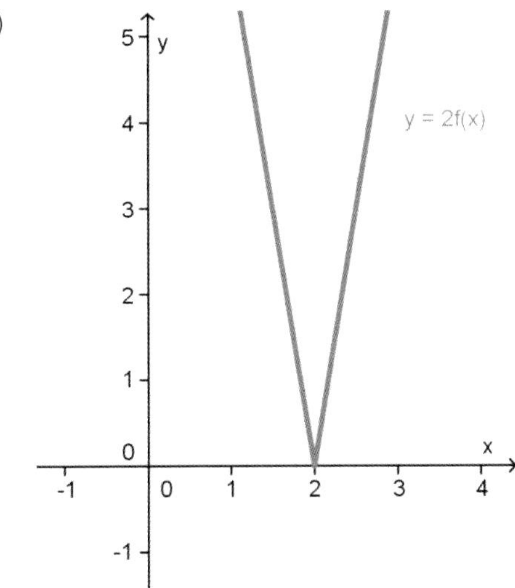

d)

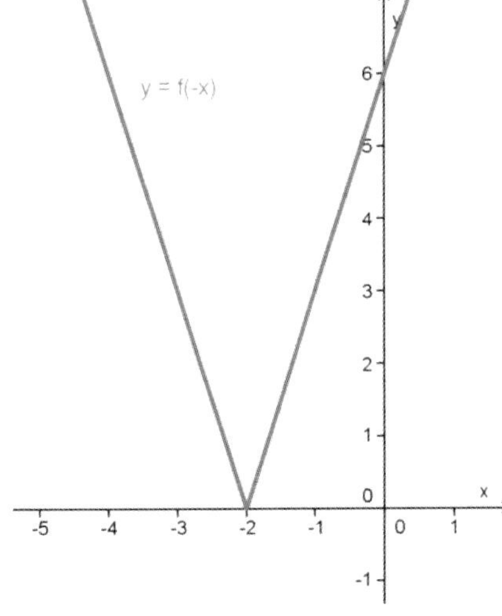

4. e)

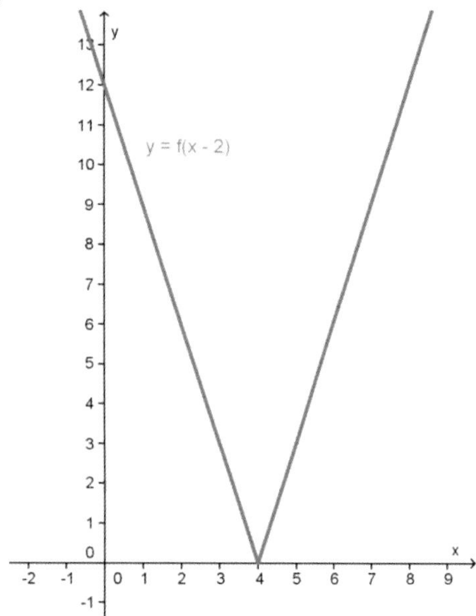

4. f)

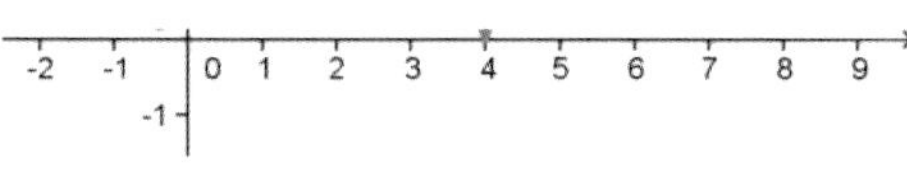

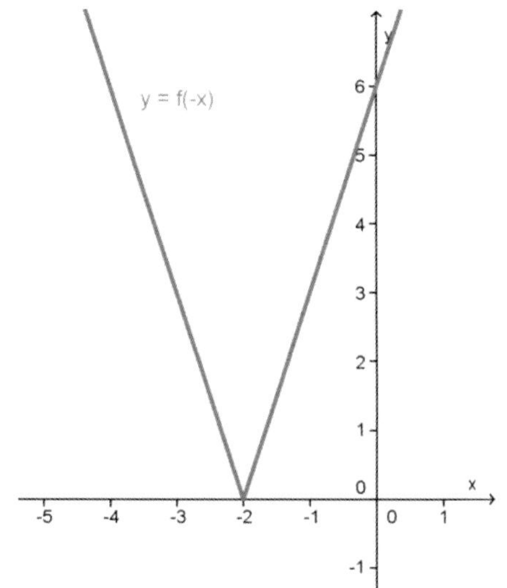

5. a)

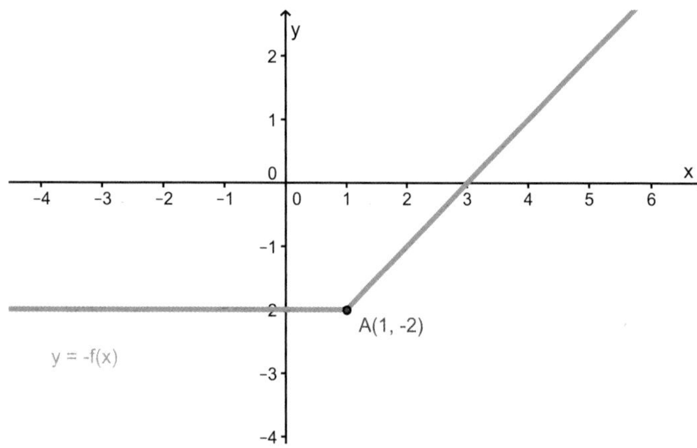

b)

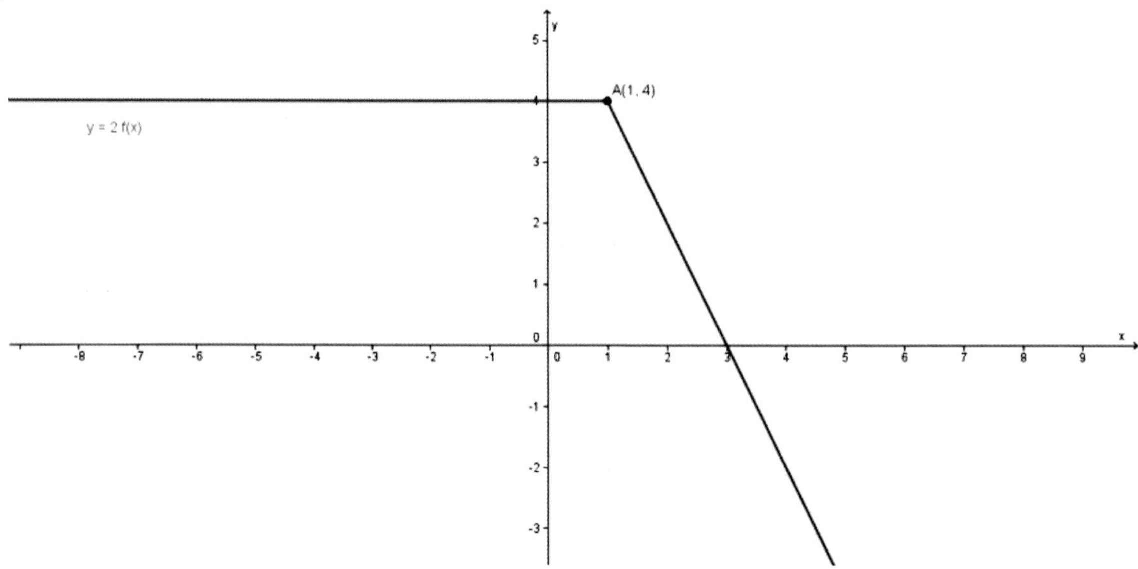

5. c)

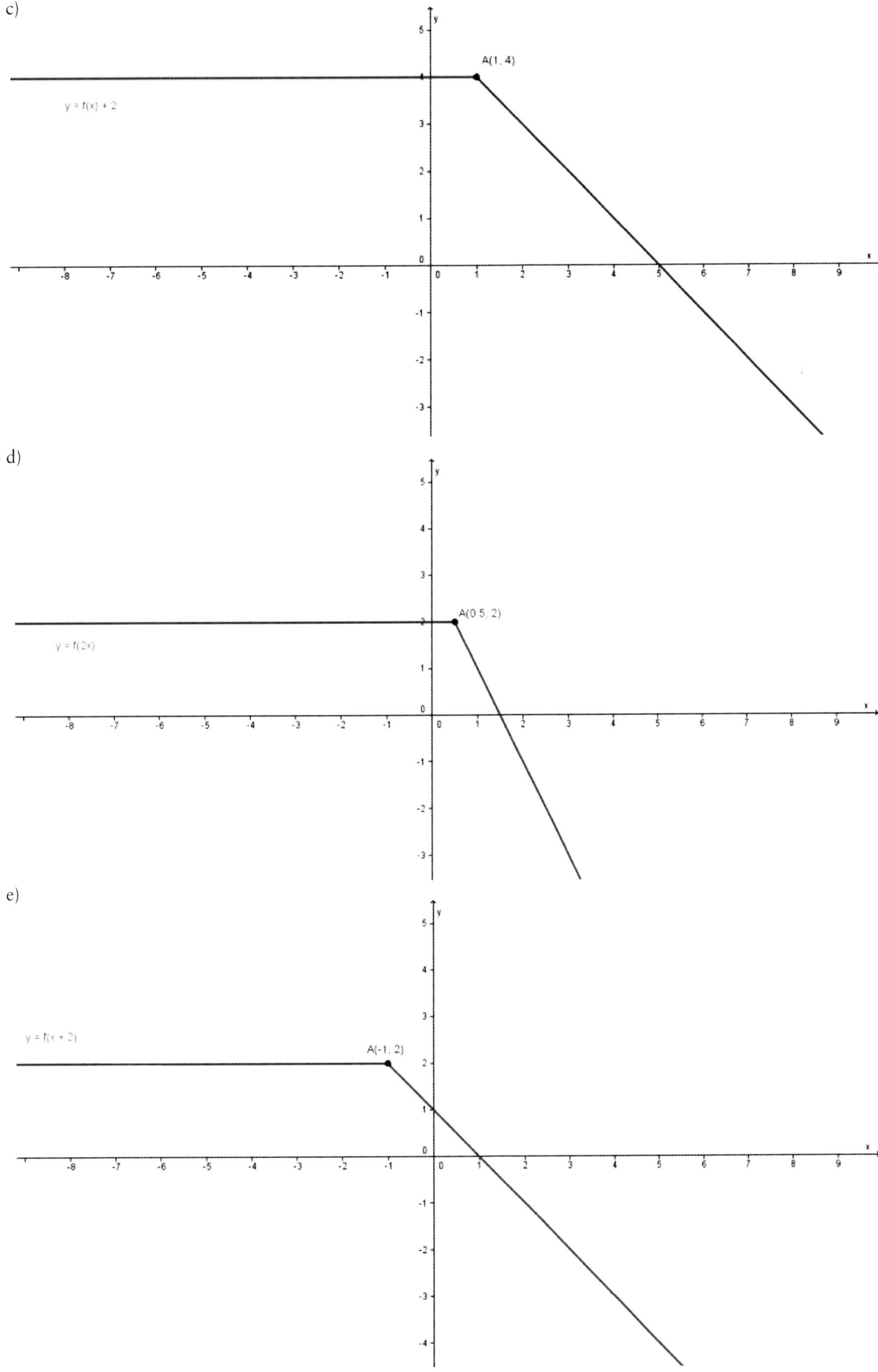

5. f)

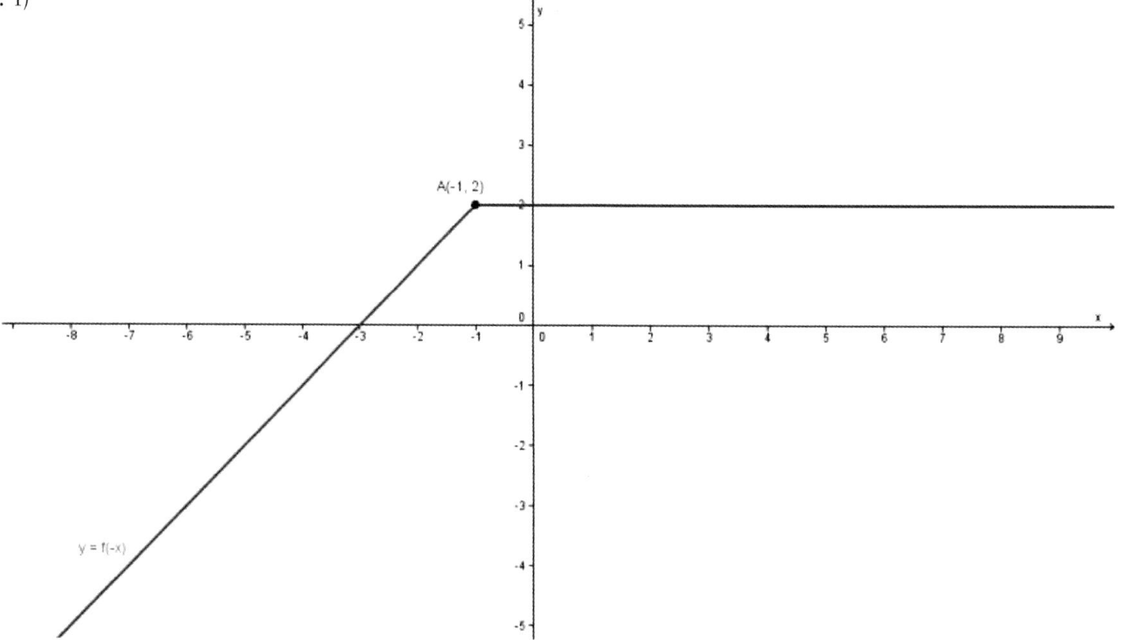

6. a)

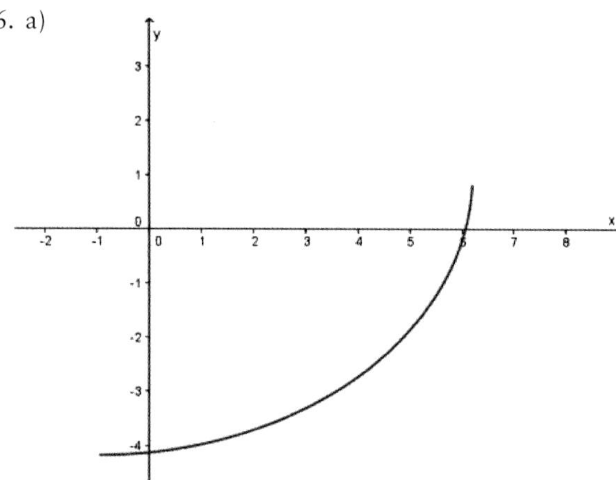

6. c)

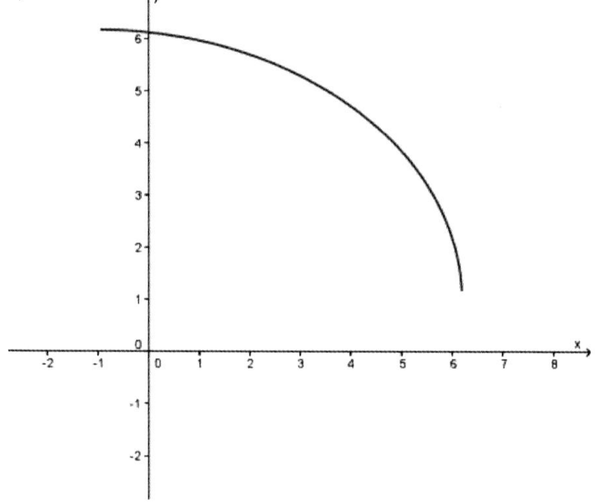

b)

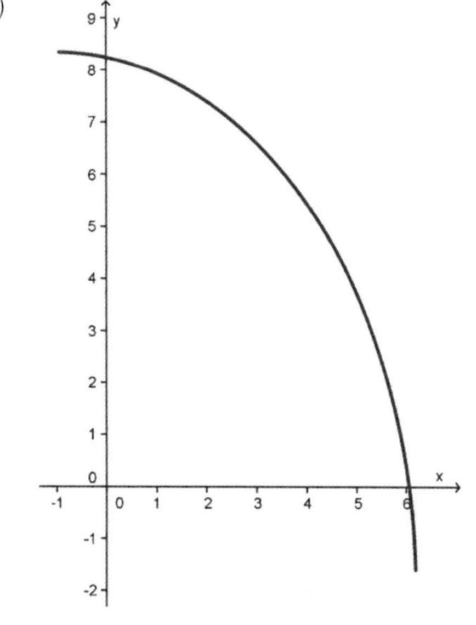

d)

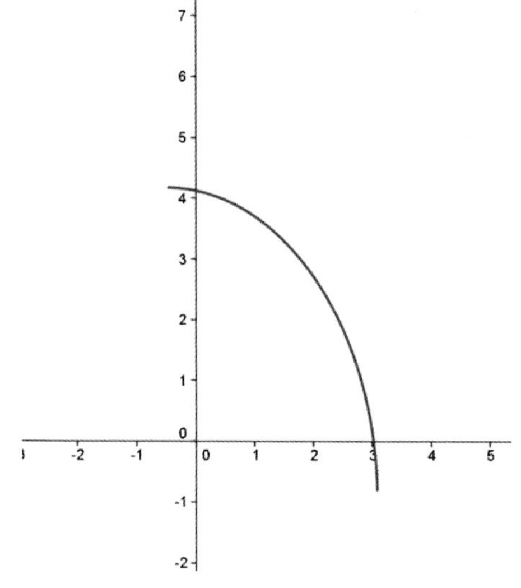

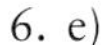

6. e)

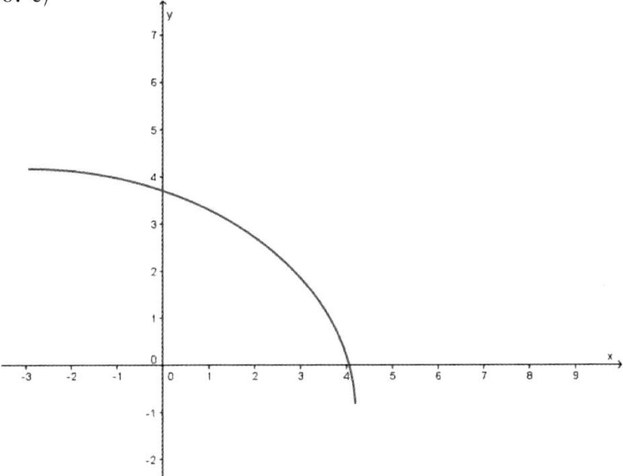

f)

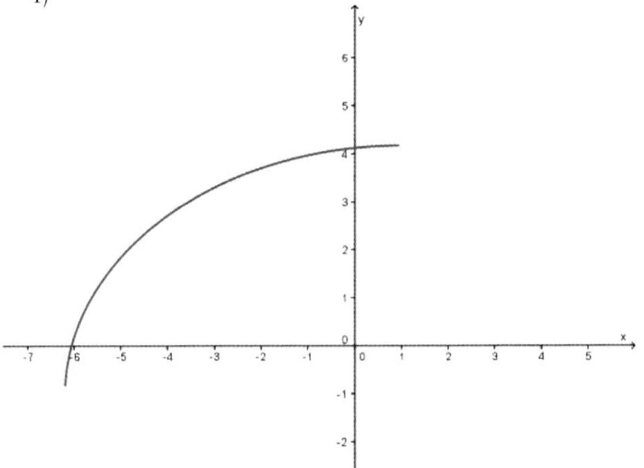

CHAPTER 5. EQUATION OF A STRAIGHT LINE

Exercise 5A

1. a) yes b) no c) yes
   d) no e) yes f) yes
2. a)

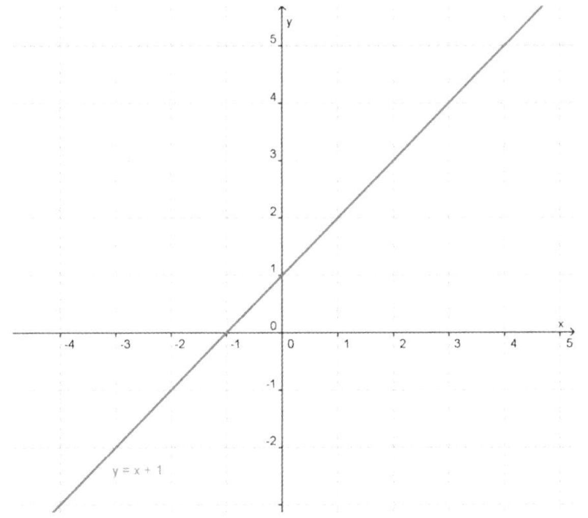

Gradient: 1, y-intercept 1.

2. b)

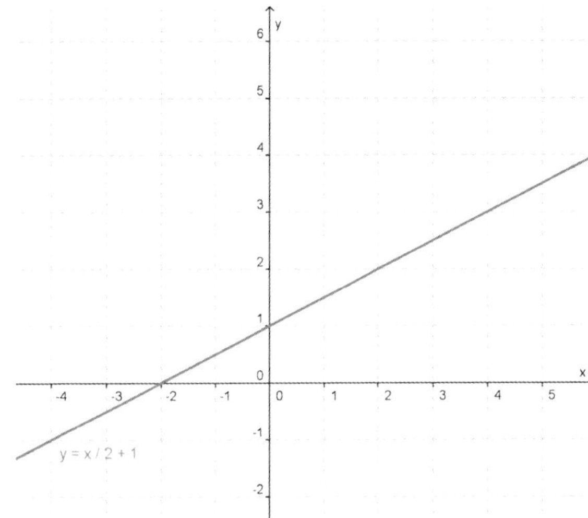

Gradient $\frac{1}{2}$, y-intercept 1.

c)

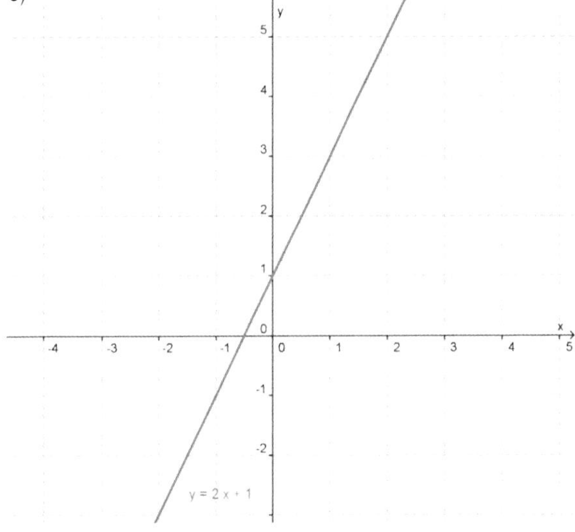

Gradient 2, y-intercept 1.

d)

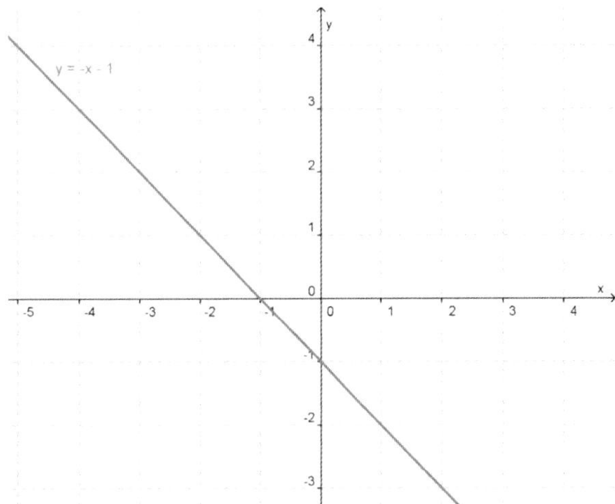

Gradient -1, y-intercept −1

3. a) Gradient 5, y–intercept 3
   b) Gradient –2, y–intercept –3
   c) Gradient 2, y–intercept $\frac{7}{2}$
   d) Gradient 1, y–intercept –1

Exercise 5B

1. a) 1 b) $-\frac{1}{2}$ c) $-\frac{4}{5}$
   d) $\frac{4}{3}$ e) $\frac{1}{4}$
2. a) $y = 2x - 3$ b) $y = x + 4$
   c) $y = 3x + 2$ d) $y = \frac{1}{2}x - \frac{5}{2}$
   e) $y = -2x$ f) $y = -x - 2$
3. a) $y = x$ b) $y = 3x - 6$
   c) $y = x + 2$ d) $y = \frac{1}{2}x + 3$
   e) $y = -3x$ f) $y = -2x - 1$
4. $y = 9x - 33$
5. $y = 4x + 3$
6. $y = -x - 1$
7. $m = 1$
8. $y = 5x - 48$
9. $y = 7x - 53$
10. $y = 2x - 7$
11. $y = 3x + 13$
12. $x = 7$
13. $y = 5x - 14$
14. $C\left(\frac{1}{5}, 0\right), D(0, -1)$

Exercise 5C

1. a) $3x - 2y + 3 = 0$
   b) $3y - 5 = 0$
   c) $x - 1 = 0$
   d) $3x - 4y - 3 = 0$
   e) $4x - 5y = 0$
   f) $4x - 25y = 0$
   g) $2x + 7y + 3 = 0$
   h) $4x - 3y + 1 = 0$
   i) $12x - 6y - 1 = 0$
   j) $7x + 6y - 1 = 0$
2. a) (3, 0) b) (0, 4)
3. a) (0, 0) b) (0, 0)
4. $2x + y - 3 = 0$
5. $4x - 6y - 9 = 0$
6. $a = 3$; $b = 1$; $3x + y - 6 = 0$
7. a) A(2, 5)
   b)

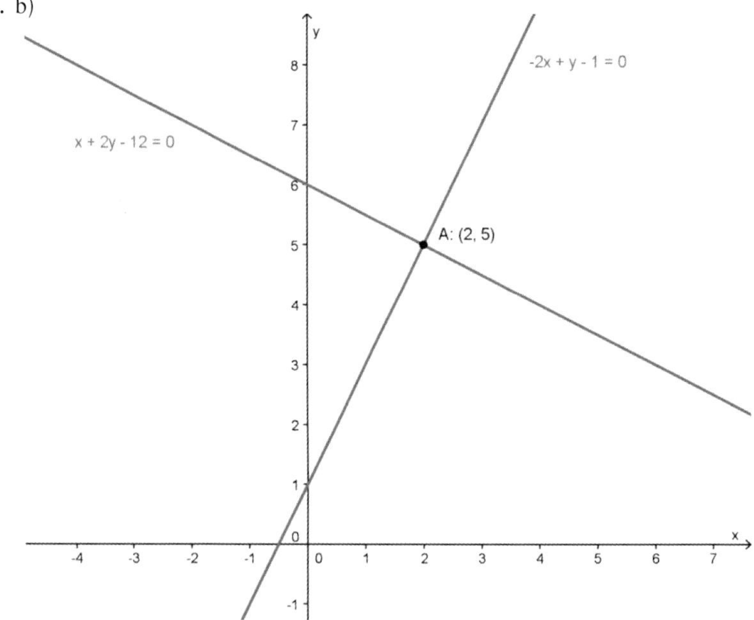

Exercise 5D

1. a) (5, 5) b) (5, 4)
   c) (–1, –5) d) (11.5, 4)
   e) (2.5, –4.5) f) (2, 1)
   g) (0, 5)
2. a) $\left(\frac{1+\pi}{2}, 11\right)$ b) $\left(\frac{5}{2}, 1+\sqrt{2}\right)$
3. a) B(–2, 6) b) B(4, 7)
   c) B(–26, 17) d) B(–21, –24)
   e) $B(2, 3\pi)$
4. a) –3 c) 1, –3

Exercise 5E

1. a) parallel b) neither
   c) parallel d) perpendicular
   e) neither f) parallel
   g) neither
2. a and c perpendicular;
   b and e parallel;
   d and f neither.
3. $p = -7$
4. a) $y = -\frac{7}{2}x - \frac{5}{2}$
   b) $\frac{2}{7}$
5. –3
6. 2
7. $2y + 3x - 9 = 0$
8. a) –10
   b) $3x + 10y - 109 = 0$
9. $2x + 3y - 3 = 0$
10. a) 1
    b) $y + x - 3a = 0$

CHAPTER 6. DIFFERENTIATION

Revision Exercise 6A

1. a) $-x$
   b) $x^2 + 2x - 4$
   c) $2x^2 + 2$
   d) $-x^3 + x^2 - x + 1$
   e) $4x^2 - 4x$ or $4x(x - 1)$
2. a) x^3
   b) $x^{3/2}$
   c) $x^{-5/2}$
   d) x^{-1}
   e) x^0 or 1
3. a) $1 - x + x^2 - x^3$
   b) $x^{-4} + x^{-1}$
   c) $4x^3 - 3x^2 - x$
   d) $2x^{3/2} + 5x^{-5/2}$
   e) $x^{-2} - 1$
4. a)

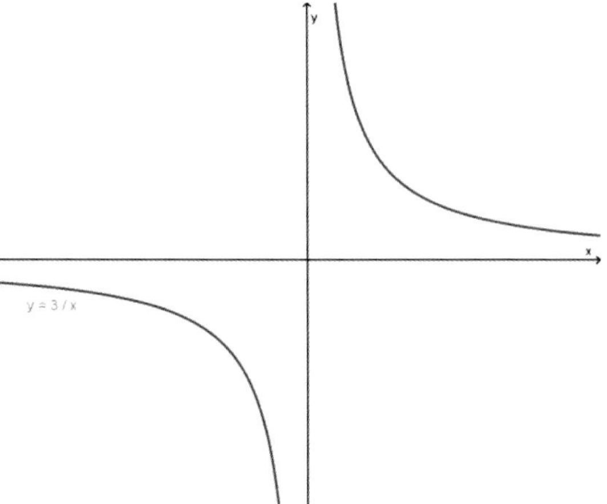

4. b)

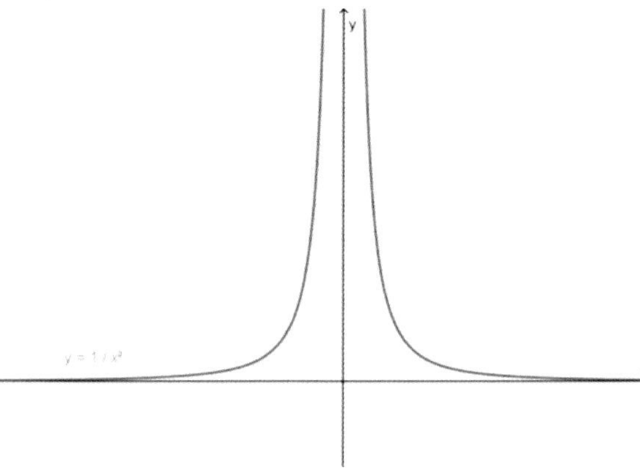

c)

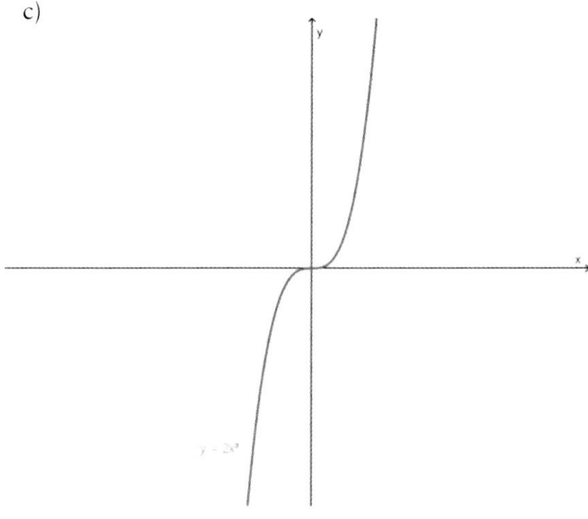

d)

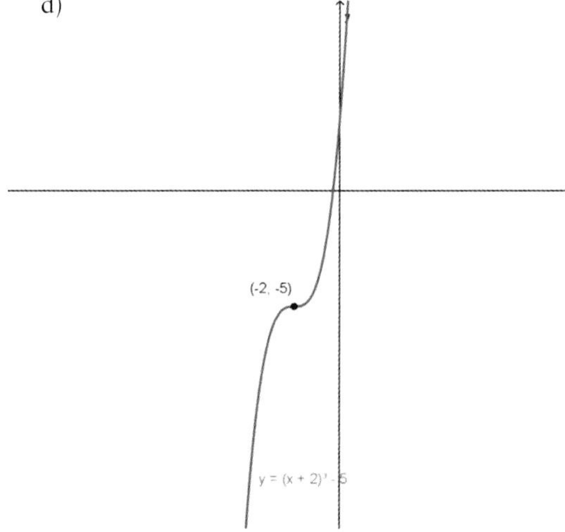

5. a) $-1 < x < 3$
   b) $x < -9$ or $x > 0$
   c) $x < -1$ or $x > \frac{1}{2}$
   d) $-3 < x < 3$

Exercise 6B

1.

x_1	y_1	m
2	8	7
1.1	1.331	3.31
1.01	1.030301	3.0301
1.001	1.003003001	3.003001

Gradient = 3

2.

x_1	y_1	m
3	2	3
2.1	–0.79	2.1
2.01	–0.9799	2.01
2.001	–0.997999	2.001

Gradient = 2

Exercise 6C

1. a) $\frac{dy}{dx} = 1$ b) $\frac{dy}{dx} = 2x$
   c) $\frac{dy}{dx} = 5$ d) $\frac{dy}{dx} = -3$
   e) $\frac{dy}{dx} = 2x - 1$
2. a) $\frac{dy}{dx} = -2x$ b) $\frac{dy}{dx} = 3$
   c) $\frac{dy}{dx} = 4x + 5$ d) $\frac{dy}{dx} = 3 - 6x$
   e) $\frac{dy}{dx} = 4x + 2$
3. a) $\frac{dy}{dx} = 2x$; $\frac{dy}{dx} = 2$ b) $\frac{dy}{dx} = 2x + 1$; $\frac{dy}{dx} = 1$
   c) $\frac{dy}{dx} = 6x + 2$; $\frac{dy}{dx} = 8$ d) $\frac{dy}{dx} = 3x^2$; $\frac{dy}{dx} = 3$
   e) $\frac{dy}{dx} = 3x^2 + 6x$; $\frac{dy}{dx} = 9$

Exercise 6D

1. a) $\frac{dy}{dx} = 6x$ b) $\frac{dy}{dx} = 2$
   c) $\frac{dy}{dx} = -7$ d) $\frac{dy}{dx} = 10x^4$
   e) $\frac{dy}{dx} = 3x^6$ f) $\frac{dy}{dx} = -6x^2$
   g) $\frac{dy}{dx} = -\frac{5}{4}$ h) $\frac{dy}{dx} = -x^{-4}$
2. a) $\frac{dy}{dx} = -x^{-2}$ b) $\frac{dy}{dx} = \frac{1}{2}x^{-1/2}$
   c) $\frac{dy}{dx} = -\frac{1}{2}x^{-3/2}$ d) $\frac{dy}{dx} = \frac{3}{2}x^{1/2}$
   e) $\frac{dy}{dx} = -\frac{3}{2}x^{-5/2}$ f) $\frac{dy}{dx} = 4x^{-3}$
   g) $\frac{dy}{dx} = -x^{-5/2}$ h) $\frac{dy}{dx} = x^{-4/3}$

3. a) 3
   b) 4
   c) –¼ or –0.25
   d) 0.25
   e) –0.25
   f) 1
   g) $-\frac{5}{64}$
   h) –0.5
4. a) $\frac{dy}{dx} = 2x$
   b) $\frac{dy}{dx} \to \infty$
   c) $\frac{dy}{dx} \to -\infty$
5. a) $\frac{dy}{dx} = 3x^2$
   b) $\frac{dy}{dx} \to \infty$
   c) $\frac{dy}{dx} \to \infty$
   d) The gradient of $y = x^2$ is negative when x is negative, whereas the gradient of $y = x^3$ is positive when x is negative.
6.

Functions:	$\frac{1}{3}x^3$	$(x+1)(x-2)$	$3x^3$	$\frac{5}{x^2}$	$5x^2$
Derivatives:	x^2	$2x - 1$	$9x^2$	$-\frac{10}{x^3}$	$10x$

2. a) $\frac{dy}{dt} = 8t + 3$
   b) $\frac{dP}{dv} = 2v + v^{-2}$
   c) $\frac{dv}{dt} = 10$
   d) $\frac{ds}{dt} = 1 + 10t$
   f) $\frac{dp}{dq} = q^{-2}$
   e) $\frac{dp}{dq} = q^{-2}$
   f) $\frac{dW}{dx} = \frac{5}{2}x^{3/2} - \frac{1}{2}x^{-1/2}$
   g) $\frac{dA}{ds} = -4s + 3$
   h) $\frac{dz}{d\theta} = 1 + \theta^{-2}$
   i) $\frac{dm}{dn} = 9n^2 - 4n + 3$
   j) $\frac{dA}{dr} = 2\pi r$

Exercise 6E

1. a) $\frac{dy}{dx} = 6x + 4$
   b) $\frac{dy}{dx} = 12x^3 - 1$
   c) $\frac{dy}{dx} = -x^{-2} - 8x^{-3}$
   d) $\frac{dy}{dx} = \frac{1}{3} + \frac{x}{2}$
   e) $\frac{dy}{dx} = 2x - 4$
   f) $\frac{dy}{dx} = 3x^2 + 6x$
   g) $\frac{dy}{dx} = 4x^3 - 3x^2 + 2x$
   h) $\frac{dy}{dx} = 4x^3$
   i) $\frac{dy}{dx} = \frac{1}{2}x^{-1/2} + 3$
   j) $\frac{dy}{dx} = -x^{-2} + \frac{1}{2}x^{-3/2}$
   k) $\frac{dy}{dx} = 3x^{1/2} - \frac{1}{2}x^{-1/2}$
   l) $\frac{dy}{dx} = -\frac{1}{2}x^{-3/2} - \frac{3}{2}x^{1/2}$
3. a) $f'(x) = -4x$
   b) $f'(x) = -x^{-2}$
   c) $f'(x) = 8x - 1$
   d) $f'(x) = 1 - 2x^{-2}$
   e) $f'(x) = 1 - 4x^{-2}$
   f) $f'(x) = -\frac{1}{2}x^{-3/2}$
   g) $f'(x) = 4x - 5$
   h) $f'(x) = 6x^2 - 2x$
   i) $f'(x) = \frac{1}{2}x^{-1/2} + \frac{3}{2}x^{1/2} + 1$
   j) $f'(x) = \frac{2px + q}{r}$
4. a) $f'(x) = 3$
   b) $g'(x) = 2x$
   c) $f'(x)g'(x) = 6x$
   d) $\frac{f'(x)}{g'(x)} = \frac{3}{2x}$
   e) $h(x) = 3x^3 + 2x^2$
   f) $h'(x) = 9x^2 + 4x$
   g) No
   h) $j(x) = 3x^{-1} + 2x^{-2}$
   i) $j'(x) = -3x^{-2} - 4x^{-3}$
   j) No

Exercise 6F

1. a) $\frac{dy}{dx} = 4x$
   b) $\frac{dF}{dp} = 4p^3 - \frac{1}{p^2}$
   c) $\frac{dA}{dr} = 5r + \frac{7}{2}$
   d) $\frac{db}{dc} = -\frac{3}{2}c^{-5/2} - c^{-2}$
   e) $\frac{dx}{dy} = -10y^{-3}$
2. a) $\frac{dy}{dx} = 2$
   b) $\frac{dy}{dx} = 12$
   c) $\frac{dy}{dx} = 9$
   d) $\frac{dy}{dx} = \frac{1}{2}$
   e) $\frac{dy}{dx} = -6$
3. $\frac{dV}{dp} = 6p - 4p^{-2}$ when $p = 2, \frac{dV}{dp} = 11$
4. a) $A = 4\pi r^2$
   b) $\frac{dA}{dr} = 8\pi r$
   c) $\frac{dA}{dr} = 16\pi$
5. 124 m s^{-1}.
6. a) $\frac{dc}{ds} = 2 + \frac{1}{3}s^{-2/3}$
   b) $\frac{1}{8}$

Exercise 6G

1. a) $\frac{dy}{dx} = 2x$
   b) 2
   c) $y = 2x - 1$
2. $y = 16x - 29$
3. $y = -8x - 11$
4. $16y + x - 66 = 0$
5. a) Gradients at A and B are both –3
   b) $3y - x + 10 = 0$
6. b) $y = 3x + 5$
7. 68
8. a) 4, –4

Exercise 6H

1. (–1, 1)
2. a) $\frac{dy}{dx} = \frac{2}{x^3}$
   b) (2, –¼)
3. a) (4, 4)
   b) (9, 6)

4. a) $\frac{dy}{dx} = 6 + 6x^2$
   b) (1, 8), (–1, –8)
5. (2, –16)
6. 4 and –4
7. (½, 2), (–½, –2)
8. (2, –34/3), (6, –70)
9. a) $\frac{dy}{dx} = 12x^2 - 84x + 125$
   b) 5
   c) $y = 5x + 116$
10. 45 metres
11. a) 45 cm²
   b) 25 seconds.
   c) 81 seconds

Exercise 6I

1. a) (0, 2)
   b) (–2, –4)
   c) (4, 16)
   d) (1, 1), (–1, 5)
   e) (–2.5, –6.25)
   f) (5, –50)
   g) (2, –2)
   h) (5, 51)
   i) (2, –63), (3, –64)
   j) $\left(\frac{\sqrt{3}}{3}, \frac{-2\sqrt{3}}{9}\right), \left(\frac{-\sqrt{3}}{3}, \frac{2\sqrt{3}}{9}\right)$
   k) (1, –1)
2. (6, –61), (2, 3)
3. a) $\frac{dy}{dx} = 18x - 12x^2$
   b) (0, 2), (1.5, 8.75)
4. b) $f'(x) = 1 + 8x^{-2} - 48x^{-4}$
5. a) $f'(x) = \frac{40}{3}x^{-1/3} - \frac{5}{3}x^{2/3}$
   b) (8, 48)
6. –18
7. a) $\frac{dy}{dx} = 2px - q$
   b) $p = 3, q = 24$
8. $b = 3, c = 3$

Exercise 6J

1. a) Gradient 12; Increasing
   b) Gradient –12; Decreasing
   c) Gradient 3; Increasing
   d) Gradient –3; Decreasing
   e) Gradient –2; Decreasing
   f) Gradient 8; Increasing
   g) Gradient 3; Increasing
   h) Gradient 5; Increasing
   i) Gradient –½; Decreasing
   j) Gradient 1; Increasing
   k) Gradient ½; Increasing
   l) Gradient $-\frac{5}{2}$; Decreasing
2. a) Decreasing for $x < -1$;
   Increasing for $x > -1$
   b) Increasing for $x < -1$;
   Decreasing for $-1 < x < 1$;
   Increasing for $x > 1$
   c) Increasing for all values of x
   d) Decreasing for all values of x
   e) Decreasing for $x < -1/2$;
   Increasing for $x > -1/2$
   f) Decreasing for all values of x (except zero)
   g) Decreasing for $x > 0$
   h) Decreasing for $x < \frac{1}{2}$;
   Increasing for $x > \frac{1}{2}$
   i) Decreasing for $0 < x < 4$;
   Increasing for $x > 4$
   j) Increasing for $x < 0$;
   Decreasing for $x > 0$
5. Always decreasing.
6. $x < 0$ or $x > \frac{8}{3}$
7. a) (1, –32), (4, –59)
   b) (1, –32) maximum;
   (4, –59) minimum
8. Minimum
9. Minimum at (0, 3);
   maximum at $\left(\frac{2}{3}, \frac{13}{3}\right)$
10. a) $\frac{dy}{dx} = 8x^3 - 12x^2$
   b) Point of inflection at $x = 0$;
   minimum at $x = \frac{3}{2}$

Exercise 6K

1. a) $f'(x) = 4x$; $f''(x) = 4$
   b) $f'(x) = x^3 + x^2$; $f''(x) = 3x^2 + 2x$
   c) $f'(x) = 1 - \frac{1}{x^2}$; $f''(x) = \frac{2}{x^3}$
   d) $f'(x) = \frac{1}{2}$; $f''(x) = 0$
   e) $f'(x) = \frac{3}{2\sqrt{x}}$; $f''(x) = -\frac{3}{4}x^{-3/2}$
   f) $f'(x) = -\frac{3}{2}x^{-3/2}$; $f''(x) = \frac{9}{4}x^{-5/2}$
   g) $f'(x) = 12x^5 + 12x^{-7}$;
   $f''(x) = 60x^4 - 84x^{-8}$
   h) $f'(x) = -4x + 1$; $f''(x) = -4$
   i) $f'(x) = 1 - 3x^2$; $f''(x) = -6x$
   j) $f'(x) = 1$; $f''(x) = 0$
2. a) $\frac{dy}{dx} = -1$; $\frac{d^2y}{dx^2} = 1$
   b) $\frac{dy}{dx} = 4$; $\frac{d^2y}{dx^2} = -12$
   c) $\frac{dy}{dx} = 5$; $\frac{d^2y}{dx^2} = 0$
   d) $\frac{dy}{dx} = -\frac{1}{2}$; $\frac{d^2y}{dx^2} = -1$
   e) $\frac{dy}{dx} = -7$; $\frac{d^2y}{dx^2} = 12$
3. a) $\frac{dy}{dx} = 2$; $\frac{d^2y}{dx^2} = 4$
   b) $\frac{dy}{dx} = \frac{3}{2}$; $\frac{d^2y}{dx^2} = -\frac{3}{4}$
   c) $\frac{dy}{dx} = 0$; $\frac{d^2y}{dx^2} = \frac{3}{2}$
   d) $\frac{dy}{dx} = -2$; $\frac{d^2y}{dx^2} = 3$
   e) $\frac{dy}{dx} = \frac{5}{2}c$; $\frac{d^2y}{dx^2} = 0$
4. Minimum (6, –63);
   maximum (2, 1)
5. Minimum (3, –36)
7. $\frac{dy}{dx} = -8x + \frac{1}{x^2}$;
   maximum at $\left(\frac{1}{2}, -3\right)$
8. a) $\frac{dy}{dx} = 6x^2 - 10x - 4$
   b) $-\frac{1}{3}, 2$
   c) $\frac{d^2y}{dx^2} = 12x - 10$
   d) Maximum at $x = -\frac{1}{3}$;
   minimum at $x = 2$
9. Minimum (0, 3);
   maximum (2, 15).
10. a) 4
   b) Minimum at $x = 1$;
   maximum at $x = -\frac{4}{3}$
11. a) $f'(x) = 1 + 12x^{-2} - 108x^{-4}$
   b) Minimum

Exercise 6L

1. a) 3 s   b) 45 m
2. a) 1s   b) 3 ms⁻²
3. 2
4. a) 50 km h⁻¹.
   b) $\frac{d^2C}{dv^2} = 2000v^{-3}$
   c) £40
5. a) 5 ms⁻¹
   b) $\frac{d^2F}{dv^2} = 4v^{-3} + \frac{2}{125}$,
   always positive for $v > 0.5$
   c) 0.6 N.
6. a) $h = \frac{300}{\pi r^2}$

c) $r = \sqrt[3]{\frac{100}{\pi}}$

7. a) $l = 200 - \pi r$

b) $A = 400r - 2\pi r^2$

c) $r = \frac{100}{\pi}$

d) $\frac{d^2A}{dr^2} = -4\pi$

e) $r = \frac{200}{\pi}$; $l = 0$; circular

8. a) $h = \frac{500}{x^2}$

c) $x = 10$; $h = 5$; cost = £3000

9. b) $0 < x < 1$ cm

c) $x = \frac{5 - \sqrt{7}}{6}$

d) $\frac{d^2V}{dx^2} = -4\sqrt{7}$

10. c) $\frac{d^2A}{dx^2} = -(100 + 25\pi)$

d) $A = \frac{200}{4 + \pi}$

REVIEW EXERCISE – CHAPTERS 4–6

1. $f(x) = x(x-3)(x-2)$ $x = 0, 2, 3$

2. a) $y = x(x-6)^2, x = 0, 6$ (repeated root)

b)

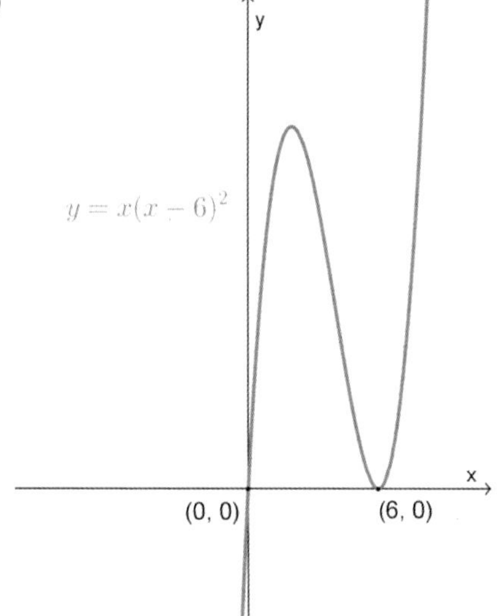

3. a) $f(x) = x(x^2 - 7x + 10x)$

3.b) $f(x) = x(x-5)(x-2)$

c)

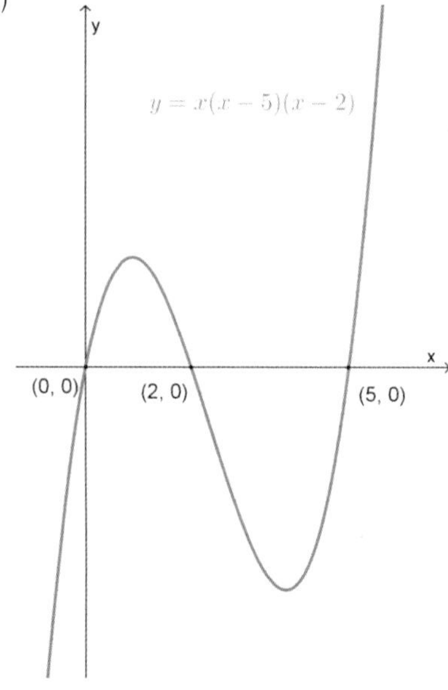

d) $x = 0, 2, 5$

4. a)

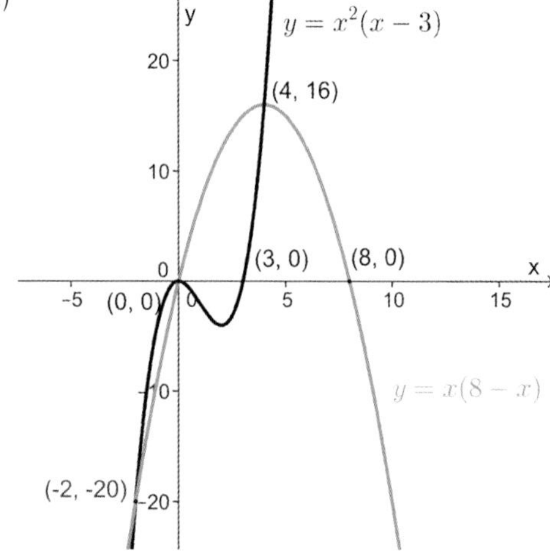

b) (4,16), (–2,–20), (0, 0)

5.

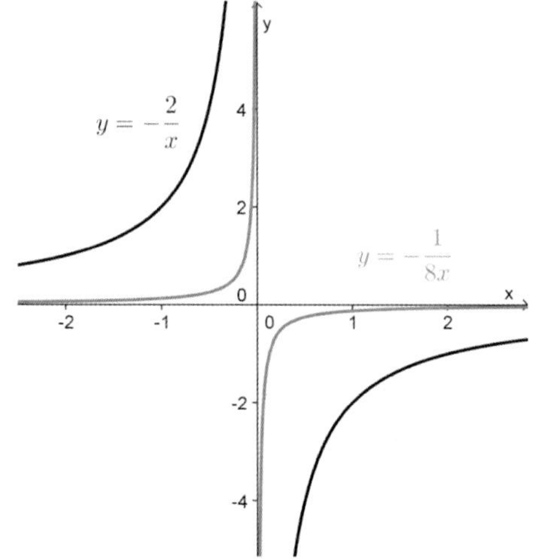

6.

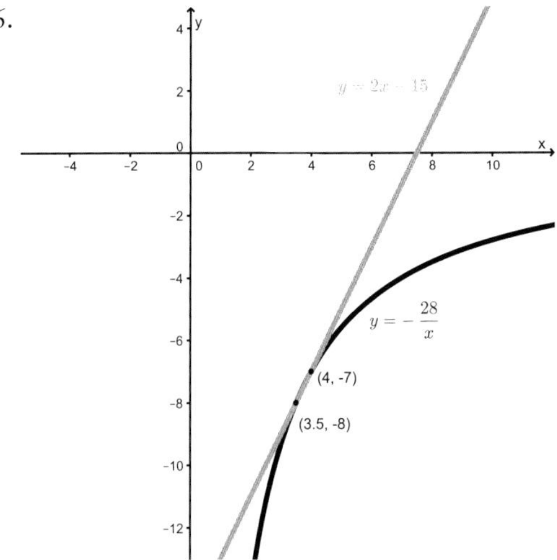

7. a) $x = 3, y = -5$ or $x = -4, y = 16$

b)

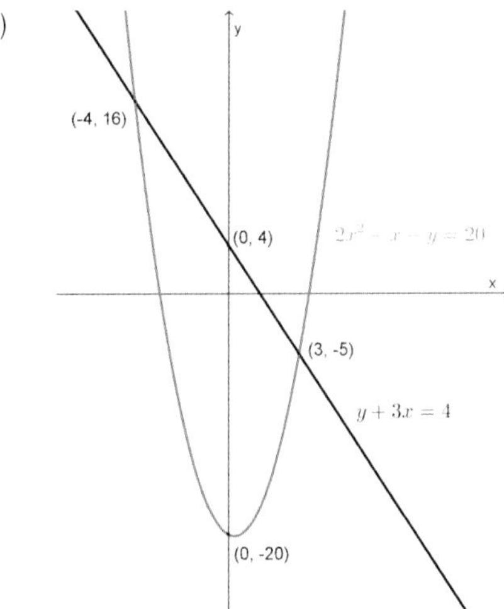

c) $x > 3$ or $x < -4$

8. a) $x^2 - 2x + 1 = 0$

b) 1 point

c)

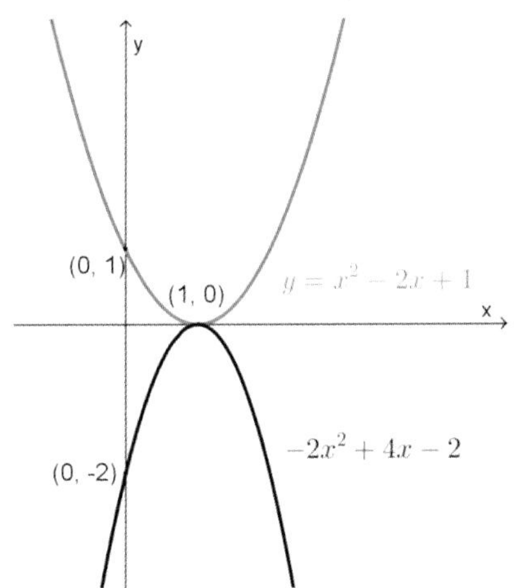

9. a) Translation 2 units in positive x-direction.

b) Translation 3 units in positive x-direction.

c) Translation one unit in negative x-direction, 2 units in positive y-direction.

10. a) Translation 2 units in positive x-direction, 4 units in positive y-direction.

b)

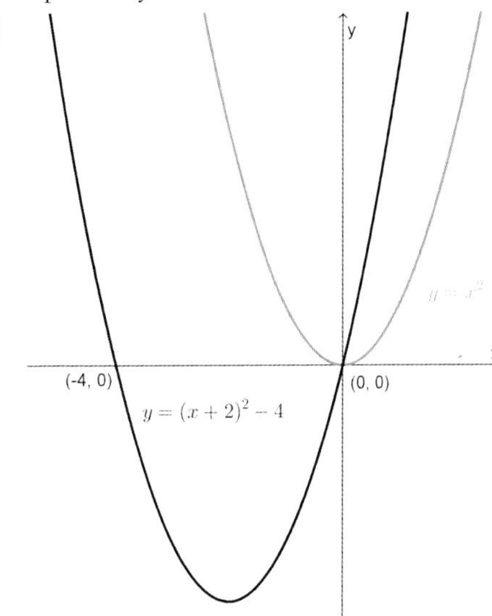

11. a)

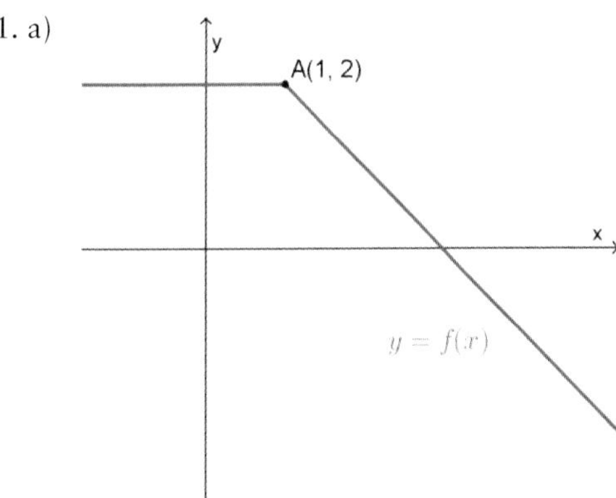

b)

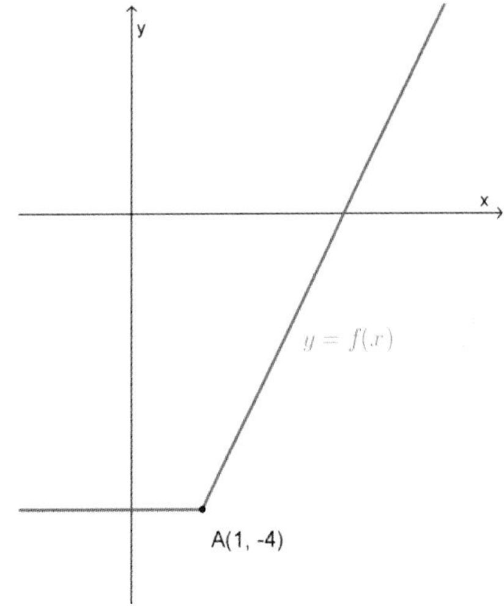

11. c)

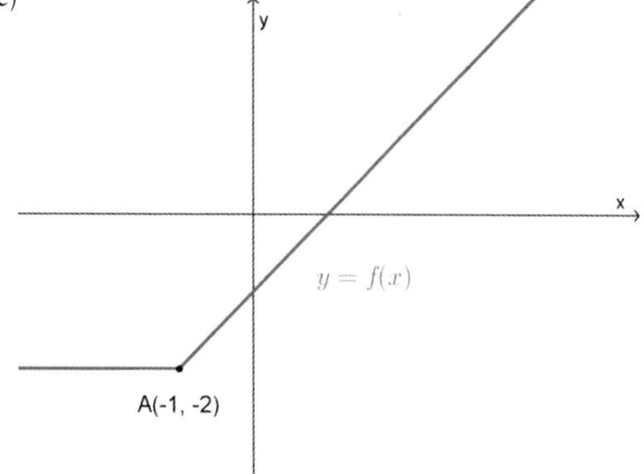

12. Yes, no, yes, no

13. $-\frac{1}{3}$

14. a) $y = 4x + 2$
 b) $y = -2x + 10$

15. a) $y = x - 6$
 b) $y = -2x + 3$

16. $y = -2x + 6$

17. a) $2x + 3y - 60 = 0$
 b) $9x - y + 12 = 0$

18. a) (–4, 0)
 b) (0, 5)

19. a) $a = 1;\ b = 3$
 b) $x + 3y - 21 = 0$
 c) $d = 1;\ e = -1/3;\ 3x - y - 3 = 0$
 d)

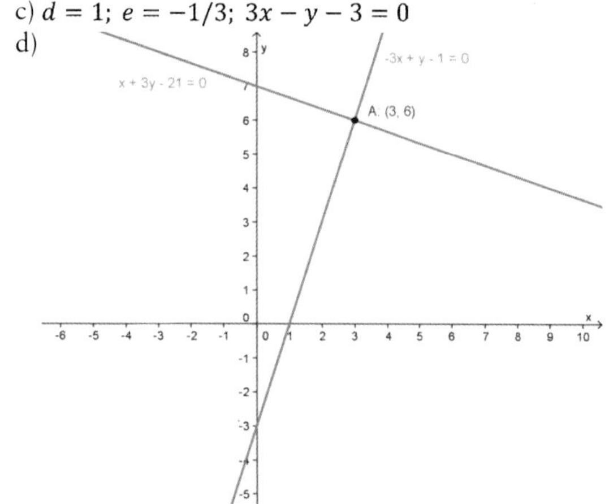

20. 3

21. a) 2
 b) $x + 2y - 7p = 0$

22. a) $\frac{dy}{dx} = 10x - 3$
 b) $\frac{dy}{dx} = x + \frac{1}{2}$
 c) $\frac{dy}{dx} = \frac{3}{2}\sqrt{x} - \frac{1}{2\sqrt{x}}$

23. a) $\frac{dy}{dx} = -\frac{1}{2}$
 b) $\frac{dy}{dx} = \frac{1}{2}$
 c) $\frac{dy}{dx} = -\frac{3}{5}$

24. a) $\frac{dv}{dt} = 20 - 10t$
 b) $\frac{dA}{dr} = \frac{14}{3}\pi r - \frac{\pi}{3}$
 c) $\frac{dz}{d\theta} = 6\theta^5 + 4\theta^3 - 2\theta$

25. a) $f'(x) = -\frac{4}{x^2}$
 b) $f'(x) = 1 - \frac{9}{x^2}$
 c) $f'(x) = \frac{1}{2\sqrt{x}} + 1$

26. $\frac{dV}{dp} = 6p^2 + 4p^{-2}$; when $p = 2$, $\frac{dV}{dp} = 25$

27. a) $\frac{db}{dq} = 3 + q^{-3/2}$
 b) $\frac{1}{4}$

28. 23

29. a) Gradients at A and B are both 8
 b) $8y + x - 34 = 0$

30. a) (1, 4)
 b) (0.25, 8)

31. –1, 5

32. a) (2.5, –12.5)
 b) (1, 4), (3, 0)

33. (1.5, –18)

34. b) $f'(x) = 1 + 4x^{-2} - 12x^{-4}$

35. a) $\frac{dy}{dx} = 2px - q$
 b) $p = -4, q = 8$

36. a) $b = 6, c = 12$

37. a) Decreasing for $x < -0.5$; Increasing for $x > -0.5$
 b) Decreasing for $-\sqrt{27} < x < \sqrt{27}$;
 Increasing for $x < -\sqrt{27}$ and $x > \sqrt{27}$

38. a) $\frac{dy}{dx} = 12x^3 - 24x^2$
 b) Point of inflection at (0, 0); minimum at (2, –16).

39. a) $f'(x) = x,\quad f''(x) = 1$
 b) $f'(x) = \frac{5}{2}x^{\frac{3}{2}} + 1,\quad f''(x) = \frac{15}{4}\sqrt{x}$

40. a) $\frac{dy}{dx} = 36,\quad \frac{d^2y}{dx^2} = 96\sqrt{2}$
 b) $\frac{dy}{dx} = 12\sqrt{2} + 1,\ \frac{d^2y}{dx^2} = 12$

41. a) $\frac{dy}{dx} = 3c^2,\quad \frac{d^2y}{dx^2} = 2c$
 b) $\frac{dy}{dx} = -\frac{2}{c},\quad \frac{d^2y}{dx^2} = \frac{2}{c^2}$

42. Minimum at $x = 8$; maximum at $x = 1$

43. a) $k = 4$
 b) Minimum at (1, –27), maximum at $\left(-\frac{4}{3}, \frac{100}{9}\right)$

44. a) 2 s b) 36 m

45. a) 10 ms^{-1} c) 6 kN

CHAPTER 7. COORDINATE GEOMETRY

Exercise 7A– Revision

1. a) $y = x$
   b) $3x + 10y = 60$
   c) $x - 3y = 1$
   d) $x + 12y = 36$
   e) $x - y = -1$
2. a) $f(x) = (x+2)^2 - 4$
   b) $f(x) = (x+4)^2 - 10$
   c) $f(x) = -(x+5)^2 + 31$
3. a) $x = -2, -4$
   b) $x = 1, -5$
   c) $x = 3\sqrt{2} - 1, -3\sqrt{2} - 1$
4. a) 2 roots
   b) 0 roots
   c) 1 root
   d) 0 roots
   e) 0 roots

Exercise 7B

1. a) (4, –3) b) (1, –1)
   c) (3, –2) d) (4.5, 5.5)
   e) (5, –3.5)
2. a) B(–7, 13) b) B(25, –6)
   c) B(0, 20) d) B(4, 12)
   e) B(6, –15)
3. a) –2 b) –10
   c) –1 d) $\frac{4}{3}$
   e) 0
4. a) $4x - 3y + 4 = 0$
   b) $3x + 5y - 12 = 0$
   c) $x - y + 5 = 0$
   d) $x = 2$
   e) $x - y = 0$
5. a) yes b) yes
   c) no d) yes
   e) no
6. a) $x + 2y - 7 = 0$
7. a) (13, 15) b) $\sqrt{34}$
8. a) $x + 4y - 12 = 0$
9. a) $-\sqrt{2}$ b) $\frac{\sqrt{2}}{2}$
   c) –1
10. a) (19, 5) b) $\frac{1}{5}$
   c) 0 d) (6, 5)
   e) East

Exercise 7C

1. a) yes b) no c) no
   d) yes e) no f) yes
   g) no h) yes i) yes
   j) no
2. a) 4 b) 64 c) 100
   d) 8 e) 5 f) 4
   g) 10 h) 2 i) 8
   j) 20
3. a) $(x+5)^2 + (y-7)^2 = 64$
   b) $(x-8)^2 + (y-7)^2 = 16$
   c) $(x+2)^2 + (y+1)^2 = 100$
   d) $(x-10)^2 + (y-5)^2 = 17$
   e) $(x-9)^2 + (y-3)^2 = 2$
   f) $(x+2)^2 + (y-2)^2 = 10$
   g) $(x+5)^2 + (y-2)^2 = 5$
   h) $(x-8)^2 + y^2 = 8$
   i) $(x-5)^2 + (y+2)^2 = 13$
   j) $(x+1)^2 + (y-9)^2 = 20$
4. a) $(x-10)^2 + (y+5)^2 = 9$
   b) $(x-4)^2 + (y-2)^2 = 13$
   c) $(x+1)^2 + (y+3)^2 = 2$
   d) $(x-8)^2 + (y+3)^2 = 8$
   e) $(x+7)^2 + (y-5)^2 = 20$
   f) $x^2 + (y-7)^2 = 5$
   g) $(x-2)^2 + (y+3)^2 = 18$
   h) $(x-6)^2 + (y-2)^2 = 10$
   i) $(x-4)^2 + (y+8)^2 = 17$
   j) $x^2 + (y-3)^2 = 13$
5. a) 2 b) 2 c) 0
   d) 1 e) 0 f) 2
   g) 1 h) 2 i) 0
   j) 1
6. $a = 1, \frac{79}{47}$
7. a) $(x - 5)^2 + (y - 13)^2 = 169$
   b) $12y - 5x + 38 = 0$
8. a) Centre (2, 4), radius 4.
   b) $y = 0, y = -\frac{4}{3}x$
9. a) Centre (4, 3), radius 3.
   b) $y = 0, y = \frac{24}{7}x$
10. a) (–1, –3), (5, 3)
   b) Centre of circle (2,0) from equation. Midpoint of AB is $\left(\frac{-1+5}{2}, \frac{-3+3}{2}\right) = (2{,}0)$

CHAPTER 8. SEQUENCES AND SERIES

Revision Exercise 8A

1. a) $x = 2$
   b) $w = -4$
   c) $z = -\frac{12}{7}$
   d) $y = -\frac{5}{4}$
   e) $v = 1$
2. a) $x = 1, -7$
   b) $x = 8, -10$
   c) $x = 2, 4$
   d) $x = 1$
   e) $x = 0, 5$
3. a) $x = 10, y = 5$
   b) $x = 10, y = -1$
   c) $x = -9, y = -8$
   d) $x = -2, y = -1$
   e) $x = -5, y = -7$
   f) $x = 2, y = -3, z = -2$
4. a) $3n - 2$
   b) $2n + 3$
   c) $4n - 7$
   d) $-10n + 5$
   e) $-20n + 37$

Exercise 8B

1. a) –1, 1, 3, 5
   b) 7, –2, –17, –38
   c) 1, 0, 1, 4
   d) –2, 4, 12, 22
   e) –6, –4, 0, 6
   f) 2, 9, 28, 65
   g) 0, 3, 16, 45
   h) 7, 22, 45, 76
   i) –2, 3, –4, 5
   j) $1, \frac{8}{7}, \frac{11}{9}, \frac{14}{11}$
2. a) $n = 11$ b) $n = 4$ c) $n = 3$
   d) $n = 5$ e) $n = 6$ f) $n = 2$
   g) $n = 3$ h) $n = 2$ i) $n = 10$
   j) $n = 3$
3. 4
4. $a = 3, b = 5$
5. $a = 4, b = 3$
6. $a = 1, b = 3, c = 2$
7. $u_n = (n-2)^2 + 4 \geq 4$ for all values of n
8. –5
9. a) $4n$ is always even, therefore $4n - 7$ is always odd
   b) Examples $u_n = 2n, u_n = 2n + 4, u_n = 4n - 2$
10. $u_n = 5n - 6$
11. a) $u_k = (3k-2)(3k-3)$
   b) $u_k = (3k-2)(3k-3) = 3(3k-2)(k-1)$
   Hence each term is multiple of 3.

Exercise 8C

1. a) 1, –3, –7, –11
   b) 1, –1, –1, –1
   c) 3, 4, 9, 64
   d) $2, \frac{3}{2}, \frac{11}{8}, \frac{43}{32}$
   e) 27, 18, 12, 8
   f) 3, 7, 43, 1807

1. g) $3, \frac{3}{4}, \frac{3}{7}, \frac{3}{10}$
   h) $\frac{1}{4}, -\frac{1}{2}, -2, -5$
   i) $-\frac{3}{4}, 2, -\frac{7}{2}, \frac{15}{2}$
   j) 2, 1, –1, –1
2. a) $u_{n+1} = u_n + 3, u_1 = 2$
   b) $u_{n+1} = u_n - 5, u_1 = -5$
   c) $u_{n+1} = u_n, \quad u_1 = 37$
   d) $u_{n+1} = -u_n, \quad u_1 = 2$
   e) $u_{n+1} = 6 - u_n, \quad u_1 = 2$
   f) $u_{n+1} = 2u_n, \quad u_1 = 2$
   g) $u_{n+1} = \frac{u_n}{2}, \quad u_1 = 1$
   h) $u_{n+1} = \sqrt{u_n}, \quad u_1 = 256$
   i) $u_{n+1} = (u_n)^2, \quad u_1 = 2$
   j) $u_{n+1} = 4u_n - 2, \quad u_1 = 1$
3. 1, 0.43, 0.39, 0.39, 0.39
4. a) 1, 4, 1
   b) 1
5. 3, –5
6. $d = \frac{16}{9}$
7. –4, 2
8. –2
9. a) 2.71, 2.81, 2.77
   b) 24
   c) 3
10. b) $q = 6$

Exercise 8D

1. a) $\frac{3}{4}, \frac{9}{16}, \frac{27}{64}$ b) Converges
2. a) $1, 3a, 9a^2, 27a^3$
   b) $-\frac{1}{3} < a < \frac{1}{3}$
3. 1, 2, 5, 26; diverges
4. a) $3, \frac{3}{5}, \frac{15}{13}, \frac{39}{41}, \frac{123}{121}$
   b) Converges and oscillates
5. 2.5
6. Diverges
7. Converges to 2.
8. a) 1, 0.3, 0.79, 0.45, 0.69
   b) yes
   c) $c = \frac{10}{17}$
9. $0 < p < 2$
10. $a > 0$

Exercise 8E

1. a) yes b) yes c) no
   d) no e) yes f) yes
   g) yes h) no i) yes
   j) no
2. 9
3. a) 59, 299
   b) 26, 146
   c) –13.3, –93.3
   d) 4.55, 34.55
   e) $23p, 103p$
   f) $\frac{29}{3}, \frac{109}{3}$
   g) $(-15y + 19), (-95y + 99)$
   h) $6.5 \times 10^4, 2.65 \times 10^5$
   i) $(-2 + 2\sqrt{2}), (-42 + 42\sqrt{2})$
   j) 1014.5, 1074.5
4. b) 346
5. 10.5
6. b) 537
7. b) £1900
8. 432

Exercise 8F

1. a) 110 b) 0
   c) 72 d) –325
   e) 63 f) 5.5×10^5
   g) 0 h) $440\sqrt{5}$
   i) $11 - 44x$ j) 142
2. 624
3. 1600000
4. a) £36750 b) £306250
5. a) £99
   c) 50 or 80 months
   d) Cannot be 80. The repayments would be negative after 50 months.
6. $a = 10, d = 0.8$
7. 15
8. a) $2n + 1$
   b) $S_n = n(n + 2)$
9. $S_n = \frac{n}{2}[2a + (n - 1)d]$
   $= \frac{n}{2}[a + (a + (n - 1)d)]$ (1)
   $u_n = a + (n - 1)d$
   $\Rightarrow l = a + (n - 1)d$ (2)
   Sub (2) in (1) $\Rightarrow S_n = \frac{n}{2}(a + l)$

Exercise 8G

1. a) $2 + 3 + 4 + 5$
   b) $\frac{3}{2} + 2 + \frac{5}{2} + 3 + \frac{7}{2}$
   c) $\frac{1}{10} + \frac{2}{10} + \frac{3}{10} + \frac{4}{10} + \frac{5}{10}$
   d) $3 + 2 + 1 + 0 + -1 + -2 + -3$
   e) $20 + 15 + 10 + 5 + 0$
   f) $9700 + 9800 + 9900 + 10000$
   g) $0 + \frac{1}{4} + \frac{1}{2} + \frac{3}{4}$
   h) $16 + 21$
   i) $\frac{3}{2} + 2 + \frac{5}{2} + 3$
   j) $1 + 1 + 1 + 1 + 1 + 1$
2. a) $\sum_{1}^{4}(r + 2)$
   b) $\sum_{1}^{7}(3r + 7)$
   c) $\sum_{1}^{20}(-2r - 3)$
   d) $\sum_{1}^{10}(1002 - 2r)$
   e) $\sum_{1}^{6}(22 - 7r)$
   f) $\sum_{1}^{10}(20r + 1)$
   g) $\sum_{1}^{5}\left(\frac{2r + 3}{2}\right)$
   h) $\sum_{r=1}^{b}(2r + 1)a$
   i) $\sum_{1}^{13}(2r + 3)\sqrt{3}$
   j) $\sum_{r=1}^{6}(rt^2)$
3. a) 75 b) 65
   c) $15 + 10x$ d) 20
   e) 77.5 f) 30.5
   g) $11y$ h) 120
   i) –19900 j) 5
4. $S_n = 5 + 11 + 17 + \cdots + (6n - 1)$
   $S_n = \frac{n}{2}[2a + (n - 1)d]$
   $= \frac{n}{2}[10 + 6(n - 1)]$
   $= 5n + 3n(n - 1) = 5n + 3n^2 - 3n$
   $= 3n^2 + 2n = n(3n + 2)$
5. $n^2 + 6n - 160 = 0;\ n = 10$
   (–16 is not possible)
6. a) 6, 4, 2, 0, –2
   d) $n = 8$ or $n = 1$

Exercise 8H

1. a) no b) yes c) no
   d) yes e) no f) no
   g) yes h) no i) yes
   j) no k) yes
2. a) 1, 3, 9, 27, 81
   b) –4, –8, –16, –32, –64
   c) –2, 4, –8, 16, –32

2. d) 64, 32, 16, 8, 4
   e) $10^3, 10^4, 10^5, 10^6, 10^7$
   f) 32, 48, 72, 108, 162
   g) $2, 2\sqrt{2}, 4, 4\sqrt{2}, 8$
   h) $\frac{1}{2}, \frac{1}{4}, \frac{1}{8}, \frac{1}{16}, \frac{1}{32}$
   i) a, ab, ab^2, ab^3, ab^4
   j) $y, 1, \frac{1}{y}, \frac{1}{y^2}, \frac{1}{y^3}$
3. £89600
4. $r = 0.4, a = 5$
5. 10000
6. 46656
7. a) 7, 35, 175, 875
   b) $u_n = 7 \times 5^{n-1}$
8. $x = -\frac{1}{2}$, Terms: $\frac{1}{2}, \frac{3}{2}, \frac{9}{2}$
9. a) $h, fh, f^2h, f^3h, \ldots$
   GP common ratio f
   b) $\frac{2}{5}$
   c) 2 metres

Exercise 8I

1. a) 121 b) $\frac{63}{64}$
   c) 11 d) $\frac{1023}{1024}$
   e) 36.0 (3 s.f.) f) 11333 (5 s.f.)
   g) 9.49 (3 s.f.) h) 3.95 (3 s.f.)
   i) 11.1 (3 s.f.) j) $6 + 3\sqrt{2}$
   k) 1
2. a) 363 b) 0.999 (3 s.f.)
   c) $7 + 3\sqrt{2}$ d) 63
   e) 40.5 (3 s.f.) f) –21
   g) 85 h) $\frac{7 + 3\sqrt{2}}{4}$
   i) 85 j) 2.00 (3 s.f.)
3. 9.57 m
4. 1,968,000
5. 36.0
6. 1555
7. a) £12400 b) £261,000
8. Any multiple of 8.
9. a) $\frac{b^2}{a}, \frac{b^3}{a^2}$ b) $\frac{b^9}{a^8}$
10. a) $x = 0$ or $x = 3$
    b) 3, 6, 12 or 12, 6, 3

Exercise 8J

1. a) 1 b) 5 c) $\frac{100}{9}$
   d) –8 e) 200 f) $2 + \sqrt{2}$
   g) 8.53 (3 s.f.) h) $\frac{16}{3}$
   i) $\frac{\pi^2}{\pi^2 - 1}$ j) $\frac{36x^2}{6x - 1}$
2. a) $\frac{8}{3}$ b) 1
   c) $\frac{(1 + \sqrt{3})}{2}$ d) $\frac{3}{2}$
   e) $\frac{a}{1 - a}$ f) 2
   g) 14 h) x
   i) 3 j) $\frac{10}{9}$
3. $\frac{50}{9}$
4. $\frac{5}{6}$
5. a) $r = 0.9, a = 5$
   b) 50
6. a) $S_\infty = \frac{a}{1 - r} \Rightarrow 700 = \frac{140}{1 - r}$
   $\Rightarrow 1 - r = \frac{140}{700} \Rightarrow r = 0.8$
   b) 9.18
   c) 582.56
7. $\frac{5}{4}$
8. b) $\frac{1}{5}, \frac{4}{5}$ c) –20, –5
9. a) 133 b) $\frac{400}{3}$
10. b) 245.277
    c) $S_n = \dfrac{1400\left(1 - \left(-\frac{3}{4}\right)^n\right)}{1.75}$

Exercise 8K

1. a) 2 b) 1680 c) $\frac{1}{20}$
   d) 1440 e) 15 f) 127
   g) 2 h) 1 i) 100
   j) 48
2. a) 8 b) 10 c) 45
   d) 56 e) 35 f) 100
   g) 70 h) 1 i) 20
   j) 1

Exercise 8L

1. a) $1 + 6x + 15x^2 + 20x^3 + \cdots$
   b) $1 + 8x + 24x^2 + 32x^3 + \cdots$
   c) $1 - 4x + 6x^2 - 4x^3 + \cdots$
   d) $1 + \frac{3x}{2} + \frac{3x^2}{4} + \frac{x^3}{8}$
   e) $1 - 10x + 40x^2 - 80x^3 + \cdots$
   f) $1 + 10x + 45x^2 + 120x^3 + \cdots$
   g) $1 + 15x + 75x^2 + 125x^3$
   h) $1 - \frac{3x}{10} + \frac{3x^2}{100} - \frac{x^3}{1000}$
   i) $1 + 40x + 600x^2 + 4000x^3 + \cdots$
   j) $1 - 4.22x + 7.43x^2 - 6.97x^3 + \cdots$
2. a) $128 + 448x + 672x^2 + \cdots$
   b) $8 + 24x + 24x^2 + \cdots$
   c) $1000 - 30x + \frac{3x^2}{10} + \cdots$
   d) $1 - \frac{3}{x} + \frac{3}{x^2} - \cdots$
   e) $256 + 768x + 864x^2 + \cdots$
   f) $16 + 32x^2 + 24x^4 + \cdots$
   g) $x^4 + 4x^2 + 6 + \cdots$
   h) $4 + 8x + 6x^2 + \cdots$
   i) $625 + 1000x + 600x^2 + \cdots$
   j) $\frac{1}{a^3} + 3x + 3a^3x^2 + \cdots$
3. a) $1 + 3x + 3.75x^2 + 2.5x^3$
   b) 1.34
4. a)
   $1 + nax + \frac{n(n-1)a^2}{2}x^2 + \frac{n(n-1)(n-2)a^3}{6}x^3$
   b) $n = 20, a = 0.7$
   c) 391.02
5. a) $1 + 9px + 36p^2x^2$
   b) $p = -1, q = 9$
6. $p = 0.125, A = 768$
7. 1280
8. $1 + 14x + 75x^2 + 180x^3$
9. a)
   $1 - nx + \frac{n(n-1)}{2}x^2 - \frac{n(n-1)(n-2)}{6}x^3$
   b) $n = 3$
10. a) $1 - 8x + 24x^2 - 32x^3$
    b) 0.961

CHAPTER 9. TRIGONOMETRY

Revision Exercise 9A

1. a) $\frac{11}{4}, -\frac{1}{4}$
   b) $4 \pm \sqrt{17}$
   c) $\frac{1 + \sqrt{5}}{4}, \frac{1 - \sqrt{5}}{4}$
   d) $\frac{3 + 5\sqrt{5}}{2}, \frac{3 - 5\sqrt{5}}{2}$
2. a) $x = \frac{1}{3}$
   b $x = \frac{4p}{3p - 2}$
   c) $x = \sqrt{\frac{2(1 + y)}{y}}$
   d) $x = \frac{2de - fc}{f - 2d}$
3. a) 045° b) 180°
   c) 225° d) 315°

Exercise 9B

1. a) 1.04 cm b) 9.76 cm
   c) 2.51 cm d) 10.7 cm
2. a) 4.8° b) 47.2°
   c) 31.4° d) 6.0°
   e) 29.4°

3. a) $A = 49.9°, C = 98.1°$ or $A = 130.1°, C = 17.9°$
   b) $B = 48.5°, C = 109.5°$ or $B = 131.5°, C = 26.5°$
   c) $C = 53.6°, A = 88.4°$ or $C = 126.4°, A = 15.6°$
   d) $A = 78.1°, B = 44.9°$ or $A = 101.9°, B = 21.1°$
   e) $C = 59.9°, B = 67.1°$ or $C = 120.1°, B = 6.9°$
4. a) 0.444 b) 26.3°, 153.7°
5. a) 80° b) 26.0 km
6. $AC = 6.29$ cm, $AD = 8.71$ cm
7. $CBF = 22.4°, BCF = 18.1°$

Exercise 9C

1. a) $a = 6.12$ cm
   b) $a = 7.48$ m
   c) $b = 4.46$ km
   d) $c = 11.4$ cm
   e) $c = 7.09$ mm
2. a) $A = 40.8°$ b) $Y = 41.0°$
   c) $P = 53.8°$ d) $C = 82.8°$
   e) $B = 69.1°$
3. a) $A = 91.0°,\ B = 59.0°,\ C = 30.0°$
   b) $A = 29.0°,\ B = 104.5°,\ C = 46.6°$
   c) $a = 9.9$ cm, $B = 63.1°, C = 73.9°$
   d) $b = 23.6$ feet, $C = 18.2°, A = 19.8°$
   e) $b = 5.2$ km, $A = 68°,\ B = 44°$
   f) $c = 1.6$ cm, $B = 26°, C = 117°$
4. No. With three angles given, it is not possible to find the lengths of the sides.
5. No. The sum of the two shortest sides must be greater than the longest.
6. a) 29.8 m b) 55.1°
7. 10.9 m
8. 74,300 km

Exercise 9D

1. a) 12.9 cm^2 b) 120,000 m^2
   c) 1.17 km^2 d) 1.44 cm^2
   e) 5.51 m^2 f) 28.1 cm^2
2. a) $b = 3.78$ cm
   b) $b = 14.5$ m
   c) $b = 6.13$ mm
   d) $b = 31.7$ km
3. a) $C = 26.7°$ b) $C = 67.8°$
   c) $C = 80.2°$ d) $C = 16.0°$
4. 5 cm^2
5. 63.23°
6. $x = -1$
7. $\dfrac{100 + 25\sqrt{3}}{4}$ cm^2
8. a) $\frac{1}{2}pq\sin\theta$ b) $\frac{1}{2}qr\sin\theta$

Exercise 9E

1. a) $\frac{\pi}{6}$ b) $\frac{\pi}{4}$ c) $\frac{\pi}{3}$
   d) $-\frac{\pi}{3}$ e) $\frac{3\pi}{4}$ f) $-\frac{\pi}{2}$
   g) $\frac{\pi}{9}$ h) -2π i) 3π
   j) 20π
2. a) 120° b) 240° c) 10°
   d) 1° e) –6° f) 450°
   g) 27° h) 225° i) 0°
   j) 80°
3. a) 4π b) 0.576 c) 0.489
   d) 3.18 e) 5.74 f) 3.12
   g) 1.19 h) 10.4 i) –1.55
   j) –4.10
4. a) 720° b) 1620° c) 810°
   d) 30° e) 150° f) –45°
   g) –900° h) $\frac{180}{\pi}$ i) $\frac{1080}{\pi}$
   j) $-\frac{450}{\pi}$
5. a) 0.5 b) 0.5 c) $\frac{\sqrt{3}}{2}$
   d) $-\frac{\sqrt{3}}{2}$ e) 0 f) $\frac{1}{\sqrt{2}}$
   g) $\frac{1}{\sqrt{2}}$ h) 1 i) 0
   j) 0
6. a) 3.14 cm b) 9.42 m
   c) 4.19 cm d) 209 m
   e) 7.85 mm
7. a) 8.38 cm^2 b) 78.5 cm^2
   c) 0.393 cm^2 d) 0.00838 m^2
   e) 21.2 km^2
8. 5.53 m
9. 47.0 cm
10. a) 66.1 cm b) 28.6 cm
11. a) 22.5 mm b) 18.6
12. b) 0.680
    c) 12.2 m^2
    d) 0.920 m^2
13. a) $2\sqrt{3}$ cm b) 2π cm^2
14. 22.9 cm^2
15. a) 24π cm^2
    b) 4 cm
    c) 8π cm^2

Exercise 9F

1.

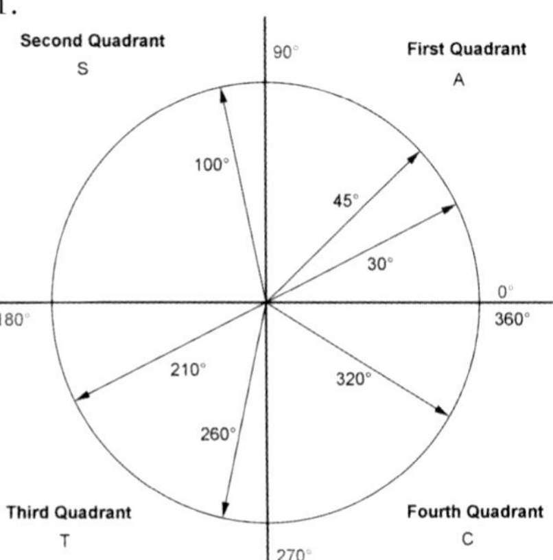

2.

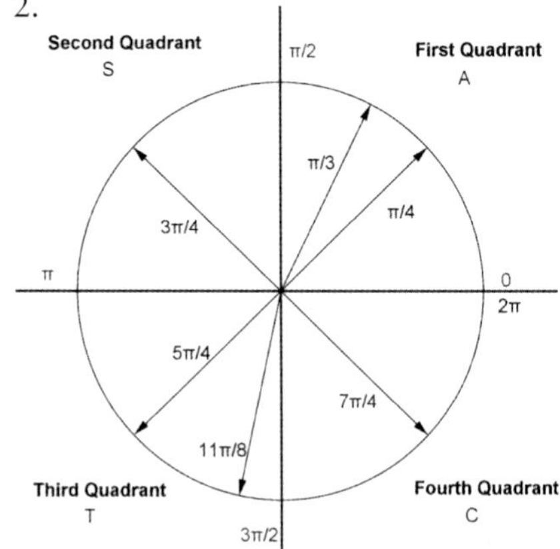

3. a) positive b) positive
   c) negative d) negative
   e) positive f) negative
   g) positive h) negative
   i) negative j) positive
4. a) $-\sin\theta$ b) $\sin\theta$
   c) $-\cos\theta$ d) $-\sin\theta$
   e) $\cos\theta$ f) $\sin\theta$
   g) $\cos\theta$ h) $\tan\theta$
   i) $\sin\theta$ j) $\cos\theta$
5. a) 0 b) $-2\cos\theta$
   c) 0 d) $2\sin\theta$
   e) 0 f) $-\tan^2\theta$
   g) $\sin^2\theta$ h) $-\cos x$
6. a) $\sin 5°$ b) $\cos 20°$
   c) $\tan 89°$ d) $-\tan 10°$
   e) $-\cos 10°$ f) $\sin 10°$
   g) $\tan(1)$ h) $\sin x$
   i) $2\sin(85°)$ j) $-\cos x$

Exercise 9G

1.

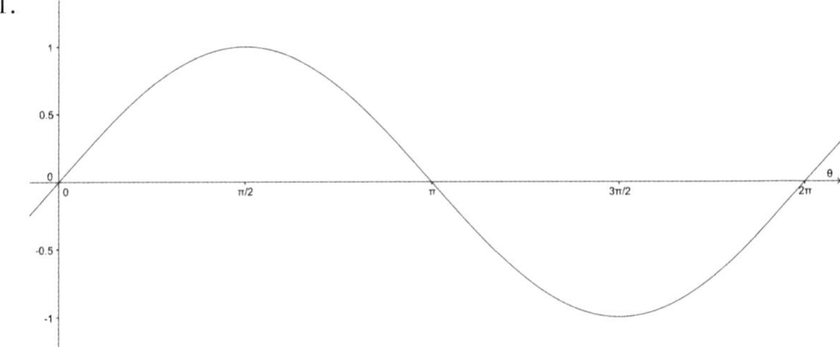

2.

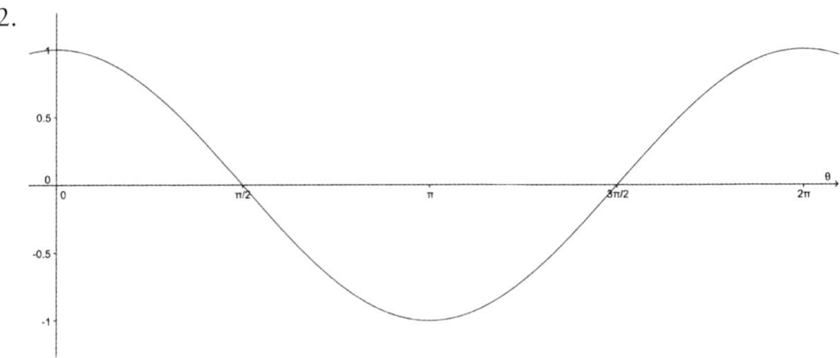

3.

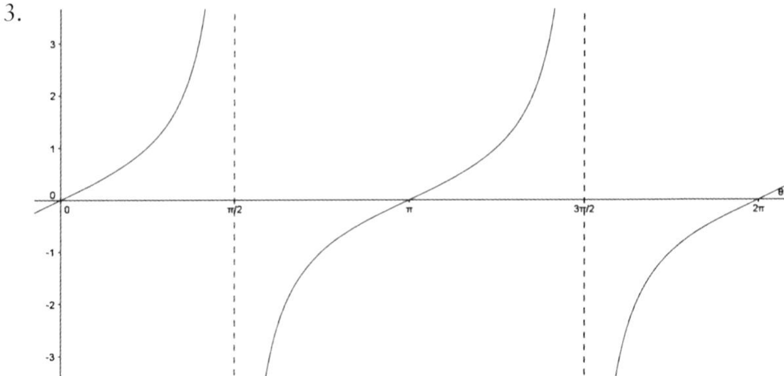

4. a) 2 b) 3
   c) 0 d) 1

5. a) 2 b) 2
   c) 0 d) 2

6. a) 2 b) 3
   c) 2 d) 2

7. a) $\frac{\sqrt{3}}{2}$ b) $-\frac{\sqrt{2}}{2}$
   c) 1 d) $-\frac{\sqrt{3}}{3}$
   e) $-\frac{1}{2}$ f) $-\frac{\sqrt{2}}{2}$

8. a) $\sin x = \frac{2\sqrt{10}}{7}$, $\tan x = \frac{2\sqrt{10}}{3}$
   b) $\cos x = \frac{\sqrt{57}}{19}$, $\sin x = \frac{4\sqrt{19}}{19}$
   c) $\cos x = \frac{\sqrt{21}}{11}$, $\tan x = \frac{10\sqrt{21}}{21}$
   d) $\sin x = \frac{2\sqrt{7}}{7}$, $\tan x = \frac{2\sqrt{3}}{3}$
   e) $\cos x = \frac{\sqrt{2}(\sqrt{3}-1)}{4}$, $\sin x = \frac{\sqrt{2}(\sqrt{3}+1)}{4}$
   f) $\sin x = \frac{2}{3}$, $\tan x = \frac{2\sqrt{5}}{5}$
   g) $\cos x = \frac{\sqrt{2}}{2}$, $\sin x = \frac{\sqrt{2}}{2}$
   h) $\sin x = \frac{2\sqrt{2}}{3}$, $\tan x = -2\sqrt{2}$
   i) $\cos x = -\frac{\sqrt{55}}{8}$, $\tan x = -\frac{3\sqrt{55}}{55}$
   j) $\cos x = -\frac{6\sqrt{37}}{37}$, $\sin x = \frac{\sqrt{37}}{37}$
   k) $\cos x = -\frac{5\sqrt{29}}{29}$, $\sin x = -\frac{2\sqrt{29}}{29}$

9. a) $x = 60°, 240°$
   b) $x = 150°, 210°$
   c) $x = 30°, 150°$
   d) $x = 45°, -135°$
   e) $x = 135°, -135°$
   f) $x = \frac{\pi}{3}, \frac{2\pi}{3}$
   g) $x = \frac{\pi}{4}, \frac{7\pi}{4}$
   h) $x = \frac{\pi}{6}, \frac{5\pi}{6}, \frac{13\pi}{6}, \frac{17\pi}{6}$
   i) $x = -\frac{7\pi}{6}, -\frac{\pi}{6}, \frac{5\pi}{6}, \frac{11\pi}{6}$
   j) No solutions

Exercise 9H

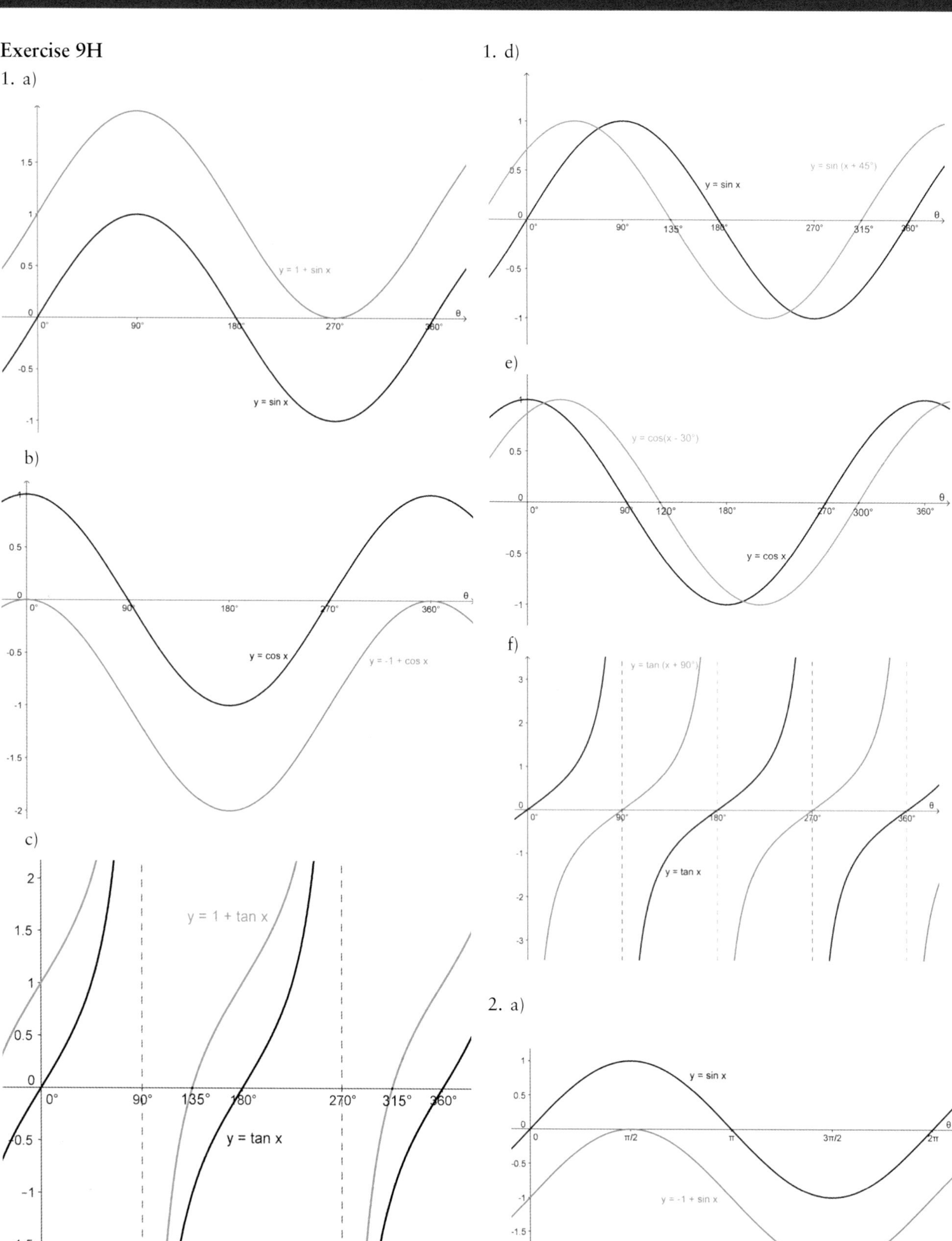
1. a)
y = 1 + sin x
y = sin x
b)
y = cos x
y = -1 + cos x
c)
y = 1 + tan x
y = tan x
1. d)
y = sin (x + 45°)
y = sin x
e)
y = cos(x - 30°)
y = cos x
f)
y = tan (x + 90°)
y = tan x
2. a)
y = sin x
y = -1 + sin x

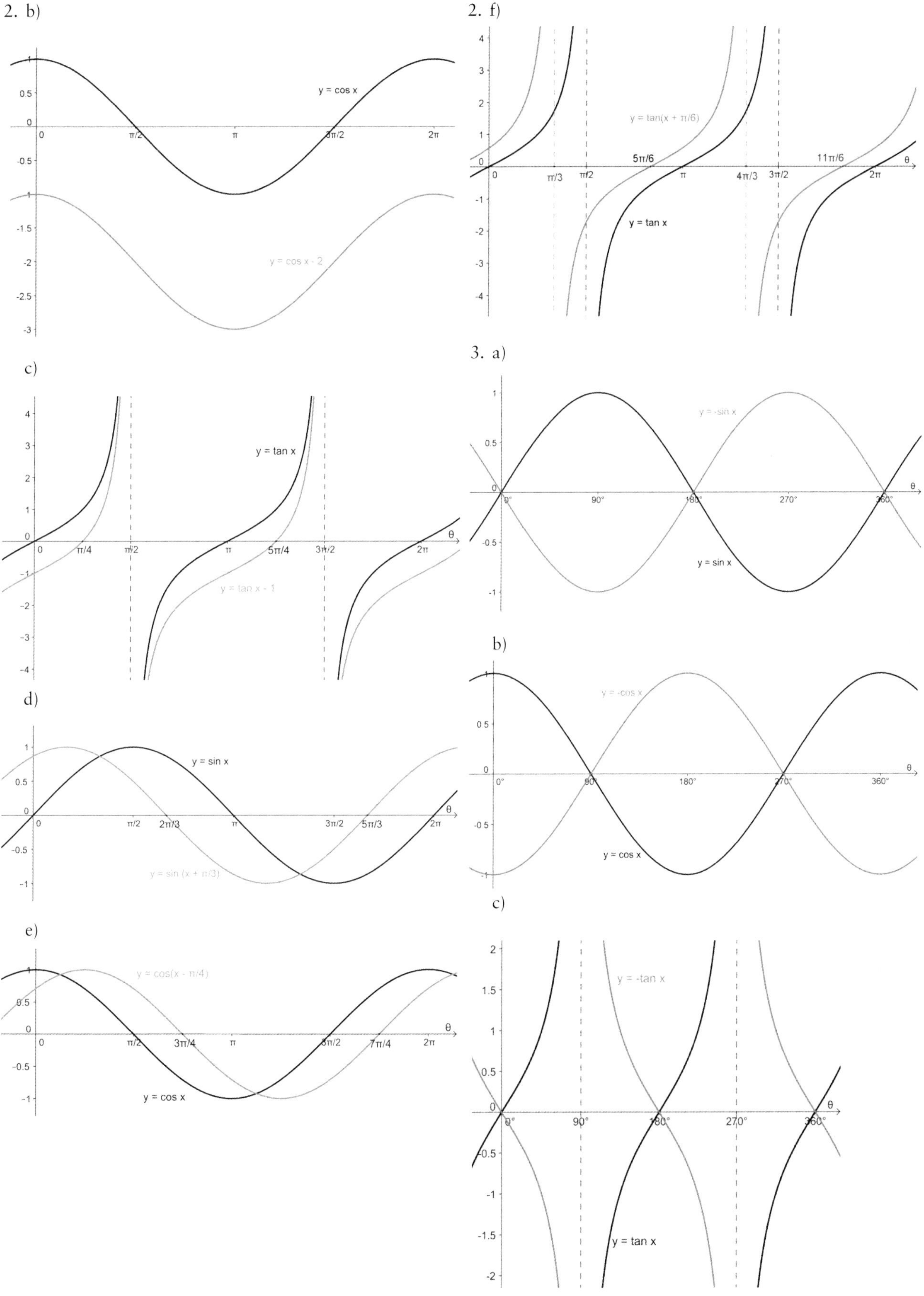
2. b)
y = cos x
y = cos x - 2
c)
y = tan x
y = tan x - 1
d)
y = sin x
y = sin (x + π/3)
e)
y = cos(x - π/4)
y = cos x
2. f)
y = tan(x + π/6)
y = tan x
3. a)
y = -sin x
y = sin x
b)
y = -cos x
y = cos x
c)
y = -tan x
y = tan x

4. a) $y = \cos x$ period 360°; $y = \cos 2x$ period 180°

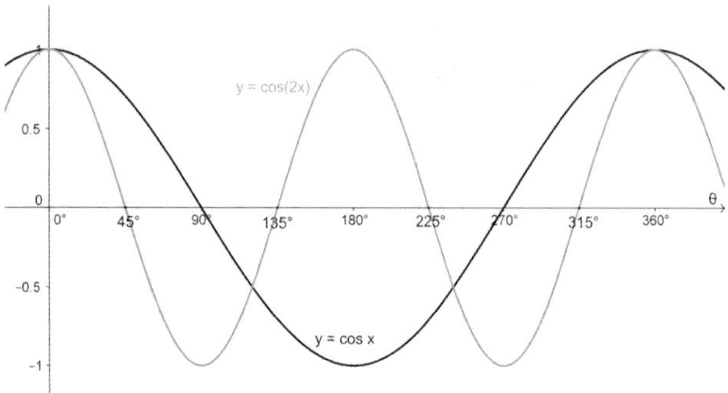

b) $y = \sin x$ period 360°; $y = \sin\frac{x}{2}$ period 720°

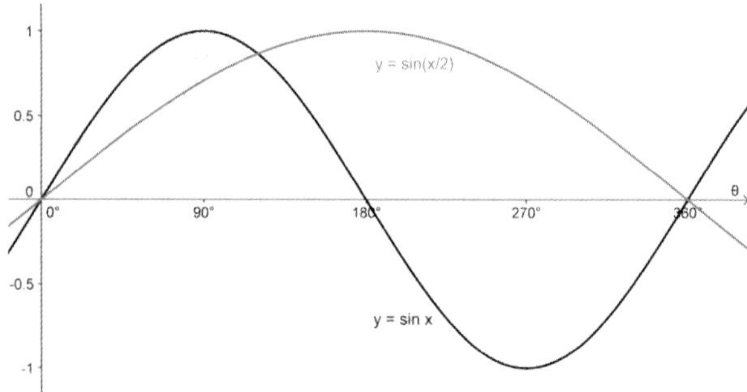

c) $y = \tan x$ period 180°; $y = \tan 2x$ period 90°

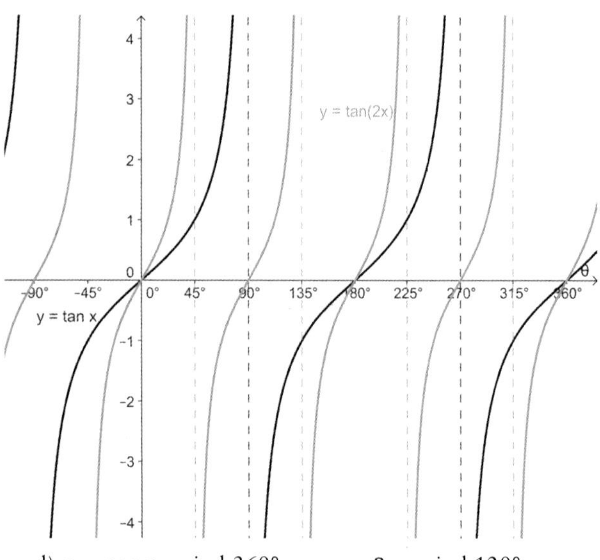

d) $y = \cos x$ period 360°; $y = \cos 3x$ period 120°

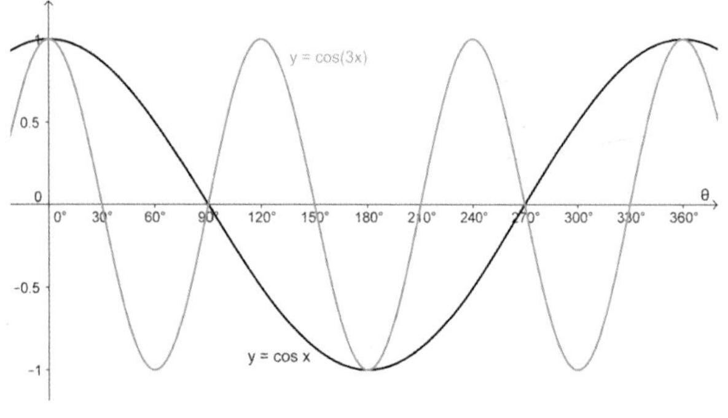

5. a)

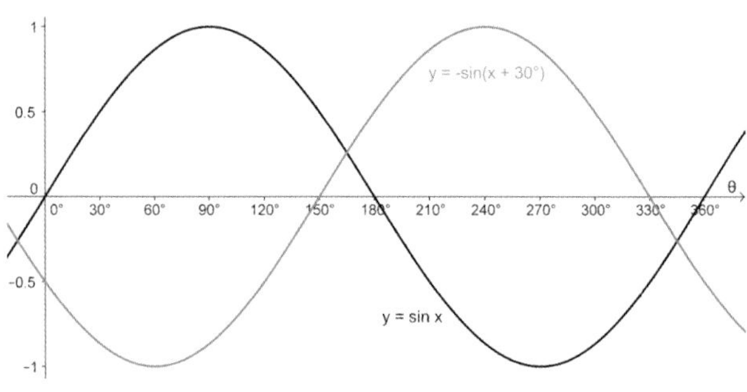

b)

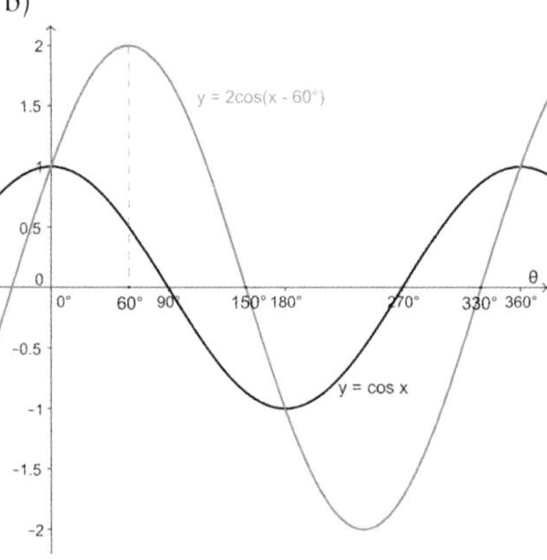

c)

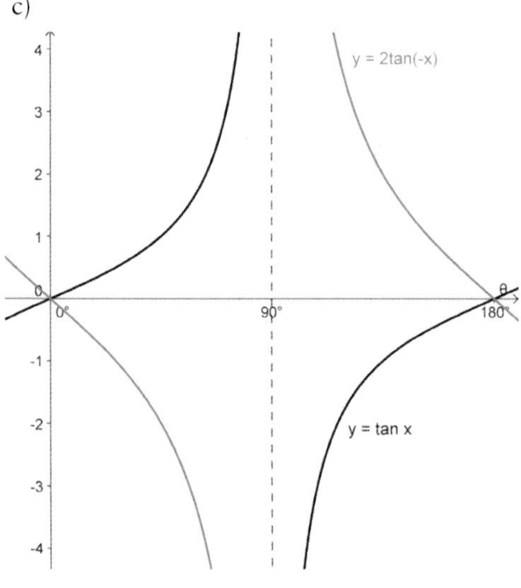

d)

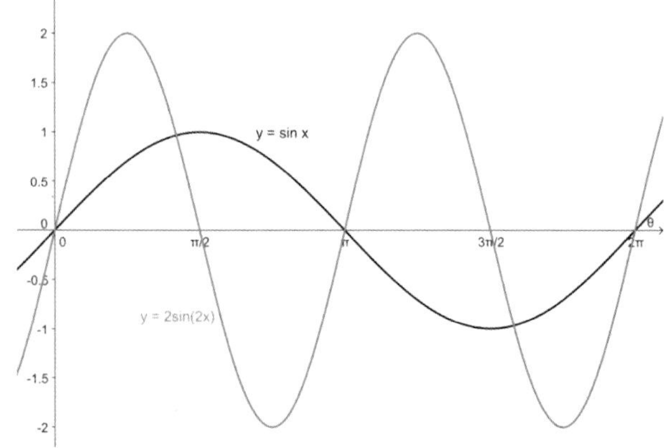

5. e)

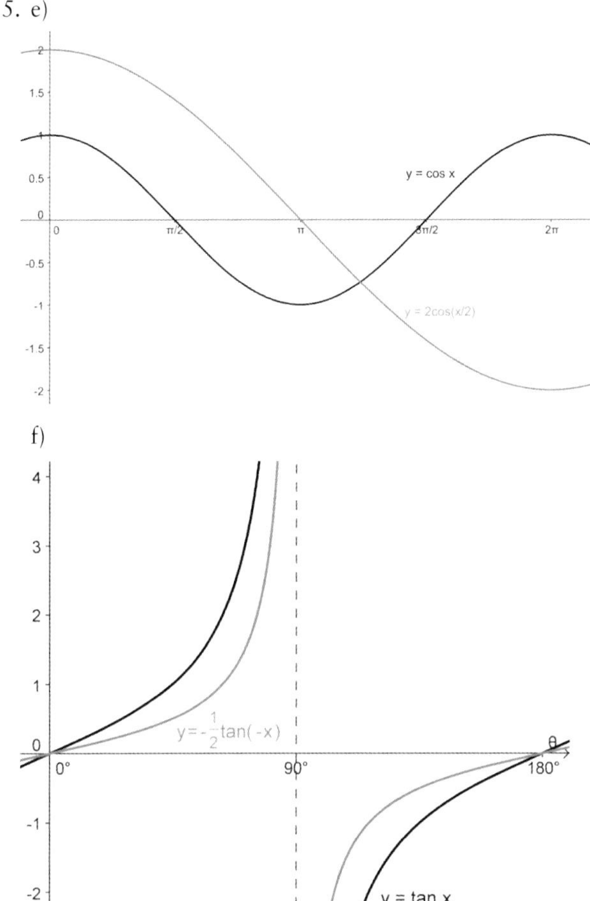

f)

6. a) $y = 1 + \cos x$
   b) $y = -\sin\left(\frac{x}{2}\right)$
   c) $y = 2 + \tan x$
   d) $y = -2\cos(4x)$

7. They are the same functions.

Exercise 9I

1. a) $\frac{1}{\tan x}$ b) 1
   c) $\sin x$ d) 0
   e) $1 + \cos^2 A$ f) 2
   g) $\frac{1}{\sin^2 x}$ h) 1
   i) $\sin^2 x \cos^2 x$ j) $\tan^2 \theta$

3. t

Exercise 9J

1. a) $x = 60°, 120°$ b) $x = 120°, 240°$
   c) $\theta = 115°, 245°$ d) $\theta = 63.4°, 243°$
   e) $A = 75.5°, 284°$ f) $y = 26.6°, 153°$
   g) $x = 11.3°, 191°$ h) $A = 39.6°, 320°$
   i) $x = 8.11°, 352°$ j) $t = 57.5°, 238°$
   k) $\theta = 70.5°, 289°$ l) $z = 201°, 339°$
   m) $y = 65.5°, 294°$ n) $\theta = 127°, 233°$
   o) $x = 8.63°, 171°$

2. a) 0.96, 2.18 b) 0.69, 5.59
   c) 2.08, 4.20 d) 6.05, 3.37
   e) 2.39, 5.53

3. a) $\theta = 31.7°, 122°$ b) $x = 26.6°, 63.4°$
   c) $x = 60°, 120°$ d) $x = 15°, 45°, 135°, 165°$
   e) $\theta = 29.4°, 89.4°, 149°$ f) $x = 97.2°$
   g) No solutions in range
   h) $15°, 75°, 105°, 165°$
   i) No solutions in range
   j) $A = 73.7°$

4. a) $x = 105°, 285°$ b) $x = \frac{11\pi}{12}, \frac{23\pi}{12}$
   c) $x = 45°, 135°$ d) $x = 0°, 240°, 360°$
   e) $x = 15.3°, 195°$ f) $x = \frac{\pi}{8}, \frac{5\pi}{8}, \frac{9\pi}{8}, \frac{13\pi}{8}$
   g) $x = 20°, 60°, 140°, 180°, 260°, 300°$
   h) $x = 15°, 105°, 195°, 285°$
   i) $x = 80°, 170°, 260°, 350°$
   j) $x = \frac{\pi}{4}, \frac{7\pi}{12}, \frac{5\pi}{4}, \frac{19\pi}{12}$

5. a) $\theta = 30°, 150°, 210°, 330°$
   b) $x = 19.5°, 161°, 199°, 341°$
   c) $y = 60°, 120°, 240°, 300°$
   d) $x = \frac{\pi}{3}, \frac{2\pi}{3}, \frac{4\pi}{3}, \frac{5\pi}{3}$
   e) $x = \frac{\pi}{2}, \frac{2\pi}{3}, \frac{4\pi}{3}, \frac{3\pi}{2}$
   f) $x = 0, \frac{3\pi}{4}, \pi, \frac{7\pi}{4}, 2\pi$

6. a) $x = 90°$
   b) $\theta = 60°, 180°, 300°$
   c) $t = 71.6°, 117°, 252°, 297°$
   d) $x = 76.0°, 135°, 256°, 315°$
   e) $y = 70.5°, 289°$
   f) $x = 90°, 180°, 270°$
   g) $\theta = 0°, 120°, 240°, 360°$
   h) $x = 270°$

7. a) $56.3°, 135°, 236°, 315°$
   b) $202°, 338°$
   c) $31.7°, 328°$
   d) $24.2°, 129°, 231°, 336°$

8. a) $\theta = 0.821, 2.32$
   b) $x = -1.30, 1.30$
   c) $y = -2.07, -0.689, 1.07, 2.45$
   d) $x = 0.896, 2.25$
   e) $\theta = -\frac{2\pi}{3}, -\frac{\pi}{6}, \frac{\pi}{3}, \frac{5\pi}{6}$

9. $x = \frac{\pi}{4}, \frac{5\pi}{4}$

10. $\theta = 5.65°, 95.65°, 185.65°, 275.65°$

11. $7\sin^2\theta + 6\sin\theta - 1 = 0, \theta = 8.21°, 172°, 270°$

12. $\theta = 78.5°, 282°$

REVIEW EXERCISE CHAPTERS 7–9

1. a) 0 b) 2
   c) 2 d) 1
2. a) no b) yes
3. a) 5 b) 2
4. a) $(x + 3)^2 + (y - 3)^2 = 9$
   b) $x^2 + (y + 1)^2 = 20$
5. a) $(x + 5)^2 + (y + 1)^2 = 10$
   b) $(x - 1)^2 + (y + 8)^2 = 5$
6. a) (2, 0), (–6, –8)
7. a) 2, 5, 10, 17
   b) 1, –4, –9, –14
8. a) $n = 4$ b) $n = 6$
9. $a = ½, b = 4$
10. a) 1, 7, 25, 79
    b) 80, 64, 52, 43
11. a) $u_{n+1} = u_n - 2;\ u_1 = 6$
    b) $u_{n+1} = 2u_n + 2;\ u_1 = 1$
12. a) 18, 51 b) 673
13. a) 1, –1.57, –0.10, –0.94, –0.46
    b) yes
    c) $c = 7/11$
14. a) yes b) yes
15. a) –7, –127
    b) –2, –22
16. a) –650 b) 21
17. a) 0 + –2 + –4 + –6 + –8
    b) –3 + –1 + 1 + 3 + 5 + 7 + 9
18. a) $\sum_{r=1}^{4}(5 - 2r)$
    b) $\sum_{r=1}^{11}(r - 1 + x)$
19. a) 60 b) $70 + 10x$
20. a) yes b) no
21. $r = 0.2, a = 9$
22. a) 2.50 (3 s.f.)
    b) 2.66 (3 s.f.)
23. a) 186
    b) $4(\sqrt{3} + 1)$
24. a) 1.35 b) 6
25. a) ½ b) ⅔
26. 10/11
27. a) 12 b) 1/20
    c) 28 d) 100
28. a) $1 - 9x + 27x^2 - 27x^3$
    b) $1 - \frac{4x}{3} + \frac{2x^2}{3} - \frac{4x^3}{27} + \cdots$
29. a) $4096 + 30720x + 96000x^2 + \ldots$
    b) $\frac{1}{16} - \frac{x}{2} + \frac{3x^2}{2} + \cdots$
30. 3.71 cm
31. 16.9°
32. $B = 42.1°, C = 103.9°$ or
    $B = 137.9°, C = 8.1°$
33. $a = 10.1$ m
34. $B = 59.2$
35. a) $A = 91.2°$, $B = C = 44.4°$
    b) $a = 7.7$ mm, $B = 19.5$ mm, $C = 11.5°$
    c) $c = 14.2$ cm, $B = 7.2°$, $C = 61.8°$
36. a) 43.3 cm²
    b) 42.0 cm²
37. $b = 6.48$ cm
38. $c = 35.5°$
39. a) $\frac{\pi}{2}$ b) $\frac{\pi}{5}$
40. a) 720° b) 6°
41. a) 0.855 b) 7.14
42. a) –0.5 b) –1
43. 34.6 cm²
44. a) negative
    b) negative
45. a) $\tan\theta$ b) $-\sin\theta$
46. a) $-\tan\left(\frac{\pi}{4}\right)$
    b) cos 80°
47. a) $\cos x = \frac{\sqrt{21}}{5}$, $\tan x = \frac{2\sqrt{21}}{21}$
    b) $\sin x = \frac{\sqrt{17}}{9}$, $\tan x = -\frac{\sqrt{17}}{8}$
48. a) $x = 60°$
    b) $x = \frac{\pi}{6}, \frac{7\pi}{6}, \frac{13\pi}{6}, \frac{19\pi}{6}$
49. a) $2 + 2\cos\theta$
    b) $\sin^4 x$
51. a) $x = 120°, 300°$
    b) $x = 16.6°, 163°$
52. a) $x = 22.1°, 97.9°, 142°$
    b) No solutions in range
53. a) $x = \frac{\pi}{2}, \frac{7\pi}{6}$
    b) $x = 139°, 221°$
54. a) $x = 0.749, -0.749$
    b) $x = -2.21, -1.08, 0.934, 2.07$
55. $\theta = 70.5°, 289°$

CHAPTER 10. LOGARITHMS

Revision Exercise 10A

1. a) x^5 b) y^3 c) z^{13}
   d) p^{-3} e) q^5
2. a) 2.5 b) 4 c) –3
3. a) $x = 0$ or $x = -3$
   b) $x = 1$ or $x = -4$
   c) $x = \frac{1}{2}$ or $x = -3$
   d) $x = 0$ or $x = 2$ or $x = -3$
   e) $x = \frac{1}{3}$ or $x = -2$
4. a)

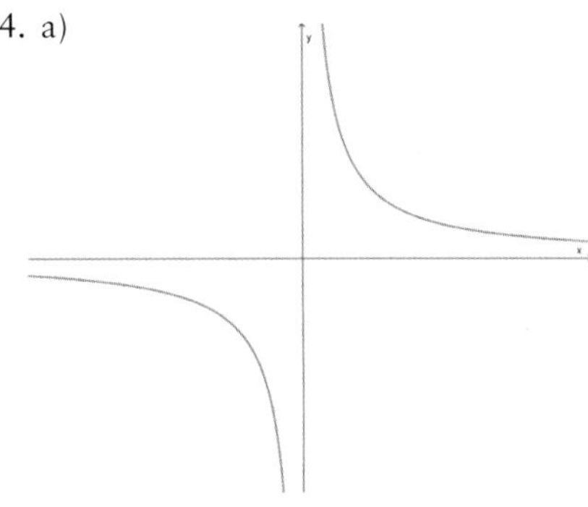

Asymptotes: $y = 0, x = 0$

b)

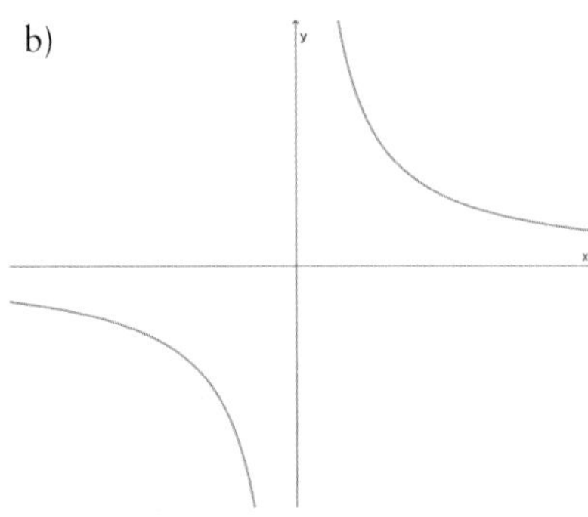

Asymptotes: $y = 0, x = 0$

c)

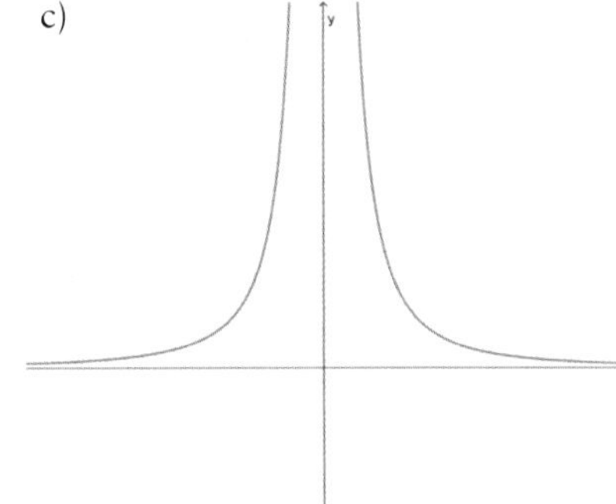

Asymptotes: $y = 0, x = 0$

d)

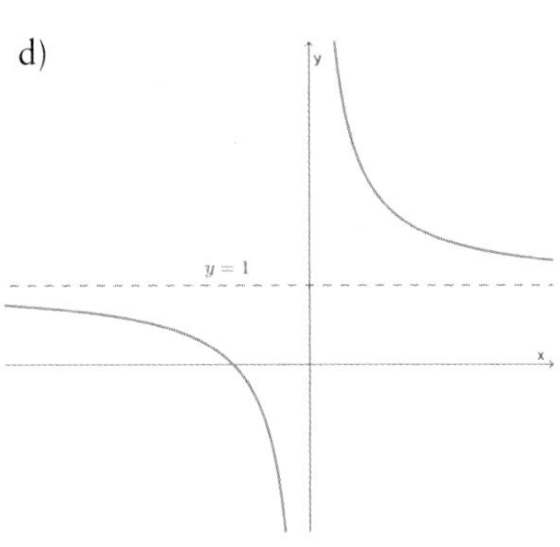

Asymptotes: $y = 1, x = 0$

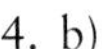

Exercise 10B

1.

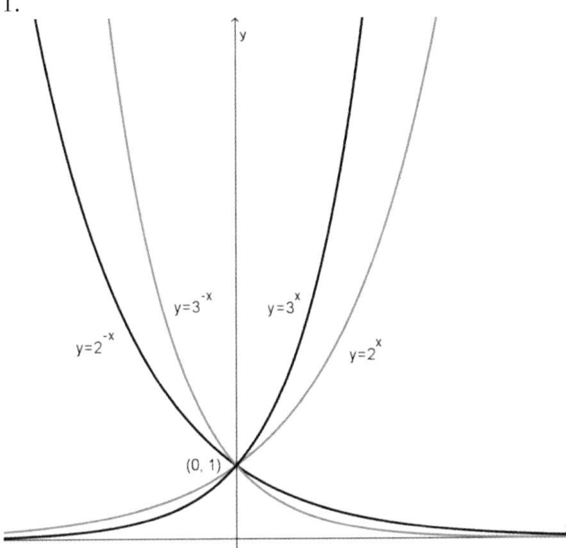

2. b)

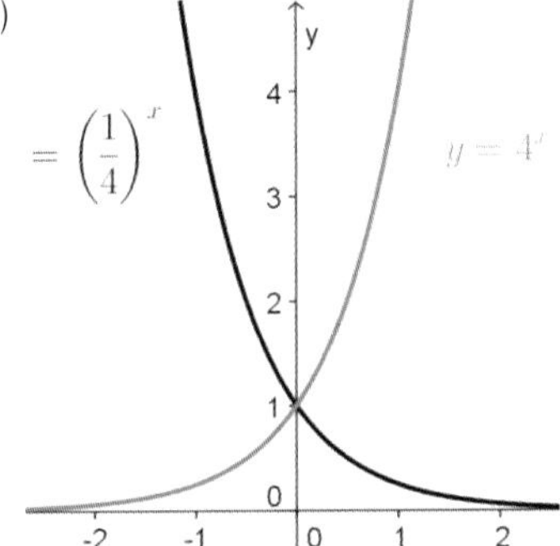

3. a)

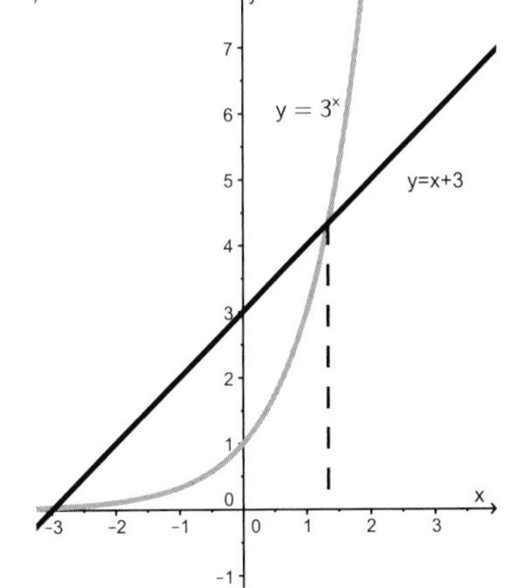

b) $x \approx 1.3$
c) $x \approx -2.9$

4. b)

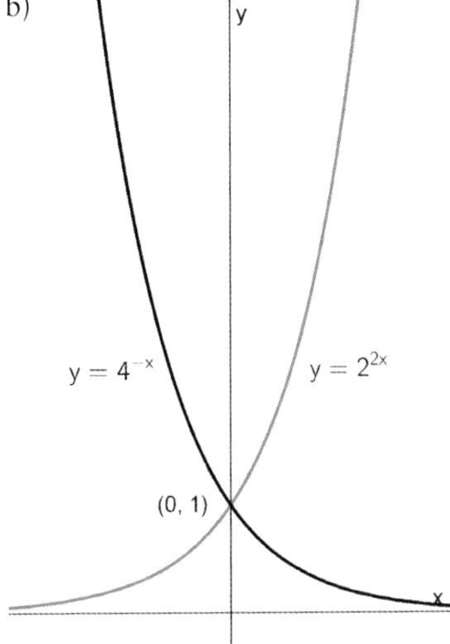

5. a)

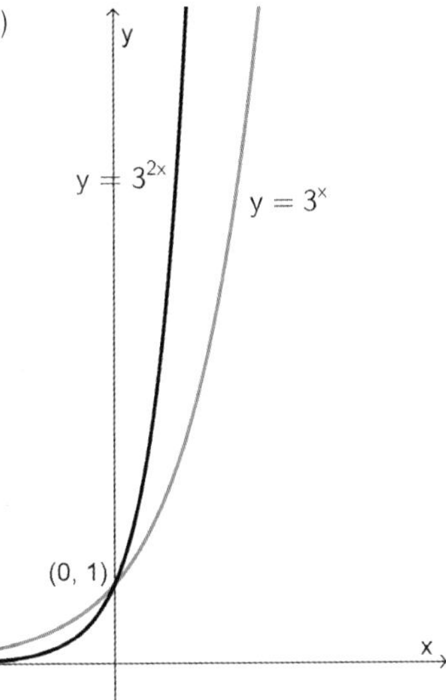

b)

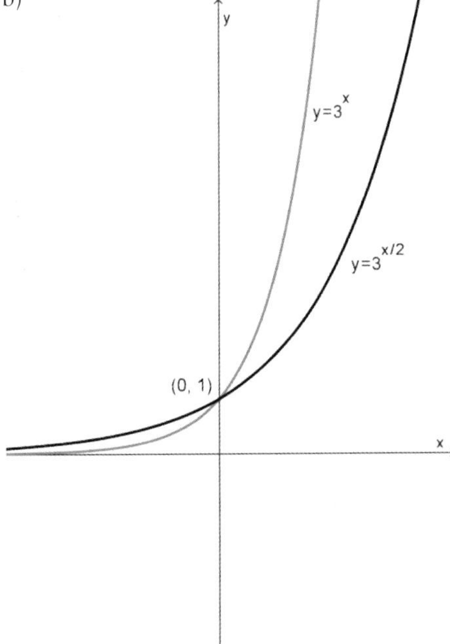

5. c)

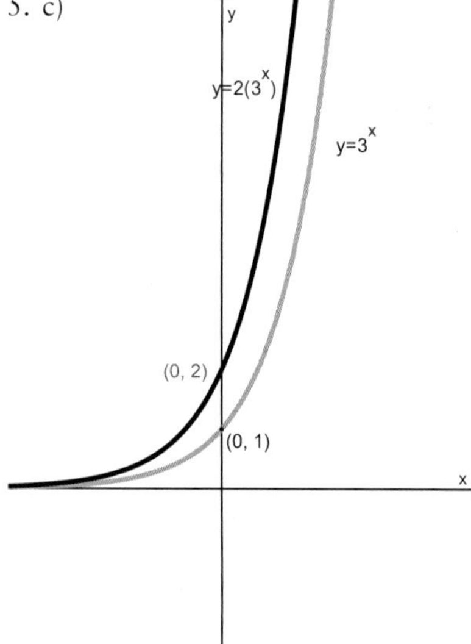

6. a)

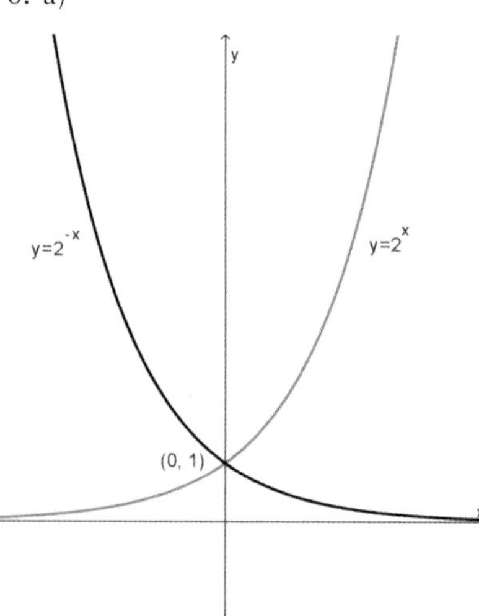

b)

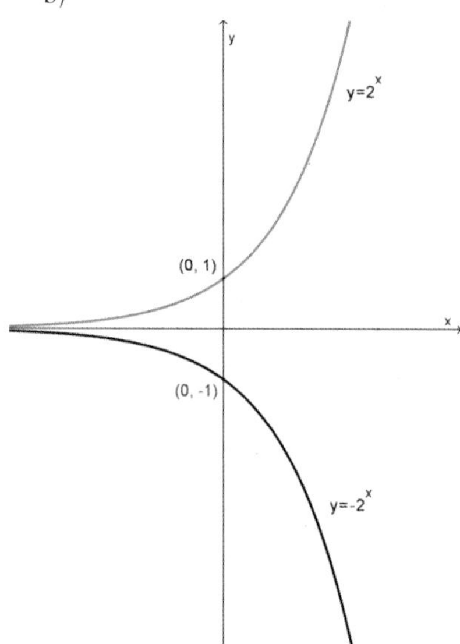

6. c)

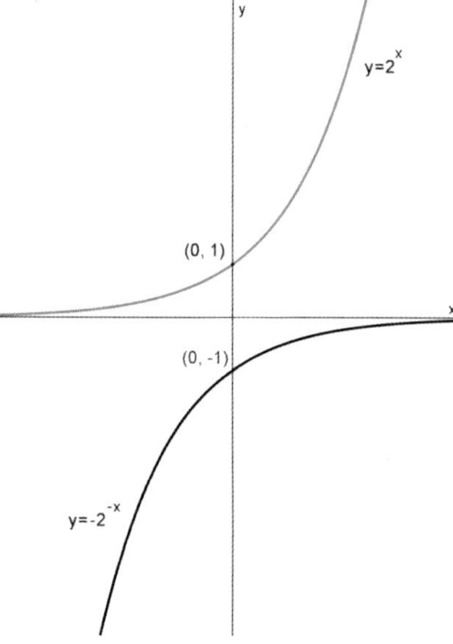

7. a)

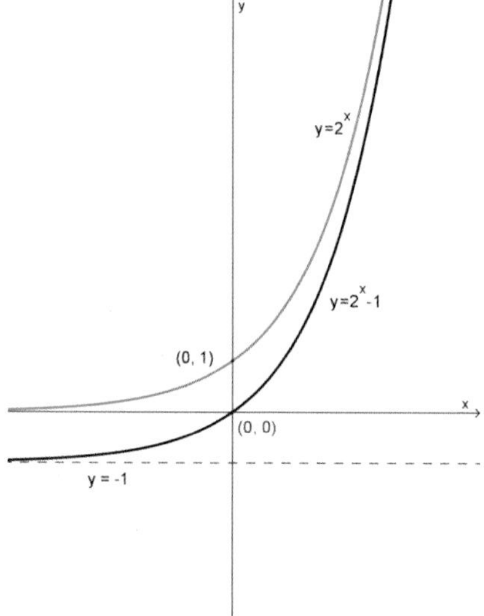

b)

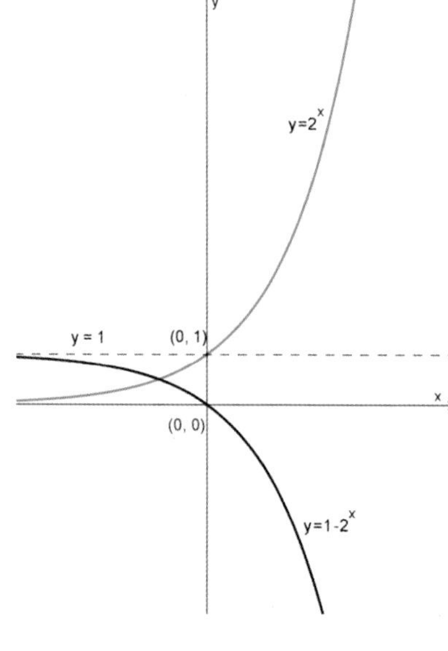

7. c)

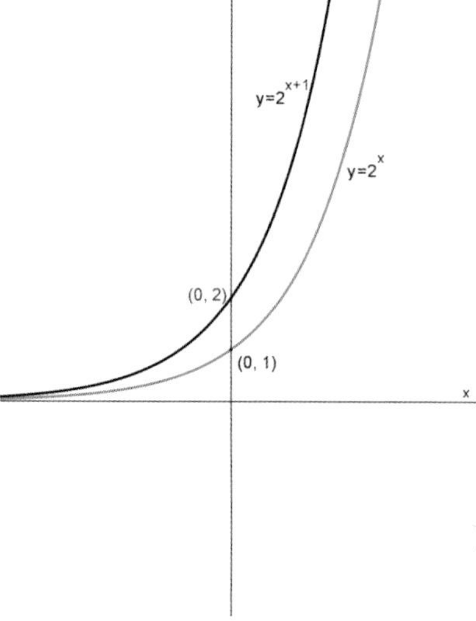

d)

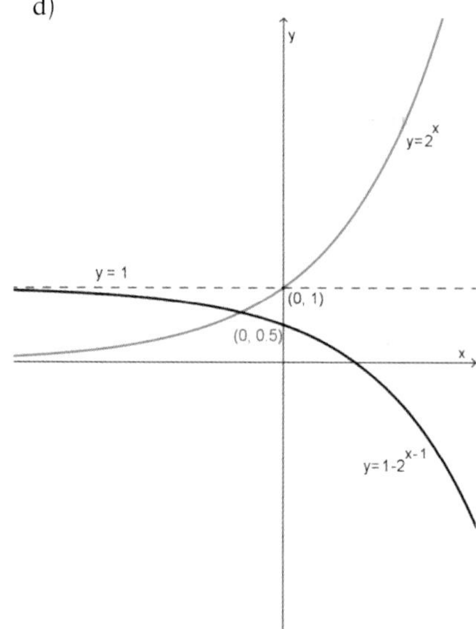

8. a) $y = 3^x$
   b) $y = -3^x$
   c) $y = 1 - 3^x$

Exercise 10C

1. a) 0 b) 3 c) 4
   d) 3 e) 2 f) –4
   g) –2 h) $\frac{3}{2}$ i) $\frac{1}{3}$
   j) $\frac{1}{2}$
2. a) 2.65 b) 2.01 c) 0.431
   d) 0.903 e) 2.10 f) 0.631
3. a) $\log_{10} 100 = 2$
   b) $\log_5 0.008 = -3$
   c) $\log_4 \frac{1}{4} = -1$
   d) $\log_9 1 = 0$

3. e) $\log_2 4 = 2$
f) $\log_8 8 = 1$
g) $\log_6 7776 = 5$
h) $\log_7 282475249 = 10$
i) $\log_{10} 10000000 = 7$
j) $\log_5 125 = 3$

4. a) $7^1 = 7$ b) $4^0 = 1$
c) $2^7 = 128$ d) $2^{-4} = \frac{1}{16}$
e) $6^{-1} = \frac{1}{6}$ f) $8^2 = 64$
g) $4^3 = 64$ h) $7^4 = 2401$
i) $5^4 = 625$ j) $3^{-10} = \frac{1}{59049}$
k) $2^{7/2} = 8\sqrt{2}$

5. a) 3 b) 9 c) 2
d) 4 e) 4 f) 2
g) 10 h) 2 i) 2
j) 10

6. a) 3 b) –1 c) 9
d) $-\frac{1}{2}$ e) 0 f) 1.13
g) 6.60 h) 1.86 i) 2.24
j) $\frac{5}{3}$

7. Makes no sense. Base 1 cannot be raised to a power to make the other number.

Exercise 10D

1. a) $3\log_2 10$ b) 5
c) $4\log_3 2$ d) $3\log_7 3$
e) –5 f) $3\log 5$
g) $4\log_4 10$ h) $16\log_2 3$
i) $-\log_4 10$ j) $-3\log_{10} 2$

2. a) $\log_a 60$
b) Not possible to simplify
c) $\log_2 90$
d) $\log_3 170$
e) Not possible to simplify
f) $\log_p 36$
g) 2
h) 2

3. a) $\log_a 15$
b) Not possible to simplify
c) $\log_2 3$
d) $\log_3 10$
e) Not possible to simplify
f) $\log_q 12$
g) $2\log 2$
h) $\log_6\left(\frac{11}{4}\right)$

4. a) $\log_2 63$ b) $\log_5 80$
c) $\log\left(\frac{3}{2}\right)$ d) 1
e) $\log_3 72$ f) 2
g) 3 h) $\log\left(\frac{a^5b^2}{c^4}\right)$

5. a) $\log a + \log b + \log c$
b) $\log a + \log b - \log c$
c) $2\log a + \log b + \log c$
d) $2\log a + \frac{1}{2}\log b + \frac{1}{2}\log c$
e) $\frac{1}{3}\log a - \frac{1}{2}\log b$
f) $1 + \log_5 a + \log_5 b$
g) $2\log_2 a - 2\log_2 c - 5$
h) $3 + 3\log_3 b$

6. a) $\log(x^6y^2)$
b) $\log\left(\frac{p^3}{q^3}\right)$
c) $\log\left(\frac{a^7b^6}{c^4}\right)$

7. a) $3 + a$ b) $2a - 1$

8. a) $\frac{p}{4}$ b) $\frac{3p}{4} + 1$

9. a) 3 b) $\log_a 891$

11.

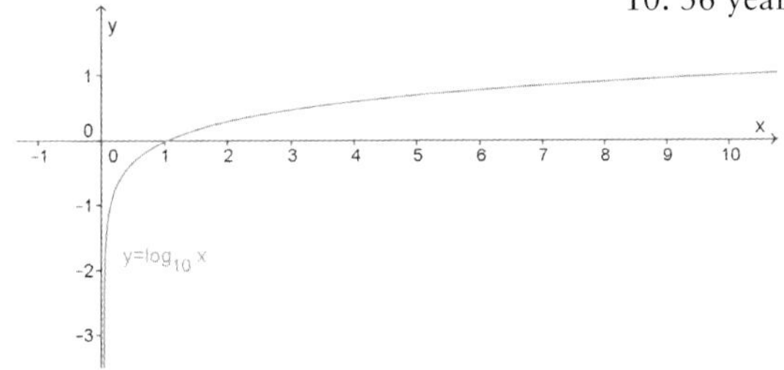

Possible observations:

a) Passes through (1, 0).

b) Vertical asymptote $x = 0$.

c) y is always increasing, but gradient of curve always decreasing.

d) Inverse of $y = 10^x$ (mirror image in line $y = x$).

Exercise 10E

1. a) 1.07 b) 0.631 c) 2.58
d) 1.11 e) –1.37 f) $-\frac{1}{2}$
g) –0.862 h) $\frac{1}{2}$ i) $-\frac{1}{3}$
j) –1.66

2. a) $\frac{1}{2}$ b) $\frac{1}{3}$
c) –1 d) $\frac{1}{2}$

Exercise 10F

1. a) 1.95 b) 3.91 c) 1.5
d) 2.18 e) –1 f) –0.232
g) 1.46 h) 1.83 i) 1
j) 6.64

2. a) 9.909 b) 2.593 c) –2.342
d) –1.390 e) –0.513 f) –0.818
g) –1.257 h) 2.269 i) –0.735
j) –0.192

3. 1.5

4. a) $5 + a$ b) $2a - 1$ c) $32\sqrt{2}$

5. $x = 2$; No, only if one base is a power of the other (e.g. 8 is a power of 2).

6. b) 2.46

7. 12

8. a) $x = 6$ or $x = \frac{1}{36}$
b) $x = 8$ or $x = \frac{1}{4}$
c) $x = 1000$ or $x = 10^{-5}$
d) $x = 5.20$ (3 s.f.) or $x = \frac{1}{9}$

9. $x = 1$

10. 36 years (rounded up)

CHAPTER 11. INTEGRATION

Revision Exercise 11A

1. a) $x^2 + x$
b) $x^4 + 2x^3 - x^2$
c) $x^2 - 4x + 3$
d) $6x^2 - x - 2$
e) $x^4 - 1$
f) $x^3 + 6x^2 + 12x + 8$

2. a) a^5 b) b^{-1}
c) c^6 d) d^9

3. a) $e^{\frac{3}{2}}$ b) $f^{-\frac{1}{2}}$
c) $g^{\frac{4}{3}}$ d) h

4. a) $\frac{dy}{dx} = 2x$
b) $\frac{dy}{dx} = -3x^2 + 8x - 2$
c) $\frac{dy}{dx} = -2x^{-3} + x^{-2}$
d) $\frac{dy}{dx} = 5x^{\frac{3}{2}} - \frac{1}{2}x^{-\frac{1}{2}}$
e) $\frac{dy}{dx} = 2x - 4$

Exercise 11B

1. a) $y = 3x^2 + c$
 b) $y = \frac{1}{7}x^7 + c$
 c) $y = x^2 + c$
 d) $y = -\frac{1}{3}x^3 + c$
 e) $y = -x^4 + c$
 f) $y = x^6 + c$
 g) $y = x^3 + c$
 h) $y = \frac{1}{2}x^{100} + c$
 i) $y = \frac{5}{4}x^8 + c$
 j) $y = 3x^4 + c$
 k) $y = -3x^3 + c$
2. a) $y = -x^{-3} + c$
 b) $y = 2x^{-1} + c$
 c) $y = -\frac{1}{9}x^{-3} + c$
 d) $y = x^{\frac{4}{3}} + c$
 e) $y = -ax^{-1} + c$
 f) $y = -\frac{1}{2}x^{-14} + c$
 g) $y = 2x^{\frac{7}{2}} + c$
 h) $y = x^{-11/5} + c$
 i) $y = 72x^{-1/8} + c$
3. a) $y = \frac{2}{3}x^{\frac{3}{2}} + c$
 b) $y = \frac{2}{5}x^{\frac{5}{2}} + c$
 c) $y = -\frac{1}{2}x^{-2} + c$
 d) $y = \frac{1}{3}x^3 + c$
 e) $y = \frac{1}{2}x^2 + c$
 f) $y = 2x^{\frac{1}{2}} + c$
 g) $y = \frac{16}{5}x^5 + c$
 h) $y = -x^{-1} + c$
 i) $y = \frac{1}{16}x + c$
 j) $y = -\frac{1}{6}x^{-6} + c$
4. Any three functions that meet the criteria, for example:
 a) $y = x^2$
 b) $y = x^2 + 2$
 c) $y = x^2 - 2$

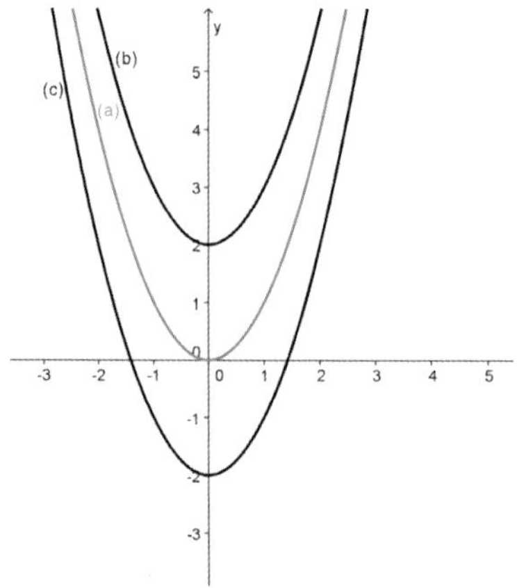

The three sketches all have the same gradient.

Exercise 11C

1. a) $2x^2 + c$ b) $\frac{1}{6}x^6 + c$
 c) $-\frac{1}{4}x^4 + c$ d) $-x^3 + c$
 e) $5x + c$ f) $\frac{3}{4}x^4 + c$
 g) $2x^{50} + c$ h) $\frac{5}{3}x^6 + c$
 i) $-2x^6 + c$ j) $\frac{3}{2}x^6 + c$
2. a) $-x^{-4} + c$ b) $4t^{-1} + c$
 c) $\frac{1}{16}x^{-4} + c$ d) $\frac{1}{2}y^{\frac{5}{4}} + c$
 e) $-\frac{b}{2}x^{-2} + c$
3. a) $y = z^{-9/4} + c$
 b) $y = \frac{1}{2}x^{-16} + c$
 c) $r = \frac{4}{3}\theta^{\frac{9}{2}} + c$
 d) $s = 10x^{-1/10} + c$
4. a) $y = \frac{2}{3}y^{\frac{3}{2}} + c$
 b) $y = \frac{1}{2}x^{-2} + c$
 c) $y = \frac{1}{8}s + c$
 d) $y = \frac{1}{5}x^5 + c$
5. a) $y = p + c$
 b) $z = \frac{2}{7}x^{\frac{7}{2}} + c$
 c) $p = -\frac{16}{3}z^{-3} + c$
 d) $y = 8x^{\frac{1}{2}} + c$
 e) $s = \frac{4}{3}t^3 + c$
 f) $I = -\frac{1}{6}x^{-6} + c$

Exercise 11D

1. a) $3x + \frac{16}{7}x^{\frac{7}{4}} + c$
 b) $4x + 2x^{\frac{3}{2}} + c$
 c) $\frac{8}{3}x^3 + \frac{7}{2}x^2 + c$
 d) $\frac{2}{5}x^5 + \frac{3}{2}x^2 + c$
 e) $\frac{3}{2}x^4 + 2x^2 + c$
 f) $4x - 3x^{-1} + c$
 g) $2x^2 - \frac{1}{3}x^3 + c$
 h) $\frac{9}{2}x^2 - \frac{1}{3}x^3 + c$
 i) $-\frac{x^{-6}}{6} + \frac{8}{3}x^{\frac{3}{2}} + c$
 j) $-\frac{x^{-3}}{3} + 4x^{\frac{3}{2}} + c$
 k) $\frac{3}{4}x^4 + \frac{5}{2}x^2 + c$
 l) $4x^2 - \frac{x^3}{3} - 8x + c$
2. a) $x^4 + x^3 + 6x + c$
 b) $4x^4 + 2x^3 + 5x + c$
 c) $3x^4 + 2x^3 + 7x + c$
 d) $\frac{1}{4}x^2 - 3x^{-1} + c$
 e) $\frac{1}{6}x^2 - 4x^{-1} + c$
 f) $\frac{x^3}{3} - 4x^2 + 3x + c$
 g) $\frac{x^4}{4} - 8x^3 + 72x^2 + c$
 h) $\frac{x^4}{4} - \frac{7}{3}x^3 + \frac{15}{2}x^2 + 3x + c$
 i) $\frac{x^3}{3} - 2x^2 + 3x + c$
 j) $\frac{x^3}{3} + \frac{7}{2}x^2 + 19x + c$
3. a) $\frac{8}{5}x^5 + 2x^2 + c$
 b) $\frac{x^3}{3} + 2x^2 + 4x + c$
 c) $\frac{x^5}{5} - \frac{4}{3}x^3 + 4x + c$
 d) $8x^2 + 48x^{\frac{3}{2}} + 81x + c$
 e) $4x - 2x^2 + \frac{x^3}{3} + c$
 f) $-\frac{x^{-3}}{3} + x + \frac{2}{x} + c$
 g) $-\frac{2}{3}x^3 + \frac{x^2}{2} + x + c$
 h) $\frac{x^4}{2} + x^3 + c$

3. i) $-4x^{-1} - 2x^{-2} - \frac{1}{3}x^{-3} + c$

j) $\frac{x^6}{6} + \frac{4}{5}x^5 + \frac{3}{2}x^4 + \frac{4}{3}x^3 + \frac{x^2}{2} + c$

4. a) $(k + 2)^2x + c$

b) $\frac{4}{3}x^3 + 2kx^2 + k^2x + c$

c) $\frac{k^2}{3}x^3 + 2kx^2 + 4x + c$

d) $\frac{(k + 2)^2}{3}x^3 + c$

5. a) $x - \frac{1}{x} + c$

b) $2\sqrt{t} - 2t + c$

c) $z + 2z^{\frac{3}{2}} + c$

d) $-x^{-\frac{1}{2}} - \frac{x^{-1}}{2} + c$

e) $-x^{-1} + x^{-2} + c$

f) $2\left(\theta^{\frac{1}{2}} + \theta^{-\frac{1}{2}}\right) + c$

g) $6s^{\frac{1}{6}} + \frac{6}{7}s^{\frac{7}{6}} + c$

6. $y = 7x - 2x^{-1} + c$

7. –4

Exercise 11E

1. a) $y = \frac{3}{2}x^2 - 3$

b) $y = \frac{x^3}{3} + 4x + 1$

c) $y = -\frac{1}{x} + 1$

d) $y = \frac{x^4}{4} + x + 1$

e) $y = \frac{x^4}{2} - \frac{x^3}{2} + \frac{x^2}{2} + \frac{3}{2}$

f) $y = -\frac{1}{x} + \frac{1}{2x^2}$

g) $y = \frac{2}{3}x^{\frac{3}{2}} + \frac{1}{3}$

h) $y = \frac{2}{3}x^{\frac{3}{2}} + \frac{2}{3}x^3 + \frac{2}{3}$

i) $y = \frac{x^3}{3} + 3x^2 + x + \frac{2}{3}$

j) $y = -\frac{2}{3}x^{-\frac{3}{2}} - \frac{1}{x} + \frac{1}{10} + \frac{\sqrt{2}}{6}$

2. a) $y = 5x - 3x^{-1} + c$

b) $y = \frac{21}{2}$

3. $y = \frac{4}{5}x^5 + 3x^2 + 8$

4. $y = \frac{4}{3}x^3 + \frac{7}{2}x^2 + \frac{7}{6}$

5. $y = -x^2 + 2x + 2$

6. a) $\frac{dy}{dx} = 2x^2 - 1$

b) $y = \frac{2}{3}x^3 - x - 5$

Exercise 11F

1. a) 9 b) $\frac{245}{3}$

c) 44.7 (3 s.f.) d) 648

e) 68 f) 8340 (3 s.f.)

g) 1330 (3 s.f.) h) 28

i) 24 j) $\frac{11}{6}$

2. a) $-4 + 8\sqrt{2}$ b) $-6 + 18\sqrt{3}$

c) $-12 + 60\sqrt{5}$

3. b) A(12, 0)

c) B(4, 256)

d) 1728

4. $A = \frac{11}{6}, B = \frac{9}{2}$, Total $= \frac{19}{3}$

5. Total = 34.25

6. 15 cm²

7. a) 2 b) $\frac{8}{3}$

Exercise 11G

1. a) $\left(\frac{11}{3}, \frac{11}{9}\right)$ m

b) 8.22 m²

2. a) A: $y = 1$, B: $y = 4$

b) $x = 2\sqrt{y}$

c) $\frac{28}{3}$

3. a) $\frac{dy}{dx} = 3x^2 - 14x + 15$

b) (3, 13)

c) y–coordinate of P is 13, the same as Q

d) $\frac{4}{3}$

4. b) 17.5

5. a) A(–5, –8), B(2, 27)

b) 57.2 (3 s.f.)

6. a) $\frac{8}{3}, 2$

b) $\frac{x^4}{4} - \frac{7x^3}{3} + 8x^2 + c$

c) 21.3 (3 s.f.)

7. a) (1, 1)

b) $\frac{1}{12}$

8. a) 1 and 2

c) $\frac{1}{4}\left(2^{\frac{4}{3}} - 1\right)$

d) 3:1

Exercise 11H

1. a) 280.5 b) 279

2. a)

x	1	1.5	2	2.5	3	3.5	4
$y = \frac{x}{(1+x)^2}$	0.25	0.24	0.22222	0.20408	0.18750	0.17284	0.16

b) 0.616 (3 s.f.)

3. 1.12 (3 s.f.)

4. 10.2 (3 s.f.)

5. a) 16.2

b) $x = \frac{y^2}{5} - 5$

c) $\frac{50}{3}$

6. a)

x	0	0.5	1	1.5	2
$y = x(2 - x)$	0	0.75	1	0.75	0

b)

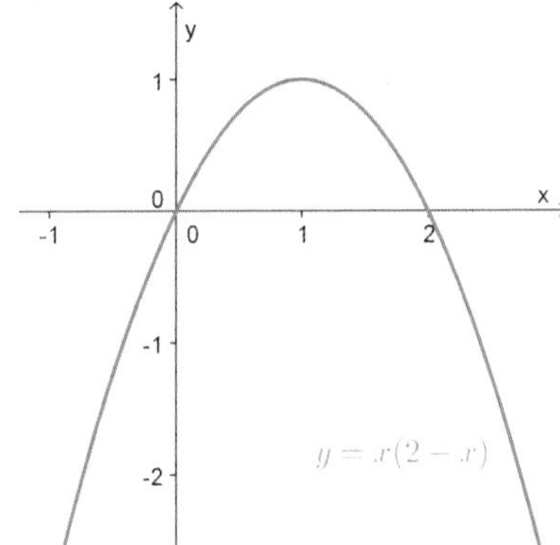

c) 1.25

d)

x	0	0.25	0.5	0.75	1	1.25	1.5	1.75	2
$y = x(2 - x)$	0	0.4375	0.75	0.9375	1	0.9375	0.75	0.4375	0

e) 1.31 (3 s.f.)

f) $\frac{4}{3}$

g) i) 6.25% ii) 1.56% (3 s.f.)

7. a)

t	0	4	8	12	16	20	24
v	0	2.71	8.29	**24.12**	69.75	**201.6**	**582.62**

b) 2390 m (3 s.f.)

8. a)

x	3	4	5	6	7
y	5.385	8.124	11.269	**14.765**	**18.574**

b) 46.14

9. a) 0.7761
   b) Multiply answer a) by 4. Gives 3.105.
   c) π

10. The approximation for the concave curve would be smaller than the true answer. The approximation for the convex curve would be greater than the true answer.

REVIEW EXERCISE CHAPTERS 10 & 11

1. a)

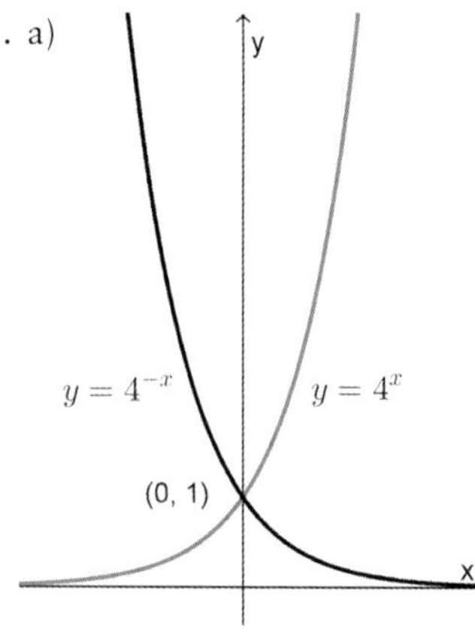

b)

y
$y = 4^x$
$y = 1 + 4^{-x}$
(0, 1)
x

c)

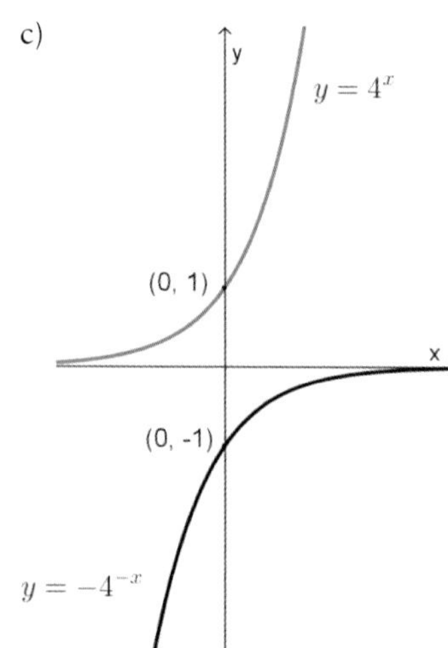

1. d)

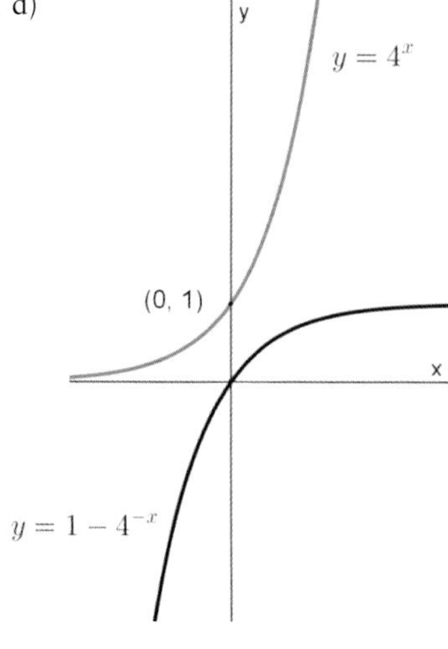

e)

y
$y = 4^x$
$y = 4^{2x}$
(0, 1)
x

f)

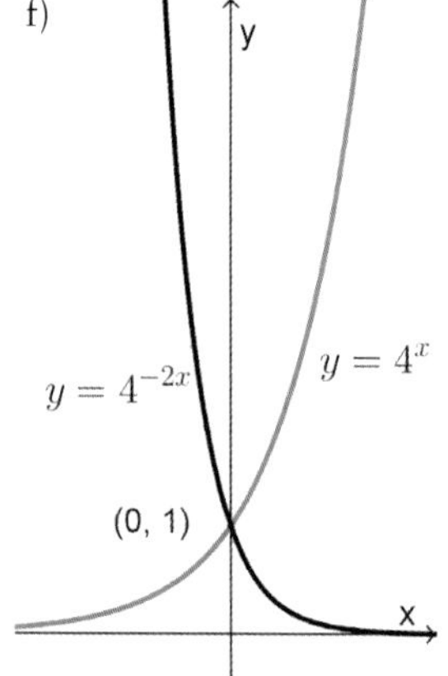

2. a) 2
   b) –3

3. a) $\log_2 16 = 4$
   b) $\log_3 \frac{1}{81} = -4$

4. a) $2^{10} = 1024$ b) $4^{-2} = 0.0625$

5. a) 6 b) 6

6. a) 2 b) 3.79

7. a) 3 b) $\log_a 96$

9. a) $2 \log_2 6$ b) –2

10. a) $\log x^5 y^5$
    b) $\log\left(\frac{p^3}{q^6}\right)$
    c) $\log\left(\frac{a^5 b^7}{c^4}\right)$

11. a) 1.21 b) –3.32

12. a) 3.58 b) –2.56

13. a) –3 b) 15.275

14. a) $4 + a$ b) $4a - 1$
    c) $2\sqrt{2}$

15. b) 2.32

16. a) $y = \frac{1}{16}x^8 + c$
    b) $y = -\frac{1}{5}x^2 + c$

17. a) $y = -t^{-\frac{1}{2}} + c$
    b) $y = -x^{-7} + c$

18. a) $z = \frac{1}{2}t^2 + c$
    b) $p = \frac{1}{2}x^2 + c$

19. a) $8x - 2x^{-1} + c$
    b) $-\frac{x^{-5}}{5} + \frac{4}{3}x^{\frac{3}{2}} + c$

20. a) $\frac{9}{4}x^4 + \frac{3}{2}x^2 + c$
    b) $\frac{x^4}{4} - \frac{2}{3}x^3 + \frac{x^2}{2} + c$

21. a) $y = \frac{x^3}{3} - x^2 + 2$
    b) $y = \frac{2}{3}x^{\frac{3}{2}} + 4x^{\frac{1}{2}} + 2$

22. $y = \frac{3}{2}x^4 + 2x^2 - \frac{1}{2}$

23. a) $\frac{46}{3}$
    b) 6.48 (3 s.f.)

24. a) A(–2, 12), B(4, 6)
    b) 36

25. 3.13